The Literature of Reconstruction

THE LITERATURE *of* RECONSTRUCTION

NOT IN PLAIN BLACK AND WHITE

BROOK THOMAS

JOHNS HOPKINS UNIVERSITY PRESS
Baltimore

Printed in the United States of America on acid-free paper
2 4 6 8 9 7 5 3 1

Johns Hopkins University Press
2715 North Charles Street
Baltimore, Maryland 21218-4363
www.press.jhu.edu

Library of Congress Cataloging-in-Publication Data

Names: Thomas, Brook, 1947– author.
Title: The literature of Reconstruction : not in plain black and white / Brook Thomas.
Description: Baltimore : Johns Hopkins University Press, 2017. | Includes bibliographical references and index.
Identifiers: LCCN 2016012791| ISBN 9781421421322 (hardback) | ISBN 9781421421339 (electronic) | ISBN 1421421321 (hardcover)
Subjects: LCSH: American literature—19th century—History and criticism. | Politics and literature—United States—History—19th century. | Literature and society—United States—History—19th century. | Race relations in literature. | BISAC: HISTORY / United States / 19th Century. | LITERARY CRITICISM / American / General. | SOCIAL SCIENCE / Discrimination & Race Relations. | HISTORY / United States / Civil War Period (1850–1877).
Classification: LCC PS217.P64 T58 2017 | DDC 810.9/358—dc23
LC record available at https://lccn.loc.gov/2016012791

A catalog record for this book is available from the British Library.

Johns Hopkins University Press uses environmentally friendly book materials, including recycled text paper that is composed of at least 30 percent post-consumer waste, whenever possible.

For my best students and teachers

Contents

Illustrations

Acknowledgments

A literary critic trying to maneuver on the terrain of what was once called the dark and bloody ground of Reconstruction studies needs an army of support. I am indebted to Elizabeth Demers of Johns Hopkins University Press for her promotion of the book. Juliana McCarthy, Mary Lou Kenney, Meagan M. Szekely, and Julia Smith have been models of congeniality during production. Publishing with Hopkins has special meaning for me. I grew up in the suburbs of Baltimore. Woodrow Wilson, Thomas Dixon, and Sidney Lanier, about whom I write, have connections with Hopkins, as do more recent scholars whose views are closer to mine. While I was immersed in research, it was an inspiration to imagine that while I was on the university's Homewood campus cheering my older brother in cross-country races sponsored by the Hopkins spiked-shoe club, doctoral students were producing groundbreaking work under the supervision of C. Vann Woodward. The year I graduated from high school, Johns Hopkins published Otto H. Olson's biography of Albion W. Tourgée, which would later prove invaluable in my research.

My ideas were shaped by stimulating exchanges at conferences bringing together historians, legal scholars, and literary critics. Sally Greene organized a symposium on Tourgée including Al Brophy, Michael Kent Curtis, Mark Elliott, and John David Smith. Carolyn Karcher was also there. Carolyn and I have shared common interests for years, and I rely heavily on her impeccable scholarship. Scott Romine and Amanda Claybaugh joined me on a panel devoted to the literature of Reconstruction in Boston. Amanda and Al Brophy later participated in a conference at the University of Maryland, College Park, on race, law, and literature, where I met face-to-face authors of work I admire: Steven Best, Jeannine DeLombard, Andrew Hebard, Hoang G. Phan, Mary Helen Washington, and Edlie Wong. I also renewed dialogue with law and literature scholars Chris Brown, Nan Goodman, and Robin West, while getting to know Peter Maillois with his extensive knowledge of the law and Woodrow Wilson. Robert Levine and I have a long history of mutual support and engagement. Scott Romine, Elaine Frantz

Parsons, and Gregory Downs highlighted a colloquium at University of California, Irvine, designed to promote discussion between historians and literary critics of Reconstruction. We were joined by Edward Blum. I frequently draw on Edward, Elaine, and Greg's historical expertise. Greg also employed his well-honed literary sensibility to improve a draft of my introduction.

Historians Laura Edwards, Eric Foner, Steven Hahn, Kate Mazur, K. Stephen Prince, Heather Cox Richardson, Lucy Salyer, Manisha Sinha, and Daniel Stowell helped me avoid blunders by graciously responding to e-mails out of the blue asking for clarification or making claims about complicated issues I did not fully understand. Legal scholars Ariela Gross and Daniel Sharfstein enlightened me on the myth of the so-called "one-drop rule." Literary scholars R. Bruce Bickley Jr., Jeffory Clymer, Jennifer Greeson, Gregory Jay, Sharon Kennedy-Nolle, Jack Kettering, Paul Petrie, Ben Railton, Peter Schmidt, and Jeremy Wells responded in different ways to queries about their work. At the University of California, Irvine, Spencer Olin, Steven Mailloux, and Richard Godden exhibited exemplary patience as I went on at length about my latest research obsessions. Alexander von Humboldt junior scholars from Germany, Birte Christ and Stefanie Mueller, made sure I did not neglect poetry in cross-examining the law and literature of the period. While working on this book, I was also directing the dissertations of Brian Fonken and Erin Sweeney. Those two have no idea how much working with and learning from them raised my spirits.

Chapters 4 and 5 expand and revise essays I published previously in the *Arizona Quarterly* and *English Literary History.* In other chapters I draw on parts of essays published in the *Mississippi Quarterly* and *English Language Notes.*

My biggest debt is to my wife, Jayne Lewis, and my son, Peter Thomas. Peter's interest in history gives me hope that I will have at least one loyal reader in the future. Jayne was a willing listener to details about the intricate plots of Reconstruction novels, especially ones having to do with romantic reconciliation.

Works Cited: Abbreviations

AC	Albion W. Tourgée. *An Appeal to Caesar.* New York: Fords, Howard, and Hulbert, 1884.
BC	John William DeForest. *The Bloody Chasm.* New York: Appleton, 1881.
BR	W. E. B. Du Bois. *Black Reconstruction: An Essay Toward a History of the Part Which Black Folk Played in the Attempt to Reconstruct Democracy in America, 1860–1880.* New York: Russell and Russell, 1935.
BS	Albion W. Tourgée. *Bricks without Straw: A Novel.* 1880. Durham: Duke UP, 2009.
CAM	Joel Chandler Harris. *The Chronicles of Aunt Minervy Ann.* New York: Scribner's, 1899.
CD	Charles W. Chesnutt. *The Colonel's Dream.* New York: Doubleday, Page, 1905.
CF	Pauline E. Hopkins. *Contending Forces: A Romance Illustrative of Negro Life North and South.* 1900. New York: Oxford UP, 1988.
CM	Thomas Dixon. *The Clansman: An Historical Romance of the Ku Klux Klan.* 1905. Lexington: UP of Kentucky, 1970.
DW	Charles W. Chesnutt. "The Dumb Witness." *The Short Fiction of Charles W. Chesnutt.* Edited by Sylvia Lyons Render. Washington, DC: Howard UP, 1981.
FD	Charles W. Chesnutt. *Frederick Douglass.* 1899. Atlanta: Clark Atlanta UP, 2001.
FE	Albion W. Tourgée. *A Fool's Errand. By One of the Fools.* 1879. Cambridge: Harvard UP, 1961.
GS	Albion W. Tourgée. *With Gauge and Swallow, Attorneys.* Philadelphia: Lippincott, 1890.
GT	Joel Chandler Harris. *Gabriel Tolliver: A Story of Reconstruction.* New York: McClure Phillips, 1902.

HBC	Charles W. Chesnutt. *The House Behind the Cedars*. Boston: Houghton Mifflin, 1900.
HD	Pauline E. Hopkins. *Hagar's Daughter: A Story of Southern Caste Prejudice*. In *The Magazine Fiction of Pauline Hopkins*. 1901–1902. New York: Oxford UP, 1988.
HH	Sutton E. Griggs. *The Hindered Hand: or, The Reign of the Repressionist*. Nashville: Orion, 1905.
ID	William Dean Howells. *An Imperative Duty*. 1891. Edited by Paul R. Petrie. Peterborough: Broadview, 2010.
IE	Albion W. Tourgée. *The Invisible Empire*. 1880. Baton Rouge: Louisiana State UP, 1989.
II	Sutton E. Griggs. *Imperium in Imperio: A Study of the Negro Race Problem, A Novel*. 1899. New York: Arno, 1969.
IK	John William DeForest. "An Independent Ku Klux." *Civil War Memories*. 1872. Edited by S. Joshi. New York: Barnes and Noble, 2009.
IL	Frances Harper. *Iola Leroy, or Shadows Uplifted*. 1892. 2nd ed. Philadelphia: Garrigues, 1893.
JE	Albion W. Tourgée. *John Eax*. In *John Eax and Mamelon, or the South without the Shadow*. New York: Fords, Howard, and Hulbert, 1882.
JM	George Washington Cable. *John March, Southerner*. New York: Scribner's, 1894.
JV	John William DeForest. *Honest John Vane: A Story*. New Haven: Richmond and Pattery, 1875.
KD	Constance Fenimore Woolson. "King David." *Scribner's Monthly* 15 (1878): 781–89.
LS	Thomas Dixon. *The Leopard's Spots: A Romance of the White Man's Burden—1865–1900*. New York: Doubleday, Page, 1902.
MA	Albion W. Tourgée. *Mamelon*. In *John Eax and Mamelon, or the South without the Shadow*. New York: Fords, Howard, and Hulbert, 1882.
ME	Albion W. Tourgée. *Murvale Eastman, Christian Socialist*. New York: Fords, Howard, and Hulbert, 1890.
MRC	John William DeForest. *Miss Ravenel's Conversion From Secession to Loyalty*. 1867. New York: Holt, Rinehart, and Winston, 1955.
MT	Charles W. Chesnutt. *The Marrow of Tradition*. Boston: Houghton Mifflin, 1901.
OG	Constance Fenimore Woolson. "Old Gardiston." *Harper's New Monthly Magazine* 52 (1876): 662–74.

PA Charles W. Chesnutt. "The Partners." *The Short Fiction of Charles W. Chesnutt.* Edited by Sylvia Lyons Render. Washington, DC: Howard UP, 1981.

PP Albion W. Tourgée. *Pactolus Prime.* New York: Cassell, 1890.

RG Albion W. Tourgée. *A Royal Gentleman [Originally Entitled "Toinette"].* New York: Fords, Howard, and Hulbert, 1874.

RK Constance Fenimore Woolson. "Rodman the Keeper." *Atlantic Monthly* 39 (1877): 261–77.

RR Thomas Nelson Page. *Red Rock: A Chronicle of Reconstruction.* New York: Scribner's 1898.

SBF W. E. B. Du Bois. *The Souls of Black Folk.* 1903. Edited by David W. Blight and Robert Gooding-Williams. Boston: Bedford, 1997.

SC Charles W. Chesnutt. "The Sheriff's Children." *The Wife of His Youth and Other Stories of the Color Line.* Boston: Houghton Mifflin, 1899.

SD María Amparo Ruiz de Burton. *The Squatter and the Don: A Novel Descriptive of Contemporary Occurrences in California.* 1885. Houston: Arte Publico Press, 1997.

SH Charles W. Chesnutt. "The Sway-Backed House." 1900. *The Short Fiction of Charles W. Chesnutt.* Edited by Sylvia Lyons Render. Washington, DC: Howard UP, 1981.

TR Thomas Dixon. *The Traitor: A Story of the Fall of the Invisible Empire.* New York: Doubleday, Page, 1907.

WW María Amparo Ruiz de Burton. *Who Would Have Thought It?: A Novel.* 1872. Houston: Arte Publico Press, 1995.

Note to the Reader

In addition to using "black" and "African American," where context dictates, I also use "colored." As founding members of the NAACP and African American writers knew, the terms "black" and even the now outdated "Negro" were not adequate to deal with the racial complexity of the times. For instance, most Jim Crow laws did not separate "blacks" and "whites." They separated "coloreds" and "whites." Those organizing the challenge to Louisiana's Jim Crow law in *Plessy v. Ferguson* considered themselves "colored" but not "blacks" or "Negroes."

The Literature of Reconstruction

- INTRODUCTION -

NOT IN PLAIN BLACK AND WHITE

William Dean Howells provides a succinct explanation of how novels can enhance our understanding of Reconstruction's politics:

> There are other reasons besides weakness of will which lead people to prefer novels to congressional documents or tables of statistics, even when both have reference to the same problems. Literature has this immense advantage over official reports: that it may take into account the forces which everyone knows to be efficient, but cannot reduce to figures, and there is the opportunity for such selection in art as shall give one swiftly the really vital points in a great political or social situation. There is no reason in the nature of things why a novel may not be a very truthful and very cogent political argument, since man is a political animal, and the novel excludes nothing which concerns the essential elements of human society.[1]

Howells, the master of American literary realism, does not claim that novelists provide accurate empirical evidence of an era. He does claim that through a process of selection they can construct political arguments by creating fictional worlds that hypothetically relate the forces of an era to one another. It is no accident that Howells makes this claim in a review primarily devoted to *A Fool's Errand* and *Bricks without Straw,* two novels about Reconstruction by Albion W. Tourgée. The era's most outspoken white advocate of African American rights, Tourgée had been a carpetbagger judge in North Carolina and would go on to defend Homer Plessy before the US Supreme Court. Through analysis of Tourgée's and others' works of literature, I hope to address a challenge that Laura Edwards poses to historians of her generation. Because legal and political matters were so central to Reconstruction, political historians dominated early scholarship. With the rise of social history in the 1960s, however, a different picture of the period began to emerge. "Moving the focus away from the nation's statehouses to southern fields and households," social historians "have argued that the outcome of people's daily struggles over economic resources and social relations is as pivotal to understanding the period as the decisions of political leaders." The challenge, Edwards argues, is to bring the concerns of social history, "which so often takes local areas as its focus," together with those of political history, "which looks to the state and national level for analytical direction." In *Gendered Strife and Confusion: The Political Culture of Reconstruction*, she does just that, beginning with a rape case that allowed politicians to use the event to spin "a dramatic allegory of Reconstruction politics."[2]

Literary figures also used vivid accounts of people's everyday lives in particular places to spin political allegories with national implications. To be sure, they wrote about fictional, not real, people. But when it comes to presenting the "slippery subjectivity of private lives," they were as well equipped as social historians. Indeed, works of fiction have the salutary function of reminding us that turning an account of local events into a political allegory will almost always involve a certain amount of speculation. Fictional stories also influenced efforts at reconstruction and how those efforts have been interpreted by historians. Even so, the amount of literary criticism on Reconstruction pales in comparison to the amount of historical analysis. That imbalance affects our historical as well as our literary understanding of one of the country's most politically complicated undertakings: reconstructing the Union on a new basis after a bloody civil war. In early 1877, Sidney Breese, chief justice of Illinois, acknowledged, "We must live in the world the [Civil] War made." Debates during Reconstruction remind us that the Civil War made possible many worlds. Historians continue to debate which world actually prevailed while the nation continues to debate which world should have triumphed. Reconstruction, C. Vann Woodward insists, constitutes "the moral core of national history." Reading the literature of the time allows us to conjure up competing visions of the worlds that might have emerged to mark the birth of a new nation.[3]

Given the important role transformations in the law played at the time, it is not surprising that a number of Reconstruction authors, such as Sidney Lanier, Thomas Nelson Page, Thomas Dixon, and Charles W. Chesnutt, were, like Tourgée, trained in the law. As important as legal issues were, however, almost all of these authors recognized that legal change could not tell the entire story of the era. The German legal thinker Carl Schmitt makes a distinction between legality and legitimacy. Proponents of the modern *Rechtsstaat* claim to found the state on rule by law. But, Schmitt argues, it is impossible to find within the law itself an adequate foundation for the state. The law may have formal coherence, but a state needs more than legality to make people believe in its authority. A state must be legitimated by a sense of tradition and by constantly reaffirmed and recreated symbols and myths. The debate about how to reconstruct the nation after the Civil War was a debate about legitimacy, as well as about specific laws. It was a question of foundational myths, as well as a question of foundational legal principles. The works I treat narrate stories that provide different senses of legitimacy for a reunited nation. Insofar as Reconstruction remains what Eric Foner memorably calls "America's unfinished revolution," that battle over legitimacy continues today. Attention to works of literature can give us a clearer sense of what is at stake in that battle.[4]

Many issues raised during the era of Reconstruction are still with us, unresolved and often controversial. We cannot properly understand current racial relations without knowledge of Reconstruction policies and their undoing. To be sure, Reconstruction's failure was due to more than the policies adopted. It was also caused by deeply engrained social and political attitudes, many of which persist. Even so, more than insight into racial relations is at stake. The period is important for showing how economic, social, and political issues became interrelated with those of race. Legal precedents for dealing with terrorism grow directly out of governmental efforts to counter the threat of organizations like the Ku Klux Klan. Reconstruction was also linked to what Alan Trachtenberg calls "the incorporation of America." Efforts to rebuild and reunite the nation after the devastation of civil war focused on the construction of railroads, the nation's first major corporate entities. Today's debates about governmental subsidies, regulation, and businesses too big to fail can be traced to this era. Speculation in railroads led to the Panic of 1873, an economic disaster that affected the prospects for Reconstruction while setting off heated arguments about credit, currency, and monetary circulation.[5]

Questions about the government's role in issues of both race and the economy were especially important because the preservation of the Union and the passage of the Fourteenth Amendment gave increased power to the national government over the states. That change led to arguments about state versus national jurisdiction that persist today. The role of the national government in education was debated then, as it is now. Many of today's attacks against welfare sound eerily similar to complaints that the Freedmen's Bureau was a paternalistic governmental institution taking away incentives for African Americans to develop self-reliance. Expansion of the national government's powers began in order to wage the Civil War. A national tax was levied, a massive national debt incurred, greenbacks printed, a national system of detectives established, and a compulsory military draft enacted with provisions for those with money to hire substitutes. Unaware of Abraham Lincoln's role in this expansion, many revere him as the nation's best president, while lamenting the powers he granted to the national government. Aware of Lincoln's role, some libertarians vilify the national hero for drastically altering the nature of the Union while claiming to preserve it.[6]

Even with its increased power, the national government was not up to the task of making Reconstruction a success. According to William Gillette:

> In the field of administration, federal resources were not equal to the nation's responsibilities. The federal bureaucracy, faced with unprecedented tasks of governance, was too small to cope, for it was scarcely larger in 1871 than it had been in 1861. It lacked money and imagination and was poorly organized and ineffectually managed. Furthermore, the army was too small and too scattered about to have been capable of preserving order. The structure of the government itself was handicapped by the federal system with its separation of powers, diffusion of responsibility, and lack of an adequate mechanism to formulate a coherent policy or to execute it consistently. Therefore very little legislation had been executed uniformly and firmly in the states.

Furthermore, Reconstruction could not overcome "a constitutional tradition that was grounded in antebellum decentralization and local autonomy."[7]

Its inability to do so is illustrated in the career of the famous lawyer David Dudley Field, an acquaintance of Herman Melville and the brother of Supreme Court justice Stephen Field. Born in Connecticut, Field practiced law in New York and is best known today for the Field Code, which codified the common law and influenced legal reform throughout the English-speaking world. Field began his career as a Democrat. But his strong antislavery beliefs led him to become a Republican. In 1866, he helped to defend Lambdin P. Milligan in the most important civil liberties case to come out of the Civil War. Milligan was a vocal critic of Lincoln and the war effort. He was accused of conspiring with the Confederacy and convicted in a military tribunal, even though civil courts were open in his home state of Indiana. Field and his fellow lawyers Jeremiah S. Black, James Buchanan's attorney general, and future president James Garfield convinced the Supreme Court to release Milligan and declare unconstitutional Lincoln's creation of military tribunals trying civilians. Clearly reining in the power of the national government, this decision is rightly hailed today by civil libertarians. At the time, however, it was strongly criticized by advocates of Radical Reconstruction for potentially undermining their policies. That did not turn out to be true. Nonetheless, in 1876, Field again defended people accused of conspiracies. This time they were members of a white supremacist organization who participated in the massacre of African Americans in Colfax, Louisiana, on Easter Sunday, 1873. William Cruikshank and two others were convicted and tried in federal, not state, courts under the Enforcement and Ku Klux Klan Acts. Once again, Field prevailed, convincing the Supreme Court that "sovereignty, for the protection of the rights of life and personal liberty within the respective States, rests alone with the States." Between these major cases defining the jurisdictions of the states and the national government, Field made a fortune as a corporate lawyer working for, among others, the railroad giant Jay Gould and William (Boss) Tweed. At the same time, he directed his skills in codification toward international law, producing *Outlines of an International Code*. Encouraged by the American Peace Society, at international meetings Field advocated using his understanding of the US federal system as a model to avoid war. In 1876, the same year the *Cruikshank* opinion was announced and Field rejoined the Democratic Party, the Centennial Exposition in Philadelphia had a space for international law. As chair of the "International Code Committee of America," Field gave an address in part about the United States' contributions to world peace.[8]

Field and others were able to convince the Supreme Court that, in ratifying the Civil War Amendments, "the people did not suppose they were thereby changing the fundamental theory of their government" and its division of state and national powers. Even so, national power expanded in other areas. Even John Tyler Morgan, an ardent advocate of states' rights and white supremacy, agreed that the national government had increased powers in foreign affairs. Herein lies one of the paradoxes of the era. Reconstruction failed in part because of the inability and at times unwillingness of the national government to assert its new power. Yet in other areas, racial injustice was furthered by the assertion of new national power. In immigration, the national government insisted on its control over the states and developed an elaborate bureaucracy to deal with newly declared illegal immigrants, mostly Chinese. The national government also reaffirmed its power in relations with Native Americans by subduing tribes in the West and working to deny them traditional cultural practices. Finally, the newly united nation embarked on a campaign of imperialism, forcing newly conquered subjects into second-class citizenship. Reconstruction needs to be understood in relation to these developments, not apart from them.[9]

The importance of these issues has produced widely varying interpretations about their significance, making Reconstruction one of the most controversial periods in US history. It has proven far more controversial than the Civil War and, perhaps in part for that reason, gets less public attention. To acknowledge that many of its issues remain unresolved undercuts the belief that the country successfully reunited after civil strife. Yet trying to build a new nation without the institution of slavery and with an altered relationship between the states and the national government proved more difficult in many ways than waging war. While many today might agree with Foner that the country needs to complete its unfinished revolution, for years the prevailing view was that the nation survived only because Reconstruction failed. A typical account comes in a textbook of American history written in 1911 and revised in 1920 by David Saville Muzzey for a series edited by Columbia's James Harvey Robinson, the founder of the New History. Robinson praises the book for narrating the past so as to "explain prevailing conditions and institutions by showing how they have come about." According to Muzzey, Congress did the southern states "an unpardonable injury by hastening to reconstruct them on the basis of negro suffrage. The South would never have cherished resentment against the North for the defeat of 1861–1865 on the fair field of battle; but all the years that have passed since the death of Abraham Lincoln have hardly seen the extinction of the bitter passion roused in the hearts of the men, women and children of the South against their fellow countrymen of the North for 'the crime of Reconstruction.'" The phrase "the crime of Reconstruction" lacks a source. It stands, uncontested, as the white South's view of the period, accepted by scholars like Muzzey.[10]

Accounts like Muzzey's dominated the first half of the twentieth century. They are repeated as late as John F. Kennedy's *Profiles in Courage* (1957). Kennedy was also influenced by progressive historians, like Pulitzer Prize winner Allan Nevins, who organized "Professors for Kennedy" and wrote the preface for the inaugural edition of *Profiles in Courage.* Nevins's first book was *The Emergence of Modern America: 1865–1878*, published in 1927 as part of a series called A *History of American Life.* The series editors Arthur M. Schlesinger Sr. and Dixon Ryan Fox note how Nevins's emphasis on "economic and social development" goes beyond earlier studies whose "principal concern was with political and constitutional problems." Praising Nevins for treating "the whole episode of Reconstruction without a single reference to either Charles Sumner or Thaddeus Stevens," they promise that his book will revise "the older ideas of Reconstruction." Nevins does not, however, revise the view that "carpetbagger and Negro rule" was full of "maladies." Both the editors and Nevins accept that as established fact. While faulting various accounts for their "Southern point of view" and giving a generally positive portrait of the Freedmen's Bureau, Nevins buys into the "story of corruption, incompetence, and extravagance."[11]

In 1927, Charles and Mary Beard also turned to economic analysis of Reconstruction, just as earlier Charles made his mark with an iconoclastic economic interpretation of the Constitution. The two Beards stressed class warfare. In *The Rise of American Civilization* (1927), the Beards called the Civil War a second American Revolution, not because of emancipation but because it displaced the southern planter aristocracy from power and marked the ascendency of northern capitalists. Radical Reconstruction, which they also saw as misrule, was orchestrated by the business interests of northern bankers and industrialists. Although the Beards welcomed the demise of the planter class, they lamented the rise of capitalists who took control over farmers and laborers. That control, for them, persisted to the time of their writing. In 1929, after Republican Herbert Hoover exploited anti-

Catholic sentiment against his opponent Al Smith to win a number of southern states, the Beards and Nevins's friend Claude Bowers published *The Tragic Era: The Revolution After Lincoln.* Having won the admiration of Franklin Delano Roosevelt for plotting the country's history as a battle between the legacies of Jefferson and Hamilton, Bowers aimed his best-selling, melodramatic account of corrupt and greedy Republican misrule at bringing "the South back into line." The next year, Howard K. Beale independently supported the Beards and Bowers's narrative of class warfare and northern capitalist manipulation, an interpretation gaining favor with the onset of the Great Depression. In 1959, Stanley Coben summarized the "Beale thesis" as the

> view that Radical Reconstruction "was a successful attempt by northeastern business, acting through the Republican party, to control the national government for its own economic ends: notably the protective tariff, the national banks, [and] a 'sound currency.'" The Radical program is also said to have been "the method by which the 'Masters of Capital' . . . expected to exploit the resources of the southern states" behind federal protection. Western hostility to these eastern business designs was avoided by large appropriations for rivers, harbors, railroads, free land, and pensions, and by use of the ever-potent "bloody shirt." Thus is supposed to have been prevented a union of western and southern agrarian opposition to the industrial and financial masters of the East.[12]

W. E. B. Du Bois's powerfully revisionist *Black Reconstruction* was part of the move to economic analysis. If today his book, deservedly, is praised for countering the prevailing racist account, Du Bois insisted, "The whole development of Reconstruction was primarily an economic development" (*BR*, 721). To be sure, there were significant differences between Du Bois and supporters of the "Beale thesis." Du Bois praised Stevens and Sumner, while Bowers and Beale vilified them and tried to resurrect Andrew Johnson's reputation. Most important, for Du Bois the masters of capital were not behind radical measures. On the contrary, in 1876, they produced a successful counterrevolution by producing a "bargain between Big Business and the South" that brought Reconstruction to an end (*BR*, 691). Although Beale was not convinced by Du Bois's Marxist framework, he was attracted to Du Bois's attack on northern capitalists. In 1940, he wrote an influential essay defending a class-based interpretation while encouraging a reassessment of the role of African Americans. Praising Du Bois while faulting him for trying "to portray the Negro and certain whites of the rural South as a typical proletariat," Beale insists that we need "to see what the Negro really was and why he did not gain more from Reconstruction." In the 1950s, Beale's, Du Bois's, and the Beards' view of a northern capitalist conspiracy was discredited by empirical analysis, but Du

Bois and Beale's appeal for a racial reappraisal won the day. Writing in the midst of the Reagan administration, Foner pays homage to Beale and the Beards, favorably citing Beale's 1940 essay and self-consciously drawing on the Beards' description of "The Second American Revolution."[13]

II

It is a truism that contemporary concerns influence interpretations of any historical period or of any work of literature. Because the political stakes are so high, that is especially true of Reconstruction and its literature. As Michael W. Fitzgerald writes, "Reconstruction in scholarship has been shaped by its utility in furthering one or another political agenda, or at least in expressing an evolving racial ethos." After early interpretations of Reconstruction justified segregation, revisionist interpretations were in line with the civil rights movement of the twentieth century. More recent interpretations implicitly—and sometimes explicitly—participate in contemporary debates. Those interpretations frequently suggest different reasons why the egalitarian ideals of Reconstruction remain unfulfilled. Some focus on the construction of a discourse of white supremacy, which, it is implied, continues to exert a powerful influence. Others look at the failure to achieve the integrationist goals that Martin Luther King Jr. saw as its legacy. Steven Hahn challenges that "liberal integrationist framework" and stresses a black liberation struggle. Yet others fault the political agenda of Radical Reconstruction for its neglect of issues of class and gender. Literary analysis includes all of these interpretations and more.[14]

It would be naive to think that we can completely escape contemporary presuppositions in scholarly work. On the contrary, as Hans Georg Gadamer powerfully argued in response to efforts to construct a method ensuring objective understanding of the past, it is precisely our "Vorurteilen," our pre-judgments or prejudices, that, as a product of the past, give us access to a world we no longer inhabit. For Gadamer, however, that is only a starting point. If our prejudices give us access to the past, then through a circular hermeneutical process our tentative understandings of the past have the capacity to alter our present perspectives. But those who stay entrenched in black and white judgments of an era or of the literary works written about it cannot participate in this movement toward a fuller understanding—which brings me to the title of this introduction.[15]

Even after passage of the Thirteenth, Fourteenth, and Fifteenth Amendments, and the Civil Rights Act of 1866, Charles Sumner felt the nation needed a more comprehensive civil rights act to supplement the one of 1866. The Civil War, he insisted to Congress, was fought over equality of rights. "Only by maintaining

Equality will you maintain the great victory of the war." Waxing eloquent, he enthused, "There is beauty in art, in literature, in science, and in every triumph of intelligence, all of which I covet for my country; but there is a higher beauty still in relieving the poor, in elevating the down-trodden. There is a true grandeur in an example of justice, making the rights of all the same as our own." He then proposed making it a federal crime to discriminate on the basis of color in public transportation, accommodations, entertainment, and education, as well as in jury duty and burial. As he lay dying in 1874, he pleaded with his friend Frederick Douglass to get the bill passed. But Democrats swept the 1874 fall elections, giving them control of the House for the first time since before the Civil War. The new Congress would be seated in March of 1875. To honor Sumner, Republicans decided to propose his bill to the lame-duck Congress. Various compromises forced elimination of the provisions for schools and cemeteries. Nonetheless, enjoying the irony, House Republicans added as a preamble a plank from the Democratic 1872 national platform pledging equal rights to all men before the law. The new, watered-down bill passed. Yet, in 1883, the Supreme Court declared the act unconstitutional, arguing that the Fourteenth Amendment prohibited the actions of states, not individuals. States, not the national government, regulated the actions of individuals.[16]

Soon thereafter, George Washington Cable, a novelist and a former Confederate soldier, argued that, despite the Supreme Court's decision, the nation had an equitable duty to treat African Americans as the citizens they had in name become. No longer should they be treated, as they continued to be treated, as aliens and menials. The Atlanta journalist Henry Grady responded to Cable by claiming that the truly equitable solution to the "race problem" was a system of separate but equal segregation. He called his response "In Plain Black and White," asserting, "Clear views, clear statement, and clear understanding are the demands of the hour. Given these, the common sense and courage of the American people will make the rest easy."[17]

My book is an extended argument against both meanings of Grady's punning title. A system of black and white segregation was not equitable. Nor did it reflect the population of the United States, which had multiple racial makeups. Indeed, most Jim Crow laws separated not blacks and whites but whites and "coloreds," with the latter comprised of a variety of admixtures. Even though I, along with almost everyone writing about nineteenth-century racial issues, will use the opposition of blacks and whites, it is important to remember that the opposition in large part grows out of the era of segregation. At the time, racial classification was by no means so clear-cut. Equally important, I argue against Grady's belief that there were commonsensical, black and white solutions to the issues of the day.

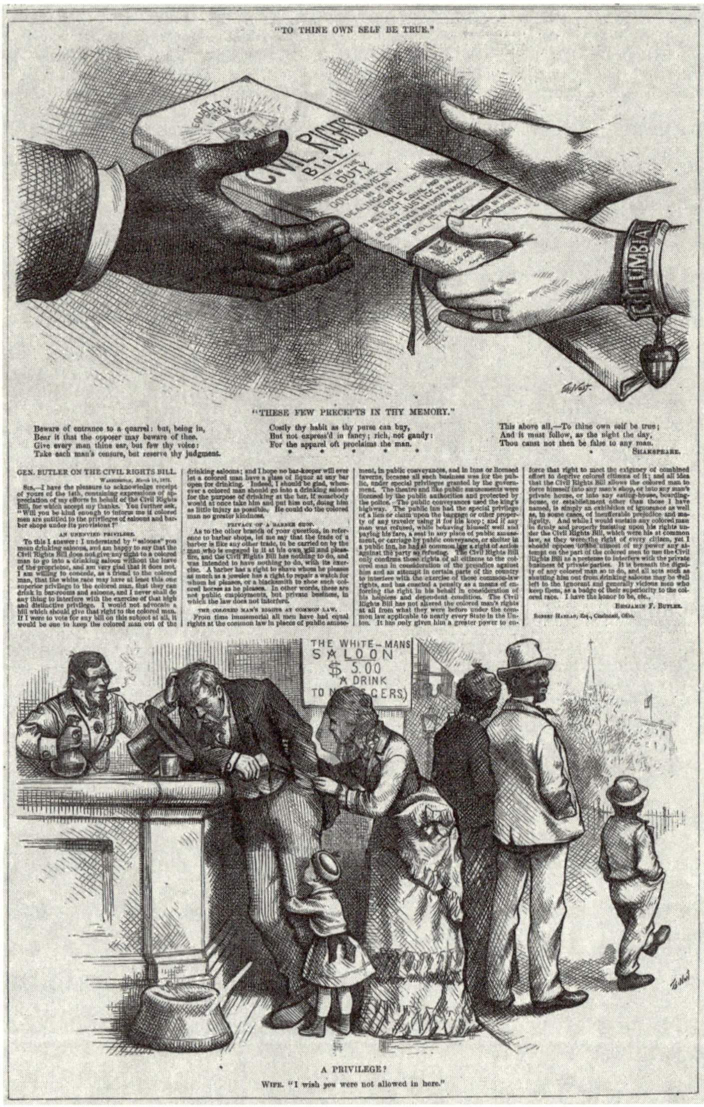

"TO THINE OWN SELF BE TRUE."

"THESE FEW PRECEPTS IN THY MEMORY."

Beware of entrance to a quarrel: but, being in,
Bear it that the opposer may beware of thee.
Give every man thine ear, but few thy voice:
Take each man's censure, but reserve thy judgment.

Costly thy habit as thy purse can buy,
But not express'd in fancy; rich, not gaudy:
For the apparel oft proclaims the man.
* * *

This above all,—To thine own self be true;
And it must follow, as the night the day,
Thou canst not then be false to any man.
*
SHAKSPEARE.

GEN. BUTLER ON THE CIVIL RIGHTS BILL.

WASHINGTON, March [illegible], 1875.

SIR,—I have the pleasure to acknowledge receipt of yours of the 14th, containing expressions of appreciation of my efforts in behalf of the Civil Rights Bill, for which accept my thanks. You further ask, "Will you be kind enough to inform me if colored men are entitled to the privileges of saloons and barber shops under its provisions?"

AN UNENVIED PRIVILEGE.

To this I answer: I understand by "saloons" you mean drinking saloons, and am happy to say that the Civil Rights Bill does not give any right to a colored man to go into a drinking saloon without the leave of the proprietor, and am very glad that it does not. I am willing to concede, as a friend to the colored man, that the white race may have at least this one superior privilege to the colored man, that they can drink in bar-rooms and saloons, and I never shall do any thing to interfere with the exercise of that high and distinctive privilege. I would not advocate a bill which should give that right to the colored man. If I were to vote for any bill on this subject at all, it would be one to keep the colored man out of the drinking saloons; and I hope no bar-keeper will ever let a colored man have a glass of liquor at any bar open for drinking. Indeed, I should be glad, whenever a colored man should go into a drinking saloon for the purpose of drinking at the bar, if somebody would at once take him and put him out, doing him as little injury as possible. He could do the colored man no greater kindness.

PRIVACY OF A BARBER SHOP.

As to the other branch of your question, in reference to barber shops, let me say that the trade of a barber is like any other trade, to be carried on by the man who is engaged in it at his own will and pleasure, and the Civil Rights Bill has nothing to do, and was intended to have nothing to do, with its exercise. A barber has a right to shave whom he pleases as much as a jeweler has a right to repair a watch for whom he pleases, or a blacksmith to shoe such colored horses as he pleases. In other words, these are not public employments, but private business, in which the law does not interfere.

THE COLORED MAN'S RIGHTS AT COMMON LAW.

From time immemorial all men have had equal rights at the common law in places of public amusement, in public conveyances, and in inns or licensed taverns, because all such business was for the public, under special privileges granted by the government. The theatre and like public amusements were licensed by the public authorities and protected by the police. The public conveyances used the king's highway. The public inn had the special privilege of a lien or claim upon the baggage or other property of any traveler using it for his keep; and if any man was refused, while behaving himself well and paying his fare, a seat in any place of public amusement, or carriage by public conveyance, or shelter in a public inn, he had at common law a right of action against the party so refusing. The Civil Rights Bill only confirms these rights of all citizens to the colored man in consideration of the prejudice against him and an attempt in certain parts of the country to interfere with the exercise of those common-law rights, and has enacted a penalty as a means of enforcing the right in his behalf in consideration of his helpless and dependent condition. The Civil Rights Bill has not altered the colored man's rights at all from what they were before under the common law applicable to nearly every State in the Union. It has only given him a greater power to enforce that right to meet the exigency of combined effort to deprive colored citizens of it; and all idea that the Civil Rights Bill allows the colored man to force himself into any man's shop, or into any man's private house, or into any eating-house, boarding-house, or establishment other than those I have named, is simply an exhibition of ignorance as well as, in some cases, of insufferable prejudice and malignity. And while I would sustain any colored man in firmly and properly insisting upon his rights under the Civil Rights Bill, which were his at common law, as they were the right of every citizen, yet I should oppose to the utmost of my power any attempt on the part of the colored men to use the Civil Rights Bill as a pretense to interfere with the private business of private parties. It is beneath the dignity of any colored man so to do, and all acts such as shutting him out from drinking saloons may be well left to the ignorant and generally vicious men who keep them, as a badge of their superiority to the colored race. I have the honor to be, etc.,

BENJAMIN F. BUTLER.

ROBERT HARLAN, Esq., Cincinnati, Ohio.

A PRIVILEGE?

WIFE. "I wish you were not allowed in here."

In the upper image from *Harper's Weekly*, Thomas Nast evokes Shakespeare's *Hamlet* to depict the nation being true to itself by passing the Civil Rights Bill of 1875, forbidding discrimination against African Americans in many public spaces. In the lower image, he ironically shows a whites-only saloon serving a drunken white man whose wife and daughter wish that he, like the respectable African American family turned away, was denied access. Between the two images is the speech that Representative Benjamin F. Butler delivered introducing the bill, including high praise for African Americans' service in the Civil War.

An alternative to Grady's way of thinking can be found in Howells's one extended treatment of race. There is strong evidence that Howells wrote *An Imperative Duty* (1891) with Grady and Cable's debate in mind. He has a character mention "Mr. Cable's books" (*ID*, 78) and another insist on "race instinct" (69), which Grady used to justify segregation. The same character worries about "social equality" (51), which Grady accused Cable of advocating and Cable called that "huge bugbear." Howells describes this character as conceiving of "what she called living up to the truth as something that might be done singly; that right affected her as a body of positive color, sharply distinguished from wrong, and not shading into and out of it by gradations of tint, as we find it doing in reality" (55–56). In a story about a mixed-race character who could pass as white, Howells's comment challenges Grady's belief that both human beings and human judgments are black and white. In doing so, it does not level all distinctions. That gradations of tint shade into one another does not mean that all individuals have the same skin color or, more importantly, that there is no space for judgment, as Howells's criticism of black and white thinking makes clear. What Howells advocates are more refined discriminations and judgments.[18]

Nonetheless, perhaps more than any other era in American history, Reconstruction has provoked black and white responses. Those responses take many forms. Most obvious is the division of races. But there are also historically fluctuating judgments as to whether Reconstruction was good or bad. Those judgments are linked to black and white accounts of causation. For instance, in 1980, Michael Les Benedict argued that historians "now agree that racial rather than economic issues determined the course of Reconstruction." To me, it makes more sense to explore the complicated interaction between racial and economic, as well as political, legal, and other causes. Black and white judgments and accounts of causation have, in turn, fostered narratives about periodization with a clear-cut divide between a time when Reconstruction was supported and when it failed. Finally, the moral judgments of Reconstruction have tended to focus on the wrongs committed, either against prostrate white southerners or abandoned freedmen. Identifying wrongs can be morally satisfying, but coming up with remedies is a much more complicated task. Indeed, one of the causes of wrongs in the era was the desire to seek black and white solutions. Works of literature can remind us of how complicated attempts to come up with remedies were and how complicated they remain today.[19]

Gregory Downs has recently taken to task scholars who underestimate the difficulties facing the nation by indulging in the myth that the time directly after Appomattox opened a "window of enormous opportunity" when the South "might have accepted anything." On the contrary, he insists, the only way to control a resistant white southern population was through military occupation and the "threat of force." The problems Reconstruction raised did not have simple solutions, in part because there was no agreement about what the goals of Reconstruction were. Although today many assume that the goal was to bring about racial equality, a proposed syllabus for teaching high school American history in 1921 does not even mention that goal. Instead, it lists "three great tasks":

1. Re-establishing broken political unity.
2. Recovery from the losses of war.
3. Re-vamping the economic life of a section which had been using an ancient and outworn labor system.

Limiting the goals to these three allowed teachers to declare Reconstruction a success and fit segregation into a narrative of the nation's continuing progress. After all, the nation did unite politically, recover from the devastation of war, and transform the economic system of the South. The description of the old economic system as an "ancient and outworn labor system" is especially significant. In addition to failing to mention slavery, it implies that the economy of the New South was a progressive advancement, not a system designed to keep most freedmen in subservient conditions. To be sure, when the syllabus goes on to note the "transition from slave to free labor system of production," it cites two essays by Du Bois. But the failure to list the goal of racial equality greatly simplifies the task at hand.[20]

At the same time, a singular focus on the goal of racial equality can also simplify the story. Bringing about racial equality was difficult enough as it was. To do so simultaneously with reuniting politically, rebuilding after the destruction of war, and transforming a region's economic system was a Herculean task. The story gets even more complicated if we add to the mix claims by some white southerners that the real goal of Radical Republicans was to exact revenge on the South by imposing "Negro rule" or the more credible claim that their primary goal was not racial equality but maintaining party dominance in the South and, thus, the nation. The goals of Reconstruction are themselves a source of historical debate.

Even the Civil War amendments that provided the constitutional basis for possible racial equality have a complicated legacy, and not only because by the end of the era their powers had been eroded. Foner provides a helpful summary of different reactions to the Fifteenth Amendment. Obviously, many white southerners adamantly opposed it, but it was also criticized by some who claimed to champion equality. Elizabeth Cady Stanton attacked it for favoring ethnic males over white women of culture and refinement. "Think of Patrick and Sambo and Hans and Yung Tung who do not know the difference between a Monarchy and a Republic, who never read the Declaration of Independence . . . making laws for Lydia Maria

Child, Lucretia Mott, or Fanny Kemble." Women were not the only people left out. Restrictions could still be made based on property, education, and literacy. Some of these restrictions were more prominent in the North than in the South. Henry Adams called the amendment "more remarkable for what it does not than for what it does contain." In contrast, for James Garfield, it was the culmination of Reconstruction. It "confers upon the African race the care of its own destiny. It places their fortunes in their own hands." But for Wendell Phillips and Tourgée, such celebrations were dangerous, since both argued that suffrage alone would not be enough.[21]

The Fourteenth Amendment, which was so important for the twentieth-century civil rights movement, has its own complicated legacy. Today's focus is almost exclusively on Section 1, with its citizenship, privileges and immunities, due process, and equal protection clauses. At the time, however, Sections 2, 3, and 4 were some of the most controversial. Section 2 got rid of the infamous three-fifths provision of the original constitution but required that if a particular group, like African Americans, was denied the right to vote, then the state's number of representatives in Congress would be determined by the state's population reduced by the disenfranchised percentage. Section 3 disqualified many former Confederates from holding national office. Section 4 had to do with the debt incurred by Confederate states during the insurrection. Barely mentioned today, these sections remind us of how partisan the amendment was.

Section 1 also had an unexpected effect. The first two clauses of Section 1 have to do with citizens. The "due process" and "equal protection" clauses refer to persons. Because corporations by a fiction of the law are legal persons, the Fourteenth Amendment was frequently used to protect corporate interests. By 1911, the Supreme Court had heard 607 Fourteenth Amendment cases. Of these, 312 involved corporations; thirty involved the rights of racial minorities.[22]

A novel approach to the Thirteenth Amendment came from Edward A. Pollard, the author of *The Lost Cause*. According to Pollard, a strict proponent of states' rights, the amendment, properly interpreted, should have little effect. Slavery, he claimed, was abolished only in those places subject to the jurisdiction of the United States, which he argued was confined in the South to customhouses and military barracks. Much more serious, the prohibition on slavery and involuntary servitude was used to justify restrictions on Chinese immigration. As Stacey L. Smith has shown, on the West Coast, Chinese coolie labor was denounced as a different brand of slavery. Likewise, Chinese women were considered either slaves to their husbands or prostitutes. Immigration of Chinese laborers and women was, therefore, against the spirit of the Thirteenth Amendment. Another effect arose out of the amendment's declaration that the only exception to abolishing slavery and involuntary servitude is "punishment for crime whereof the party shall have been duly convicted." Jeannine DeLombard points to how one way in which African Americans in the antebellum period gained legal status was through the criminal justice system. The Thirteenth Amendment, unintentionally, contributed to the post-emancipation association of African Americans with crime.[23]

III

I began this introduction arguing that attention to works of literature can enhance our historical understanding of Reconstruction. Even though there is an imbalance between literary and historical analysis of the era, I am, of course, not the first person to deal with its literature. But I approach the topic differently than historians and literary critics who came before me. Harvard historian Paul Buck won a Pulitzer Prize in 1939 for *The Road to Reunion: 1865–1900*, which gives substantial attention to literature. But his emphasis on reconciliation generates a sanitized defense of segregation. Edmund Wilson's *Patriotic Gore* (1962) is misleading for a variety of reasons. Writing a hundred years after the outbreak of the Civil War, he was more influenced by the Cold War than the civil rights movement. Understandably skeptical of concentrated power in the national state and the rise of the imperial presidency, Wilson traced the cause of civil strife to the desire to establish a centralized government. Afterward, he claims, the "needling and meddling of Reconstruction" imposed the new order on the South. Furthermore, as authoritative as Wilson tries to sound, his literary judgments are idiosyncratic. He dismisses Cable's *John March, Southerner* as a thorough "bore" and faults Page's *Red Rock* for being "as boring as Cable's *John March.*" Anyone relying on Wilson has a ready excuse to avoid reading these long but, to my mind, important novels. To be sure, more recently historians Nina Silber and K. Stephen Prince have written compelling books about the era's literature. Silber's *The Romance of Reunion* (1993) has become a standard reference for literary critics.[24] Nonetheless, despite the diminished difference between cultural historians and literary critics doing cultural studies, historians rarely read works as closely as those trained in literary studies.[25] For instance, in his accomplished *Race and Reunion: The Civil War in American Memory*, David Blight has a chapter called "The Literature of Reunion and Its Discontents." With the exception of W. E. B. Du Bois, his canon resembles that of Wilson, and although he praises Tourgée's writing as "the literary equivalent of Frederick Douglass's oratory" in keeping emancipatory memory alive, he spends far more time on Tourgée's essay about the South in fiction than on the fiction itself. The devil is in the detail. We need to pay attention to the details of authors' competing imaginative visions, not simply make historical points.[26]

Of course, both historians and literary critics need to generalize. Yet some commonly accepted generalizations need to be challenged. For instance, recently Dixon has received considerable critical attention, but too many scholars continue to agree with Nicholas Lemann's claim that Dixon expresses "the standard views of white Southerners of his generation and class." A close reading reveals that, in fact, Dixon was often at odds with other white southerners politically and economically. Works by Dixon and Page, which would seem to be allied, have significant differences. At the same time, despite their obvious differences, those by Dixon and Tourgée have some surprising similarities. To make Dixon representative of the South is to simplify him and the multiple voices of the South. "Cultural production," as Prince notes, "is seldom neat and tidy." Close readings of individual works can play havoc with our efforts to generalize. Close readings of multiple works are almost certain to do so.[27]

One reason for the relative neglect of the literature of Reconstruction by literary critics is that, as much as any literature written at any time, it demands close attention to history. It is difficult to keep straight all of the complicated details of Reconstruction while also keeping up with new advances in historiography. I have tried my best to do both. On the one hand, I hope that my close attention to works of literature complicates at least some historical generalization about both the literature and the era; on the other, I hope to enhance our understanding of Reconstruction literature by drawing on some long neglected historiography, as well as excellent work done since Foner's brilliant synthesis. Thus, although I am sure to commit errors along the way, I do not, as even accomplished literary critics have, assume that the "one-drop rule" was the legal norm at the time; claim that the Fourteenth, not the Fifteenth, Amendment addressed the right to vote for African American men; or define "carpetbaggers" as "scavengers who moved South with all their belongings in nineteenth-century suitcases made of carpet."[28]

Another reason for the relative neglect of the literature of Reconstruction is the traditional definition of the postbellum era as the age of literary realism. The realists rarely depicted Reconstruction directly, causing some critics to prefer confronting the issues it raised through readings of *The Bostonians*, *Adventures of Huckleberry Finn*, or even *Billy Budd*, rather than through engaging works about Reconstruction itself. To be sure, the last generation has extensively revised the period's canon by adding works by women and minorities, and the African American writers I include have received extensive critical scrutiny. Some white male writers have not. In his classic study of the society and culture of the times, Trachtenberg has a chapter on "The Fictions of the Real" but pays almost no attention to the writers I treat in this book. Similarly, although Kenneth W. Warren's groundbreaking first book, *Black and White Strangers: Race in American Literary Realism* is indebted to

Tourgée's criticism of the realists, Warren does not read any of Tourgée's literary works. He does, however, engage Francis Harper's *Iola Leroy*, certainly not a work of realism. In the profession, even African American writers are treated selectively. Frederick Douglass's antislavery writings are regularly taught, but for many of our students, he may as well have died with Emancipation, even though he continued to write and play a major role until his death in 1895.[29]

I should not exaggerate. Critics like Robert Levine are devoting more attention to Douglass's postbellum writing. Tourgée is undergoing a revival of sorts. De-Lombard has produced an excellent chapter on the relation of postbellum novels and the Reconstruction amendments. Sharon D. Kennedy-Nolle has written a recent book with a writer representing each military district. In addition, there is an established field of southern literary study. Outstanding critics such as Lewis Simpson, Louis Rubin, and Fred Hobson addressed many works that remain neglected today, even though, in a version of institutional segregation, for years these critics' work was featured most prominently in journals of southern literature. Recently, that situation has been addressed by the "new southern studies," which has placed works of Reconstruction literature in a national and transnational context. With its transnational emphasis, the new southern studies tries to go beyond Foner's insistence that Reconstruction is a national, not a regional, issue.[30]

As much as I have learned from literary critics associated with this new field, however, I share Downs's sympathetic caution about an almost revivalist enthusiasm for transnationalism. Downs acknowledges that we can understand domestic politics in this period "only through the lens of transnationalism." But he counters Sven Beckert's claim that transnationalism is a "way of seeing" by suggesting that it is a "way of looking." Transnationalism is a "method, not an outcome." In terms of politics, looking transnationally during the era of Reconstruction did not always produce a transnational result. On the contrary, "A powerful U.S. exceptionalism arose in the stabilization of the 1880s not from blind breast-beating but, among other factors, from meaningful engagement with anti-exceptionalist analogies advanced in transnational circulations. Just as transnationalism produced surprising outcomes in the historical past, so too should its practice now be open to nuance, contradiction, and even affirmation of the importance of national political histories, albeit stranger and more surprising ones." To be blunt, it used to be commonplace to point out how politicians distracted people's attention from domestic problems by, in Shakespeare's words, busying "giddy minds with foreign quarrels." Recently, it has become fashionable to argue that a focus on domestic issues blinds us to their true transnational significance. We need to look transnationally, but doing so should not keep us from seeing the continued importance of domestic conflicts.[31]

I can focus on my differences with some work in the new southern literary studies, transnational and other, by turning to one of its most celebrated practitioners. The third and last section of Jennifer Rae Greeson's *Our South: Geographic Fantasy and the Rise of National Literature* is "The Question of Empire/The Reconstruction South." Like me and a number of other literary critics, Greeson reads turn-of-the-century works of Reconstruction fiction in relation to the US's imperial adventures. Like me, she also challenges a black and white account of the era. There was, she argues, at one time a hybrid account. But, about the time of the Spanish-American War, sparked by the "infamous 'Dunning school'" and its revisionist historiography, an "epochal shift" occurred in which a "rigidly biracial story of Reconstruction" emerged in conjunction with "the increasingly hegemonic belief that the United States was, explicitly, a 'white man's nation.'" "This aggressive reinterpretation of the Reconstruction South was ensconced in mainstream discourse," she concludes, "when the *Atlantic Monthly* devoted its entire 1901 volume to articles on the subject by Dunning's adherents."[32]

The primary basis for Greeson's argument linking an "epochal shift" to a transnational moment is her reading of Page's *Red Rock* in a section called "Retelling Reconstruction during the Spanish-Philippine-American War." Many works of literature at this time have links to the war in the Philippines, but *Red Rock* is not one of them. Although Page's novel about Reconstruction appeared in 1898, he completed it before the Spanish-American War and certainly before the United States' civil war with the Philippines after its annexation. In fact, he had been working on his story for over a decade. To read Page's novel allegorically as creating "forms for the affective assimilation of the occupation of the Philippines into U.S. culture" is to force a transnational reading when one is not appropriate. The problem is exacerbated when Greeson pairs *Red Rock* with Pauline Hopkins's *Contending Forces*. Because the action of Hopkins's novel begins on the island of Bermuda, Greeson insists that her protagonists' fates resonate with those of Filipinos and the "deposed Queen Lilioukalani of Hawai'i," seeming to forget that Hopkins's chosen subtitle highlights the domestic scene: "A Romance Illustrative of Negro Life North and South."[33]

Greeson's argument about an "epochal shift" also relies on a misreading of the *Atlantic Monthly* series she cites. Although Dunning was given the honor of concluding the series, other contributors were not his adherents. On the contrary, the editors sought a variety of perspectives. In addition to asking Dunning, they invited a former Confederate, who was President Grover Cleveland's secretary of war; a former carpetbagger governor of South Carolina who had earlier helped to prosecute members of the Ku Klux Klan but by 1901 had second thoughts about his policies; a southern expert on Louisiana; a Massachusetts congressman; a historian from Alabama working at Harvard; the Virginian novelist Page; and Woodrow Wilson, who was trained at Johns Hopkins, noted for rivaling Dunning's Columbia and Harvard as a center for the study of American history. Some of these contributors shared Dunning's negative view of Reconstruction, but one of the most notable contributors did not. Du Bois was asked to write on the Freedmen's Bureau. His essay begins by stating for the first time in print: "The problem of the twentieth century is the problem of the color line."[34]

The editors seem to agree with Du Bois as much as with Dunning. Prior to Dunning's concluding essay, there is a short, anonymous piece, "Reconstruction and Disfranchisement," that expresses their point of view. "The Southern negroes," it argues, "in spite of every shortcoming and disadvantage, are slowly, but surely, making headway. Every consideration, whether of economics or of humanity, demands that they should have an open road. They will do the traveling." The essay explicitly disagrees with Page, who had used his contribution to argue that whites should have political control. Quoting Page, the editors insist that "'intelligence, virtue, and force of character' are not the endowment of the Anglo-Saxon exclusively. Their roots sink deeper than those of racial peculiarity into the soil of our common humanity." Granted, the piece comes off as conservative today because it favorably quotes "Booker Washington's famous sentence, 'in all things purely social as separate as the fingers, yet one as the hand in all things essential to mutual progress.'" But the essay concludes by expressing faith "that the plain people, of whatever blood or creed, are capable of governing themselves." If the *Atlantic* series was representative of popular opinion, that opinion was much more conflicted than Greeson claims.[35]

Even her dismissal of the "Dunning school" needs complicating. Without a doubt, Dunning and those working with him gave an account of Reconstruction that legitimated the regime of legalized segregation taking hold at the end of the century. Nonetheless, Greeson's dismissal is based more on reputation than a close reading of what Dunning and his colleagues actually wrote. Like many today, she couples the adjective "infamous" to "the Dunning school" and then cites a representative racist comment. Whereas usually the citation is one Du Bois called attention to years ago, Greeson lifts hers from Peter Novick in *That Noble Dream*, and it is not by Dunning or one of his students but by Ellis Paxson Oberholtzer. As much as we may disagree with Dunning and his colleagues, a recent collection has shown that there are a number of reasons for giving their work the attention that Du Bois gave it. For one, much of the empirical evidence they uncovered from countless hours in the archive, while selective, is accurate. That evidence can be used, as Du Bois used it, to provide a different interpretation of the times. In addition, Dunning's students constitute a "school" only in a loose sense. One of his most famous was Charles E. Merriam Jr., who did not write on Reconstruction but became the "father" of behavioral political science. Other students wrote on Reconstruction's effect in northern states. Even the scholars writing on southern states who are lumped together as a "school" have important differences from one another. Dunning himself anticipates Greeson and other advocates of the new southern studies by understanding Reconstruction in a national and a transnational context. His *Reconstruction: Political and Economic, 1865–1877* (1907) was part of "The American Nation" series edited by Albert Bushnell Hart. In 1909, Hart, who saw himself in the abolitionist tradition, worked to have Du Bois, his former student, deliver a talk at the American Historical Association that became the basis of *Black Reconstruction*. In the preface to his own book, Dunning insists that, whereas in most studies of Reconstruction "the South bulks largest . . . we must regard the period as a step in the progress of the American nation. In this aspect the North claims our principle attention. The social, economic, and political forces that wrought positively for progress are to be found in the record, not of the vanquished, but of the victorious section." Dunning also includes a chapter called "A Critical Period in Foreign Relations," with a map of "North America and the West Indies," including Mexico and Central America. Indeed, Dunning's interests at the time transcended national boundaries. Between his first book of Reconstruction essays and his 1907 book, he published two volumes on the history of political thought, which occupied much of his teaching.[36]

It seems to me that those studying the literature of Reconstruction have a special obligation to understand Dunning. For instance, his 1898 collection of essays is reputed to have inaugurated his "school," which painted a picture of corrupt carpetbagger and African American rule. Yet, the preface to that collection claims that its essays challenge the prevailing idea that Reconstruction is "merely a synonym for bad government." Indeed, while generally critical, Du Bois favorably cites Dunning in *Reconstruction, Political and Economic* and his insistence that "the form and manner of this corruption, which has given so unsavory a connotation to the name 'reconstruction,' were no different from those which have appeared many another time and place in democratic society" (*BR*, 618). Distancing himself from others, Dunning tried to convey an "idea of the profound problems of statecraft that had to be solved between 1865 and 1870." We may not agree with his assessment of how those problems were solved, but we can benefit from understanding the problems he identified. After all, the work of Dunning and his dissertation advisor John W. Burgess is part of the context in which a number of literary authors wrote. Even Henry James reviewed Dunning's *Essays on the Civil War and Reconstruction*, commending it, finding it "irresistible to read" the professor's account of the "immense social revolution," and expressing nostalgia for "the romantic idea" of state sovereignty. Some authors drew on the works of Dunning and his colleagues; others contested them. In either case, it is important to know what they actually wrote.[37]

Dunning's work may be part of the context in which various authors wrote, but there are numerous ways to relate works to their context. Greeson uses that relationship to support her claim about an epochal shift taking place "in just a few years at the turn of the twentieth century." She selects representative works to stand for the period before and the period after the shift. Various references to the Africanization of the South and the "locally colored Creole zone" of Cable's Louisiana fiction are her evidence of the earlier hybrid account. Page's *Red Rock* is evidence of the black and white account. But there is a problem with using any work to represent a period. At the same time that Cable was writing his creolized fiction, people North and South insisted that the United States was a white man's nation. Likewise, at the same time that Page was insisting on a rigidly biracial story of the Reconstruction South, writers like Hopkins were contesting it and affirming Cable's creole vision. In arguing for an epochal shift, Greeson does what many critics do. She turns what is a synchronic, if varying, conflict that persists throughout an era into a diachronic narrative about the sudden emergence of one element of that conflict. Intent on undercutting a black and white racial account of Reconstruction, Greeson produces a black and white narrative about periodization in which one view replaces another. A much more difficult challenge is to account for change without relying on black and white narratives of periodization. That challenge arises in defining the period of Reconstruction itself, which I need to do to clarify what I mean by the "literature of Reconstruction."[38]

IV

Is the literature of Reconstruction written during the period? Or is it about the period? Or is it both? These questions are even more complicated because it is not completely clear how we should define the period. During the Civil War, the president and Congress began planning for Reconstruction. Once the war ended, Lincoln's relatively mild plan was in large part taken over by Johnson and prevailed until 1867, when Congress asserted its powers and initiated radical measures. Then, Reconstruction, it is commonly assumed, ended when President Rutherford B. Hayes came into office on March 5, 1877, following the disputed election of 1876. With Hayes's "New Departure" federal troops were no longer called upon to prop up Reconstruction governments. Thus, Foner dates Reconstruction in his book from 1863 to 1877.[39]

But the dates of Reconstruction are not as certain as they are frequently taught. Even if there is general agreement that Reconstruction began before the war ended, few know the official end of the conflict. Most people think it was Lee's surrender to Grant at Appomattox on April 9, 1865. With its handshake between a southern gentleman and a rough northerner who granted generous terms to defeated troops, this event has such symbolic power that it will never be dislodged from the popular imagination. But seventeen days later a larger army under General Joseph F. Johnston surrendered to General William T. Sherman near Durham Station, North Carolina. A week later a small force in Alabama capitulated, and a month after that Kirby Smith's Trans-Mississippi Army surrendered at New Orleans. Even then the war was not officially over. As late as April 2, 1866, President Johnson declared the insurrection at an end everywhere but Texas. Finally, on August 20, 1866, he proclaimed the Civil War over. The end of hostilities was much messier than the image of an honorable southern surrender created by what Gregory Downs calls the "dangerous myth of Appomattox."[40]

Designating 1877 as the end of Reconstruction has created its own myths. Because we know that momentum for Reconstruction's policies was never successfully restored after the Compromise of 1877, Hayes's election marks a logical endpoint. In a book about the *Plessy* case, I wrote, "A compromise was worked out in which Hayes was given a one-vote majority in the electoral college in return for an end to Reconstruction." In 1877, however, people did not have our retrospective knowledge, and the year had a different significance. Literature can help us here. Cable's *John March, Southerner* (1894) extends from just after the Civil War into the 1890s, with most of the action occurring after 1877. Yet a contemporary review called it "the most careful and thoroughgoing study of the reconstruction period in the South which has yet been offered the world in the form of fiction." Cable's "The Freedman's Case in Equity" distinguishes between "the days of compulsory reconstruction" and "these days of voluntary reconstruction." In Hopkins's *Contending Forces* (1900), during a conversation set at the turn of the century, a visiting Englishman responds to an African American's lament that "constitutional equality is a political fiction" by asking, "Reconstruction is a failure, then?" (297)—*is* a failure, not *was* a failure. The response: "Reconstruction is not a failure, although the whole South will tell you so, and the North is being persuaded to so believe; the Negro was the living force which rent asunder the old methods of the slave-holding states and brought them out into the healthful light of decent, God-fearing living." The editors of the 1901 *Atlantic Monthly* series on Reconstruction note, "Reconstruction began with enfranchisement; it is ending with disfranchisement."[41]

Tourgée's novels provide ample evidence for why we should not think of 1877 as marking a black and white divide. In a *Fool's Errand*, he writes how, "in the winter of 1868–1869 . . . The wise men were jubilant over the success of the Great Experiment, when it was said that already Reconstruction had become an approved success" (182). If the "wise men" prematurely think that Reconstruction succeeded so rapidly, Tourgée himself marks a preliminary ending, not with success but with the "redemption" of North Carolina as early as 1870. He describes how, "as soon as the reconstruction period had passed," the southern press relaxed its caution and began a "verbal crusade" against anyone "engaged in the work of reconstruction" (173–74). In *Bricks without Straw*, he reaffirms the importance of 1870 by having his narrator note, "The period of actual reconstruction had passed and independent, self-regulating states had taken the place of Military Districts and Provisional Governments. The people of the South began, little by little, to realize that they held their future in their own hands—that the supervising and restraining power of the General Government had been withdrawn" (200). In other words, well before Hayes's inauguration, many states had been redeemed. Thus, in *Division and Reunion: 1829–1889*, Woodrow Wilson titles chapter 11, "Reconstruction (1865–1870)." The importance of 1877, as Tourgée notes in *A Fool's Errand*, is that "the last of the governments organized under the policy of reconstruction fell into the hands of those who had inaugurated and carried on the war against the nation" (314). Even so, for Tourgée and others, 1877 did not mark an end. His book goes on for one hundred pages after 1877 arrives. While writing *A Fool's Errand* and *Bricks without Straw*, Tourgée did not believe that chances for a renewal of the goals of Reconstruction were over. On the contrary, he wrote hoping to convince the nation that there was still a chance that the former Confederate states would be truly "re-constructed," not simply "re-created" (*FE*, 236). His hopes soared when his novels helped elect his friend James Garfield president. Garfield's inaugural address suggests that Tourgée's hope might not have been completely unfounded had Garfield avoided assassination.[42]

Although he had a different view of Reconstruction policies, in his *Atlantic Monthly* essay Dunning confirms Tourgée's account of its dates. Like Tourgée, he designates 1870 as the date when "the process of reconstruction was, from the technical point, complete." For Dunning, the crucial event was passage of a law entitling the final former Confederate state, Georgia, to representation in Congress. The events of 1877 are significant for marking the "first period in the undoing of reconstruction." A second period lasts until the 1890s. Even after 1877, he notes, "negroes were precisely equal in rights with the other race, and the Republican party was a powerful organization in the South." According to Dunning, it was not until Democrats controlled both houses of Congress and the presidency in 1893 that these conditions came near to an end. In 1901, with the Supreme Court yet to act on the constitutionality of disfranchising enactments, he says that "the undoing of reconstruction is nearing completion." Published the same year, Chesnutt's *The Marrow of Tradition* reminds us that fusion governments of whites and blacks won election in the South after 1893. Even the fact that Joel Chandler Harris, Page, and Dixon felt compelled to write turn-of-the-century novels with negative portrayals of events prior to 1877 indicates that debates over Reconstruction were still alive, demanding intervention. As Dixon wrote in 1905, "No man can understand current politics or the conditions of the Race Problem unless he knows the history of the awful years of 1865 to 1870."[43]

It is not completely clear when Hayes's election became entrenched as marking the end to Reconstruction. Drawing on the rhetoric of revolution, Du Bois may have contributed to that view despite dating *Black Reconstruction* from 1860 to 1880. Unable to resist the temptation of making an implied negative comparison between the events of 1876 and those of 1776, in *The Souls of Black Folk* he twice refers to the "Revolution of 1876" (41, 66). Whereas 1776 started a revolution against colonial rule, 1876 led to what Du Bois in a chapter in *Black Reconstruction* calls "Back Toward Slavery" (670–710). Hayes's victory meant that "Southern landholders and capitalists would be put in complete control of disfranchised black labor" (692). "The revolution of 1876 was, in fine, a victory for which the South has every right to hang its head" (707). For others, the election of 1876 was significant because it furthered the goals of 1776. For instance, in *The Reconstruction Period* (1905), Peter Joseph Hamilton, a lawyer from Alabama, celebrates the compromise making Hayes president for reuniting the country. "The Federal Union had been reconstructed. The people were a Nation, ready to take part in world politics and to meet the questions of internal policy which nationalization brings in its train. The period of Reconstruction was at an end."[44]

One myth to grow out of this black and white periodization is that Hayes immediately withdrew federal troops from the South after his inauguration. In fact, when Hayes first came into office, not one soldier was ordered from the South as a result of Reconstruction policies. Hayes did redeploy some troops to the West to fight Indians and to put down a railroad strike, but others remained in the South. What Hayes did was order the military to stop propping up Republican governments. Even that difference was not so great, since Grant had already halted military support in most states. When the 1876 election took place, troops were actively involved only in Louisiana, South Carolina, and Florida, where Republicans felt they could win elections because of large African American populations. These were the states (along with Oregon) with disputed returns. With Hayes's inauguration, only South Carolina and Louisiana remained, since Grant had ordered the end of military support in Florida. A few days before Hayes's inaugural, Grant himself conceded that military support of the two remaining states was no longer justified, but he left it up to the new president to issue the orders, which he did on April 10 and April 20. Those orders involved a small number of troops, who were returned to their barracks.[45]

Dunning and Burgess are careful to say that Hayes withdrew the support of the military power of the United States, not troops. Nonetheless, the belief that 1877 coincided with the withdrawal of federal troops has become what one historian calls a "durable item of our national mythology." That myth persists in high school and college textbooks, popular accounts of the period, and literary criticism. It began to take force fairly early and served political purposes as it continues to serve them today. For instance, in *Division and Reunion*, Wilson writes, "Very soon after his inauguration, President Hayes ordered the withdrawal of the federal troops from the South." Hamilton, in the table of contents to *The Reconstruction Period* has a subhead: "Federal troops leave the South." In the text, he more accurately writes, "The troops were withdrawn from the capitals [of South Carolina and Louisiana] and southern affairs were left to settle themselves." But the inaccuracy of the subhead remains. The effect has been to create the image of a national government abandoning its support of Reconstruction almost overnight by withdrawing a much larger military presence than actually existed. Wilson and Hamilton feed the myth because it conjures the image of a conquering army finally leaving the South, which is once again welcomed back into the nation. As the sexual imagery of withdrawal implies, no longer will the national government thrust itself into southern affairs by force. Today, the image serves the opposite purpose. For many lamenting America's unfinished revolution, it allows them to point to one decisive moment in the nation's calculated abandonment of the cause of freedmen rather than pay attention to the complicated details of a much messier process.[46]

One example illustrates the confusion such misunderstanding can produce for literary criticism. In the only textbook edition of Howells's *An Imperative Duty* in print, Paul Petrie provides superb editorial commentary, marred only, but significantly, by his understanding of Reconstruction. Following Edwin H. Cady, Petrie dates the book's action soon after the Panic of 1873 because Dr. Olney, the protagonist, has to return to Boston from Europe after a severe drop in the value of his Union Pacific stock.[47] Howells's apparent decision to set his story in Boston during the middle of Reconstruction elicits two comments. In the introduction, Petrie writes:

> Reconstruction, the ambitious post-Civil War federal program of reform that briefly promised civic and economic opportunity to newly freed African-American slaves, had abruptly ended as part of a political deal between white Northern Republicans and Southern Democrats to resolve the contested presidential election of 1876: in exchange for Democrats' acquiescence in awarding the presidency to the Republican candidate, Rutherford B. Hayes, who had lost the popular vote but prevailed by a slim margin in the electoral college tally, the Republicans had promised to withdraw the federal troops that had been stationed throughout the South to enforce Reconstruction laws and policies after the close of the war. (*ID*, 15–16)

Later Petrie claims that the 1873 timeframe "places the novel's events squarely during the nation's abandonment of the racially egalitarian Reconstruction program for rehabilitating the South after the Civil War" (42n2).

Because he mistakenly asserts that Reconstruction "abruptly ended" in 1877 when troops were withdrawn "throughout the South," Petrie contradicts himself. The year 1873 cannot be in the midst of retrenchment if Reconstruction was abruptly abandoned with Hayes's election. In fact, Reconstruction's promise of egalitarianism was indeed being abandoned prior to 1877, although it was not completely abandoned even then. To analyze the action of Howells's work, we need more precision. For instance, when the mixed-race heroine learns she has "black" blood, she vows to go to Louisiana where she was born to find and uplift her black relatives. Writing in 1890, Howells would have known that in 1873, Louisiana, unlike most southern states, was not yet "redeemed," but in a few years it would be.

The situation is, however, more complicated. Petrie and Cady's dating of the book's action is most likely wrong. The heroine was born around 1866. If the book is set in 1873, she would be seven years old as she is being courted by two different lovers. Women were courted much younger then than now, but seven is stretching it. Furthermore, Howells makes a point of referring to the "moony glare of an electric globe" and the "moony pallor of an electric light" (*ID*, 84, 91). The first electric lights were installed in Boston in 1882, which would set the action around 1883, when Howells conceived of his story and when there was an economic downturn, if not a panic. The year 1883 is, of course, significant because of the *Civil Rights Cases*. Setting his action in the summer, before the court's October ruling, Howells goes out of his way to note that African Americans had "the same civil rights" (38). Indeed, an 1883 date puts added pressure on an overlooked comment by Dr. Olney. Almost all critics assume that Howells agrees with his protagonist when he convinces the heroine to marry him rather than to go south to elevate her unknown colored relatives. Because she has never known them and has never "voluntarily chosen [her] part with them," he tells her, "there is no more specific obligation upon you to give your life to their elevation than there is upon me" (117). But, as Howells knew, Cable in his debate with Grady had argued that in the wake of the *Civil Rights Cases* the duty of individuals—North and South—to aid freedmen increased. Just prior to returning to *An Imperative Duty*, Howells had published *The Hazard of New Fortunes*, a fictional response to social Darwinist William Graham Sumner's 1883 claim that social classes had no duty to one another. It is possible that in his new work he explored the duty races owed to one another at the same time that he pondered what duty individuals owed to a race that could not be defined in plain black and white. In any case, the dating of the action of his book reminds us that 1877 makes a difference, but it does not mark a black and white divide.[48]

In a collection on Reconstruction studies up to 2006, the editor notes that "over half of the essays emphasize that fundamental adjustments to the consequences of the war continued after the 1877 date traditionally used to mark the end of Reconstruction." Heather Cox Richardson goes so far as to argue, "Reconstruction is a process, not a time period." This does not mean that 1877 has no significance. But we would be wise to heed Gregory Downs's description of the election of 1876 as "less an end than a pivot." For the purposes of this book, I distinguish between the period of Reconstruction, which we recognize today, and the era of Reconstruction, in which its influence was still powerful and hope for its renewal was still alive. So defined, the era of Reconstruction extended into the first years of the twentieth century. It was only then that any glimmer of hope for continuing the goals of Reconstruction in the present completely died out.[49]

No one event can mark the point when this occurred. We could point to the Spanish-American War and its aftermath, which symbolically brought northern and southern troops together under the national flag. Or we could point to the 1912 election of the first southern Democrat since the Civil War, with Wilson even winning some New England states. Or the fiftieth anniversary of the Battle of Gettysburg, which Blight so brilliantly analyzes for bringing troops of the blue and the gray together in a show of white supremacy. For me, however, if we want a symbolic event to mark an end to the era of Reconstruction, it should be the founding of the NAACP on February 12, 1909, the one-hundredth anniversary of Lincoln's birth. The NAACP clearly did not give up on the hopes of Reconstruction, but it acknowledged that to fulfill its dreams it needed to overcome not only the heritage of slavery but also the betrayal of the promise of the Civil War amendments as disfranchisement and legally supported Jim Crow prevailed. It also needed to overcome the extensive power of a generally reconciled northern and southern white population. Few in the nation were willing to risk a hard-won reconciliation of former enemies for the cause of freedmen. The founding of the NAACP marked a new long-term struggle. In this book, the literature of Reconstruction is any work written during the era of Reconstruction that portrays the entanglement of issues raised during the period of Reconstruction.

V

In addition to expanding the standard temporal definition of Reconstruction, I want to follow the lead of Richardson, Smith, and Elliott West who expand it spatially. Noting that "Reconstruction of the North receives less attention than its Southern counterpart," Foner urges "attention to its distinctively Northern and national dimensions." Yet he himself slights the West, consigning his discussion of the West's "'politics of development' akin to that of the Reconstruction South" to a chapter called "The Reconstruction of the North." But the West plays a role in a number of Reconstruction works. In the novels of Page and Dixon, Klan members and others persecuted by carpetbaggers and Freedmen's Bureau agents escape to the West. In the novels of Tourgée, scalawags and freedmen threatened by the Klan escape to the West. In a novel by Sutton Griggs, African Americans find an alternative world in Texas. In all of these works, the West plays a role similar to the one imagined in the founding document of western history: Frederick Jackson Turner's "The Significance of the Frontier in American History."[50]

Turner's "Frontier Thesis" should be read in the context of the Civil War and its Reconstruction aftermath. Rather than construct a narrative that focuses on the Mason-Dixon line separating North and South as did his friend Wilson, Turner focuses on a frontier common to both. A safety valve allowing America to avoid conflicts that plagued European history, the West served "as a consolidating agent in our history." Not a fixed boundary like the one that created an absolute division between free and slave states, the frontier allowed for expansion rather than internal conflict. "The economic and social characteristics of the frontier worked against sectionalism." A space of consensus, it produced people who "had closer resemblances to the middle region than to either of the other sections." Twice, Turner challenges Herman W. Edward von Holst, the German historian of the US Constitution, who insisted that the dispute over slavery shaped the national character. "When American history comes to be rightly viewed," Turner insists, "it will be seen that the slavery question is an incident." To signal his consolatory message, Turner cites John C. Calhoun to define the "distinguishing feature of American life": "we are great, and rapidly—I was to say fearfully—growing." Turner's Calhoun is one who would have embraced national reconciliation. To make this point he quotes Mississippi's Lucius Lamar dedicating a monument to Calhoun in

Charleston on April 26, 1887. Once an outspoken secessionist, Lamar praises Calhoun while trying to convince his audience that the famous defender of states' rights would have supported the nation that emerged after the "redemption" of the southern states. Noting that Calhoun's argument was correct for the original thirteen colonies, Lamar insists that it was altered because of westward expansion. As Turner quotes him, "In 1788 states were creators of the Federal Government: in 1861 the Federal Government was the creator of a large majority of the states." Equally important, Turner cites as his ultimate authority "the greatest of frontiersmen," Abraham Lincoln. Lincoln, the westerner, was a prime figure of reconciliation for Dixon and for Grady, who in his 1886 address to the New England Club of New York entitled "The New South" anointed Lincoln the "first typical American," one who united "Puritans and Cavaliers" by "straightening" their purposes and "crossing" their blood. Dudley H. Miles in "The Civil War as Unifier" cites the conciliatory power of Lamar and Grady without once mentioning slavery, and he is careful to locate "control of the machinery of national government" in "the Western democracy" following Andrew Jackson rather than in the North. To celebrate national harmony in the centennial year of 1876, southerner Sidney Lanier wrote a centennial ode called "The Psalm of the West."[51]

The West offered people on all sides of Reconstruction debates an escape because of economic opportunity. In *John March, Southerner,* Cable has a northern capitalist compare investment opportunities between the South and the West. In both regions massive public and private capital was invested in building railroads that promised to connect the nation after the divisions of the Civil War. Surveying the extensive network of railroad lines extending west and giving a new sense of the nation, Hamilton, in the last chapter of his 1905 *The Reconstruction Period,* enthuses, "To a large degree the West reacted upon the East and reconstructed American ideals. The war abolished slavery, but the West afterwards carried through the policy of nationalization." I will explore the importance of the West for understanding Reconstruction in chapter 5.[52]

Appeals to the West tried to overcome the divide between North and South. That divide was real. Writers as different as Page and Tourgée insisted that the North and the South were different civilizations. But when we refer to the North-South divide, as we must in any account of Reconstruction, we should keep in mind that it was not a black and white opposition. There were, after all, divisions in North and South. Not all northerners were Radical Republicans, and not all white southerners were reactionary supporters of the KKK. There were numerous Democrats in the North, and the Republican Party itself split during the election of 1872. In the South, for a while at least, there was a viable Republican Party, made up of former southern Unionists, freedmen, and carpetbaggers. Southern Republicans were often at odds with northern Republicans, just as southern Democrats at times came into conflict with northern Democrats. Of course, the most obvious problem with referring to the South in opposition to the North is the implied exclusion of African Americans from the South. As Tourgée notes, one "faction, unquestionably a minority, assume for themselves the term 'Southern' with a sublime disregard of the weak and ignorant majority. This use of the term 'Southern' has become so general that its absurdity is almost forgotten. That which is favored by this element is said to be 'Southern,' and that which is opposed to it, 'anti-Southern.' A national policy which is thoroughly approved by every member of the actual majority of the people of that section is denounced by this element as one hostile to 'the South.'"[53] That "South," as Tourgée insists, is an imaginary construct, a "mystically-bounded region" (*BS*, 339). Cable has his two southern lovers in *John March, Southerner* express a similar sentiment. They agree that "our South isn't a matter of boundaries, or skies, or landscapes . . . It's a certain ungeographic South—within—the South—as portable and intangible as . . . our souls in our bodies" (*JM*, 326–27).

Tourgée and Cable anticipate many recent scholars who argue, in K. Stephen Prince's words, that "the South was not just a place. It was also an idea." As Prince shows, the "reconstruction of southern identity" after the Civil War was largely the result of cultural production, including literary works written in the North and the South. I simply add that northern and western identities were similarly reconstructed and with them the identity of the nation. By concentrating on the works that I do, I want to show how such cultural acts of reconstruction were in turn influenced by authors' different understandings of issues raised by Reconstruction itself, which is another way of saying that the significance of the nation that emerged from the period of Reconstruction was continually reimagined and contested during the era of Reconstruction.[54]

VI

This is a book about Reconstruction literature, but I do not offer encyclopedic coverage. I do not, for instance, treat a number of long-forgotten responses to the success of *A Fool's Errand*. Nor do I treat many of the popular writers analyzed so masterfully by Kathleen Diffley; or the Reconstruction stories of Grace King, an admirer of Page, who responded to Cable's depictions of Creole society; or the friend of Thomas Nast, David Ross Locke, and his scathing satire in the voice of Petroleum V. Nasby. Instead, with the exception of Melville's *Battle-Pieces*, examined so productively by Deak Nabers, I focus on what could be called the "major" works, even if some have been relatively neglected. I pay substantial attention to works by Harper, Hopkins, Griggs, and Du Bois, as well as to a short novel by John

William DeForest, some short stories by Constance Fenimore Woolson, and some poems by Lanier and John Greenleaf Whittier. My primary works are novels by Tourgée, Cable, Page, Harris, Dixon, and Chesnutt that respond to one another. An outlier might seem to be María Amparo Ruiz de Burton. Her works have primarily been studied by scholars of Chicano/Latino literature. But *The Squatter and the Don* is set in the period of Reconstruction and is about the attempt to build the Texas Pacific Railroad, connecting the West and the South, to complement the transcontinental link between the West and the North. Ruiz de Burton's novel is a poignant reminder of Reconstruction's role in rebuilding the nation after the devastation of war. That economic project fed much of the infamous corruption of the era, which frequently involved investments in railroads. An acquaintance of many of the key figures of Reconstruction debates, Ruiz de Burton gives us a view of the period from Western eyes.[55]

Most of these works were written in dialogue with one another, and to understand them we need to read them in the context of one another. Dixon cannot be understood without a prior reading of Tourgée. The same is true of Page. In 1888, Tourgée published "The South as a Field for Fiction." Page responded with a speech, "The South as a Field for Literature, 1888." As much attention as has recently been paid to Chesnutt, he cannot be understood without appreciating his engagement with Tourgée and Cable, whom he considered mentors, and his refutation of Grady, Harris, and Page, whom he had read closely. In a letter to Booker T. Washington, Chesnutt claimed that "the medium of fiction offers a golden opportunity to create sympathy throughout the country for our cause" and added, "It has been the writings of Harris and Thomas Nelson Page and others of that ilk which have furnished my chief incentives to write something upon the other side of this very vital question."[56]

The importance of reading works in relation to one another dictates my organization. Each chapter is devoted to a topic. I look at how different works treat the thorny questions of reconciliation and reunion, debates about state versus national authority, about the Ku Klux Klan, about African American manhood and governmental paternalism, and about the economics of railroads. I end with two chapters comparing the significance of the inheritance plots in a number of the works I treat. This organization is designed to bring works into close dialogue with one another. A disadvantage of this organization is that my readings of individual works extend over a number of chapters. As a consequence, I risk compromising their aesthetic integrity. One exception is *The Squatter and the Don*, which is the primary, if not exclusive, focus of the chapter on railroads. Despite drawbacks, I adopt this organization because it best fits my subject matter. For instance, I self-consciously avoid the commonplace strategy in literary studies of using a chapter-by-chapter analysis of individual works or individual authors to produce a narrative of progress or decline. That organization places too much pressure on a work or an author to stand for each stage of the narrative. For me, no one work is representative of a moment in the era, even if some have more influence than others. In fact, at times I do not even organize an individual chapter chronologically. While staying attuned to changes that take place, I want to create an interplay between a variety of perspectives on crucial issues.

Because I cannot expect readers to remember everything I said about a work in previous chapters—and also because not everyone reads a work of criticism linearly but sometimes focuses on a couple of chapters at the expense of others—I provide occasional moments of repetition when I reintroduce a work or an issue in a new chapter. I hope that when I return to a work or an issue, such as the debate over the Civil Rights Act of 1875, it will accrue new significance as it is placed in a new context. In addition, because I cannot assume that all readers are acquainted with the works I treat, I indulge in much more plot summary than I normally do. Frequently, however, these summaries are as interpretive as they are descriptive. Indeed, as we will see, even accomplished critics sometimes have difficulty getting the action of some of these works straight.

Some literary critics might consider an organization by topics methodologically reactionary for being too thematic. But I am less interested in being fashionable than in adding to our understanding of the literature of Reconstruction. Also, my organization is calculated to emphasize a formal problem. In his review of political novels, Howells stressed the importance of selecting the forces that produce a political or social situation. The formal problem of shaping a plot, as he puts it elsewhere, requires a selection that puts those forces in "their true proportion and relation." To take one example, in *Red Rock*, Page portrays the military as omnipresent. In contrast, in Tourgée's works, the military is in the background and rarely intervenes in the action. That selection creates different accounts of what life was like during Reconstruction. Page presents a southern people oppressed by an occupying army; Tourgée depicts a South too extensive for a relatively small military presence to police action outside of a few strategic locales. As the narrator of *A Fool's Errand* puts it, "Here and there throughout the subjugated land were detachments and posts of the victorious army, gradually growing smaller and fewer as the months slipped by" (130).

Literary authors were not the only ones confronted with the formal problem of selection and proportion. James read Dunning; Dunning and other historians read literature. Indeed, Dunning seems to have read Howells. In the preface to his 1907 *Reconstruction: Political and Economic, 1865–1877*, Dunning notes that an accurate account requires attention to "social, economic, and political forces." Then, perhaps with Page and Dixon in mind, he adds: "Moral and dramatic values must not have greater weight in the writing of history than they have had in the making of history. Our narrative, therefore, while it may seem to slight the picturesque details of Ku-Klux operations and carpet-bag legislation and fraud, will be found, I trust, to present in something like their true relations the facts and forces which, manifested chiefly in the politics of the North and West, transformed the nation from what it was in 1865 to what it was in 1877." Today, we feel that Dunning himself got the relations between those facts and forces wrong. But the task of putting them in their proper proportion remains. Reading the era's fictional accounts of Reconstruction can aid us in that task.[57]

- 1 -

RECONCILIATION AND REUNION

Clasping Hands over the Bloody Chasm

In his extensive study of *The South in American Literature: 1667–1900*, Jay B. Hubbell argues that national reconciliation following the "Compromise of 1877 . . . owed more to the work of men of letters than to that of the politicians." One example he gives is a letter the New England abolitionist poet John Greenleaf Whittier wrote on March 17, 1870, to Paul Hayne, the leading southern writer after the death of William Gilmore Simms. Whittier mused, "I think the time is near at hand when Charleston & Boston—long centers of opposing ideas—both in advance of their respective sections . . . will understand each other better & do justice to each other. At any rate, their literary men should have no prejudices." Indeed, northern men of letters played an important role in creating a climate of reconciliation by publishing many southern writers for a national audience. Even Albion W. Tourgée published Joel Chandler Harris in his *Our Continent.* Whereas there was often disagreement between authors writing about Reconstruction, there was also mutual admiration. María Amparo Ruiz de Burton, who mocks "black" Republicans, uses lines from Whittier as her epigraph in *Who Would Have Thought It?* Late in his life George Washington Cable wrote an appreciation of Thomas Nelson Page. Years earlier, southern poet Sidney Lanier enthused to his brother on reading Cable's *The Grandissimes*, "a work of art, and [Cable] has a fervent and rare soul." Later, the first issue Cable edited of *The Symposium* "was in a sense a Sidney Lanier number." Writing to John Muir, Cable gushed, "There are in Lanier such wonderful odors of pine and hay, and salt sands and cedar, and corn, and such wonderful whisperings of Eolian strains and every outdoor sound—I think you would have had a great joy in one another's personal acquaintance." In 1883, when Cable made a trip north and with much fanfare met major writers, it was seen as a sign of North-South reconciliation, with northerners hopefully, but mistakenly, believing that he represented the southern point of view. His meeting with Whittier was hailed in the press as the "literary bridging of the bloody chasm."[1]

Because of examples like these and others, Hubbell, writing in 1954, joins many before him in praising men of letters for taking the lead in promoting reconciliation. Writing in 2001, David Blight takes a very different view of national reconciliation. Even though he calls reconciliation "a noble and essential human impulse," he condemns numerous celebrations of unity because they erased from national memory the egalitarian promise of Reconstruction. For instance, he insists that reports of members of the Army of Northern Virginia and the Grand Army of the Potomac embracing one another at the fiftieth anniversary of Gettysburg, "indicate just how much a combination of white supremacist and reconciliationist memories had conquered all others by 1913."[2]

Powerfully argued and eloquently written, Blight's *Race and Reunion: The Civil War in American Memory* is the high-water mark of a group of works, written a decade and a half ago, intent on showing how racial justice was undercut by a desire for reconciliation. In recent years, that argument has not been overturned, but it has been qualified. Mark Wahlgren Summers notes that "Reconstruction" is frequently used to mean "The Reconstruction of the South," which "is shorthand for 'The Reconstruction of Southern Society with a particular emphasis on Southern Race Relations.'" Summers acknowledges the important reasons for this focus but reminds us that in a climate of bitter antagonism caused by a bloody war, "to most Americans in 1865 'the Reconstruction of the Union' was more important." In *The Ordeal of Reunion,* he shows how difficult that act of reconstruction was, even without getting the nation to agree on racial equality. K. Stephen Prince argues that, "despite the importance of work by Blight and others, overreliance on the language of reunion is problematic . . . , implying that the post-Reconstruction era saw the reconnection of two static, unchanging regions. . . . The North did not find reunion with a fixed and timeless South. There was no such thing. The South was always a moving target. . . . Before reunion could occur, the story of the South needed to be rewritten."[3]

In addition, Caroline E. Janney has shown that the desire for reconciliation was not quite as pervasive as Blight implies. The public acts he brilliantly analyzes had great symbolic power, but many from North and South did not share the sentiment they embodied. From our present perspective, that is good and bad. Blight condemns the move toward reconciliation because it gets interwoven with white supremacist ideology. Some white southerners, however, condemned reconciliation because it was not supremacist enough. Many African Americans and their supporters resisted reconciliation because it meant that the North had not truly embraced the egalitarian ideals for which it had fought. Equally important, the question of reconciliation was not always linked to issues of white supremacy. In 1897, John W. Burgess, from Tennessee but teaching at Columbia University, was uncompromising about the terms necessary for reunion. The South needed to admit that there was "not one scintilla of justification for secession and rebellion. . . . It will not improve matters to concede that the South had right on its side and the North might, or, even, that both were equally right and equally wrong. Such a doctrine can only work injury to both, and more injury to the South than to the North. Chewing the bitter cud of fancied wrong produces both spiritual misery and material adversity, and tempts to foolish and reckless action for righting the imagined injustices." The truth is that the South was wrong, and "unless we are men enough to hear and accept and stand upon the truth, it is useless to endeavor to find a bond of real union between us. In a word, the conviction of the South in its error in secession and rebellion is absolutely indispensable to the establishment of national cordiality." But Burgess also stood upon the truth that "in a state whose population is composed of a variety of nationalities, the Teutonic element, when dominant, should never surrender the balance of political power, either in general or local organization, to other elements."[4]

Burgess's demand illustrates Janney's further point that reunion and reconciliation are not the same. Reunion is a legal condition; reconciliation has an affective component. The significance of acts of reconciliation depends upon the terms of reunion. If for some reconciliation meant selling African Americans down the river, others made gestures of reconciliation hoping to promote egalitarianism. To be sure, these latter efforts rarely proved successful. Nonetheless, it is important to respect the position of actors at the time, unaware of how history would turn out. To do so, I adopt oscillating perspectives. On the one hand, I join Blight in emphasizing how the terms of reunion compromised Reconstruction's egalitarian goals. On the other, I remind us that for Reconstruction to be a success—as many at the time understood—the nation needed to forge some sort of reconciliation. Of course, the definition of what constituted success varied from person to person, which means that acts of reconciliation had multiple motives and modes.[5]

In the next section of this chapter, I provide four case studies of individuals—Frederick Douglass, Lucius Quintus Cincinnatus Lamar, Adelbert Ames, and Charles Sumner—who do not easily fit into recent accounts of reconciliation. Then I turn to the 1876 Centennial Exposition in Philadelphia. The centennial's celebration of national reconciliation is easy to dismiss as a dress rehearsal for the Compromise of 1877. But a look at a few poems by Whittier and Lanier, who participated in the celebration, reveals both a utopian hope for full reconciliation and a realistic assessment of what would be needed to bring it about. The last two sections examine two works by authors associated with the rise of literary realism: John William DeForest and Constance Fenimore Woolson. Their stories confirm Summers's view of how difficult reunion was, although DeForest's does so in a comic mode that exposes the limits of what has come to be known as the romance of reunion, while Woolson's does so in a tragic mode that leaves the romance unfulfilled. Woolson's story especially helps us understand why so many people at the time preferred personal rather than political acts of reconciliation. To balance that perspective, I conclude by evoking Tourgée's response to such acts.

II

For Blight, a notable exception to those participating in the politics of reconciliation is Douglass, who "did not want national reunion; he wanted racial justice, promised in law, demonstrated in practice, and preserved in memory." In contrast, William McFeely, one of Douglass's biographers, condemns Douglass for capitulating to the reconciliationist agenda of Rutherford B. Hayes's administration: "The stances on various issues that Douglass was to take between 1877 and 1881 were the least honorable and least helpful to his fellow former slaves of any in his long life. They were, in fact, entirely consistent with the betrayal of promises that ended Reconstruction." The first step in reconciling these conflicting interpretations of Douglass is to recognize that Blight and McFeely are united by their shared condemnation of the politics of reconciliation. If all acts of reconciliation were as reactionary as they believe, Douglass should be condemned. Yet, the events McFeely points to during the Hayes administration suggest that Blight's account of Douglass is exaggerated. Douglass wanted reunion, but, like his opponents, he wanted it on his terms. At the same time, McFeely's condemnation of Douglass for temporarily abandoning his ideals depends on the historian's awareness that momentum for Radical Reconstruction was never successfully revived after the compromise of 1877.[6]

McFeely insists, "It is not a matter of twentieth-century twenty-twenty hindsight to accuse [Douglass] of [his] myopia." Nonetheless, describing the bust of Douglass on display at the 1876 Centennial Exposition in Philadelphia, he writes, "It was a great tribute to the runaway, but a tombstone for Reconstruction. The effort to rebuild a nation along a fundamentally more egalitarian line was over, and the bust an ironic memorial to a job not done." Hayes's election, for which Douglass campaigned, "spelled the end of federal responsibility for the rights of black people in the South, a responsibility that Douglass had committed his life to furthering." In fact, for Douglass, Hayes's election by no means marked the end of federal responsibility. In his inaugural address, Hayes assured the South that he believed in "home rule" only if "Southern whites agreed to recognize the political and civil rights of the Negro." Even Wade Hampton of South Carolina promised to "secure to every citizen, the lowest as well as the highest, black as well as white, full protection in the enjoyment of all his rights under the Constitution." After the 1878 elections, Hayes admitted that his "experiment was a failure," but in 1877 he did not know that Hampton and others would break their promises.[7]

Furthermore, the Civil Rights Act of 1875 was still on the books. Not as comprehensive as Douglass had wanted, the act still gave the national government responsibility to protect the rights of black people in many aspects of public life in the North and the South. Douglass was far from silent about the need to uphold the American ideal of rule by law by enforcing its provisions. In an 1878 Memorial Day speech, he warned that "a lawless and revolutionary spirit is still abroad in the country. . . . [T]he Constitution and the laws are . . . dishonored and disregarded," while "duly elected State Governments" have been "overthrown by violence." Douglass was not naïve about reasons for resistance to the 1875 act. In an August 1, 1880, speech at Elmira, New York, he acknowledged: "Liberty came to [freedmen], not in mercy, but in wrath; not by moral choice, but by military necessity, not by the generous action of the people among whom they were to live, and whose goodwill was essential to the success of the measure, but by strangers and foreigners, invaders, trespassers, aliens, and enemies. The very manner of their Emancipation invited to the heads of the freedmen the bitterest hostility of race and class. They were hated because they had been slaves, hated because they were now free, and hated because of those who had freed them." Realistically aware that the goals of Reconstruction had little chance of success as long as those "whose good will was essential to the success of [emancipation]" actively resisted laws like the Civil Rights Act of 1875, Douglass might have felt the need to work with influential members of the southern white community to eliminate their resistance and with the administration to urge it to enforce the law of the land. Such an attitude would help to explain three trips Douglass made from 1877 to 1881 to the Eastern Shore of Maryland, where he had been born and raised a slave.[8]

In June 1877, Douglass visited St. Michaels. One purpose of the trip was to meet with Thomas Auld, his former master. Auld's daughter and son-in-law welcomed Douglass as an honored guest. Douglass and Auld, a dying man, had a short, emotional visit during which amends were made, including an apology from Douglass for misportraying Auld's treatment of the former slave's grandmother. In June 1881, Douglass visited Wye House, the home of the Lloyd family, owners of the largest plantation in the area. Lloyd's son entertained Douglass on the veranda and gave him a tour of the grounds where he had spent part of his youth. Both visits were widely reported in the press, and Douglass was certainly aware of their symbolic significance. Nonetheless, citing only an anonymous letter, McFeely insists, "members of the black community who read about the visit to Auld in the press criticized Douglass for what was seen as obsequious obeisance to a slave master he had once denounced."[9]

Quick to condemn Douglass, McFeely does not mention the activities of another well-known African American at the time—Martin Delany. Called the "Father of Black Nationalism," Delany is read primarily for his antebellum writings, including his 1859 novel *Blake; or, the Huts of America*. The standard contrast between Douglass, the integrationist, and Delany, the radical separatist, who in the 1850s advocated emigration neglects Delany's post-emancipation activities. Having served as the first black major in the Union army, after the war he worked on the state level while Douglass concentrated his efforts in Washington, DC. Delany moved to South Carolina and worked with local white leaders, hoping to forge a government that would grant freedmen full citizenship. By 1874, disillusioned by corruption associated with Republican rule, he joined the independent Republican movement that promised to restore honest government and was nominated for lieutenant governor. His campaign stressed the need for cooperation between the races, which he saw as necessary for the success of Reconstruction. After losing his bid for office, he continued to campaign for cooperation, breaking completely with the Republican party in the crucial election of 1876 and backing former slave owner Hampton. In hindsight, Delany came to regret his support of Hampton, just as with hindsight McFeely faults Douglass for his efforts in the Hayes administration.[10]

There is, for example, Douglass's trip to Easton, Maryland, in November 1878, sponsored by the local Republican Party. Douglass gave two speeches at local African American churches. He also delivered a paid address at the Talbot County Courthouse on "self-made men." One of five speeches he gave on the lecture tour, it celebrated blacks and whites who had started low and had risen to fame through hard work and courage. Condemning a similar speech for having "the worst elements of [Douglass's] pull-up-your-socks sermon," McFeely does not mention that in his speech at Easton Douglass interrupted his standard delivery to exclaim spontaneously, "When asked, 'What do we do with the Negro?' my reply always has been 'Give him fair play and let him alone! Let him have every chance that every other man has. No more, no less!'" Although this sounds like an argument against governmental intervention, for Douglass it was only through the Civil Rights Act of 1875 that equal opportunity was possible. And in 1878 he had personal evidence of its effect. Rallying support for Sumner's Civil Rights Bill when it was first proposed in 1872, Douglass and other prominent black leaders cited their humiliating experiences with racial discrimination in public accommodations. Yet in 1878, when Douglass sailed to Talbot County on the *Highland Light*, he was the first

African American to have a stateroom on that steamboat. In Easton, he was the first African American to stay at the Brick Hotel, which in 1836 he had seen from the nearby prison after being arrested for trying to escape bondage. In 1883, when the Supreme Court declared the 1875 act unconstitutional, Douglass returned to his role as a protestor and delivered a stirring speech denouncing the decision. Looking back, he wrote, "The future historian will turn to the year 1883 to find the most flagrant example of this national deterioration." For him, 1883, more than 1877, marked the end of the promise of Reconstruction. Even though the 1875 act was not effectively enforced, its existence created hope for Douglass, who worked so hard for its passage.[11]

About this time of his life, Douglass, like Delany, may well have felt that calculated acts of reconciliation with former slave owners could advance racial justice, not block it. Likely, Douglass was willing to reconcile himself with his former master because he was aware of the symbolic effect of their reunion. Douglass was no longer a slave but a famous public figure. With the press reporting every detail, he showed that he was generous enough to forget and forgive. At the same time, he also hoped that this symbolic act would convince powerful whites to cooperate with him to advance the political ideals that he dearly held. In his 1899 biography of Douglass, Charles W. Chesnutt praises that strategy: "Nowhere more than in his own accounts of these meetings [with Auld and Lloyd's son] does the essentially affectionate and forgiving character of Douglass and his race become apparent, and one cannot refrain from thinking that a different state of affairs might prevail in the Southern States if other methods than those at present in vogue were used to regulate the relations between the two races and their various admixtures that make up the Southern population." In *The Souls of Black Folk* (1903), W. E. B. Du Bois himself advocates a strategy of interracial cooperation similar to the earlier ones of Delany and Douglass: "Only by a union of intelligence and sympathy across the color-line in this critical period of the Republic," he wrote, "shall justice and right triumph" (147). Not shy about condemning racial injustice, Chesnutt throughout his life and Du Bois at this time of his career understood Douglass's use of biracial reconciliation as a strategy to advance their goals.[12]

Lucius Quintus Cincinnatus Lamar was about as different from Douglass as one can imagine. He was important enough to make his way into the period's fiction as a source for Henry James's Basil Ransom in *The Bostonians* and as himself in María Amparo Ruiz de Burton's *The Squatter and the Don*. Of Huguenot ancestry, Lamar was born in Georgia, attended Emory College, and moved to Mississippi. He was an ardent secessionist and after the war was elected to the House of Representatives and then appointed senator. He was a major spokesman for redeeming the South through legal, not violent, means, and his career tends to confirm the belief that reconciliation spelled doom for the egalitarian ideals of Reconstruction. When Grover Cleveland became the first Democrat elected president after the Civil War, he appointed Lamar secretary of the Interior. Later, Cleveland appointed him the first former Confederate soldier to serve on the Supreme Court. Nonetheless, Lamar does not always live up to the image of a redeeming southerner. In his own way, he, like Douglass, worked for interracial cooperation. When he was named to the Senate, Mississippi's other senator was the African American Blanche K. Bruce. Describing a meeting with Bruce, Lamar wrote a friend:

> I told [Bruce] that I regarded him as the legitimate representative of the colored people of Miss. And myself as that of the whites; that however distinct the two races unquestionably were, they were one indivisible community; that in my opinion the happiness & prosperity of his race were just as important as the happiness and prosperity of the whites; that I had no desire to ignore, disregard, or subordinate the interests or rights of the colored people of Mississippi; that of course in case of conflict for mastery or power between the two my feelings & actions would be for the white race; but that true patriotism & statesmanship would aim to prevent such conflict & seek to bring about a harmonious cooperation & development of their social forces, & that he & I might by unselfishly acting in concert do great good for our state.[13]

In addition to working across the racial divide, in his first important speech in Congress, Lamar surprised his constituency and impressed the nation by delivering a moving eulogy for Douglass's ally, Radical Republican Charles Sumner. According to John F. Kennedy, who devotes a chapter to Lamar in *Profiles in Courage,* his speech "marked a turning point in relations between North and South." Kennedy goes on to praise Lamar's courage for two other unpopular stands with whites in Mississippi. During the dispute over the 1876 election, Lamar stood by the Electoral Commission that delivered the presidency to Hayes. He also opposed the proposal for free silver so popular in the South and defied expectations through alliances he made in Congress. He frequently worked with Republican James G. Blaine, going so far as to stop a House investigation into Blaine's questionable railroad dealings. In return, as speaker in 1875, Blaine helped to derail a new, tougher Enforcement Act that would have given the national government more power to prevent intimidation of black voters. Lamar was more intent on blocking the Enforcement Act than the Civil Rights Act, especially after Blaine helped to water down the latter. Blaine proved even more helpful to his southern colleague two years later after Lamar was appointed a senator. Claiming that the Mississippi state legislature that appointed Lamar came to power illegitimately by violently suppressing the freedmen's vote, Republicans refused to seat him. But Blaine, himself now in the Senate, used his influence to get Lamar seated.[14]

If we focus only on the racial issues of Reconstruction, Blaine and Lamar's alliance is puzzling. It makes perfect sense, however, if we remember their shared interest in developing railroads. Lamar supported the 1876 Electoral Commission in part because he felt that Hayes, more than his opponent Samuel Tilden, would underwrite the Texas Pacific Railroad designed to connect the South with California. As important as racial politics were, there were other interests that forged alliances between southerners and northerners, such as railroads and economics. Even in the realm of racial politics, Lamar, like Douglass, knew that gestures of reconciliation could be an effective political strategy. When Lamar's eulogy for Sumner transformed him from a sectional loyalist into a national statesman, he gained an advantage in his fight with the carpetbagger governor of Mississippi, Adelbert Ames.

Ames, who tried unsuccessfully to convince Douglass to become the first president of the state's new African American university, was perhaps the most notorious carpetbagger. In his chapter on Lamar, Kennedy gives a standard anti-Reconstruction portrait.

> No state suffered more from carpet-bag rule than Mississippi. Adelbert Ames, first senator and then governor, was a native of Maine, a son-in-law of the notorious 'Butcher of New Orleans,' Benjamin F. Butler. He admitted before a Congressional committee that only his election to the Senate prompted him to take up his residence in Mississippi. He was chosen Governor by a majority composed of freed slaves and radical Republicans, sustained and nourished by Federal bayonets. One Cardoza, under indictment for larceny in New York, was placed at the head of the public schools and two former slaves held the offices of Lieutenant Governor and Secretary of State. Vast areas of northern Mississippi lay in ruins. Taxes increased to a level fourteen times as high as normal in order to support the extravagances of the reconstruction government and heavy state and national war debts.

Kennedy's elevation of Lamar and denigration of Ames was in part motivated by his own politics of reconciliation. With his eye on the White House, Kennedy needed the support of southern Democrats. Attacking New Englanders like Ames helped to reassure southerners that Kennedy would not act as other Yankees had. Praising Lamar's eulogy for Sumner, he goes out of his way to call that former Massachusetts senator "the South's most implacable enemy, the Radical Republican who helped make the Reconstruction period a black nightmare the South would never forget." At the same time, by blaming white New Englanders rather than African Americans for the black nightmare, Kennedy could avoid the explicit, if not implicit, discourse of white supremacy.[15]

His description of Ames did, however, elicit a protest from Ames's daughter Blanche, who wrote to her senator from Massachusetts, demanding a correction in subsequent editions. No revision took place, but her grandson George Plimpton, editor of the *Paris Review*, knew Kennedy personally and tried unsuccessfully to exert his influence. Nonetheless, recent historians have restored Ames's reputation, a task made easier because of earlier work by James Wilford Garner, one of William A. Dunning's students. If stereotypes had prevailed, Garner ought to have vilified Ames. On the contrary, he had extensive correspondence with the former carpetbagger and exonerated him of all charges of corruption. Although in 1957 Kennedy bought into the myth that Ames's policies created a massive debt, Garner in 1901 proved that the rumored "$20,000,000 debt was in fact only $500,000." From today's perspective, Garner's book would still be accused of having a southern bias, but Du Bois himself acknowledges that Garner "conceives of the Negro as an integral part of the scene and treats him as a human being" (*BR*, 720).[16]

Garner was writing in the immediate wake of the Spanish-American War, celebrated at the time as proof of North-South reconciliation. According to Dudley Miles, "North and South were drawn into relations of exultant brotherhood. The sacrifice of blood and gold in the cause of an oppressed people fostered an intensity of patriotic fervor that lifted national life from the individualism and sectionalism that had lingered on since the Civil War." Like others, Miles highlighted the symbolism of southerners marching under the flag they once denounced. Most celebrated was the enlistment of Confederate cavalry hero "Fighting Joe" Wheeler. In Miles's volume for *The Photographic History of the Civil War in Ten Volumes*, marking the fiftieth anniversary of the outbreak of the war, he includes two popular poems about Wheeler in the section called "Brotherhood": John Jerome Rooney's "Joined the Blues" and Wallace Rice's "Wheeler's Brigade at Santiago." By northerners, both poems praise Wheeler's patriotism. What gets erased from the historical record is Ames's superb military record and his return to the army as brigadier general in his sixties to fight in the same conflict. The lack of celebratory poems about Ames's reenlistment feeds Blight's argument that national memory embraced the southern point of view. At the same time, the enthusiastic participation of this notorious carpetbagger shows that not all at the time thought joint participation of northern and southern soldiers signaled white supremacy.[17]

Ames's motivation was most likely the same patriotic spirit that prompted him to become a carpetbagger governor. Similarly, when war broke out in 1898, Edward Everett Hale brought out a special edition of "The Man Without a Country" with an introduction applying its patriotic message to the new war. Hale had written the story in 1863 to rally support for the northern cause. No proponent of white domination, he had strongly opposed slavery and established Hale House for immigrants, such as the Russian Jew Mary Antin, who wrote *The Promised Land*. Nonetheless, in 1898 he eliminated passages from his story that might have offended southerners. In contrast, white supremacist John W. Burgess opposed the war and its imperialist aftermath. He acknowledged that northerners and southerners fighting under the same flag had "buried the hatchet forever between them," but he insisted that the real reason the South no longer feared "interferences of the Republican party with regard to the Negro question" was "to some the pleasing, though to others, the startling, fact, that the Republican party, in its work of imposing the sovereignty of the United States upon eight million of Asiatics, has changed its views in regard to the political relations of races and has at last virtually accepted the ideas of the South upon that topic."[18]

Just as Wheeler's participation in the Spanish-American War is commemorated while Ames's is rarely mentioned, so Lamar's eulogy for Sumner is frequently cited while Sumner's acts of reconciliation are often ignored. Yet, as David Donald reports, in December 1872 in order to promote "the national unity and good-will among fellow-citizens," Sumner proposed a resolution "that the names of battles with fellow-citizens shall not be continued in the Army Register, or placed on the regimental colors of the United States." In 1862, Sumner had proposed a similar resolution, and he continued to feel that the nation should not celebrate battles between brothers. Likewise, in 1866 he opposed hanging paintings of Civil War battles in the Capitol rotunda. But in 1872, his effort to "promote true reconciliation" caused the Massachusetts House of Representatives to condemn it as "an insult to the loyal soldiery of the nation." They were upset with Sumner because of his feud with Grant, which led him to join Liberal Republicans and Democrats in support of Horace Greeley in the 1872 campaign. Memory is selective. When Kennedy praises Lamar's eulogy for "the South's most implacable enemy," he conveniently fails to mention Sumner's own efforts at reconciliation, even though Lamar makes a great deal of them. Kennedy is not alone. Although this is a perfect example of a controversy over how the Civil War should be officially remembered, Blight does not touch on Sumner's role. Whittier, however, was very much aware of it. He organized a petition to rescind Sumner's censure by the legislature. Henry Wadsworth Longfellow, Oliver Wendell Holmes Sr., and Harvard president Charles W. Eliot supported him. Whittier also wrote to Douglass, who, while not agreeing with Sumner's resolution, emphatically declared, "No censure of Mr. Sumner should be allowed to stain the annals of Massachusetts."[19]

To call attention to acts of reconciliation by radical egalitarians like Douglass, Ames, and Sumner does not completely undermine Blight's general claim about national memory and white supremacy. But that memory was not as collective as it might seem. Furthermore, there were multiple motives and possible outcomes for acts of reconciliation. Douglass could use them to try to rally support for racial justice. Blaine and Lamar could work for them to further shared railroad and economic interests. Ames could participate in them for patriotic reasons; others did so for humanitarian reasons or out of self-interest. There was even a sense of gentlemanly solidarity that contributed to a spirit of reconciliation. The Maryland lawyer and poet Severn Teackle Wallis, imprisoned as a copperhead during the Civil War, wrote a book honoring George Peabody, the philanthropist who gave millions for educating freedmen. He quotes Peabody: "Never . . . during the war or since have I permitted the contest, or any passions engendered by it, to interfere with the social relations and warm friendships which I had formed for a very large number of people of the South. . . . And now, after the lapse of those eventful years, I am more deeply, more earnestly, more painfully convinced than ever of our need of mutual forbearance and conciliation, of Christian charity and forgiveness, of united effort to bind up the fresh and broken wounds of the nation." And, of course, acts of reconciliation could have multiple motives. It would, for instance, be naïve to think that ambition for personal advancement played no role in some of Douglass's actions during the Hayes administration or that the desire to embarrass his enemy, President Grant, played no role in Sumner's flag proposal. But Douglass also sincerely believed that Hayes, while not perfect, was the best available hope for African Americans, just as Sumner sincerely felt that their best hope was in supporting Greeley. Indeed, Sumner's acts of reconciliation nicely fit Greeley's platform of "universal amnesty and universal suffrage."[20]

Recently, Horatio Bateman's 1867 engraving "Reconstruction," which imagines a multicultural nation with universal suffrage based on the principles of justice, liberty, and education, has been cited to illustrate the egalitarian ideals driving reform. We should not forget, however, that scenes of North-South reconciliation are also an integral part of Bateman's utopian imagination. By linking these two meanings of "Reconstruction," Bateman's engraving does more than express the egalitarian ideals of radicals. It also expresses his and others' hope in 1867 that radical egalitarianism and reconciliation could be accomplished simultaneously. Scenes of blacks and whites mingling are juxtaposed with ones of former enemies embracing.[21]

Predictably, one scene illustrates the famous handshake between Lee and Grant at Appomattox. That handshake was iconic for advocates of reconciliation. On December 23, 1886, in New York, Atlanta journalist Henry Grady delivered his speech, "The New South," to the New England Society. Grady's speech was hailed from Atlantic to Pacific for bringing North and South together. In *Poetry and Eloquence of Blue and Gray,* Miles reprints "The New South" in full in his "Brotherhood" section. A 1921 Riverside edition of "The Man Without a Country," designed for school use, lists it as an example of patriotic literature. The speech ends with Grady asking his audience if New England will "permit the prejudices of war to remain in the hearts of the conquerors, when it has died in the hearts of the conquered? Will she transmit this prejudice to the next generation, that in their hearts which never felt the ardor of conflict it may perpetuate itself? Will she withhold, save in strained courtesy, the hand which straight from his soldier's heart, Grant offered to Lee at Appomattox?"[22]

The scene of Lee and Grant shaking hands is predictable, but Bateman's portrayal of Ben Butler shaking hands with former Confederate John C. Breckenridge is not. We have already seen how Kennedy refers to Butler, Ames's father-in-law, as the "notorious 'butcher of New Orleans.'" Butler got that nickname, as well as that of "Beast" Butler, for his actions while imposing martial law on New Orleans after the Union captured it in the Civil War. Resisting occupation, southern belles, among other actions, poured the contents of chamber pots on soldiers' heads. In *Miss Ravenel's Conversion,* set in part during wartime New Orleans and published in 1867, DeForest alludes to those actions when southern Dr. Ravenel counsels his daughter to follow the "Christian example" of "these low Yankees whom we all hate so. . . . I have seen a couple of officers shamefully insulted by a woman who calls herself a lady. They returned not a word, not even a look of retaliation" (133). But Butler did retaliate. He declared, "Any lady who shall by word or gesture express contempt of any Federal officer or soldier shall be liable, without protection or redress, to be treated as a woman of the town plying her avocation." It was soon reported in the South that the latter part of the sentence was "as common prostitutes are treated," and Butler became infamous for insulting southern womanhood. Jefferson Davis denounced Butler's "contumelious" behavior and called him "a fellow deserving of capital punishment, . . . an outlaw and common enemy of mankind." Butler also gained the nickname "Spoons" Butler when he confiscated silverware from a woman illegally carrying it across Union lines. This incident led to the widespread accusation that he encouraged the looting of local homes.[23]

After the war Butler's reputation in the South got worse. In 1868 he replaced an ailing Thaddeus Stevens as the lead prosecutor in President Johnson's impeachment trial. A few years later, while speaking to the House about the Ku Klux Klan, he displayed the bloodied shirt of a carpetbagger beaten by the Klan. This act was said to have led to the coinage of the phrase "to wave the bloody shirt." In fact, the phrase was used earlier. Nonetheless, it is a sign of Butler's notoriety in the South and the historical connotations of the phrase that its origin is associated with his attempt to counter the Klan. "Waving the bloody shirt" recalls Mark Antony's famous speech in Shakespeare's *Julius Caesar* when he displays Caesar's bloody mantle to the crowd. For many northerners, southerners, like the conspirators against Caesar, claimed noble aims but generated a civil war and assassinated the head of state. Even though the war was over, the Klan constituted another conspiracy against the state. Most white southerners, of course, disagreed and had no desire to shake hands with Butler. As Thomas Dixon writes in *The Clansman*, Butler's name "was enough to start a riot in any assembly in America" (167).[24]

In contrast, Breckenridge had been vice president under James Buchanan. In the 1860 campaign, when the Democratic Party split, he was its candidate of the South, while Stephen A. Douglas was its candidate of the North. After losing the election, Breckenridge was named senator from Kentucky. When Lincoln called a special session in July 1861 to deal with secession, Breckenridge walked out and joined the Confederacy, prompting Congress to declare him a traitor. At the end of the war, he was secretary of war and escaped to Cuba and then Europe. In 1867, he remained in exile. It seems inconceivable that Bateman could imagine Butler reconciling with any southerner, especially Breckenridge. Yet, in the 1860 election, Butler, then a Democrat, after voting fifty-seven times unsuccessfully to nominate Davis, supported Breckenridge. Thus, in 1867, Bateman held out hope that the "Beast" and the traitor would again shake hands.

If Butler is an unlikely figure for reconciliation, Bateman's image of Jefferson Davis and Greeley embracing is even more telling. This reconciliation actually occurred, but not with the effect Bateman imagined. The war over, vocal abolitionist Greeley advocated sectional healing, going so far as to help post bail for Davis, who was in prison. Indeed, in *Poetry and Eloquence of Blue and Gray*, Miles includes in the section "Brotherhood" a photograph of the signatures on Davis's bail bond, singling out Greeley's and praising him for his "unusual courage." What Bateman could not have known was that, even with the events of 1877, Davis refused to "accept the situation." Nor could he have known the accommodationist politics Greeley would adopt as the Democratic and Liberal Republican candidate for president in the 1872 election.[25]

It is tempting to explain Greeley's opposition to Radical Reconstruction by referring to the two components of Bateman's engraving and concluding that he abandoned the egalitarian ideals that made him a fervent abolitionist in favor of reconciliation. But that explanation is misleading. As Bateman would have known, although Greeley opposed slavery, initially he did not oppose secession. On December 8, 1860, he wrote, "When over six or eight contiguous States shall have formally seceded from the Union, and avowed the pretty unanimous and earnest resolve of their people to *stay* out, it will not be found practicable to coerce them into subjection." Bateman was not naïve for thinking that Greeley and Davis had common views. He was naïve for thinking that Greeley's former abolitionism would necessarily lead him to support racial egalitarianism. When Greeley dismissed Radical Reconstruction as the partisan agenda of one wing of one political party, he was being consistent, not abandoning previously held egalitarian views. Indeed, the famous abolitionist and feminist orator Anna Dickinson justified her support for Greeley in 1872 by declaring, "the war was only an act in a drama. . . . What men did then they did not for the life or success of a party, but for the life and success of the nation."[26]

Politically, Greeley's major mistake was believing that slavery alone divided North and South. In *A Fool's Errand*, Tourgée notes that northerners thought emancipation would make North and South the same. That was, the Fool concludes, "a strange mistake" (*FE*, 140). North and South were, in fact, "two divergent civilizations" (168). "The ideas of generations," the Fool warns, "do not perish in an hour. Divergent civilizations can not be made instantly identical by uprooting a single institution" (140). Because reunion was not easy to accomplish even without insisting on radical egalitarianism, Bateman's engraving has a double message for us. On the one hand, the failure to realize its utopian image confirms Blight's conclusion that "the tragedy of Reconstruction is rooted in this American paradox: the imperative of healing and the imperative of justice could not, ultimately, cohabit the same house." On the other hand, its utopianism reminds us that, without the nation truly coming together, Reconstruction had no chance of success. And it was not only North and South that needed to come together. Butler and Greeley needed to shake hands with one another as much as with southerners. In 1869, Greeley used the *Tribune* to write an open letter to Butler, claiming that his radical policies were undermining reconciliation by delaying the return of prosperity in the South. Butler responded that Greeley's appeasement undermined true reconciliation by encouraging violent southern resistance.[27]

It is so easy for us today to see that Bateman's egalitarian ideals were hampered by the pervasive persistence of white supremacist prejudice that we are prone to forget his idealization of reconciliation. Likewise, with our focus on wrongs, we tend to forget that there was no clear consensus on remedies. Reconstruction will remain America's unfinished revolution if we fail to acknowledge how complicated the situation was for the actors at the time. Remembering that even some radicals understood the need for compromise, so long as it was not compromising, should help us better understand both their situation and ours.

III

As the nation's one-hundredth anniversary approached, it was southerners who initially refused to compromise. The continued failure to reach agreement about terms of reunion caused southern Democrats to oppose congressional funding for a national celebration. Nonetheless, there was sufficient support within and without Congress to go ahead with plans to have a centennial celebration coincide with a World's Fair. Honoring foundational myths, the celebration took place in Philadelphia, where the Continental Congress had met and the Declaration of Independence had been endorsed. There were exhibits from around the globe showing off Japanese porcelains and lacquer ware, jewels of India, South African ivory, peasant costumes of Sweden and Austria, Swiss watches, and French textiles. Two buildings were devoted to introducing Americans to kindergarten training in Germany, Belgium, and Switzerland. There were also art exhibits. Although the French and Germans did not send their best, the British did. Many Americans for the first time saw originals by Gainsborough, Reynolds, and Turner. American exhibits showed the nation and the world that the Union stood firm despite the recent bloody Civil War. The most visited venue was Machinery Hall, with American inventions such as the telephone, the typewriter, and the mighty Corliss engine displaying the nation's growing economic and technological power and its resilience in recovering from the Panic of 1873, the effects of which continued to plague the world economy. In an issue of the *Atlantic Monthly* serializing Henry James's *The American,* William Dean Howells reported, "It is still in these things of iron and steel that the national genius most freely speaks."[28]

Other American venues represented various segments of the nation's population. North American Indians had their own exhibit. There was a Woman's Pavilion showing an acre of products of feminine labor, including embroidery by Queen Victoria. Some products emphasized women's domestic work, while others pointed to expanded roles. There were textile designs by women trained at MIT and health care devices from the Women's Medical College of Philadelphia. African American women commissioned two sculptures by Edmonia Lewis, one of Cleopatra and one of Richard Allen, who bought his freedom from his Delaware owners, fought in the Revolutionary War, and founded the African Methodist Episcopal Church. As we have seen, Frederick Douglass, who once gave a powerful speech asking "What to the Slave is the Fourth of July?," was honored with a bust. The Italian sculptor Francesco Pezzicar sent a statue called "The Abolition of Slavery in the United States." Its rendition did not impress Howells, who described "a most offensively Frenchy negro, who has broken his chain, and spreading both his arms and legs abroad is rioting in a declamation of something (I should say) from Victor

Hugo; one longs to clap him back into hopeless bondage." Religious toleration was suggested by the presence of Catholic artist John La Farge's painting of St. Paul. The largest American painting was Peter Frederick Rothermel's "Battle of Gettysburg," hung in Memorial Hall. Depicting Pickett's Charge, this massive sixteen-by-thirty-two foot canvas had been commissioned by the lawyer who initiated efforts to establish a national cemetery for the decisive battle that took place in the exhibition's host state of Pennsylvania.[29]

An ode for the Fourth of July was commissioned for the exhibition, as well as a hymn and cantata for the opening ceremony on May 10, 1876. E. C. Steadman was invited to write the cantata and James Russell Lowell the hymn. Steadman was away in Panama, and Lowell declined. Lowell, along with William Cullen Bryant and Henry Wadsworth Longfellow, also declined to write the ode. That Lowell was invited might seem surprising. The year before he had published "The World's Fair, 1876," which mocked the United States' pretention to serve as a democratic model to the world. When Miss Columbia asks Brother Jonathan what she should display at the centennial, he responds:

> Show your State Legislatures: show your Rings:
> And challenge Europe to produce such things
> As high officials sitting half in sight
> To share the plunder and fix things right:
> If that don't fetch her, why, you only need
> To show your latest style in martyrs—Tweed.

Attacked for his lack of patriotism, Lowell pointed not only to the corruption of Boss Tweed but also to that of Butler, who was trying to dominate the politics of Lowell's home state of Massachusetts. Lowell considered his satire patriotism of the highest order. The period's corruption, he felt, risked undermining the most important result of the Civil War: "the assertion of our indivisible nationality." For him, "an indissoluble Union is the chain that holds us to our anchor. Its disjointed links would be old iron for the junkshop."[30]

Despite his satire, in two 1875 centennial odes Lowell had expressed his sense of the nation. One was for the Battle of Concord, the other for Washington taking command in Cambridge, Massachusetts. The ode on Washington used the perspective of the founding father to cast light on the present. To a journalist born in the South, Lowell wrote, "I took advantage of the occasion to hold out a kindly reconciliation to Virginia. I could do it with the profounder feeling, that no family lost more than mine by the civil war. Three nephews (the hope of our race) were killed in one of the Virginia battles, and three cousins on other of those bloody fields." According to Horace Elisha Scudder, Lowell was convinced that "the war was fought for nationality, and that emancipation was a welcome incident. Hence he is inclined to lay the emphasis in reunion on the need of reconciliation with the Southern whites rather than on the protection of blacks." At the Republican convention in 1876, Lowell supported the reformist Benjamin Bristow of Kentucky, who as the country's first solicitor general had helped convict members of the Ku Klux Klan and as secretary of the Treasury helped to clean up the Grant administration. On his initial support of Bristow, Lowell wrote, "I believed that a Kentucky candidate might at least give the starting-point for a party at the South whose line of division should be other than sectional, and by which the natural sympathy between reasonable and honest men at the North and South should have a fair chance to reassert itself." When Hayes was nominated instead, Lowell was, nonetheless, proud of blocking the aspirations of Blaine, whom he identified with corruption. The Massachusetts poet was chosen an elector for Hayes. With the disputed election hanging on one elector's vote, a rumor surfaced that Lowell would switch to supporting Tilden. Although Lowell forcefully quashed the rumor, it indicates the extent to which his belief in reunion based on reconciliation gave him a reputation for independence. Lowell's efforts at reconciliation were ideal for the organizers, who wanted the public ceremonies to dramatize a reunited nation.[31]

With Lowell, Longfellow, Bryant, and Steadman unavailable, Bayard Taylor of Pennsylvania agreed to write the Fourth of July ode. His recitation would go along with a speech by Senator William M. Evarts of New York and a reading of the Declaration by Richard Henry Lee, the namesake of the Virginian who proposed independence to the Continental Congress. For the opening ceremony, Whittier of Massachusetts agreed to write the "Centennial Hymn." To balance Whittier, Lanier, a former Confederate who lost his health imprisoned at Point Lookout, composed a cantata: "Centennial Meditation on Columbia." Lanier's poem was set to music by Dudley Buck from Connecticut, and the tenor soloist came from Boston. Dismissing the funding controversy, Lanier wrote, "All this will die out in a couple of months, and *then* everyone will be in a temper to receive a poem of reconciliation." "The Southern people," he added, "make a great deal more of my appointment to write the cantata poem than I had ever expected, and it really seems to be regarded by them as one of the most substantial tokens of reconciliation yet evinced by that vague *tertium quid* which they are accustomed to represent under the general term of 'The North.'" As Lanier acknowledges, most southerners had a distorted notion of their sectional rival. Lanier believed that the South would change as its image of the North was corrected, and vice versa. Ten years after the centennial, Grady, Lanier's fellow Georgian, seemed to prove him right with his speech, "The New South." Grady thought that Lanier was the "most artistic and cultivated poet this side of Swinburne and Tennyson." In "The Civil War as Unifier," Miles highlights Lanier's selection along with Lamar's eulogy for Sumner two years earlier as answering the prayer "for a fuller understanding and a closer union." At about the same time, Lanier's son became the managing editor of *The Photographic History of the Civil War in Ten Volumes*. Hammering home the message of reconciliation in his volume, Miles includes a photograph of Lanier and a number of his works along with Grady's speech.[32]

Joining President Grant at the opening ceremony was the governor of Pennsylvania, which had contributed substantial funds. Two other governors were invited, one from Massachusetts and one from Louisiana. Douglass, invited to sit with the dignitaries, was initially stopped by police, then allowed to proceed when recognized by a senator. There was a 150-piece orchestra and a chorus of 800 directed by German-born Theodore Thomas. The "Centennial Inaugural March" was composed by Richard Wagner, and its performance was followed by the hymn and the cantata. Whittier and Lanier agreed that there should be no "spread eagle" patriotism. Both stressed a common past leading to a common future. Whittier addresses his hymn to "Our fathers' God" and ends with:

> Oh make Thou us, through centuries long,
> In peace secure, in justice strong;
> Around our gift of freedom draw
> The safeguards of thy righteous law:
> And, cast in some diviner mould,
> Let the new cycle shame the old.

As Lanier contemplates the nation's past and future, he writes in the spirit of reconciliation, purposely evoking the *Mayflower* before mentioning Jamestown, even though Virginia was settled first. He also has the Huguenots in dialogue with the Puritans. For today's readers, the choice of Huguenots might seem surprising, but in his "Centennial Ode" Quaker Taylor also includes Huguenot grace along with Puritan will, Cavalier honor, Quaker truth and sweetness, and Dutch reformed strength as examples of American virtues. Huguenots were ideal symbols for those intent on reconciliation because they had immigrated to both the North and the South. Lanier's father came from "Virginia farmers of ancient Huguenot origin," and, as we have seen, Lamar also had Huguenot forefathers. So did Tourgée, and both he and Dixon created fictional characters with Huguenot ancestry. To be sure, Lanier's effort at religious inclusiveness was still criticized. Someone wrote to him complaining that Catholic settlers of Saint Mary's County, Maryland, were omitted. No poem could please everyone.[33]

Turning to the future, Lanier raises the question of how long the nation will last. An Angel responds:

Long as thine Art shall love true love,
Long as thy Science truth shall know,
Long as thine Eagle harms no Dove,
Long as thy Law by law shall grow,
Long as thy God is God above,
Thy brother every man below,
So long, dear Land of all my love,
Thy name shall shine, thy fame shall glow!

Miles quotes Daniel Coit Gilman, the president of the Johns Hopkins University, on the crowd's response: "The devotional exercises awakened no sentiment of reverence. At length came the cantata. From the overture to the closing cadence it held the attention of the vast throng of listeners, and when it was concluded loud applause rang through the air. A noble conception had been nobly rendered." Miles adds, "Lanier was the first southern poet to give full, clear voice to the spirit of nationality." Noting England's presence at an exhibition planned to celebrate its defeat, Woodrow Wilson hailed the centennial as "a festival of reconciliation. It spoke of peace and goodwill with all the world. It surely is not fanciful to regard it, besides, as a type and figure of the reconstruction and regeneration of the nation. . . . The national spirit was aroused, and conscious now at last of its strength. The stage was cleared for the creation of a new nation." Alabama lawyer Peter Joseph Hamilton enthused, "Political reconstruction had accomplished something, a railroad and commerce more, but the reconstitution of a common patriotism was due especially to the Centennial Exposition."[34]

Despite such praise, it is easy to dismiss Whittier's and Lanier's poems of reconciliation for covering up existing tensions. On July 4 of the centennial year in Hamburg, South Carolina, two white men in a buggy ordered a parading black militia company off the road. A few days later, when the militia captain was tried for obstructing a public highway, the company was confronted by hundreds of armed whites demanding that it relinquish its guns. Six blacks were murdered, and homes were looted. Dixon combines details from the Hamburg massacre and the 1898 Wilmington, North Carolina, massacre for a culminating scene in *The Leopard's Spots*. Five southern states did not send exhibits to Philadelphia. It is no wonder that many today agree with Michael A. Bellesiles that the "celebratory tone of the centennial" was empty rhetoric and that "there was no national harmony."[35]

In this context, Lanier's theory of poetry's basis in music is revealing. When Lanier's "Centennial Meditation on Columbia" was published prior to the big event, its language was criticized for being obscure and imprecise. Lanier defended himself by pointing out that his words were intended to be set to music. "I had to compose for the musician as well as the country, and had to cast the poem into such a form as would at once show well in music (where contrast of movement between each adjacent part, in broad *bands of color,* was, from the nature of the art, a controlling consideration) and in poetry." Lanier's success in composing for both musician and country is exhibited in the concluding stanza.

> O Music, from this height of time my Word unfold:
> In thy large signals all men's hearts Man's heart behold:
> Mid-heaven unroll thy chords as friendly flags unfurled,
> And wave the world's best lover's welcome to the world.

At the same time that God's Word unfolds from the orchestra's music, Lanier enacts in music's broad bands of color the unfurling of the American flag with its red and white stripes to welcome the world to the Centennial Exposition.[36]

Music also plays a conciliatory function for the nation. An accomplished musician, Lanier knew that music is not capable of representing "shades of meaning save those which are very intense, and very highly and sharply contrasted." Lanier turned that weakness into a strength. "The musician," he felt, "will become quite as substantial a figure in everyday life as the politician." Existing in a higher, spiritual realm, music can express a harmony disrupted by too much attention to the quotidian. Its power is freedom from "the weight and burden of realism," allowing "the spirit of man" to "call upon it for relief from the pressure and grind of Fact." Thus, in his cantata, he "tried to make the whole as simple and as candid as a melody of Beethoven's: at the same time expressing them in such a way that could not be offensive to any modern soul." Given the differences in the country, harmony was more likely to be found in music than in a realistic attention to fact.[37]

Those differences are on display in poems Whittier and Lanier wrote prior to the centennial. In 1867, Whittier published "Howard at Atlanta" about General Oliver O. Howard, the head of the Freedmen's Bureau, visiting African American children attending newly established schools in a city that had been burned to the ground during Sherman's march through the South. In the middle of the poem, Howard asks,

> "What shall I tell the children
> Up North about you?" . . .

And a little boy stood up, "General,
Tell 'em we're rising!"

The narrator then adds:

O black boy of Atlanta!
But half was spoken:
The slave's chain and the master's
Alike are broken.
The one curse of the races,
Held both in tether:
They are rising,—all are rising,
The black and white together!

Describing Atlanta rising phoenixlike out of the ashes of war, Whittier's poem, like Bateman's engraving of the same year, expresses an optimistic view of a South reconstructed with black and white rising together.[38]

Seven years later, Lanier wrote a dialect poem called "Civil Rights" that was published in a number of southern newspapers. Consisting of twenty-eight couplets in iambic hexameter, it expresses a southern cracker's response to Sumner's proposed comprehensive Civil Rights Act of 1874, not the compromised version of 1875. The speaker of the poem describes a conversation with "Old Uncle Johnny Stiles," who stops by every Sunday. Johnny recollects how Yankees had killed his son in the war: "Sherman's folks had broke my dam and burnt my mill;/And stole my watch, and mules, and horses, and my cotton and my corn,/And left my poor old Jane and me, about as we was born!" Nonetheless, he admits, "But then I tried to set it right, allowin' all along/They saw *their* side as we saw *our'n*, and maybe both was wrong." But "when I jest had come to see/My way was clear to like 'em, and treat em brotherlee," along comes the proposed Civil Rights Act, which people like Uncle Johnny saw as an attempt of the national government to impose on the South social equality between African Americans and whites.

"Hit seems as ef, just when the water's the roughest here of late,
Them Yanks had throwed us overboard from off the Ship of State.
Yes, throwed us both—both black and white—into the ragin' sea,
With but one rotten plank to hold; while they, all safe and free,
Stands on the decks, and rams their hands into ther pockets tight,
And laughs to see we both must drown, or live by makin' fight!"

Worked up, Johnny concludes:

"Yes, Jeems," says he, "they'll make it so that both of us cain't float.
Now, ef I'm drowned, I'd like to know who'll gather in my grain,

> And feed my gals, and care for wife—my dear old faithful Jane?
> (And here I'll say I've knowed him now for fifty year or more,
> And never heerd him swear, nor cuss a single cuss before:)
> I tell you, Jeems, I *kin* not help it—*maybe* it's a sin;
> *By God! ef they don't fling a rope, I'll push the nigger in!*"

Lanier's final image of Johnny throwing an African American into the raging sea to save himself is in direct opposition to Whittier's vision of blacks and whites in the South rising together.[39]

As much as these two poems seem to expose Lanier and Whittier's centennial harmony as a sham, it would be a mistake to assume that there was no room for reconciliation. In different ways, both of these earlier poems were attempts to bring North and South together. Whittier's poem is explicit. The last stanza reads:

> O brave men and fair women!
> Ill comes of hate and scorning:
> Shall the dark faces only
> Be turned to morning?—
> Make Time your sole avenger,
> Meet Fate half-way, and make it
> A joy and blessing!

Implicit rather than explicit, Lanier's message is easier to miss unless we distinguish him from his speaker and Johnny. Lanier uses both to send a message to the North, not through a utopian appeal but through a realistic appraisal of southern attitudes. Mocking Johnny's bigotry, Lanier also makes it clear that Johnny has a sincere desire for reconciliation, even though Yankees devastated his life during the war. Passage of the Civil Rights Act of 1874, the poet warns, will undermine that desire. Equally important, it will worsen the conditions of African Americans in the South, not improve them.[40]

Of course, from today's perspective, to heed Lanier's warning would have been to compromise the egalitarian ideals of Reconstruction. We get a better sense of how conditions looked at the time, however, if we remember that on this issue Lanier had an unexpected ally. Tourgée opposed the 1874 act as well. Acknowledging the bill's "beneficent purposes," Tourgée lamented that "Sumner knew no more of the actual condition of the colored man here than he realized his condition on the Gold Coast. . . . The idea of a visionary quack who prescribes for the disease without having made a diagnosis." According to Tourgée, Sumner's bill would destroy the public school system in the South because whites would close them before integrating them. Granted, when the watered-down Civil Rights Act of 1875 was challenged and sent to the Supreme Court, Tourgée defended it because of the important legal precedents involved. Nonetheless, his opposition to the 1874 bill reminds us that a policy that today seems so clearly a proper remedy might have been unwise at the time. Tourgée was not giving up on the egalitarian promise of Reconstruction in the long term, but he was making strategic decisions based on a realistic assessment of people's attitudes. In a related but different vein, neither Lanier nor Whittier were naïve about differences in the country when they wrote celebratory poems for the centennial, but they felt that there was something to be gained by working to find common ground.[41]

IV

Fiction writers as well as poets imagined reconciliation, although the ground on which it was based varied from writer to writer. As Blight points out, in a series of 1884–85 fictional pieces called "The Veteran and His Pipe" and elsewhere, Tourgée "dissented repeatedly from sectional reconciliation if it meant the obliteration of the emancipationist meaning of the war." Yet in his fiction Tourgée also draws on the fictional convention most commonly used to promote national reconciliation: a marriage plot between a northerner and a southerner. Nina Silber, the acknowledged expert on the "romance of reunion," focuses on the northern view of reconciliation. At first, she argues, women appeared in northern works as the most unforgiving of all southerners. But, "by the 1870s . . . the southern female had become the tempestuous and romantic belle, the object of the northern man's desires, and ultimately the female partner in a symbolic marital alliance which became the principal representation of sectional reunion. This image of marriage between northern men and southern women stood at the foundation of the late-nineteenth century culture of conciliation." This "formula" relied on a "gendered metaphor to make a political statement about power relations between sections in the postwar period," with the suggestion that the North "had tamed and subdued and would now control the South, in much the way that husbands were assumed to take control in marriage." But not all North-South marriages fit Silber's formula. Once conventions were established, authors could use them in a variety of ways. Just as acts of reconciliation by Douglass, Sumner, Ames, and Lamar had different significances, so too do North-South romances in works of fiction.[42]

In *A Hazard of New Fortunes* (1890), William Dean Howells comes close to Silber's formula when he has the savvy business manager of a New York literary periodical marry the daughter of a southern colonel so reactionary that he defends slavery a generation after the passage of the Thirteenth Amendment. The couple is perfectly matched, as the southern woman is attuned to the need to adapt to a commercial society, and the northern man needs her moral compass to guide him. In *The Bostonians* (1886), however, Henry James has an impoverished Mississippian, with the charisma of Lamar, successfully court a beautiful and spellbinding feminist speaker. The final scene suggests that their possible marriage promises many tears to come. Henry Adams's *Democracy* (1880) has a virtuous but no longer wealthy Virginia gentleman win the affections of a rich New York widow who has come to Washington, DC, fascinated by power and temporarily under the spell of a northern politician modeled on the corrupt James Blaine. In a twist, the northern widow is related to the Virginia Lees. In *A Fool's Errand* and *Bricks without Straw*, Tourgée has southern gentlemen court northern women, not vice versa. Subsequent chapters explore how other authors depict North-South romances, but I want to end this one by looking at how DeForest and Woolson creatively deploy the conventions of the romance of reunion—DeForest in a comic mode that stretches readers' sense of verisimilitude and Woolson in a tragic mode that draws on all of her skills as a realist.

DeForest's neglected *The Bloody Chasm* (1881) has a complicated plot that stretches credibility and playfully exposes the limits of the conventions of the romance of reunion. The book starts with a poignantly realistic description of devastated Charleston, South Carolina, soon after the end of the war. Silas Mather, a rich New England Puritan, returns to the city where he was married and walks past the destroyed Catholic and Huguenot churches. As a young man, he had been a tutor for the proud and prominent Beaufort family. Over its protest, he married one of the daughters. After a wedding in the Huguenot church, he and his wife moved north. Having made a fortune, the capitalist never forgives the South for its rebellion but feels compelled to honor his beloved wife's dying wish that he take care of her family. Childless, he also comes south intent on keeping his dead sister's son from marrying into an Irish working-class family. Col. Henry Edwards Underhill is infatuated with Norah Macmoran's beautiful voice and follows her after her diocese sends her to Charleston to help revive its Catholic Church through song.

Mather meets South Carolina's General Hilton, a lawyer he knew before the war. A true gentleman, now bankrupt and with a wooden leg, Hilton remarks, "We are a crushed, beggared, prostrate people" (*BC*, 23). He then helps the capitalist find one of two living Beauforts, the beautiful nineteen-year-old Virginia, who has a voice as lovely as Norah's. All four of Virginia's brothers were killed in battle. In addition, her father took ill and died building forts for the Confederacy, and her sister died of a broken heart after firing upon Sherman's advancing troops. Virginia is so poor that she is living in the shanty of two of her ex-slaves, Aunt Chloe and Uncle Phil. Mather wants to adopt Virginia, take her north to finish her education,

"IN VAIN IS THE STRIFE"

THE ROMAN CATHOLIC CATHEDRAL OF ST. JOHN AND ST. FINBAR, DESTROYED BY THE FIRE OF DECEMBER, 1861—MOST OF THE ABLE BODIED CITIZENS WERE SERVING AS SOLDIERS, AND THE FLAMES RAGED UNCHECKED.

DeForest's *The Bloody Chasm* begins in 1865 with a northerner walking through conquered and devastated Charleston, South Carolina: "As he strolled on toward the Battery, the desert became desolation. The well-remembered Huguenot Church was a ruin. The Catholic Cathedral was a ruin" (6). This photograph is of the Catholic Cathedral. Before its destruction the three African American figures would have been excluded or segregated in the balcony.

and leave her part of his considerable fortune. She, however, refuses to "touch one Yankee dollar" from those who killed her brothers and ruined her "country" of South Carolina (46).

Rebuffed, Mather comes up with a plan to fulfill his "double duty of converting his rebellious niece to Unionism and saving his bewildered nephew from Popery" (*BC*, 52). He announces that he will write a will leaving one-fifth of his fortune to the community, $500,000 to Underhill, and $500,000 to Virginia, if, in a specified time, Henry and Virginia marry. Aunt Chloe, Uncle Phil, and General Hilton are enthusiastic about the plan, but Virginia is not. Henry will inherit substantial money even if the marriage does not take place. Nonetheless, he is willing at least to meet Virginia, who refuses out of pride. Uncle and nephew head back to Boston, and Virginia's widowed aunt Anna Dumont moves from her shanty in Columbia to share the one in Charleston. Hearing of Mather's offer, she praises Virginia for acting like a Beaufort but then has second thoughts.

Indeed, we learn from General Hilton that acting like a Beaufort is not always the wisest course of action. The great patriarch was General Beaufort, who fought in the Revolutionary War and who both made the Beauforts and unmade them. "That venerable ghost . . . has been a sort of vampire, sucking the blood of prosperity out of the family" because "every Beaufort since has tried to live in his lordly style" (*BC*, 76). The family's financial decline started long before the defeat of the Confederacy. By 1860, although he was in substantial debt, Virginia's father was living "as if he were worth $500,000." When word comes to Virginia that Mather is dead, but his will is intact, she comes up with her own plan to inherit the sum her family feels it is worth. She writes Underhill proposing that they marry but immediately separate. Although he has little to gain financially, Henry returns to Charleston to ponder the proposal. His interest is sparked when General Hilton shows him Virginia's photograph. The general assures Underhill that, if he marries, Virginia will eventually come to love him, even though she refuses to meet him before the wedding. Somewhat improbably, Henry agrees to marry, sending his own photograph to his intended, even though it is of his brother who died at Gettysburg.[43]

Virginia's terms are harsh. The ceremony is to take place in a darkened church, so that the couple cannot see each others' faces. She also plans to wear a black veil and a black crepe dress, since she considers the marriage a funeral. The day of the wedding, Henry gets cold feet and seeks Norah, whom he has long ignored, asking her to forgive him and to save him from his fate. Putting aside her feeling for him, she refuses. Accompanied by the general, Henry proceeds to the church, putting on fake whiskers to look like his brother in case his betrothed glances at him. The ceremony over, the two go their separate ways. Virginia hopes that the uncouth northerner will seek a divorce soon after the wedding, an option a proud Beaufort cannot initiate. Instead, Henry decides to put himself in the bizarre position of wooing his own wife. He announces to Hilton:

> "I will win her as surely as the North won the South."
>
> "You are the North incarnate."

> "And my wife is the South."
>
> "Yes—a woman," sighed the General, "a generous and impassioned woman. The South has been just that, and only that, all my lifetime." (*BC*, 145)

Henry instructs his friend to tell Virginia that he has given her his hand and now gives her his heart, but she wants neither. To avoid any chance of meeting her husband, she, her aunt, Aunt Chloe, and Uncle Phil head to Europe, where they set up temporary residency in Paris.

With the bizarre terms of the will and the marriage in full force, the plot takes on the characteristics of a Hollywood screwball comedy or a Molière comedy of manners. Like the woods in a Shakespearian romance, Paris becomes a liminal space in which identities transform. As one character puts it, "Paris is wonderfully converting" (*BC*, 201). Avoiding the northern expatriate community, Virginia and her aunt meet the Baltimore widow Mrs. Fitz James and her brother, who pretend to know all of French society. Young, rich, and caught up in the atmosphere of Paris, Virginia thinks less and less of the past, immersing herself in the present and insisting on using her maiden name while always aware that she can never fully participate in the romantic intrigues because she is married. Catching up on her education, she studies French, improves her music, and becomes enamored of poetry. Aunt Chloe and Uncle Phil visit the Louvre, thinking it is a well-decorated hotel. Figures from the past assemble. Norah is in Paris studying with Virginia's voice teacher, Professor De Buthene, an impoverished Belgian reputed to have a noble lineage. The two beautiful women establish a bond while singing together. General Hilton visits, and with his arrival allusions to the romance of reunion resume. The object of Mrs. Fitz James's attention is the dashing Virginian Colonel Peyton, who, on meeting Virginia, is infatuated with her. Catering to Virginia's new love of poetry, Peyton writes her a poem about Pickett's Charge, which he observed and in which Virginia's youngest brother died. Moved, she has De Buthene set it to music and sings it for her admirer. Afterward, General Hilton and Virginia wax nostalgic about the Lost Cause, while the reader remembers that Underhill's brother also died at Gettysburg. Indeed, it is no surprise that Colonel Peyton turns out to be Underhill, who did see Pickett's Charge—as a Union officer. Henry should be upset with his wife for flirting with another man, but since he is the object of her affections, he is not. Only two people know his true identity: Norah and General Hilton. Norah promises to keep the secret, and General Hilton is his ally. As the flirtation progresses, Hilton insists to Virginia that she has to tell Peyton she is married. She tries to tell but enjoys the attention too much to do so. Forced by a jealous Mrs. Fitz James, she finally confesses; her husband reveals himself; and all is right with the world. The two provide Norah a dowry so she can marry the Catholic De Buthene, and the poor Irishwoman becomes the noble she deserves to be.

Silber cites *The Bloody Chasm* as an example of her formula. What she does not note is the serious fun DeForest has in evoking it. In addition to calling Underhill and Virginia the North and South incarnate and the South a woman, DeForest litters his book with comments like Underhill's remark that his future wife will be "a desperate case for reconstruction" (*BC*, 55) or General Hilton's to Virginia that "You are just like the South. You make yourself miserable by refusing to recognize an accomplished fact" (276). Through exaggeration, DeForest reminds us that the complexity of national reunion is one thing; the complexity of marriage is another. The basis of DeForest's allegory is Mather's will, which is so strange that Hilton exclaims, "It is a common saying among lawyers that a man frequently saves up all his lunacy for his last will and testament. Well, it *was* a cruel will" (104). Once the will is announced, DeForest transforms into a fanciful romance what started as a serious description of the conditions of the South and Mather's efforts to help a region he cannot forgive. When told of his uncle's will, Henry worries, "What if my wife should secede?" (57). Later, Hilton assures him, "When [Virginia] once begins to forget, she will begin to forgive." To Henry's, "Forgive *me*—her husband!," the general exclaims, "It will be a fine moment—that moment of reconciliation" (112). But what does Virginia have to forget and forgive? Henry, after all, graciously allows her to inherit half a million dollars. Unlike the North and the South, husband and wife have never had a sundering that they need to reconcile. When Henry notes that his future wife will be "a desperate case for reconstruction" (55), he is right. Their affair is about marriage, not about Reconstruction. By having a husband court a wife who does not even know what he looks like, DeForest renders the romance of reunion unrealistic.

Even so, DeForest has his cake and eats it, too, as he uses Mather's incredible will to mock prevailing prejudices and to put forth a complicated understanding of the dilemmas the Union faced during Reconstruction. When General Hilton commends Mather's plan for trying to bring about "reconciliation between the families and a resumption of intercourse" (*BC*, 61), the New England Puritan—recalling how the Beauforts resented the marriage of one of them to him, a northern tutor—replies, "There never had been any intercourse" (62). North and South, DeForest reminds us, did not get along long before the Civil War. Abolitionist Mather and his southern wife seem to have had a loving marriage, but the haughty Beauforts could not reconcile themselves to it. In contrast, Virginia, acting like a Beaufort, solely for the money enters into a union she insists remain loveless. At the same time, Mather himself is a hypocrite for condemning the Beauforts' sense of class superiority, while opposing the marriage of his nephew to the daughter of a working-class, Catholic family. In the end, southerner can reconcile with northerner, but Catholic has to marry Catholic.

Southerner and northerner can reconcile, but they must overcome barriers to do so. In DeForest's allegory, North and South, like Virginia and Henry, are legally united, but true reconciliation has not yet occurred. For DeForest, the South is primarily to blame. With the older generation of unforgiving northerners dying out, a younger generation, including those who fought in the war, is willing to give its heart as well as its hand. Furthermore, both the young southerner and northerner owe a debt of gratitude to the dead northerner whose wealth helps get the former out of poverty and gives the latter a life of leisure. As we have seen, DeForest demystifies the southern myth that the war alone was responsible for its destitution. Living beyond their means, the Beauforts were already in debt when war broke out. And yet, even though northern wealth is footing the bill for reunion, the South is so caught in the past that it refuses to be grateful. Naïvely, abolitionist Mather predicts that within a year of marriage, Virginia will become a "black republican" (59). On the contrary, to achieve the affective reconciliation needed to cement legal reunion, the North is put in the awkward position of having to woo the South it defeated.

There are, to be sure, people in the South who help with that wooing. Devoted to their former mistress and identifying their worth through association with the Beauforts, Aunt Chloe and Uncle Phil nonetheless welcomed the arrival of Sherman's troops and emancipation. Uncle Phil greets Mather with "Gin us our freedom, you folks did. . . . We know it, Boss, an' 'members it" (31). Aunt Chloe serves as a sort of Greek chorus, commenting on the action and providing a practical corrective to the overblown Beaufort code of honor while advocating Henry's cause. When Virginia initially refuses to consider marriage, Aunt Chloe responds: "'Pears to me dar's things be said what'd fotching mo' vittle. What we wants is words what has got some nourishment in 'em" (81). On Virginia's hope that her refusal will hurt Underhill's feelings, she comments, "Mus' hurt him powerful to keep his dollars" (83). She is also not shy about weighing in on the conjugal aspect of marriage when Virginia reveals her plan to her aunt: "Is you a grown woman, or a baby? Does you s'pose a grown-up man—a man as wears britches an' tails-coats—is a-gwine ter agree not to marry his wife? You two's jess talkin' like folks in a dream" (101).

General Hilton also helps Henry. Benefiting from the Beauforts having money to pay him old debts, Hilton starts to understand the folly of southern resentment and sense the advantages of belonging to a nation. As he tells Virginia, "It is a great country, my dear. I feel mightily protected with an American passport in my pocket. *Civis Romanus sum.* What a country it is" (*BC*, 205). When Virginia accuses him of becoming a federalist for considering the nation, not his state, his country, he responds that he talked to Robert E. Lee, who shares his sentiments. Appalled, Virginia blurts out, "The soldiers have abandoned the fight, and only the women continue it" (205). As the action makes clear, DeForest believed that women would be wise to follow the lead of soldiers and accept the terms of surrender. A former soldier himself, DeForest was one of many who saw soldiers as models for the spirit of reconciliation. For instance, Hilton feels that he and Underhill are natural allies because "soldiers are comrades. . . . They may fight under hostile flags, but still they are comrades" (24). DeForest certainly agrees with Hilton when he counters Virginia's praise of women for refusing to participate in national reconciliation: "The women and the politicians—the politicians on both sides. May God confound them" (205).

With his condemnation of politicians, DeForest indulges in a standard complaint about the barriers to true reconciliation. As a writer and a former soldier, he thought—or at least hoped—that he could transcend political divides. Enraptured by Peyton's "Pickett's Charge"—actually written, of course, by DeForest—Virginia wonders if her admirer could write a poem celebrating Yankees. Underhill responds, "I find I can write with sympathy about any subject, if I think of it long enough" (239). Proud Virginia finds this hard to believe. But, thinking it over and "insatiably curious about poetry," she realizes: "Oh it must be the impartiality of genius. I have read of that somewhere. Like Shakespeare and Homer. They wrote kindly about both sides—heroes and villains—Greeks and Trojans." Not wanting to put himself in the company of genius, Underhill attributes his capacity to "the impartiality of a soldier. A soldier learns at last to worship valor, no matter where found" (239). Virginia wishes that she could develop the same capacity and, after some hesitation, admits that out of curiosity she would even be willing to read a poem about Yankee courage.

Poetry, it turns, out is Henry's ultimate weapon in the battle for his wife's affection. With a poet's ability to adopt the perspective of the Lost Cause, this former Union officer begins to win his southern wife's heart as his poetic celebration of Pickett's Charge initiates the process of her surrender. Likewise, Virginia's desire to understand the mysterious art of poetry renders her willing to entertain the possibility of seeing the world from another point of view. Just as the beauty of music allows Protestant Henry to fall for a Catholic and northern Henry to fall for a southerner, so poetry allows Virginia to bridge the bloody chasm.

Of course, she is prepared for her change of heart by her vastly improved economic circumstances. DeForest clearly has a northern point of view, but he is no radical. Instead, he comes closer to Greeley's belief that the South will reconcile itself to reunion if the North helps it prosper economically. DeForest, like Greeley, prided himself in his ability to understand the southern point of view. When Mather and Underhill get to Charleston, they insist on seeing Fort Sumter. In January 1861, a month after South Carolina seceded, DeForest visited Charleston for the *Atlantic Monthly* and reported, as impartially as he could, on the atmosphere of secession and the possibility that Fort Sumter would be attacked. In *The Bloody Chasm,* Hilton praises Underhill's generosity as the act of a Bayard, an allusion to the Bayard family of Delaware, which consisted of peace Democrats during the war and those who actively sympathized with the white South during Reconstruction. In 1880, as DeForest was writing his book, Senator Thomas Bayard was a leading contender to become the Democratic nominee for president. The best way to win the heart of the South, DeForest suggests, is for northerners like himself to display their sympathetic understanding through literature. *The Bloody Chasm* seems to have been written with that purpose in mind. Nonetheless, because Henry's and Virginia's happy ending takes place in a self-conscious work of romance, DeForest cautions us that literature and poetry might not have the same power in real life. Furthermore, even if an individual North-South marriage works out, that does not mean that national reconciliation will occur. DeForest's novel might be no more than what Virginia calls Henry's plot to win her: "a regular Yankee trick" (*BC*, 299). Then again, earlier in the discussion of poetry's power, Virginia's aunt admits that the North won the war through "some Yankee trickery" (239).[44]

V

By exploiting the conventions of the romance of reunion at the same time that he exposes their limits, DeForest produces a seriously comic work of Reconstruction literature. Another work that creatively plays with the conventions of the genre is Woolson's tragically realistic "Rodman the Keeper." Neither writer trusts politicians, but that distrust leads to different emphases. DeForest warns readers that individual acts of reconciliation do not guarantee national reconciliation; Mather, who insists that he has "no spite toward individuals," is unforgiving toward the South for its rebellion (*BC*, 23). In contrast, Woolson focuses on the failure of even individuals to come together.[45]

"Rodman the Keeper" was published in the *Atlantic Monthly* a year after the centennial celebration and the same month as Hayes's inauguration. Woolson had established a reputation as a local color writer in the Great Lakes region. When her mother's health forced her to move South, she applied her skills to her adopted home. In addition to drawing on the conventions of intersectional romance, Woolson employs a less-noted device to mark North-South reconciliation. The warm climate of the South, it was felt, could quite literally help heal the national divide as ailing northerners sought its benefits. A late nineteenth-century nonliterary example is the development of the community of Pinehurst, North Carolina, still famous for its championship golf course. In 1895, James Walker Tufts, the Boston philanthropist who made his fortune by inventing a device for the soda fountain, bought up acres of land near Fayetteville to create a health resort for people of moderate means. The land was cheap, and Tufts was convinced that respiratory illnesses suffered by many northerners because of industrialization could be cured in an atmosphere of pine ozone found in the region. He hired Frederick Law Olmsted's firm to create a New England–style village in the middle of the South. Soon he had a golf course designed, which hosted the United North and South Amateur Championship, one of the first of various athletic contests signaling a united nation by staging North-South or Blue-Gray events. The literary equivalent is the plot in which a northerner goes South to take advantage of the region's healing powers. Once the conventions of that plot became commonplace, authors could use them, as they could the conventions of the marriage plot, for a variety of purposes. For instance, Dixon has his villain Stoneman go south for his health, and he ends up converting to the southern cause. In contrast, Tourgée's Fool goes south for his health, and he ends up dying from yellow fever.[46]

Woolson interweaves the plots of intersectional romance and health with one focused on how both sides of the conflict felt the need to honor the Civil War dead. DeForest touches on this topic when he subtly counters Virginia's resentment that she lost her brothers in the war with the reminder that Henry also lost a brother. But Woolson puts the issue at the center of her plot and explores whether that common need will bring together the two sides or divide them. John Rodman is a Union soldier from New England who moves south in part for his physical health. As he tells another character, "Like many another Northern solider, I remembered the healing climate of the South; its soft airs came back to me when the snow lay deep on the fields and the sharp wind whistled around the poor tavern where the moneyless, half-crippled volunteer sat coughing by the fire" (RK, 274). He also moves south for his psychological health. When the war began, he was twenty-eight and engaged to eighteen-year-old Mary, the minister's daughter, who nursed him back to health after he suffered wounds in his first battle. During his next enlistment, his mother died, and Mary broke her promise and married another. Never returning home, Rodman sold the family estate by mail and promptly lost his profit in a bad investment. The action begins about 1870 when he takes a position as the keeper of a national cemetery next to a former prison camp in the South. Rodman recognizes that the South "is part of a great problem now working itself out." That, however, is not his concern. "I am not here to tend the living, but the dead," he tells himself. His duties are to take care of the grounds, oversee the register of the fourteen thousand buried, and raise the flag, not out of "patriotism so-called, or rather miscalled," but as a duty to the dead soldiers (262). He confines himself to the cemetery, which is separated from the community by a "massive granite wall" (263). Nonetheless, he cannot maintain his isolation and learns that, as the first line of the story tells us, "It is easier to keep the dead than the living" (261).

On a hot day he wanders from the cemetery to find a cool spring that a black boy told him was near the old Ward plantation, now dilapidated and inhabited by a relative of the former owner. Ward De Rosset is a Confederate Army veteran, missing one arm and severely ill. Having been wounded himself, Rodman tries to help, despite resistance from the proud southerner. When De Rosset reaches a crisis, Rodman, aided by Pomp, a former slave and now a loyal servant, moves him to his cottage to care for him constantly. This act of generosity is frowned upon by Bettina Ward, the daughter of the former owner, who returns from trying to earn a living teaching closer to the coast. Unforgiving of those who killed her father and brothers and ruined the land, Bettina considers the cemetery "enemy's country" (RK, 270). She insists on returning her uncle to her place, but, lacking the resources to nurse him, she agrees to let him stay until he is ready to be moved.

> Then began a remarkable existence for the four: a Confederate soldier lying ill in the keeper's cottage of a national cemetery; a rampant little rebel coming out daily to a place which was to her anathema-maranatha; a cynical, misanthropic keeper sleeping on the floor and enduring every variety of discomfort for a man he never saw before—a man belonging to an idle, arrogant class he detested; and an old black freedman allowing himself to be taught the alphabet in order to gain permission to wait on his master—master no longer in law—with all the devotion of his loving old heart. For the keeper had announced to Pomp that he must learn his alphabet or go; after all these years of theory, he, as a New-Englander, could not stand by and see precious knowledge shut from the black man. So he opened it, and mighty dull work he found it. (270)

This incongruous assembly breaks up when De Rosset dies. Before he dies the cemetery gets unexpected visitors. In May, African Americans, dressed in mourning, "old uncles and aunties, young men and girls, and even little children" (272), singing "swing low, sweet chariot," come to decorate the graves with flowers to honor the dead who "had done something wonderful for them and their children" (273). It is Memorial Day. "The keeper had not much sympathy with the strewing of flowers, North or South; he had seen the beautiful ceremony more than once turned into a political demonstration." But there is none of that here, and he joins the procession. After it is over, he returns to his cottage, where Miss Ward is tending her uncle. When Rodman notes that there was not one "white face" even though in the North some women honored the southern dead buried there, she responds, "You are fortunate. They must be angels. We have no angels here" (273).

The two see each other one more time. On a warm night in August, Rodman interrupts a stroll to lie down under the flagpole "gazing up into the infinite sky" (RK, 275). Thinking that he is away, Bettina enters the grounds and walks past the flagpole without seeing him, although her robe erotically brushes his arm. Rodman watches as "she moved to and fro among the mounds, pausing often, and once he thought she knelt." Leaving, she sees Rodman and announces to him that she has sold her place and is going to Tennessee, alone, to teach. "A miserable life," Rodman responds, "God help the woman who must be that dreary thing, a teacher from necessity." With tears in her eyes, she turns to leave. Rodman implores her not to depart in anger and asks her to sign the visitors' registry. "The Government had it prepared for the throngs who would visit these graves; but with the exception of the blacks, who can not write, no one has come, and the register is empty" (RK, 276). She refuses to sign, insisting, "The South *is* our country, and not your icy North." As she leaves, he kisses her hand and wishes her luck. A week later Rodman learns that an energetic man from Maine has bought the Ward estate and is tearing it down to build a new dwelling.

This is not a story of reconciliation. On the contrary, it undercuts conventions of the romance of reunion. A northerner comes south for his health and ends up nursing a southerner who dies. Romantic possibilities between a northerner and a southerner are raised, but no marriage ensues. Both end up alone and friendless, their ancestral homes sold. Precisely through this failure, however, Woolson makes a case for reconciliation.

When the story was reprinted in a collection, Woolson introduced it with some lines from Thomas Bailey Aldrich's "Spring in New England," published in the *Atlantic Monthly* in 1875. Later, as the journal's editor, Aldrich would publish some of Chesnutt's conjure woman stories. In his poem, from the perspective of New England, he describes the graves of northern soldiers "far away to the South." In lines not quoted by Woolson, Aldrich ends with winter turning to spring, marked by North-South reconciliation, in which southerners honor the northern graves.

> But hush! For the strife is done.
> Forgiven are wound and scar;
> The fight was fought and won
> Long since, on sea and shore,
> And every scattered star

Set in the blue once more:
We are one as before,
With the blot from our scutcheon gone!

So let our heroes rest
Upon your sunny breast:
Keep them, O South, our tender hearts and true,
Keep them, O South, and learn to hold them dear
From year to year!
Never forget,
Dying for us, they died for you.
This hallowed dust should knit us closer yet.[47]

Woolson's story is both an ironic comment on Aldrich's hope and a wish that it will be fulfilled. Furthermore, from another *Atlantic Monthly* poem written by a northerner about graves in the South, Woolson would have known that some southern women did indeed honor Union graves. Francis Miles Finch's "The Blue and the Gray" (1867) was introduced by a passage from Greeley's *New York Tribune* describing an event April 25, 1866. "The women of Columbus, Mississippi, animated by nobler sentiments than are many of their sisters, have shown themselves impartial in their offerings made to the memory of the dead. They strewed flowers alike on the graves of the Confederate and National soldiers."[48]

Woolson, like Aldrich and Finch, hopes for impartial reconciliation. Like them, she imagines it on a personal, not a political, level. Rodman is a northerner in the South, but he does not take part in the political efforts of Reconstruction. On the contrary, he "despise[s]" carpetbaggers (RK, 268). If fourteen thousand dead, "could arise and walk," he thinks, "the whole state would be filled and no more carpetbaggers needed" (267). He is in the military but has no role enforcing Reconstruction governments. As he tells himself when asking the fourteen thousand for permission to help De Rosset, he is helping him on purely humanitarian grounds. It is "merely a question between man and man" (268). Reconciliation on this level seems so easy to achieve that its failure is all the more poignant.

Woolson does not, however, make it easy on her *Atlantic Monthly* readers. In "The New South," Grady evokes his hometown of Atlanta to bring North and South together. With General Sherman in the audience, he announces to his northern audience that his message comes from

> consecrated ground. Every foot of soil about the city in which I live is as sacred as a battle-ground of the republic. Every hill that invests it is hallowed to you by the blood of your brothers who died for your victory, and doubly hallowed to us

> by the blow of those who died hopeless, but undaunted, in defeat—sacred soil to all of us—rich with memories that make us purer and stronger and better—silent but staunch witnesses in its red desolation of the matchless valor of American hearts and the deathless glory of American arms—speaking eloquent witness in its white peace and prosperity to the indissoluble union of American States and the imperishable brotherhood of the American people.

Woolson's use of a Georgia landmark threatens to undermine the "white peace" of an "imperishable brotherhood." She models her cemetery on the one next to the notorious prison camp of Andersonville. The fourteen thousand dead corresponds to the number at Andersonville. Andersonville also had a famous registry of death, kept and recovered by Dorane Atwater, one of the prisoners. Clara Barton aided in the reburial efforts and was given the honor of raising the flag during the celebration of Andersonville as a national cemetery June 25, 1865. When Bettina Ward tells Rodman, "We have no angels here" (RK, 273), it is an allusion to Barton, "the Angel of the Battlefield."[49]

The misconduct at Andersonville was so egregious that its commander was tried and convicted in one of the first war crimes trials ever held. A commissioner at the military tribunal was Gen. Lew Wallace, who would go on to write *Ben-Hur.* Whenever a northern politician wanted to wave the bloody shirt and block reconciliation, he simply had to evoke Andersonville. For instance, early in the election year of 1876, Blaine, hoping to get the Republican nomination, did just that. With Democrats in control of the House, a bill was proposed in the centennial year to remove all of the disabilities of former Confederates under the Fourteenth Amendment. Looking for an issue to rally the base of his party, Blaine moved to exempt Jefferson Davis, whom he blamed for the atrocities at Andersonville. Southern Democrats took the bait and responded by condemning northern cruelty to prisoners at places like Point Lookout in Maryland. Thus, Blaine was successful, temporarily at least, in drawing party lines based on conflicted memory of the war, not on Reconstruction policy or the economy.[50]

Nonetheless, Woolson seems to place primary blame for the failure of reconciliation on Bettina's obstinate loyalty to the Lost Cause. Rodman appears to have learned the lesson the narrator attributes to the fourteen thousand: "while ye have time, do good to men . . . we are beyond your care" (RK, 262). In contrast, Bettina stays trapped by memory of the dead. "I remember the tears of my mother, and the grief all around us. There was not a house where there was not one dead" (276). Bettina's continued dwelling on the fallen distinguishes her from DeForest's Virginia. Virginia, too, begins wedded to the dead, but then she goes to Paris and starts to immerse herself in the present. Admitting her enjoyment to General Hilton, she

Woolson's "Rodman, the Keeper" is set in a national cemetery modeled on the one next to the notorious prisoner-of war camp in Andersonville, Georgia. In the 1872 presidential campaign, Democratic and Liberal Republican candidate Horace Greeley advocated North and South "clasping hands over the bloody chasm." Thomas Nast depicts Greeley unsuccessfully reaching to find a hand over the bloody chasm of the Andersonville cemetery in *Harper's Weekly.*

guiltily worries, "It is like forgetting the dead; it *is* forgetting them." The general gently replies, "It may be best. . . . Probably it is best to remember chiefly living facts and living men" (*BC*, 240). Bettina never seems to learn that lesson. To be sure, her nighttime visit to the cemetery displays her potential for forgiveness. But even that gesture is to the dead, and she refuses to make her visit public for the living.

The situation is, however, not quite that simple. Rodman, after all, stays as keeper of the cemetery while Bettina tries to "begin a new existence" as a teacher (RK, 275). And even her uncompromising loyalty has a double significance. Soon before Bettina enters the story, we are told of the one decoration on the wall of Rodman's cottage. It is a verse "Inscribed in ornamental text":

> Toujours femme varie,
> Bien fou qui s'y fie;
> Une femme souvent
> N'est qu'une plume au vent.
>
> [Woman always varies
> He who puts his faith in her is really crazy

A woman often
Is only a feather in the wind.] (RK, 269)

Later, Rodman explains the verse to the dying De Rosset with Bettina listening. The verse, which Rodman got from a Frenchman, encapsulates his sense of betrayal by his former lover. When De Rosset asks if he really believes it, Rodman responds, "I do. But they cannot help it, it is their nature" (275). He then begs Bettina's pardon, aware that he might have offended her, as he later does when he ridicules her plan to start a new life as a teacher. These two moments strongly suggest that Rodman does not want Bettina to go to Tennessee because he hopes she will stay and be courted. Just when the misogynist renews romantic interest in a woman, he is rejected again, not because Bettina is too fickle, but because she is too steadfast in her loyalty.

This irony directed against the protagonist is only one of many in the story, large and small. Rodman goes South for its healing powers and ends up trying to nurse a southerner who can find comfort only in the confines of a Union cemetery. He claims to honor education but disparages Bettina's effort to be a teacher. Bettina speaks of the icy North, yet it is she who is icy—though not always. Whereas she refuses to lay flowers on the Union graves, when she enters the Ward estate "the room bloomed at once." This blossoming occurs immediately after Rodman thinks, "the whole thing reminds me of a funeral," with its display of flowers (RK, 271). Bettina hates the North for causing death in southern homes but seems unmoved by the horrible deaths of fourteen thousand in the prison camp next to her own home. When her nighttime visit shows that she is indeed moved, she unwittingly demonstrates that there are angels in the South after all. Even the name "Ward" carries ironic significance. Reconstruction policy was criticized for turning freedmen into wards of the state, but in this story a member of the leisure planter class becomes the ward of a governmental official.

These and other ironies emphasize the story's complex depiction of competing loyalties. Even Pomp has his loyalties tested. He wants to help his former master but has to disobey him and Bettina in order to do so. Then, on Memorial Day, he sneaks out at night to decorate the graves of the Union dead. He does so secretly because of the risk of betraying his loyalty to his old master. In that sense, Pomp is similar to Bettina, who also privately displays her reverence for the dead soldiers. Most of all, however, Woolson uses Bettina to depict the conflict southerners faced between being loyal to their state or region or to the nation. Describing the "conflicting loyalties" involved in the Civil War, Nathaniel Hawthorne notes the "anomaly of two allegiances" in the American federal system. Whereas the state "comes nearest to home to a man's feelings, and includes the altar and the hearth," the nation "claims his devotion only to an airy mode of law, and has no symbol but a flag." Like many southerners, Bettina increases her hostility to the nation because a war waged in its name laid waste to the people and soil that commanded loyalty to the state.[51]

But a national cemetery complicates Hawthorne's characterization of what constitutes allegiance to the nation. For friends and relatives of the many who died waging war in the name of the Union, loyalty to the nation was related to memory of the dead. In his First Inaugural Address, Lincoln, trying to hold the Union together, counters sentiments like Hawthorne's and appeals to the "better angels of our nature" by evoking, as "our bonds of affection," "the mystic chords of memory, stretching from every battle-field, and patriot grave, to every living heart and hearthstone, all over this broad land." Woolson echoes Lincoln when she describes how on Memorial Day "spring blossoms were laid on the graves of the soldiers, from the little Maine village to the stretching ranks of Arlington, from Greenwood to the far western burial-places of San Francisco" (RK, 273).[52]

For many southerners, however, the North did not honor the words of Lincoln nor his plea in the Second Inaugural "to bind up the nation's wounds." At one point an elderly, caring southern doctor comes to the cemetery to treat De Rosset. "Cursing the mismanagement of the entire medical department of the Confederate army" that led to so much suffering, he, nonetheless, has no love for the nation. Having made "his first and last visit to a national cemetery," he disparagingly mutters, "National! . . . national!" (RK, 271). From the doctor's point of view, his contempt is justified. The cemeteries the government created in the wake of the Civil War were called "national," but no Confederates were allowed to be buried in them. Not until the Spanish-American War did President McKinley, while visiting Atlanta, declare the care of Confederate graves a national duty. The fictional De Rosset may be nursed in a national cemetery, but in real life he would not have been allowed to be buried there. For southerners, the exclusion of the Confederate dead raised questions about what "national" meant. Indeed, as Catherine W. Zipf has argued, national cemeteries were established in the South not only to honor the Union dead but also to display national sovereignty in the conquered territory.[53]

To be sure, from a Union perspective at the time, it was completely fair to deny a rebellious enemy burial next to the loyal dead, especially since many white southerners insisted that African Americans could not be interred in white cemeteries. Woolson knows this and is by no means an advocate of the "lost cause" (RK, 262). But she does her best to understand the feelings of the white southerners she met during her stay in the midst of Reconstruction. For Henry James, that effort was a literary success. Reviewing Woolson's southern stories, he wrote that they were "the fruit of a remarkable minuteness of observation and tenderness of feeling on the part of one who evidently did not glance and pass, but lingered and analyzed." Her stories have "a high value . . . when regarded in the light of the *voicelessness* of the conquered and reconstructed South. Miss Woolson strikes the reader as having a compassionate sense of this pathetic dumbness—having perceived that no social revolution of equal magnitude had ever reflected itself so little in literature, remained so unrecorded, so unpainted and unsung. She has attempted to give an impression of the circumstance, among others, and a sympathy altogether feminine has guided her pen. She loves the whole region, and no daughter of the land could have handled its peculiarities more indulgently, or communicated to us more of the sense of close observation and intimate knowledge."[54]

Written in 1887 for *Harper's Weekly*, James's review might have caught the attention of Tourgée, who also had lived in the South and prided himself on trying to understand the southern point of view. Perhaps prompted by James's review, Tourgée, the next year, wrote "The South as a Field for Fiction." Whereas James worries about the South's voicelessness, Tourgée insists that the preferred subject of our literature "has become not only Southern in type, but distinctly Confederate in sympathy." Tourgée even goes out of his way to attack "Mr. Howells and Mr. James," who avoid representing southern life only because it does not lend itself to the "trivialities which both these authors esteem the most important features of real life." Tourgée certainly would have looked askance at James's praise of Woolson's portrayal of African Americans, some of the " 'natural objects' of the region." Observing that Woolson "preceded Uncle Remus by a considerable interval," James claims that "she has noted scientifically the dialect of the freedman" and produced a "careful philological study." Tourgée admits that the "Negro" has become a "stock character of fiction" but faults those portrayals. "About the Negro as a man, with hopes, fears, and aspirations like other men, our literature is very nearly silent. Much has been written of the slave and something of the freedman, but thus far no one has been found able to weld the new life to the old. This indeed is the great difficulty to be overcome. As soon as the American Negro seeks to rise above the level of the former time, he finds himself confronted with the past of his race and the woes of his kindred."[55]

Tourgée thought enough of Woolson's literary talent to publish her in *Our Continent*. Even so, he would have considered Pomp a stock character. To be sure, on Memorial Day, Pomp sneaks out at night to decorate the graves, and when he learns to read, his primer is the placard honoring the dead who freed him. But even this gesture is at odds with Tourgée. Woolson confirms the widely accepted belief that slaves were freed by white soldiers. Tourgée, in contrast, stressed the extent to which African Americans contributed to the war effort. Just as Tourgée would have faulted Woolson's portrayal of Pomp, so he would have disagreed with Rodman's and, seemingly, Woolson's belief that the Union dead would have endorsed an apolitical reconciliation of northerners and southerners.

A soldier himself, he celebrated acts of individual caring between former enemies. In a work written shortly after "The South as a Field for Fiction," he retells Woolson's story, with a twist. "A Conflict Between Church and State" depicts a Union soldier imprisoned not in Andersonville but in a camp near Salisbury, North Carolina, not far from where Tourgée lived as a carpetbagger. "Taken prisoner and confined in the fetid, overcrowded pen, he had sunk rapidly into consumption, and but for an almost miraculous escape would have been one of the twelve thousand nameless dead who sleep beneath the long ridges on the sunny hillside beyond where the famous prison stood" (GS, 171). After his escape, the soldier makes his way to northern Virginia. There, reversing Woolson's account in which a Union soldier nurses a dying, aristocratic, one-armed Confederate, Tourgée has his Union soldier cared for by a working-class, one-armed Confederate. In Tourgée's account, it is the dying Union soldier who comes from the well-to-do family of a New York attorney. Twenty years later, the former Confederate, in need of legal advice, seeks it from the wealthy attorney, who is eternally grateful to the southerner who cared for his son as he died. As much as Tourgée is moved by such individual acts, for him reconciliation could not be, as it was for Woolson, "merely a question between man and man" (RK, 268). Tourgée felt that the best way to honor the Union dead was to perpetuate the ideal for which they fought. In 1885, he has a fictional veteran regret that Decoration Day, "a day of jubilee," has become Memorial Day, "a day of mourning." According to Tourgée, the holiday should be like the Fourth of July, a day of celebration proclaiming the victory of a nation's dedication to new values of equality.[56]

Woolson's story is not dedicated to these values. Like Greeley and many others at the time, she thought that the "great cause" (RK, 268) for which Union soldiers fought was confined to emancipation. That belief affects her sense of the goals of reunion and thus the significance of reconciliation. Even so, "Rodman, the Keeper" compellingly shows how bringing the nation together required northerners and southerners to overcome hostility toward those who had killed loved ones. It also lets us see that, if reconciliation demanded loyalty to the nation, what that meant was not clear. One reason the nature of the formally reunited nation was open to a variety of interpretations was that the definition of its federal system was up for grabs. The Civil War had made it clear that primary sovereignty lay in the nation, not in the states, but precisely how much power would remain with the states still needed to be negotiated. Although that negotiation took place largely in what Hawthorne calls the "airy mode of law," the era's writers also influenced people's views. Tourgée, for instance, makes clear where he stands when he has his fictional veteran answer Hawthorne's characterization of loyalty to the state by declaring that he did not fight for "our altars and our fires" but for a nation that stands for "freedom and the right." For Woolson, the issue is not so clear, as suggested by the image of Rodman raising the national flag over a national cemetery in the South. Pointing to the infinite, the flag dominates the landscape, but its sovereignty seems confined to the space within the granite wall of the cemetery. With this image Woolson anticipates Gregory Downs and Kate Masur's claim that in the South the US government was "less a 'Yankee Leviathan' than a Stockade State, a collection of outposts—both military and civilian—powerful within narrow geographical boundaries but limited in their reach." The next chapter looks at how other writers imagine the relation between individual states and the nation.[57]

-2-

FEDERALISM

Thinking Nationally, Acting Locally

Although after the war many southerners shared Bettina Ward's view that the South was their country, none of the writers I treat completely endorse it. All, in some form or another, embrace nationalism. Nationalism, however, took many forms. In this chapter, I explore how the national visions of various writers were distinguished by different portrayals of the country's complicated system of federalism, which had been transformed by the Civil War.

That change is marked grammatically. In the antebellum years, most people said "The United States are . . . "; after the war, more and more said "the United States is . . . . " The change is also marked by the Civil War Amendments. Earlier amendments restricted the activity of the national government. All three Civil War Amendments gave it new enforcement powers. Reconstruction's failure is due at least in part to the inability—or unwillingness—of the national government to assert its authority as extensively as radicals hoped. In the midst of a crisis in Charles W. Chesnutt's *The Marrow of Tradition* (1901), Dr. Miller proposes: "We might call on the general government. . . . Surely the President would intervene." But an African American lawyer responds: "Such a demand would be of no avail. . . . The government can only intervene under certain conditions, of which it must be informed through designated channels. It never sees anything that is not officially called to its attention. The whole negro population of the South might be slaughtered before the necessary red tape could be spun out to inform the President that a state of anarchy prevailed. There's no hope there" (*MT*, 192). The process by which African Americans could no longer count on the general government to protect their rights began long before 1877.[1]

Historians traditionally distinguish between two programs for Reconstruction: presidential and congressional. The presidential program grew out of Lincoln's insistence that the Union had never been split asunder because, lacking the right to secede, no "state" had left the nation. Presidents Lincoln and Johnson believed in the "perdurance" of individual "states," the doctrine that "once a State, always a

State." For them, rebellion had been the act of combinations of disloyal persons, not "states." Since "states" themselves had never left the Union, once legitimate civil government was restored to them and they acknowledged terms established by the executive branch, Reconstruction would be accomplished. For many congressional Republicans, however, the presidential plan would have led only to the restoration of the Union, not to a true reconstruction of the nation. Radical Republicans also denied the indestructibility of individual "states." Thaddeus Stevens argued that rebellious states were conquered provinces. If this was a realistic assessment of what happened, legally it led to the contradiction of a country conquering its own territory. Thus, Charles Sumner advocated the more logically consistent doctrine of "state suicide." When the southern states voted to secede, Sumner argued, they lost their status as "states." The territory over which they previously had jurisdiction was not lost to the United States, but it did come under control of Congress, as did any other US territory that was not a "state."[2]

The doctrines of "conquered territory" and "state suicide" justified the creation of military zones in the South until Congress agreed to recognize the governments of the formerly rebellious "states." But with the "redemption" of the South, states regained power they seemed to have lost. They were helped by various Supreme Court decisions. For instance, in *Texas v. White* (1869), Chief Justice Salmon Chase, Lincoln's former secretary of the Treasury, memorably declared, "The Constitution, in all of its provisions looks to an indestructible Union, composed of indestructible States." Then, in the *Slaughter-House Cases* (1873), the court made a clear distinction between state and national citizenship, restricting the privileges and immunities of US citizenship to such an extent as to make them of little use in protecting African American rights.[3]

This chapter begins with a comparison of two staunch supporters of national supremacy over the states: the radical Albion W. Tourgée and the conservative John W. Burgess. Both faulted various court cases and Reconstruction measures for continuing to recognize the sovereignty of individual states. Despite that agreement, Burgess, unlike Tourgée, was a harsh critic of the governments formed in the South before "redemption." Burgess's views make clear that belief in national supremacy did not necessarily entail support of African American rights. I then turn to how two southern writers, Thomas Nelson Page and Joel Chandler Harris, made a case that, for the good of the nation, the national government should not interfere with local control over the "race problem." Despite that agreement, the two imagined different class structures for local control. The next section focuses on Thomas Dixon. Often said to represent the white southern point of view, this scathing critic of Reconstruction came closer to Tourgée than to his fellow southerners in embracing the advantages of centralized power. Dixon's Reconstruction trilogy constructs a narrative in which, as repressive as it was, Reconstruction was necessary for the triumph of nationalism and America's imperial mission for the white race. Dixon's imperialism reinforces a paradox I identified in the introduction. If, on the one hand, Reconstruction failed in large part because the national government did not exercise its newly won powers, then, on the other hand, that failure was accomplished by increased national power in the realms of immigration and imperialism. I conclude by showing how Sutton Griggs imagines a world in which African Americans can appropriate to their advantage a federal system that gives states control over race relations.

II

Tourgée's works have traditionally been read as a Radical Republican's attack on the South's resistance to Reconstruction. In fact, they are just as critical of northern Republicans' lack of understanding of the conditions of the South, conditions that Tourgée as a carpetbagger knew firsthand. *A Fool's Errand* employs a variety of metaphors for proper reconstruction of the nation. Pruning vines, a worker worries that "it seems a clar waste" to cut back too severely. The Fool responds:

> Cut it down. It seems a pity, as you say, to destroy that beautiful growth, but, when vines have run wild for a time, the only way to bring them back to sober, profitable bearing, is to cut them back without scruple . . . It's wasting the past, but saving the future. And it's my notion that the same thing is true of peoples and nations, Andy. For instance, when a part of a country rebels, and runs wild for a time, it ought to have the rank wood, the wild growth, cut away without mercy. They ought to be held down, and pruned and shaped, until they are content to bear "the peaceable fruits of righteousness," instead of clambering about, "cumbering the ground" with a useless growth. (*FE*, 115)

Earlier the narrator notes that the "social conditions of three hundred years are not to be overthrown in a moment" and that, having "ripened into war," they "are never healed by simple victory." Instead, "the broken link can not be secured by mere juxtaposition of the fragments, but must be fused and hammered before its fibers will really unite" (24–25). Later, describing how the Fool parceled out some of his land to sell to freedmen so that they could be self-sufficient farmers, the narrator notes, "He purchased some Confederate buildings which were sold by the government, tore them down, and, out of the materials, constructed a number of neat and substantial little houses on the lots which he sold" (56). Reconstruction for Tourgée did not mean simply repairing existing structures. It meant dismantling old institutions and building new structures. Most important was the need to dismantle the states that had rebelled against the Union. Not to do so would allow "those who had inaugurated and carried on war against the nation" to regain power (305).

For Tourgée, the Civil War occurred not only because of a dispute over slavery but also because of the "fallacy" in our federal system of applying "the word 'State,' in its original or international sense, to one of the subordinate commonwealths of our nation" (*FE*, 233). A "*State of the Union*" (232) for him was precisely that, an entity depending on the nation for its existence. Nonetheless, he argued that, except for the right to secede, "the doctrine of 'State Rights' is altogether unimpaired and untouched" by the Civil War (357). To be sure, Radical Republicans temporarily divided the South into military districts, but those districts were comprised of states. Rather than follow Sumner's doctrine of "state suicide," the country adopted a plan of "forfeited rights." The boundaries and jurisdictions of the formerly rebellious states remained in place but were temporarily in "suspended animation."[4]

Tourgée's sense of federalism is poignantly dramatized in "A Conflict Between Church and State" in *With Gauge and Swallow, Attorneys* (1890). The chapter is about a former Confederate soldier who lost his arm during the Civil War. Despite his lost limb, he works diligently to make his northern Virginia farm an economic success. That success is due not only to his hard labor but also to the efficient management of the farm by his housekeeper, a former slave. After a while, the two start to produce children as well as crops. Scandalized, neighbors send a minister to let the former soldier know that he has to put a halt to his immoral ways. For the minister, this means giving the former slave some money to convince her to leave the house and the state. But the soldier, who has come truly to love his housekeeper, misunderstands and thinks that the minister wants him to make the mother of his children an honest woman by marrying her. Virginia, however, has an antimiscegenation law, so the two go to Washington, DC, and get married. When they return, they are promptly arrested for violating the Virginia statute. The former soldier's brother seeks aid from the firm of Gauge and Swallow, which files a suit challenging the Virginia law. In the end, a bargain is reached, and the couple is freed from jail after agreeing to go to the "great West" where no one will "inquire about the pedigree of [the] wife" (GS, 178).

This story makes a variety of legal points. One is about the hypocrisy of antimiscegenation laws. As Tourgée frequently argued, interracial love is bound to happen. Laws banning interracial marriage, therefore, turn love into an illegal act. His most obvious point, however, has to do with the relation between individual states and the national state. Although the chapter is called "A Conflict Between Church and State," it is also about a conflict between state and national jurisdiction. Why is it, after all, that a marriage recognized in the national capital is not recognized by all of the states in the Union? As the narrator remarks in the last line of the chapter, with the case dismissed, "those lawfully wedded in one State may still be adjudged malefactors in another" (GS, 178). Working within the federal system, northern Republicans assumed they could rule southern states by enfranchising freedmen, but, according to Tourgée, they misunderstood the situation in the South. In the chapter "Out of Due Season," the Fool reviews four proposals for Reconstruction. "The *first* was, that the State machinery of the *ante bellum* days in the lately denationalized sections should be set in motion, and the re-organized communities restored to their former positions without change, except as to individuals; just as you renew a wheel in a worn-out clock, and, starting the pendulum, set it again to its work" (*FE*, 131). This was the president's plan. The second, also avoiding necessary changes, was "to allow the vagrant States to come back into the national fold" but not to count freedmen in figuring population for the House of Representatives and the Electoral College unless they were enfranchised. Holding out hope for the first plan, the South rejected this one. The third plan, which the Fool favored, pointed to the doctrine of state sovereignty as the "root of evil" and acknowledged the nation's obligation to prepare freedmen for the responsibilities of liberty.

> So it proposed that the States which had been in the infected region should be quietly left to molder in the grave of rebellion,—the bed they had themselves prepared; that the region they once embraced should be divided up into Territories without regard to former statal lines, and so remain for a score of years under national control, but without power to mold or fashion the national legislation—until time should naturally and thoroughly have healed the breaches of the past . . . It recognized as an undeniable fact the idea that men who had gazed into each other's faces over gleaming gun-barrels, by the fateful blaze of battle, were not so fit to adjust the questions arising out of the conflict as those yet unborn. It was based upon the fact, too, that the slave was not made fit for unrestrained political power by the simple fact of freedom. Slavery might be ended as a legal status by proclamation, but as a living fact it could not. The hands could be unshackled by a constitutional amendment; but heart and brain must have an opportunity to expand, before the freedman could be capable of automatic liberty. (132)

The fourth plan was a compromise of the first three. No one, the Fool complains, thought it was the best plan. Because of the need to win an election, it prevailed but was, nonetheless, doomed to fail. For Tourgée, Radical Reconstruction was not radical enough.

In *Black Reconstruction*, W. E. B. Du Bois affirms Tourgée's belief that the strategy of retaining Republican rule in the South by enfranchising African

Americans was insufficient. Industrialists in the North, he argues, were more willing to "accept immediate Negro suffrage" than "pay the cost of social uplift" (*BR*, 222). Uplift could occur only if the social and economic structures of the South were truly reconstructed. That required much more than the abolition of slavery and the enfranchisement of freedmen. It required creation of a political system that did not allow a few influential families to control politics. According to the narrator of *A Fool's Errand*, "Leadership, in the sense of a blind, unquestioning following of a man, without his being the peculiar exponent of an idea, is a thing almost unknown at the North: at the South it is a power. Every family there has its clientage, its followers, who rally to its lead as quickly, and with almost as unreasoning a faith, as the old Scottish clansmen, summoned by the burning cross" (*FE*, 141). Given the continued power of the southern oligarchy, it was naive to believe that "enfranchisement was all that was required to cure all the ills which hitherto had afflicted, or in the future might assail," newly emancipated slaves (250). On the contrary, "The freedman is," the Fool writes to his former northern mentor, "just as impotent now of all power of self-protection as he was before the ballot was given him" (170).

"The spirit of the dead Confederacy," the Fool laments, "was stronger than the mandate of the nation to which it had succumbed in battle" (*FE*, 142). That spirit found expression through control of individual southern states. For the Fool, it was incomprehensible that the Wise Men of the North, "without guaranties for the future, or without power of reversal or modification, should restore this territory, this people, these States, to the position of equal, independent, and co-ordinate sovereignties" (173). Truly to bring about the goals of Reconstruction, southern civilization had to be dismantled. The only way to do that, Tourgée thought, was to treat the South as a conquered territory. "The North is simply a conqueror; and, if the results she fought for are to be secured, she must rule as a conqueror" (171). Instead, Reconstruction failed because northern Republicans joined white southerners in discrediting carpetbaggers, like himself, as well as southern whites and blacks trying to create a new southern society. For perhaps the only time in history, "the conquering power has discredited its own agents, denounced those of its own blood and faith, espoused the prejudices of its conquered foes" (180).

Tourgée's argument is partially confirmed by William A. Dunning. According to Dunning, "By 1867 it seemed clear that there were three ways available for settling the issues of the war in the South: first, to . . . permit the Southern whites themselves, through the Democratic Party, to determine either chiefly or wholly the solution of existing problems; second, to maintain Northern and Republican control through military government; and third, to maintain Northern and Republican control through negro suffrage." The first was "from the standpoint of

"We regard the Reconstruction Acts (so called) of Congress as usurpations, and unconstitutional, revolutionary, and void."—*Democratic Platform.*

The caption of "This Is a White Man's Government" quotes the Democratic Party's claim in the 1868 presidential campaign that the Reconstruction Acts are "usurpations, and unconstitutional, revolutionary, and void" because they violate the Constitution's division of powers between the states and the national government. Thomas Nast offers, in *Harper's Weekly*, representatives of three wings of the Democratic Party trampling on an African American veteran reaching for a ballot box: a simian Irish American worker from the Five Points area of New York City; former Confederate general Nathan Bedford Forrest, responsible for the slaughter of captured African American soldiers at Fort Pillow and an organizer of the Ku Klux Klan; and August Belmont, the rich, Jewish national chair of the Democratic Party, holding bribery money. In the background are sketches of atrocities committed against African Americans.

the great national issues demanding settlement grotesquely impossible." The choice, therefore, "had to be made between indefinite military rule and negro suffrage. The traditional antipathy of the English race toward military power determined resort to the second alternative. It was proved by the sequel that the choice was unwise."[5]

Today, we tend to see military rule and African American suffrage as two prongs of radicals' strategy. Dunning reminds us that at least some initially saw them as alternative solutions. Ironically, however, the choice of suffrage could work only so long as the military intervened to protect black voters. Dunning's view was shared by his dissertation advisor, John W. Burgess, who hired Dunning at Columbia University. Called the "father of American political science," Burgess is best known today for his racist comments cited by Du Bois in *Black Reconstruction*. Yet even Du Bois concedes that Burgess's account is "more than fair in law" (*BR*, 720), adding, "subtract from [him] his belief that only white people can rule and he is in essential agreement with me" (726). Indeed, Burgess insists that Sumner's doctrine of "state suicide" is "sound political science and correct constitutional law." Like Dunning, he felt that the wisest course would have been placing the South "under Territorial civil government and keeping [it] there until the spirit of loyalty to the Nation was established and the principle and practice of civil equality among all citizens was made thoroughly secure." Sounding like Tourgée, Burgess claimed that the architects of Congressional Reconstruction failed to take "this course, the only true and sound course," because of the fallacious idea that "these communities were 'States' of the Union, notwithstanding their rebellion against the United States and their attempted secession from the Union."[6]

Burgess's strong belief in the supremacy of the national sovereignty caused him to mock Supreme Court decisions reasserting "state" sovereignty. For instance, when Justice Stanley Matthews in the 1884 *Virginia Coupon Cases* cited Chase on "an indestructible Union composed of indestructible States," Burgess compared his logic to "Dogberry's charge to the watchmen in *Much Ado*." Burgess's criticism of *Texas v. White* struck at the heart of the constitutional doctrine of southerners who affirmed the federal system while criticizing a policy of national intervention into southern affairs. The Alabama lawyer Peter Joseph Hamilton, whom Woodrow Wilson later appointed a federal judge for Puerto Rico, cited *Texas v. White* as the "cornerstone of American constitutional law." Likewise, Burgess's response to the *Slaughter-House Cases* (1873) majority's distinction between national and state citizenship is similar to that of Frederick Douglass. According to Douglass, "Two citizenships mean no citizenship. The one destroys the other. It is the folly, as Franklin would have it, of harnessing a horse at each end of the wagon. The one defeats the efforts of the other. The nation affirms, the state denies and there is no progress. The true doctrine is one nation, one country, one citizenship and one law for all the people." Calling the majority's opinion entirely erroneous," Burgess argues that, by restricting national citizenship, the court had "thrown aside the great gain in the domain of civil liberty won by the terrible exertions of the nation in the appeal to arms." For Burgess, the past of slavery proved that we cannot trust individual states, which are only local forms of government, to protect civil liberties. On the contrary, "if history has taught anything, it is that civil liberty is national in origins, contents, and sanction." The Civil War was a turning point in history because, prior to it, the United States was "lagging in the march of civilization," due to "slavery" and "'state' sovereignty." But with "emancipation" and "nationalization," the United States asserted "its supremacy, forevermore." Tourgée makes a similar point in *A Fool's Errand* when he mocks a wise man of the North for insisting that "all these questions of the rights of citizens are regulated, by the fact of reconstruction, to the tribunals of the States, and must be settled and determined there, according to the spirit of the Constitution" (234).[7]

Tourgée and Burgess might have agreed on the need to keep the South under territorial government and on the supremacy of the nation over mistakenly named "states," but they disagreed on many other issues. For instance, Tourgée defended Reconstruction governments, whereas Burgess accused them of "plundering the treasury, increasing the taxes, selling franchises, issuing bonds, and celebrating high carnival everywhere and all the time." Their difference is registered in their response to monetary Reconstruction. It is no accident that important cases maintaining what Edward S. Corwin would retrospectively call "dual federalism" involved financial issues. One of the most forceful proponents of drawing a line between state and national powers was David Dudley Field. He could find almost all the judicial precedents he needed in *Collector v. Day* (1871), in which the court ruled that the national government did not have the power to levy an income tax on a Massachusetts judge, who was a state official. Other cases reasserting "state" sovereignty, such as *Texas v. White* and the *Virginia Coupon Cases*, involved questions of state debt and currency. As today's term *sovereign debt* and the old reference to Britain's gold coins as *sovereigns* indicate, sovereignty is tied to a nation's financial system. Inefficient finance was a major cause of the abandonment of the Articles of Confederation and the adoption of the Constitution. The Civil War raised issues old and new. Most obviously, the Confederacy needed its own system and its own currency. Both sides incurred heavy debts waging war, which led to the printing of paper money. In *The Lost Cause Regained*, Edward A. Pollard argued that a major reason for the South's defeat was the inability of its government to match the "wonderful success of Federal finances." "While the unbroken finances of the North enabled it to keep immense armies in the field, and to spread a factitious prosperity through the country, the utter failure of the Confederate currency did more to demoralize the war than any other single cause, and hurried the final catastrophe. . . . The evils of a depreciated currency are of the most various descriptions; they pervade all the channels of public life and are felt in every daily care of the people. In the South they produced universal distress and penetrated every home; they were named as the prime cause of desertion from the army."[8]

Printing large amounts of paper money also attracted counterfeiters. Both sides of the conflict printed counterfeit bills to undermine the opposition's economy. Counterfeiting inevitably raises questions about the difference between "real" and "fake" money, since a counterfeit bill has, after all, a real existence. Two bills can be materially identical, but one is counterfeit if it is not backed by an invisible act of authorization by the sovereign power. Searching for a material manifestation of sovereign authority, many people insisted that paper money be backed up by gold or silver, which raised the question of specie payment. With the end of the war, a question also arose over the status of the debts of the former Confederate states. In the early years of the Republic, Alexander Hamilton had shrewdly secured support for the national government by absorbing debts incurred by states while fighting for independence. Section 4 of the Fourteenth Amendment made it clear, however, that the national government would not extend its claim of sovereignty so far as to absorb the debts Confederate states incurred in rebelling against the Union. The status of greenbacks was an equally pressing concern. Prior to the Civil War, only banks, as private corporations, issued paper money. After the war, the controversial *Legal Tender Cases* first denied and then affirmed the authority of the national government to do so. But those cases did not decide whether to resume specie payment and, if so, whether to use a gold or silver or both. The question of a metallic standard was influenced by a variety of factors, including international agreements and the discovery of large deposits of silver in the West. Lurking in people's minds were also the financial advantages of southerners who hoarded gold over those who held onto now worthless paper money. After heated debates, the country adopted the gold standard recommended at the 1867 Paris International Monetary Conference. The Coinage Act of 1873 discontinued the silver dollar, and in 1875, specie payment in gold for greenbacks was resumed.[9]

These tight money policies primarily hurt the poor and those in debt and created new sectional and class divisions that persisted into the Great Depression. Silver advocates denounced the Coinage Act as the "Crime of 1873." Tight money also recalled the long-standing controversy about the national banking system. Printing greenbacks was not the only way to increase the money supply. Deposits in banks had a similar effect. "The amount of currency in dollars in 1867 was only slightly smaller than the amount of bank-deposit dollars, but because of the remarkable growth of banking in the next five years, deposit dollars were double the amount of currency dollars just before financial panic occurred in 1873." Banks were concentrated in the Northeast, and tight-money policies were understandably condemned as furthering that region's interests at the expense of the nation. With the collapse of the Freedman's Saving and Trust Company in 1874, freedmen in the South were especially affected.[10]

Progressive historians Charles and Mary Beard and Howard K. Beale linked monetary Reconstruction with Radical Reconstruction, claiming that the radical policies were dictated by northeastern financial interests. In fact, the two did not align. Monetary Reconstruction was launched by Andrew Johnson's Democratic secretary of the Treasury Hugh McCulloch. McCulloch, unlike Johnson, was a proponent of hard money, but that did not make McCulloch an ally of Radical Republicans. As Walter T. K. Nugent puts it, "Johnson's greatest persecutors among the Radical Republicans were at least as [greenbackish] as he; the President and his impeachers were closer on financial questions than either of them were to Secretary McCulloch or to the less militant Republicans who frequently had charge of congressional monetary affairs." During the Grant administration, hard-money policies were engineered by moderate Republicans like Senator John Sherman, who would later become Rutherford Hayes's secretary of the Treasury. After the Panic of 1873, this wing of the party gained increasing control over greenbackers like Benjamin Butler.[11]

A strong advocate of hard money, Burgess celebrated the triumph of monetary over Radical Reconstruction within the Republican Party. Describing the events of 1877, he attributed Hayes's election as much to his promise of "a sound money Republican administration" as to his promise of a new departure. According to Burgess, many "who had usually voted with the Republicans," even though they disapproved of their southern policy, "were on the point of turning against [the party]" until Republicans passed the Resumption of Specie Act on January 14, 1875. With that legislation, "the financial policy of the Republican party, and of the country, was dragged to the front, and the Southern policy was forced backward, and made to constitute a less prominent issue in the campaign of 1876."[12]

Tourgée, in contrast, lamented the Republican Party's embrace of dimes and dollars at the expense of rights for freedmen. He was neither a supporter of the growing Greenback Party nor an advocate of silver, but he was acutely aware of the effect tight money had on the economy. In 1896, the year the Supreme Court decided the *Plessy* case, he published two essays that expressed his economic views: "The Reversal of Malthus" and "The Best Currency." Having lived in the South directly after the war, he also identified with the plight of southerners. In the same chapter in which he describes options for Reconstruction, the narrator of *A Fool's Errand* sympathizes with the financial condition of southerners after the war.

> Sadness and gloom covered the face of the earth. . . . The good things of the past were apples of Sodom in the hand of the present. The miser's money was as dust of the highway in value; the obligor, in his infinite promise to pay, had vanished, and the hoarder only had a gray piece of paper stamped with the fair pledge of a ghostly nation. The planter's slaves had become freedmen while he was growing into a hero, and no longer owed fealty or service to him or his family. The home where he had lived in luxury was almost barren of necessities: even the ordinary comforts of life were wanting at his fireside. . . . While he had fought, interest had run. War had not extinguished debt. What was a mere bagatelle when slaves and stocks were at their highest was a terrible *incubus* when slaves were no more, and banks were broken. The army of creditors was even more terrible than the army with banners, to whom he had surrendered. (*FE*, 129–30)[13]

As sympathetic as Tourgée was, he also knew how white southerners used questions of currency and debt to malign carpetbaggers. One of the best satiric moments in *A Fool's Errand* occurs when he explains the etymology of the term. In the chapter "Balik and Balaam," we are told: "'Carpet-bagger,' which was in some sense the lineal descendent of 'abolitionist,' was, as was very proper for a second edition, a considerable improvement on its immediate predecessor" (*FE*, 179). If in the North, "abolitionist" meant simply "one who favors the emancipation of slaves," in the South it meant that "+infidel+murderer+thief+ravisher+incendiary+all hell's accumulated horrors, 'not otherwise appropriated'" (178). Nonetheless, for southerners "abolitionist" had the disadvantage of having a specific meaning traced to its etymology that "sometimes interfered with its perfect application" (178). In contrast, "carpetbagger" was "undefined and undefinable" (179). Most likely, it had its origin in the days of "wild-cat money" during the antebellum period. There was so little regulation that banks could be established and print their own paper notes without having a specific location for their business. Agents "carried the bills around in *carpet-bags,* and were hence denominated, 'Carpet-baggers'" (177). One of the most unscrupulous of these agents, a Wisconsin editor, became a Copperhead during the Civil War. Searching for an epithet to disparage northerners who moved South after the war, he "bethought himself of his own nickname. . . . The name itself was a stroke of genius." It had "all the essentials of a denunciatory epithet in a superlative degree. It had a quaint and ludicrous sound, was utterly without a defined significance, and was altogether unique. It was susceptible of one significance in one locality, and another in another, without being open to any etymological objection. This elasticity of signification is of prime importance in a disparaging epithet: there is almost always a necessity for it" (177–78). In the North "carpetbagger" usually referred to "those, who without any visible means of support, lingering in the wake of a victorious army, preyed upon a conquered people." In the South, it meant "a man of Northern birth" and carried with it all of the former connotations of "abolitionist," plus the "incarnation of Northern hate, envy, spleen, greed, hypocrisy, and all uncleanness" (180).[14]

Carpetbaggers' original association with wildcat money complemented southerners' condemnation of them for their lack of a home base, greed, and irresponsible financial policies leading to debt and high taxes. Tourgée tries to show that, on the contrary, the Fool and his kind helped to promote industry and a developing economy. But he also had to combat the power of the northern press. The New York editor Horace Greeley launched a campaign blaming carpetbag rule for ruining his vision of a prosperous South supported by northern capital. Most northerners, like Burgess, bought into the stereotype of carpetbaggers as fiscally irresponsible. Thus, a national government intent on using gold to back the paper money it issued to win the Civil War failed to back carpetbaggers with the support they needed to make Reconstruction a success.

Differing on views of finance, Republicans Tourgée and Burgess also strongly disagreed on rights for African Americans. Burgess believed that, for the government to fulfill the nation's duty to protect the civil liberties of its citizens, political rights had to be restricted. Convinced that the Teutonic people were "particularly endowed with the capacity for establishing national states," he concluded that the "exercise of political power" was not "a right of man" and that non-Teutonic elements should be allowed to exercise it "only after the state shall have nationalized them politically." Whereas it was unfair to delay such nationalization, it was unwise to "hasten the enfranchisement of those not yet ethnically qualified." One reason Burgess advocated a period of territorial civil rule was because he so strongly opposed African American suffrage. To be sure, there is some truth to his claim that Radical Republicans insisted on giving the vote to freedmen in order to guarantee Republican rule in the South. Yet Burgess's response to that political maneuver was extreme. "From the point of view of sound political science, the imposition of universal negro suffrage upon Southern communities, in some of which the negroes were in a large majority, was one of the 'blunder-crimes' of the century. There is something natural in the subordination of an inferior race, even to the point of enslavement, but there is nothing natural in the opposite." Abstractly, Tourgée agreed that "the elective franchise" is a "privilege," not a "right." Once it had been granted, however, it became a "right which the sovereign must maintain and enforce, or submit to nullification of the law." Granting freedmen suffrage was not sufficient to make Reconstruction a success, but it was necessary for the United States to call itself a democracy and not perpetuate an oligarchy. In *A Fool's Errand,* Tourgée describes the Fool's unwillingness to accept the belief of "the judicial philosophers of our American bench" that "suffrage is not a right, but a privilege" (336–37).[15]

If Burgess's stance on political rights clearly aligns him with opponents of Reconstruction, his criticism of the *Slaughter-House Cases* marks a difference from them on civil rights. But even here his views are complicated. For him, it was important to distinguish sovereign power from governmental power. Although he denied state sovereignty, he did recognize that the Constitution divides powers between the national and state governments and that the nation cedes to states particular roles in protecting civil liberties. Thus, he condemned the "noted, not to say notorious, Ku-Klux-Klan Act of April 20, 1871, in which Congress simply threw to the winds the constitutional distribution of powers between the 'States' and the United States Government in respect to civil liberty, crime and punishment, and assumed to legislate freely without limitation for the preservation of civil and political rights within the 'States.'" In contrast, as we see in chapter 3, Tourgée strongly supported the Ku Klux Klan Act.

Burgess and Tourgée also disagreed about the scope of civil rights. In the *Civil Rights Cases,* when the Supreme Court ruled that the Fourteenth Amendment allowed the national government to act only in cases of state action, Burgess did not protest. On the contrary, he agreed with the court that the 1875 act was unconstitutional, citing its Thirteenth, not its Fourteenth, Amendment argument that acts of individual racial discrimination are not a perpetuation of the institution of slavery. For Burgess, such acts were in the realm of social rights, and he adamantly opposed any notion of "social equality." Civil rights, for him, were primarily the economic ones guaranteed by the Civil Rights Act of 1866.[16]

Tourgée had warned against passage of Sumner's 1874 Civil Rights Act because it would stir up resentment and be unenforceable. Nonetheless, he had an expansive sense of what civil rights entailed, and when the 1875 act was challenged, he defended its constitutional basis. His friend Samuel Phillips, to whom he dedicated a book and who helped him defend Homer Plessy, argued the government's case for the 1875 act before the Supreme Court. As we saw in chapter 1, for Frederick Douglass the government's defeat was far more devastating than the implementation of Hayes's "New Departure" in 1877. After all, until the court's decision, the national government still had the right to crack down on individual acts of discrimination. In contrast, segregationists were delighted with the decision. Henry Grady wrote an editorial for the *Atlanta Constitution* praising the court's decision. It is one of the few editorials from that time that he saved in his scrapbook. He titled it "Where to Draw the Line" and began, "The line has been drawn just where it should be," referring not only to the color line but also to the powers between states and the national government. In his response to George Washington Cable's "The Freedman's Case in Equity," Grady crowed that the "revolutionary" effort to impose equal social and civil rights "stands null and void by the highest court," leaving "the Southern people, temporarily at least, in control of the race problem."[17]

Prior to the Civil War, states had the power to decide whether or not to have slavery. The Thirteenth Amendment took away that power. With the *Civil Rights Cases,* the court returned to the states the power to control social relations between the races. The *Civil Rights Cases* also set the stage for legislation mandating segregation and instituting disfranchisement. Written after Grady's essay, Thomas Nelson Page's *Red Rock* (1898) and Joel Chandler Harris's *Gabriel Tolliver* (1902) helped legitimate that legislation through their portrayal of local conditions in two southern communities.

III

According to Tourgée, for white southerners, "the state is first," and "the Nation is a thing remote and secondary" (*BS*, 338). "The 'Southern' man is proud of the Nation chiefly because it contains his section and state; the 'Northern' man is proud of his section or state chiefly because it is part of the Nation" (339). As accurate as that characterization may have been for many white southerners, it does not completely account for Page and Harris. Local-color writers, who exerted a powerful influence on northern views of the South, both were confirmed nationalists. Thomas Nelson Page served his country as ambassador to Italy during World War I. Many thought that Woodrow Wilson would appoint him ambassador to the United Kingdom, but that position went to another southern man of letters, Walter Hines Page, who published both Chesnutt and Dixon. In 1905, Wilson's political rival Theodore Roosevelt visited Atlanta to demonstrate his love of the entire country. He insisted on meeting Harris and publicly proclaimed, "Presidents may come and presidents may go, but Uncle Remus stays put. Georgia has done a great many things for the Union, but she has never done more than when she gave Mr. Joel Chandler Harris to American Literature. . . . Where Mr. Harris seems to me to have done one of his greatest services is that he has written what exalts the South in the mind of every man who reads it, and yet what has not even a flavor of bitterness toward any other part of the Union." In an editorial written the same year A *Fool's Errand* was published, Harris proclaimed, "We have no Southern literature worthy of the name, because an attempt has been made to give it the peculiarities of sectionalism rather than to impart to it the flavor of localism." For Thomas Nelson Page and Harris, loyalty to section led to national division; attention to local conditions could easily accommodate itself to the federal system. Launching the publication of *Uncle Remus Magazine*, Harris wrote Page, hoping he would contribute: "It will be a Southern magazine by being first of all an American magazine. It will not have to bid good-bye to sectionalism, or to prejudice, or to intolerance of any kind, for it will never know them."[18]

North-South reconciliation was foremost on both authors' minds. In 1883, Harris condemned "stalwarts" in the North for waving the bloody shirt and "strutters" in the South for continuing to support the Confederacy. His position was similar to that of Mark Twain. Also in 1883, Twain published *Life on the Mississippi*, with his description of meeting "Uncle Remus" and George Washington Cable in New Orleans. Twain's criticism of intolerant southern strutters in that book is well known. Less acknowledged is his dislike of those who waved the bloody shirt. A Mugwump, Twain sided with the Democrat Grover Cleveland in the 1884 election against James Blaine, who tried to rally support by waving the bloody shirt. In *Adventures of Huckleberry Finn*, published soon after the election, Twain quietly parodies that strategy. Late in the book, Twain mocks Huck and Tom's overblown attempt to free a slave who is already free by having Tom insist that illiterate Jim keep a diary of his captivity. Since no paper is allowed, Huck steals a white shirt from Aunt Sally's clothesline for Jim to mark with his own blood. Harris also supported Cleveland, and his model for reconciliation was Cleveland's appointment to the Supreme Court, L. Q. C. Lamar, because of "his remarkable eulogy upon Charles Sumner." Lamar's views, Harris insists, "have become the views of the Southern people. . . . He is as liberal and progressive now as he was when he made the Sumner speech, and he has lived up to his highest ideal of American statesmanship, which means love for the whole country." Page shared that love. In the preface to the Plantation Edition of his works, he insisted that he had "never wittingly written a line which he did not hope might tend to bring about a better understanding between North and South, and finally lead to a more perfect Union."[19]

Both Page and Harris felt that a more perfect Union was one whose federalism allowed the nation to relinquish control on racial matters to southern states. Their view on federalism is almost identical to that of Harris's friend and colleague at the *Atlanta Constitution*, Grady. In June of 1889, Grady gave a speech at the University of Virginia called "Against Centralization." He began by alluding to *Texas v. White* and affirming that the republic was "an indissoluble union of indestructible states." Disavowing any desire to return to what he considered the doctrine of states' rights, he, nonetheless, decried "the increasing tendency to concentrate in the federal government powers and privileges that should be left with the states and to create powers that neither the state nor the federal government should have." Grady, Page, and Harris's position was foreshadowed by Pollard. In *The Lost Cause* (1866), Pollard defended the justness of secession and slavery. Two years later, with the election of 1868 approaching and a desire to support the Democratic Party, he published *The Lost Cause Regained*, in which he revised his view of what the "lost cause" stood for, in hopes of giving it a realistic chance of victory. Abandoning his insistence on the right to secede, Pollard redefined the "lost cause" to conform with the position of many northern Democrats during the Civil War who supported the Union but resisted changes in the relation between the national government and the states. Brandishing war Democrats' slogan "The Union as it Was," Pollard, in a chapter called "The True Nature and Service of the Union," declared, "The Union may be more effectually destroyed by consolidation than by secession." Pollard's redefinition of the "lost cause" helped him form an alliance with loyal northern Democrats, like Horatio Seymour, wartime governor of New York and his party's 1868 presidential candidate. Later, no longer intent on rallying behind the lost cause, Grady adopted Pollard's attack on centralization as a way to ally himself with Liberal Republicans skeptical of centralized power. When it came to racial matters, however, the popularity of Page and Harris's African American dialect stories gave the two writers of fiction more credentials to lecture northern audiences than anyone in that alliance, including Grady. Page claimed that "no man who has ever written has known one-tenth part about the negro that Mr. Harris knows," and he tried to get Harris to join him for a national reading tour to match the one just completed by Cable and Twain. Twain enthused that Harris "is the only master the country has produced" in writing the "negro dialect." Harris and Page are best known for their short stories, but both felt the urgency to write Reconstruction novels. Harris was so identified with Uncle Remus that his never took off and remains neglected today. Identified as the defender of the Old South, Page produced a best seller, which has come to epitomize the response of the "Plantation School" to Reconstruction. Both works deserve a close look.[20]

Page and Harris shared Grady's belief that the solution to the "Negro problem" was a system of black and white segregation, but the two had different visions of the New South. Page responded to Grady's nationally influential speech, "The New South" with one called "The Old South," which he revised for an 1892 collection. In praising the Old South, Page did not defend slavery. Although he felt that it benefitted "uncivilized" Africans, he condemned it as a "horror" and "a great barrier which kept out the light" and "did not admit of argument." He did, however, defend the gentlemanly civilization the South produced. In this respect, Page, the descendant of two governors of Virginia, is quite different from Harris, an illegitimate child born in Georgia. Harris had a much more populist streak. Both he and Page would have endorsed Grady's view that governmental centralization was a "paternalism gone mad" that allowed "the centralist and the monopolist" to serve one another: "the strong government protecting the money power, and the money power the political standing army of the government." But Harris would been much more inclined to agree with Grady, who said in a speech delivered to farmers that "the government can protect its citizens. . . . It can top off these colossal fortunes and, by an income tax, retard their growth. It can set a limit to personal and corporate wealth. It can take trusts and syndicates by the throat. It can shatter monopoly; it can equalize the burden of taxation; it can distribute its privileges impartially." Page and Harris's class difference is registered in their fiction.[21]

Both start their Reconstruction novels with idyllic pastoral scenes prior to the Civil War. Neither describes the war itself, focusing instead on the memory of it and the disruption of antebellum harmony caused by Reconstruction. Harris's antebellum Shady Dale in *Gabriel Tolliver* is characterized by its "serene repose" (*GT*, 18). After the war, the place, on the surface, seems to maintain some tranquility. "But behind the appearance of repose there was a good deal of restlessness and uneasiness" (116), which comes to the surface with the reign of Radical Reconstruction. Reconstruction, we are told, imposed "conditions that had no precedent or parallel in the history of the world" (121). Similarly, in *Red Rock*, Reconstruction brings "the disorganization of the plantations" and an "unwonted amount of lawlessness" (*RR*, 139). The once well-kept landscape is despoiled and in disarray.

In both novels, this disruption is linked to the intrusion of the national government into local affairs through the Freedmen's Bureau. Page's bureau agent, Jonadab Leech, is far more corrupt than Harris's Gilbert Hotchkiss. Leech is a power-hungry hypocrite, a coward who avoids service in the war, and a husband who abandons his wife. Hotchkiss believes in what he is doing and considers it his duty. He is even granted a degree of moral scruples when he resists the advances of an African American woman. Nonetheless, he "belonged to that large and pestiferous tribe of reformers, who go through the world without fixed principle," mistaking "his opinions for first principles" (*GT*, 290). He is an abolitionist who supported John Brown, not Garrison, and believes that "philanthropy, and reform, and progress generally are worthless unless it be accompanied by strife, and hate, and, if possible, by bloodshed" (291). During Reconstruction, those like him "succeeded in dedicating millions of human beings to misery and injustice, and warped the minds of the whites to such an extent that they thought it necessary to bring about peace and good order by means of various acute forms of injustice and lawlessness" (291).

In *Red Rock* and *Gabriel Tolliver*, the effect of the Freedmen's Bureau is similar. The harmony that could have prevailed between freedmen and whites is disrupted by the activities of this wing of the national government. In *Gabriel Tolliver*, African Americans are "no longer cheerful" (114). One exception is Uncle Plato, who, ignoring the temptations of the Freedmen's Bureau, continues to operate within the bonds of communal affection established between whites and blacks and maintains his status and good humor. In *Red Rock*, the bureau's effect is to make freedmen unwilling to work, leaving the once pastoral fields in unproductive disarray.

The intrusion of the national government into the local scene also severs the local community's institutions from their proper functions. Harris depicts the school that Gabriel attended transformed into the site of Union League meetings. In *Red Rock*, the courthouse, the symbol of the community's control over questions of justice, is corrupted. Judge Bail, who is appointed by the federal government through the influence of a railroad lobbyist, is in cahoots with Leech. The old customs of this venerable system of justice are abandoned, and the African American sheriff cannot keep order in the court. Biased results are inevitable. In addition, the intrusion of the national government into local customs disrupts the relation between the community and the state.

The action of each novel is primarily based in one state. Harris's Shady Dale has for years held a retreat for Georgia's most distinguished politicians, who benefitted from its pastoral harmony. Trying to evoke the aura of myth, Page does not name a particular state. The region he describes "lies too far from the centres of modern progress to be laid down on any map that will be accessible. And, as 'he who maps an undiscovered country may place what boundary he will,' it need only be said, that it lies in the South, somewhere in that vague region partly in the old Southern States and partly in the yet vaguer land of memory" (*RR*, vii). As Fred Hobson points out, Page does not explicitly set his novel in his home state because Virginia did not experience Reconstruction as harshly as he wanted to depict it. Page's major sources described corruption in South Carolina. Even so, the 1869 election that helped Virginia avoid much of the conflict experienced in other southern states did play a role in the political debates of the time. In Washington on railroad business in May 1869, Robert E. Lee met with President Grant and assured him that Virginia would not resist the Fifteenth Amendment. Prior to its ratification, however, the 1869 elections saw northern-born Conservative Gilbert C. Walker defeat Republican Henry H. Wells, a carpetbagger who had been appointed provisional governor by the military commander. Wells advocated disfranchising Confederate veterans. Walker opposed—while claiming to support—the Fifteenth Amendment and an influx of white northerners to develop the state's economy. Worried that this election would spell the end of the Republican Party's rule in the state, George S. Boutwell, secretary of the Treasury, tried to get Grant to oppose the results. He failed, but his efforts caused Horace Greeley to complain in the *Tribune* that Boutwell was taking "more account of the unity and coherence of the Republican Party than the triumph of its cardinal principle." This debate is behind the action of *Red Rock*, whose landscape and terrain are unmistakably those of Page's home state. The book's best families once influenced politics in the state capital, but with the new order, the mutually beneficial relation between the state government and the local community breaks down. Page dramatizes that breakdown through scenes of corruption in the state capital. He also stretches the historical record by claiming that, with the division of the South into military districts, "the old State, with all others like it, ceased to exist" (*RR*, 198). As we have seen, in fact, the doctrine of "state suicide" was never fully implemented.[22]

Harris gives a vivid, if distorted, portrait of what it meant for states temporarily to forfeit their rights. Blaming politicians for exploiting "sectional prejudice . . . to feed and grow fat upon," his narrator insists:

> It is impossible, even at this late date, for any impartial person to read the debates in the Federal Congress during the years of 1867–68 without realizing the awful fact that the prime movers in the reconstruction scheme (if not the men who acted as their instruments and tools) were intent on stirring up a new revolution in the hope that the negroes might be prevailed upon to sack cities and towns, and destroy the white population. This is the only reasonable inference; no other conceivable conclusion can explain the wild and whirling words that were uttered in these debates: unless, indeed, some charitable investigator shall establish the fact that the radical leaders were suffering from a sort of contagious dementia. (*GT*, 242–43)

To explain "the passionate and blind resistance of the whites of the South and their hatred of everything that bore the name or earmarks of Republicanism," the narrator recalls "the facts" (243). A "mongrel convention" was assembled "to frame a new constitution for the State. . . . It was made up of political adventurers from Maine, Vermont, and other Northern States, and boasted of a majority composed of ignorant negroes and criminals. . . . When the military commandant who had charge of affairs in Georgia, found that the State government established under the terms of Mr. Lincoln's plan of reconstruction, had no idea of paying the expenses of the mongrel convention out of the State's funds, he issued an order removing the Governor and Treasurer, and 'detailed for duty as Governor of Georgia,' one of the members of his staff" (243–44). An election was held in April 1868 to elect new state officers and to ratify or reject the new constitution. "No safeguard whatever was thrown around the ballot-box, and it was the remembrance of this initial and overwhelming combination of fraud and corruption that induced the whites, at a later day, to stuff the ballot-boxes and suppress the votes of the ignorant" (244).

Darwin Turner has shown that Harris's "facts" are fabricated: "In Georgia's constitutional convention of 1867–68, only thirty-three delegates were Negroes. Nine were Northern whites, and 128, or 74%, were white Georgians. . . . In 1868, only three members of the Georgian Senate were Negro; thirty-three were white. Twenty-nine members in the House were Negro; 105 were white. This 'Negro-dominated' body in 1868 forced the resignation of one Negro senator, and expelled the other two senators and twenty-five of the twenty-nine Negro members of the House." Harris had no need to distort the facts to portray southerners losing local control. For both him and Page, justice is restored when communities regain control over their own affairs. Gabriel, falsely accused of murdering the Freedmen's Bureau agent, escapes with the help of the entire community. Families fraudulently dispossessed in *Red Rock* regain partial control of their estates, and the hero escapes an unfair conviction. In championing local control, however, both authors are careful to display their unequivocal loyalty to the nation.[23]

One way they do so is through their depiction of the occupying military. The military is as much an arm of the national government as the Freedmen's Bureau. Nonetheless, individual members are depicted as sympathetic to the local white community. In *Gabriel Tolliver,* young Captain Falconer is from Kentucky, and "he's not fond of these carpet-baggers and scalawags at all" (259). He comes "from a family of Democrats, who never voted anything but the Democratic ticket, except when Henry Clay was a candidate, and when Lincoln was running for a second term" (319). In *Red Rock,* the military's sympathy goes even further. In a dramatic scene, Captain Lawrence Middleton from Massachusetts recognizes the need to keep African Americans under control and viciously whips a self-proclaimed prophet and leader named Moses, causing an entire group of African Americans to abandon their air of defiance and submit. Middleton and his fellow officers readily socialize with the local whites, leading to a well-received marriage. It was fictional scenes like this, more than any empirical study, that caused Burgess to proclaim that the northern army officers "mingled socially with the old families, and, in many cases, married their fair daughters. The common soldiers from the Northern 'states' also fraternized with their race relatives in the South."[24]

The problem, therefore, is the northern political elite in control of the national government. By the time Harris and Page were writing, that sentiment had become commonplace. Hilary A. Herbert, President Cleveland's secretary of war, a former Confederate soldier from Alabama, contributed an essay to the *Atlantic*

Monthly's turn-of-the-century series on Reconstruction. According to him, the "feeling of vindictiveness . . . was far more intense among non-combatants than in the returned soldiers. These had learned to respect their foes. . . . And now, thirty-five years afterwards, it may be affirmed without reserve that if the soldiers of the two armies had been allowed of themselves, uninfluenced by politicians, to dictate the terms of reconstruction, the history of the United States during the past three decades would have been widely different." In the novels by Page and Harris, the effect of the politicians' actions is felt locally through the heads of the Freedmen's Bureau. Harris's Hotchkiss knows he is "playing with fire" but is confident because he "had the Government behind him" (*GT*, 290). Page's Leech goes further. In *Red Rock*, "the two words heard were 'the Government' and 'Leech.' Suddenly the two had become one. Leech was the Government, and the Government was Leech: no longer merely the State—the Carpet-bag Government—but *the* Government" (*RR*, 488). For both authors, the problem was not the general idea of government but the misuse of government by Radical Republicans. At the end of Harris's book, Gabriel marks himself as a future leader by delivering a speech that addresses the question, "Why should a parcel of politicians turn us against a Government with which we are compelled to live?" (*GT*, 441).[25]

Whereas Page and Harris agree that partisan politicians should not have that power, they differ on how to remedy the problem. Page idealizes the old southern system of governance that defers to a group of elite, gentlemanly families. Harris, in contrast, is more populist, celebrating "the salt of the earth" (*GT*, 5) who inhabit Shady Dale. Walter Hines Page might have gone too far when, almost two decades before *Gabriel Tolliver*, he claimed that Harris "hardly conceals his scorn for the old aristocracy." Harris, after all, expresses his admiration for the gentlemanly son of Shady Dale's founder. He does, however, make it clear that transmission of the southern political tradition need not be carried out by "gentlemen." Harris's heroes, in addition to Gabriel, are Major Tomlin Perdue and Mr. Billy Sanders, both of whom served in the Confederate Army. Gabriel's grandmother initially thinks that Major Perdue is a "hard and cruel man" because she has "heard of several of [his] shooting scrapes." But when she sees him tenderly nurse a friend who has been burned, she realizes that his tough code of "turn-about is fair play" makes him a just and honorable man (*GT*, 73). Sanders is a reformed alcoholic with rough manners, who believes that Lincoln was "one of the greatest men the country ever produced" (112). He has an uncanny ability to deal with the conditions the South faced under Reconstruction. His character was so attractive to Harris's audience that, when he created *Uncle Remus Magazine*, Harris had regular columns by Mr. Billy Sanders, the philosopher from Shady Dale. In *Gabriel Tolliver*, Sanders conducts shrewd detective work in order to engineer a scheme to free Gabriel from prison. Whereas in *Red Rock* leadership in the New South rests in the hands of descendants of the landed gentry, in *Gabriel Tolliver* Gabriel comes from humbler origins.[26]

In both novels, the South is also threatened by the increased commercialism that came with the North's victory. Disagreeing with those who "mistake repose and serenity for stagnation," Harris's narrator insists, "what is called progress is nothing more nor less than the multiplication of the resources of those who, by means of dicker and barter, are trying all the time to overreach the public and their fellows, in one way and another" (*GT*, 18). Elsewhere, he adds, "the atmosphere of commercialism is unfavorable to the growth of sentiments of an ideal character. That is why wise men who believe in the finer issues of life are inclined to be suspicious of what is loosely called civilization and progress" (110–11). Even so, Harris recognizes that, although Silas Tomlin, a money lender, is not the most sympathetic character, he is probably right when he tells Gabriel, "We'll all have to work now, we'll have to buckle right down to it. The way I look at it, the man who is doing nothing is throwing money away" (102–3).

A major reason Gabriel becomes the spokesperson at the end of the book is that, although he is forced to live in a commercial world, he has managed to stay in touch with the sense of repose and serenity associated with Shady Dale. He does so through contemplative moments on the town's old Bermuda grass hills. Those moments evoke the memory of his prewar childhood, when he, his best friend Nan, and the other children played on those hills. As Gabriel grows older and is troubled by a transformation in his feelings for Nan, we are told:

> He had his own world to fall back upon—a world of books, the woods and the fields. And he was far from unhappiness; for no human being who loves Nature well enough to understand and interpret its meaning and its myriad messages to his own satisfaction, can be unhappy for any length of time. Whatever his losses or his disappointments, he can make them all good by going into the woods and fields and taking Nature, the great comforter, by the hand. . . . So Gabriel confined his communications for the most part to his old and ever-faithful friends, the woods and the velvety Bermuda fields. (*GT*, 248)

It is no accident that the perspective Gabriel achieves from those hills helps him uncover a conspiracy plotted by the Union League. Nor is it an accident that he has no alibi for the murder of which he is accused because at the moment of the crime he is alone on the hills. The quality that makes him vulnerable to a false accusation of crime against a representative of the Reconstruction regime also makes him a representative for the new way of life the South faces. It is this connection to a threatened world of repose and serenity that gives the community of

Shady Dale the authority to work out the problems—racial and otherwise—it faces in the postbellum world.

Page does not share Harris's romantic sensibility of solitude in nature. His vision is more Virgilian and classical, with an orderly landscape linked to a civilized order. In *Red Rock*, the check against rampant commercialism is disinterested gentlemanly virtue, not a romantic sensibility cultivated in nature. Appropriately, the novel's antebellum moment of harmony is not children playing imaginative games in nature but the ceremonious staging of a ball, a leisure-class activity that engages the entire white community and two northern guests, with proper class hierarchy and custom observed. In Cable's *John March, Southerner*, a southern woman depicts the conflict of Reconstruction as "decency in the wrong and vulgarity in the right" (62). In Page's world, there is no such conflict. Decency is not only in the right; it is the right. Vulgarity is not only in the wrong; it is the wrong. This is a major reason why Page's Freedmen's Bureau agent is so much more despicable than Harris's. To Leech's claim to be the government, Page opposes Steve Allen. Faced with poverty after the war, Steve nonetheless refuses to work with his hands and instead trains to be a lawyer. When Leech assumes that Steve will cower before him because he is "the Government of the United States," Leech's local ally warns, "He ain't afeard of the Government or nothin' else" (*RR*, 190). Steve's lack of fear does not stem from a disdain for governance but from the fact that, in Page's world, no government is above the quality of the people in charge. A proper government is defined less by its institutions than by the code of self-sacrifice and virtue held by its governors. "War," we are told, "cannot plunder Virtue" (246). Thus, when Reconstruction leads to a condition in which "all civil government had disappeared" (80), the phrase has a double meaning. The local institutions of government have been suspended, and civility no longer exists. Harmony prevails when the entire society recognizes the virtues of proper conduct. For instance, in court, General Legaie, acting as an attorney, is insulted by the judge's violation of custom and walks out, abandoning his client. Even those who are not gentlemen themselves do "not see how a gentleman could have done otherwise" (*RR*, 457). The gentlemanly code is so pervasive that it even affects the African American community. There are "quality niggers" and vulgar ones (129). When loyal Tarquin is asked by Leech to expose the whereabouts of Steve Allen, he responds that even if he did know he would not tell. "If I betrayed a gentleman, I couldn't look my master in the face." Leech responds, "'I'm the Government, and I'll make you tell.' But Tarquin was unmoved" (491).

In "The Civil War as Unifier," Dudley Miles claims that novels of Reconstruction "had the salutary influence in acquainting the whole country with Southern civilization and conditions, and in setting the Southern people before the reading public in a new light. . . . the prophecy of Lamar 'know each other and you will love each other' was proving true." Trying to educate northerners about southern affairs, Harris and Page both include characters who model a desired northern response. Harris's implied northern reader appears in the book's frame. The novel starts with the northern wife of the fictional narrator being invited to his hometown of Shady Dale. She returns, full of praise for the inhabitants and their way of life. Page highlights the Welch family, which relocates to Red Rock from the North and ends up integrated into the community. Major Welch is also Page's reminder to southerners that gentlemanly behavior is not confined to the South. Another northern gentleman is Senator Rockfield, a college classmate of the Grays' honorable neighbor Dr. Cary. Harris has Shady Dale returned to local control without outside help. He only asks that northerners understand why that was necessary. In contrast, in *Red Rock*, the vulgar, illegitimate rule of Reconstruction is overcome with the gentlemanly help of Major Welch and Senator Rockfield. Through their efforts, Page suggests that the creation of a more perfect union requires a coalition of northern and southern gentlemen. In his account, such a coalition existed prior to the disruption of the war and Radical Reconstruction. When Major Welch and Middleton visit Red Rock before the firing on Fort Sumter, young Jacquelin inadvertently insults their home state of Massachusetts. Making up for the mistake, Dr. Cary "proceeded deftly to name over a list of great men from Massachusetts, and to link their names with those of the men of the South whom she most delighted to honor" (*RR*, 21).[27]

According to Page, most northerners are unaware of the South's belief in this code of mutual respect because their understanding of the South has been distorted. In Page's mind, local self-governance is impossible without local self-representation in literature and history. Convinced that, if those outside the South understood, they would allow the South to control its own affairs, he insists that "no mind will be able to produce the delicate and subtle phases of [southern] civilization but one who has received its spirit into the warp and woof of thought." Unfortunately, however, the South has not projected its own image to the world. By letting others misrepresent southern civilization during the Civil War, the South failed to attract the European and northern support it needed to prevail, making it "conquered by the pen rather than the sword." History, Page worries, might repeat itself in the era of Reconstruction. "Contemporary history," he writes, "is being recorded by writers organically disabled to comprehend the action of the South." The result is an image of the South as "the breeder of tyrants, the defender of slavery, the fomenter of treason." Issuing a challenge to southern men of letters, he warns, "We must either leave our history to be written by those who do not understand it, or we must write it ourselves."[28]

Tourgée is perhaps the prime example of those Page felt were "organically disabled" from telling the story of the South. When Tourgée published "The South as a Field for Fiction" in 1888, claiming that literary representatives of the South were confederate in sympathy, Page responded with "The South as a Field for Literature," playfully remarking, "it may be left for some writer styling himself a novelist to tell the story and perpetuate the life that is gliding so rapidly into the irrevocable past." *Red Rock*, which he worked on for over a decade, is Page's answer to those like Tourgée. In *A Fool's Errand*, we are told that the South, although "a republic in name," was "an oligarchy in fact" (168). Page does not disagree. In the preface to *Red Rock*, he admits that the system he so admires was indeed "an Oligarchy" (viii). But whereas Tourgée insists that progress demands dismantling the oligarchy, Page feels that progress is possible only if the South retains the best of the old system. At stake for both is how the honored American ideal of local self-governance is best served within its system of federalism.[29]

Tourgée disputes the South's claim to champion local control. According to Hesden Le Moyne in *Bricks without Straw*, local officials in the South are not directly elected by the community; they are appointed by either the state legislature or the governor. "The South," he insists, "is to-day and always has been a stranger to local government" (425). In the 1868 North Carolina constitutional convention, Tourgée pushed through a reform allowing local control over local offices. This measure allowed communities where freedmen constituted a large percentage of the population to practice self-governance. For Tourgée, therefore, the issue was not local governance versus unwarranted interference by the national government, but state governance versus an alliance of the local and the national.

Tourgée's model for true local self-government was the New England township system: a "nursery of democratic freedom" (*FE*, 168). According to Le Moyne, "Each township is itself a miniature republic," in which "the inhabitants," all equal citizens, "control and manage for themselves, directly and immediately, their own local affairs" (*BS*, 423). These miniature republics are the foundation for democratic rule in the country, then the state, and finally the nation. Tourgée's account of the New England township system is, it should be clear, as idealized as Page's account of the benevolence of the southern oligarchy. Indeed, when Tourgée portrayed the conditions in the North in *Murvale Eastman, Christian Socialist*, he was much more realistic about its political corruption. Nonetheless, his evocation of the township system, bolstered by a reference to Alexis de Tocqueville, rhetorically challenges southern pretentions to virtuous local control. Essential to Tourgée's argument is the fact that, under the southern system, freedmen were denied any possibility of local self-governance.

Page's belief that proper self-governance could be ensured only if the pillars of the community were in charge might seem reactionary. But it was easily adapted to the doctrine of governance by the "best men" espoused by Mugwumps when they abandoned the Republican Party to support Grover Cleveland in the 1884 election. The Mugwumps' faith in men of virtue and professional training was in turn taken over by the progressivism Page would come to embrace. It is no accident that progressivism, with its celebration of professionalism and its attack on corruption, coincided with the disfranchisement of most African Americans in the South. Nor is it an accident that Tourgée vilified Mugwumps and opposed their campaign for extensive civil-service reform as a way to combat governmental corruption. For Tourgée, civil-service reform threatened to transform a republic directly responsible to the people into a bureaucracy of professional administrators, a transformation that Page's friend Wilson would help to implement.[30]

Given these differences, we would expect Tourgée and Page to be on opposite sides in every election. But, as we look back on these figures from the judgment seat of the present, it is important to remember that the American political system often creates strange alliances when it comes to electing a president. Confronted with the political choices of the day, Tourgée, Page, and Harris ended up supporting the staunch nationalist Teddy Roosevelt. That Tourgée, a loyal Republican, backed Roosevelt is no surprise. By the time the Rough Rider assumed the presidency, Tourgée had already been appointed US consul to Bordeaux. From France, he wrote Roosevelt, praising him for inviting Booker T. Washington to the White House and providing advice on foreign affairs. Page's support of a Republican is much more surprising. But both he and Roosevelt were gentlemen. Remarrying after his first wife's death, Page moved to Washington, DC, where he lived in a stately mansion built with his new wife's fortune. The two were at the center of the capital's social scene, and Page was a personal friend of Roosevelt. He supported the Spanish-American War and bucked the South by voting for Roosevelt and his imperialist policies in the 1904 election. By 1912, Page switched his support to his fellow Virginian Wilson, but so did W. E. B. Du Bois.

Harris also supported the Spanish-American War, although it is not clear how he voted in 1904. He was a strong supporter of "free silver," which Republicans opposed, and in an interview he once said, "I am not a politician. I am a Democrat on election day, but that is as far as I go." Nonetheless, Harris was clearly moved by Roosevelt's praise of him during the president's trip to Atlanta in 1905. Sincere, Roosevelt's praise was also politically shrewd, as he tried to win southern support. Earlier that year in a speech called "Lincoln and the Race Problem," Roosevelt cited the Great Emancipator in order to stake out a position that Harris certainly would have supported. Condemning racism, he preached the need for northerners to respect the views of their fellow countrymen of the South. With an eye to the South, Roosevelt invited Harris to the White House. That Harris, like Page, came to support a northern Republican is suggested when he has Billy Sanders come away from a visit to the White House, "feelin' that Teddy is the President of the whole country, an' not of a party." Sanders does not mention Roosevelt's imperialism, but he does praise his willingness to take on "the men in Wall Street." In 1907, Harris went so far as to have his fictional Sanders mock how the South used to fetishize states' rights. In the past, the South acted as if "a state was somethin' alive an' wigglin'—somethin' that could crawl about an' git its feelin's hurt." But now it realizes that "a state aint nothin' but a passel of people livin' in boundary lines that nobody can p'int out except by hearsay." Given the solid South's allegiance to the Democratic Party, it took courage for Page and Harris to embrace Roosevelt. Their independence of party helped to establish their credentials as lovers of the nation first.[31]

IV

Another southerner with links to Roosevelt was Dixon. Agreeing with Harris and Page that most northerners did not understand the "race problem," Dixon had a different view of the relationship between states and the nation. He did not simply want the nation to relinquish racial control to the states; he wanted the nation to take control and establish a white republic. Page and Harris's racism was paternalistic. They professed sincere kindness and respect for African Americans, with Harris advocating uplift within the confines of segregation. Dixon's racism was of a different order. At times, he advocated excluding African Americans from the nation. At other times, he expressed sympathy for Booker T. Washington's plans for manual education in a segregated world. Although in his works there is occasionally an African American like Jake in *The Clansman*, who is loyal to his former master and meant to be a sympathetic character, there is no lovable and shrewd Uncle Remus. Nor is there anything like Page's claim that, prior to the disruption of Reconstruction, "the blacks were generally in full sympathy with the whites, and the ties of personal association and affection were recognized on both sides." Dixon believed instead in racial antagonism. Establishing his ideal white republic was a task requiring centralized power, and centralized power was justified only if it promoted white supremacy.[32]

Dixon's first Reconstruction novel, *The Leopard's Spots*, begins in the spirit of Harris and Page. Like their works, it is in part a bildungsroman tracing the growth of a hero, Charles Gaston, from his youth in the Civil War to the turn of the century. It is also set primarily in one state—North Carolina. On the first page,

General Lee pays homage to the Tar Heel state when he praises the bravery of its troops with "God Bless old North Carolina" (*LS*, 3). Dixon even reminds us that the major fighting of the Civil War did not end at Appomattox but near Durham Station, North Carolina, where Gen. Joseph Johnston surrendered on April 26, 1865. Praised as "the typical American Democracy," North Carolina "had loved peace and sought in vain to stand between the passions of the Cavalier of the South and the Puritan fanatics of the North" (*LS*, 51). In the course of this book and his Reconstruction trilogy, however, Dixon moves from focusing on North Carolina to making a case for a strong national state.

After voting Republican in 1900, Dixon toyed with switching to the Democrats in 1904. But on economic matters and concentrated governmental power he was closer to the party of Lincoln. His views are suggested by Charles Gaston in *The Leopard's Spots*. At one point, a scalawag tries to convince Gaston to join forces with a pact formed by the Republican Party and the Farmers' Alliance, noting that "the Southern people have nothing in common with these Northern Democrats who make your platforms and nominate your candidate" (*LS*, 195). Gaston admits to himself that "on the issue of the party platforms he was in accord with the modern Republican utterances at almost every issue, and so were his associates in the Southern Democracy" (199). Nonetheless, the one principle his party stood for was "the supremacy of the Anglo-Saxon." For Gaston, that principle trumps all. Dixon's task is to link that principle to a vision of centralized power that rivals and supplants the one put forth by Tourgée defending African American equality.

Growing up in North Carolina, Dixon knew Tourgée. After Tourgée left the state and became a well-known author, the ambitious Dixon sought and accepted advice from him. Later, having become a successful minister in Boston and learning of the former carpetbagger's financial difficulties, Dixon sent a letter gratefully acknowledging Tourgée's help and inviting him to his home. Tourgée did not take him up on the offer, but when Dixon embarked on his literary career, he knew he had to discredit the image of Reconstruction created by his one-time mentor. Including figures from *Uncle Tom's Cabin*, *The Leopard's Spots* explicitly refutes Stowe's novel. Likewise, *The Clansman* is a self-conscious rebuttal to *A Fool's Errand*, which was considered the *Uncle Tom's Cabin* of Reconstruction. Just as Stowe verified the accuracy of her novel by writing *A Key to Uncle Tom's Cabin*, so Tourgée followed *A Fool's Errand* with *The Invisible Empire*, his factual documentation of the activities of the Ku Klux Klan. Dixon, a former minister, one-time graduate student of political science, and a trained lawyer, was at pains to convince a turn-of-the-century audience that Tourgée's firsthand fictional and nonfictional accounts were wrong. The parallels between the novels are hard to miss.[33]

In *A Fool's Errand*, Tourgée calls the Klan's tactics of violent intimidation a new "Reign of Terror" (250); a generation later, Dixon reserves that designation for carpetbagger rule. Tourgée faults the South for its hostility to immigrants from other regions; Dixon insists that the "power of assimilation has always been a mark of Southern genius" (*CM*, 276). The most horrifying moment in *A Fool's Errand* is a vindictive lynching. In *The Clansman*, a lynching is fully vindicated. The most exciting chapter in *A Fool's Errand* is "A Race Against Time," describing the carpetbagger's daughter on a courageous horse ride to save her father from the Klan. Dixon counters with "A Ride for Life," in which the sister of the Klan's leader braves danger while riding to save her lover from hanging at the hands of Austin Stoneman, his carpetbagger father. In *A Fool's Errand*, the southern lover of the carpetbagger's daughter converts to the Fool's point of view. In *The Clansman*, Stoneman's daughter converts to her southern lover's point of view. Even Dixon's carpetbagger might owe a debt to Tourgée. Although Stoneman is modeled primarily on Thaddeus Stevens, Stevens was dead by the time of *The Clansman*'s action. Furthermore, Stevens never moved South for his health as Stoneman does and Tourgée did.

Dixon's self-conscious response to *A Fool's Errand* would seem to support the widespread assumption that Dixon and Tourgée are polar opposites. In many ways they are. In a Memorial Day speech after the *Plessy* ruling, Tourgée called the court "the consistent enemy of personal liberty and equal right." In a 1907 novel, Dixon praised it as "the last bulwark of American liberties" (*TR*, 330). Whereas Tourgée attacked the doctrine of states' rights, Dixon joined many southerners in holding Reconstruction responsible for threatening those rights. To counter Representative Stoneman's claim that the rebellious "states" of the South are "now but conquered provinces" (*CM*, 43), Dixon offers President Lincoln's belief that the Union had never been split asunder because, lacking the right to secede, no "state" had left the nation. His fictional Lincoln proclaims, "These states must be immediately restored to their rights, or we shall betray the blood we have shed. There are no 'conquered provinces' for us to spoil. A nation cannot make conquest of its own territory" (*CM*, 44). As the words he puts into Lincoln's mouth indicate, Dixon was an advocate of Presidential Reconstruction. But Dixon also shared Lincoln's belief in the unquestionable primacy of the Union. On the issue of centralized power, Dixon was closer to Tourgée than we might suspect.[34]

We have already seen how Burgess, a firm believer in national sovereignty, could dismiss carpetbag rule for its "career of corruption, shame, and vulgarity." Dixon does not go so far as Burgess and argue that the alternative should have been indefinite state suicide, but he is much less skeptical of centralized power than Harris or

Page. One of the strongest arguments for dual federalism was that the states were protectors of civil liberties against the centralized national government. In his play *A Man of the People*, however, Dixon defends Lincoln's crackdown on civil liberties by fictionalizing the arrest of Clement Vallandigham. Siding with Lincoln against the Ohio Copperhead, whose motto was "The Constitution as it is, the Union as it was," Dixon refuses to indulge in nostalgia about a lost federalism. In the same work, Dixon has Jefferson Davis and Robert E. Lee discuss the possibility of arming slaves to fight for the Confederacy. Lee insists that, "led by their masters—they'll fight to a man." Davis counters that states with a "majority of Negro population will never agree to the arming of half a million slaves." When Lee asks if Davis will "allow Mississippi, Louisiana, and South Carolina to defeat a plan necessary to save the life of the Confederacy," Davis exclaims, "The States are sovereign, General Lee—for this purpose we are fighting." Discouraged, Lee responds, "Then I think it may be time to ask ourselves, heart to heart, the question whether the Confederacy, as organized, does not carry within its own body the seeds of death. The rights of a state must somewhere yield to the supreme power of a nation."[35]

Dixon also demonstrates this attitude in his portrayal of governmental detectives, the use of which during and after the Civil War was a sore point with the South, which regarded it as a sign of increased governmental intrusion into the lives of private people. In *Bricks without Straw*, Tourgée mocks that paranoia when the neighbors of Hesden Le Moyne falsely claim that he has hidden detectives in his house and has used them to find out the identity of each participant in a raid by the Klan. Nonetheless, the government did use detectives to combat violence against freedmen. For instance, a detective was instrumental in bringing charges against some of the men participating in the Colfax Massacre of 1873. In *Red Rock*, Page exploits this concern by having governmental detectives entrap the rash younger brother of one of the book's protagonists. In *Gabriel Tolliver*, Harris shows that proper detective work is best done by private citizens, as Billy Sanders undoes the government's case against Gabriel. Dixon adopts a different strategy. In *The Traitor*, a detective is sent to investigate crimes committed in Independence, North Carolina, and by the end of the novel he relocates to the South, joining Dixon's former head of the Klan in a profitable business venture. For Dixon, the power of the federal government can be harnessed to protect white interests, not undermine them. In *The Clansman*, a friend of Dr. Cameron, watching the corrupt state legislature operate, observes, "Once more we are a sovereign State—a sovereign Negro state" (*CM*, 270). States' rights are no good if the national government overseeing the states is not controlled by those dedicated to white supremacy.

The question of control obsesses Dixon. Page puts his faith in a class of virtuous gentlemen personally linked to the community, who he believes disinterestedly govern in its best interest. Although Dixon also champions virtue, he is much more authoritarian. Page's virtuous leaders can disagree politically as Mr. Gray, a Democrat, and Dr. Cary, a Whig do. In the end, for Page, virtue will prevail. In contrast, Dixon puts his faith in a leader who has power akin to that of a military commander or a dictator. Even Congress, where debate supposedly takes place, is completely controlled by Austin Stoneman. In Dixon's works, if the wrong leader is in charge, then the entire system becomes corrupt. For Page, however, virtue can thrive even alongside poor political leadership. We see that difference in their portrayal of military rule during Reconstruction. Both condemn arming black militias, but Page is careful to distinguish Leech's black militia from the occupying army, which he portrays sympathetically as a pocket of virtue, even though it is charged with maintaining carpetbagger rule. In contrast, in the chapter "At the Point of the Bayonet," Dixon makes no distinction between the black and white troops as Ben Cameron and his father are arrested. In Dixon's eyes, these occupying forces are completely corrupt because they are under the wrong command. As Phil Stoneman tells the white captain who has imprisoned Ben, "I'm an officer of the United States Army, of the fighting corps—not the vulture division" (*CM*, 225). Southerners in Dixon's world are more than willing to submit to national authority, so long as it is properly commanded. Arrested for defying authority, Dr. Cameron protests, "The war is over; the South is conquered; I have no country save America. For the honor of the flag, for which I once poured out my blood on the heights of Buena Vista, I protest against this shame" (230). Instead, he is shackled by an African American, who causes a "spurt of bruised blood from the old Mexican War wound [to stain] the iron" (231). Later, Stoneman accuses Dr. Cameron of "Resistance to the authority of the National Government." He responds: "No; resistance to the travesty of government and the mockery of civilization under which we are being throttled! The tyranny of military martinets was child's play to this. . . . Eighty thousand armed Negro troops, answerable to no authority save the savage instincts of their officers, terrorize the state" (289).

Dixon's account of the Civil War confirms his belief in centralized power. He does not agree with many southerners that it was a "War between the States." In fact, according to Dixon's commander-in-chief, Lincoln, "The war has been a giant conflict of principles to decide whether we are a bundle of petty sovereignties held by a rope of sand or a mighty nation of freemen" (*CM*, 48). As Stoneman's daughter, who becomes Ben's lover, puts it, the Civil War, "which seemed to her a wicked, cruel, and causeless rebellion, was the one inevitable thing in our growth from a loose group of sovereign states to a United Nation" (148). *The Clansman's* portrayal of that possibility is why D. W. Griffith could turn it and parts of *The Leopard's Spots* into a film called *The Birth of a Nation.* Strong nationalist that he was, Tourgée also believed that the Civil War should have led to the birth of a new nation through Reconstruction. As the Fool puts it, "Races, nations, and classes must be born again, must see another generation, before that result is ever obtained" (*FE*, 167).

Of course, Dixon and Tourgée advocate the birth of very different nations. The most important difference is the role they envision for African Americans. Alluding to Lincoln's "House Divided Speech," Dixon has the Man of the People proclaim, "The Nation cannot exist half white and half black, any more than it could exist half slave and half free" (*CM*, 47). In contrast, for Tourgée, African Americans are a vital component of "We, the People." It would be a mistake, however, to account for the difference between these writers' views by imposing today's distinction between homogeneity and diversity. In fact, both writers stress the need for a homogeneous citizenry. According to the Fool, "The first great prerequisite of successful Reconstruction is to break down the legal barriers to a homogeneous development of the country" (*FE*, 168). Likewise Dixon, appropriating the language of advocates of African American rights, has Lincoln declare, "We can have no inferior servile class, peon or peasant" (*CM*, 46). Lincoln follows up with a comment that could be an allusion to Tourgée's book, dedicated to the citizen kings of the country, *Letters to a King* (1888): "The American," Dixon's Lincoln says, "is a citizen king or nothing" (*CM*, 46).

Despite Dixon's refusal to grant African Americans the status of citizen kings, Tourgée can share the belief that a nation must have a homogeneous citizenry because the two writers have different views about the relation between a nation's people and its institutions. For Dixon, the racial character of a nation's people determines whether or not it can have a strong central government. Dr. Cameron tells Stoneman, "This Republic is great . . . because of the genius of the race of pioneer white freemen who settled this continent, dared the might of kings, and made a wilderness the home of Freedom. Our future depends on the purity of this racial stock" (*CM*, 291). In contrast, for Tourgée institutions shape the character of a nation's people, not vice versa. "The seventy-odd millions of people who constitute the population of the American Republic," he claimed, "whether white, black, Celt or Slav, or from whatever European stock they may be descended, in political ideals are purely American and derivatively Anglican." For Tourgée, northerners and southerners, shaped by different institutions, are different peoples, and a homogenous nation can be created only if the character of the southern people, black and white, is changed by the intervention of a strong national government.[36]

Dixon, of course, opposed any plan that would turn blacks into Americans. But his difference with Tourgée was not about centralized power, which he approved if the people are properly commanded. Early in *The Leopard's Spots*, the narrator warns that "Government threatened to become organized crime instead of the organized virtue of the community" (94). Nonetheless, Gaston holds on to the ideal that government can fulfill its proper purpose. Working to redeem North Carolina, he insists, "I believe that the Government is the organized virtue of the community, and that politics is religion in action" (284). Attracted to power, Dixon saw too much potential in the nation not to want to control it as well. As Gaston adds, "I believe that the State is now the only organ through which the whole people can search for righteousness, and that the progress of the world depends more than ever on its integrity and purity" (284). Gaston's "State" is clearly not simply the state of North Carolina. Dixon has moved from a focus on an individual state to a vision of the world's progress.

The role Gaston attributes to the nation-state is influenced by contemporary political theory. After graduating from Wake Forest with the highest honors ever achieved there, Dixon received a scholarship for the graduate Seminar in Historical and Political Science at the Johns Hopkins University. Dixon soon abandoned his studies to pursue a career first in theater and then in the ministry. Before he left, however, he studied political theory and was introduced to the ideas of fellow student and friend Woodrow Wilson. Wilson indicated some of those ideas on April 18, 1884, during a formal debate over the Blair Bill providing federal money to help educate African Americans. Professor Herbert Baxter Adams favored the bill. Wilson strongly opposed. He was countered by another student, John Dewey. A few years after Dixon left Johns Hopkins, he recommended Wilson for an honorary degree from Wake Forest. The publicity Wilson won was the first national attention he received.[37]

Wilson's views, like those of his rival political scientist Burgess, were profoundly influenced by his understanding of the Civil War and Reconstruction. For both men, those events led to a spirit of progressive nationalism, but their accounts of how that came about reveal competing views of constitutionalism and federalism. In 1892, Wilson published *Division and Reunion: 1829–1889* as part of a series called "Epochs of American History." In his preface, he acknowledges that the period was controversial, but he insists on "impartiality of judgment; for impartiality is a matter of the heart, and I know with what disposition I have written." At the 1896 American Historical Society meeting, however, he made his point of view clear when, fed up with northern accounts, he defended the South. "There is nothing to apologize for in the past of the South, absolutely nothing to apologize for." Burgess responded by insisting that it was "unmanly" for the South not to apologize for its "attempt to destroy the Union." In Wilson's 1901 "The Reconstruction of the Southern States," his differences with Burgess are again on display when he embraces *Texas v. White*'s ruling that the Constitution created an indestructible Union of indestructible states. To Burgess's objection that a "state" was not really a state because a nation could have only one sovereign power, Wilson, from the "Old Dominion State," had earlier responded by granting sovereignty to the nation and dominion to individual states. Because Lincoln agreed with the sentiment expressed in *Texas v. White*, Burgess was highly critical of his plan for Reconstruction. In contrast, Wilson, as does Dixon and so many others, speculates on how different Reconstruction would have been under Lincoln. "Had Mr. Lincoln lived, perhaps the whole of the delicate business might have been carried through with dignity, good temper, and simplicity of method."[38]

Of course, Lincoln had not lived, and Wilson goes on to describe the horrible conditions of the southern states under carpetbagger rule. He does not stop there, however. In a significant turn that would have caught Dixon's eye, he writes, "But that dark history is not part of our present story. We are here concerned, rather, with the far-reaching constitutional and political influences and results of Reconstruction. That it was a revolutionary process is written upon its face throughout; but how deep did the revolution go? What permanent marks has it left upon the great structure of government, federal, republican; a partnership of equal states, and yet a solidly coherent national power, which the fathers erected?" Reconstruction unfolded the way it did because the Civil War "discovered the foundations of our government to be in fact unwritten." Despite what the Constitution said, "the ultimate foundation of the structure was . . . physical force, sustained by the stern loves and rooted predilections of masses of men, the strong ingrained prejudices which are the fiber of every system of government." The sentiments sustaining that force are ones that "constitutions can neither originate nor limit."[39]

Wilson's account is a direct challenge to Burgess. For Burgess the national state was sovereign, which he had famously defined as "that which imposes the limitation." Whereas he was careful to distinguish the sovereign state from the government and the Constitution, he nonetheless thought that, in the United States, the Constitution was the state's way of asserting its limits. An earlier review of Burgess's work by Wilson highlights their difference. While praising Burgess's understanding of "such part of political life as it is operative within the forms of law," Wilson faults his understanding of "the actual facts of political life, the actual phenomena of state growth." Political science, Wilson insists, has to deal with aspects of political life "lying entirely outside the thought of the lawyer," such as the way "states come into existence, take historic shape, create governments and institutions and at pleasure change or discard what forms or laws they must in order to achieve development." Burgess, he claims, writes in the "language of science," but comprehensive political science demands the "language of literature" to deal with those sentiments that constitutions can neither originate nor limit.[40]

In Burgess's language of science, "the modern national popular state" was the "product of the progressive revelation of human reason through human history." In Wilson's language of literature, the state was founded on ingrained prejudices, and when the Civil War came, the Constitution, written "for lawyers, not for soldiers," could provide no answers. Burgess acknowledges that in order to conduct the war Lincoln did not always adhere to the strict letter of the Constitution. Nonetheless, Burgess argues that the Constitution implies the powers of a temporary constitutional dictatorship when necessary to preserve the state. In contrast, Wilson saw no constitutional basis for various wartime acts. "Whenever the law clogged or did not suffice it had to be laid aside or ignored." Likewise, there was no constitutional basis for Reconstruction. "The Constitution knew no such process as this of Reconstruction, and could furnish no rules for it." As bleak as this account is, Wilson, like Dixon, turns the dark days of Reconstruction into a happy fall that leads to the modern progressive state.[41]

Reconstruction was illegitimate, but, like the Civil War, it was motivated by the progressive sentiment of "union and nationality." To be sure, the physical force used to support that sentiment in the Civil War and Reconstruction was sustained, according to Wilson, by the ingrained prejudices of only one section of the country: the North. Nonetheless, the sentiment of nationality, hitherto "unorganized" and "a thing above the law," gained force and with the redemption of the southern states expressed the "stern loves and rooted predilections" of white North and South. The "revolution of consciousness" brought about by the Civil War and Reconstruction transformed a government whose "spirit" was "federal" into one "national in temper and point of view." At that point, the state could become what Gaston envisions it to be: "the organized virtue of the community" (*LS*, 284).[42]

For Dixon and Wilson, organization is a key concept. Registering and influencing the views of his day, Burgess defined a state as a "particular portion of mankind, viewed as an organized unit." Appropriately, in stressing the difference Lincoln would have made to Reconstruction, Wilson claims that he would have allowed the states to "organize themselves and set up governments made comfortable to the new order of things." Similarly, listing arguments about why southern states had "forfeited their rights," Wilson adds to Stevens's doctrine of conquered territory and Sumner's doctrine of state suicide an argument about their "temporary disorganization." Indeed, for Sumner that disorganization continued into Reconstruction and justified federal control and African American suffrage.

"Nothing is clearer," he argued, "than that of the absolute necessity for suffrage for all colored persons in the disorganized states." Dixon explicitly and Wilson implicitly draw on the importance of organization to turn arguments like Sumner's on their heads and assert the illegitimacy of Reconstruction governments. After all, they believed, it was African Americans' inability to organize virtue that made them incapable of proper government. For Wilson and Dixon, the new order should not simply be a return to an earlier federalism. It should organize the people nationally. With that organization in place, the United States was poised for what Wilson calls "novel enterprises at the threshold of an unlooked for future." "Empire," he concludes, "is an affair of strong government, and not of the nice and somewhat artificial poise or of the delicate compromises of structure and authority characteristic of a mere federal partnership."[43]

Supplementing Wilson's account with an explicit doctrine of white supremacy and Burgess's Hegelianism that saw the progressive unfolding of reason through human history, Dixon urges a reunited United States to embark on a project of worldwide imperialism for the white race. The subtitle of *The Leopard's Spots* is "A Romance of the White Man's Burden: 1865–1900," an allusion to Rudyard Kipling's famous poem, published on Lincoln's birthday in 1899 and dedicated to the United States in its civil war to suppress Filipinos after it acquired their islands from Spain. Knowing that most southerners opposed imperialism, Dixon has Gaston contrast the Old South with his "progressive" vision. "Our old men dreamed of local supremacy. We dream of the conquest of the globe" (*LS*, 439). That conquest must be racial. "The Anglo-Saxon is entering the new century with the imperial crown of the ages on his brow and the scepter of the infinite in his hands" (439).[44]

For the nation to carry this imperial crown to the world, it needed to remain white. That meant controlling immigration, which was made easier by the transformation of a mere federal partnership into a strong centralized government. Burgess, for instance, insisted that a nation had a right to protect "its nationality against the deleterious influence of foreign immigration." For most of the country's early history, individual states were primarily in control of immigration. But with the Chinese Exclusion Acts of 1882 and 1892, a national state apparatus to control immigration developed, and it was supported by a number of Supreme Court decisions. In one of his unacknowledged debates with Tourgée in *The Clansman*, Dixon alludes to the debates over Chinese exclusion. In *A Fool's Errand*, Tourgée calls St. Paul's proclamation that "God hath made of one blood all the nations of the earth" a "living principle in the Northern mind" (140). Indeed, the phrase had been a rallying call for abolitionists. After emancipation, Sumner cited it in his 1866 speech, "The Equal Rights of All." New Englanders also used it to combat anti-Chinese sentiment. In 1870, Congress revised the 1790 Naturalization Act to allow those of

African descent, as well as whites, to become naturalized citizens. Sumner unsuccessfully tried to include Chinese immigrants by making the act color-blind. He was supported by Frederick Douglass.[45]

An 1881 Senate debate over a treaty with China led to the first exclusion act. Senator George Frisbie Hoar of Massachusetts, Sumner's friend and editor of his papers, rose and quoted St. Paul to defend the right of Chinese people to immigrate. Senator John Miller of California, a leader of the anti-Chinese faction, interrupted: "Go on—quote the remainder of the sentence." Flustered, Hoar murmured: "There is no more of it." "Oh, yes, there is," rejoined Miller, "for the apostle added to the words the Senator has just quoted, 'and hath determined the bounds of their habitation.'" Miller's response shows how effectively opponents of equal rights had managed to appropriate the authority of St Paul for their own cause. In *The Clansman*'s fictional debate between Stoneman and Lincoln, Dixon reenacts Miller's correction of Hoar. Significantly misquoting Paul by substituting "races" for "nations," Dixon has Stoneman proclaim, "God hath made of one blood all races," only to be interrupted by Lincoln's "Yes. But finish the sentence. 'And fixed the bounds of their habitation'" (*CM*, 47).[46]

At the time that Dixon was composing his Reconstruction trilogy, Hoar and Miller's exchange was back in the news. Hoar's sharp criticism of the Philippine-American War during the nation's imperialist expansion in the wake of the Spanish-American War and his defense of the Filipino people recalled his passionate defense of the Chinese. Imperialist, yet fearful that Filipinos might be made US citizens, Dixon, as he worked on *The Clansman*, would have been aware of Hoar's positions and the publicity accompanying the senator's death on September 30, 1904. Furthermore, in 1892 Dixon engaged in a heated debate with the agnostic Robert Ingersoll. When Douglass delivered his stirring condemnation of the *Civil Rights Cases* in 1883, Ingersoll had been the main speaker. In the same year Ingersoll engaged Dixon, he debated Representative Geary over the wisdom and fairness of the Californian's extension of the 1882 Exclusion Act. In addition to restricting Chinese immigration, the Geary Act made provisions for deporting Chinese illegally in the country—after one year of hard labor. Attacking the legislation, Ingersoll proclaimed, "When the rights of even one human being are held in contempt, the rights of all are in danger. We cannot destroy the liberties of others without losing our own." Nonetheless, as Dixon would have known, Geary's bill was enacted. If this external evidence is not enough to prove that Dixon is alluding in his fiction to the exchange between Hoar and Miller, there is even more compelling internal evidence. In the paragraph preceding his correction of Stoneman, Lincoln argues that eventually the nation would have to get rid of African Americans. "If the Negro were not here," he asks the Radical Republican, "would we allow him to land?" He then adds, "The duty to exclude carries the right to expel" (*CM*, 46), precisely the rationale the Supreme Court gave in *Fong Yue Ting v. United States* (1893), upholding various provisions of Geary's 1892 Exclusion Act.[47]

Although Tourgée would have acknowledged the nation's power to exclude and expel, he opposed the Chinese exclusion acts, praising President Chester A. Arthur's veto of the 1882 bill and calling the bill a "wall to prevent foreigners from entering our territories" comparable to the Great Wall of China. To be sure, Tourgée thought that some Chinese communities were degraded, but he did not fear foreigners of all races entering the country. He believed that, exposed to American institutions, they would transform into loyal and competent citizens. Nonetheless, in the 1880 presidential campaign, he strongly supported James Garfield who, on the one hand, advocated using the power of the national government to assure rights of freedmen, and, on the other, urged use of that same power to consider restricting Chinese immigration in order to keep the country free of the servile labor it had fought a war to eliminate.[48]

Two decades later, Tourgée, like Dixon, supported the United States' imperial expansion. Like many Republicans, Tourgée denounced the Mexican-American War. When the Spanish-American War broke out, however, he supported it and even annexation of Puerto Rico, Guam, and the Philippines, even though he disagreed with Kipling's belief "that the woeful 'burden' which the 'White Man' is compelled to bear, is to rule the colored races of the world and to compel the brown 'half-devil and half-child' to serve his interests, promote his comfort, and enhance his wealth." Tourgée supported acquisition of the insular territories for the same reason he advocated imposing northern institutions on the South. Given his faith in the power of institutions to transform populations, Tourgée encouraged nation building. An imperial policy, he felt, would extend free institutions to the former Spanish colonies and, thus, create a "new civilization in the gloom of Oriental darkness." Dixon dismisses similar arguments for imperialism as "shallow cosmopolitanism" (*LS*, 445). Even so, Tourgée's imperial vision helps to explain why, at the end of *A Fool's Errand*, his carpetbagger protagonist is "engaged by a company of capitalists in one of the republics of Central America" to aid in "that strange contest between civilization and semi-barbarism which is constantly being waged in that wonderfully strange region" (390). Tourgée's belief in the power of free institutions to shape virtuous citizens made him want to spread their benefits not only to the South but to all areas of the globe.[49]

Taken together, the views of Burgess, Wilson, Harris, Page, Dixon, and Tourgée on federalism confirm a paradox I identified in the introduction. On the one hand, supported by the Supreme Court and public opinion, the national government increased its power to limit immigration and to extend imperialism overseas.

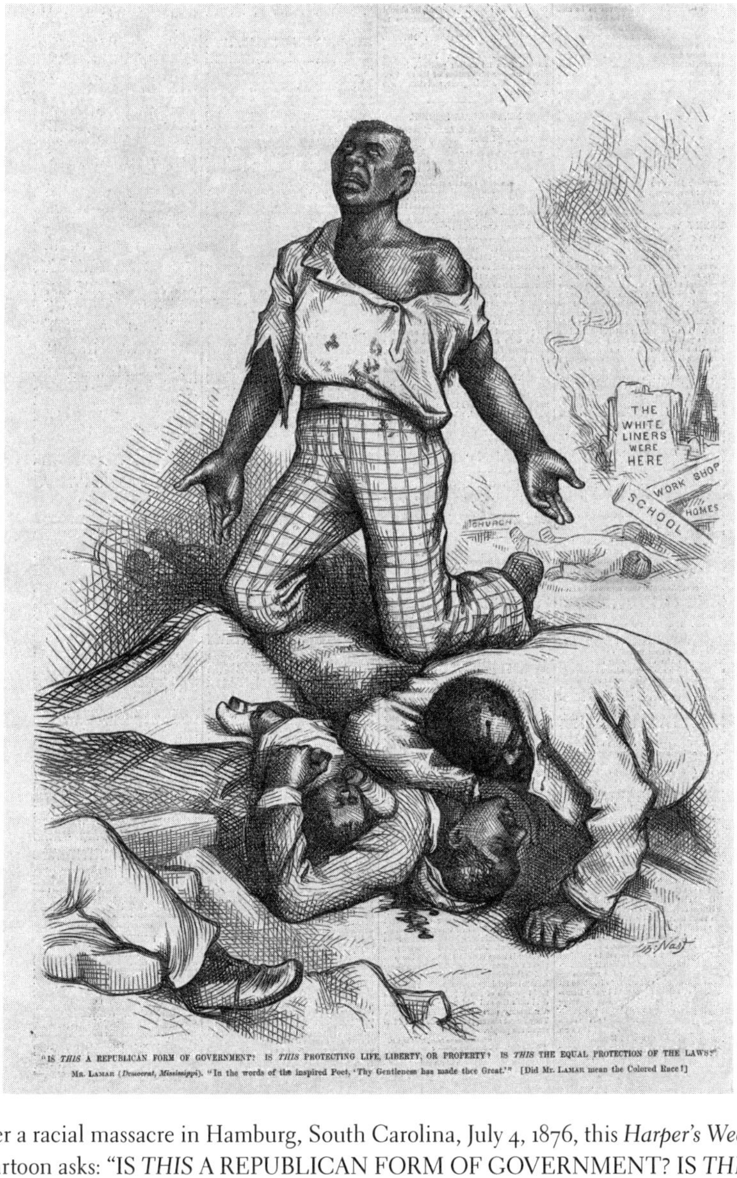

After a racial massacre in Hamburg, South Carolina, July 4, 1876, this *Harper's Weekly* cartoon asks: "IS *THIS* A REPUBLICAN FORM OF GOVERNMENT? IS *THIS* PROTECTING LIFE, LIBERTY, OR PROPERTY? IS *THIS* THE EQUAL PROTECTION OF THE LAWS?" Mr. Lamar (Democrat, Mississippi). "In the words of the inspired poet, 'Thy gentleness has made thee Great.'" [Did Mr. Lamar mean the Colored Race?] In addition to evoking parts of the Fourteenth Amendment, Thomas Nast cites a constitutional basis of the Reconstruction Acts: Article IV, Section 4: "The United States shall guarantee to every State in the Union a Republican Form of Government."

On the other hand, restricted by the Supreme Court and lacking substantial public support, it failed to exercise the power that would have given Reconstruction a better chance for success. Although the national government never heeded Dixon's call officially to endorse white supremacy, federalism was fashioned to give individual states the control over racial issues that Page and Harris wanted.

V

This vision of federalism did not go unchallenged by African American writers. Two of Pauline Hopkins's novels culminate with trials, in which she implies the need for the national government to intervene in order to produce justice. *In Contending Forces,* Hopkins counters the historical record and has the federal Supreme Court give redress to an African American family wronged in the state of North Carolina. In *Hagar's Daughter,* she presents a murder trial in Washington, DC, in which the falsely accused is defended by the former governor of Massachusetts. A key witness for the defense is an African American woman, who points the finger at a former Confederate soldier, now a chief at the Treasury Department. When the prosecution is about to win the day by discrediting the testimony of the African American woman against an honorable white man, the defense turns to a governmental detective employed by the Secret Service. Providing her own account of the proper role of governmental detectives, Hopkins has this converted slave owner, who was willing to marry a woman he thought had mixed blood, reveal all and make sure justice is done, even though it means convicting the former Confederate soldier, who turns out to be his brother and one of the conspirators in the Lincoln assassination.

The most interesting African American literary response to debates about federalism, however, is that of Sutton Griggs. In Griggs's *The Hindered Hand; or, The Reign of the Repressionist* (1905), two characters discuss a book by "a rather conspicuous Southern man who had set himself the task of turning the entire Negro population out of America" (206). One of them thinks that "a policy of misrepresentation was the necessary concomitant of a policy of repression" (206). In the book's third edition, the characters' discussion of the book is expanded and becomes an appendix called "A Hindering Hand. Supplementary to *The Hindered Hand*: A Review of the Anti-Negro Crusade of Mr. Thomas Dixon, Jr." Griggs self-consciously wrote his novels to intervene in the racial debates of the time.

Six years earlier, Dixon had not yet published his first novel, but there were plenty of issues for Griggs to explore. As the national government waged imperialist wars while conceding to the states control over African Americans' lives, *Imperium in Imperio* (1899) imagines a world in which African Americans take over a state to create their own empire within the larger American empire. Because of the date of its publication and its title, most recent criticism of *Imperium in Imperio* has looked at its relation to the Spanish-American War. More central to its plot, however, are debates about federalism growing out of Reconstruction. As poignantly as anyone, Griggs points out the problems with how the powers between the national and state governments were drawn.[50]

Griggs imagines a secret organization of African Americans located in Texas. There are two possibilities for this empire within the empire. One, advocated by Harvard-educated Bernard Belgrave, is for the organization to be in vigilante opposition to the United States. The other, advocated by Belgrave's onetime friend Belton Piedmont, is more complicated. In a long speech, Piedmont insists that "the relation of the General Government to the individual state" is "the one serious flaw in the Constitution of the United States."

> The General Government says to the citizen: "I am your sovereign. You are my citizen and not the citizen of only one state. If I call on you to defend my sovereignty, you must do so even if you have to fight against your own state. But while I am your supreme earthly sovereign I am powerless to protect you against crimes, injustices, outrages against you. . . . The Negro must therefore fight to keep afloat a flag that can afford him no more protection than could a helpless baby. . . . The Negro finds himself an unprotected foreigner in his own home. Whatever outrages may be perpetrated upon him by the people of the state in which he lives, he cannot expect any character of redress from the Central Government." (*II*, 181–82)

Calling the Supreme Court "the chief bulwark of caste prejudice in a democratic America," Piedmont cites as examples the *Civil Rights Cases* and *Plessy v. Ferguson* (*II*, 213, 193).

Piedmont's plan is to appropriate this inherent flaw in the federal system by taking over the state of Texas. African Americans would, therefore, be able to use state power for their own protection. This plan, Piedmont implies, is true to the spirit of the founding fathers of the organization, who instructed its leaders "to pay especial attention to the history of the United States during the revolutionary period" (*II*, 193). Indeed, during that period, the idea of imperium in imperio played a crucial role. A major point of contention between the colonies and Great Britain was whether the colonies could have substantial local control. The British response was to insist on the impossibility of having an empire within an empire. Sovereignty, the mother country insisted, could not be divided. William Blackstone clarified the colonies' legal status by relying on the same distinction Wilson would later use between sovereignty and dominion. Because Britain's American colonies had been obtained either by conquest or by treaty, they were not "part of the mother country" but were instead "distinct (though dependent) dominions." That position provoked the colonists into uniting and declaring independence to establish their own sovereignty. Once they did, the debates over imperium in imperio influenced how the founding fathers determined the relationship between individual states and the national government. Denying that imperium in imperio was by nature a solecism, the federalists developed a theory of divided sovereignty. Nonetheless, Blackstone's distinction remained a useful one for the United States' own imperial adventures. Chief Justice John Marshall drew on Blackstone in *Cherokee Nation v. Georgia* (1831) to designate Native American tribes "domestic dependent nations." Aware of how within its empire Great Britain had created white dominions that still owed sovereignty to the monarch, Justice Edward Douglass White in *Downes v. Bidwell* labeled the newly acquired insular territories "foreign to the United States in a domestic sense." In *Imperium in Imperio*, however, Piedmont's plan to exploit the federal system's dual sovereignty is opposed by Belgrave, who, following the rules of the organization, sentences his rival to death.[51]

Griggs's own position is not completely clear. His sympathies seem to lie with Piedmont, and it is possible that he sees his protagonist's plan as a serious alternative. It is much more likely that he is using Piedmont's plan to encourage the national government to eliminate this flaw in the federal system and provide African Americans with the protections they need. This possibility is reinforced by the existence of Belgrave's radical alternative for an empire within an empire, one that, as Peter Schmidt observes, "ironically comes to mirror the obsessions of another invisible empire, the Ku Klux Klan." In fact, Griggs, who read Tourgée, may well have known that in *A Fool's Errand* the staunch critic of states' rights called the Klan "an *imperium in imperio* (*FE*, 257). In the next chapter, I compare representations of the Klan in various works of the time.[52]

-3-

THE KU KLUX KLAN

The Necessity of Extreme Measures

The extralegal violence of the Ku Klux Klan and other white supremacist groups caused the national government to respond with its own extreme measures. In 1870 and 1871, the US Congress passed three different Enforcement Acts, the last one known as the Ku Klux Klan Act. Deemed necessary to combat the threat of domestic terrorism, these acts were the era's most explicit challenge to the tradition of dual federalism. They gave power to police the actions of individuals in some circumstances to the national, rather than to the state, government. For instance, the Ku Klux Klan Act of April 20, 1871, allowed President Grant to suspend habeas corpus, declare martial law, and use federal military force to suppress terrorist organizations violating civil rights. Offenders were tried in federal, not state, courts. Even some moderate Republicans, including Carl Schurz, claimed that the acts threatened the capacity of the states to protect the rights of the individual. If the time ever comes "when a part of the Republic will be so deeply sunk in anarchy and rule of violence that nothing but a strong, consolidated central Government, invested with arbitrary powers, can remedy the evil," he warned, "we should have manliness enough to declare that this great experiment of local self-government has failed." Coming to the United States from Germany after the failed revolution of 1848, Schurz had been an avid abolitionist and became a prominent turn-of-the-century anti-imperialist. But these measures along with other issues caused him to join liberal Republicans and oppose Grant in the 1872 election.[1]

The provision authorizing the suspension of habeas corpus points to how complicated the legal efforts to combat the Klan became. In 1867, Radical Republicans had passed the Habeas Corpus Act so that blacks and white Unionists in the South could appeal to federal, not state, courts. But in 1870, when the Republican governor of North Carolina cracked down on the Klan, suspected members appealed to the same 1867 act. The Ku Klux Klan Act recognized that the protection of blacks and white Unionists now depended on the possibility of suspending habeas corpus. The Enforcement Acts also recognized the need to nip in the bud unlawful conspiracies. After all, according to Lincoln, since states did not have the right to secede, the rebellion against the union was conducted by conspiracies of individuals. Then Lincoln himself was assassinated by a group of conspirators. Linking individuals to conspiracies, however, is no easy matter.

As the Enforcement Acts were being debated, Sidney Lanier wrote a dialect poem called "Them Ku Klux" that dramatizes the difficulty of identifying conspirators. The poem's southern narrator is engaged in his Sunday activity of reading newspapers on his porch when he receives a visit from James Munro, a neighbor from the North who has bought a local farm. The narrator praises the carpetbagger's work ethic and calls him "a fust-rate honest neighbor." James reports that he has been reading an account of the Klan in a Pennsylvania newspaper. Skeptical, the narrator responds,

> And so I says, "Now James Munro,
> You air a man of gumption,
> You know that two and two make fo;
> And you ain't much on presumption;
> And now that you've lived in Bibb fo' year,
> Did you ever see, er feel, or hear,
> Or taste, or smell, or think you was near,
> A Ku Kluxin assassin?"

By way of contrast, he tells his neighbor of reading about a congressional speech by Charles Sumner, condemning President Grant's effort to annex Santo Domingo. According to the narrator, "[Sumner] *says Grant's their leader— /That Grant his-self's a old be-Ku Klux / —A regular Ku Klux breeder!*"[2]

The speech referred to is "Violations of International Law, and Usurpations of War Powers," delivered March 27, 1871. Sumner had consistently opposed Grant's efforts at annexation, blocking them in the Senate. Sumner and Grant's animosity became so great that in 1872 Sumner joined Schurz and other liberal Republicans, as well as Democrats, in supporting Horace Greeley for president. Sumner's stand on Santo Domingo also pitted him against his friend Frederick Douglass, who supported Grant. In his speech, Sumner claims that Grant's plan violated international law and the Constitution. "How can we expect to put down the Ku-Klux at the South," he asks, "when we set in motion another proceeding kindred in constant insubordination to Law and Constitution?" If Grant had spent "one quarter of the time, money, zeal, will, personal attention, personal effort, and personal intercession" on protecting "Southern Unionists, white and black" that he spent unlawfully trying to obtain Santo Domingo, then "our Southern Ku-Klux would have existed in name only." Instead, Grant, like the Klan, strikes "at the African race. . . . Lawlessness is the common element."[3]

Having alluded to this speech by Sumner, the narrator offers to read the newspaper account for his friend. But he cannot find his spectacles, which, it turns out, are on the top of his forehead. James and the narrator's wife have a laugh at his expense. Then James, jokingly, says the incident may prove Sumner right about Grant.

> "Which makes me b'leeve that Sumner's right
> And Grant's like you, so full o' spite
> A fumblin' and a gruntin'
>
> To find out whar the Ku Klux was
> (And you for your old spectikles) . . .
> That he clean forgot (what Nancy see)
> To feel *hisself* right keerfullee;
> Then p'raps he's 'a' found that hisself might be
> Th' identickel thing he was huntin'!"[4]

Read superficially, Lanier's poem seems a typical white southern refutation of accounts of the Klan's atrocities reported in northern papers. Why trust those accounts when James, living in the South, has no empirical evidence that the Klan exists? But the use of Sumner suggests that more is going on. If in Lanier's "Civil Rights" Sumner is the implied villain, in this poem he is appealed to as an authority three years before Lucius Lamar's 1874 eulogy for him. Certainly, many white southerners would have delighted in Sumner's accusations against the Republican president presiding over Reconstruction. First, Grant's imperialist efforts to take over Santo Domingo reinforced southern complaints that Reconstruction was itself an imperialist campaign. Second, Sumner's claim that Grant acted against the interests of the "African race" fed arguments that northerners had no real concern for people of color. Finally, Sumner's comparison of Grant to the Klan gave ammunition to charges that the government adopted terrorist tactics in its efforts to combat alleged terrorism.

But the poem does much more. As the playful mocking of the narrator's inability to find his spectacles indicates, the poem is about how we see and how we read. Specifically, it is about how we come up with evidence to identify members of conspiratorial organizations, like the Klan. How do we detect a conspiracy? Is empirical evidence enough? That question is especially relevant for the Klan, which appeared at night, its members disguised as ghosts who could disappear into the air. Indeed, one provision of the Ku Klux Klan Act forbade people from going "in disguise upon the public highway or upon the premises of another for the purpose, either directly or indirectly, of depriving any person or any class of persons of the equal protection of laws." Lanier evokes the spectral possibility of disappearing ghosts with a series of dialect puns. "Ain't" is sometimes rendered "h'aint," a suggestion that "haints," "haunts," or "ghosts" might inhabit the poem. Similarly, "are" is rendered "air," a suggestion that evidence of the Klan is "in the air," with its multiple meanings. In fact, the title of the poem was originally "Where Air Them Ku Klux."[5]

On the one hand, this aspect of the poem reinforces the narrator's skepticism about northern reports of the Klan's widespread existence. It also reminds us (as we should know all too well from today's "war on terrorism," if not from reading Thomas Pynchon) that attempts to identify conspiratorial groups can foster conspiratorial paranoia. On the other hand, the poem creates a dilemma for the reader. Although there is no conclusive empirical evidence, it is possible that the narrator himself is a member of the Klan. Like Grant, he might be identical to the thing he is hunting. That this possibility can only be suggested, not definitively proven, is, of course, part of the point. Such a reading can be dismissed as paranoia, but it suggests just how widespread the Klan's membership might be and how effective members are at disguising their identities.

Lanier's poem dramatizes how hard it was to legislate against an organization whose membership was by nature elusive. Since the premise of the legislation was that these groups constituted an unlawful conspiracy, it was in the interests of the perpetrators not to leave any traces of self-conscious organization. At the same time, since those intent on keeping African Americans in their place wanted their efforts to have a major effect, they also hoped to create the impression of a widespread movement. These almost contradictory goals help explain the function of disguises. Obviously, disguises helped to conceal the identity of members. They were also ostensibly designed to frighten superstitious freedmen. At times, that might have happened, but more often than not freedmen knew that human beings, not ghosts, were intimidating them. More important, disguises gave the group a collective identity. The costumes were not as uniform as they became in the twentieth century after the circulation of images from *The Birth of a Nation*. But the fact that the Ku Klux Klan Act had a provision about disguises shows how much the Klan was identified with them.[6]

Of course, it is one thing to identify someone as a member of the Klan while in disguise. It is quite another to identify him in everyday life without his disguise, which is why we can only speculate if the narrator of Lanier's poem is a member of the Klan. Indeed, when it comes to identifying individual members of the Klan in a particular locale, even today's best historians have to rely on a certain amount of speculation. For instance, in her fascinating account of Klan activity in Union County, South Carolina, Elaine Frantz Parsons acknowledges that conspirators were never reliably identified and tried. Even though we have the names of people arrested under the Enforcement Acts, the government lacked the reliable local information consistently to arrest the right men. Trying to reconstruct Klan membership, Parsons relies on the most sophisticated network analysis available to experts in the digital humanities. In the end, however, her most important identifications are still speculative.[7]

What Parsons and others have conclusively shown is that, just as today's terrorists rely on the Internet to expand their activities, so the Klan relied on newspapers. Local journalists used the press to send coded messages about meetings. Even the northern accounts of Klan violence that Lanier's narrator dismisses provided Klan wannabes with models of intimidation and assurance that violent response to "carpetbagger and negro rule" was successful elsewhere. The press also waged a heated debate over the extent and legitimacy of Klan violence which was never completely resolved. After the Klan's peak activity, that debate was retroactively waged in fiction, which provided competing political allegories about local Klan activities.

In many works of the period sympathetic to the plight of African Americans, the Klan is either mentioned or makes a brief appearance. For instance, in Chesnutt's *The Marrow of Tradition*, the African American laborer Josh Green recalls a visit by the Klan when he was ten years old. Hiding in the bushes, he watched as they murdered his father, causing his mother to lose her mind. This event is, he tells the black physician Dr. Miller, "branded on my memory, suh, like a red-hot iron bran's de skin" (*MT*, 111). The leader of the Klan on that visit of death was Captain McBane, the son of a former slave overseer, who reaps a profit after the war through the convict lease system. As Dr. Miller listens to Josh's story, he recalls the "timeworn explanation that the Ku-Klux movement, in the main, was merely an ebullition of boyish spirits, begun to amuse young white men by playing on the fears and superstitions of ignorant negroes." Josh's story, however, reminds him of "its tragic side,—the old wound still bleeding, the fruit of one tragedy, the seed of another" (*MT*, 112). Indeed, Josh lives, waiting for a chance to have revenge.

Whereas the Klan is mentioned or makes a brief appearance in works like *The Marrow of Tradition*, in Tourgée's *A Fool's Errand* and *Bricks without Straw*, it is central to the plot. Tourgée wrote both novels after Congress, with Republicans in control of both houses, produced a report on the Klan in 1871. Describing the report in his 1901 *Atlantic Monthly* account of "The Ku Klux Klan Movement," William Garrett Brown notes that for the Republican majority, "'Ku Klux' meant simply outlaws." The Klan's success "seemed to nullify the Emancipation Proclamation, and the constitutional amendments which were meant to seal forever the victory of the North over the South, and of liberty over slavery." In contrast, for the Democratic minority, that success "seemed to reassert the great principles of the American Revolution. . . . [T]he first Ku Klux in history were disguised men who, against the law, threw tea overboard in Boston harbor." With Republicans no longer in control of both houses and Hayes's "New Departure" underway, Tourgée hoped his novels would convince the public of the accuracy of the majority report and convince a wavering national government that intervention was still needed. Because some questioned his fictional account, Tourgée added to a subsequent edition of *A Fool's Errand* the nonfictional *The Invisible Empire,* just as Harriet Beecher Stowe had felt obliged to produce *A Key to "Uncle Tom's Cabin."* A major task of southern revisionist fiction at the turn of the century was to refute the account of the Klan so memorably created by Tourgée two decades before.[8]

To a large extent, the fictional responses to Tourgée tried to confirm the Democratic minority report of 1871. But to varying degrees they also share similarities with accounts by people like Brown, who in their minds, if not ours, thought they were providing a balanced view. For instance, in his study of North Carolina, J. G. de Roulhac Hamilton insisted that the Klan "furnished protection to the oppressed. . . . The women of the South once more could leave their doors without the accompaniment of a deadly terror. Property became fairly safe again. . . . Certain it is that no open revolt could ever have accomplished so much good as did the secret operations of the so-called Klan, and few to-day would deny that there was necessity for some remedy for the conditions then existent." But Hamilton goes on to admit that the Klan, "degenerating from its high purpose and estate, as might have been expected from its nature and organization, . . . was often violent and sometimes oppressive, and in the end, fell into the control of reckless spirits who used it for private vengeance rather than public punishment." Likewise, although Brown felt that "the end attained was mainly good. Southern society was righted," he concludes by lamenting, "The method of [the Klan] survives in too many habits of the Southern mind, in too many shortcomings of Southern civilization, in too many characteristics of Southern life." Southerners had "kept their solidarity unimpaired by any healthful division on public questions. . . . [T]hey learned to set men above political principles, and good government above freedom of thought." To be effective, turn-of-the-century responses to Tourgée's earlier representation of the Klan had to address such concerns.[9]

In the rest of this chapter, I first look at Joel Chandler Harris and Thomas Nelson Page. Unified in their opposition to Reconstruction, they give portrayals of the Klan that imply different views of what the postbellum South should strive for. Those views of the future are narratively linked to the past. As Brown pointed out, those who tried to justify the Klan appealed to the nation's revolutionary founding. Harris and Page's different portrayals of the Klan help to distinguish the two authors' foundational myths for the nation. I then turn to Dixon and show how his account of the Klan constructs a foundational myth that places the United States in a progressive narrative about world history that fits into his view of nationalism, which we explored last chapter. For Dixon, the Klan enables the redemption of the South, leading to the birth of a new nation to carry out an imperial mission for the white race. Having dealt with these three responses to Tourgée, I return to his works to show their ongoing capacity to respond to those who came after him. But even Tourgée shares with his opponents a sense of redemptive history.

II

Responding to one of Tourgée's later novels, Joel Chandler Harris exclaimed, "What shall we say of such a writer? Is he a monomaniac, or simply a refugee from his race?" In *Gabriel Tolliver,* Harris offers an alternative account to Tourgée's when thirteen white riders disrupt a Union League meeting at a church. "Three times this ghostly procession marched around the church," until the leader breaks the silence by asking his fellows, "Brothers, is all well with you?" (*GT,* 252). They reply, "All is not well," and claim to see "Trouble, misery, blood." The leader responds that if they see blood, then all is in fact well. After repeatedly riding around the church, the riders "suddenly disappeared in the darkness" (252). Gabriel, who is watching, unobserved, feels as if "he had been dreaming. If ever there were goblins, these were they. The figures on horseback were so closely draped in white that they had no shape but height, and their heads and hands were not in view" (252).[10]

Initially paralyzed by this visitation, the African Americans in the church soon rush in panic to escape. Pistol shots signal a message, and the white horsemen reappear to chase the "fleeing negroes," taunting the black minister who organized the meeting with repeated utterances of "Blood" (*GT,* 254). Abandoning the frightened minister in town, they depart with the warning "Beware!" (255). Through all of this activity, the white Freedmen's Bureau agent stays in the church undisturbed. When finally he leaves, the leader of the group, the "Knights of the White Camellia" (257), finds Gabriel and reveals his identity. It turns out to be Major Tomlin Perdue, one of the book's more sympathetic characters.

The major had already appeared in Harris's *The Chronicle of Aunt Minervy Ann* (1899). In that book, he saves a black man elected to the Georgia legislature from an attack by a "would-be Ku-Klux" (*CAM,* 28). Orchestrated by Perdue, the scene of salvation is one of humor, as a pretentious member of this "amateur Ku-Klux" appears in town the next day with buckshot in his butt (16). In *Gabriel*

Tolliver, the major returns home after the war "thoroughly reconstructed. He was full of admiration for General Grant's attitude toward General Lee." But "when he saw the unexpected turn the politicians had been able to give to events, he found it hard to hold his peace" (*GT,* 117). The major assures Gabriel that his group was simply having some fun: "They don't belong to the Ku Klux that you've read so much about" (260). In fact, the major does not "believe that there's any danger of a nigger-rising" (261). He is, however, afraid of scalawags and carpetbaggers who organize freedmen for their own purposes. The chapter with the visitation begins with the narrator's vivid description of the constitutional convention imposed upon the state, and its aftermath. Even Gabriel, who believes the freedmen pose no danger, feels that those events require "that something must be done to convince the misguided negroes that the whites were not asleep" (245). Justifying his own actions, the major laments, "But men of my sort will be misjudged. . . . Violent men will get in the saddle, and outrages will be committed, and injustice will be done" (262).

To be sure, Shady Dale wakes "up the next morning to find the walls and the fences in all public places plastered with placards, or handbills, printed in red ink," with "a grinning skull and cross-bones," endorsed by "the Venerable, the Grand Cyclops, in behalf of the all-powerful Klan" (*GT,* 263). Because the handbills refer to "White Riders" being "abroad," it is never completely clear whether Shady Dale experiences a visitation from the real Klan, or whether the Knights of the White Camellia are cleverly using the specter of the Klan and its violence to cause more fright. In either case, the major, while distancing himself and his group from the Klan, clearly lays the blame for the Klan's violence on Radical Reconstruction. As he tells Gabriel, "You will live, my son, to see some of these same radicals admit that all the injustice and all the wrong is due to the radical policy." The narrator intrusively adds, "This prophecy came true. Time has abundantly vindicated the Major and those who acted with him" (262).

Without denying the violence of the Klan, Harris exonerates the major and, by implication, the "good people" of the South by blaming the formation of the Klan on radicals and by distinguishing between those involved in admittedly unjust violence and those asserting control through good, old-fashioned fun. That Harris had an audience more than ready to accept this distinction is made clear by Tourgée's description of the northern press's initial response to reports of the Klan. The "newspapers of the North," he reports, "unwittingly accustomed their readers to regard it as a piece of the broadest and most ridiculous fun. . . . What could be funnier, or a more appropriate subject of mirth, than that the chivalric but humorous and jocose Southrons should organize a ghostly police to play upon the superstitious fears of colored people, who were no doubt very trifling, and needed a good deal of regulation and restraint?" (*FE,* 181).

In *Gabriel Tolliver,* we never see the Klan, only a group of pranksters controlling African Americans by harmlessly playing on their superstitions. In *Red Rock,* however, Page depicts the activities of the Klan directly. Not distinguishing between the Klan and other, harmless, groups, Page challenges Tourgée's account by differentiating between legitimate and illegitimate actions. In the first half of the book, Steve Allen, one of the protagonists, joins the Klan and serves as its leader to disarm a black militia organized by the Freedmen's Bureau agent Jonadab Leech. By arming the local African Americans, Leech has broken down the social and economic fabric of the community. African Americans "became insolent and swaggering. The fields were absolutely abandoned. Should they handle hoes when they could carry guns! Should they plough when they were the State guard!" When the companies drilled, "they filled the streets and took possession of the sidewalks, yelling, and hustling out of their way any who might be on them. Ladies walking on the street were met and shoved off into the mud" (*RR*, 232).

Faced with this situation, "ghostly riders" meet one night at an old, dilapidated hospital, intent on restoring health to the community. Because of Leech's hold on the county, people had discounted the possibility that "the Ku Klux might reach there," and the African Americans took home "their arms and accouterments, with all the pride and pomp of newly decorated children." Then, "in the dead of night," with "the most perfect organization" the "visitation" comes (*RR*, 237). In most cases, the disarming is accomplished quietly by "awful forms wrapped like ghosts in winding-sheets." But "in some few places there had been force extended and violence used" (238). As the narrator sums up, "A new and unknown force had suddenly arisen. The negroes were paralyzed with terror. Many of them believed that the riders were really supernatural, and they told, with ashy faces, of the marvelous things they had done" (239).

Once the disarming is complete, Steve Allen quits the Klan. Nonetheless, some ruthless characters continue to operate in its name. The group's illegitimacy is made clear by its new leader, the villain McRaffle, who is the only member who seriously injured someone in the disarming raid. Earlier, McRaffle had gratuitously killed a "half dozen negroes" (*RR*, 192). By the end of the book, he has become a scalawag with a governmental appointment. Committing acts of personal vengeance, McRaffle's group also threatens to burn a colored school. By attributing that threat to a sham Klan, Page counters testimony to Congress on the Klan's attacks against schools. In *The Invisible Empire,* for instance, Tourgée, relying on that testimony, includes a chapter called "Hostility to Schools and Teachers" (71–83). In *Iola Leroy,* Harper gives us a chapter called "Flames in the School-Room," in which the first school Iola teaches in the South becomes a "smoldering ruin, . . . the cruel work of an incendiary's torch" (147). In *Red Rock,* the sham Klan's

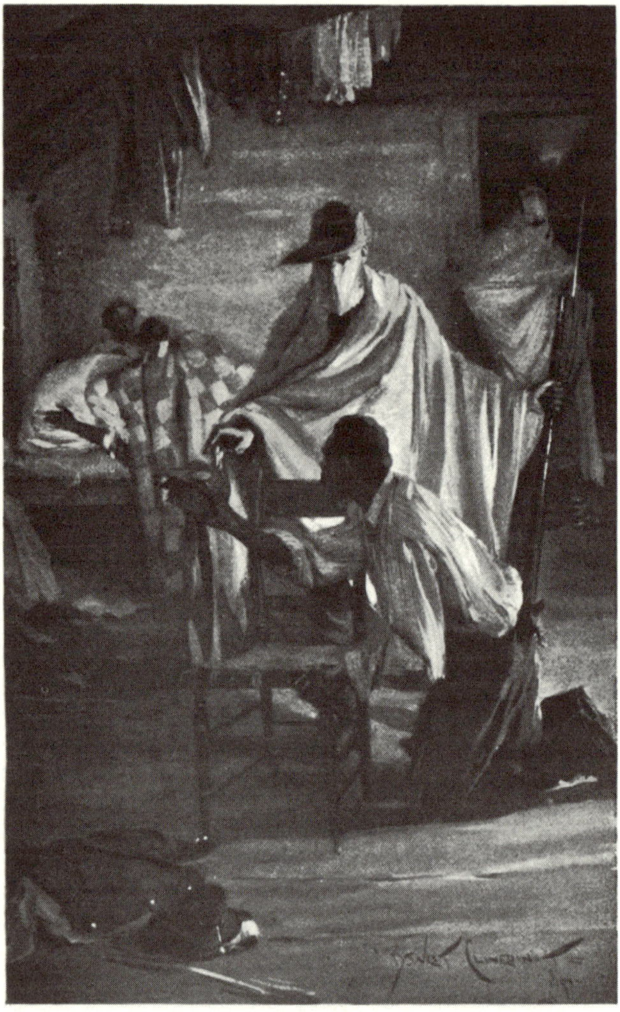

KU KLUX—" AWFUL FORMS WRAPPED LIKE GHOSTS IN WINDING-SHEETS."

This illustration from *Red Rock* depicts the Klan disarming a member of the African American militia. Stripped of his uniform and deprived of his rifle, the man cowers before the Klan members. His children lie frightened in bed as their mother hides under covers, hoping to escape this visitation from figures associated in her mind with the return of the Indian-killer. The Klan figure in the foreground evokes phallic masculinity, while the one in the background has a ghostlike aura.

attempted raid on the school is foiled by two southern women claiming that "you ain't so much against niggers and carpetbaggers as you make out." McRaffle insists that they "leave the Invisible Empire to execute its dread decrees." Not cowed, one of the women pulls the mask off McRaffle's face, telling the group, "I know every mother's son of you" (407). Unmasked, this group of ruffians has no identity other than that of cowards.[11]

Although Steve Allen opposes the Klan's actions under McRaffle, he does, one more time, feel obligated to act outside the law. Rupert Gray, the hotheaded younger brother of the legitimate heir to the Red Rock estate, unwisely associates with McRaffle and is tracked down and arrested by governmental detectives. Steve organizes a group to free Rupert from prison. Before the rescue takes place, however, Steve has a probing exchange with Dr. Cary, a former Whig who opposed secession but remained loyal to his state once it joined the Confederacy. Dr. Cary is the one notable resident who did not participate in disarming the black militia. Sympathetic to Steve's cause, he opposes the method Steve chooses to combat the injustice of Rupert's arrest. Acknowledging that he would give his life to save Rupert, he goes on:

> "But I could not kneel to my God to-night if I did not declare to you my belief—my profound conviction—that this is not the way to go about it. I know that the wrongs we are suffering cry to God, but I urge you to unite with me in trying to remedy them by law, and not by violence. Let us unite and make an appeal to the enlightened sense of the American people, of the world, which they would be forced to hear. Violence on our side is the only ground which they can urge for their justification. It is a terrible weapon we are furnishing them, and with it, not only can they defeat us now, but they can injure us for years to come." (*RR*, 429)

Steve disagrees, and the rescue continues successfully.

This dispute over the appropriate use of violence to correct injustice is crucial for an understanding of *Red Rock*. Dr. Cary is an extremely sympathetic character, but the action of the book backs Steve Allen. It does so by linking the restrained, but necessary, use of violence in the Klan's disarming of the black militia with the founding myth of Red Rock. On the first page of the novel, we are told that Red Rock takes its name from "the great red stain . . . which appeared on the huge bowlder in the grove, beside the family grave-yard, at the far end of the Red Rock gardens." This stain was believed to be "the blood of the Indian chief who had slain the wife of the first Jacquelin Gray who came to this part of the world: the Jacquelin who had built the first house at Red Rock, around the fireplace of which the present mansion was erected, and whose portrait, with its piercing eyes and fierce look, hung in a black frame over the mantel, and used to come down as a warning when any peril impended above the house." The husband "had exacted swift retribution, for the murderer, on that very rock, and the Indian's heart blood had left that deep stain in the darker granite as a perpetual memorial of the swift vengeance of the Jacquelin Grays" (*RR*, 1). There are two elements of this initial description: the story of Red Rock's founding and the legend of supernatural vengeance. The historical event gets a form of independent confirmation when, prior to the war, the father of the present Jacquelin Gray tells the story of the founding ancestor to Major Welch, a visiting northerner. A scholar, the Indian-killer "had been a soldier under Cromwell and lost all his property" (27). Red Rock's dissenting founding father married the daughter of a loyalist over her family's objection, immigrated to the New World, and built his house in the midst of the frontier. His murdered wife left him one child, and he reputedly exacted revenge on the Indian chief with his bare hands. As opposed to the historical account, the supernatural legend is met with some skepticism. As a young boy, Steve Allen said "that the stain was nothing but a bit of red sandstone which had outcropped at the point where that huge fragment was broken off, and rolled along by a glacier thousands of years ago" (2). Nonetheless, the legend "was asserted and believed by the old negroes (and, perhaps, by some of the whites, too, a little)." The narrator then adds, "And if the negroes did not know, who did?" (1).[12]

It is not clear whether we are supposed to believe in the supernatural powers of the Indian-killer to enact revenge for future generations or not. On the one hand, we have Steve's skepticism. On the other hand, the portrait does fall down at crucial moments when the Grays' possession of Red Rock is in peril. What is certain is that, during the disarming raid, the Klan exploits the African Americans' belief in the legend by leaving behind "a picture drawn with red chalk on the floor of the portico, a fairly good representation of the 'Indian Killer'" (239).[13]

African Americans are not the only ones to connect the Klan's raid with the myth of the Indian-killer. The former overseer Hiram Still also believes in the swift vengeance of the ghost of the original Jacquelin Gray. While the present Jacquelin is away on a long voyage for his health and protection, Still, using fraudulent proof of a debt owed him by Jacquelin's father, takes possession of Red Rock, causing Mrs. Gray to suffer mentally and face the prospect of not being buried next to her husband. By calling in another debt, Still has also taken Dr. Cary's home. Living in his ill-begotten home, Still is haunted by the portrait of the Indian-killer. One night he sees "the outline of a man on horseback . . . clearly defined against the skyline on the crest of a hill . . . apparently . . . just behind the dark clump of trees where lay the old Gray burying-ground" (*RR*, 440). Though Still does not know it, this "ghostly horseman" turns out to be Steve Allen, riding at night to court his lover. Steve has quit the Klan, but this association of him as a "night rider" (441) with the righteously vengeful Indian-killer serves to legitimate his belief in necessary, if restrained, violence to bring about justice.

Page was so taken with the idea of ghosts returning from the grave to remedy situations in the present that, as war threatened to break out with Spain in April the year *Red Rock* appeared, he published a poem in the *Washington Post* called "The Dragon of the Seas." Responding to reports that a Spanish fleet was assembling, the poem recounts the tale of the Spanish Armada that threatened the English nation three centuries before. Despite having the power to drench the earth "With Saxon blood," the Spanish were repulsed when their attack awoke the "Dragon of the Seas," embodied in Sir Francis Drake. The poem ends by returning to the present and warns: "If Spain fire a single shot/Upon the Spanish Main, /She'll come to deem the Dragon dead/Has waked to life again."[14]

In *Red Rock,* a returning ghost also commits violence in the name of the nation. Indeed, Page legitimates his foundational myth by evoking two of the North's most famous writers. *Red Rock*'s ghostly horseman recalls Washington Irving's "The Legend of Sleepy Hollow"; its house Nathaniel Hawthorne's *The House of the Seven Gables.* All three works raise the specter of the supernatural and treat it with skepticism. Page especially draws on Hawthorne. Both writers decorate their houses with intimidating portraits of their founders, which conceal secret vaults containing documents essential to the plot. Both also acknowledge the prior inhabitation of Native Americans: Page through his founding legend, Hawthorne through the Pyncheons' Indian deed. One crucial difference is that Page insists on his founder's legitimate title to his estate, whereas Hawthorne exposes the Pyncheons' deceitful claim to their land. Despite this difference, both novels have founding myths of violence and blood. Cheated out of his land and condemned to hang as a witch, Matthew Maule points to Colonel Pyncheon and declares: "God will give him blood to drink!" Evoking Salem's infamous witchcraft trials, Hawthorne demystifies myths of the Puritans as noble founding fathers. Thus, in New England's most famous author, Page finds confirmation for his challenge to narratives about the Puritan origins of the American self. Indeed, Page clearly wanted to give a different story about the founding of the country. In "The Want of a History of the Southern People," he lamented that everyone knows the name of the *Mayflower* but very few remember the names of the three ships that brought the founders of Jamestown, even though "the men borne hither by these three vessels, and not the passengers on the *Mayflower,* were the Argonauts who first took the Golden Fleece, this golden land."[15]

To be sure, in *Red Rock* the original Jacquelin Gray was a soldier for Cromwell. But he married the daughter of a Cavalier. America, Page suggests, results from the marriage of the two opposing forces in England and also from a tradition of Puritan violence. By dramatizing that violence, the legend of Red Rock challenges the founding myth of Plymouth Rock, especially as supplemented by the story of Thanksgiving. Tourgée in *A Fool's Errand* reminds us that some southerners dismissed Thanksgiving as that "new Yankee holiday, which has been added to the governmental calendar since the first year of Lincoln's reign" (54). The New England story of the Puritans celebrates a peaceful coming together of Native Americans and white settlers. In contrast, Page gives us a story about the rise of the nation through conflict and necessary violence with the Indians. To reinforce this point, he has the regiment of Union soldiers who alienate Leech because of their sympathy with the local inhabitants shipped "to the Northwest to keep the Indians down" (*RR*, 183). At that safe distance from the South, African American cavalrymen are allowed to be part of the force. When Rupert, freed from jail, joins the battle against the Indians, he distinguishes himself by saving an African American trooper. In contrast, responding to the claim that foreclosure of old landed estates because of high taxes is "robbery," Leech proclaims, "Then it is only paying robbery for robbery. You have been the robbers! You robbed the Indians of these lands, to start with" (211).

In Page's founding myth, the taking of Indian land is not robbery but is necessary to allow the triumph of civilization, as embodied in the gentlemanly code of honor exhibited by the descendants of the Indian-killer. Likewise, early in the first chapter we are assured that the Mexican-American War was necessary "to establish the security of the United States" (*RR*, 3). Jacquelin's "father, and his father's cousin, Dr. Cary, of Birdwood, and Mr. Legaie" (3) won renown fighting for their country, while Steve Allen's father "was killed in Mexico, leading his company up the heights of Cerro Gordo" (5). Southern participation in the Mexican-American War is important for Page, as it will be for Dixon, because that war united sides that would fight against one another during the Civil War. Grant, Lee, and Jefferson Davis all participated. Page associates this national venture to the Klan's disarming of the black militia as one more example of the legitimate use of violence to secure the well-being of the nation.

Once the blacks are no longer a threat, however, all further actions by those claiming to be the Klan are illegitimate, even if the legend of the Indian-killer remains in play. After the "Ku Klux raid" (*RR*, 241), Page gives us two chapters with seemingly different responses. In the first, the Freedmen's Bureau agent Leech and the former overseer Still go to the nation's capital to get the government's support in suppressing the threat of the Klan. They are well received and return "with the conviction that their mission had been completely successful" (241). To counter their lobbying, Dr. Cary and General Legaie make their own visit to

Washington, DC. Through a chance meeting with Dr. Cary's college roommate, now a northern senator, they get an audience with the president. Though treated with "great civility," they come away from this meeting "somewhat downcast" (245). But they have procured a sympathetic ally in Senator Rockfield. This chapter describes a response through established governmental and legal channels, whereas the next chapter returns us to a response connected to the founding myth of the Indian-killer.

The next chapter is about the return of Jacquelin from his voyage. Reminiscent of Philip Nolan in Edward Everett Hale's "The Man Without a Country," Jacquelin, "on the high seas or in a foreign land," has yearned to see "the flag of the nation" (*RR*, 257). "He had begun to realize the idea of a great nation that should be known and respected wherever a ship could sail or a traveler could penetrate: of a re-united country in which the people of both sides, retaining all the best of both sides, should vie with each other in building up the nation, and should equally receive all its benefits. He had pondered much on this, and he thought he had discovered the way to accomplish it, in a complete acceptance of the new situation" (257). But the "extraordinary changes" that "had taken place in the county" while he is away make him realize that work still needs to be done before the new situation is acceptable (258). On his arrival Jacquelin is met by the African American Waverley, who remarks, "Marse Jack, you done riz f'um de dead. Ef I didn't think 'twas my ole marster—er de Injun-Killer" (252). Describing how the time is out of joint in Red Rock, Waverley exclaims, "[D]e debble is done broke loose, sho! . . . De overseer is in the gret house, and de gent'man in the blacksmiff shop. I wonders sometimes dat old Injun-Killer don' come down out de picture sho 'nough—like so many o' dem dead folks what comin' out dey graves" (253). Waverley's reference to dead folks coming out of their graves is to the recent raid by the Klan. And it will be Jacquelin, an avatar of the Indian-killer, working with Steve Allen, who resists Leech and Still and tries to set things right in Red Rock. Indeed, the chapter in which he returns is called "Jacquelin Gray Comes Home and Claims a Graveyard." Jacquelin, however, never joins the Klan. Instead, like Dr. Cary and General Legaie, he works primarily through the legal system. To be sure, when Still threatens to get rid of the family graveyard, Jacquelin warns him that he will, like the Indian-killer, enact revenge with his bare hands, a reminder that there are acts that require a violent response. But when Still relents, Jacquelin and Steve pursue legal remedies.

Jacquelin's rejection of the Klan and respect for the law are on display in an episode late in the book. Leech accuses almost all the reputable southern whites with breaking Rupert out of jail and has them arrested. Steve Allen, however, escapes and kidnaps Leech to bargain for their release. In prison, Jacquelin and a friend are visited by the northern teacher of the colored school that McRaffle tried to burn. She turns out to be the same woman who nursed them in the prison hospital at Point Lookout during the war. She confides to them that she is Leech's abandoned wife. Despite his disloyalty to her, she asks Jacquelin and his friend to save her estranged husband. Southerners, they cannot refuse. Jacquelin, somewhat incredibly, gets the military officer in charge to set them temporarily free, promising to return to prison once their secret mission is accomplished. That mission is complicated because McRaffle and his band of ruffians, masquerading as the Klan, are looking for Leech with the aim of lynching him. Eluding the illegitimate Klan, Jacquelin and his friend rescue Leech and fulfill their promise to return.

As improbable as this episode is, Page includes it for a variety of reasons. Illustrating the southern code of honor, it is also designed to promote North-South reconciliation. Northern kindness, shown by Leech's wife, is repaid by southerners, while both northerners and southerners suffer at the hands of immoral carpetbaggers. In addition, the episode suggests Jacquelin's preference for the law over vigilante justice, as he goes so far as to return himself to prison. Confronted by scenes like this one, the reader is meant to see how exceptional the use of legitimate violence is for the virtuous people of the South. It is justified only if it leads to the restoration of law and honor, just as the Indian-killer's founding act of violence made possible the development of southern—and national—civilization.[16]

Page's justification of the Klan's legitimate use of violence distinguishes him from Harris. Their difference is registered in their foundational myths. These myths have some common features. Like the original Jacquelin Gray, Raleigh Clopton, the founder of Shady Dale, has a double character. "It was said of Raleigh Clopton that his sense of justice was as strong as his temper, which was a stormy one. He espoused the cause of young Eli Whitney, who had been despoiled of his rights in the cotton-gin in Georgia, and this led him into a series of difficulties without parallel in the history of the state. Raleigh Clopton's attitude in this contest brought him in conflict with some of the most powerful men and interests in the commonwealth" (*GT*, 40). In his fight against "knavery, fraud and corruption," he once "dragged one judge from a buggy, and plied him with a rawhide" (40). Clopton's feuds with powerful men create difficulties for his son Meriwether. Nonetheless, Meriwether transforms his father's roughness into gentlemanly refinement: "He was neither hardened nor embittered by the violence with which he had to deal. On the contrary, his character was strengthened and his temper sweetened; so that when the lads, who listened to his mellifluous translations from the Latin poets, were old enough to appreciate the qualities that go to make up a good man and an influential citizen, the fact dawned upon their minds that Meriwether Clopton was the finest gentleman they had ever seen" (41). But such similarities obscure important differences.

As in *Red Rock*, in Shady Dale an "old court-house, the temple of justice, had been reared in the centre of the town" (*GT*, 37). But whereas Page celebrates the antebellum legal system of the South for guaranteeing justice, Harris uses the example of Eli Whitney to show that powerful forces often corrupted the courts to advance private interests. The most important difference, however, involves the moment of foundation itself. Shortly after the treaty ending the Revolutionary War, Raleigh Clopton entered hostile Creek territory. The Creeks' hostility raises the specter of violence, and Harris alludes to the "bloody contests between the white settlers and the Creeks" (*GT*, 38). Shady Dale, however, is a sanctuary from such violence. The Creeks' chief is General McGillivray, "one of the most remarkable men of his time," who negotiated a treaty with George Washington, causing the "Father of his country" to refer to him as "my friend" (34). Clopton has one stormy interview with the chief, but then the two come to terms, just as McGillivray did with Washington. Forging a friendship with the founding father of Shady Dale, McGillivray deeds Clopton two thousand acres. Clopton then contacts "the choice spirits who had fought by his side in the bloodiest battles of the War for Independence" (35) and gives each one "a part of his domain." Tested by the hardships of the Revolutionary War, these men are "for the most part . . . men of substance and character" (36).

What Harris does not mention is that American infringement on Creek territory had caused McGillivray to ally himself with the British during the Revolutionary War and with the Spanish later on. He did sign the 1790 Treaty of New York, the first under the Constitution, but the details of the treaty let us see what Harris's foundational myth obscures. The treaty established clear boundaries of Creek territory and promised to remove illegal American settlers. In exchange, the Creeks agreed to return fugitive slaves who had sought refuge with them. Whereas the United States did not honor either of its two terms, fugitive slaves were betrayed. McGillivray personally profited, establishing a large plantation farmed by his own slaves. Of course, in the version of the story that Harris gives us, there is no mention of slavery or broken US promises. On the contrary, Clopton founds Shady Dale through peaceful negotiation and friendship without the violence necessary to establish Red Rock.

Whereas Red Rock's name reminds us of bloody violence, "from the time of the First Settler, the Clopton Place had been dedicated and set apart to uses of hospitality" (*GT*, 38). The deed that, "in name of the Creek Nation, conveyed the domain to Raleigh Clopton, distinctly set forth the condition that the Clopton Place was to be an asylum and a place of refuge for the unfortunate and for those who needed succour" (38). During the Creek Wars, white prisoners were delivered to Shady Dale and allowed to recover. Not commenting on the irony that General

McGillivray insists on this space of refuge while refusing sanctuary to fugitive slaves, Harris offers a story of foundation consistent with his condemnation of the Klan's violence.

That condemnation would seem to make his views closer to Tourgée's than to Page's. Unlike Tourgée, however, Harris blames the Klan's actions on the radicals it attacked, while implying that the majority of southerners were simply involved in harmless fun, playfully exploiting African Americans' superstitions as a means of social control. In this regard, Page turns out to be closer to Tourgée than to Harris. In *Red Rock*, the disarming raid leads to the Ku Klux Klan Act when Leech and Still report to the national capital that there is "a new rebellion" calling for "the suspension of writs of privileges and the exercise of the strongest powers of the Government" (*RR*, 241). That description of the Klan's activities is similar to the one Tourgée, a real carpetbagger, reported to Washington and reinforced through his fiction. Of course, for Tourgée, this legislation, except for the suspension of habeas corpus, was justified as a means of containing illegitimate violence. In contrast, for Page, this particular act of violence was justified to overcome illegitimate rule. Unlike Harris, Page acknowledges that the majority of respectful white southerners occasionally condoned extralegal violence. On that matter, he anticipates the author considered the Klan's most powerful advocate: Thomas Dixon.

III

Dixon's reputation comes from the popularity of his most famous book, *The Clansman*, and its incorporation into D. W. Griffith's film *The Birth of a Nation*. Based on those representations, it would seem that Dixon gave the Klan unequivocal support. Indeed, publication of *The Clansman* inspired the Klan's rebirth at the start of the twentieth century. But *The Clansman* focuses solely on the Klan's role in "redeeming" the South. Once redemption was accomplished, Dixon believed that the Klan was no longer needed. Thus, he follows Page in distinguishing between what he considers the Klan's legitimate and illegitimate activities. For instance, in *The Leopard's Spots*, a novel with a longer historical reach than *The Clansman*, Dixon has Major Dameron, the local leader of the Klan, disband his order. As he notes, "the Klan has done its work. The carpet-baggers have fled. The state is redeemed from the infamies of Negro government, and we have a clean, economical administration" (*LS*, 171). The dissolution of the order comes in a chapter called "The Danger of Playing with Fire." It is prompted by a plot by "a lot of drunken devils, masquerading as Ku Klux" (169), to kill an African American. When the major hears of this plan, he laments, "It's too easy for vicious men to abuse [the Klan]. Its power is too great" (170). What was once a necessary organization, according to him, is now "full of wild youngsters and revengeful men" masquerading as real Klansmen (171). Just as in *Red Rock*, McRaffle, the leader of the disreputable Klan, becomes a scalawag with a governmental appointment, so in *The Leopard's Spots* does Allan McLeod, who reorganizes the disbanded Klan, become a scalawag and the leader of the local Republican Party.[17]

The illegitimate Klan after redemption plays a major part in the plot of *The Traitor* (1907), the last and least read book of Dixon's Reconstruction trilogy. The novel's protagonist is John Graham, the former leader of the Klan in the county of Independence, North Carolina. Graham orders the disbandment of the Klan and is appalled when it is reorganized and becomes nothing more than "an engine of personal vengeance and criminal folly" (*TR*, 95). One of its most despicable acts is an attack on a Jewish merchant who is protected by Graham. Then a scalawag judge of the US Circuit Court is murdered. As in *Red Rock*, this local act leads to passage of the Ku Klux Klan Act. Graham is framed and charged with conspiracy as a member of the Klan and with the murder the judge. Whereas John is considered a traitor, the real traitor turns out to the self-serving leader of the illegitimate Klan. At the beginning of the book, Steve Hoyle is engaged to the judge's beautiful daughter, Stella. Hoyle saves himself by revealing the order's secret membership, leading to five hundred arrests. Like McRaffle in *Red Rock*, he is a scalawag. By the book's end, he becomes "one of our fattest, most solemn and most dignified judges of the Federal Courts" (*TR*, 331). Before that appointment, he helps to arrest Graham, who has fallen in love with Stella. Stella turns out to be a legal liability to Graham because he has secretly confessed to her his former leadership of the Klan.

The possibility that Stella will prove an unwitting traitor to her lover again recalls *Red Rock*. Page's novel culminates in the trial of Steve Allen. After breaking Rupert out of jail, Steve escapes Leech's efforts to track him down. But when Leech arrests most of the men in the community and offers to free them in exchange for Steve, Steve turns himself in. In the process, his lover, the daughter of Major Welch, intent on proving that Steve is no longer a member of the Klan, inadvertently reveals that he participated in the disarming raid. The charges for freeing Rupert are dropped, and Steve is charged under the Ku Klux Klan Act. He seems doomed to conviction, but, then, secretly, his lover marries him in jail, allowing her to avoid testifying. Although, in *The Traitor*, Dixon does not go so far as to stage a secret marriage between Graham and Stella, in *The Leopard's Spots*, he does have Charles Gaston secretly marry his lover in prison. In *The Traitor*, Stella proves her love by standing by Graham despite public attempts to humiliate him.

When Graham comes to trial, his attorneys are fictionalized versions of Reverdy Johnson and Henry Stanberry. In real life Johnson had been attorney general under Zachary Taylor and Stanberry attorney general under Andrew Johnson. In addition, though opposed to slavery, Reverdy Johnson successfully argued the case against Dred Scott and was one of the most prominent lawyers before the Supreme Court. Stanberry gave Johnson his legal arguments in vetoing the Civil Rights Act of 1866 and the Reconstruction Act. Through the efforts of a federal Secret Service agent sent to investigate the case, Graham is cleared of the charge of murder, actually committed by a carpetbagger. But he is convicted of conspiracy under the Ku Klux Klan Act for his previous activities. Given the chance to escape from the local prison, he refuses, fully intent on respecting federal authority, and is sent to a federal prison in Albany, New York. In the meantime, a suit on his behalf challenges the constitutionality of the act under which he was convicted. After serving time in prison, Graham is pardoned so that authorities can avoid having his case brought before the Supreme Court. He returns to Independence and, a proponent of the New South, establishes a successful cotton mill, supervised by the retired Secret Service agent.

As much as Dixon steals from Page, their fictional trials reveal important differences with respect to their views on the national government. Unlike Steve, Graham does not go free. Given a chance to escape, he insists that he must respect the decision of the federal court, even though he considers the act under which he is convicted unconstitutional. In addition, whereas both writers portray the Ku Klux Klan Act as responding to a particular event, not a generalized threat across the region, in *The Traitor* the attack is on a federal judge rather than on local African Americans. Thus, in Page the Ku Klux Klan Act results from activity by the real Klan that is not committed directly against a federal official, whereas in Dixon the act results from a direct attack on a governmental official that is not committed by the real Klan. Indeed, in *The Clansman*, Ben Cameron, the local leader of the real Klan, attempts from the first to avoid a "clash with the authority of the United States . . . as a matter of principle" (354). "A battle with United States troops," Dixon emphasizes, "might mean ruin for the South" (363). Another significant difference is that, unlike Page, Dixon bases his fictional trial on ones that actually took place.

During the 1868 election, the Klan successfully repressed the African American vote in the Piedmont counties of South Carolina. As the 1870 election approached, South Carolina's Republican governor vowed that history would not repeat itself. He formed an African American militia to protect voters, disregarding a warning that to do so "would most unquestionably lead to a war of races." The governor's tactics worked in the short term, but when Republicans prevailed in 1870, it was white supremacists' turn to vow that history would not repeat itself. The Klan embarked on a new, more severe, reign of terror to "reinstitute constitutional liberty—

Southern style." As the insurrection grew beyond the governor's capacity to contain it, President Grant's attorney general Amos Akerman, the only former Confederate in the cabinet, went south to view the situation personally. Concluding that no community "nominally civilized, has been so fully under the domination of systematic and organized depravity," he recommended to Grant national intervention under the new Enforcement Acts. Strictly following the letter of the law, Grant issued a proclamation on October 12, 1871, commanding all involved in unlawful combinations to surrender their arms and return home. When they failed to do so, on November 17 he declared the nine counties in a state of rebellion and suspended habeas corpus. US troops broke the back of the Klan, with numerous arrests and many other Klansmen escaping to the West or Canada.[18]

So many were arrested that Akerman divided them into different categories, with only the most severe cases brought to trial in the Fourth Federal Circuit Court. These are the trials Dixon fictionalizes in *The Traitor*, even though he adds verisimilitude to Graham's disbanding of the Klan by moving the action to North Carolina, where redemption occurred earlier than in South Carolina. In a not-so-subtle dig at Akerman, Dixon names the federal secret agent, who clears Graham of murder charges and later becomes his business partner, Mr. Ackerman. Reverdy Johnson of Maryland and Henry Stanberry of Ohio were indeed defense attorneys hired with $10,000 raised by Wade Hampton. Even these two skilled attorneys could not save most of those brought to trial. Convicted by predominantly black juries, many, like Graham, were sent to federal prison in Albany. The rationale for their convictions was, however, a defeat for the prosecution. The major constitutional issue raised by the trials was over those provisions of the Enforcement Acts allowing the national government, rather than states, to convict individuals of common law crimes, such as murder, committed while depriving African Americans of their rights. No conviction resulted from those provisions. Instead, like Graham, who is absolved of charges of murder, members of the Klan were convicted for participating in a conspiracy. To be sure, by strategically disagreeing on larger issues, the circuit court judges created the opportunity for the Supreme Court to rule on these issues. Dixon has authorities grant Graham a pardon to avoid that review. In fact, when George H. Williams replaced Akerman as attorney general, he hesitated to involve the higher court. On the one hand, he was more sympathetic than Akerman to southerners' complaints about bayonet rule. On the other hand, he faced a budgetary crisis. Congress had passed rigid enforcement measures without providing enough money to implement them. Worried about the cost of the trials, Williams urged "rigid economy."[19]

Dixon alters the historical record in other significant ways. Akerman's hope to convict the leaders of the Klan fell flat because most had the means to escape the state before arrest. With a few exceptions, "the men who stood trial, confessed, or pleaded guilty were poor, young, illiterate, unimportant, and guilty of lesser offenses." Many claimed to have joined the Klan out of fear. Noting that they lacked the "manliness" to defy the pressure of their neighbors, one of the two presiding judges wrote privately that a second proclamation of emancipation was needed to free poor whites in the South from the gentlemen who ruled their lives. In contrast, Dixon has his noble leader take the rap for the men under him.[20]

A more accurate sense of how class affected the arrests and trials comes in John William DeForest's "An Independent Klan" (1872), published in the wake of these events. A former Freedmen's Bureau agent in Greenville, South Carolina, DeForest had an intimate understanding of the area. His story is about Selnarten Bowen, an illiterate "cracker," whose only contribution to the household is the neighborhood pigs he kills, claiming they are wild. His weapon is an Enfield rifle left over from the war, during which it was frequently dropped. In the first line, Selnarten worries to his tobacco-chewing wife, "These niggers is gone in for stealin' worse 'n ever. Hev we lost anythin?" (IK, 224). Although he has nothing worth stealing, pig-stealing Selnarten decides to join the Ku-Klux, which he hears is being organized by respectable whites. His wife, "who is the better man of the two," simply tells him not to come home without another pig. Selnarten finds Squire Anderson, hoping to join the Klan. The Squire is not a Klan member, but he decides to have some fun at his poor neighbor's expense, making him go through ridiculous rituals to become a sworn member. Fortified with what he thinks is membership in the secret order, the cracker decides to kill the hog of a "fellow-citizen and elector who was as simple and ignorant as Selnartin himself": the one-legged African American Ham Irvine, who makes ends meet as a cobbler (232). "Holding himself to be a true member of the Ku-Klux society, and supposing that every Ku-Klux had a right to 'go for niggers' in any way that pleased him, [Selnartin] had no more scruples of conscience about his person than if he had been a sheriff duly provided with a warrant" (233). While Ham is away, Selnartin breaks into his cabin and kills the pig. Before he can leave, Ham returns and, despite his handicap, is about to overwhelm the thief, until Selnartin uses his Civil War rifle to kill him. Selnartin had never killed anyone in his pig raids, "But this evening he believed he was a Ku-Klux, and that as such he had a right to kill whosoever resisted him." The story ends a few weeks later when martial law is declared and federal troops arrive "to stamp out a silly and savage reign of terror." As "high-toned and low-toned members of the famous order were confessing their atrocities and surrendering themselves for trials, this almost incredibly ignorant creature came into military headquarters and gave himself up as a Ku-Klux, revealing for the first time who it was that had killed Ham Irvine" (236). Written in a comical vein with underlying pathos, "An Independent Ku-Klux" gives an account of someone who is in neither the legitimate nor the illegitimate Klan. It also provides poignant insight into how the aura of the Klan gave poor whites a sense of empowerment, legitimating their petty and not-so-petty crimes.

Although not focused on the major atrocities that took place, DeForest's story makes it clear that freedmen were murdered. Thus, he calls attention to the most important distortion of the historical record in *The Traitor*: the failure to depict murders committed against freedmen and carpetbaggers. Graham is falsely accused of murdering a white judge, actually killed by a carpetbagger. In *The Clansman*, however, Dixon draws on the same events as *The Traitor* and does portray violence against freedmen. Book IV reenacts the Klan activities that prompted President Grant to invoke the most extreme provisions of the Enforcement Acts and proclaim a condition of lawlessness in nine Piedmont counties of South Carolina. Dixon alludes to this historical context with a few well-placed details. Faced with the efficiency of the Klan, his villain, Austin Stoneman, realizes the folly of relying on "the negro, the carpetbagger, and the scalawag" (*CM*, 346). As a result, he sends a telegram to Washington, DC. "President Grant the next morning issued a proclamation declaring the nine Scotch-Irish hill counties of South Carolina in a state of insurrection, ordered an army corps of five thousand men to report there for duty, pending the further necessity of martial law and the suspension of the writ of *Habeas Corpus*" (350). Suffering another setback, Stoneman sends a second telegram to the White House, "and the Writ of *Habeas Corpus* was suspended and Martial Law declared" (353). Whereas *The Clansman* is more accurate than *The Traitor* in portraying the object of the Klan's violence, in other ways it revises history even more starkly. Most obviously, Dixon turns a decisive setback for the Klan into a glorious triumph that allows him to fit the events of 1871–72 into a narrative about white global rule. Whereas Page has the legitimate Klan confirm his myth about the necessity of violence in the nation's founding, Dixon fashions a myth in which the Klan's violence against African Americans is essential to world historical progress. In order to see how he does so, we need to understand his resolution of three seeming contradictions in the plot of *The Clansman*.

Two of these contradictions are suggested by a debate early in the book between President Lincoln and Representative Austin Stoneman about a future policy for the rebellious southern states. Sympathetic to the South, Dixon's Lincoln opposes Stoneman's plan to treat those states as conquered territory. Impatient, Stoneman interrupts, "But we are acting outside the Constitution." To which Lincoln replies, "Congress has no existence outside the Constitution" (*CM*, 44). If Dixon endorses Lincoln's assertion that Congress and Stoneman cannot act outside the Constitution, how, later in the book, can he condone the activities of the

Klan, which also acts outside the law? The second seeming contradiction comes from the fact that Lincoln's reply to Stoneman is about more than Reconstruction politics. Dixon, trained as a lawyer, takes this comment almost word for word from Justice John Marshall Harlan's dissent in *Downes v. Bidwell*, the first of the Insular Cases in which the Supreme Court established the constitutionality of the US's rule over territories recently conquered in the Spanish-American War. *Downes v. Bidwell* was decided in 1901, shortly before Dixon composed his trilogy. Harlan disagreed with the opinion of Justice Henry Billings Brown, just as he had five years earlier in *Plessy v. Ferguson*. To Brown's argument that Congress had plenary power over people living in the newly won territories and need not be constrained by the Bill of Rights, Harlan countered, "In my opinion, Congress has no existence and can exercise no authority outside the Constitution." Why would Dixon, who was pro-imperialist, have his Lincoln quote from Harlan's anti-imperialist dissent?[21]

The answer to that question requires resolving a third seeming contradiction. Dixon advocates global Anglo-Saxon supremacy, but *The Clansman* champions not Anglo-Saxons but Scotch-Irish. The victims of Anglo-Saxon imperialism in the British Isles, the Scotch-Irish played a leading role in freeing the American colonies from the British Empire. It was Scotch-Irish Patrick Henry who "had swept the aristocracy of the Old Dominion into rebellion against the King and into triumphant Democracy" (*CM*, 187). Likewise, the Scotch-Irish of North Carolina "issued the first Declaration of Independence in Mecklenburg, and lifted the first banner of rebellion against the tyranny of the Crown" (188). It is the same Scotch-Irish who resist Stoneman's Reconstruction efforts. As Dixon tells us, members of the Klan are not only in the guise of the Confederate dead; they are also "the reincarnated souls of the Clansmen of old Scotland" (2). Why does Dixon champion opponents of Anglo-Saxon rule in *The Clansman*?

The answer to why Dixon has Lincoln respond to Stoneman with Harlan's anti-imperialist quotation is, on one level, simple. For Dixon, as for many other southerners, Reconstruction was an imperialist imposition of the North upon the South. Even some northerners agreed with this view. Charles Sumner, for instance, in an 1867 speech entitled "Are We a Nation?" claimed that the United States deserved that designation only if it insisted on one sovereignty and one citizenship, with equal civil and political rights for all. Anticipating objections from the South, he goes on, "Call it imperialism, if you please: it is simply the imperialism of the Declaration of Independence with all of its promises fulfilled." The Scotch-Irish may be perfectly suited for Dixon's anti-imperialism during Reconstruction, but to understand how their resistance generates worldwide Anglo-Saxon imperialism at the turn of the century, we need to reconstruct Dixon's understanding of transatlantic history.[22]

In *The Clansman*, Dixon restages the British Civil War on American soil. The Scotch-Irish, we are told, were a race that "had defied the Crown of Great Britain a hundred years from the caves and wilds of Scotland and Ireland, taught the English people how to slay a king and build a commonwealth, and driven into exile into the wilderness of America, led our Revolution, peopled the hills of the South, and conquered the West" (*CM*, 342). The name of Dr. Richard Cameron, the father of the southern family that is the book's heroic center, alludes to the Scotch martyr Richard Cameron. Cameron was known as the Lion of the Covenant for ruthlessly defending the National Covenant of 1638, which opposed Charles I's attempt to impose episcopacy upon Scotland. "Covenanters" created the Reformed Presbyterian Church of Scotland. Ulster County, South Carolina, where the action of Book IV takes places, was, according to Dixon, "settled by the Scotch folk who came from the North of Ireland in the great migrations which gave America three hundred thousand people of Covenanter martyr blood, the largest and most important addition to our population, larger in numbers than either the Puritans of New England or the so-called Cavaliers of Virginia and Eastern Carolina; and far more important than either, in the growth of American nationality" (187). Initiating resistance against Charles's tyranny, Covenanters successfully banded with Cromwell and the Puritans during the British Civil War, only to suffer when Cromwell himself became an imperialist military dictator who marched ruthlessly into Ireland and ruled England, Scotland, and Wales with an iron hand. The Restoration, however, brought no relief for the Scotch-Irish, who found Charles II repeating efforts to impose episcopacy, thus provoking the armed resistance of Cameron, who was killed in battle in 1680. His followers, known as the Cameronians, acknowledged the rule of neither James II nor William III, who took over the throne after the Glorious Revolution of 1688. Indeed, the Scotch-Irish in Ulster suffered economically when Parliament, pressured by English merchants, imposed high taxes and tariffs, while restricting the trade of Irish wool to England.

When the religious Test Act of 1715 supplemented this repressive economic policy, numerous Scotch-Irish escaped to America. "Full of bitter feeling toward the British government," the Scotch-Irish played a key role in the Revolutionary War. King George III reportedly said that the revolution was caused by "those pestiferous Presbyterians. They are always in unrest and will be until they are wiped out." Horace Walpole quipped, "I hear that our American cousin has run away with a Presbyterian parson, and that is the end of it." In his account of independence, George Bancroft claimed that "the first voice publicly raised in America to dissolve all connection with Great Britain came, not from the Puritans of New England, nor the Dutch of New York, nor from the cavaliers of Virginia, but from the Scotch-Irish Presbyterians."[23]

These stories were revived, reinforced, and elaborated with a resurgence of Scotch-Irish identity in the late nineteenth century. In 1889, the first of many Scotch-Irish Congresses met in Tennessee. The Scotch-Irish Society of America was established the same year. *The Clansman* relies upon and contributes to the resulting flurry of patriotic publications preserving Scotch-Irish history, keeping alive the "esprit de corps of the race" and promoting "social intercourse and fraternal feeling among its members now and hereafter." At the American Historical Association meeting in 1896, Woodrow Wilson, himself Scotch-Irish, gave a talk about writing United States history. Alluding to the talk without naming Wilson, John W. Burgess reported, "I recently heard a distinguished professor of history and political science say he thought the history of the United States [immediately before the war] could be truthfully told only by a Scotch-Irishman." In *The Clansman*, Wilson's acquaintance tells a story in which the Scotch-Irish, having banded together with the Puritans of New England to defeat George III, find themselves, after the Civil War, persecuted by their former allies in the North. A major premise of that story, one shared by many British at the time, was that the North's motive in preserving the Union was imperial. According to this version of the past, the South was treated like a colony and, like the Scotch-Irish in Ulster in Northern Ireland, suffered repressive economic measures. Prior to the Civil War, the South was victimized by high tariffs. After the war, it faced confiscation of property and high taxes, including a cotton tax that, Dr. Cameron says, "was an act of stupid vengeance on the South," since "no other farmers in America have their crops taxed by the National Government" (*CM*, 194). A poignant moment in the novel comes when a widow must sell her home to pay the cotton tax. "Every dollar of this money," Dr. Cameron says, "bears the stain of the blood of a starving people" (288–89). Similarly, Dixon implies that the effort to disarm southern whites was similar to the Disarming Act of 1756 that took away the Scots' right to bear arms. The force behind these repressive measures is Stoneman, who, in Dixon's account, is an American Cromwell.[24]

Stoneman is clearly based on Thaddeus Stevens, the congressman behind much of Radical Reconstruction, but he is a composite figure. As we saw in chapter 2, like carpetbagger Tourgée, Stoneman moves South for his health. In using Stoneman to evoke Cromwell, Dixon provides a lesson in moral history. Characterized by his "iron will," Stoneman, like Stevens, makes his fortune as the owner of iron mills. But Cromwell's nickname was "Ironsides," and he and Stoneman share personal qualities. As inflexible as he was in public life, Cromwell doted on his children. An 1899 account reports that Thomas Carlyle "made it possible to behold the Protector as a compound of the tenderness of a woman and the fierceness of the Numidian lion." Stoneman, despite his "unconquerable will," would do anything for his son and daughter (*CM*, 185). "There was one weak spot in his armour. . . . the consuming passion with which he loved his two children" (96). Beneath his "cruelty," there is a "gentle" personality (181). But even though "all individual pain hurt him," Dixon's "Puritan," like Cromwell, is a political despot (293, 342). Just as Cromwell convened Parliament, offering to join with it to serve the people, so Stoneman evokes popular authority as a leader of the House of Representatives. Cromwell, however, soon dissolved Parliament when it questioned his "Instrument of Government." Similarly, Stoneman, the people's master, not their servant, follows Cromwell in establishing a military dictatorship that relies on a secret service, with agents reporting directly to its ruler.[25]

With Lincoln's assassination, "Vice-President Johnson took the oath of office, and men hailed him Chief; but the seat of Empire had moved from the White House to a little dark house on the Capitol hill" (*CM*, 79). Ostensibly the voice of the people, Congress bends to Stoneman's will as he forces through bill after bill outside the Constitution. From Dixon's perspective, he continues his unconstitutional activities when he moves South. He is, however, defeated by the Klan. As we have seen, in staging Stoneman's defeat during the government's successful crackdown on the Klan, Dixon distorts history—but only by a few years. In fact, Dixon merely foreshortens time. After the events of 1871–72, the national government failed to invoke the most extreme provisions of the Enforcement Acts. As a result, white supremacists regained control of the South Carolina counties in the 1876 election through a supposed policy of "force without violence." In *The Clansman*, Dixon reports that a "white rifle-club was organized in every town, village, and hamlet" (351). Supposedly formed for social purposes, these clubs displayed weapons to intimidate African Americans with a fresh memory of earlier violence. Re-armed white supremacists often went beyond a show of force and committed racial massacres to speed South Carolina's redemption.[26]

In addition to foreshortening the time it took to redeem the state, Dixon makes it look as if violence is a justified response to oppression. What from one perspective is extralegal violence, from Dixon's point of view is a legitimate response to the attempt to force upon the South the social equality of blacks. In this regard, Dixon's narrative is uncannily similar to that of the avowed defender of law, John W. Burgess. Burgess, who attacked the Ku Klux Klan Act for undermining the constitutional distribution of power between states and the nation, justified the Klan's activities based on accounts by those he termed the "most trustworthy men in South Carolina." These men "affirm[ed] to this day" that the Klan organizations

> had no traitorous intent, whatsoever, but were simply defensive in their nature; that the wholesale pardoning of criminals by the Governor and the vagrancy of the negroes had filled the country with desperadoes who made the life, property,

> and female honor insecure; and that, as the militia was composed of the friends of those fiends and the "State" government itself would not protect the white citizens, it was absolutely necessary for the white people to create some means of united action in self-defence and take the law into their own hands.[27]

In *The Clansman*, the violation of female honor is the straw that breaks the camel's back. Just as Page in *Red Rock* has Dr. Cary and Steve debate the use of violence, Dixon has Dr. Cameron debate his son about the necessity of the Klan. Arguing that "two wrongs never make a right," Dr. Cameron insists that "a secret society such as you have planned means a conspiracy that may bring exile or death. I hate lawlessness and disorder. We have had enough of it." Ben prophetically responds that the Klan is "the only way. The next step will be a black hand on a white woman's throat!" (*CM*, 262). The rape occurs two chapters later, and Stoneman is indirectly responsible. Upset at the freedmen's docility, he insists that every one of them be taught "to stand erect in the presence of his former master and assert his manhood" (207). Asserting his manhood, the former slave Gus rapes young Marion Lenoir. Holding its own trial, the Klan convicts and lynches Gus, an extralegal act justified by Dixon's belief that the Enforcement Acts and other Reconstruction legislation were invalid. The historical Grant might have declared a state of lawlessness and the fictional Stoneman might order a rally to proclaim the "supremacy of law," but since that law is coupled to the unconstitutional effort to impose the "enforcement of the equality of every man under the law," the law is actually on the Klan's side (*CM*, 355).[28]

Drawing on historical documents, Dixon presents "The Prescript of the Order of the Invisible Empire," which is addressed "To the lovers of law and order, peace and justice." It vows "to protect the weak, the innocent, and the defenseless from the indignities, wrongs and outrages of the lawless, the violent, and the brutal," while promising "to protect and defend the Constitution of the United States, and all the laws passed in conformity thereto, and to protect the states and the people thereof from all invasion of any source whatever" (*CM*, 320–21). Crucial to this constitutional argument are the phrase "in conformity thereto" and the implied link between the protection of the people and the protection of the states. Claiming to adhere to the true Constitution, the Klan feels compelled to combat the Enforcement and the Ku Klux Klan Acts by protecting individual liberty through the protection of states' rights. When Stoneman's daughter Elsie, who has fallen in love with Ben, accuses him of being "guilty of murder" for the extralegal execution of the black rapist, he replies, "The judge who pronounces sentence of death on a criminal outlawed by civilized society is not usually called a murderer, my dear." When she asks, "And by whose authority are you a judge?" he proclaims,

"By the authority of the sovereign people who created the State of South Carolina. The criminals who claim to be our officers are usurpers placed there by the subversion of the law" (333–34).

In fact, Ben evokes an authority that predates South Carolina's sovereignty. The Klan carries on the spirit of the martyred Scotch-Irish of centuries ago. Those Covenanters, in turn, represent the "remains of Aryan civilization" (*CM*, 264). As Ben tells local members of the Klan, "There are laws of our race, old before this Republic was born in the souls of white freemen. The fiat of fools has repealed on paper these laws" (338). Ben's contempt for paper laws might seem to contradict the reverence Lincoln earlier expresses for the Constitution, but, from Dixon's point of view, it does not. First, the Constitution that Dixon's Lincoln reveres exists prior to Reconstruction. It does not support the Enforcement Acts that Dixon and others felt were unconstitutional. Second, for Dixon, the true Constitution, created by a "legislative body of the Aryan race" (*CM*, 152), expresses the same spirit of liberty that inspires the Klan. When Stoneman passes paper laws betraying that spirit, the Klan has a duty to resist so that the higher principles of civilization will prevail.

In the world turned upside down created by his subversion of the law, Stoneman's disregard of higher law backfires. Intent on making an example, Stoneman has Ben arrested for killing a black man. "Within thirty minutes he was tried by drum-head court martial and sentenced to be shot" (*CM*, 357). What Stoneman does not know is that his son Phil, who sympathizes with the Klan, was responsible for the murder. Assuming that his father will never allow him to be executed, Phil disguises himself and changes places with his friend. But, to assure Ben's execution, Stoneman orders that any appeal for a stay of execution has to be made through him, at which time he goes into hiding. The result, as Ben notes, is that "the old fool has entrapped his son in the net he spread for me!" (361). Ben, however, rallies the Klan to save Phil, without bloodshed, bringing about the miraculous transformation of Phil's father, who praises the Klan for saving his boy.

With Stoneman's embrace of the Klan, order is restored, and the book ends as Ben proclaims, "Civilisation has been saved, and the South redeemed from shame" (*CM*, 374). Stoneman's conversion shows that Dixon may rewrite Reconstruction as a replay of the aftermath of the seventeenth-century British Civil War, but he rewrites it with a difference. Cromwell's reign ended with the restoration of the crown, not the triumph of the Scotch-Irish. On the American side of the Atlantic, the Scotch-Irish do triumph. In fact, they do more than triumph; they unite a divided nation and the long-divided Anglo-Saxon race. The union of this white nation is symbolized by Stoneman's dramatic conversion and the love affairs of the Stoneman and Cameron children. The promised intermingling of northern and southern blood means first of all that the South has become incorporated into the

"'The Fiery Cross of old Scotland's hills!'"

This illustration from *The Clansman* celebrates the Klan's execution of the African American prostrate in the foreground. It shows the extent to which Dixon is responsible for the iconography associated with the Klan today: the fiery cross, the hooded figures in the background, the white uniforms. Whereas the illustration in *Red Rock* evokes Page's legend of the ghostly return of the Indian-killer, this illustration reinforces Dixon's link between the Klan and the Scotch-Irish.

larger mission of the nation. But it also means that the Scotch-Irish have become incorporated into the more expansive race of Anglo-Saxons.

Although it is commonplace to emphasize the value white supremacists place on racial purity, for Dixon the Anglo-Saxon race is an amalgam of white races. In *The Leopard's Spots*, Gaston calls to "the men of my race, Norman and Celt, Angle and Saxon, Dane and Frank, Huguenot and German martyr blood!" (441). But the Scotch-Irish transform the Anglo-Saxon race as they get absorbed by it. Just as the nation born out of *The Clansman*'s action finds its true mission only when the Puritan Stoneman's nationalism is absorbed into the southern cause, so Anglo-Saxon imperialism is justified only when it is guided by the liberty-loving spirit of the Scotch-Irish. Within Gaston's global Anglo-Saxon Imperium lurks the invisible empire of the Klan.

The link between *The Clansman*'s anti-imperialism and *The Leopard's Spots*'s imperialism is made clear by the similarity between Ben's view of the law and Gaston's. In a fiery speech, Gaston declares, "Nations are made by men, not by paper constitutions and paper ballots. We are not free because we have a Constitution. We have a Constitution because our pioneer fathers, who cleared the wilderness and dared the might of kings, were freemen. It was in their blood, the tutelage of generation on generation beyond the seas, the evolution of centuries of struggle and sacrifice" (*LS*, 442). As Gaston's reference to "the evolution of centuries" indicates, Dixon subscribes to a progressive theory of history in which past struggles and sacrifices lead to a better world ruled by Anglo-Saxons.

Critics often misunderstand the action of *The Clansman* because they fail to see it in the context of the progressive view of history that Dixon's trilogy expresses. Each of the three works is driven by the conflict of a young woman forced to choose between two men. The heroine of *The Leopard's Spots* has to choose between a father who represents a noble, but no longer viable, Old South, and a lover who symbolizes the new nation of the future. The other two works focus on important synchronic conflicts within this progressive, diachronic framework. In *The Clansman*, the woman's choice is again between a father and a lover, now representing a sectional conflict between North and South, a conflict already resolved in *The Leopard's Spots*. In *The Traitor*, the choice is between two southern lovers who represent different views about the Klan. Successful resolution of the conflicts in the last two works is necessary for the triumphant Anglo-Saxon imperialism anticipated by the first work of the trilogy. In *The Traitor*, the scalawag's daughter's choice of Graham confirms that the Klan is not a conspiracy of traitors but a group of patriots of the highest order. In *The Clansman*, Elsie's choice of Ben makes way for the redemption of the South and, therefore, of the nation.

Alluding to how the British viewed the founding fathers, Ben defends himself against Elsie's charge that he is a "conspirator" by calling himself a "revolutionist" (*CM*, 335). As he tells his fellow Clansmen, "Your fathers who created this Nation were first Conspirators, then Revolutionists, now Patriots and Saints" (338). Declaring himself a "successful revolutionist" (374) at the end of the book, Ben no longer needs to operate outside the law. Dixon's sense of a progressive history is so powerful that in *The Clansman* it sweeps Stoneman along with it.

Even before Stoneman's conversion, he is given begrudging admiration. Almost in awe, the narrator describes how "the sheer wonder of the man's personality held the imagination of [his] audience" (171). Stoneman's talent for leadership calls attention to one of the most overlooked aspects of *The Clansman*: the similarity between its villain and its hero. Both are charismatic. We first see Ben's charisma through Elsie's irresistible sexual attraction to him. Looking "defiantly" into Ben's "brown eyes, about which a smile was constantly playing," she is carried away by "his contagious laughter. She had to join in spite of herself. He laughed with boyish gaiety. It danced in his eyes, and gave spring to every moment of his slender wiry body. She felt its contagion infold her" (128). The "contagion" of Ben's fun," we are told, "could not be resisted" (149). Similarly, Ben's political ambition is sparked for the first time when he sees Stoneman speak in Congress. Just as Elsie cannot resist Ben's eyes, so Ben is held "spellbound" by Stoneman's eye. "It could thrill to the deepest fibre of the soul that looked into it . . . It could dominate, awe, and confound." Not "bent to persuade or convince," Stoneman's oratory is "haunted" by a "contagious" force (132–33). Admiring Stoneman's ability to wield political power, the redeeming southerner adopts the northern radical's methods.

Ben Cameron justifies his revolutionary actions by appealing to the sovereignty of the people and by evoking laws higher than those written on paper. In the first half of the book, Stoneman does the same. Having earned the label "revolutionist" (*CM*, 40, 153) for his imperial designs on the South, Stoneman too claims that the "will of the people . . . is supreme" (160) and justifies his violation of the Constitution by proclaiming that "there are higher laws than paper compacts. We are conquerors treading conquered soil. Our will alone is the source of law" (160). Even Ben and Stoneman's motives sound the same. Elsie warns her lover, "This wild vengeance is a crime you are doing, however great the provocation" (334). Likewise, in the last pages, her father acknowledges that he was motivated by a "quenchless desire for personal revenge" (371) set in motion when Lee's troops caused his financial ruin by destroying his iron mills.

What distinguishes the two characters are the causes for which they fight, not their methods. Phil Stoneman makes this clear in a heated exchange with his father. "It is," he explains, "a question of who possesses the right of life and death over the citizens, the organized virtue of the community, or its organized crime" (*CM*, 329). Dixon leaves no doubt that Stoneman is aligned with crime. Most obviously, his revolutionary rule leads to crimes by blacks against whites. But Stoneman is also a gambler. With him in control of the "Ship of State," the "pirate captains of the boldest criminals who ever figured in the story of a nation" have free reign (153). Stoneman's corruption is linked to the spell his mistress Lydia Brown has over him. "No more curious or sinister figure ever cast a shadow across the history of a great nation than did this mulatto woman in the most corrupt hour of American life. The grim old man who looked into her sleek tawny face and followed her catlike eyes was steadily gripping the Nation by the throat" (94). Lydia's power starts to unwind when Stoneman moves South and becomes infatuated with virginal Marion Lenoir. Lydia's spell is finally broken when the Klan saves Stoneman's beloved son. With Stoneman's last-minute conversion, everything changes. Once the Puritan's ambitions have been turned to the cause of virtue, the qualities he displays in ruling the nation are potentially available to advance worldwide, white imperialism.

History for Dixon is Hegelian: conflict ridden, but forward moving. It includes one battle after another between different factions of whites, the unsuccessful resolution of each spawning a new conflict. If the British Civil War resulted in the successful overthrow of the king, it also generated the exploitation that led to the immigration of the Scotch-Irish to America, who then spearheaded a successful War of Independence from Britain, only to find themselves in conflict with the Puritans and Cavaliers with whom they had banded, thus provoking the American Civil War. As bloody as that war was, it was necessary for history to move forward. Reconstruction threatened once again to divide the nation, but with the redemption of the South, Stoneman's conversion, and the disbanding of the Klan, the union of Puritan, Scotch-Irish, and Cavalier has finally become a reality, poising the United States for its twentieth-century imperial mission. Whereas many at the time considered the Spanish-American War the final battle of the Civil War because it united northern and southern troops under one flag, Dixon saw it as the culmination of a centuries-long transatlantic struggle.

Dixon's portrayal of Stoneman was influenced by the revival of interest in Cromwell as the three-hundredth anniversary of his 1599 birth approached. That revival produced conflicting assessments, but the one that would have most caught Dixon's eye turned Cromwell into a hero for advocates of US imperialism. In a 1904 speech to the Naval War College, Brooks Adams promoted imperialism while comparing George Washington to Cromwell for his "organizing and administrative intellect," as well as his "personification of the principle of consolidation." Even more telling was a 1900 biography of Cromwell by arch-imperialist and hero of San Juan Hill Theodore Roosevelt. In the book, Roosevelt, like Dixon, makes frequent comparisons between Cromwell's time, the American Revolution, and the Civil War. Admitting Cromwell's flaws, Roosevelt nonetheless paints a generally positive portrait. Summarizing the complicated events following Charles I's surrender, Roosevelt writes, "After much warfare of factions, some strong man, a Cromwell or a Napoleon, is forced or forces himself to the front, and saves the factions from destroying one another by laying his iron hand on all." Similarly, Dixon writes, "Behind the tragedy of Reconstruction stood the remarkable man whose iron will alone had driven these terrible measures through the chaos of passion, corruption, and bewilderment which followed the first assassination of an American President" (*CM*, 343).[29]

Immediately preceding his account of Cromwell's iron hand, Roosevelt notes, "Any revolutionary movement must be carried through by parties whose aims are so different, or whose feelings and interests are so divergent, that there is great difficulty in the victors coming to a working agreement to conserve the fruits of their victory. Not only the leaders, but more especially their followers—that is, the mass of the people—must possess great moderation and good sense for this to be possible." Sharing Dixon's sense of progressive but conflict-ridden history, Roosevelt sees the white American people as those finally in possession of that moderation and good sense. The fitness to govern, he asserts, "is not a God-given, natural right, but comes to a race only through the slow growth of centuries, and then only to those races which possess an immense reserve of strength, common sense and morality." Or, as Dr. Cameron, named after a fiery revolutionary, puts it, "The sober common sense of the Nation will yet save us" (*CM*, 262).[30]

For both Roosevelt and Dixon, the leader who most embodied that common sense was Lincoln. In the early years of the twentieth century Lincoln became the hero of those championing the modern progressive state that, they felt, had to take on powers previously deemed beyond its reach in order to make the United States the preeminent world power in the new century. Roosevelt called Lincoln the first "progressive," the founder of a "party of dynamics, not a party of stasis," and compared his "iron will" to that of Cromwell. But Lincoln could serve as the figure for the modern state only because he was revered as a man of the people who, better than Congress, embodied the will of the people. Indeed, for Dixon, he literally becomes what Burgess called "the modern national popular state," the true "source and support" of "individual liberty." In a 1920 play called *The Man of the People*, Dixon defended Lincoln's violation of civil liberties and his suspension of habeas corpus as constitutionally necessary to save the Union. Why, then, if Dixon celebrated Lincoln and supported Roosevelt's turn-of-the-century imperialism, did he put in his hero's mouth the words of Justice Harlan's anti-imperialist dissent in *Downes*?[31]

First of all, Dixon would have delighted in the irony that *Dred Scott* was the precedent for Harlan's anti-imperialist argument. Most people think that *Dred Scott* was only about slavery and that with the Thirteenth and Fourteenth Amendments it no longer had any force. In fact, Justice Taney also directly addressed the question of whether Congress had plenary power over the territories. Ruling that it did not, Taney rendered the Missouri Compromise unconstitutional. The relevance of that decision is noted by another literary figure trained as a lawyer: Edgar Lee Masters. In his iconoclastic biography of Lincoln, the anti-imperialist Masters points out that the "colonial adventures" Republicans undertook in 1899 "in the name of Lincoln" would have been impossible had the court heeded Taney's claim that "a power . . . in the general government to obtain and hold colonies and dependent territories, over which they may legislate without restrictions would be inconsistent with its own existence in its present form." Dixon also would have relished the irony that Justice Harlan, the lone dissenter in the Civil Rights Cases and *Plessy*, furnished the language for his fictional Lincoln to protest the sectional imperialism of North against South. The burden of Dixon's narrative is to show that those constitutional checks on congressional power are outdated when a reborn and united white nation tries to spread the spirit of liberty to the world. This sense of history is perfectly registered in *Downes*, as the once-necessary anti-imperialist constitutional position of Justice Harlan is contained in its pages only to be superseded by the new pro-imperialist position of Justice Brown. Countering objections that his ruling gives unchecked power to Congress, Brown, sounding like Ben Cameron and Charles Gaston, declares, "There are certain principles of justice inherent in the Anglo-Saxon character which need no expression in constitution or statute to give them effect." Making constitutional Dixon's anticonstitutional constitutionalism, Justice Brown's ruling sanctions the anti-imperialist imperialism of the minister's Reconstruction trilogy.[32]

That constitutional sanction was refined in further rulings by the court penned by Justice Edward White, an expert in Roman law and questions of empire. In 1910, White was appointed chief justice by President Taft, the chair of the first civilian commission to study the problems of governing the Philippines. In a sentiment that Dixon would have shared, White once remarked of the Insular Cases, "If we had not decided them as we did, this country would have been less than a nation." Indeed, seeking an audience at the White House for *The Birth of a Nation*, Dixon also persuaded Justice White to screen the film, only to learn that in his youth, White had been a member of the Klan—fitting confirmation for Dixon that the Anglo-Saxon imperial mission White legitimated was animated by the same spirit of liberty that helped the Scotch-Irish redeem the South.[33]

IV

Dixon sent a copy of *The Leopard's Spots* to Tourgée, who by this time was serving as US consul in Bordeaux, France. Disillusioned and fearful of losing the post that finally provided him with financial security, Tourgée vowed to remain publicly silent on political issues. Nonetheless, in a private letter he wrote a scathing rebuttal to Dixon's romance. He died before he could read *The Clansman*, but his wife responded in part for him. The same year that Dixon published the second of his trilogy, he wrote an article about the crackdown on the Klan in North Carolina, accusing Tourgée of supporting the suspension of habeas corpus. Emma Tourgée wrote Dixon providing solid evidence to the contrary. Dixon responded condescendingly, never admitting his error.[34]

Tourgée did not read *The Clansman*, but twenty-six years before its publication he had already provided a response in *A Fool's Errand*, which Dixon self-consciously tries to refute. Whereas Dixon argues that the Klan's role in "redeeming" the South was necessary to save civilization, Tourgée insists that the Klan blocked its progress. He exposes a central contradiction in Dixon's—as well as Page's—narrative of legitimation. For the two southerners, African Americans needed to be kept in their place because they were incapable of self-government in the political and economic spheres and thus were socially inferior to whites. Even in Harris's *Gabriel Tolliver* the victim of the Knights of the White Camellia is a superstitious, uneducated freedman easily led astray by the Freedmen's Bureau agent. But in Tourgée's works, the Klan targets freedmen who achieve economic independence or exert independent leadership in their community. Freedmen are not kept from advancing because of an inherent lack of intelligence or motivation. They are stymied by extralegal violence the moment they try to assert themselves.

Almost halfway through *A Fool's Errand*, Tourgée introduces the Klan in a chapter called "A New Institution." The action takes place in "the winter of 1868–69 when the wise men were jubilant over the success of the Great Experiment; when it was said that already Reconstruction had been an approved success, the traces of the war been blocked out, and the era of the millennium anticipated" (*FE*, 182). A group of colored men approach the Fool and ask him if he has heard "bout de Klux." They are not fooled by the Klan's disguises, describing the band as "dem folks what rides about at night a-pesterin' pore colored people an' a-pretendin' to be jes from hell, or some battlefield ob ole Virginny." The Fool's initial response is dismissive. "There is nothing in the world in it," he says. "Probably a parcel of boys now and then take it into their heads to scare a few colored people, but that's all. It is mean and cowardly, but nothing more. You needn't have any trouble about it boys" (182). But then Bob Martin, the group's spokesman, "an industrious and thrifty blacksmith . . . noted as being one of the most independent and self-reliant of his people in all political and pecuniary matters," shows the Fool his back, which from "the nape down and to below the waist, was gashed and marked by repeated blows. Great farrows were plowed in the black integument, whose greenly-livid lips were drawn back, while coagulated fabrine stretched across, and mercifully protected the lacerated flesh. The whole back was livid and swollen, bruised as if it had been brayed in a mortar" (183).

By having this "severe and deliberate flagellation" administered by a former overseer, Tourgée makes the obvious point that the regime of slavery continues to exert its force. Through his bone-chilling description, combining clinical precision with a metaphorical comparison of Bob's back to a plowed field, he makes a more subtle point. The image of a mortar evokes the healing powers of the medical profession. Rather than create a healthy economy by expertly applying skills to plough the soil, though, the Klansman "scientifically" wields his lash to turn a fellow human being's back into a bloody wasteland (*FE*, 184). All Bob had done was contribute to the economy as he "wukked honestly and fa'rly" to provide a home for his family and "to give the boys an' gals a little eddication, and let em hav a fair start in life wid de rest ob de worl'" (185). When he told other freedmen that they had the right to vote and refused to do more work for a white man who never paid him, the Klan felt he had to be put in his place.

In *Bricks without Straw,* Tourgée again portrays victims of the Klan as economically self-sufficient African Americans. Through the combined efforts of the physically powerful Nimbus and his intellectually shrewd, physically handicapped childhood friend Eliab Hill, African Americans build a thriving community called Red Wing, whose economic engine is Nimbus's tobacco farm. At the center of the community is a combined church-schoolhouse built with the aid of northern philanthropy and presided over by Mollie Ainslie, a white New England teacher. The community's success and the leadership of Nimbus and Eliab is rewarded with a vicious attack by the Klan while Nimbus and Mollie are away. Nimbus's wife, Lugena, and his children are abused, and Eliab brutally beaten. In the middle of the attack, Nimbus returns, wielding his Union army saber as an "ebon angel of wrath," and severely wounds one masquerader and causes the others to retreat (*BS*, 276). As one aims his pistol at Nimbus, Lugena strikes him in the head with an axe. Even though the Klan abandons the scene, taking the wounded bodies, it is too late. The church-schoolhouse has been torched, and Nimbus knows that he must leave the state, separated from family and farm. But first he carries nearly dead Eliab to the book's white protagonist, who secretly nurses him back to health.

Tourgée stitches this scene together from factual accounts, including those of the Klan's deadly beating of a man named Elias Hill and of a black wife courageously

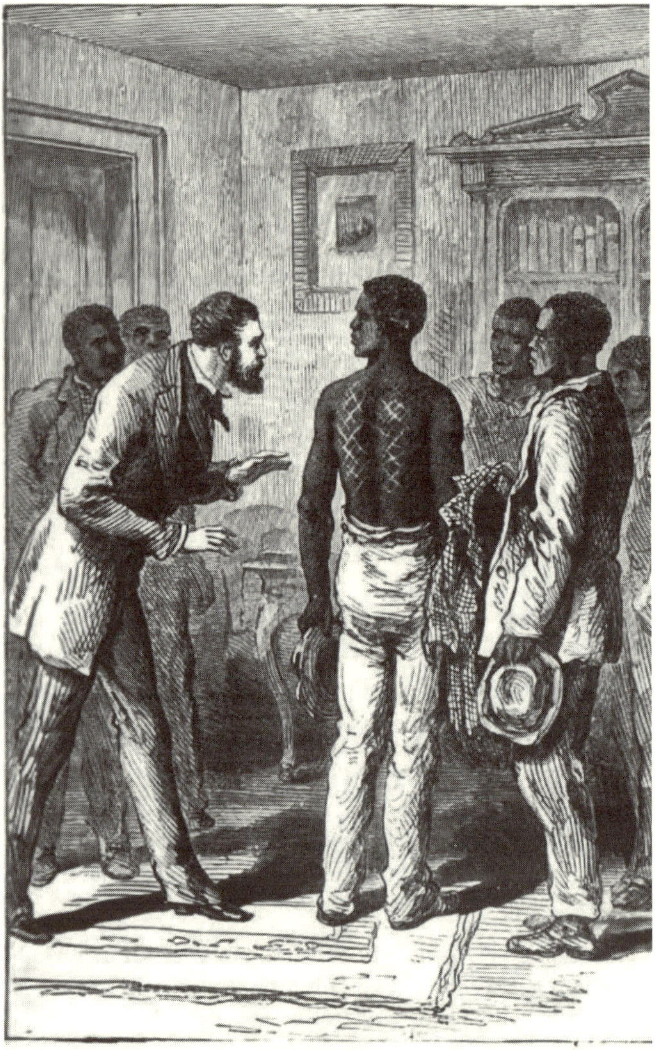

Bob Martin's Experience.

This illustration from A *Fool's Errand* shows Comfort Servosse examining the lacerated back of former soldier Bob Martin, who was brutally whipped by the Klan for demanding payment for his services as a blacksmith and for encouraging African Americans to vote.

protecting her husband. The scene Tourgée creates is so powerful that Page, Harris, and Dixon have to contest it. In *The Chronicles of Aunt Minervy Ann* (1899), Harris gives us, instead of Lugena, an African American wife who promises to protect her husband but stutters and flees when she learns that the Klan has threatened him. He is protected by his wife's former owner. Page insists that schools were never attacked by the legitimate Klan, and Harris blames the Union League for transforming a former school into a meeting place. Whereas Tourgée has the most reputable citizens of the white community participating in the Klan's gratuitous violence, Page and Dixon portray it as the action of morally suspect people, who often become scalawags. In *A Fool's Errand*, Tourgée makes it clear that carpetbaggers and scalawags were in fact victims of Klan violence.[35]

The chapter following the introduction of the Klan consists of excerpts from letters the Fool receives, describing attacks on or threats to carpetbaggers, like himself, or to locals sympathetic to African Americans. That chapter is followed by one about the Klan whipping the son of the Fool's neighbor for defending the Fool's ideas. The neighbor, who had once condoned the whipping of abolitionists who came to the South to preach their cause, now seeks the Fool's help for his son to escape to the West, where he will be welcomed by the same abolitionists. Then comes a chapter dedicated to the murder of John Walters. A staunch supporter of the Union, Walters had resisted conscription into the Confederate Army. After the war, opposing the ex-slaveholding gentry's effort to retain power, he worked to create a coalition of freedmen, white laborers, and small farmers. A man of little education but great courage and ability, he is seen by the Klan as a threat. Walters is based on John W. Stephens, who tried to convince seemingly moderate Frank Wiley to run for sheriff in 1870. While Stephens was observing a Conservative political meeting, Wiley suggested that they go to another room to discuss plans. Stephens never returned. Wiley, a secret member of the Klan, had him strangled and stabbed to death.[36]

The historical basis of Tourgée's account cannot, however, explain the power of his fictional narration. He provides no direct account of Walters's murder. Instead, we are given various mediated versions in a chapter called "A Thrice-Told Tale." The first of three sections consists of widely divergent newspaper reports, some from the conservative press, one from the radical press. The effect of this section is similar to Lanier's poem about the Klan. There is no certainty about who committed the crime, if there even was one. But Tourgée follows up with two perspectives lacking in Lanier's poem. The second section introduces a white eyewitness, not to the murder but to the convention and Walters's departure. A thrice-told tale in itself, the third account has the narrator relate the report of an African American servant who overhears his master describe to a visitor his role in the murder. The servant tells the religious leader Uncle Jerry, who brings the servant to the

Fool. The Fool conducts his own investigation and concludes that the account is accurate, although there is not enough direct evidence to bring the case to trial. While giving an African American the privilege of revealing the truth, Tourgée also reminds us that his testimony will never be heard in court.

Uncle Jerry is so upset by the Klan's activities that, frustrated by the "impotency of the law," he "openly and boldly declared the monstrous doctrine that the colored people ought to defend themselves and each other" (*FE*, 192). In the next chapter, some whites intent on intimidating Jerry for his defiance attend one of his religious meetings. Jerry welcomes them so long as they show respect but rebukes them when they persist in mockery. With his "finger pointing toward them as steady as a rifle-barrel," he goes into a trance and in vivid detail tells the story of Walters's murder, "giving the names of those engaged, and the part taken by each in the bloody dead" (226). When the "spell" is over, Jerry is informed that one of the whites at the meeting was the ringleader the servant had overheard. For his revelation of the truth, Jerry is brutally lynched on a moonlit night in front of the local courthouse.

Like the murder of Walters, the lynching of Jerry is based on an actual event. But the real-life Wyatt Outlaw was lynched before Stephens's murder. In recreating the event, Tourgée does more than document Klan violence; he comments on the revelatory power of fiction and Jerry's power to harness it. Jerry's spell is an allusion to the phenomenon of glossolalia, or speaking in tongues, described in Acts 2.4. During Pentecost, "They were all filled with the Holy Ghost, and began to speak with other tongues, as the Spirit gave them utterance." As Jerry begins to speak, we are told, "When at length his tongue was loosed . . . , he poured forth one of his wonderful rhapsodies" (*FE*, 226). Inhabited by the Spirit, Jerry has the gift of a writer of fiction to use the rhetorical power of *enargia* to create a scene with enough vividness to move an audience, even though he was not actually present to witness it. "He painted as by magic the scene of the murder and gave the very tone and manner of each of those engaged in it, even though he had never seen them" (226–27). Tourgée, like Jerry, paints vivid scenes calculated to move his audience. In this case, when he does, the spirits of Wyatt Outlaw, John Stephens, and other of the Klan's victims speak through him.

Tourgée's attempt to recover the past recalls Walter Benjamin's "Theses on the Philosophy of History." Intent on describing a historical method for a "redeemed mankind," Benjamin writes, "Only that historian will have the gift of fanning the spark of hope in the past who is firmly convinced that *even the dead* will not be safe if [the enemy] wins." Tourgée, however, is not alone in sharing this sense of redemptive history. Both Page and Dixon portray the legitimate Klan redeeming spirits from the past: whether the reincarnated spirit of the Indian-killer or the reincarnated spirit of the clansmen of Old Scotland.[37]

Reconstruction seems to invite thoughts of redemption. In the aftermath of its Civil War and Cromwellian rule, Great Britain experienced "The Restoration." "To restore" means to preserve an essence, as when a damaged painting is restored. Many white southerners would have been happy with a period of restoration after the American Civil War. Robert E. Lee proclaimed, "I believe it to be the duty of everyone to unite in restoration of the country, and the reestablishment of peace and harmony." Restoration would have confirmed the slogan: "The Union as it was; the Constitution as it is." But for most in the victorious North, restoration was not enough. The Union needed to build a new structure on the basis of an amended Constitution. For radicals, like Tourgée, Reconstruction meant redeeming the nation from its sin of slavery. In an 1867 speech praising the Civil War for having turned "Nullification and Secession" into "extinct monsters" and creating "One Nation" with "no North, no South, no east, no West," Charles Sumner rejoiced, "All hail to the Republic, redeemed and regenerated, One and Indivisible." For many white southerners, however, Reconstruction itself threatened to betray everything the Union stood for. Thus, they felt the need to be redeemed from its sins. They used "redemption" rather than "restoration" for the same reason Benjamin did: it has economic and primarily religious significance. Someone could redeem a piece of land under the law by repaying a forfeited mortgage or unpaid taxes within an allotted period of time. In religion, "redemption" refers to Christ's sacrifice of himself in order to save human beings from their sins and thus give them a new life. In the King James Version of the Bible, "redeem" translates from the Greek "*exagorazo*," which means to buy back or to rescue from loss. According to Lewis Simpson, for Page, the "metaphor of the destiny of Southern civilization became Christian Resurrection." In "The Old South," Page describes how the "destruction" of the South fell "under the euphemism of reconstruction": "She was crucified; bound hand and foot; wrapped in the cerements of the grave; laid away in the sepulchre of the departed; the mouth of the sepulchre was stopped, was sealed with the seal of government, and a watch was set. The South was dead, and buried, and yet she rose again. The voice of God called her forth; she came clad in her grave-clothes, but living, and with her face uplifted to the heavens from which had sounded the call of her resurrection."[38]

Although Page published this essay while working on *Red Rock*, in the final version of the novel he does not use this imagery so explicitly. One reason may have been that he did not want to be accused of sectional prejudice. In the novel, the victory of virtue leads to the redemption of the nation as well as the South. Indeed, "redemption" works for Page and Dixon because in their different ways both want to move forward materially and spiritually, not simply to restore a lost order. Indeed, the plot of *Red Rock*, in which the Grays regain ownership of most of their land and the South is reborn as it and the nation are saved from their sins, unites the economic and religious meanings of "redemption."

For Page and Dixon, the Klan played a key role in redeeming the South. For Tourgée, it generated new sins requiring redemption in the future. Nonetheless, Tourgée, Page, and Dixon agree on one aspect of the Klan. In *A Fool's Errand*, Tourgée describes it as "the desperate effort of a proud, brave, and determined people to secure and hold what they *deemed to be their rights*" (254). Dixon favorably, if partially, quotes this passage. Indeed, Page, Dixon, and Tourgée agree that the "real" Klan was made up of former soldiers of the Confederacy, who promoted discipline and organization. When the Klan lynches Uncle Jerry in *A Fool's Errand*, it acts with "the regularity and ease of a practiced soldiery" (229). This image of discipline suits the novelists' ends more than it accurately registers most Klan activity. More often than not, the Klan operated like Page and Dixon's sham Klans. Evoking a larger cause but settling local scores, they were somewhat scattered and not rigidly disciplined. Nonetheless, Tourgée, Page, and Dixon all have a stake in representing the Klan as more organized than it frequently was.[39]

To be legitimate alternatives to illegitimate Reconstruction rule, Dixon and Page's Klans have to represent the organized "intelligence, virtue, and force of character" that Page insists will eventually rule "in the states in the South . . . as certain as the operation of the law of gravity." Both writers consider the Klan legitimate when it consists of the virtuous members of the local community and illegitimate when they are not involved. Dixon, however, demands more. Page's Klan grows almost spontaneously out of the community. In contrast, Dixon's Klan has an elaborate interstate and hierarchical chain of command beyond the local. "The organization was governed by the Grand Wizard Commander-in-Chief, who lived at Memphis, Tennessee. The Grand Dragon commanded a State, the Grand Titan a Congressional District, the Grand Giant, a County, and the Grand Cyclops a Township Den" (*CM*, 1). Before organizing his den, Dixon's Ben travels to Tennessee, ostensibly and appropriately, "on some important legal business" (*CM*, 192). Then, before Ben calls the den into action, General Forrest, "a great Scotch-Irish leader of the South from Memphis" (295), visits South Carolina.[40]

Tourgée needs an organized and disciplined Klan for a different reason. Intervention by the national government required proof of an organized conspiracy carrying on the spirit of rebellion. Denying Harris's distinction between "The Knights of the White Camellia" and the Klan, Tourgée argues that the Ku Klux Klan was a generic term that embraced a variety of orders. Even though groups varied from place to place, Tourgée, like Dixon, implies that they were a coordinated effort, mostly coming into existence after Forrest visited nearly all of the southern states between January and May of 1868 (*IE*, 27–28). For Tourgée, such a widespread conspiracy, inspired by a former Confederate, needed a national response. When Bob Martin tells the Fool about his beating, the Fool damns a government "too timid or too weak to put down this new rebellion" (*FE*, 191).

To be sure, in *A Fool's Errand* the Klan is broken on the state level when a one-time member converts to the Fool's point of view while under the spell of his daughter. This defection prompts a former leader of the Klan publicly to renounce his membership. That act convinces another former member, who participated in Uncle Jerry's lynching, to alleviate his bad conscience by confessing and naming other participants. In democratic fashion, the Klan unravels from the bottom up. In contrast, for Dixon, the Klan is dissolved by command of the leader. Furthermore, whereas in *The Traitor* Dixon depicts Steve Hoyle as the vilest coward for betraying the Klan's membership, Tourgée emphasizes the courage it took for individuals to buck their community and their leaders to tell the truth, even though it comes too late. The state is already back in white supremacist hands, and the legislature passes a law giving "amnesty and pardon for all who had committed acts of violence in disguise, or at the instigation of any secret organization" (*FE*, 317). In its zeal it also, the narrator satirically reports, "*even pardoned the victims!*," members of the Union League who were among the Klan's targets and committed no secret violence.

From Tourgée's point of view, national intervention was clearly needed, and, as we have seen, Congress finally provided it. But in *Bricks without Straw*, we see the fate of that legislation. There are no confessions or conversions. Instead, Tourgée gives us the conclusion of Nimbus's story. Forced by the Klan to abandon his family and farm, Nimbus goes from state to state. Later in the book, we learn that in his wanderings he participated in the Colfax Massacre. In Colfax, Grant Parish, Louisiana, white supremacists resented the local Reconstruction government controlled by a mixture of whites and coloreds. On Easter Sunday, April 13, 1873, they organized a paramilitary group to attack colored officials and take control. Outmatched in arms, the colored community tried to defend itself but was overwhelmed. As a historical marker by the Colfax Courthouse still on display puts it, "On this site occurred the Colfax Riot in which three white men and 150 negroes were slain. This event marked the end of carpetbag misrule in the South."[41]

In addition to showing the brutality of white supremacist violence, the Colfax massacre led to an important Supreme Court case. Two of the whites involved were arrested and convicted under the Enforcement Acts. They were accused of a conspiracy to "injure, oppress, threaten, or intimidate" African Americans trying to exercise their rights. One of their attorneys was David Dudley Field. Another was Reverdy Johnson, who had tried to get the Enforcement Acts declared unconstitutional in the South Carolina Ku Klux Klan trials. In *United States v. Cruikshank* (1876), he had more success. The Supreme Court overruled the convictions of the two by maintaining the *Slaughter-House Cases'* strict distinction between national and state citizenship and its drastic limitation of the privileges and immunities of US citizenship. In order to convict under the Enforcement Acts, the government had to prove that the conspirators violated a right "granted or secured by the constitution or laws of the United States." One of the privileges retained by the *Slaughter-House Cases* was for people "peacefully to assemble, for the purpose of petitioning Congress for a redress of grievances." But the defendants were convicted more generally of violating a group's right "peacefully to assemble for lawful purposes." Because that right existed "long before the adoption of the Constitution," it was a right to be protected by the states, not the national government. Furthermore, whereas the defendants were convicted of violating the due process and equal protection clauses of the Fourteenth Amendment, the court ruled that the amendment "adds nothing to the rights of one citizen against another." Protection of existing rights remained with the states, and the national government could intervene only if the states themselves, not individuals, denied those rights. The US government also claimed that the defendants had violated the victims' Second Amendment rights. But the court ruled that "the right to bear arms is not granted by the Constitution; neither is it in any manner dependent on that instrument for its existence. The second amendment means no more than that it shall not be infringed by Congress, and has no other effect than to restrict the powers of the national government." Finally, the defendants were accused of violating the right to vote. But the court insisted that the "Constitution of the United States has not conferred the right of suffrage upon any one. . . . The right to vote in the States comes from the States." All the Fifteenth Amendment did was prohibit "discrimination in the exercise of the elective franchise on account of race, color, or previous condition of servitude." Since white Republicans were also intimidated from voting, the prosecution, the court alleged, had not established that the attack was racially motivated. Unable to "specify any particular right," which the national government had the authority to protect, the prosecution presented charges that "are too vague, and general" and "lack the certainty and precision required by the established rules of criminal pleading, and are therefore not good and sufficient in law."[42]

Frederick Douglass called *United States v. Cruikshank* "the Dred Scott case of the new dispensation." The court's retreat from protecting the rights of African Americans was so egregious that it needs to be put in context. That can be done in part by tracing the shifting meaning of "civil rights" at the time. Prior to the Civil War, "civil rights" encompassed what today we call "civil liberties." In the United States' system of federalism, the national government was considered their primary threat and states their protector. By placing restraints on the national government, the Bill of Rights codified that belief. But states' authority to legalize slavery complicated that view. In the wake of *Dred Scott,* which drew on the Bill of Rights to declare that African Americans had no rights that a white man had to respect, some southern states started to define civil rights as those reserved for whites. Thus, with the abolition of slavery, Congress passed various civil rights bills guaranteeing equal civil rights for African Americans. Because of the role states played in denying those rights to African Americans, the Founders' vision of the national government threatening civil rights and the states protecting them was reversed. The Civil War Amendments were the first to grant the national government new powers rather than limit them. In the Thirteenth and Fourteenth Amendments, those powers protected civil rights; in the Fifteenth they allowed the federal government to protect people from being denied the right to vote on the basis of race. Nonetheless, the old view that states were the protectors of what today we call civil liberties, guaranteed by the Bill of Rights, did not die out. Many people—not just southerners—were concerned that individual civil liberties were threatened by the new enforcement powers given the national government. The national protection of civil rights thus came into conflict with the traditional view that national power had to be reined in to protect civil liberties. Indeed, when the court insisted that in criminal cases, "the accused has the constitutional right 'to be informed of the nature and cause of the accusation,'" its ruling was hailed by some as a victory for civil liberties. Affirming traditional federalism, the court declared, "Sovereignty, for the protection of the rights of life and personal liberty within the respective States, rests alone with the States." Field wanted the court to declare that "state inaction is no cause for federal action." Not going that far, the court on almost all other grounds legitimated Field's sense of federalism, just as ten years earlier it sided with him in the landmark civil liberties case of *Ex Parte Milligan.* As Michael Kent Curtis puts it, for most justices on the court and for many US citizens, "national protection of civil rights would be the end of federalism."[43]

Tourgée felt that traditional federalism, not the protection of civil rights, had to go. In his brief to the court in the *Plessy* case, he insisted that "the opinion in Cruikshank's Case cannot stand," because it ignores the Fourteenth Amendment's creation of "a *new citizenship*" with new protections to the individual. In *A Fool's Errand,* composed shortly after *Cruikshank* was decided, Tourgée offers a slightly different rebuttal to the court's decision. Trying to inform the "wise men" of the North about the conditions in the South, the Fool writes a politician, asking the national government to help combat the Klan. The politician responds that, because the states "are now fully restored, and are sovereign republics," it is their responsibility to deal with the Klan, not the national government's. "The States must protect the lives, persons, and property of their own citizens from aggression on the part of others. The National Government can not act, so long as *its* existence or *its* authority is not assailed or interfered with" (*FE*, 234). Later in the book, the narrator responds to this claim. If the Klan had simply attacked the "poor colored man," he notes, its actions would have been "cowardly" (254). But the Klan and other white supremacist groups took on not only the freedman but also "the Nation, which had given the victim citizenship and power. . . . It was not the individual negro, scalawag, or carpet-bagger, against whom the blow was directed, but the power—the Government—the idea which they represented" (254–55). Because these groups attacked the authority of the nation, the nation was justified in passing legislation allowing a national response.[44]

Much to Tourgée's dismay, the court failed to allow the nation to defend itself, and in doing so rendered African Americans' attempts to defend themselves hopeless. In *United States v. Harris* (1883) the Supreme Court went further than it had in *Cruikshank* and struck down the section of the Ku Klux Klan Act allowing the federal government to protect individuals from private conspiracies. In fact, most Democrats never accepted the constitutionality of the 1870 and 1871 acts, and, in the 1890s, controlling Congress and the White House for the first time since the Civil War, they repealed most, if not all, of their other provisions. In his novels, however, Tourgée makes more than a legal argument. He wants to make it clear that the Klan's success was not due to the cowardliness of African Americans. As he portrays them, they display exceptional bravery. He also wants to make it clear that redemption was not justified because freedmen were incapable of advancing economically and politically. They were making exceptional progress. Without governmental support, however, their resources were no match for the overwhelming resources mobilized against them. Responding to the Fool's letter asking for help, a "wise" northern politician responds, "The government has done all it can be expected to do,—all it had power to do in fact. It has given the colored man the ballot, armed him with the weapons of the freeman, and now he must show himself worthy to use it. . . . The capacity for self-government is proved, first of all, by its inclination and capacity for self-protection. . . . If people are killed by the Ku-Klux, why do they not kill the Ku-Klux" (*FE*, 235)? In chapter 4, we will see how the court's and most of the public's belief in individual self-reliance and their distrust of governmental paternalism undercut freedmen's efforts to achieve equality.

- 4 -

OF MULES AND MEN

African American Manhood and the Paradox of Paternalism

Near the end of Stephen Crane's *The Red Badge of Courage*, Henry Fleming, having demonstrated his bravery in battle, "felt a quiet manhood, nonassertive but of a sturdy blood. . . . He was a man." As is well known, Henry's confidence in his manhood is potentially, if not necessarily, undercut. Although his company does not know it, on the first day of combat his badge of honor is inflicted by a fellow soldier who, like Henry, is in cowardly retreat. What is less often noted is that the courage Henry displays on the second day of battle is set in motion when he overhears an officer tell a general that his regiment fights "like a lot 'a mule drivers." This derogatory comparison to "mule drivers," rather than a hatred of the enemy, gives Henry his Emersonian "new eyes" and sparks his heroic deeds. The significance of that comparison is illuminated by the book's first scene, which features the only African American in the book. "A negro teamster who had been dancing upon a cracker box with the hilarious encouragement of twoscore soldiers" is "deserted" the moment the possibility of battle arises and the serious business of war begins.[1]

Even if Crane suggests something cowardly about this desertion, it is telling that in the most famous fictional portrayal of the war that ended slavery in the United States Henry asserts his military manhood in response to being compared with those coded as African Americans. According to authors as different as Mark Twain and W. E. B. Du Bois, slavery had taken away African American manhood. In the same year that *Adventures of Huckleberry Finn* was published, Twain wrote a friend, "We have ground the manhood out of them & the shame is ours not theirs & we should pay for it." Almost twenty years later, Du Bois wrote of the sudden emancipation of "black men emasculated by a peculiarly complete system of slavery" (*SBF*, 50).[2]

Today, manhood is usually considered a gendered category, but, at the time, male African Americans, even old ones, were denied manhood because they were considered childlike. "Manhood" in this context was more a generic than a gendered term, and African American women writers, such as Francis Harper and

Pauline Hopkins, were some of the strongest advocates of African American manhood. To be sure, as a number of scholars have shown, the gendered implications for ideals of manhood were of extreme importance in the period, and these affected and were affected by Reconstruction. I touch on some of those implications, especially on what they meant for courtship and the role of fathers as breadwinners. But my primary focus will be on the portrayal of African Americans as perpetual children.[3]

Of course, African Americans were not the only ones who had their manhood questioned. In *The Clansman,* Ben Cameron is arrested by the military. A white officer confines the "blue-blood" to a dungeon-like cell with "two big white drunks . . . half-fighting drunks," instructed to "work on his teeth and manicure his face a little to initiate him into the ranks of the common people." Within seconds, Ben has the drunks calling him "Marster" and referring to themselves as "A common—stump-tailed—cur dog" (*CM,* 223–24). A true man, Dixon implies, can make others feel as if they do not belong to the same species as human beings. But, whereas the drunks are depraved individuals, African Americans were portrayed as lacking manhood as a race. Just as scientific racists considered the "African race" "outcasts from evolution," incapable of developing beyond a primitive stage, so it was felt that African Americans could not grow into true manhood. That deficiency affected how their military valor was depicted. Having lost the war, southern whites themselves were vulnerable to having their manhood questioned, as manifested by the North's delight in accounts of Jefferson Davis trying to escape the downfall of the Confederacy dressed like a woman. The need to counter that story is behind Dixon's portrayal of Simon Legree in *The Leopard's Spots* escaping military service by dressing as "a German emigrant woman. He wore dresses for two years, did house work, milked the cows and cut wood for a good-natured old German" (*LS,* 86). Similarly, in *Red Rock* at the start of the war, Freedmen's Bureau agent Leech loudly encourages all to enlist but fails to volunteer himself, claiming that he has a wife. Hearing Leech's excuse, a volunteer responds, "All right—send her in your place. I guess she'd do as well" (*RR,* 37). Because white men as a group are considered capable of achieving full manhood, gendered comparisons serve well to undercut these cowards' military manhood. Such gendered comparisons were not considered necessary in the portrayal of childlike African American males.[4]

The alleged childlike nature of African Americans was used to justify the paternal institution of slavery. African American military service during the Civil War challenged that stereotype. The three Civil War Amendments to the Constitution laid the groundwork for its complete overturn. These amendments allowed former slaves to become legal husbands and fathers with the right to enter into contracts and become breadwinners for their families. They could also develop their manhood through education and through participation in the political sphere. In this chapter I look at a variety of literary works of the time to illustrate African Americans' efforts to assert their manhood. I also look at how, around the time that *The Red Badge of Courage* appeared, those efforts were questioned in many works of fiction. These works helped to foster and to reinforce views, like those in a 1905 volume on Reconstruction that African Americans were "an affectionate, credulous race, which followed the new masters and enabled them to wreck States for the resulting plunder—a child-race, but unable to grow above a child's intelligence."[5]

African Americans' attempts to assert their manhood were also undermined by various Supreme Court decisions. Frequently dismissed for simply replicating the dominant racism of the time, those cases are, in fact, more complicated. Although their effect was to strip the Civil War Amendments of their egalitarian potential, they did so while professing to foster the ideal of equal opportunity. African Americans, they assumed, would be denied the opportunity to become self-reliant individuals, if they continued to benefit from the governmental protections promoted by their advocates. By ruling that African Americans needed to be treated like other men and not be the special favorites of governmental policy, these cases illustrate what Aviam Soifer has called the "paradox of paternalism." Even former abolitionists feared that governmental paternalism would simply replace the former paternalism of slavery. Nowhere was this new form of paternalism more evident than in the slogan "40 acres and a mule," attributed to the Freedmen's Bureau. This chapter shows how the association of African Americans with mules implied that they were incapable of equal citizenship. In the most famous speech to come out of the Civil War, Abraham Lincoln starts by alluding to how the founding fathers "brought forth" a new nation "conceived in liberty." He ends by imploring his generation to become founding fathers themselves by giving the nation a "new birth of freedom." Mules do not make very good fathers.[6]

II

Soon after the Thirteenth Amendment was enacted, Justice Noah Swayne on circuit declared that it forbade not only the institution of slavery but also its badges and incidents. In the years soon after the Civil War, many northerners felt that African Americans had earned their freedom by exchanging their former badges of servitude for red badges of courage. After all, the Thirteenth Amendment completed the work of the Emancipation Proclamation, which was a military measure, constitutionally justified by the president's executive powers as commander-in-chief. At the start of the conflict, freed slaves were considered contraband of war. After the Emancipation Proclamation, Congress issued a call for African Americans to enlist to fight for the freedom of their race. In his eulogy for Lincoln, the historian George Bancroft asserted that the proclamation "decided the result of the war. It took from the public enemy one or two millions of bondsmen, and placed between one and two thousand brave and gallant troops on the other side of the Union." Although his opinion undercut protections for African Americans under the Fourteenth Amendment, Justice Samuel Miller in the *Slaughter-House Cases* (1873) said of them, "And when hard-pressed in the contest, these men (for they proved themselves men in that terrible crisis) offered their services and were accepted by thousands to aid in suppressing the unlawful rebellion." Benjamin Butler introduced the 1875 Civil Rights Act to Congress by appealing to the obligation "to defend the rights of those men who have given their blood for me and my country."[7]

Numerous works of literature praise African American soldiers. Frances Harper's *Iola Leroy* (1892), one of the first novels written by an African American woman, starts with scenes of wartime emancipation peopled with brave African American soldiers. Harper was influenced by William Wells Brown. In his post–Civil War 1867 version of *Clotelle*, Brown added four chapters extolling the wartime heroism of black troops. Lawyer-novelist Albion W. Tourgée was so impressed by the bravery of his fellow African American troops that, after the war, a southern newspaper complained that, according to him, "the niggers alone 'crushed the rebellion.'" He began an 1868 speech at the North Carolina Constitutional Convention by praising the "dusky martyrs" of Fort Pillow, who imparted the "noble lesson of manhood." In *Bricks without Straw* (1880), Tourgée describes the defeated South, "stricken at last most fatally by the dark hands which she had manacled, and overcome by their aid whose manhood she had refused to acknowledge" (105). In the same work he gives us the courageous African American soldier Nimbus. In *Toinette* (1874), the heroine's brother is a color-bearer who wraps the flag around his body rather than surrender at Ft. Pillow. Along with his body is discovered his deed of manumission, a photograph of Lincoln, and a copy of the Emancipation Proclamation covered with his blood. In *A Fool's Errand* (1879), there is Bob Martin, who fought at Fort Wagner. To a group of southerners, the Fool proclaims that the black man "was allowed to testify on the battlefield, and will be allowed to testify in courts of justice. When he took the oath of service, he acquired the right to take the oath of witness" (*FE*, 65).[8]

By the time Tourgée defended Homer Plessy before the Supreme Court in 1896, however, much fiction of the time shared Henry's attitude in *The Red Badge of Courage*. The popular image was that African Americans had been incapable of participating in their own liberation, which had been brought about by the Great Emancipator and the valor of white soldiers. In *Black Reconstruction*, Du Bois quotes a biographer of Grant who proclaims that "the American Negroes are the only people in the history of the world, so far as I know, that ever became free without any effort of their own" (*BR*, 716). Even Sutton Griggs, celebrated by some as a militant African American writing at the turn of the century, subscribes to that stereotype. Although he imagines a secret black army at the time of the Spanish-American War, he has his protagonist in *Imperium in Imperio* proclaim, "When at last the war came to set us free we stayed in the field and fed the men who were reddening the soil with their blood in a deadly struggle to keep us in bondage forever. . . . We know that our patient submission in slavery was due to our consciousness of weakness; we know that our silence and inaction during the civil war was due to a belief that God was speaking for us and fighting our battle" (242–43).

Of course, not everyone accepted such portrayals. In Pauline Hopkins's *Contending Forces* (1900), a character argues that African Americans earned their rights at "Wagner and Fort Pillow" (*CF*, 232). In *Hagar's Daughter* (1901–1902), she has an old African American impress his audience with exaggerated accounts of both battles, including details of Colonel Shaw's death. His tales are obviously fabricated, a device to cover the identity of the speaker, who turns out to be a real veteran who served at the less mythologized battle of Honey Hill and is now on a dangerous mission as an agent of the secret service. Even so, his stories reveal how much African American bravery at Fort Wagner and Fort Pillow had become part of African American folklore. Similarly, in his *Plessy* dissent, Justice John Marshall Harlan praised "citizens of the black race in Louisiana, many of whom, perhaps, risked their lives for the preservation of the Union." But Justice Harlan held a minority position in the nation as well as on the court. Around the time of *Plessy*, questions about southern military manhood no longer existed. Revisionist Reconstruction literature is full of images of brave southern men who lost the war not because they lacked bravery but because of the North's overwhelming resources. At the same time, African Americans, who contributed greatly to the North's victory, are dismissed as cowards. If black troops are portrayed at all, they are stripped of their bravery. In *Red Rock*, *The Leopard's Spots*, and *The Clansman*, black militias used to enforce Reconstruction rule are, without resistance, disarmed and disbanded by members of the Klan.[9]

To be sure, Joel Chandler Harris praises Qua, a former African prince turned slave, for his bravery in the American Revolution. Fighting "in behalf of liberty . . . He was in his element when war was at its hottest" (*CAM*, 3). More directly, in his

1911 volume of the *Photographic History of the Civil War*, Dudley H. Miles includes a few photographs of African American troops and praises the "brilliant fighting" of the famous 54th and 55th regiments of Massachusetts. He also mentions regiments "organized out of plantation negroes," noting that, although "they lacked, as was quite natural, individual initiative," they almost always fulfilled "their duty pluckily and persistently." Even so, the photographs and Miles's sincere, if condescending, account appear in a section called "The Lighter Side," which includes examples of comic poems and pieces produced by the war. The section begins with Irish American Charles Graham Halpine's defense of the right of African Americans to serve, but it takes the form of a dialect poem called "Sambo's Right to Be Kilt." The last two photographs of African Americans are one showing former slaves on a freed Mississippi plantation, titled "De Darkeys Got So Lonesome," and one of African American teamsters called "Contraban."[10]

Even Dixon in *The Leopard's Spots* acknowledges that in the Spanish-American War, "the well-drilled Negro regulars . . . acquitted themselves with honor at Santiago" (413). According to Dixon, however, that is because they were led by white officers. In contrast, "The Negro volunteers were the source of riot and disorder wherever they appeared." When a black regiment camps in Independence, North Carolina, waiting to be mustered out of service, one of the troops insults a young white lady and is immediately beaten to death by her escort. In an ensuing altercation, the black regiment is easily routed by armed whites. In conjunction with this racial battle, whites compose a new Declaration of Independence, demanding that all black officials resign their positions and that the local black newspapers shut down. When Charles Gaston delivers this document to a group of black leaders, a black minister rightly responds that the group does not have the authority to execute such orders. Gaston replies, "Your authority is equal to ours—the authority of elemental manhood" (*LS*, 417).

The widespread association of African Americans with mules fostered the image of blacks lacking elemental manhood. Around this time, the US Military Academy adopted the mule as its mascot because of the pack mules that served real soldiers. In contrast, the nation's ideal of military valor was linked to horsemanship, as evidenced by the equestrian statues of George Washington and Civil War heroes, North and South. The popular genre of the Western drew on and developed that ideal. It is, for instance, no accident that in *The Red Badge of Courage*, the officer comparing Henry's regiment to mule drivers rides a horse "with the skillful abandon of a cowboy." Historically, Crane's cowboy looks forward to Teddy Roosevelt's "Rough Riders" and the Spanish-American War much more than he represents how anyone would have thought of the Civil War at the time. As one account put it, Roosevelt's "dashing band of Western cowboys," his "sturdy frontier-heroes,"

These African American soldiers are proudly posing for an 1864 photograph that was reprinted in *The Photographic History of the Civil War* (1911). Editor Dudley Miles uses it to illustrate a line from Irish American Charles Graham Halpine's wartime dialect poem "Sambo's Right to Be Kilt": "And his eye runs sthraight [*sic*] on the barrel sights." Although replete with stereotypes, Halpine's poem stresses the bravery of African Americans to mock the fears of those who protested their enlistment as soldiers.

were the epitome of self-reliant manhood, possessing "their own mounts, their own arms," and, knowing "how to take care of themselves, live under any circumstances and fight all the time."[11]

Tourgée anticipates this turn-of-the century description when he calls the typical southerner who joined the Klan a "rough rider" (*BS*, 251). An African American in *Bricks without Straw* reports seeing a gathering of the Klan: "Dey wuz all good men. I seed de hosses, when they mounted ter go 'way. I tell ye dey wuz good 'uns! No pore-white trash dar; no lame hosses ner blind mules" (259). Despairing at the freedmen's chances of combatting the Klan, he adds, "Dey's got the hosses an' de guns." The Klansmen's potency, like that of Roosevelt's Rough Riders, is in part established by their horsemanship. In contrast, African Americans are almost always portrayed with a mule. In *Red Rock,* an African American encouraged by Leech joyously proclaims, "We've got the Gov'ment behind us, and we'll put a gun in every colored man's hand and give him, not a mule, but a horse to ride." To which another freedman responds, "A *mule's* good 'nough for me—I b'lieve I ruther have a mule 'n hoss, I'se fotched up wid mules" (*RR,* 321–22).

A well-known travel writer, New England's Reverend Henry Field was the brother of Supreme Court justice Stephen Field, lawyer David Dudley Field, and Cyrus Field, the driving force behind the transatlantic cable. Confirming that there was a color line in New England as well as the South, he insisted:

> Social intercourse cannot be regulated by law; it must be left to those natural attractions and affinities which the Almighty has planted in our breasts. That the whites should desire to keep to themselves, is not to be ascribed to arrogance; it does not even imply an assumption of superiority. It is not that one race is above the other, but that the two races are different, and that, while they may live together in the most friendly relations, each will consult its own happiness best by working along its own lines. This is a matter of instinct, which is often wiser than reason. We cannot fight against instinct, nor legislate against it; if we do, we shall find it stronger than our resolutions and our laws.

In 1886 Henry published *Blood Is Thicker than Water,* recording the minister's train trip through the South and stressing North-South reconciliation. Intent on assuring northerners that African Americans were no longer in a servile position in the South, he wrote: "Now they are free, and show it in every motion. Look at that young buck mounted on a mule! His garments can hardly hold together, and yet he bestrides the beast as proudly as if he were Alexander the Great. There is a dash of independence in every kick of his long legs, and the rags that wave from his tattered coat seem as if they float in the air of freedom."[12]

Mules were also used to associate carpetbaggers and scalawags with African Americans. An 1868 *Greensboro Patriot* cartoon exploits a dispute between Tourgée and the local William Henderson over the Republican nomination for Congress by juxtaposing an image of "Judge Tourgee," labeled "Carpet-bagger," with one of "Windy Billy," labeled "Scalawag." Henderson is depicted on his way to Congress on a mule saying "I'll ride Darr's mule to Congress yet!" Tourgée is riding a pig, accompanied by a childlike African American carrying a banner with "Ruin or Rule In Spite of the Mule" and quoted as saying "Hold' on, little 'manhood' we'll beat the mu-el man!" Having been associated with mules, Tourgée works to counter stereotypes of African Americans and mules. In *A Fool's Errand*, he has his fictional carpetbagger promote self-sufficient freedmen farmers by helping them "buy horses" (56). But in doing so, he violates a social code. As one southerner warns him, there are two things that "are more sacred than any other to the Southern mind; to wit, to *buy and hold land* and to *ride their own horses*" (108–9). Thus, the Fool's actions are opposed by "organizations in some parts of the State instituted to prevent the colored people from buying land and owning horses" (56). Indeed, a number of African Americans are beaten when they "become owners of horses and houses in their own right" (98). The horses of two are stolen; those belonging to others are "cut and mangled."[13]

Acknowledging that possession of a horse rather than a mule marked one's economic status, Tourgée also makes it clear that ownership of a mule could be a move toward economic self-sufficiency, not reliance on governmental paternalism. Nimbus, for instance, uses some of his military earnings to buy a mule that will help him work the land. "It's gwine ter be great times fer us niggers," he declares, "now we's free. Yer see dat mule out dar? . . . Dat ar mule b'longs ter *me*" (*BS*, 132–33). But, even though "according to the common law, the possession of personal property is *prima facie* evidence of its ownership," Nimbus has to take great care to prove his purchase, because one of the "black codes" enacted in the early days of Presidential Reconstruction declared that a freedman must produce a bill of sale to establish ownership over "any horse, mule, hog, cow, steer, or other stock" (134). As the narrator notes, "It was well for Nimbus that he was armed with his 'dockyments.'"

Like Tourgée, George Washington Cable challenges stereotypes of African Americans and mules. In *John March, Southerner* (1894), John's manhood is confirmed when a beautiful southern belle spies him riding a mare and exclaims to an equally beautiful friend how "well-mounted" he is (*JM*, 264). In another scene, Cable depicts "two shabby black men . . . on plough mules" (59). Between them, riding a "poor smart horse," is the African American politician Cornelius Leggett. By placing Cornelius, decked out in "store clothes, watch-chain, and shoe-blacking" on a horse, Cable establishes him as the pretentious, corrupt, oversexed figure he is (59). But the status of riding on a horse also marks Cornelius as different from similarly corrupt African American politicians in the works of Page and Dixon. Cornelius is incredibly shrewd. Secretly in league not with carpetbaggers and scalawags but with his former owner, a white supremacist who outdoes him in corruption and hypocrisy, Cornelius justifies his actions with "Niggers steals with they claws, white men with they laws" (95). And, despite all of his corruption, he makes sure that with every railroad deal that feathers his nest, provisions are made for building schools to educate his fellow freedmen. African Americans felt they had established their manhood as soldiers in the war; in peacetime they hoped to enhance it through schooling.

III

Literacy's importance for freedmen is dramatized negatively in *Gabriel Tolliver.* Gabriel learns that Reverend Jeremiah Tomlin is organizing a Union League meeting at Gabriel's old school and decides to hide inside and observe the meeting. When Gabriel is discovered, he concocts an excuse and tries to please Tomlin by writing on the blackboard, "Rev. Jeremiah Tomlin will lecture here to-night, beginning at early candlelight" (*GT,* 161). Tomlin is pleased, but he has to take Gabriel's word for what he wrote, since he cannot read. After Gabriel leaves, the Reverend approaches the blackboard and, "with the most patient curiosity examined the inscription or announcement Gabriel had written. With his forefinger, he traced over the lines, as if in that way he might absorb the knowledge that was behind the writing. Then, stepping back a few paces, he viewed the writing critically. Finally, he shook his head doubtfully, exclaiming aloud: 'Dat's whar dey'll git us—yes, suh, dat's whar dey sho' will git us'" (16). Indeed, mastery of language plays a crucial role in the plot. When Gabriel is falsely accused of murdering the Freedmen's Bureau agent, he is sprung from prison after receiving a secret message delivered by a young boy in pig Latin.

Harris sincerely believed that he was an advocate for African Americans. Late in his life, he and his son established *Uncle Remus Home Magazine,* whose goal was the obliteration of prejudice against blacks. In the fiction that made him famous, however, Uncle Remus, like Mark Twain's Jim, is loveable despite his illiteracy. Similarly, in *Gabriel Tolliver,* Harris's model freedman is Uncle Plato, who relies on the paternal protection of whites while being mocked for his inability to read. Harris counters the view of "historians" who claim that the situation during Reconstruction was "full of peril" because freedmen were dangerous (*GT,* 114). On the contrary, "Gabriel could never be brought to believe that there was anything to be dreaded in the attitude of the blacks" (115). That "was clear to Gabriel, but it was not clear to his elders. And what a pity it was not! How many mistakes would have been avoided! What a dreadful tangle and turmoil would have been prevented if these grown children could have been judged from Gabriel's point of view!" (114). For Gabriel, blacks are not dangerous precisely because they are "grown children."

African Americans, however, knew that they needed education in order to advance. In the midst of his memorable portrait of the souls of black folk, Du Bois makes a plea for the proper training of black men. For him, the "paths of peace winding between honest toil and dignified manhood call for the guidance of skilled thinkers, the loving reverent comradeship between the black lowly and the black men emancipated by training and culture" (*SBF*, 101). Of course, Booker T. Washington also viewed education as a vehicle toward African American manhood, but he and Du Bois disagreed on the scope of that education. At the time, Washington's manual education had far more support than Du Bois's insistence on higher education for a talented tenth. For instance, in *Education in America*, compiled for the 1900 Paris Exposition and edited by N. Murray Butler, the future president of Columbia University, Washington contributed the essay on African Americans. Even Dixon has Charles Gaston recommend disfranchisement but advocate "large appropriations for the industrial training of Negroes along the lines of the new movement of their more sober leaders" (*LS*, 463). To be sure, Gaston is opposed by Reverend John Durham, whom many take to be Dixon's spokesperson in *The Leopard's Spots*. But the novel never resolves this disagreement between two racists, and given Gaston's role in the book, he could as easily represent Dixon's view as Durham. Dixon himself praised Washington in a 1905 article for the *Saturday Evening Post*.[14]

Such connections help explain why Du Bois is favored over Washington today. Nonetheless, as important as the debate between these two is, it has been emphasized, especially by scholars at institutions of higher education, at the expense of other important issues that become apparent if we look at the portrayal of education in works of Reconstruction literature. Plans for education occur in every pro-Reconstruction novel. Toward the end of *Iola Leroy*, a former black soldier heads south to become a teacher and uplift the race. Toward the end of *A Fool's Errand*, the Fool marks the transition from soldiering to schooling with, "Make the spelling-book the scepter of national policy" (387). Indeed, no one pushed for education more than Tourgée. The young heroine of *Bricks without Straw* comes south from New England to educate freedmen, training a talented African American to be a teacher himself. Written in time for the 1880 election, *Bricks without Straw* influenced President Garfield, who expressed a number of Tourgée's ideas in his inaugural address. For the 1884 campaign, Tourgée produced *An Appeal to Caesar*, a nonfictional book outlining the need for educational reform. In *Pactolus Prime* (1890), a novel set in Washington, DC, the title character is an African American bootblack who served in the Union army as a color bearer. While shining shoes, he debates congressmen on various issues, most notably national educational policy.

Tourgée's argument was not about manual versus higher education; instead, he highlighted the nation's need to wipe out illiteracy. In doing so, Tourgée raised important questions about how to finance that effort. There were three main sources of funding: philanthropy, local taxes, and support from the national government. Intent on establishing southern whites' generosity, Henry Grady uses the local tax burden to argue that "though the whites pay nineteen-twentieths of the [school] tax, they insist that the blacks shall share its advantages equally." In fact, the use of local taxes sparked resentment in many white southerners. Dixon plays on this resentment in *The Leopard's Spots* when he describes a Reconstruction government that "sold and divided the school fund" rather than using it for education (116). Responding to what they perceived as northern misperception, other southern whites argued that they supported African American education and bore the financial costs through tax dollars. In Sidney Lanier's dialect poem "Civil Rights," "Uncle Johnny Stiles" expresses his resentment toward Charles Sumner's proposed Civil Rights Act of 1874, which would have required integrated schools, lamenting: "When every nigger's son is schooled (I payin' the tax, / For not a mother's son of 'em had more than's on ther backs)."[15]

Continuing his debate with Grady, Cable in *John March* stresses southern whites' resentment rather than their generosity. He has an Englishman listen with dismay as locals describe how they countered Cornelius Leggett's use of tax dollars for public education. Even as they insisted that the main support of schools came from counties and townships, they changed the state constitution "to forbid the levy of any school tax by a county or township except on special permission of the legislature" (*JM*, 153). It was, the Englishman is told, the "property-holder's only protection." Thus, black and white students too poor to afford the local private academy are denied any public support. Indeed, in a final act of benevolence, the locals transfer to the private academy the three thousand dollars earned from public land and earmarked by the federal government for education. "Public funds to a private concern," comments the shocked Englishman, "That's a steal" (154).

Aware of such tactics, the Freedmen's Bureau established colored schools in Kentucky that, until 1882, were paid for by a black poll tax kept separate from other state funds. Washington's Tuskegee Institute had widespread support in part because it was financed primarily by philanthropists, such as the railroad tycoon Collis Huntington. But even philanthropic support was questioned if it undercut local community control. In *Red Rock*, Page contrasts two colored schools. One was established by the daughter of a southern gentleman-doctor, who feels the responsibility to help teach black children. Supported locally, it "had been talked over and deliberated on until it was in some sense the outcome of the concert of the neighborhood"(*RR*, 398). A fancier school was founded by a transplanted northern woman, who consulted none of "the county people" but sought support only from rich northern friends. "This school came to be considered as a foreign institution, conducted on foreign principles, and in opposition to the school already established by the neighborhood" (398–99). Even so, as we have seen, displaying exemplary southern courage, the teacher of the local school foils a plot by a now-corrupt Klan to burn the rival school.[16]

Southern writers were not alone in expressing skepticism about northern philanthropic efforts to educate freedmen. In "King David" (1878), Constance Fenimore Woolson tells the story of David King, a schoolteacher in New Hampshire. During the war, extreme nearsightedness and a delicate constitution kept him out of the army, but with victory he feels that there is "work fitted to his hand." He conceives of "a glorious idea" to go south to teach freedmen. His farmer neighbors tell him not to go: "We've paid dear enough to set 'em free, goodness knows, and now they ought to look out for themselves." He goes anyway, "with such aid and instruction the Freedmen's Bureau could give him." He finds "tens of thousands of ignorant children's irresponsible souls . . . that not long stay childish, and that have in themselves all the capacities for evil" that others have (KD, 781). He fails in the classroom and also in buying a cotton farm to teach his students work habits: "There is . . . no overseer now, and no lash; no slaves, and way little toil. The negroes would work only when they pleased and that was generally not at all" (782). Eventually, the schoolteacher admits defeat and retreats to New Hampshire. Before he leaves, Uncle Scipio makes it clear to him that northerners, even blacks, are not wanted in the South. "You see, suh, how it is, you see, Mars King David . . . a color'd man will unnerstan us 'specially ef he hab libed at the Souf; we don't want no Northern free niggahs hyar. But a 'spectable color'd preacher" would get their attention (789).[17]

Nonetheless, the perceived threat to local control posed by northern philanthropic support paled in comparison to that posed by national governmental support. Even in *John March, Southerner,* Cable has outside support come from "Yankee missiona'y teachers" (152). But in 1884, 1886, and 1888, the Senate passed bills for national funding of schools to wipe out illiteracy. About 75 percent of funds would have gone to the South, where illiteracy was the highest, especially among the African American population. Each time, however, the legislation failed in the House. Opposition came from the North as well as from the South. George William Curtis, the editor of the formerly abolitionist *Harper's Weekly,* predicted the "inevitable demoralization of the community." Extolling the virtues of "local self-government," he denounced any legislation that would encourage individual states to turn to "the national government for results which it should owe to its own industry, sacrifice, intelligence, and energy." Not surprisingly, in 1890, when

Senator Henry W. Blair of New Hampshire proposed a new bill, it was defeated. What is surprising is that Tourgée also opposed the Blair Bill. He did so for a good reason. The Blair Bill gave money to the states. Controlled by whites, those states, Tourgée warned, would distribute it disproportionately to white schools. Instead, Tourgée proposed giving the money directly to local schools. Doing so would truly ensure local community control. But his plan challenged a pillar of the country's legal structure: federalism, in which the national government had to work through the states. Tourgée's plan had no chance of succeeding. Soon after the Blair Bill failed, the country plunged into an economic depression, leaving the national government with no money in its coffers even if a bill were to overcome legal objections. By the time that Du Bois argued in *The Souls of Black Folk* "that the national government must soon step in and aid popular education in some way," the cause was long lost (143).[18]

That lost cause drove Tourgée to despair. To compensate for whites grinding the manhood out of African Americans, Twain paid for an African American to attend Yale Law School. This lawyer would go on to help Thurgood Marshall in his early legal career. Generous as he was, Twain, a private person, paid tuition at a private school. In contrast, in *Pactolus Prime,* when a young, light-skinned black man wants to receive an education to become a lawyer in order to do "something for the race," Pactolus counsels him to pass as white for the advantage and prosperity of his children (140). A few years later, Tourgée would turn this fictional encounter into a legal argument in his brief to the Supreme Court in the *Plessy* case. Insisting that the "*reputation of being white*" is property because it confers earning power, Tourgée claimed that the Louisiana statute gave conductors arbitrary power to take away property without due process of law by assigning someone like Plessy with "white blood" to a colored car. "How much would it be *worth,*" he asks in his brief, "to a young man entering upon the practice of law, to be regarded as a *white* man rather than a colored one?"[19]

Of course, the *Plessy* case was not about education. In fact, in his brief to the Supreme Court, Tourgée's friend and co-counsel, Samuel F. Phillips, acknowledged that segregation in public schools was different from segregation in public transportation. Because schooling was an extension of parental duty, "parental sentiment of the community upon this interesting and delicate subject" must be taken into consideration. Justice Harlan, although never explicitly condoning segregated schools, may have made a similar distinction. In his *Plessy* dissent, he points to Blackstone's assertion that "personal liberty . . . consists of the power of locomotion." There was no long-standing common-law principle about public schools. The lack of such a principle and the issue of tax dollars may explain why Justice Harlan felt free to write the opinion for the court in *Cumming v. Richmond County*

Board of Education (1899), which refused to prohibit a school board with limited funds from closing a colored high school to support a colored elementary school, even though it left a white high school open. Certainly, for Tourgée, providing quality education for African Americans had priority over insistence that schools be integrated. As we have seen, he criticized Sumner's 1874 Civil Rights Bill because, while well intentioned, it risked undermining African American education. Most whites in the South, he argued, would close down public schools before integrating them. Indeed, when the Civil Rights Bill was finally approved in 1875 by a lame-duck Congress after Sumner's death, the controversial school provision was dropped, and the bill confined itself to addressing public accommodations, amusement, and transportation.[20]

Even so, *Plessy* remains a landmark case in terms of African American manhood. As much as any case of the era, it demonstrated the court's willingness to condone what Du Bois called the "emasculating effects" of "caste distinction," that offspring of slavery (*SBF*, 72). One of the most devastating portrayals of the emasculating effects of caste distinction on education comes in the novels of Charles W. Chesnutt. Chesnutt, who could have passed as white, was the son of a Union army mule driver. He began teaching school in North Carolina when he was fourteen. At nineteen he earned an administrative position training teachers for colored schools, only to abandon his educational career to take a job on Wall Street, followed by legal training. Finding it more financially rewarding to work as a legal stenographer than as a black lawyer, he harbored an ambition to be a writer. He was encouraged by Tourgée and Cable, who served as mentors. In the wake of the *Plessy* decision, he published three novels. His first, *The House Behind the Cedars* (1900), has many details that show Chesnutt's familiarity with the *Plessy* opinion as well as with Tourgée's argument to the court. To take one example, he has an African American pass as white and develop a lucrative legal practice. Soon his sister joins the young lawyer on the other side of the color line, and she is courted by George Tryon, her brother's aristocratic friend, who displays his love through his expert horsemanship in a medieval jousting tournament. George's last name evokes thoughts of Lanier, who died in Tryon, North Carolina, and wrote a poem about jousting called "The Tournament," which in 1876 he incorporated into his centennial ode to portray the conflict between North and South in the Civil War. Fittingly, when his lover's racial heritage is revealed, chivalrous Tryon abandons her, and she becomes a teacher at a colored school. Coveted by a mulatto politician and member of the school board, who, like Cable's Cornelius Leggett, owns a horse, gold watch-chain, and fancy clothes, she dies trying to escape his advances. The book ends as she is carried, dying, to her mother's home in a mule cart by a loyal, illiterate, colored friend. Her position in the school remains vacant.

Similarly, in Chesnutt's last novel, *The Colonel's Dream* (1905), the prejudices of the color line force the lone African American schoolteacher to quit his job and take a position as a porter for a railroad company, his career as an educator sacrificed to economic necessity and the spirit of caste.

IV

The Colonel's Dream ends with its white protagonist grieving over the death of his son. Chesnutt's previous novel, *The Marrow of Tradition* (1901), also ends with a father grieving for his son. In this case, however, the father is black. Critics have faulted Chesnutt's Dr. Miller because at a crucial moment he fails to lead African American resistance against the overwhelming force of whites intent on killing all blacks in sight. As a result, Josh Green, a stevedore employed by Miller's brother, has to take on the role of leader himself and dies avenging the brutality inflicted by the Klan on his parents when he was a child. Given the portrayal of African Americans at the time, however, Miller's role as a father and husband should not be underestimated. First, Chesnutt makes it clear that Miller's decision is not due to cowardice. "Every manly instinct urged him to go forward and take up the cause of these leaderless people, and, if need be, to defend their lives and their rights with his own" (*MT*, 282). Nonetheless, Miller recognizes that it is useless to die for a lost cause when, alive, he will be able to help shape a more just future. Thus, Chesnutt confronts us with a paradox. Josh, still thinking of himself as a son, is intent on vengeance for an act in the past. In contrast, Miller, who identifies himself as a father, is focused on the future. Indeed, in his final act in the book he overcomes his own sense of past injustice and tries to save the life of the son of the racist newspaper editor whose press campaign helped to spark a massacre that led to his own son's death.

Chesnutt's portrayal of a black man as a father and husband is a welcome corrective to the perception of African Americans as childlike. Du Bois understood the importance of portraying black men as fathers when he strategically includes his brief, moving chapter about the loss of his son in *The Souls of Black Folk*. Elsewhere, Du Bois features the sorrow songs of slaves, but in this chapter he insists that black men experienced sorrow as fathers, not just as slaves. In contrast, in the works of Page and Dixon, we never encounter a responsible black father, grieving or otherwise. Page, to be sure, includes powerful black women, but their positive portrayal is due to their loyalty to the white children they raise. Their husbands are either absent or irresponsible drunks.

Portraits of African American men as manly suitors were even harder to find than as responsible husbands and fathers. As pervasive as the romance of reunion was, it almost always involved whites. Authors discrediting Reconstruction used romance to assert white southern manhood. On the one hand, manly heroes protect southern womanhood. On the other hand, as if to make up for the South's defeat in the war, almost every novel has a scene in which a woman surrenders to her protector. Sometimes the conquered woman is from the North, like Ruth Welch in *Red Rock* or Elsie Stoneman in *The Clansman*. Other times she is from the South, like Blair Cary in *Red Rock*, Sally Worth in *The Leopard's Spots*, or Nan Dorrington in *Gabriel Tolliver*. As Stella Butler in *The Traitor* exclaims, seeing John Graham riding a stallion in Klan attire, "I could surrender to such a man!" (49). Similarly, *Gabriel Tolliver* ends with the chapter "Nan Surrenders."

Not surprisingly, scenes of black men courting black women in works by Dixon, Page, and Harris are either absent or aimed at comedy. No true manhood is allowed. For instance, in *The Traitor*, while a three-hundred-pound woman is being whipped by her diminutive husband, her former husband "saves" her by pummeling his rival. Soon both males find themselves trapped under the weight of the wife as she hurls herself on top of them, only to have a white man break up the altercation. *Gabriel Tolliver* gives a more serious scene. Ike Varner, the most popular African American in town, has to cope with an oversexed wife. One night, thinking Ike is in town, she flirts with the Freedmen's Bureau agent as he walks past her home. The agent rebuffs her, but Ike, hiding, shoots him, a murder attributed to Gabriel. Harris's works also add a twist to the portrayal of African Americans as children. As Darwin T. Turner pointed out years ago, an alternative is to depict them as docile old men: "The old-time male darkies are sexless. Uncle Remus is ancient. After tending to Miss Sally when she was a child, he is a nurse and companion for Miss Sally's son and grandson. Uncle Plato and Hamp Perdue have wives, but romance and sensuality cannot be associated with their marriages. Among the Negro men, only aging Daddy Jack courts a woman, but his flirtation with teen-aged Tildy suggest comedy rather than romance. Whether young or old, Harris's Negro men give their love only to their masters." Even Cable, the courageous author of "A Freedman's Case in Equity," draws on stock stereotypes in describing Cornelius Leggett's courtships of far too many women. To be sure, Leggett's promiscuity matches that of his former owner, Reverend John Wesley Garnet, but the stereotypes remain. They dominate an unsuccessful scene when Cornelius woos his latest flame one night while she is working as a servant for the Marches, who are away. Ahead of him, a white townsman intent on courting John's widowed mother comes to the window to kiss her, but he kisses instead the black servant wearing Mrs. March's finest dress. Cornelius uses the occasion to exact a bribe for his silence.[21]

Portraying responsible African American husbands and fathers, neither Tourgée nor Chesnutt indulge in the stereotypes used by Cable. But even in *The Marrow of Tradition*, *The Colonel's Dream*, *A Fool's Errand*, and *Bricks without Straw*, the scenes of romance involve whites, with Tourgée's two works having a northern woman courted by a southern male, who significantly is the one who surrenders. To be sure, Tourgée and Chesnutt wrote novels featuring characters within the tradition of the tragic mulatta, who can pass as white. But in Tourgée's *Pactolus Prime* and Chesnutt's *The House Behind the Cedars*, which in part responds to Tourgée's romance, we have unmanly white suitors who abandon their lovers once they learn about their racial status; there are not manly African American suitors. In Tourgée's earlier *Toinette*, revised and retitled *A Royal Gentleman*, a southern plantation owner is fully aware of his lover's racial status and refuses to marry her. A courageous soldier, who was "first over the walls of Fort Steadman," he would "rather have faced Fort Hell at its hottest" than marry Toinette. As she asks, "Where was his manhood, that he should sit down like a child and say 'I would, but I dare not'?" (*RG*, 450, 449, 446).

William Dean Howells's *An Imperative Duty* and Harper's *Iola Leroy* counter those plots by depicting white men—both doctors—whose love triumphs over any lingering racial prejudice. In *Iola Leroy* we finally get an honorable black male suitor, Dr. Latimer, for whom Iola rejects the white doctor. Hopkins's *Contending Forces* and *Hagar's Daughter*, as well as Griggs's *Imperium in Imperio*, follow Harper in portraying black courtships. Even so, the courtships in all four novels either draw on the romance of mixed race or emphasize factors other than romance. Dr. Latimer's courtship occupies a small part of a short chapter called "Wooing and Wedding," whereas Harper devotes pages to the courtship of Iola's white planter father and her mixed-race mother, who was born a slave. What brings Iola and Dr. Latimer together is not so much romance as their shared commitment to elevate their race. The same is true of the Booker T. Washington figure Dr. Lewis, who marries Dora Smith in *Contending Forces*. In contrast, Will Smith's romantic courtship of the mysterious Sappho is firmly entrenched in conventions associated with the tragic mulatta. Indeed, the action of the book is framed by the tragic story of an allegedly mixed-race marriage under the reign of slavery. Similarly, in *Hagar's Daughter* almost all the scenes of courtship and marriage involve allegedly mixed-race women. In Griggs's novel, courtships are also dominated by questions of racial mixture. The marriage of the mulatto Bernard Belgrave is thwarted by the suicide of his lover, who adheres to an ideology of racial purity. Belton Piedmont's courtship culminates in marriage but is subverted when the light skin of the couple's child causes Belton unjustly to accuse his wife of having an affair with a white man. Belton eventually recognizes his mistake and becomes a loving husband and father. Nonetheless, at the book's end, he abandons wife and son and returns to be executed, devoted more to a cause than to his family.

This paucity of scenes of romantic courtship most likely results from the felt need to counter stereotypes of oversexed African Americans. Dr. Miller's manhood as a father devoted to his family also challenged the figures of Harriet Beecher Stowe's Uncle Tom and Harris's Uncle Remus, neither of whom were fathers. Once again Tourgée proved innovative. In almost all novels of passing, the protagonist's mother is of mixed race or colored and the father is white. But in *Pactolus Prime*, Pactolus is the father of a beautiful daughter passing as white. Although to protect her station in life he cannot reveal his relationship to her, he is a devoted father, providing her with financial security and love. Equally poignant are Tourgée's portraits of faithful and responsible African American fathers and husbands in *A Fool's Errand* and *Bricks without Straw.*

Most notable is Nimbus in *Bricks without Straw.* Immediately after the war, Nimbus avails himself of a new law allowing him to marry in order to legitimate his children. In signing the marriage contract, he tries, unsuccessfully, not to record what people assume to be his last name, hoping to keep his children from inheriting the name of a slaveholder. As he tells a friend, "I ain't a-gwine ter brand my chillen wid no such slave mark" (*BS*, 119). Dixon alludes to a similar sentiment in *The Traitor,* when the husband of the three-hundred-pound Aunt Julia changes "his name several times after the war" for fear that retaining his master's name would serve as "the badge of slavery" (65). Indeed, Dixon might have laughed at Tourgée's African Americans' response to Nimbus's attempt to sever his nominal connection to slavery. "'Yah! Yah! Yah!' echoed the dusky crowd behind him. 'You's jes' right dah, you is! Nigger mighty little use fer heap o' names. Jes' like a mule—one name does him, an' mighty well off 'ef he's 'lowed to keep dat'" (*BS*, 113). Forced by the law to retain his nominal connection to slavery, Nimbus nonetheless goes to work to become a breadwinner for his family by buying land with his military savings and, with his mule, turning it into a productive tobacco farm.

A husband and father's role as breadwinner recalls how important self-reliant labor was for the period's model of manhood. In a transformed economy, northerners, like Tourgée, questioned the manhood of the leisure, planter class, while southerners emphasized their own tradition of self-sufficient, Jeffersonian yeoman farmers. Complicating matters was the transformation of African Americans from slaves to freedmen, expected to conform to the manly ideals of contractually based free labor. Women's increased presence in the labor market added yet another complication. In his most famous speech, Booker T. Washington extolls the virtues of self-reliant labor and praises the managers of the Atlanta Exposition for recognizing the "value and manhood of the American Negro." Nowhere, however, does he refer to African Americans as breadwinners for their own families. Instead, he emphasizes their former loyalty to white families, "nursing your children, watching the sickbed of your mothers and fathers." Without noting the irony, Washington appeals to his white audience by assigning to African Americans the traditional feminine role of nursing. That slippage is revealing. Former slaves were not the only ones affected by the new reign of contract. Under the law of coverture, married women were supposedly not allowed to enter into contracts. Until the passage of married women's earnings acts, the wages they earned legally belonged to their husbands. Although husbands and fathers were still considered the breadwinners for their families, women played a larger role.[22]

In Reconstruction fiction, many white southern women, either widowed or having inherited a family estate, continue to hope that marriage will solve their financial difficulties. But there are exceptions. Woolson's Bettina Ward opts to be a teacher. Page gives us Blair Cary, who helps put bread on the table for her impoverished family by also becoming a teacher, and Miss Bush, Leech's abandoned wife, who has to make ends meet by teaching. During the war, Leech's wife served as a nurse, that other traditional female occupation. Chesnutt has the white Laura Treadwell give piano lessons. He also depicts African American women joining the labor market. Rena tries to support herself by teaching, and Dr. Miller opens a school for African American nurses. Harper's Iola serves as a nurse and then turns to teaching, after her efforts to work as a saleslady fail because of racial prejudice. Hopkins's Ma Smith runs a boarding house, and Sappho takes on Hopkins's profession as a stenographer. New England schoolteachers occupy the background of *A Fool's Errand*, and *Bricks without Straw* foregrounds the teacher Mollie Ainslie. In a generally positive review of Tourgée's two novels, Howells goes out of his way to praise the portrayals of Nimbus and Eliab Hill while claiming that Tourgée misses a "fine opportunity for dramatic success and poetic justice" in his portrayal of Mollie. She is, for Howells, too unambiguously positive. A more "honest" characterization of her motives would have helped the novel. But Howells fails to note how Tourgée was, again, ahead of his time. Mollie does more than occupy the traditional female role of a teacher. She becomes an entrepreneur, making money through shrewd investments. Tourgée, who defended the right of women to practice law, had earlier depicted a strong white southern woman from the yeoman class. In *Toinette*, Betty Certain takes control of a plantation when her aristocratic husband is murdered. She runs it with great skill and efficiency. Possessing exceptional physical strength and courage, when she is attacked she fights one man with an ax and wrestles another to the ground. She is a white version of Nimbus's wife

Lugena, who bravely protects her children with an ax and then supports them when her husband has to flee the state to protect himself. Indeed, Betty forms an alliance with Toinette, who has served as a nurse during the war and later becomes a successful singer.[23]

The new contractual economy may have created possibilities for women as well as for freedmen, but, having once touted the advantages of paternalistic chattel slavery over contractual "wage slavery," white southerners quickly learned how to exploit contracts to thwart black's self-reliant manhood. Laws were passed declaring anyone without a contract for labor a vagrant subject to a fine. Those unable to pay the fine had to work for the state to settle their debt. Unfair in themselves, such laws were made even worse when combined with the convict-lease system dramatized in *The Colonel's Dream*. With slavery formally abolished, the convict-lease system created a new form of slavery by exploiting a loophole in the Thirteenth Amendment to contract the involuntary labor of prisoners to private parties without the paternalistic obligations of the old system. Chesnutt exposes the system by having the colonel paternalistically rescue a former family slave by bidding at public auction for the involuntary labor of the man who watched over him when he was a young boy.

For Du Bois the forces keeping African Americans from becoming manly, self-reliant workers were more systematic. Like Chesnutt, he calls attention to the convict-lease system. But the major problem for him is "the written and unwritten law of peonage" (*SBF*, 127). Nowhere was peonage more apparent than in the system of sharecropping. Arguing that the South found a way to prosper despite carpetbagger mismanagement, the historian Allan Nevins in 1927 claimed that "the number of small farmers continued to increase, partly through the break-up of old plantations, partly through the occupation of neglected lands. It was a section in which the poor man, white or black, found it remarkably easy to establish his independence." "The share system," he insisted, "was decidedly to the advantage of the Negroes as a whole." In contrast, Du Bois shows how the contracts African American sharecroppers entered into were decidedly to their disadvantage. Peonage was perpetuated by migration-agent laws, restricting employers from enticing workers to move from one state to another, and by the legally enforced system of credit and debt. Debt was the reason why African Americans could not fulfill the "dream of philanthropist and statesman" (*SBF*, 128) and become self-sufficient landowners: "The keynote of the Black Belt is debt" (118). Debt condemns freedmen to a position of dependency and encourages black laborers to remain "shiftless." "They are careless because they have not found that it pays to be careful; they are improvident because the improvident ones of their acquaintance get on about as well as the provident" (128).[24]

As Du Bois knew, the system that kept African Americans in debt was not confined to the South. Sharecropping primarily produced cotton, and subjection to King Cotton despoiled the land and people's lives. Introducing his reader to "the Cotton Kingdom,—the shadow of a marvelous dream," Du Bois goes on: "And where is the King? Perhaps this is he,—the sweating ploughman, tilling his eighty acres with two lean mules, and fighting a hard battle with debt" (107). But the ploughman is losing the battle because "cotton is down to four cents." During the Civil War, faced with the blockade of the South, Great Britain encouraged cotton production in India. Thus, after the war, the South faced stiff competition for its primary cash crop. In Du Bois's account, "Debt," capitalized and personified, stares the freedman in the face.

Scholars attending to the economics of Reconstruction continue to debate how to characterize the sharecropping system. Did a farmer pay half of his crop to the landowner as rent for tenancy or did the landowner pay half of the crop to a farmer-employee as wages? If the former is true, the system was consistent with peonage and perpetuated the tradition of a slave economy. If the latter is true, the system marked an economic revolution, which, as Charles Beard's student Louis M. Hacker argued, was the "triumph of American capitalism." If farmers were wage earners, they should be seen as "rural" proletariats, not peons. Given these choices, Du Bois's description of African American workers as proletariats within a system of peonage might seem a contradiction. In fact, it suggests that the economy of the New South was a hybrid, not yet full-blown capitalism but also not simply a vestige of slavery. As the convict-lease system showed, that economy relied on the capitalistic assumptions of contractual labor to maintain control over the labor of former slaves. Whereas, prior to Emancipation, defenders of slavery pointed to its benevolent paternalism to resist any interference from the national government, in the new economy the paternalism of the national government was needed to protect freedmen from a contractual system with the potential to perpetuate peonage.[25]

For Du Bois, the only way to escape an economic system that deprived African Americans of their proper manhood was through the agency of suffrage, which would force politicians to respond to their interests. "Negroes must insist continually, in season and out of season, that voting is necessary to modern manhood" (*SBF*, 70). Du Bois's link between suffrage and manhood can be traced to a February 5, 1866, speech by Charles Sumner that, for Du Bois, "laid down a Magna Charta of democracy in America" (*BR*, 193). According to Sumner, "The ballot is a *schoolmaster*. Reading and writing are of inestimable value, but the ballot teaches what these cannot teach. It teaches manhood. Especially is it important to a race whose manhood has been denied" (*BR*, 195). To Sumner's belief that the ballot educates people "into the principles of government," (*BR*, 195), Du Bois adds that, in modern society, it is through the "power of the ballot" that men exercise the right of "self-defence" (*SBF*, 43). In identifying the right to vote as a form of self-defense, Du Bois echoes the utilitarian philosophers Jeremy Bentham and John Stuart Mill, but he is also working within an African American tradition inaugurated by Frederick Douglass. Condemning Booker T. Washington's failure to insist on the right to vote, Du Bois praises Douglass for having "bravely" stayed true to "the ideals of his early manhood" (*SBF*, 66). As Douglass's famous autobiography reveals, that manhood was achieved, as a slave, on the one hand, when he learned to read, which opened him to education, and, on the other hand, when he courageously resisted the brutality of the slave master Covey by fighting him. For one generation of African Americans, self-defense manifested itself in military service; for Du Bois's generation, it corresponded to suffrage. Yet, by 1903, when he published *The Souls of Black Folk*, the right to vote was almost universally denied African Americans in the South.

Not surprisingly, Dixon turns disfranchisement into a question of manhood. In *The Leopard's Spots*, an order goes out to the Klan to threaten each African American the night before the election. Dixon's narrator assures us that, in fact, any African American who showed up to vote would be allowed to do so. But, "Any man, black or white, who can be scared out of his ballot is not fit to have one. . . . The ballot is a force. This is simply a matter of manhood" (*LS*, 162–63). In an age when the franchise was restricted by literacy tests, Dixon would have preferred tests of manhood.

For a collection called *The Negro Problem*, published in 1903, Chesnutt contributed an essay called "The Disenfranchisement of the Negro." Likewise, the final section of his "The Courts and the Negro" is called "The Right to Vote." It describes the judiciary's response to disfranchisement, paying close attention to the 1903 case of *Giles v. Harris*. On behalf of himself and five thousand African Americans in Montgomery County, Alabama, Giles brought forth a bill in equity, demanding relief for being denied the right to register to vote. Writing for the majority, Justice Oliver Wendell Holmes Jr., denied the request, noting that "equity cannot undertake now, any more than it has in the past, to enforce political rights." If the conspiracy to keep blacks from voting was as powerful as alleged, he concluded, "unless we are prepared to supervise the voting in the state by officers of the Court, it seems to us that all the plaintiff could get from equity would be an empty form." Having stripped the Enforcement Acts of their power, the court had already registered its unwillingness to support such supervision even if the executive branch was willing to provide it. Now it used that lack of supervision to deny appeals to correct the injustice.[26]

V

For African Americans, the court's decision in *Giles* was devastating. But it points to an issue that must be addressed in any account of African American manhood in this period: the role of governmental paternalism. If, in order to exercise their right to self-defense, African Americans had to seek governmental protection, was the right to suffrage a sign of self-sufficient manhood or proof that they could not advance without special help from the government? During argument for the *Cruikshank* case, one of the defendants' attorneys, David Dudley Field, was asked about the implications of his argument for *United States v. Reese,* which involved voting rights. He responded, "If eight hundred thousand voters cannot secure the rights to which they have been declared entitled, then that is the best argument that they are not worthy of them." Similarly, education may have been a vehicle to manhood, but, as we have seen, it seemed dependent on what some considered unconstitutional aid from the national government. In his argument against the Blair Bill, G. W. Curtis cited Armstrong's maxim, "Take out the self-help, and the rest is not worth much." By the end of the nineteenth century, the popular image was that African Americans had not even helped emancipate themselves. In 1890, Alabama senator John Tyler Morgan expressed the widely held opinion that, unlike Native Americans, African Americans had passively submitted to slavery. For Morgan, the Fourteenth and Fifteenth Amendments themselves were proof of African Americans' "natural inability to preserve their freedom, and to enjoy in its blessings" without the government giving "them higher and more definite security for their liberties than was provided for the white race."[27]

Whereas many white Americans were not as virulent in their racism as Morgan, most did think that African Americans owed their legal rights to governmental paternalism. The Supreme Court's response was, however, quite different. Sincerely convinced that emancipation had transformed the southern economy into a full-fledged capitalist one, most of the justices were not prepared to deal with the hybrid economy that actually existed. Along with racism, that economic assumption, and a desire to maintain dual federalism guided the court's logic. Thus, with a majority of the justices staunchly antipaternalistic, in a series of decisions, it refused to grant freedmen more security for their liberties than it provided for white men. In 1883, the watered-down Civil Rights Act of 1875 was challenged. Phillips, then solicitor general, defended the bill before the Supreme Court. But Justice Bradley, who in 1873 had notoriously argued that the Fourteenth Amendment did not give women the right to practice law, insisted that freedmen must "take the ranks of a mere citizen" and cease "to be the special favorite of the law." Thus, "his rights as a citizen and a man are to be protected in the ordinary modes by which other men's rights are protected." The *Plessy* court agreed, adding that the law is incapable of guaranteeing social equality of the races.[28]

The court's rejection of paternalism is most explicit in *Hodges v. U.S.* (1906). In Arkansas a group of whites used violent intimidation to keep African Americans from entering into contracts for their labor. The African Americans appealed to the federal government, citing the Thirteenth Amendment and claiming that these actions imposed upon them a badge of servitude. Justice David Brewer wrote the court's opinion. Of all the justices on the court, Brewer, a relative of the Fields and the son of missionaries, was most sympathetic to Chinese immigrants' claims for rights. He had also dissented in *Giles v. Harris*, along with Justice Harlan and Justice Brown, who wrote the *Plessy* opinion, a case in which Justice Brewer did not take part. Even so, Justice Brewer in *Hodges* ruled that the Thirteenth Amendment did not apply. "When the problem of the emancipated slave was before the Nation," he insisted, it "might have left them in a condition of alienage, or established them as wards of the Government like the Indian tribes, and thus retained for the Nation jurisdiction over them, or it might, as it did, give them citizenship." They were given citizenship because the nation "doubtless believed that in the long run their best interests would be subserved, they taking their chances with other citizens in the States they should make their homes." For Justice Brewer, citizenship did not entail governmental protection in private relationships; it meant achieving the status of individual self-reliance that made special governmental protection unnecessary.[29]

A few years before Justice Brewer's ruling, Dixon has his scalawag politician in *The Leopard's Spots* justify manipulation of the freedmen's vote by claiming that the African American "is the ward of the Republic—our only orphan, chronic, incapable. That wardship is a grip of steel on the throat of the South. Back of it is an ocean of maudlin sentimental fools. I am simply making the best of the situation" (264). The situation changes "when the Anglo-Saxon . . . [is] united into one homogeneous mass" by the Spanish-American War (413). Now, "The Negro was no longer the ward of the republic. Henceforth, he must stand or fall on his own worth and pass under the law of the survival of the fittest" (418).

Dixon's novel affected public opinion. *Hodges v. U.S.* influenced the law by rendering the Thirteenth Amendment almost powerless to combat racial discrimination. Many today would agree with *Jones v. Mayer* (1968), in which the court restored some of the amendment's power by declaring, "Insofar as *Hodges* is inconsistent with our ruling today, it is hereby overruled." Favorably viewing *Jones v. Mayer* as finally fulfilling the intention of the Civil Rights Act of 1866, one scholar claims that the benefits of the Freedmen's Bureau and the Civil War Amendments were produced by a "sort of federal welfare" philosophy. Nonetheless, it is important to remember that the majority in *Hodges* felt that the decision was properly treating African Americans as equal citizens before the law, not as wards of the government. There were, of course, problems with that view. As we have seen, starting with the *Slaughter-House Cases* (1873), the court defined the privileges and immunities of US citizenship so narrowly that the protection of almost all fundamental rights was left to individual states, with the national government refusing to intervene. When the national government tried to intervene by passing the Civil Rights Act of 1875, the court declared it unconstitutional. In fact, for many people in the country, intervention by the US government would have been interpreted as a sign of paternalism and proof that African Americans were incapable of achieving full manhood on their own.[30]

Remedies, I have said, are harder to identify than wrongs. We will search literature in vain for solutions to the paradox of paternalism. Even so, as "the language of paradox," it does register its complexities. Portraying black professionals more than any writer of the period, Chesnutt challenges stereotypes that African Americans could not rise. Nonetheless, his focus on professionals has opened him to charges of class bias that legitimates laissez-faire arguments opposing governmental interference into the market. The most vocal critic of Chesnutt's class-consciousness is Walter Benn Michaels, who condemns him for portraying racial discrimination while neglecting economic inequality. Significantly, Michaels bases his argument on a scene in a Jim Crow car from *The Marrow of Tradition* with allusions to the *Plessy* decision, a perfect example of the paradox of paternalism. At the same time that the majority endorsed the laissez-faire doctrine that the government was powerless to help African Americans advance socially, it upheld a state's right to impose racial segregation in the name of the welfare of "the people." Michaels's misreading of Chesnutt's use of *Plessy* shows how, even today, critics are unprepared to deal with the paradox of paternalism. I quote at length.

> One of the most important and even alluring facts about racism is that even CEOs and doctors and lawyers can be its victims. No scene more vividly captures this phenomenon than the famous and controversial train chapter in Charles Chesnutt's novel *The Marrow of Tradition*, written in 1901, a few years after the decision in *Plessy*. Two doctors, a black one and a white one, friends and colleagues back in Boston, are traveling south together. When they reach the Virginia border, the conductor tells the black one that the car he's riding in is now for whites only and he is made to move to the colored car, where he finds himself among a group of what Chesnutt calls "noisy, loquacious, happy, dirty and malodorous" "farm laborers." . . . And [the doctor] wishes that the "classifica-

> tion of passengers" on the trains "might be made on some more logical and considerate basis than a mere, arbitrary, tactless, and, by the very nature of things, brutal drawing of the color line." . . . [Chesnutt's] point is that the doctor—as doctor—doesn't belong to a race, and if there's a line to be drawn between him and the other passengers, it should not be the arbitrary and illogical color line but rather the "more logical" method of classification the text hopes for. Indeed, that classification is the one already in place before the train arrives in Virginia (and it's the classification that resisted Jim Crow laws the longest). Its method is economic: it divides the world not into black and white or white and Jew but into first class and coach, into rich and poor. And its logic is the logic of the market: you get what you are willing and able to pay for. The color line, from this standpoint, is arbitrary because it interferes with the efficiency of the market. And, by the same token, Chesnutt criticizes the state that enforces Jim Crow as insufficiently liberal, since its police power is invoked against rather than on behalf of what he himself called "liberty of contract"—his right to buy whatever ticket he wants. . . . The injustice in Chesnutt, then, is that racism and the drawing of the color line interfere with the market. If you're forced to ride with the malodorous farm laborers because you're poor, that's unfortunate but not unfair. If you're forced to ride with them because you're black, that's another story. So the poor are not victims of discrimination; they are the unfortunate by-products of an essentially just mechanism—the market. Poverty, in other words, is not a civil rights issue. . . . The problem in Chesnutt is not that the farm laborers can't afford to ride in the clean comfortable car; it's that some people who can afford to (like Dr. Miller) aren't allowed to.[31]

Michaels's fundamental flaw is to claim that Chesnutt endorses a contractually based market economy. To be sure, a staunch Republican, Chesnutt believes in the ideal of free labor. Nonetheless, he is fully aware of how the South's hybrid economy used contract to perpetuate peonage. According to Michaels, Chesnutt embraces "the logic of the market: you get what you are willing and able to pay for." In fact, that is the logic of the laissez-faire *Plessy* majority. Anticipating the majority, Henry Field wrote, "There is a plain rule of justice, which ought to be recognized and enforced, viz: that every man is entitled to what he pays for. If there be on the part of whites an unwillingness to occupy the same cars and sit in the same seats with blacks, let them be separate, only let equally good cars be provided for both, if both pay for them." Far from agreeing with such logic, Chesnutt strongly disagrees with it. To be sure, Miller, unlike most blacks and whites, can afford to pay for a first-class ticket. But when he is not allowed to sit with his professional peer, there is no equally good car for him to occupy, Chesnutt's reminder that blacks are considered so economically inferior that a first-class car is not even provided for them.[32]

Chesnutt emphasizes this point by dramatizing how allegedly fair separate-but-equal laws are arbitrarily enforced. When Miller enters the colored car, it is not, as Michaels reports, occupied by farm laborers. Instead, it is empty until uncouth, but rich, Captain McBane enters, smokes, spills ashes, and spits. McBane is one of three white supremacists intent on disfranchising African Americans. When Miller insists that he be removed from his car, the conductor refuses, undercutting his earlier insistence that the separate-but-equal law must be enforced. "The beauty of the system lies in its strict impartiality—it applies to both races alike" (*MT*, 55). Chesnutt knows that this was an important legal argument. The *Plessy* majority ruled that the Louisiana Jim Crow law did not violate the equal protection clause of the Fourteenth Amendment because it applied equally to both races. In showing that in fact the law was administered unequally, Chesnutt likely had in mind the case of *Yick Wo v. Hopkins* (1886), cited by the *Plessy* court. In the earlier case, a California law regulating laundries was declared unconstitutional because, although it seemed to apply equally to all, it was administered unfairly. Chesnutt tries to make a similar case for Jim Crow laws.

Michaels's criticism of Dr. Miller's lack of class awareness is similar to attacks that legal historians Kenneth Mack and Barbara Welke have made against black professionals in general for complaining about their exclusion from first-class accommodations rather than focusing on improving the lot of black workers. Kate Masur answers Mack and Welke by defending protests that, admittedly, stressed caste more than class. "The denial to elite African Americans of first-class accommodations or integrated seating arguably epitomized racial expression better than did the exploitation of black laborers. For even if African Americans could escape the drudgery of labor and a hand-to-mouth existence, the racial 'caste' system meant they could never command the same respect as their white counterparts." Furthermore, there is ample evidence that Chesnutt is aware of the problems faced by working-class blacks. For instance, Miller is not told to sit in the "colored" car at the Virginia border but "far down in Virginia . . . at a station beyond Richmond" (*MT*, 52). Miller is confronted here because he has bought a ticket in the "sleeping-car, where the separate-car law does not apply" (54). It is only when the sleeper is disconnected that Miller and Burns have to move into day coaches, and the conductor approaches them. If Chesnutt had wanted to have Miller and Burns separated the moment they entered a Jim Crow state, he would have had the conductor interfere at the Maryland border, not the Virginia border. But he wanted to point out the arbitrariness of Jim Crow laws. Miller can travel through the entire state of Maryland and most of Virginia unaffected by laws mandating segregation, so long as he can afford a ticket for a sleeping car. Without that economic privilege, he would have been separated the moment the train entered Maryland. The racism behind Jim Crow can tolerate a black man having first-class accommodations in a private sleeping car, but it cannot tolerate him sitting publicly in any car for whites, whether first class or coach, unless he is in a subservient position. The conductor, after all, would have allowed Miller to sit in the "white" car, if he were Burns's servant. This point is reinforced later in the episode in a scene that Michaels neglects. At a station, Miller observes as a "coloured nurse found a place [in the white car] with her mistress" (*MT*, 59). This detail alludes to a provision in the 1890 law challenged by *Plessy* that exempted nurses from separate car restrictions. Miller's response mirrors Tourgeé's argument in his brief to the court. "White people . . . do not object to the negro as a servant. As the traditional negro—the servant,—he is welcomed, as an equal, he is repudiated" (*MT*, 59).[33]

After McBane leaves the colored car and before the farm laborers enter, there is another important moment that Michaels neglects. At a stop, Miller sees "a huge negro, covered thickly with dust," who is dangerously hitching a ride on "one of the rear trucks" (*MT*, 58–59). Climbing off to get a drink, the man sees McBane and casts "a glance of intense ferocity" (59) toward the white racist. So poor that he cannot afford a ticket, this man is Josh Green. Later, we learn that as a young boy Josh hid and watched as McBane, leading the Ku Klux Klan, murdered his father. Indeed, with conscious irony, Chesnutt turns to Josh and his vow of violent revenge on McBane directly after Miller consoles himself about the fate of African Americans by quoting, "Blessed are the meek, for they shall inherit the earth" (62). Michaels assumes that Miller's point of view is Chesnutt's point of view, that what Miller hopes for, "the text hopes for." As this passage makes clear, though, Chesnutt complements Miller's professional point of view with Josh's. Indeed, working-class Josh is so important for the episode's dramatic action that the chapter ends with him, not with Miller. If Miller is a victim of race, Josh is a victim of both race and class.[34]

Despite Josh's importance, Michaels mentions him only briefly, calling him "one of the 'malodorous' farm laborers." In fact, Josh is a stevedore. Alert to issues of class, Chesnutt is attuned to the labor his characters perform. Whereas black farm laborers were in a position of dependency in the agrarian economy of the South, Josh is vulnerable to the New South's industrial economy. Both economies use contracts to keep African Americans in subservient positions. Michaels claims that Chesnutt embraces "liberty of contract," which was the laissez-faire doctrine used to restrict governmental interference into the economy. But the only time "liberty of contract" appears in the novel, it is used by the African American journalist Barber to describe the marriage contract, not a labor contract (*MT*, 85).

Although cautious Dr. Miller questions Barber's boldness, Chesnutt uses the radical journalist to point out the hypocrisy of laissez-faire advocates who support the state's right to prohibit interracial marriage but deny the state's right to regulate labor contracts. In making that point, Chesnutt is by no means advocating contract as the basis for all economic relations. On the contrary, he recognizes that the contractual system replacing the slave economy continued to make African American laborers vulnerable. At its worst, it underlay the convict lease system. The son of a slave overseer, McBane, "had held, until recently, as the reward of questionable political services, a contract with the state for convict labor, from which in a few years he had realized a fortune" (34). But more is at stake than the convict lease system. Lacking the paternalism of the old system of chattel slavery, the hybrid economy of contract and peonage had no new safeguards. As General Belmont, another white supremacist, gloats, "we are better off without slavery, for we can get more out of the free negro, and with less responsibility" (88).

Chesnutt depicts a full range of working-class African Americans after slavery's paternalism. In addition to agricultural laborers and industrial laborers like Josh, there are servants. Sandy is employed by Mr. Delamere, an old southern gentleman, who provides him with paternalistic protection. This trusted relationship between master and servant is one we could find in Page or Harris. But with Delamere's death Chesnutt signals the demise of that tradition. As in Dixon, the representative of the Old South is replaced by one of the New South. In Chesnutt, the result is decline rather than progress. Just as honorable, paternalistic Judge Straight of *The House Behind the Cedars* is replaced by *The Marrow of Tradition*'s Judge Everton, who will not intervene to stop a possible lynching, so the lawyer Delamere is survived by the political demagogue and lawyer General Belmont, another of the white supremacists. Servants in the new regime, Chesnutt makes clear, can expect no paternal protection. As Major Carteret, the third white supremacist, tells Delamere, who is trying to protect Sandy, "This man is no longer your property. The negroes are no longer under our control, and with their emancipation ceased our responsibility" (*MT*, 212). A sign of the new regime is the fate of Carteret's loyal, deferential servants Mammy Jane and her grandson Jerry. "If all the colored people were like you and Jerry," the major tells Jane, "there would never be any trouble. You have friends upon whom, in time of need, you can rely implicitly for protection and succor" (44). Instead, both are slaughtered in the massacre set off by Carteret, Belmont, and McBane's campaign of racial hatred.[35]

A young nurse temporarily caring for Carteret's infant son represents an alternative to employment as a servant. A graduate of a mission school, with "some instruction in Dr. Miller's class for nurses" (42), her relationship with the Carterets is based solely on a contractual cash nexus. "They gave her nothing but her wages, and small wages at that, and she owed them nothing more than equivalent service. It was purely a matter of business; she sold her time for their money. There was no question of love between them" (42). Recognizing that something is lost in this new arrangement that lacks the bonds of affection controlling Mammy Jane's loyalty, Chesnutt describes the young nurse as "in what might be called the chip-on-the-shoulder stage, through which races as well as individuals must pass in climbing the ladder of life" (42). During this transitional period, the question is: Who will care for working-class blacks?

The answer seems to be the African American professional class. Josh works not for a white but for Miller's brother, who inherited their father's thriving business. Whereas Michaels claims that Dr. Miller and Dr. Burns are traveling together from Boston, where they are "friends and colleagues," Miller is in fact returning from New York where he has purchased equipment for his hospital that will provide medical services for the African American community. Even though working-class blacks are economically more vulnerable than Dr. Miller and his brother, the prosperous Miller brothers cannot provide the paternal protection they would like because racial discrimination is not confined to class. In the book's culminating racial massacre, Miller's hospital is burned to the ground. Lacking anyone to turn to for paternal protection, African Americans understandably looked to the government. But in a country that considers, even to this day, provisions for the health of all of its citizens a paternalistic governmental intrusion, they found little support.[36]

One period that did not distrust governmental intervention and economic redistribution was the New Deal. Writing at that time, Howard K. Beale retrospectively pondered a solution to the condition of freedmen that highlights how pervasive the paradox of paternalism remained. "Suppose," he wondered, "that, on some such plan as the Dawes and Burke acts for Indians, the Negro had been given land and then been treated as a ward? Suppose he had gradually been given control of land distributed to him to become economically experienced?" Today, almost all scholars agree that the Dawes Act, while well intentioned, was a disaster for Native Americans. It was in part a response to the court's decision in *Elk v. Wilkins* (1883), which denied a Native American man birthright citizenship after he renounced tribal loyalty and tried to register to vote. Designed to encourage Native Americans to integrate into white society, the act rewarded them with private land if they left their tribes. Of course, much of that governmental land had once belonged to tribes, and the effect was to create conflict within the Native American community and to undermine traditional customs. Even so, since the situations of African Americans and Native Americans were different, maybe Beale's solution would have helped. Certainly, giving freedmen land would have been a positive measure. But another work of fiction helps us see why similar plans at the time failed.[37]

John William DeForest served as a Freedmen's Bureau agent in Greenville, South Carolina. *Miss Ravenel's Conversion* (1867) gives a sense of the conditions he faced. Dr. Ravenel of Louisiana is firmly convinced of the moral necessity of emancipation. In the chapter "Re-Organize Southern Labor," set in the midst of the war, the occupying army gives him oversight of a plantation and assigns former slaves to work for him, for which they "receive some remuneration—not for the bygone centuries of forced labor and oppression—but for what they will do hereafter" (*MRC*, 229). The doctor tells his laborers: "You can become useful and even influential citizens if you will. But you must be industrious and honest, and faithful to your engagements. . . . You will work ten hours a day during work season. You will be orderly, honest, virtuous, and respectable. In return, I am to give you rations, clothing, quarters, fuel, medical assistance, and instruction for your children. I am also to pay you as wages eight dollars a month for first-class hands, and six for second-class. Each of you will have his little plot of land. Finally, I will endeavor to see that you are all, old and young, taught to read" (243). The difficulties the doctor faces are registered in a letter he receives from Captain Colburne, the book's protagonist, who is also a convinced abolitionist. Having been assigned a lazy African American aide, Colburne writes the doctor and warns him that many freedmen are not trained to work. His aide, Colburne ironically notes, made Wendell Phillips a prophet when he proclaimed that "the negro is the only man in America who can afford to fold his arms and quietly await his future." Dr. Ravenel responds that Colburne is "too impatient. . . . God has chosen to allow himself a hundred years to free the negro. We must not grumble if He chooses to use up a hundred more in civilizing him. . . . What right has Captain Colburne to demand roses and potatoes of land which has been sown for centuries with nothing but thistles? We ought to be thankful if it merely lies barren a while" (252–53). Later, when rebel forces take over the plantation, Colburne and a freedman give Dr. Ravenel and his daughter cover as they escape with the former slaves in their charge. In an act of bravery, shouting "like a lion," the freedman sacrifices himself to help the others (292).

Despite its obvious caution, this incident seems to endorse the task DeForest faced as a Freedmen's Bureau agent. In fact, it raises serious questions about how to accomplish that task. Dr. Ravenel's efforts are based on a program instituted by General Nathaniel Banks in occupied Louisiana. Assigning former slaves to a plantation, it treated them as wards of the state in which they underwent a transition period of apprenticeship. For instance, it did not allow them to bargain for other employment, and it required a pass system, ostensibly designed to stop the spread of smallpox, restricting free movement. Banks defended his policy as the best way "to *prepare* the Negro for as perfect an independence as that enjoyed by any other class." As Du Bois pointed out, however, the military's plan was in competition with those proposed by planters, "immigrant Northern capitalists," and the long-standing community of free people of color in Louisiana. The latter advocated putting the system of labor on a "democratic footing" by leasing plantations to "'gangs' of laborers working for their own account. Seeds, mules, and agricultural implements were distributed among these freedmen—not as a gratuitous gift, but in the character of a loan, leaving to the laborer all his dignity and independence." In contrast, Banks's plan was a "system of serfdom with schools and many excellent features, but with other provisions which insulted the free Negroes and hindered real emancipation" (*BR*, 457–58).[38]

The response Phillips made to Banks (to which Colburne alludes) grew out of this debate. "If there is anything patent in the whole history of our thirty years' struggle," Phillips insisted, "it is that the Negro no more needs to be *prepared* for liberty than the white man." Frederick Douglass unequivocally sided with Phillips, claiming that Banks's policy "practically enslaves the Negro, and makes the Proclamation of 1863 a mockery and delusion. What is freedom? It is the right to choose one's own employment." Banks's policy determines for "the so-called freedman, when, and where, and at what, and for how much he shall work, when he shall be punished, and by whom punished. It is absolute slavery. It defeats the beneficent intentions of the Government, if it has beneficent intentions, in regard to the freedom of our people."[39]

The controversy over how to reorganize the system of labor in Louisiana points to numerous complications. Clearly, the plan Du Bois mentions of long-standing freed people of color leading "freedmen toward economic emancipation" is abstractly the best. Nonetheless, as even Du Bois recognized, it had to confront the practical problem of dealing with laborers conditioned by years of slavery. Many, like Colburne's aid, lacked an internalized work ethic. To be sure, this plan provided incentives for them to work for their own profit. But to reap profit from their labor, they needed to market their goods. That required training and experience. Indeed, although the plan eliminates the paternalism of both former planters and the military, it depended on a Freedman's Aid Association financed by wealthy members of Louisiana's substantial community of free people of color. Commendable, that paternalism, according to the military, had to contend with a tradition of "bitterness of feeling among the slaves and the free people of color" (*BR*, 459). Whether such class antagonism existed or not, few southern states outside of Louisiana could rely on a wealthy community of free blacks. In those states, former slaves making the transition to free labor turned to the national government and the Freedmen's Bureau as an alternative to the paternalism of planters, carpetbaggers, or the military. Douglass's criticism of Banks's plan encapsulates the ideological dilemma the bureau faced. On the one hand, Douglass embraced the ideal of free labor. Workers should be free to choose their own employment. On the other, he insisted that government should display beneficent intentions toward freedmen. But how can the labor market be free if the government has policies designed to favor a particular group? On the one hand, Douglass wanted newly emancipated slaves to be free to contract their labor with whomever they wanted. On the other, he certainly supported provisions by which the Freedmen's Bureau could interfere with labor contracts it considered unfair.

VI

No institution raised the specter of paternalism more than the short-lived Freedmen's Bureau. Writing in 1902, the political scientist John W. Burgess acknowledged that "it would have been a moral outrage" for the government not to have provided freedmen some assistance "during the transition into the new status." Nonetheless, he contended that the bureau's administration did as "much harm as good" precisely because it did not allow for a transition period modeled on the apprentice system of the sort Banks proposed. Instead, according to Burgess, the freedmen got something for nothing.

> When the government began to furnish them with food, clothes, fuel and shelter gratis, they, like the children that they were, conceived of this, to them, a very agreeable state of things as something that was to last forever, as the New Jerusalem. They gathered about the depots of the Freedmen's Bureau and could not be induced to go away in search of work or a livelihood. The belief became quite general that the Government intended to give every man forty acres of land and a mule, and otherwise support him permanently. The danger was that the newly emancipated would quit work altogether and throw themselves entirely upon the charity of the United States Government. Many did do so, and formed thus a sort of privileged class throughout the whole South under the protection of the Government of the United States.[40]

Burgess's belief that the paternalistic protection of the bureau turned former slaves into a "privileged class" was widely shared. In much of the period's fiction, corrupt agents were to blame. The *New York Times* called Page's villainous Leech in *Red Rock* an accurate description. If Harris's agent in *Gabriel Tolliver* is not quite as corrupt, he is responsible nonetheless for leading African Americans astray and depriving them of their "child-like gaiety" (*GT*, 114). The freedmen themselves "ain't no more to blame for all of this than a parcel of two-year-old children" (258). In *The Leopard's Spots,* Dixon repeats typical attacks on the bureau. "If the devil himself had devised an instrument for creating race antagonism and strife he could not have improved on the Bureau in its actual workings." Even so, with his belief in a possible positive role for the government, Dixon does admit, "Had clean-handed, competent agents been possible [the Bureau] might have accomplished good." Instead, "these agents were as a rule the riff-raff and trash of the North. They were lifted from penury to affluence and power. The possibilities for corruption and downright theft were practically limitless" (*LS,* 75). These lowly characters "have absolute power over all questions between the Negro and the white man" (42), including the power to dictate the terms of labor contracts and to prohibit freedmen from working for a white person. In one scene General Worth has to lose four days of labor because he is summoned by the bureau on the charge of an African American who has a grudge against him. When Worth arrives, the African American is so intimidated that he drops his charges. But when it comes time to settle annual contracts, the general is forced to pay an extra fifteen hundred dollars, despite explicit language to the contrary. The agent delivering the judgment is Reverend Ezra Perkins, a man with "Mormon whiskers" (78), who after losing "his church because of unsavoury rumors about his character" had become a "book agent and then an insurance agent" (75). All is not lost, however, because the general seeks the help of a Union soldier, Major Grant, who has "learned to like you Southerners" (77) and promises to fix things with Ezra.

In *The Clansman,* Dixon's indictment of the bureau is accomplished in a few pithy sentences. Linking false promises by the bureau, misguided education, voter corruption, and shiftless African American workers, he writes, "Everyman was to receive forty acres of land for his vote, and the enthusiastic speakers and teachers had made the dream a resistless one by declaring that the Government would throw in a mule with the forty acres. Some who had hesitated about the forty acres of land, remembering that it must be worked, couldn't resist the idea of owning a mule." He goes on, "The Freedman's Bureau reaped a harvest in $2 marriage fees from negroes who were urged to make their children heirs of landed estates stocked with mules" (*CM,* 238–39). Turning the bureau's effort to remedy the prohibition on marriages under slavery into a hypocritical ploy to "reap" a profit rather than encourage freedmen to harvest crops, Dixon also mocks its effect on African American manhood, through his reference to mules. Under the paternal influence of the bureau, African Americans will bequeath to their heirs estates teeming with animals unable to reproduce themselves.

In *The Souls of Black Folk,* Du Bois offers a different account of mules and inheritance. Trying to make a living raising cotton as a sharecropper, an African

This cartoon was used in the 1866 Pennsylvania gubernatorial campaign. It plays on the fears of whites that the Freedmen's Bureau encouraged African American idleness at the expense of hard-working white taxpayers, depicted in the background chopping wood and ploughing the field. The bureau is imagined as a building resembling the US Capitol with the inscription: "Freedom and No Work." Library of Congress.

American man laments that his "mule died last week." He then adds, hopefully, "but a white man loaned me another." The hope fades, however, as the loan generates more debt. When the man's son in the city asks the "struggling father" for money, there is none. "And so the son rose in the night and killed his baby, and killed his wife, and shot himself dead. And the world passed on" (*SBF*, 114–15).

For Du Bois, the Freedmen's Bureau helped people avoid tragedies such as this account of fathers and sons. He defends the bureau without denying some of its flaws. Significantly, he admits its paternalism. In the sentence before his comment on the emasculating effects of slavery, he acknowledges that the government, through the bureau, assumed "charge of the emancipated Negro as the ward of the nation" (50). In doing so, it risked having its "paternalistic methods" discourage "self-reliance" (58). Nonetheless, Du Bois insists, a period of paternalism was necessary to give freedmen time to grow into self-reliant manhood. Unfortunately, the Bureau was prematurely disbanded "before its work was done" (60). The vote, Du

Bois argues, became the primary source of self-defense only because the bureau no longer existed. Du Bois admits that after emancipation "every sensible man, black and white" would have agreed to "restricted Negro suffrage," based on education, but that option was never possible. Instead, there was a "choice between suffrage and slavery" (59–60). Even so, Du Bois does not place the entire blame on racists. Some responsibility lay with the bureau itself. "It came to regard its work as merely temporary, and Negro suffrage as the final answer to all present perplexities" (60). "So," Du Bois laments, "the Freedman's Bureau died and its child was the Fifteenth Amendment" (60).

For Du Bois, the paradox of paternalism is captured in this image of African Americans forced to exercise the manly art of self-defense by relying on "the child" of a prematurely dead paternal institution. If suffrage had been protected and nourished by a biracial coalition, it could have become the avenue to African American power that someone like Sumner hoped it would become. But that development was not allowed because "many a scheme of friendliness and philanthropy, of broadminded sympathy and generous fellowship between the two [races] has dropped still-born because some busybody has forced the color-question to the front and brought the tremendous force of unwritten law against the innovators" (*SBF*, 145). As a result, the vote as a "child" was not sufficient to provide adequate protection. Yet the North turned to it, "rather than pay the cost of social uplift on the scale which an efficient Freedmen's Bureau evidently demanded" (*BR*, 222). Ending *Souls* by returning to metaphors of birth, Du Bois pleads with his reader that "my book fall not still-born into the world-wilderness" (*SBF*, 195).

No more able to solve the paradox of paternalism than Du Bois, Tourgée uses similar imagery for a different effect. Although the court insisted that African Americans were not wards of the state and needed to be treated the same as other citizens, Tourgée, like Du Bois, recognized the need for a transitional period. Thus, a chapter in *A Fool's Errand* is called "Citizens in Embryo." "Slavery might be ended as a legal status by proclamation," he writes, "but as a living fact it could not. The hands could be unshackled by a constitutional amendment, but heart and brain must have an opportunity to expand, before freedom could be capable of automatic liberty" (*FE*, 132). The paternal function of the Freedmen's Bureau allowed for that expansion: "When the war ended there were four millions of men, women, and children without homes, houses, lands, money, food, knowledge, law, right, family, friends, or possibility for self-support. All these the Bureau adopted. They constituted a vast family of foundlings, whose care was a most difficult and delicate matter, but there was not one among them all who complained of the treatment they received" (*BS*, 158). The bureau accomplished this difficult feat in large part because of the motivation of the freedmen and the integrity of its agents. Most agents "were chosen from among the wounded veteran officers of our army, or were detached from active service by reason of their supposed fitness on account of character or attainments. Almost every one of them had won honor with the loss of limb or of health; all had the indorsement [*sic*] and earnest approval of men in command of our armies, who had personal knowledge of their character and believed in their fitness" (157). With the bureau's demise, however, that character and fitness came under attack. "The poor thing is dead now, and, like dead humanity, the good it did has been interred with its bones. It has been buried, with curses deep and bitter for its funeral obsequies. Its officers have been loaded with infamy" (155), depicted as "thieves and vagabonds—corrupters of the blacks and oppressors of the whites" (158). Blacks had been branded inferior by the institution of slavery; now service in the bureau was an "ineffaceable brand of shame" (156).

The works of Page, Harris, and Dixon prove Tourgée right. Dixon goes so far as to have General Worth ask Major Grant, "Why couldn't they put soldiers into the Bureau if they had to have it, instead of these skunks and wolves" (*LS*, 77). In contrast, Du Bois acknowledges that "the qualities that make a good soldier do not necessarily make a good social reformer" (*BR*, 223). Although both Du Bois and Tourgée lamented the premature death of the bureau, Tourgée, more explicitly than Du Bois, acknowledged the inadequacy of freedmen relying only on the Fifteenth Amendment for self-defense. Tourgée fought for African Americans' right to vote, but he also chastised Charles Sumner for "exulting too quickly when he declared that by giving the ballot to the freedman we had 'chained him to the chariot-wheel of American progress'" (*AC*, 72). Given the continued power of the southern oligarchy, it was naïve to believe that "enfranchisement was all that was required to cure all the ills which hitherto had afflicted, or in the future might assail," newly emancipated slaves (*FE*, 250). On the contrary, "the freedman is," the Fool writes to his former northern mentor, "just as impotent now of all power of self-protection as he was before the ballot was given him" (170). The right of suffrage needed to be complemented by the protection and training provided by the Freedmen's Bureau.

Like Du Bois, Tourgée blames more than white southerners. His primary target is northern Republicans, who, motivated by the political goal of winning elections in the South, devised a Reconstruction policy that enfranchised African Americans, assuming that the right to vote was all freedmen needed to protect themselves. "From this womb of party necessity and political insincerity came forth this abortion, or rather, this monster, doomed to parricide in the hour of its birth" (*FE*, 133).

With his charge of parricide, Tourgée switches the terms of the debate, questioning the manhood not of African Americans but of those controlling the national government after the fratricide of the Civil War. Charged with giving the nation a new birth of freedom, they instead gave birth to a monstrous policy that undercut the paternal function every government has to protect the rights of its citizens. It was, in short, lack of manhood in the "Wise Men" of the North that undercut efforts of freedmen to develop as men. For Tourgée, Reconstruction's only chance of success was for the "Wise Men" to support a coalition of carpetbaggers, scalawags, and freedmen. Instead, they abandoned all three to the overwhelming power of the entrenched southern establishment. As a result, the responsibility for Reconstruction's failure "will rest now and for all time with the Republican party of the North,—a party the most cowardly, vacillating, and inconsistent in its management of these questions, that has ever been known in any government" (*FE*, 171). In the aftermath of war, southerners displayed far more manhood than their northern counterparts.

Nowhere was this more apparent than on the question of state versus national sovereignty that we examined in chapter 2. Supposedly the Civil War had decided the question, but for Tourgée, except for the right to secede, "the doctrine of 'State Rights' is altogether unimpaired and untouched by what has occurred" (*FE*, 377). In continuing to recognize the sovereignty of individual states, the nation failed to assert its own right of self-defense. For instance, responding to the Fool's call to "make the spelling-book the scepter of national policy," a character asks, "But how shall these citizens of the States be educated by the Government without infringement of the rights of the States?" (*FE*, 388). Tourgée's answer is slightly different from Du Bois's. Like Du Bois, he feels that in a republic the right to vote must be considered a right of modern manhood. But for him, it is in the nation's, not simply the individual's, self-defense to educate all voters—white and colored. As Pactolus Prime puts it, arguing with a congressman, "Does not the whole theory of National aid to education rest in the idea that the ignorant voter is a source of actual peril—less likely to know what he ought to do and quite powerless to do even what he may perceive ought to be done?" The "Nation," Pactolus insists, has "the right, in order to provide for the 'general welfare of the United States,' to declare that every man who holds a ballot shall be enabled to read it" (*PP*, 119–20).

Failing to defend itself through education, the nation was even more lacking in manhood in its response to the Ku Klux Klan. Whereas it could have declared the Klan's "acts treasonable" (*FE*, 189), it reacted to the "potent instrumentality" of the Klan with the "impotency of the law" (191). The major cause of that impotency was the failure of the national government to assert the sovereignty it won in the war. "The South surrendered at Appomattox," Tourgée quipped, but the nation "has been surrendering ever since."[41]

Tourgée's claim that the nation, not African Americans, lacked manhood raises the thorny issue of agency. Confronted with orthodox accounts that dismissed freedmen's role in Reconstruction, Du Bois amassed a vast amount of evidence in *Black Reconstruction* to prove how instrumental they were. Under Du Bois's sway, many critics today rightly condemn works of fiction that portray freedmen as pawns in the hands of ruthless scalawags and carpetbaggers. But, as Du Bois knew, agency is not a black and white issue. Too much stress on agency can feed the myth of self-reliance used to deny governmental aid to freedmen. A prime target of Tourgée's ire was Horace Greeley's admonition: "Root, hog, or die!" (FE 137). Through Bob Martin, Nimbus, and Uncle Jerry Hunt, Tourgée shows how mistaken Greeley and others were. Despite displaying considerable independence and courage, all three characters are defeated. Uncle Jerry suffers the worst fate. Confronted with violence from the Klan, he has "an idea that his race must, in a sense, achieve its own liberty, establish its own manhood, by a stubborn resistance to aggression" (225). Jerry's view should "have been the correct and proper one," but holding it turns out to be a "fatal error" (252, 192). Given the conditions at the time, African Americans did not have the resources to combat the entrenched white elite in the South. Linking Uncle Jerry to the Fool and his errand, the narrator notes that the black minister's "appeal to arms may be heroic, but it is the heroism of folly, the faith—or hope, rather—of the fool" (225). For his folly, Uncle Jerry is lynched.

Faulting Tourgée for denying African Americans agency in education in *A Fool's Errand* but praising him for recognizing it in *Bricks without Straw,* Peter Schmidt writes, "Within the space of one year . . . , Tourgée rethought both how his fiction represented blacks and how it defined the aims and methods of black education. His portraits of black leaders shift significantly, from stressing dependency to stressing agency, the right of blacks to define their own destiny." Without a doubt, *Bricks* has a fuller portrait of an African American community than *A Fool's Errand.* But it is highly questionable that "within the space of a year" Tourgée had an epiphany that moved him from blindness to insight on black agency, especially since he began *Bricks* before *A Fool's Errand.* As much as he was concerned about African American rights, he would not have considered agency a "right." People do not have a right to "define their own destiny"; they have to define it within concrete historical circumstances. The circumstances that freedmen faced make the opposition between dependency and agency far too simple.[42]

We see this in *Bricks* when Tourgée advocates blacks taking over their own school. Nonetheless, the preacher Eliab Hill, who is earmarked to become the teacher, first has to be taught by Mollie, the New England schoolteacher. When the Klan brutally beats Eliab for what it considers his pretensions, he survives only because Hesden Le Moyne, the southern planter turned radical, defies the community by secretly nursing him back to health. Regaining minimal health, with white financial support, Eliab still has to go north for a professional education. On Christmas morning, Hesden "rode to the depot nearest his home, purchased two tickets to a Northern city, and, when the morning train came in, . . . lift[ed] from a covered wagon which stood near by, the weak and pallid form of the long-lost 'nigger preacher,' Eliab Hill, and place[d] him upon the train. It was noticed by the loungers about the depot that Hesden carried but half concealed a navy revolver which seemed to have seen service" (*BS*, 358).

Eliab's agency, like everyone's, depends on support from others. Given their historical circumstances, freedmen needed governmental support to exercise their agency. It is precisely such support that Eliab's best friend Nimbus lacks in his battles with the Klan and, later, white supremacists in Colfax. Nimbus, however, does not give up. At the end of *Bricks without Straw*, Tourgée, insisting on Nimbus's unflinching manhood, has him reunited with his family, heading west to start a new life, riding not a mule but the iron horse of a newly constructed railroad.

VII

Eliab's and Nimbus's escapes from the South on railroads add yet another complication to the paradox of paternalism. The supposedly free market replacing the regime of slavery was dominated more by businesses formed through combinations than by self-reliant individuals. Chesnutt hints at this complication in "The Partners," which appeared in the *Southern Workman*, published by the Hampton Institute in 1901 and intended primarily for African American readers. The story traces the lives of two freedmen who are "among the human flotsam and jetsam that followed in the wake of the Civil War" (PA, 253). William Cain and Rufus Green want to be self-sufficient, but they lack proper training. "Slavery had not been a good school for training in self-reliance" (253). Noting how white folks do business, they decide to enter into a partnership, with a legal contract sealing the deal. For a while they work at odd jobs just to survive. Then an opportunity arises. "A Northern philanthropist, filled with the fine, post-bellum zeal for the freedmen, purchased at a low price an extensive plantation in the vicinity of the town, which he cut up into small farms, and, for the encouragement of industry and thrift among the Negroes, sold to them at prices little more than the nominal" (254). William and Rufus buy the last two lots but are told that a partnership is "incompatible with the development of self-reliance and strength of character, and that their best interests would be promoted by their learning each to fight his own battle" (254). Both marry and try to develop their farms independently. William succeeds, and Rufus does not. Their friendship is marred by a feud between their wives, and eventually they have a dispute over water rights. They hire a surveyor, who is the previous owner of the plantation, resentful over the present state of affairs. Finding a flaw in the title to Rufus's farm, he travels north to locate a descendent of the philanthropist, who "had died in comparative poverty." For a small sum he procures a quitclaim deed to the land, including all of Rufus's improvements, and begins an action in ejectment. Rufus's attorney loses the suit on a technicality, even though "a better advocate might have won it" (258). Without a home, Rufus is abandoned by his wife, who starts to take in laundry for white people. When William hears about the fate of his former friend, he reconciles with him, loading Rufus's belongings on a cart—led by a horse, not a mule—and takes him in. They renew their partnership, with William confident that his attorney can win back Rufus's land on appeal.

The story has a clear lesson. As the narrator points out, the philanthropist's original idea "was a contradiction" (PA, 255). At the same time that he paternalistically told the freedmen what sorts of agreements they could reach with one another, he preached self-reliance. But, "A thoughtful student of history might have suggested to the philanthropist that the power of highly developed races lies mainly in their ability to combine for the better accomplishment of a common purpose" (254). As William W. Cook put it in 1893, "It is true that the wonderful success of modern business is dependent upon combination; that by combination capital is obtained, enterprises of magnitude conducted, great results accomplished; and that every partnership and every corporation is a combination." Freedmen, Chesnutt suggests, were held to a standard of self-reliance that did not apply to the white business community.[43]

Having studied law while working as a stenographer in the Cleveland office of the Nickle Plate Railroad Company, Chesnutt knew that the major business combinations at the time were railroads. In his novels, they usually play a progressive role, bringing commerce and new ideas to isolated and provincial parts of the South. Tourgée also supported building new railroads. In *Bricks without Straw,* they do more than provide blacks with a lifeline out of the South. Mollie makes a fortune after she moves to Kansas by wisely investing in property near a proposed new line. As much as Tourgée was attracted to the progressive potential of railroads, however, he also knew they had been allowed to undermine the democratic ideals of a truly reconstructed nation. In the preface to *Murvale Eastman, Christian Socialist,* he writes, "Transportation, by far the greatest business of the country, is controlled by fewer individuals than any other. There are many railroads, but all are parts of or dependent upon a few 'systems.' Probably less than a score of men actually control the transportation of the United States, the earnings of those engaged in it and the profits of those dependent upon it. So much power over the comfort and prosperity of so many has never been wielded by so few" (*ME,* ii). Indeed, during this age that celebrated self-reliance, the prime example of governmental paternalism was not the Freedmen's Bureau but the massive governmental subsidies to build railroads for the profit of a few. Freedmen never got their forty acres and a mule, but railroads got huge stretches of governmental land—and more. Granting subsidies to attract railroads was arguably more a cause of financial corruption and overspending in Reconstruction governments than handouts to freedmen. Once lines were built, redeemed regimes worked hard to make sure that these symbols of national progress were segregated. In the next chapter, I turn to the works of María Amparo Ruiz de Burton, recognized as the first important Mexican American author, to explore her and other authors' portrayal of railroads. Having socialized with a number of the major figures of the times, Ruiz de Burton shows how important railroads were in the era of Reconstruction and how they connected the West to the issues it raised.

-5-

RUIZ DE BURTON AND RAILROADS

The Westward Course of Reconstruction

At the end of *Who Would Have Thought It?*, María Amparo Ruiz de Burton alludes to a rift in the Republican Party during the crucial election of 1872, the year the book was published. The year before, faced with Charles Sumner's opposition to his plan to annex Santo Domingo, President Ulysses S. Grant sent the Radical Republican's close friend Frederick Douglass to the Caribbean with a team of negotiators. On the return voyage, Douglass was forced to dine separately, an affront heightened when Grant failed to invite him to a White House dinner with the commissioners. Sumner exploited the incident, questioning Grant's commitment to African Americans and trying, unsuccessfully, to convince Douglass to join him and Liberal Republicans in supporting Horace Greeley. Ruiz de Burton clearly sides with Grant, ridiculing any suggestion that Douglass had been offended and mocking Sumner's highly publicized speech "Republicanism v. Grantism" by including one called "Cacklism v. Grantism."[1]

The book's ending shows how closely Ruiz de Burton followed the details of Reconstruction politics. It also indicates how idiosyncratic her political positions were. They followed as much from self-interest and personal acquaintance as from principles of political economy. For instance, in *Who Would Have Thought It?* Cacklism is identified with the massive corruption that Ruiz de Burton, the wife of a career military officer trained at West Point, knew accompanied the war effort. Promotions frequently were awarded because of political connections, not military competency, and unscrupulous officers channeled governmental expenditures into private bank accounts. For Ruiz de Burton, as for John William DeForest, who chronicled similar corruption in *Miss Ravenel's Conversion* (1867), the graft of the Gilded Age followed directly from such wartime practices. A major motive for Liberal Republicans' break with Grant was the corruption associated with his administration. By linking Cacklism with Sumner, whose integrity was rarely questioned, Ruiz de Burton reverses that opposition, associating a "black"

Republican she hated with corruption and a West Point graduate and personal acquaintance with impeccable honesty.[2]

Ruiz de Burton's idiosyncratic political positions deserve our attention in part because the personal acquaintances that helped to shape them were so extensive. She was born in Baja, California. During the Mexican-American War, she met and married the American military officer Henry S. Burton while he was commanding occupying forces. The new Catholic bride moved with her New England Protestant husband to Alta, California, in 1847. Because of his military deployment, for a while before and after the Civil War, she lived in Georgetown and Washington, DC. She became friends with Mary Todd Lincoln, frequently attended White House events, and was close enough to Grant to ask him to find her son a job in the New York Custom House or an appointment at West Point or Annapolis. After the war, her husband took command of Fortress Monroe where Jefferson Davis was imprisoned. The Burtons became friends with the Davises. Mrs. Davis later commented on how graciously they treated her husband after he had been abused by the former commander. "Very soon after my arrival [at Fortress Monroe] General Burton called with his cheerful, affectionate wife, and they were, from the first day until the last, most kind and considerate to us." After her husband died in 1869, she maintained these connections and added others. Although she would villainize Collis Huntington and Leland Stanford in her fiction, in California she dined with the former and her daughter spent time with Stanford's wife. She also knew prominent figures in her native country of Mexico, including members of its delegation to Washington, DC.[3]

In addition to being important because of the contacts that formed them, Ruiz de Burton's views are worthy of our attention because they help counter the tendency in political criticism to make literary works conform to positions that, after the fact, we decide are representative of a period. That tendency is especially strong with Reconstruction, whose politics seem so black and white by today's standards. But individuals do not adopt political positions to fit our retrospective sense of what is representative. Although seemingly inconsistent, Ruiz de Burton's views give us access to different positions available at the time, reminding us, for instance, that an admirer of Grant could criticize Reconstruction or that even a Radical Republican like Sumner could find reasons to ally himself with a candidate whose proposed New Departure, when taken over by President Hayes four years later, would lead to the Compromise of 1877.

Ruiz de Burton's positions are equally revealing in *The Squatter and the Don: A Novel Descriptive of Contemporary Occurrences in California*, originally published in 1885 but set during the years 1872 to 1876. The late twentieth-century republication of this novel inaugurated a national project aimed at reconstructing the literary history of Hispanics in the United States. In the book, Don Mariano Alamar, the don of the title, describes the conquered Mexicans of California as having "no one to speak for them" (*SD*, 66). The editors of this 1992 edition celebrate Ruiz de Burton for giving voice to those Californios by exposing how, despite provisions in the Treaty of Guadalupe Hidalgo (1848), they lost their land to Anglo squatters backed up by corrupt legislators and judges. The book details even more governmental corruption, as the squatters and the Don become victims of the corporate greed of the Big Four who helped to build the transcontinental railroad and who exercise monopolistic control of lines in California. Written from the vantage point of 1884, the final chapter, "Out with the Invaders," looks back on the book's action and urges the people to resist the "*imperium in imperio*" set up in California by the Central Pacific (341). "The very act of writing and publishing this historical romance," the editors claim, "was a form of empowerment for the collectivity" that created "a narrative space for the counter-history of the subaltern" (7).

It did not take long, however, for José Aranda to question this "subaltern thesis." For instance, set in the period of Reconstruction, *Squatter* also sympathizes with the South. When the squatters invade San Diego County to make spurious claims for Don Mariano's land, they carry "carpet-bags" (*SD*, 69). Later, the Don, complaining about the lack of "right and just legislation," fears that "the Congressmen from the north do not seem to feel all the interest they should in reviving the south" (166). Congress, we are told, does not "respect the rights of the Southern people" (203). Most important is that Ruiz de Burton champions the Texas Pacific Railroad designed to connect the South with San Diego. Proposed by Colonel Tom Scott, the Texas Pacific promises to transform the sleepy town of San Diego into a prosperous center of trade and commerce. It will also allow the South to flourish economically. "The construction of the Texas Pacific," we are told, "ought to be advocated by every honest man in the United States, for it is the thing that will help the exhausted South to get back its strength and vitality" (274). Yet, trying to maintain its monopoly on transcontinental traffic, the Big Four work to block Scott's plans, deafening Congress to the "wail of the prostrate South, or the impassioned appeals of California" (200).[4]

The members of the Big Four are such obvious targets that even Aranda has been taken in by the populist fervor of Ruiz de Burton's attack on the Central Pacific. But her anticorporate rhetoric is misleading. After all, she attacks one corporate giant only to advocate another. Nonetheless, *Squatter*'s portrayal of railroads reminds us that Reconstruction was more than a program for advancing the rights of freedmen. It was also supposed to reconstruct materially a South devastated by war. In DeForest's *Miss Ravenel's Conversion*, almost all of southerner Dr. Ravenel's money is tied up in railroad stock. When those railroads are destroyed by the Union Army, he and his daughter lose their entire investment. After the Civil War, railroads throughout the South had to be rebuilt. But more than rebuilding had to take place. No longer based on a slave economy, the South needed new lines to restore prosperity. New lines would also help heal the wounds of war by easing sectional divide and linking former enemies as part of an interconnected web of markets. The effect was not only economic. The completion of the transcontinental railroad in 1869 played an important symbolic role in reassuring the nation that unity had been restored. Along with quotations from former presidents, Martin Luther King Jr., Anna Julia Cooper, and a Mohawk prayer, every US passport contains the inscription on the monument to the Golden Spike at Promontory Point: "May God continue the unity of our country as the railroad unites the two great oceans of the world." As a character in DeForest's *Honest John Vane* (1875) counsels a congressman, "Unite the North and South. . . . Close up the bloody chasm. Bind together the national unity in chains of cast-iron" (*JV*, 90).[5]

New England's Reverend Henry Field agreed. Field had one brother working for railroad giant Jay Gould, another delivering a notorious Supreme Court opinion favorable to Huntington, and another famous for using new technology to connect distant lands. Henry became friends with Henry Grady in 1880 after his brother Cyrus loaned the Georgian twenty thousand dollars to buy an interest in the *Atlanta Constitution*. At the same time, H. Victor Newcomb, president of the Louisville and Nashville Railroad, agreed to guide Grady's stock speculation to help him pay back the loan. Newcomb befriended Grady after the reporter wrote glowing stories about him, calling Newcomb "the Napoleon of the railroad world," who saved the Louisville and Nashville during the Panic of 1873 by securing loans in London. In *Blood Is Thicker than Water* (1886), a record of his train trip through the South, Henry insisted that railroads helped reconcile former enemies. "In our country railroads had a political as well as commercial value. They, and only they, could prevent our Union of States from becoming unwieldy the larger it grew, and dropping apart by the fact of enormous extension." For Ruiz de Burton that unity was possible only if a transcontinental line connecting the South to the West complemented the one connecting the North to the West.[6]

Squatter, with its political battles over railroads, is an ideal work of fiction to trace the impact of Reconstruction on the West and vice versa. To do so we have to look both from West to South and from South to West. We need, in other words, to bring the resources of Reconstruction studies usually applied to literature of the South to bear on a work whose criticism has been dominated by those trained in Hispanic/Latino or Western literary studies. We also need to look at novels of Reconstruction from an economic perspective. The Gilder Lehrman Institute of

American History dates "The Civil War and Reconstruction" from 1861 to 1877, followed by "The Rise of Industrial America" from 1877 to 1900, with the Gilded Age as part of the latter. Similarly, literary critics frequently bring economic analysis to bear on novels of the Gilded Age, while focusing on issues of race for the literature of Reconstruction. But the Gilded Age is not separate from Reconstruction; it overlaps with it. Charles Warner and Mark Twain published the novel that gave the Gilded Age its name in 1873. Economic issues, like the devastating Panic of 1873, affected racial politics, and racial politics affected responses to economic problems. Unless we want to follow the logic of one of Thomas Dixon's characters in *The Leopard's Spots* (1902), who thinks that questions of race are "more important than any theory of tariff or finance," we need economic analysis of works associated with Reconstruction as much as racial analysis of works associated with the Gilded Age (*LS*, 161).[7]

II

Vincent Pérez attempts economic analysis of *The Squatter and the Don* by arguing that Ruiz de Burton sympathizes with the lost plantation culture of the South because of her nostalgia for a lost hacienda culture of Alto, California. But that comparison does not hold for a variety of reasons. For Ruiz de Burton, one of the supreme examples of legislation that helped "law-breakers" (SD, 64) is the new fence law passed in California. By this law, the burden of protecting crops from grazing animals passed from owners of crops to owners of stock. As a result, the Don complains, "any man can come to my land . . . plant ten acres of grain, without a fence, and then catch my cattle which, seeing the green grass without a fence, will go eat it. Then he puts them in a '*corral*' and makes me pay damages and so much per head for keeping them, and costs of the legal proceedings and many other trumped up expenses, until for such little fields of grain I may be obliged to pay thousands of dollars" (64). That, or the squatters simply shoot his cattle. There were also fence laws in the South. In *The Souls of Black Folk*, W. E. B. Du Bois remarks, "I think I never before quite realized the place of the Fence in civilization" (108). But fence laws in the South had a different effect from those in California. In the South, they disadvantaged non-landowning poor whites and blacks. "Access to forage enabled landless whites and blacks to raise work animals and other livestock of their own. With a horse or a mule, a cow and some hogs, a tenant could strike a better contract and meet part of his family's basic needs." The new laws spelled ruin for people whose economic independence relied on the tradition of common grazing land, even as part of private plantations. As Du Bois writes of a poor African American, if not for "the new fence law . . . he might have raised a little stock and kept ahead"

(*SBF*, 113). The same laws that disadvantaged hacienda owners in California advantaged plantation owners in the South.[8]

As this example shows, Ruiz de Burton is not an agrarian. Her vision is for the New South, not the Old South. With most of her southern allies former Whigs, her economics are developmental and commercial, not agrarian. Although she associates squatters with carpetbaggers, Clarence, the book's hero, proudly identifies himself as a "money-making Yankee" (*SD*, 332). He accumulates wealth by investing in mines and stocks, even though his father, the "Squatter" of the book's title, "thinks stock gambling is next to robbery" (109). Clarence also feels that "it is a pity that such men as Don Mariano and his sons do not have some other better-paying business than cattle-raising" (152). The Don himself speculates in real estate and tries to convince the squatters that they "can make more money by following other laws that are more just, more rational" (90). The most obvious indicator of Ruiz de Burton's developmental vision is, however, her strong support of the Texas Pacific. For Ruiz de Burton, railroads effected a temporal transformation, accelerating time as if years were "condensed into the space of a few days." That new sense of time distinguished prosperous and productive economies from backward and stagnant ones, such as those in Mexico and San Diego without the Texas Pacific.[9]

Tom Scott's railroad stirred southern memories of J. C. Calhoun's plan to ally South and West through a program of internal improvements. It also recalled antebellum debates over the best transcontinental route. At a commercial convention in Memphis in 1845, prominent southerners met and proposed a southern route that would open the "West to southern influence and settlement." Momentum picked up during the administration of Franklin Pierce, who surrounded himself with southern expansionists. He dispatched one to Spain to negotiate the purchase of Cuba. Mexico was also a target. The Mexican-American War did not satisfy the United States' designs on its southern neighbor. Mexico's mineral wealth in northern states was always on expansionists' minds, who also hoped for either a canal or a railroad connection through the Isthmus of Tehauntepec as an east-west trade route. Furthermore, the path for a southern transcontinental railroad would be easier to build with acquisition of more Mexican territory because it would allow the route to avoid mountains close to the existing border. Secretary of War Jefferson Davis favored a line along the thirty-second parallel and pushed for negotiations that led to the Gadsden Purchase.[10]

President of the South Carolina Railroad Company, James Gadsden was one of the most influential figures at the 1845 Memphis convention. He was an ardent advocate of slavery and in 1831 supported the nullification movement. Failing to divide California into a free and a slave state, he tried to get permission to set up a colony in the state using slave labor. Davis got him appointed to negotiate for the purchase of the Mesilla Valley between the Gila and Rio Grande Rivers. The plan gained momentum when the French seemed intent on working a deal to control the Mexican state of Sonora. In 1854, Gadsden convinced President Santa Anna, whose country was in financial difficulty and needed money, to agree to sell more land. Santa Anna also knew that the southern filibuster William Walker had recently led an armed force into Baja, California, and declared himself the first president of Lower California and then the first president of the Republic of Sonora. His filibustering was disavowed by the US government, but when put on trial, he was acquitted. His actions reminded Santa Anna of how vulnerable Mexico was to US force. In negotiations Gadsden warned him that the spirit of the age would eventually lead to the secession of his northern states. With the Gadsden Purchase and favorable surveys commissioned by Davis, the South seemed ready to get its southern route. But it had competition from those advocating a northern route and from Stephen Douglas, who wanted a central route that would favor his home state of Illinois.[11]

Douglas is best known for his debates with Lincoln and his support of the Kansas-Nebraska Act. Prior to the Civil War, southern planters who wanted to extend slavery to the West were constrained by the Missouri Compromise. As Kansas and Nebraska neared statehood, they got support from Stephen Douglas, who argued that the people of the respective territories should have the right to decide about slavery. His doctrine was known as "Squatter Sovereignty." In *Squatter*, Ruiz de Burton mocks this doctrine by claiming that those occupying the Don's lands believe in "*Squatter's Sovereignty*" (*SD*, 62). This mockery might seem inconsistent with Ruiz de Burton's support of the South, but Douglas's primary aim was to appease southerners to get them to support his central transatlantic route.

As even this brief summary shows, the South's proposal was, as C. Vann Woodward puts it, "part of the struggle for control over the Western territories, and part of the contest for sectional balance of power; it was behind the Kansas-Nebraska Act and the repeal of the Missouri Compromise." With the Civil War over and Reconstruction underway, one reporter labeled the renewed effort for a southern route "A National Highway along the Path of Empire." A New Orleans newspaper hailed a South-West line as the "great panacea" that would "release the South from the bondage of the North." Like Grant's imperialist designs in the Caribbean, the proposed lines were motivated by hopes of financial development and profit. Many southerners agreed with a Port Royal editor who thought the annexation of Santo Domingo would bring enough trade to his town to help build a new railroad that would bring even more trade.[12]

Through her connections in Mexico and California and with Davis, Ruiz de Burton knew the details of this entire history. She also knew that railroads played multiple roles in the cultural debates of the times. In addition to being a symbol for a reunited and reconstructed nation, they were also icons of material prosperity and progress. At the same time, they were blamed for the Gilded Age's notorious corruption and the Panic of 1873. All of these views are expressed in Reconstruction fiction. As we saw at the end of the last chapter, although both had concerns about the political power railroads commanded, Albion W. Tourgée and Charles W. Chesnutt generally recorded their positive effects. George Washington Cable's portrayal is more negative. In the chapter "The Golden Spike" in *John March, Southerner,* the townspeople celebrate the opening of the "Pulaski City, Suez, and Great South Railroad." Sounding a bit like Nathaniel Hawthorne in "The Celestial Railroad," Cable observes the people gathered "to hail the screaming herald of a new destiny: a destiny that openly promised only wealth, yet freighted with profounder changes; changes, which, ban or delay them as they might, would still be destiny at last" (*JM,* 142). Railroads do not play much of a role in *Gabriel Tolliver,* but Joel Chandler Harris was highly critical of them. In a 1907 column, Billy Sanders exclaims, "Party don't amount to shucks. The railroads don't belong to no party, an' they're the ones that's doin' what little governin' that is to be done." Sanders goes on to mention Democrat William Jennings Bryan's suggestion that "the gener'l government would have to own the railroads." Thomas Nelson Page did not endorse national ownership. Nonetheless, in *Red Rock* he attacks his fictional carpetbagger government for guaranteeing bonds that will finance a private corporation's construction of a railroad. When someone raises "a question as to the danger to the credit of the State if it should go into the business of endorsing private enterprises," the carpetbagger governor says that the answer is simply to raise taxes, which will force genteel landowners to lose their property (*RR,* 209). Similarly, Thomas Dixon exploits populist sentiment against railroads by blaming their power and the corruption associated with them on Reconstruction governments and carpetbaggers' fiscal irresponsibility.[13]

Dixon's portrayal did not go unchallenged. In his response to *The Leopard's Spots,* Tourgée claims that, whereas the North Carolina "legislature did indeed . . . authorize the issue of railroad bonds in immense quantities, . . . no taxes were levied to pay the interest on them." In fact, the promise of economic benefits garnered bipartisan support for railroads in the South during the early days of Reconstruction. Anticipating the completion of the transcontinental railroad, Edward A. Pollard in *The Lost Cause Regained* (1868) enthuses over a network "forming a great connecting link between Europe and Asia, opening to the Old World the shortest route to China and Japan." Such bipartisan support is documented by Du Bois and William A. Dunning, who includes a map of the national trunkline system of 1875 in *Reconstruction: Political and Economic, 1865–1877.* Dunning's student

J. G. de Roulhac Hamilton reports that in North Carolina, "practically all the bonded debt had been incurred in aiding in the construction of railways and other channels of communication" prior to the Civil War. After the war and before Radical Reconstruction, "in 1866, and 1867, in spite of the economic and financial depression in the State, the public debt was increased by $3,015,000 in aid of railways."[14]

In his negative portrayal, Cable makes it clear that his fictional railroad is strongly supported by both his corrupt African American politician and his equally corrupt southern redeemers. By not acknowledging bipartisan support, Page's criticism, like Dixon's, is hypocritical. As a young attorney, Page worked in the law offices of a railroad. His first cousin, William Nelson Page, was a prominent engineer who helped build the Chesapeake and Ohio Railroad, which is the model for Page's fictional line. Historically, the Chesapeake and Ohio was developed with the aid of Collis Huntington, the supreme villain of *Squatter.*[15]

Ruiz de Burton includes positive and negative views of railroads found in other Reconstruction works. On the one hand, she decries the corrupt and monopolistic practices of the Big Four and the Central Pacific. On the other, she feels that Congress should have subsidized the Texas Pacific to benefit San Diego and the South. For her, then, there were good railroads and bad ones. For Ruiz de Burton, the difference has to do with "fundamental morality" (*SD*, 201). A political economy, for her, is a moral one. As her authority on this point she cites, somewhat surprisingly, Herbert Spencer. Most of us today think of Spencer, who coined the phrase, "survival of the fittest," as a proponent of social Darwinism, which was used to justify the unfair economic divisions of the Gilded Age and beyond. But if laissez-faire advocates cited Spencer to point out the folly of legislating against a naturally ordained economic order, Ruiz de Burton reminds us that for Spencer those laws were the expression of a moral economy. Legislators, according to Don Marino, should not succumb to interest politics but be "the guardians of public morality, the teachers of what is right and just. They should never enact laws that are not founded upon rectitude, as Herbert Spencer says" (*SD*, 161). Later, we are told, "If our legislators could only be induced to adopt Herbert Spencer's view of the *duties of law-givers*, there would be far less misery in the United States" (200). This is because, and here the novel quotes Spencer, what we call "*moral law* is simply a statement of the *conditions* of beneficial action" (201). Conforming to moral law, the Texas Pacific will create conditions of beneficial action. Opposed to moral law, the Big Four's monopoly increases misery in the world.[16]

The Big Four's disruption of the moral order of the world explains why, in rapid succession, one character after another suffers severe illness or disability. At the start of the book, San Diego is portrayed as a bastion of health. Even John Gasbang, one of the worst squatters, proudly proclaims that San Diego is a "most healthy city" with a "perfect climate" (*SD*, 70). Having lost his health by "too close application to business," New York financier James Mechlin had vainly sought recovery in Florida, Italy, and the south of France. Then, on a short visit to San Diego, "his health improved so rapidly that he made up his mind to buy a country place and make San Diego his home" (67). He becomes friends with the Don, and marriages between their families raise the possibility of a harmonious and profitable union of eastern and western interests. Appropriately, Mechlin and the Don invest in the Texas Pacific, which promises to increase the prosperity of all by connecting the two coasts. By the end of the book, however, Mechlin has committed suicide, and his son is crippled, having been shot in the legs by a squatter, who then goes mad. In the meantime, the Don dies of a lung disease, one of his sons contracts a mysterious paralysis, and another son nearly dies in an accident. At one point, Mrs. Mechlin, the Don's wife, and one of the Don's daughters are "in their beds, suffering with nervous prostration and night fevers" (312). Likewise, Clarence's father is a broken man, one of his daughters contracts a severe fever, and Clarence himself nearly dies of typhoid.[17]

Ruiz de Burton is not subtle about the cause of all of this misery. Her world is governed by a natural law that, if followed, will lead to productive harmony. "God intended it should be," she writes (*SD*, 87). "No legislation can change it" (91). But animals and human beings have different relations to it. Cows grazing on crops simply "obey the law of nature" (172). Humans have the freedom to violate natural law. Violations by an influential man can produce "the 'palsy,' the moral stagnation of the man whose power for good or evil extends to millions of people, to unlimited time" (190.) Through his opposition to the Texas Pacific, Huntington brings physical as well as financial misery into the world.

A chapter in the midst of the most intense outbreak of the book's maladies is called "The Snow Storm." It begins with Mechlin's recently crippled son explaining how the fates of his and the Don's families are "entirely based on the success" of the Texas Pacific. If it fails, he observes, "my father will, and Don Mariano will be sadly crippled" (*SD*, 275). To be sure, in that "winter of '74–'75—everybody's hopes were bright. No clouds in San Diego's horizon meant misfortune. Not yet!" (276). The rest of the chapter describes the Don and his sons driving cattle over a mountain when a snowstorm erupts, leading to the Don's pneumonia and the son's paralysis. The next chapter begins with a quotation from Thomas Carlyle about how great men are the "revealed embodied Possibilities of human nature" (281). But the "'*great men*' in California," we are told, "are upas trees, blighting life, spreading desolation, ruin, death upon all they overshadow" (281).

Near the book's end, the chastened squatter Darrell admits responsibility for the Don's death. Clarence, however, insists that the Don's own family believes that "the disappointment of the failure of the Texas Pacific was what killed Don Mariano" (*SD*, 331). Ruiz de Burton does not let Darrell completely off the hook. As Mechlin's genteel New York sister- in-law puts it, "bad-mannered people . . . spread discomfort and discord wherever they are" (187). Darrell is bad mannered toward the Don's family and his own. As the proposed marriages between the two families suggest, the Squatter and the Don could have worked out a productive alliance had the Big Four not destroyed Tom Scott's plans to bring prosperity to San Diego and the South. Instead, there is a "blight, spread over Southern California, and over the entire Southern states" (343).

Ruiz de Burton's Spencerian moralism may generate political positions at odds with ones we generally recognize, but it continues to portray the events of the period in black and white terms. Ruiz de Burton's black and white portrayals grow in part out of her use of satire. She has characters named Gasbang, Colonel Hornblower, and Judge Lawlack. The judge suggests the absence of justice in San Diego. In league with the squatters, he renders judgment after judgment that is overturned by the state Supreme Court. But the process takes years, tying up the Don's land and his financial resources. To illustrate the extent of the corruption that takes place, a lawyer for the squatters tells the story of two litigants. One says, "See here; you had better compromise this suit. Don't you see, on my side I have the law, the equity, the money and the talent?" The other agrees: "You have the law, the equity, the money, and the talent, but *I have the Judge*" (*SD*, 269).[18]

When Ruiz de Burton uses historical figures, however, her black and white satire has a different effect. Even though the Don has legitimate title to his land, as long as it is in dispute, the squatters get to stay. Grant's attorney general has had the suit for two years, but no action is forthcoming. Visiting Washington, DC, with two of the Don's daughters and some of his East Coast relatives, George Mechlin visits the attorney general, who is supportive and surprised that the case was not dismissed by his predecessor. He is about to visit his home state of Oregon but assures Mechlin that he will instruct the solicitor general to ask the Supreme Court to dismiss the suit immediately. When Mechlin finds out that the solicitor general has failed to do so, he meets with him and they argue. Mechlin accuses the official of failing to follow orders. The solicitor general claims that he has the discretion to execute the order or not. The following exchange ensues, starting with Mechlin's response:

> "Ah, I see. The chief might issue an order, but the subaltern might only execute it if he deems it proper."
>
> "I am not a subaltern—I have as much authority—"
>
> "Yes, in the absence of the Attorney General."

"Always—when absent or present."

"Then the department has two heads." (*SD*, 138)

Mechlin goes away without getting any action.

Clearly, the solicitor general is linked to the corruption that frustrates the Don. But neither he nor the attorney general is simply a fictional character. Ruiz de Burton refers to Attorney General Williams, making it clear that she has fictionalized Attorney General George Henry Williams of Oregon, Grant's replacement when Amos Akerman resigned (*SD*, 210). Some historians speculate that Akerman was forced to resign because of his uncompromising prosecution of the Klan, which Williams did not pursue as rigorously. When Grant unsuccessfully nominated Williams for chief justice in 1873, the bar protested that he lacked the requisite "qualities of intellect, experience and reputation." Having ruled against the Union Pacific and under pressure from the railroad lobby, Williams was himself forced to resign as attorney general. Ruiz be Burton portrays this man known as one of Grant's "chief flatterers and hangers-on" as a stellar character and his solicitor general as a scoundrel. Historically, the solicitor general was Samuel F. Phillips, Tourgée's friend from North Carolina, who helped argue the government's case in *Cruikshank* and the *Civil Rights Cases*. Later, with Tourgée, he represented Homer Plessy. To turn Phillips into a character akin to Judge Lawlack and Williams into a hero is an ideological distortion.[19]

When Ruiz de Burton has mixed views of institutions, she tends to have black and white fictional responses. Just as she has two views of railroads, so she has two views of government. California's governmental corruption in *Squatter* parallels that of carpetbagger regimes in the novels of Harris, Page, and Dixon. For Ruiz de Burton, however, California's corruption is not imposed by the national government. On the contrary, she has her characters seek remedy in Washington, DC. In part, her faith in the national government stemmed from her friendship with Grant. The Don's dispute over the title of his land is loosely based on a title dispute Ruiz de Burton had over a piece of land she called Jamal. That dispute was finally resolved in 1876 by a direct order from Grant giving her clear title. But Ruiz de Burton's friendship with the president does not completely account for her belief in the moral power of a central government. Fully to understand Ruiz de Burton's political attitudes, we need to consider her views of Mexico before, during, and after the Civil War. Having grown up in Baja, California, which felt neglected by the central government in Mexico City, Ruiz de Burton, like Confederates, was inclined to champion the sovereignty of individual states. That attitude was modified starting in October 1861, when Great Britain, France, and Spain took advantage of civil war in the United States to send troops to Mexico, demanding that the government under Benito Juárez pay its foreign debt and protect the property rights of European subjects and citizens in Mexico. The European powers made it clear that they would resist any efforts by the United States to bail out Mexico's debt, fearful that this would be a ploy to take control of Mexican affairs. In early 1862, ships with troops entered the harbor at Vera Cruz. The British and Spanish came to an agreement with Mexico, but the French had other designs. They landed troops and engaged Mexicans, with Napoleon III installing Austrian Maximilian on the throne in December 1863. Initially, Ruiz de Burton supported Juárez and the liberals. Then she dramatically reversed her stand.[20]

Her reversal is registered in *Who Would Have Thought It?* when she stages a dialogue between two aristocratic Mexicans after rumor of Maximilian's pending installation gets out. One Mexican is a native, the other is an Austrian immigrant. With the initial invasion by French troops, the two provided financial assistance to Juárez and the youngest joined the military, but both are willing to become loyal subjects of Maximilian. As the native Mexican explains, "Not only will I consider such an act perfectly honorable and patriotic, but I would consider it wrong to oppose the re-establishing of a monarchy in Mexico under a Hapsburg, for the Hapsburgs were, and are, the legitimate and lawful heirs of the glorious Isabella and the great Charles V" (*WW*, 197). During the Mexican war for independence earlier in the century, Spain was ruled by a Bourbon. For Ruiz de Burton's characters, because of improper succession, that monarch was illegitimate and revolution was justified. But the "Mexicans did not want a republic; they wanted a good and just prince" (197). With Maximilian they will have one, and he will provide the Mexican people with what they need most: "a stable government, which would bring to them peace and prosperity and raise them to a high rank among the civilized nations of the world" (196). To be sure, Ruiz de Burton's two characters agree that people would simply laugh at arguments about the right to succession. So they endorse the plan by which a group of Mexicans would claim the authority to invite Maximilian to rule. "To base his throne upon the will of the people is more suitable to the ideas of the present time. . . . A republican form of government is not suited to Mexicans, and it is well that the change be made with *their free approval*" (198).

Ruiz de Burton seems unconcerned that Texas was taken over by the United States when a group claiming to be the voice of the people invited annexation. The sham Bear Flag Republic of California tried to use the same strategy. So did filibusters intent on taking even more Mexican territory. Nonetheless, she would have been aware, as Gregory Downs has recently shown, that the political instability in southern states and the threat of armed conflict over the results of the 1876 election caused many to fear that the United States was undergoing a "Mexicanization" of its politics. She was also acutely aware that in the United States, where the people were supposedly king, there was no hope of restoring a monarchy. Even so, her desire for a strong, morally just figure—or central government—to ensure stability remained, especially because in both Mexico and the United States that stability, in her eyes, would protect her financial investments. In *Squatter*, the Mechlin party makes a patriotic visit to Mount Vernon and Washington's grave the day after they climb the recently completed capitol dome for a "beautiful panorama" of Washington, DC (*SD*, 198). These excursions take place in a chapter called "Looking at the Receding Dome," which all members of the group do from a train departing the capital. Collectively, they share George's worry that Congress will not support the Texas Pacific in its efforts to help the South and free California from the "clutches of a grasping monopoly" (200). The image of the receding dome registers Ruiz de Burton's homage to the national government, which she feels should support "good," as well as her fear that the "chief of the lobby" under the dome will make it support "bad"(200). In *The Americans*, Spencer claimed that "the republican form of government is the highest form of government; but because of this it requires the highest type of human nature—a type nowhere present at present existence." With the type of human nature needed to make a republic work not yet in existence, Ruiz de Burton puts her faith in government by a morally enlightened elite.[21]

As elitist as her political views were, Ruiz de Burton's distrust of the lobbying power of railroad monopolies was fully justified. For instance, the Big Four's graft is well documented, having come to light when a number of Huntington's letters were made public in an 1882 suit filed by the wife of Charles Crocker, another member of the Big Four. Even so, Ruiz de Burton does not tell us that, while living in San Diego in the 1850s, she and her husband invested in one of the lines, hoping to profit from a route along the thirty-second parallel. After her husband's death, she was forced to sell much of the stock at a loss. Nor does she provide an accurate account of the Texas Pacific. Historically, Tom Scott was not the agent of beneficence that Ruiz de Burton makes him out to be. He earned the title "colonel" during the Civil War, when he was named assistant secretary of war for transportation because of his experience with the Pennsylvania Railroad. After the war, he unscrupulously developed and took over railroad lines in the Reconstruction South to serve the Pennsylvania's network. Because of his lobbying, the Pennsylvania legislature was reputedly the nation's most corrupt. No enemy of corporate monopolists, Scott invented the holding company, a legal instrument that greatly aided corporate giants. Even so, he overextended himself with his plans to develop the Texas Pacific.[22]

In large part, Scott's problem was timing. In September 1873, Jay Cooke's bank collapsed, bursting the bubble caused by railroad speculation and setting off a massive financial panic that endured as a long-term depression affecting all aspects of Reconstruction policy. The Panic of 1873 made it impossible for Scott to get adequate private financing and forced him to seek governmental subsidies for the Texas Pacific to match those granted earlier to the Big Four's Central Pacific. Briefly mentioning this catastrophic panic, Ruiz de Burton attributes Scott's failure to Huntington's unscrupulous opposition (*SD*, 180, 188, 299). To be sure, Huntington worked tirelessly to block the construction of a competing transcontinental line and vowed, as Ruiz de Burton repeatedly tells us, "to see the grass grow over Tom Scott" (256, 297, 339, 342). But Scott was perfectly capable of matching Huntington's bribes with bribes of his own, frequently winning lobbying battles. Outmaneuvered politically, Huntington, according to Woodward, "resorted to a flank attack on the field of engineering and construction." In the original Texas Pacific grant, Huntington's Southern Pacific had rights to build in California, meeting Scott's line at the Arizona border. With capital reserves to start construction, Huntington built to the border and added a bridge across the Colorado River. He did not stop there. He began laying track on the Arizona side, through the Indian reservation at Fort Yuma. Although ordered to halt, he instructed his workers to continue at night while the military men who might have stopped them slept. Despite the government's displeasure with his defiance of orders, Huntington had completed a crucial stretch of the line without the governmental subsidies demanded by Scott. Thus, by 1876–77, when the action proper of *Squatter* ends, Huntington was well on his way to defeating Scott, despite his rival's continued political victories.[23]

Huntington and Scott had more in common than a corrupting influence on legislators. As railroad tycoons, they had numerous shared interests. For instance, in contrast to Ruiz de Burton, both men would have supported the fence laws that relieved railroad companies of liability if trains struck livestock that strayed onto tracks. One railroad ally went so far as to argue that the open range "impedes business" by slowing rail traffic. More importantly, both Huntington and Scott wanted trained but cheap labor. With emancipation, former slaves became a possible source of such labor. It is, therefore, no accident that Huntington became a major supporter of Colonel Samuel Armstrong's Hampton Institute. Ruiz de Burton might have known Armstrong from her husband's days commanding nearby Fortress Monroe. Hampton was also located next to the port terminal of Huntington's Chesapeake and Ohio Railroad. The initial route of the Chesapeake and Ohio completed in 1873 stretched from Richmond to West Virginia. In the early 1880s, Huntington added a connection to give West Virginia coalmines an outlet to the sea, prompting citizens to name a major West Virginia town after their benefactor. Huntington even had plans to connect the Chesapeake and Ohio with the northern transcontinental railroad, giving him control of Virginia's best route to the West and sparking his interest in Armstrong's plans for educating freedmen.[24]

Armstrong, the Hawaiian-born son of a missionary, had commanded a black regiment in the Civil War and along with his troops received US citizenship as a result of his service. After the war, be became an agent of the Freedmen's Bureau. Armstrong got his idea for Hampton from schools his missionary father had established for native Hawaiians at the request of King Kalakaua. In turn, Armstrong's views of education influenced educational policy for inhabitants of the Insular Territories, acquired after the Spanish-American War, and even for inhabitants of the British Empire. Along with John Greenleaf Whittier, Huntington's partner Mark Hopkins was a trustee of Hampton. Huntington gave so much to Hampton that, after his death, its library was named in his honor. A featured speaker at its dedication was Booker T. Washington, Hampton's most famous alumnus, whose Tuskegee Institute also benefited from Huntington's generosity. Praising the robber baron's concern for "the Indian, the Chinaman, the negro," Washington called Huntington "one of the princes of the earth." It is worth taking some time to compare Huntington's "interest and faith" in what, according to Washington, "the world calls the weaker races" with Ruiz de Burton's depiction of those groups, whose economic status was influenced by the emergence of corporate culture.[25]

III

Huntington demonstrated his concern for African Americans and Native Americans through his philanthropic contributions. He supported "the Chinaman" more directly. His railroads employed so many Chinese laborers that resentment against monopolies became entangled with anti-Chinese sentiment and vice versa. Prior to the Civil War white laborers in the North feared competition from African American slaves. After the war, white laborers in the West feared competition from Chinese immigrants. In 1875 Congress passed the Page Act, which banned entrance of Asian "coolies" and prostitutes. Denying that any racial prejudice was involved, the bill's sponsor, California's Horace Page, cited the Thirteenth Amendment, claiming that the Chinese were forced into involuntary servitude. Stacey L. Smith summarizes Page's rationale.

> He claimed that he had no "prejudice against any people on account of race or color" and that he was "willing at all times and under all circumstances to accord to every people, of whatever nationality or color, the equal protection of the laws." The Chinese were an exception. They introduced immorality, paganism, disease, and poverty into California. Most damning, they undermined the

> nation's new birth of freedom. Chinese immigrants arrived under conditions "in comparison to which African slavery was a paradise." They came to California "as slaves to the companies which pay their passage." More distressing, slavery defined nearly every aspect of family life among the Chinese. "Woman, when not used as a slave, is something worse," Page confided. "The relations between parent and child are like those of master and slave" because the Chinese father "sells his son into servitude and his daughter for prostitution." Chinese should not be excluded merely because they were Chinese but because they practiced types of slavery inimical to the postemancipation nation.

A few years later, fed up with corruption in state government, the people of California convened a constitutional convention. The Constitution of 1879 combined some progressive reforms with both anticorporate and anti-Chinese provisions. One, for instance, forbade corporations from hiring "Chinese or Mongolians." When Chinese challenged these provisions and later national exclusion acts, they frequently had the support of Huntington's railroad corporations and the best attorneys money could buy.[26]

A case with direct allusions to Reconstruction is *U.S. v. Wong Kim Ark* (1898), which determined who was eligible for birthright citizenship under the Fourteenth Amendment. There are two ways to become a citizen—through naturalization and by birth. Naturalization is controlled by Congress; birthright citizenship by the language of the Constitution. The first naturalization act passed by Congress in 1790 limited naturalization to "free whites." After the Civil War, a new act passed in 1870 made way for those of African descent, but no provision was made for those of Asian descent. Thus, the only path to citizenship for Asians was through birth. That path would seem to have been opened by the citizenship clause of the Fourteenth Amendment. Designed to overturn Justice Taney's refusal in *Dred Scott* to grant US citizenship to anyone of African descent, free or slave, the citizenship clause states, "All persons born or naturalized in the United States, and subject to the jurisdiction thereof, are citizens of the United States and the state wherein they reside." Born in San Francisco of Chinese parents who could not be naturalized citizens, Wong Kim Ark assumed that he was a citizen of the United States. But in 1895 when he tried to reenter the country after visiting his parents, who had returned to China, he was denied entry by US officials who said he was not a citizen and thus came under the 1892 Geary Act that had extended the 1882 Chinese Exclusion Act. Wong Kim Ark disagreed and claimed birthright citizenship under the Fourteenth Amendment.

Arguing against Wong Kim Ark was Solicitor General Holmes Conrad from Virginia. A former Confederate cavalry officer, Conrad could not resist noting

"When Will This Ass Kick: A Case for the Society for the Prevention of Cruelty to Animals," by G. Frederick Keller, appeared May 20, 1881, in the *WASP*, a San Francisco magazine edited by Ambrose Bierce. Collis Huntington, Leland Stanford, and Charles Crocker of the Big Four, along with their Chinese ally, ride a donkey representing the people of California. (Mark Hopkins had died in 1878.) On the donkey's tail is California's 1879 constitution. In the cage labeled "Santa Clara County," which lost its case against the Southern Pacific Railroad, are "The Poor Mussel Slough Settlers."

that the Fourteenth Amendment existed only because southern states were forced to ratify it. He also insisted that the amendment had not expanded national power over citizenship. Such power, he told the court, recalled efforts during Radical Reconstruction, "that unhappy period of rabid rage and malevolent zeal when corrupt ignorance and debauched patriotism held high carnival in the halls of Congress." In the *Slaughter-House Cases*, he argued, the Supreme Court had "forever shattered the idol of national citizenship which the 'reconstruction Congress' had placed upon so lofty a pedestal." To bolster his case he cited a Kentucky case prior to *Dred Scott* that denied free African Americans citizenship even though they were born in the United States. He also relied on *Cruikshank*, which defined citizens as "the people who compose the community." Because of race and culture, he argued, Chinese could not be part of such a community in the United States.[27]

Opposing this former Confederate were two prominent northeastern attorneys. An expert in international law, Joseph Hubley Ashton had been assistant attorney general under Presidents Lincoln and Johnson. Maxwell Perkins Evarts came from a distinguished New England family. His father, William Maxwell Evarts, had been Johnson's attorney general and Hayes's secretary of state. His grandfather, Jeremiah Evarts, was the most vocal opponent of Jackson's Indian removal policy. Evarts represented Wong Kim Ark because he was an attorney for Huntington's Southern Pacific Railroad.

Evarts and Ashton had unsuccessfully represented Chinese litigants in *Fong Yue Ting v. U.S.* (1893). As Dixon alluded in *The Clansman*, the Supreme Court upheld provisions under the 1892 Geary Act, which gave Congress plenary power to deport aliens at will. Having lost at trying to restrict national power over issues of immigration, in *Wong Kim Ark* Evarts and Ashton opposed Conrad by stressing national authority over citizenship. Evarts, the Southern Pacific attorney, ended his brief by quoting Charles Sumner. Sumner had unsuccessfully tried to have the word "white" removed from the 1870 Naturalization Act so as to make those of Asian descent eligible for naturalization. Evarts turned to him to define the meaning of the Fourteenth Amendment: "Here is the great charter of every human being, *drawing vital breath upon this soil*, whatever may be his condition and *whoever may be his parents*. He may be poor, weak, humble or black—he may be Caucasian, Jewish, Indian, or Ethiopian race—he may be of French, German, English or Irish extraction; but before the Constitution all those distinctions disappear . . . He is one of the children of the State, which, like an impartial parent, regards all of its offspring with equal care."[28] In a six-to-two ruling, the Supreme Court ruled in favor of Wong Kim Ark. Its ruling prevails today, meaning that, except for some common-law exceptions, such as the children of diplomats, all people born in this country, no matter what the status of their parents, are US citizens.

Despite the Exclusion Acts, Sumner's friend Douglass felt that in 1886 the US government was protecting Chinese immigrants better than African American citizens. Lynchings in the West, culminating with the massacre of numerous Chinese miners in Rock Springs, Wyoming, prompted the military temporarily to declare martial law. In his speech "Southern Barbarism," given on the twenty-fourth anniversary of the Emancipation Proclamation, Douglass alludes to that protection and President Cleveland's condemnation of the violence and then insists that the "persecuted and murdered black citizens of Mississippi" deserve the same treatment. Indeed, William E. Birkhimer, a lawyer and West Point graduate who would later be awarded the Medal of Honor during the Philippine-American War, was on the staff of the commanding office at the time. The declaration of martial law prompted him to write *Military Government and Martial Law* (1892), which went through three editions. According to him, the Reconstruction Acts were justified only under martial law. To the objection that Reconstruction was a time of peace, he responded that, on the contrary, the South was in a "state of latent rebellion."[29]

Although by the 1870s San Diego had a large Chinese community and by 1880 Ruiz de Burton had a Chinese cook, Chinese are absent from *The Squatter and the Don*. Clearly, Ruiz de Burton was not impressed by Huntington's support of African Americans at Hampton and elsewhere. In *Who Would Have Thought It?*, she consistently mocks expressions of sympathy for African Americans, including those for Douglass. Although African Americans do not play much of a role in *Squatter*, Ruiz de Burton does satirize Huntington's antislavery credentials by describing the merchants and farmers under his control as "hushed and made docile under the lash" (*SD*, 343). The book ends with the people "wait[ing] and pray[ing] for a Redeemer who will emancipate the white slaves of California," an allusion not only to Lincoln's freeing of the slaves but also to the redeemer governments that freed southern states from the "Negro rule" imposed by Reconstruction (344). In Ruiz de Burton's world, that Redeemer did not care very much for the Native Americans trained alongside African Americans at Hampton.[30]

In *Who Would Have Thought It?* Dr. James Norval and his loyal banker Sinclair are on a scientific expedition to the Southwest Territory when they come across a band of Indians holding captive a white woman and her young daughter. The mother, a Mexican with pure Spanish blood, is married to an Austrian. In Ruiz de Burton's political allegory, the mother suggests the legitimacy of Maximilian's ascendance to the throne. She is captured in Sonora, Mexico, by Apache Indians and sold to Mohaves, who force her to marry their chief. Lola is born five months after her mother's capture. The mother is so ashamed that she wishes only to die after having Norval rescue Lola from these "horrid savages" and promising to raise her daughter a Roman Catholic (*WW*, 36). Ruiz de Burton clearly has no sympathy for barbaric Indians who wander back and forth between Mexican and US territory without proper respect for national borders. Although she condemns Anglo squatters for taking possession of Californios' land, she has no problem with Anglo settlers taking Indian land. Like Page, she considers dispossession of the Indians necessary to advance civilization.

As we saw in chapter 4, African Americans and Native Americans occupied different positions in the world of Reconstruction. Native Americans who retained tribal loyalty were considered wards of the national government, which had the direct control over territories that Sumner wanted it to have in the South under his doctrine of "state suicide." In contrast, African Americans were given citizenship and expected to make their own way in the world at the same time that courts

"The Reconstruction Policy of Congress, As illustrated in California" was directed against 1867 gubernatorial candidate George C. Gorham, who advocated extending suffrage. Gorham is depicted supporting an African American, a Chinese, and a Native American. To his left, someone proposes adding a monkey. To his right, Brother Jonathan, protecting a ballot box, informs him that in the country's history suffrage "was dedicated to the white race alone." Library of Congress.

undercut the national government's power to protect them. In the South, African Americans futilely hoped that they would receive forty acres and a mule from property taken from former slaveholders. In the West, Indians were deprived of their lands, which were redistributed to white settlers and railroads. In the South, for a while, national troops protected African Americans against members of the native white population. As that support wound down, many troops were transferred to the West, where, with the rare exception of protecting the Chinese, they primarily supported migrating whites against members of Native American tribes. In *Who Would Have Thought It?*, when Norval and Sinclair encounter the "rascally" Indians holding Lola and her mother, "they were returning from a fight with an emigrant train and some government troops" (*WW*, 34).[31]

In *Squatter*, the situation is different because much of the action takes place within a state. Whereas the national government retained control over tribal lands, Indians not residing on those lands were in a subservient position to private landowners, similar to African Americans in the South. Ruiz de Burton describes Indians working for the Don as "stupid," "lazy," and "great thieves" (*SD*, 240, 258, 292). "Lazy" as they are, they are a source of cheap labor. When some squatters resist the Don's proposal that they raise cattle, one protests that he does not want to become a vaquero tending to livestock. The Don's response: "You can hire an Indian boy to do that part" (*SD*, 89). In contrast, the Don's genteel sons are not equipped for manual labor. The one who is paralyzed driving cattle in a snowstorm slowly recovers only to suffer another attack of lameness when forced to help with plowing. "He is so unused to labor" that "work broke him down" (317). The other son loses his job in a bank and has to become a brick mason. When he almost dies in a workplace accident, we are told, "Oh, it was so inexpressibly sad to think that his precious life was risked for the pitiful wages of a hod carrier!" (326). We might recall that Booker T. Washington learned the trade of a brick mason at Hampton Institute and tried to make African Americans proud of earning the wages Ruiz de Burton dismisses as "pitiful."

The point is not simply the obvious one that Huntington was more supportive of people of color than Ruiz de Burton. As offensive to our standards as Ruiz de Burton's mockery of expressions of sympathy for people of color is, she calls attention to the limits of some of those sentiments. Washington may have praised Huntington for supporting the so-called weaker races, but they remained subservient in the railroad tycoon's corporate world. Huntington, like Washington, was much more intent on turning freedmen, Native Americans, and Chinese immigrants into productive economic workers than equal political citizens. Ruiz de Burton attacks Huntington's unscrupulous means of stopping the Texas Pacific, but she shares his vision of a hierarchical labor force.

IV

There are, of course, differences between Ruiz de Burton and her villain other than their attitudes toward people of color. In *Squatter*, the Big Four's business practices depend on the belief articulated by Leland Stanford that "there will always be misery in the world, no matter who causes it" (*SD*, 296). The Big Four's world is one of cutthroat competition. In contrast, Ruiz de Burton, decrying a politics dictated by self-interest and lobbying, holds onto the classical republican ideal of a virtuous politician standing above the fray, serving as "mentor, guardian and trustee of the people" (*SD*, 166). Thus, in the final chapter, she calls for "*the people of California [to] take the law into their own hands,* and seize the property of [the Big Four], and confiscate it, to reimburse the money *due the people*" (338).

As Ruiz de Burton knew, this populist rhetoric would find a favorable audience with many Californians fed up with Huntington and his friends' control over the state. "Monopoly," the National Anti-Monopoly League declared, "is growing in all the States. It has completely subjected only one. In California it has ripened its fruit. There, Monopoly is King. There, a few men control steam transportation. They have annihilated competition. . . . There is not a producer that does not pay heavier tribute than conquered people ever paid their conquerors." Like almost all of Huntington's enemies at the time, Ruiz de Burton evokes the bloody events of Mussel Slough. In May 1880, a local marshal serving eviction notices killed seven men in Tulare County who had refused to vacate Southern Pacific land. With the railroad's permission, they had occupied the land with the promise that they would be able to buy it later at its original value. Because the Southern Pacific had been given the land as a free governmental subsidy, it would still make a substantial profit from such a sale. But, when the farmers added irrigation systems, orchards, and vineyards, the railroad demanded payment for the land's improved value. Feeling betrayed, these squatters of a different kind refused to leave.[32]

Ruiz de Burton's allusion to Mussel Slough recalls similar populist rhetoric that the Klan used to legitimate its recourse to vigilante justice. In calling for the confiscation of property and reimbursement of money due the people, she is no more demanding public ownership of railroads than the Klan was advocating socialism. She is simply referring to the railroads' refusal to "to pay taxes on their gigantic property" (*SD*, 337). Those taxes were made possible by the anticorporate and anti-Chinese 1879 California Constitution, which prohibited railroads from deducting mortgages from the taxable value of their property, as individuals were able to do. When Huntington's railroads refused to pay the excess, claiming that the provision violated the equal protection clause of the Fourteenth Amendment, various counties sued. In the 1882 case of *San Mateo County v. Southern Pacific Railroad,* the California Supreme Court sided with the county, but it was overruled in a federal circuit decision by Henry Field's brother, US Supreme Court justice Stephen Field. Ruiz de Burton was, understandably, upset about this reversal. Even so, her economic vision remained Spencerian.[33]

Spencer, for instance, helped her counter arguments favoring monopolies. An 1883 article in the *Popular Science Monthly* offered a scientific argument ostensibly proving that monopolies were good for the people. Acknowledging that, "the Central Pacific Railroad Company owns; or controls, with a few exceptions, all the railroads in California, and the western termini of three transcontinental lines," the author produces figures showing a drop in rates for transporting goods in the decade from 1872 to 1881. If the 1872 rate had been in effect in 1881, he asserts, the company would have reaped an excess profit of over 5.8 million dollars. Noting that a similar reduction in rates did not take place in the East, which lacked a monopoly, he concludes, "The railroad, heretofore generally untrammeled by restrictive legislation, has been productive of more beneficial results to the country at large than the most sanguine enthusiast a generation ago would have dreamed. As it is a human institution, it has contained faults common to humanity. These, experience and interest will in time reduce to a minimum, and, guided by the same laws which in the past have produced so favorable results, its future operations must consistently work toward the greatest good for the greatest number." Ruiz de Burton agrees that railroads can produce beneficial results, but not if monopolies are allowed to flourish. Enlisting the scientific authority of Spencer, she insists that Huntington's monopoly is not aligned with natural laws leading to a productive economy but is, instead, an unnatural "Hydra-headed monster" that must be destroyed (*SD*, 276).[34]

Ruiz de Burton's use of Spencer puts in perspective her calls for beneficent legislation. Whereas her references to him at first seem surprising, her belief in a distribution of labor according to class lets us see why they make perfect sense. For her, an economy spreading benefits to all depends on a naturally hierarchical system of labor, and it would be a violation of moral law to legislate against that system. Ruiz de Burton may call for the "people" to take the law into their own hands, but the hands of many of those people are, in her world, assigned to economically subservient roles in service of a genteel ruling class. Although Ruiz de Burton socialized with Huntington and Stanford, neither their corporate world nor Scott's is governed by her genteel ruling class. But the hierarchical vision remains. To recognize this similarity between the two corporate monopolists Ruiz de Burton turns into protagonist and villain, we need to understand the role of the Texas Pacific in the "Compromise of 1877."

To understand the so-called Scott Plan, we have to go back to 1875, when Scott turned for help to the Republican Party's floor leader, Representative Benjamin Butler of Massachusetts. Like Sumner, Butler was part of the radical wing of the party, and he had argued the case against President Johnson at his impeachment trial. Butler and Sumner were, however, political rivals, with Butler coveting the stately intellectual's Senate seat. When Sumner died, Butler was charged with getting his prized Civil Rights Bill through the 1875 lame-duck House before the Democratic majority swept into office in the 1874 election would prevail. The bill became part of a comprehensive legislative package designed to increase the Republican Party's influence in the South. Other measures gave the president increased power to suppress white supremacists and provided another two years of funding for troops in the South. These measures were, of course, controversial. The package became even more controversial when Butler added Scott's request for railroad subsidies. Unlike Sumner, Butler was deeply implicated in railroad intrigue. Suspicious of Butler, some congressmen thought his "hidden purpose" was passage of the Texas Pacific bill. With even Republicans afraid that passage of Scott's bill would set the stage for "every conceivable scheme of public plunder," Butler's allies deemed it necessary "to promote economic recovery and to align railroad capitalists and big business with the Republican Party in the forthcoming election." In the end, the only measure to pass was the Civil Rights Bill, which was stripped of the provision banning segregated cemeteries and schools.[35]

When his alliance with the radical wing of the Republican Party ended in failure, Scott saw another opportunity with the disputed election of 1876. Knowing that a number of southerners wanted his railroad to be built, he encouraged them to create a behind-the-scenes alliance with the conservative Hayes under the assumption that he would support the Texas Pacific and the southern economy more than Samuel Tilden. Although Tilden, like Hayes, was a friend of Scott's, he had vowed with other northern Democrats in the wake of the Panic of 1873 to save taxpayers' money by putting an end to the corrupt practice of subsidizing monopolists. Some former southern Whigs went along with Scott. One was Lucius Quintus Cincinnatus Lamar, who, as we have seen, had railroad interests that transcended party lines. For his support, Ruiz de Burton praises Lamar in *Squatter* (*SD*, 340). Hayes never gave official support to the Texas and Pacific, and he did not favor it after he became president. Nonetheless, Scott did his best to play a role in brokering the election. He could do so only because he and Huntington had declared a temporary truce, having recognized their common interest in supporting a president who hoped to forestall tumult among workers—North, South, East, and West—who, in Hayes's words, might "make war on property." Thus, about the time that the action proper of *The Squatter* ends, Ruiz de Burton's two antagonists were aligned. Their truce did not last long, but while it did, soon after elected, Hayes, advised by Scott, helped put down the 1877 railroad strike.[36]

The role played by the Texas Pacific in the "Compromise of 1877" was made famous by C. Vann Woodward, who, it has been shown, somewhat exaggerated Scott's influence. Nonetheless, the Texas Pacific was a factor, and Woodward's account remains an important corrective to earlier economic explanations of Reconstruction. As we have seen, Woodward's mentor, Howard K. Beale, as well as Charles and Mary Beard, Claude Bowers, and William Hesseltine, attributed Radical Reconstruction to northern corporate and financial interests. Committed to the "Beale thesis," these New Dealers and socialists claimed that most members of the Republican Party had no real interest in the welfare of freedmen. Instead, Republicans wanted to wrest power from the planter class and in the process created class alignments that dominated US politics for the rest of the century. Beale and the Beards went so far as to claim that Republicans had intentionally worded the Fourteenth Amendment to protect corporate interests. According to this conspiracy theory, the amendment's framers used the word "person," not "citizen," in the due process and equal protection clauses, knowing that by a fiction of the law corporations were legal persons. In contrast, Woodward shows that corporate and financial interests, North and South, played a major role in engineering Radical Reconstruction's demise. The class alignments that Beale and his allies claimed led to Radical Reconstruction, in fact, helped lead to the "Compromise of 1877."[37]

Certainly, the architects of radical measures in 1867 did not represent a united economic front. Thaddeus Stevens supported a stiff tariff but advocated greenbacks. In contrast, Sumner supported "sound money" but voted for reduced tariffs. Benjamin Butler, who pushed through the 1875 Civil Rights Act, was a friend of railroads and became a presidential candidate of the Greenback Party. At the same time, New York congressman William W. Phelps, director of four large banks and eight railroads, was one of only three Republicans to vote against the Civil Rights Act of 1875, arguing, "You are trying to do what it seems to me this House everlastingly tries to do—to legislate against human prejudice, and you cannot do it." Prior to the Panic of 1873, many manufacturers saw themselves as producers whose "natural allies were farmers and laborers." After 1873, many manufactures, "shocked by depression-fed strikes and riots, fundamentally revised their self-image" and began to believe that their "natural allies were other men of means such as bankers, merchants, and transporters." Prior to 1873, manufacturers frequently supported monetary policies that provided ample money and low interest rates to fuel production. After 1873, most abandoned support of greenbacks and, with bankers and railroad magnates, embraced the gold standard. As John W. Burgess, confirms, this view and this alliance came to dominate the Republican Party with Hayes's election.[38]

Reconstruction is America's "unfinished Revolution" not only because it failed to bring about full political and civil rights for freedmen but also because reaction to it helped to make comprehensive economic reform under Republican rule unthinkable. Du Bois recognized this, which is one reason he abandoned the party of Lincoln to support Woodrow Wilson in the 1912 election. Trapped in his Marxist framework, however, Du Bois failed to see that such reform had been conceivable in 1867 when Radical Republicans passed the Reconstruction Act. Most who imagined it were southern Republicans who had a better sense of conditions in the South. They were convinced that the rights of freedmen could be advanced only if all citizens were free from the domination of both planters and big business. As plans for Radical Reconstruction were underway, members of this wing of the party formed the National Anti-Monopoly Cheap-Freight League. Hoping to stimulate internal trade and industry, the league's president, Lorenzo Sherwood, a former antislavery Whig from Texas, drafted legislation designed to guarantee cheap freight rates on railroads. Rather than continue handing out lucrative governmental subsidies to private railroads, Sherwood proposed that the government build the lines itself. Once built, they would be available, at the same rate, for any company to use. Modeled on earlier projects for building canals, the league's plan allowed for competition between private companies but gave no one company exclusive control of a particular line. Nor did it allow for the expensive land grants and construction subsidies doled out to railroad after railroad. Providing a vision for developing the country economically at the same time that plans were underway to give freedmen equal civil and political rights, Sherwood's proposal was considered by its backers essential for the success of Reconstruction.[39]

It had a notable group of supporters. One was Grant's attorney general George H. Williams. Another was James Speed of Kentucky, attorney general under Lincoln and Johnson, before he resigned over Johnson's Reconstruction politics. Others included former Union generals Ambrose Burnside and Daniel Sickles, one a railroad man, the other commander of the second military district of North and South Carolina created by radical legislation; Governors William Holden, Francis Pierpont, and William Brownlow of North Carolina, Virginia, and Tennessee; and Senator James Nye of Nevada, who briefly employed Mark Twain as his secretary and is mocked in Twain's *Sketches Old and New*. Other senators who supported Sherwood's proposal were James Harlan of Iowa, who as Johnson's secretary of the interior fired Walt Whitman, then working as a clerk in Harlan's department; Joseph Fowler of Tennessee, who broke party ranks and voted for acquittal at Johnson's impeachment trial; and John Henderson of Missouri, a coauthor of the Thirteenth Amendment, who likewise voted to acquit Johnson. Sherwood's plan also had the backing of Henry Charles Carey, a chief economic advisor to President Lincoln and perhaps the most famous American economist of his generation.

Carey made his name as the theoretic proponent of Henry Clay's "American System," which hoped to overcome sectional differences by harmonizing the interests of manufacturing, commerce, and agriculture through an activist government that stimulated the economy with internal improvements and tariff protection. To work, Carey's "system" had to be self-contained. Funded by homegrown capital, production using native materials would generate profits that, when reinvested, would stimulate further production. Convinced that reliance on foreign capital or use of profits to encourage production in other countries would ruin the system, Carey strongly opposed the "English System" of laissez-faire economics and free trade. He also speculated that, if Henry Clay had won the 1844 election, manufacturing would have flourished in the South, leading to the gradual abandonment of slavery, a drop in sectional tensions, and the ultimate prevention of civil war. Fearful that the country would become dependent on English capitalists investing in bonds needed to pay off the massive debt incurred during the war, Carey advocated continuance of Lincoln's "greenback" policy. He outlined his program in a series of letters to the speaker of the House of Representatives Schuyler Colfax. Those letters were published in 1865 under the title *The Way to Outdo England Without Fighting Her.* Colfax would become Grant's first vice president. In 1867, Carey wrote another series of letters to Massachusetts senator Henry Wilson, who would become Grant's second vice president. Strongly disagreeing with Wilson's laissez-faire, free-trade politics, Carey collected these letters as *Reconstruction, Industrial, Financial, and Political.* He signed on to Sherwood's National Anti-Monopoly Cheap-Freight Railway League because it linked a Reconstruction policy to the American System.[40]

We will never know whether Sherwood's plan would have succeeded. Unmentioned in almost all accounts of Reconstruction, his legislation did not pass. Certainly, history—and the Republican Party—went in a different direction. As we have seen, convinced that speculation leading to the Panic of 1873 could be controlled by backing up the nation's currency with something "real," Congress stopped issuing greenbacks and passed the Coinage Act, which moved the country toward the gold standard. One result was, as Carey predicted, the destruction of any possibility for a self-contained, productive national economy. Without the government's ability to create money to stimulate the economy, development became increasingly dependent on foreign investment, much of it by the same English capitalists who had helped finance the Confederacy. From 1873 until the outbreak of World War I, the United States became the world's largest debtor nation, with the majority of foreign money going to railroads. There were dealers for American railroad securities in Amsterdam, Frankfurt, Paris, and London, the last of which set aside a special section of its stock market for American lines.[41]

This destruction of hopes for the American System is registered in a work of fiction published the same year as *Squatter* and also set in the age of Reconstruction. The title character in William Dean Howells's *The Rise of Silas Lapham* owns an Italian statue depicting Lincoln freeing the slaves. Nonetheless, with his fortune on the rise, he tells his future son-in-law, "I hate to see them stirring up those Southern fellows again. . . . Seems to me it's time to let those old issues go." But, with the Panic of 1873, the value of Silas's investments plummets. One hope for rebound is "a big milling property" in the Midwest that his nemesis, Milton Rogers, has given him to cover past debts. There is only one railroad line to the mills, owned by a small company with which Silas can do business, but that company has just been leased to a railroad giant. Because the giant will be able to dictate its price for the mills or tell the owner "to carry his flour and lumber to market himself," Silas thinks of the railroad moguls "Vanderbilt, Jay Gould, and Tom Scott," not Huntington. Of course, if Sherwood's plan had been enacted, no single company would have had the giant's power. Even though in the novel one company does, Silas seems to have a chance when Rogers produces an alleged group of English investors who want to purchase the mills at a favorable price. Before Silas can decide if he will sell to them, however, the railroad makes its offer, rendering any other deal impossible. In the meantime, Silas's New England–based paint business is brought to its knees by a new company in West Virginia. By the end of the novel, Silas has been forced to sell out to the new firm, which employs his son-in-law to open new markets in South America.[42]

In *Squatter,* Ruiz de Burton registers the demise of the American System in a different way. In her final attack on the Central Pacific, she almost sounds like Carey as she scolds Huntington for shamefully extracting profits from the people of California to "build roads in Guatemala" (*SD*, 343). Once again, however, her populist rhetoric is misleading. Whereas Silas condemns Tom Scott as a corporate monopolist who strangles individual businessmen like himself, Ruiz de Burton turns Scott into a savior, not telling us that in 1873 he was abroad, trying to get foreign investors to buy into the Texas Pacific. When the Panic struck, its international impact was so severe that he returned home empty-handed, intent on having the government finance his dream. Championing Scott, Ruiz de Burton endorses a moral economy developed through a global, not a national, circulation of capital. Celebrated by some critics as anti-imperialist, Ruiz de Burton's transnationalism is most obvious in her portrayal of the banking industry.

Few authors give as positive an account of bankers as Ruiz de Burton. Hamlin Garland's "The Return of a Private" (1890) gives a typical view of banks at the time. After risking his life to preserve the Union, Garland's Private Smith returns to his Wisconsin farm in ruined health only to fight an "insatiable mortgage." His fate is compared to "the millionaire," who sat out the war and "sent his money to England for safe-keeping." *Squatter* presents a different view. For instance, Clarence celebrates saving a huge amount of money while buying a ranch because "the bank was going to foreclose on the farm for a loan of forty thousand dollars" (*SD*, 141). In *Who Would Have Thought It?*, New York banker William Sinclair is a model of integrity in a world of corruption. In *Squatter*, the honorable Mechlins are also New York bankers. Pointing to lucrative profits made financing the Civil War debt, Carey warned Wilson that the banking system was "a great monopoly for the especial benefit of the Trading States." Large banks exploited connections forged while financing the Civil War debt to manage foreign investments of the sort Scott sought to build his railroad. Assuming that the Texas Pacific will be a success, Clarence plans to link San Diego to this global network of capital by starting a West Coast bank that will employ members of the Mechlin and Alamar families. The failure of the Texas Pacific ruins his plan, but in Ruiz de Burton's world, that failure is caused by corrupt legislators influenced by Huntington's greed much more than it is due to the systematic problems that led to the failure of Jay Cooke's bank and ushered in the Panic of 1873.[43]

As devastating as that panic was in actuality, it hardly affects the Mechlins in New York, who maintain their luxurious, globe-trotting lifestyle. Nor does it affect Clarence's ability to reap profits as he continues to amass a fortune while traveling to Mexico, South America, and England. After a long absence from the book, he reappears in Paris and accidentally bumps into the Mechlins, who have been visiting spas in Germany. Their meeting leads to the novel's culminating action: the reconciliation of the Alamar, Mechlin, and Darrell families—or what is left of them. This reconciliation is Ruiz de Burton's way of bringing together the forces she feels are needed to battle Huntington's monopoly. She calls the chapter in which these forces come together "Reunited At Last," which is a suggestive title in a book set during the period in which the United States was trying to overcome sectional differences after the Civil War. Yet her reunion of forces within California is made possible by a rendezvous of rich Americans outside US borders.

V

We get a different view of transnationalism, especially in the western hemisphere, if we turn to Tourgée. Tourgée is understandably associated with the South, but he also had knowledge of the West. When he left North Carolina in 1879, he took his family to Denver in the midst of the Colorado silver rush. His wife Emma caught silver fever, and the family invested in real estate and mining. In *With Gauge and Swallow*, he drew on his western experience to portray the fictional Colorado case of the *New Aryan Mine v. Nobels*, which required extensive "knowledge of Spanish law and Mexican grants" (155). A year after *The Squatter and the Don* was published, he reviewed Helen Hunt Jackson's *Ramona* and Hubert Bancroft's *History of the Pacific States*. Like Ruiz de Burton, he criticizes Anglo settlers for their failure to respect titles granted under Spanish and Mexican rule. This new people to the land

> has little regard for others rights, and looks with infinite scorn on all that was before it came. When the mines fail, it turns its greedy eye upon the soil itself. It represents not only a conquering people but an alien people, a strange and hostile impulse. It construes the rights of the conquered by the laws and maxims of the conqueror. Prescriptive right is flouted with contempt. Titles confirmed by two hundred years of use and occupancy are nailed down to the strict requirement of English law, with its stern demand of "visible marks and boundaries." The lust for gold is succeeded by the lust for land. The landgrabber follows hard upon the footsteps of the prospector. On the heels of both comes the railroad.[44]

Unlike Ruiz de Burton, Tourgée also criticizes the dispossession of Native Americans. He praises *Ramona* for depicting California as the "Indian's lost inheritance and the Spaniard's desolated home." The United States, he laments, "never found anything better to do with our own Indians than to kill them." Tourgée's comment recalls Page's condemnation of carpetbagger Leech for protesting the stealing of Indian lands. Indeed, Tourgée denounced the Mexican-American War supported by Page and Dixon. "There are few intelligent Americans," Tourgée writes, "who do not look forward either with hope or apprehension to the future relations between the United States and Mexico. There are few who do not regard the movement which resulted in the acquisition of California and New Mexico as one of the most shameless and disgraceful episodes of our history." Given his later support of the Spanish-American War, Tourgée's condemnation of the Mexican-American War might seem inconsistent, but for him there was a clear difference. One war was against a European imperial power; the other was against a liberty-loving multiracial society in the Americas. Bancroft teaches us, he reports, that the Mexican love of liberty, which has no "European root," has been chiefly supported by "the aboriginal element of its population." Noting the United States' imposition of the color line despite considerable racial mixing, Tourgée praises Mexico's toleration of and recognition of its own racial intermixture. "The Mestizo and the mulatto—sometimes even the representative of three races—stand side by side with the purest Creole blood in rank, social position, and opportunity, as with the most abject of the aboriginal population. These races and classes live together in comparative harmony." In contrast, in the United States, "race-prejudice is so intense that no consideration of justice, humanity, or religion has been sufficient to compel us to recognize the civil or political equality of the Indian." Paradoxically, "Spanish arrogance" has lent itself "to tolerance in regard to distinctions of race, while Anglo-Saxon liberalism stumbles always at the color-line."[45]

Whereas Ruiz de Burton loves poking fun at Anglo-Saxon liberalism, she has a different sense of the racial situation in Mexico. Far from celebrating the liberty-loving aboriginal element of the population, she feels that Mexico could have best risen to a high rank in the civilized nations of the world by accepting a European monarch. Without Maximilian, "the government of Mexico, being a free and independent government, lets its Indians live as they please, and its more civilized citizens take care of themselves as best they may" (*WW*, 194).

Ruiz de Burton also had a different view of economic relations between the United States and its southern neighbors. Prior to and during the Civil War, southern states looked south to expand slavery and regional trade. To appease southerners, President James Buchanan proposed and Ruiz de Burton supported the McLane-Ocampo Treaty of 1859, which would have granted the United States "perpetual right to transit across the Isthmus of Tehuantepec, access to land to build two railroad routes in the north, [and] the right to protect these railroad lines with or without Mexican consent in case of imminent danger." These lines would have opened Pacific trade for southern ports. Afraid that the South hoped to annex more territory and opposed to any competition for a northern transcontinental railroad, northerners defeated the treaty. During the Civil War, westward expansion was part of the Confederate strategy. It recognized the Confederate territory of Arizona, which included land acquired by the Gadsden Purchase, and planned expansion into Mexico. In the final years of the war, Senator William Gwin of California, a native of Mississippi, travelled to France and proposed to Napoleon III "Gwin's Dukedom of Sonora." This plan involved the colonization of Sonora by slaveholders. Napoleon III approved, but Maximilian did not. After the war, ex-Confederates founded a number of colonies in Mexico. After the war, six-term senator John Tyler Morgan, a member of the Ku Klux Klan, who publicly debated Tourgée on the race question, avidly supported an inter-ocean canal through Nicaragua that would benefit Alabama's port of Mobile. Once the Texas and Pacific was defeated, to the chagrin of Huntington, he also proposed controlling railroad rates. A member of the Senate's foreign relations committee, he worked closely with Ruiz de Burton's friend Matías Romero, Mexico's minister in Washington, DC. His first major foreign policy speech in May 1878 was for improved relations with Porfirio Díaz's Mexico. In 1883, he unsuccessfully advocated a new trade agreement supported by Ruiz de Burton's friend Grant. Making a case for the "sisterhood" between the two nations, Morgan claimed that "Mexico holds a relationship with the United States which no other government or people can occupy." His views on Mexico may have been one reason why, despite the evidence, Ruiz de Burton felt that the major threat to Central America and Mexico was from "black" Republicans.[46]

Tourgée disagreed. For him, the major threat was the South, "which has always been the home of the filibuster." He ends his review warning that Otto von Bismarck's designs on Mexico might spark more intervention by the United States. Even without the Monroe Doctrine, "which has more than once offered excuse for American wrong-doing," the Cleveland administration could find cover by claiming to protect the "semi-international" railroads in northern Mexico, "built by American capital and controlled by American influence." Interference into Mexico's internal affairs, Tourgée speculates, would bring about the alliance of West, South, and commercial interests in the North that Ruiz de Burton hoped the Texas Pacific would promote. Tourgée predicts that southern members of Cleveland's Democratic Party and of his cabinet, including Lamar, would lend "solid" and "enthusiastic" support in order to "becloud in the public memory" their party's record during the Civil War. They would then be free "to make new political combinations," such as one with "leading Republicans" supporting "the practical disfranchisement of the colored race in the Southern States." Lurking behind all of these maneuvers is the "'Duke of Sonora's' famous estimate of the marvelous wealth of the northern provinces" and the opportunity to appropriate "a larger or smaller portion of Mexican territory." Given the political power of a "very considerable moneyed interest," Tourgée fears that once again the lure of "marvelous mineral wealth" will disable the moral compass of the nation.[47]

Ruiz de Burton's sense of the role that the area's mineral wealth played in a transnational economy is suggested by a detail in *Who Would Have Thought It?* Lola's mother gives Norval and his banker friend a vast amount of gold that makes her daughter a rich heiress. The mother also gives Norval some rough pebbles that turn out to be emeralds, diamonds, rubies, and opals. A product of the American soil, recently taken from Mexico, these stones are "sent to Europe to be made into jewelry," where, turned into "first-class gems," they achieve their true value before being shipped back to America (WW, 47).

Two years after Ruiz de Burton published *Who Would Have Thought It?*, Tourgée produced his own economic allegory about mineral wealth. While still a carpetbagger in North Carolina, he composed two works that tried, as their subtitle puts it, to imagine a future "South Without the Shadow." They are dedicated:

To

THE NEW SOUTH

That Is to Be.

When the Fire of Self-Sacrifice Shall Have Burned Away

The Dross of the Past and Left Only Its

GOLD

This commonplace reference to gold has special meaning for an author who knew that the term *carpetbagger* took on its first derogatory connotations when applied to wildcat bankers carrying suspect paper currency. Still intent on reconstructing the South and the nation one year after the country had moved toward the gold standard, Tourgée writes his second novella to dramatize the effects of the Panic of 1873. It tells of Paul Dewar, a southerner, whose wife inherits a plantation called Mamelon, named after a prehistoric mound, the relic of an unknown race that once inhabited the land. After fighting for the South in the Civil War, Paul tries to transform himself from a leisurely gentleman to a productive man of enterprise. He first puts his hands to plowing the land and planting tobacco, earning the disdain of his wife, who, like Ruiz de Burton, feels that such labor is unsuited for a gentleman. When tobacco farming fails, Paul joins forces with Captain Dickson from Massachusetts to turn the persimmon and hickory trees growing on the property into hardwood handles for tools that will help build the nation. Mortgaging his wife's plantation to build a factory, Paul and his partner soon have a thriving business that employs many workers.[48]

Then the Panic of 1873 hits, destroying the market for their goods, causing Paul to lay off workers, and leaving them heavily in debt. Going north to seek financial support, Paul returns empty-handed. With the mortgage on Mamelon about to be called in, he appears to shoot himself so his wife can collect his life insurance. But the bullet goes astray, and Paul is struck with a case of apoplexy. He is brought back to health by Professor Ware, who has come with him from the North. The professor finds the stray bullet, lodged in a piece of rock that is part of a collection that Paul has found at the ancient mound. The force of the bullet exposes the core of the rock, which turns out to be corundum. "It is," the professor tells us, "but a step from corundum to sapphire and the ruby . . . I should not be surprised, if this very specimen were properly cut and worked, to find a perfect crystal ruby, without a flaw in its heart" (*MA*, 297). Soon Captain Dickson returns, "with his engines and machinery . . . grinding the faulty crystals to powder to be used in polishing other jewels and hard substances—glass and the like. Every day the hopes of the great 'New York Corundum Company' have been growing brighter" (298). It is even possible that they will soon be taking out "rubies, sapphires, and . . . other jewels there" (298).

A romance, told on Valentine's Day, this tale is a political allegory at odds with those told by Ruiz de Burton. Ruiz de Burton portrays Native Americans as savages, threatening civilization most identified with Europe; Tourgée, anticipating José Marti, is an exceptionalist, tracing the unique value of the American soil to its ancient inhabitants. He also endorses a political economy quite different from Ruiz de Burton's. Tourgée imagines a prosperous New South shaped by an updated version of Carey's American System. Paul's effort to make Mamelon productive dramatizes Carey's view that land has value as the result of the labor—past and present—expended on it. The leisure class that so fascinates Ruiz de Burton does not, for Carey or Tourgée, aid the nation's productivity. Nor does help for Paul come from northern bankers. Loyally trying to rebuild the South, he finds no financing there, even though, as Tourgée angrily noted in 1868, northern bankers and their Wall Street associates and foreign friends maintained the South during the days of rebellion by buying its bonds. Most important, the mineral wealth found on the land has a practical use and achieves its full value not by being shipped to Europe but through the scientific knowledge and enterprising spirit of northerners helping a southerner move beyond sectional prejudice.[49]

Given Tourgée's belief in the American System, it is not surprising to find that seven years before writing this novella he had strongly supported the National Anti-Monopoly Cheap-Freight Railroad League. Having met Sherwood at the 1866 Southern Loyalist Convention in Philadelphia, Tourgée was a member of the league's national council. For him, the plan was essential for what he thought should be the Republican Party's goal of generating a new economy in the South that would free both African Americans and poor whites from subservience not only to the old planter class but also the corporate interests of railroads. "There is nothing which can ever secure a genuine, hearty, and valuable reconstruction," the carpetbagger declared, "but a full, thorough, and efficient system of national development." Enthusiastically praising the league's program as "Steam Reconstruction," he waxed eloquent: "Hourly it has grown more and more stupendous in its proportions and more and more beautiful in its harmony."[50]

The harmony of interests Tourgée imagines was never realized. If it had been, we might have had a very different New South from the one Ruiz de Burton champions through completion of the Texas Pacific in her black and white romance about the westward course of Reconstruction. In the next chapter, I look at how various writers depict the New South's inheritance from the past.

- 6 -

WORKING WITH THE HERITAGE OF THE OLD SOUTH

As different as *The Squatter and the Don* and *Mamelon* are, both dramatize the possible disinheritance of established families. Questions of inheritance are a staple of Reconstruction fiction, as authors make different cases for who should inherit the South and the nation. This chapter and chapter 7 focus on inheritance plots that interweave a number of topics we have already treated. When freedmen are viewed as perpetual children, they are not considered worthy heirs of the nation's past. The issue of federalism is often portrayed as a clash between the South's effort to maintain local control over its political and cultural inheritance and its need to break with the sins of the past. Not all inheritance plots involve the Klan, but when they do, the Klan is seen either as necessary for white southerners to retain their rightful inheritance or as an illegitimate force denying freedmen and carpetbaggers their fair share. As *Squatter* and *Mamelon* show, the outcome of these plots is almost always influenced by authors' economic visions, including their sense of the proper role for northern capital. Finally, connecting past to future, inheritance plots are frequently linked to different authors' foundational myths. Plots about inheritance, in other words, are not simply questions of the legal execution of a will. They also indicate their authors' sense of how the nation should legitimately be reconstructed.

In this chapter, I proceed more or less in reverse chronological order, starting with Thomas Nelson Page, Joel Chandler Harris, and Thomas Dixon, moving to George Washington Cable, and ending with Albion W. Tourgée, whose works established the traditions to which the others respond. In chapter 7, I turn to African American writers, starting with Frances Harper and Pauline Hopkins and ending with an extended discussion of the novels Charles W. Chesnutt published in his lifetime.

II

In Page's *Red Rock*, the inheritance plot involves the estate that gives the novel its name. In the antebellum period, Red Rock's pastoral harmony, presided over by a

In "The New South," Henry Grady describes a Confederate soldier returning home from war, his trade destroyed and his home in ruins. This is a photograph of the ruined mansion of the Pinckney family of Charleston, South Carolina. After studying at Westminster and Oxford, Charles Cotesworth Pinckney returned to South Carolina and later served in the Revolutionary War as an aide-de-camp to George Washington. The family home was ruined by fire during the Civil War. For many at the time a major task of Reconstruction was to repair the physical destruction suffered by the South.

guardian class of virtuous gentlemen disinterestedly maintaining the public good, embodies the epitome of civilization, marred only by the institution of slavery. As we have seen, through his account of Red Rock's origin, Page implies that this civilized order had a foundation in violence, as Jacquelin Gray, scholar turned fierce Indian-killer, carves a home out of the wilderness and bloodily defends it. With Reconstruction, Red Rock and its civilized order are again under attack. With the aid of the villainous Freedmen's Bureau agent Jonadab Leech, the estate's former overseer, Hiram Still, dispossesses the Grays of their inheritance.

The dispossession occurs in the chapter "Jacquelin Gray Goes on a Voyage," which interweaves three strands of action. The chapter starts by describing the condition of the present-day Jacquelin Gray, who returns from the war fatherless and in broken health after imprisonment in Point Lookout. Before he went off to war, his father explained his will. The elder Jaquelin Gray leaves everything to his wife, but, as he tells his elder son, "it would be the same thing as if he left it to him and Rupert. . . . I leave it to her, and I leave her to you." This responsibility marks Jacquelin's passage into manhood. "Jacquelin listened, his mind suddenly sobered and expanded to be a man's measure." His father goes on: "Keep the old place. Make any sacrifice to do that. Landholding is one of the safeguards of a gentry. Our people, for six generations, have never sold an acre, and I never knew a man who sold land that throve" (*RR*, 47). But, even though Jacquelin has assumed his father's place at the head of the family and taken his place in the regiment when he falls, Jacquelin has to abandon Red Rock temporarily after Leech invades the family home to arrest him on trumped up charges. With his war wounds made worse by rough handling, Jacquelin goes on a long Pacific voyage to recover his health and to avoid further conflict with Leech. The voyage also allows him to recover from the psychic wounds of war, and he learns how to reconcile his love of the South with allegiance to the nation. That allegiance is tested when he returns to find the effects of the Radical Republican measures of 1867 on the "old country" (198). The second strand of action describes those effects, which include an election that "gave the ballot to the former slave, just as it was taken away from the former master" (199). Even "more arbitrary . . . the State itself was suddenly swept out of existence, and a military government was substituted in its place." As we have seen, the "old State" (199) did not in fact completely disappear, but Page perpetuates the myth that it did. In his account the absence of a legitimate state government to protect the people corresponds to the absence of a male descendent of the Indian-killer to protect Red Rock. To make the connection clear, the third strand of action describes Still's maneuvers to take possession of Red Rock. The combined action of the chapter shows how "the years of the carpetbagger's domination well-nigh destroyed the South" (198).

When war broke out, Still avoided military service by claiming an attack of rheumatism. Nonetheless, he displayed his loyalty by lending money "to help to equip the companies" (*RR*, 43); that is, "he lent it not to the county, . . . but to Mr. Gray and Dr. Cary on their joint security" (43–44). During the war he "turned all them Confed. notes into gold and greenbacks" (87), ending up rich while those who fought ended up poor. After the war, he tries to play both sides, courting favor with Leech while generously lending locals money when they need it to stay afloat. But he reveals his hand by becoming the "only white man of note in the upper end of the county who took the new 'ironclad' oath" (202), swearing that he never gave aid or comfort to the Confederacy. His alliance with Leech clear, he starts to call in his debts, ruining the lives of many. The most substantial debt is a bond for over fifty thousand dollars that he claims Jacquelin Gray's deceased father owed him. Before the war, the elder Gray signed the bond when he sent Still to buy land and slaves for a sugar plantation in the deep South. With Jacquelin not present to protect Red Rock, Still calls in the bond from Mrs. Gray, who cannot pay it. As a result, Still, with Leech as his attorney, enforces the bond and then buys the estate at a secret "public" auction for far less than fifty thousand dollars. Seemingly triumphant, Still takes possession but is haunted in the house by the eyes of the portrait of the Indian-killer, which "pierced him wherever he went" (205). When Jacquelin comes home, his mother, undone by the stress, dies, and Still will not let her be buried in the family cemetery next to her husband. In fact, prompted by Leech, Still threatens to "get rid of the old grave-yard altogether" (260). Unannounced, Jacquelin confronts him in his old home in the dim darkness after sunset. Looking up, Still thinks he sees "tall and gray, the 'Indian-killer,' his eyes blazing like coals of fire" (261). Jacquelin warns him, "You will not be in this place always. We are coming back here, the living and the dead" (262).

Still's acquisition of Red Rock is complicated even more in the next chapter when the northerner Major Welch decides to locate in the area for his health. Welch's wife is a proponent of Reconstruction and has been in correspondence with Leech. The Welches' beautiful daughter Ruth shares her mother's ideals. Major Welch is more cautious, having been a guest of the Grays prior to the war and having seen the pastoral harmony of Red Rock while entertained at the ball described at the beginning of the book. When Welch and Ruth come south to look for a place to live, Still hosts them for a night. Welch cannot help but compare this night with the one almost a decade earlier, and he notes how unfit Still is to be the owner of Red Rock. Still's vulgarity is even more evident when he tries to impress the Welches with a grand ball. Nonetheless, Major Welch buys a substantial portion of Red Rock for his southern home. With Still violating his former owner's wish and selling part of the old estate, it is now in possession of a scalawag and a northerner.

BEFORE HIM STOOD, TALL AND GRAY, THE INDIAN-KILLER.

When Jacquelin Gray, unarmed, confronts Hiram Still about his usurpation of the family mansion and his threat to destroy the family graveyard, Still pulls a pistol out of his desk. Jacquelin, reinforcing Still's fear that he is facing a resurrected Indian-killer, coolly tells him, "If you attempt to draw that pistol on me, . . . I will kill you right where you are." When a servant enters with a light, he mutters to himself, "Good Lordy!" (*RR*, 262).

Before purchasing his land, Welch goes with Still to the courthouse to check on the validity of the title. At the courthouse, they meet Jacquelin Gray, who has returned from his voyage, intent on recovering his family's lost estate. Gray has joined Steve Allen in a law partnership, and he is inspecting the documents Still used to take over Red Rock. After Gray leaves, Still tries to take the documents, claiming they are his. The clerk refuses, saying that they are part of the legal record. Still relents but remains upset because he claims the clerk has smeared the fifty-thousand-dollar bond with red ink. The clerk, however, insists that the "stain was on that bond when Leech filed it" (*RR*, 312). Gray and Allen do not doubt the existence of the bond, but they think they can amass enough evidence to show that Mr. Gray would have paid it or a substantial portion of it. Thus, they file a suit, which must also name Major Welch, since he has bought a large portion of the estate. Subsequently, Jacquelin learns that Steve Allen is in love with Ruth Welch, and he feels that Steve should not sign the suit, but Steve does anyway.

When the suit comes to trial, Still and Major Welch are represented by the venerable Mr. Bagby, while Still alone is represented by Leech and the former Klansman, turned scalawag, McRaffle. Against them are aging General Legaie, Steve, and Jacquelin. Presiding is Judge Bail, whose appointment has been suggested by a northern lobbyist. The judge clearly sides with Still, and no evidence of fraud comes forward, leaving the defense with the task of simply verifying that the date of the bond corresponds with Still's visit to buy and stock the sugar plantation. The only person alive able to confirm that visit is the Grays' former slave, Doan. Doan does not remember calendar dates, but he knows that Still returned a day before the portrait of the Indian-killer fell down before the war. Doan remembers vividly because the portrait of "de ghos'" (*RR*, 460) fell while he was painting the hearth red and overheard Mr. Gray and Still talk about the overseer's trip South. According to Doan, Still told his employer that he was returning the bond and others because he had not been able to buy as much land or as many slaves as expected. Before he could hand over the papers, however, a thunderstorm erupted, knocking down the portrait and blowing the bonds to the ground, where the one for fifty thousand dollars was smeared by the blood-red paint with the toe-print of young Rupert Gray, who was playing nearby. Mr. Gray then deposited the bond with others in a hole in the wall exposed by the fallen portrait, and Doan and Still nailed the Indian-killer's portrait back in place.

Doan's testimony is damning, and Still tries to stop it. But McRaffle asks another question, prompting Doan to describe how, years later, Still took the papers out of the hole when the portrait fell again on the day Leech came to Red Rock to arrest Jacquelin Gray. With this revelation, Still leaps up and calls it a lie. Leech calms him down and gets Doan to admit that he cannot read and, thus, cannot tell one bond from another. Nonetheless, Doan confidently claims to be able to identify this bond because of Rupert's red toe marks. In the meantime, Steve produces the bond and shows it to Major Welch, who asks Doan to identify it. He does so, seconded by the stately African American Tarquin, who also saw Still remove it.

Despite overwhelming evidence of Still's deceit, the judge rules that Doan's testimony is out of order, declining "to hear ghost stories" (*RR*, 465). He orders the jury to rule that no fraud has been committed. Major Welch, however, appalled at the injustice committed and embarrassed that he is aligned with Still in the suit, addresses the court. Although he bought his property from Still in good faith, he now realizes that Still did not properly hold title. Indeed, the careful reader will remember that Welch knows Doan's ghost story is true because the man from Massachusetts had been told the story of the portrait and the red paint during his visit to Red Rock before the war. As a result, Major Welch conveys his part of the land to the Grays. Even though this entails a substantial financial loss, he insists, "I am not willing to hold another man's property which he lost by fraud" (467). All he asks is that the Grays agree to declare that every action Major Welch made "was free from any taint of suspicion" (468). The next day Gray visits Major Welch and tells him he does not want to take advantage of an impulsive act. Welch insists that he acted out of a sense of right, and the two arrange for Welch to lease the land.

Based on the evidence of the red-stained bond, Steve and Jacquelin prepare to file a new suit. Page makes no secret of its significance: "On the decision depended everything. It was recognized on both sides that it was not a mere property question, but a fight for supremacy" (*RR*, 473). Aware of how important it is to win this battle, Leech plays his trump card before the next trial can take place. As we saw in chapter 2, he has almost all notable white southerners arrested for having broken Rupert out of jail. Leech's primary target, Steve Allen, escapes until a deal is reached that everyone will be released if Steve turns himself in. Steve is then arrested for his former Klan activities, which he has revealed to Ruth Welch, who inadvertently tells Leech. With Ruth's secret marriage to Steve, however, she escapes having to testify, and Steve goes free. It is this trial marking the failure of the Ku Klux Klan Act to convict Steve, not a new suit over possession of Red Rock, that culminates the action of the book.

Page does not, however, leave the inheritance plot unresolved. In a final chapter, he ties up loose ends. Jacquelin, we learn, gives Ruth a wedding present of the property her father had bought from Still. In the meantime, having seen the ghost of the Indian-killer again, Still proposes a deal with Jacquelin. Gray hesitates, thinking that he has enough evidence to win in a new trial. But with Judge Bail still in office and Leech retaining some power, the outcome of a trial would be uncertain. So Jacquelin accepts Still's offer, with the Grays taking over the Red Rock home and much of the surrounding land, while Still retains his former overseer's house and substantial property. Jacquelin's first act is to bury his mother next to his father in the family graveyard also containing the body of the old Indian-killer.

Page's plot is designed to convince a national audience of the justness of the southern response to Reconstruction. For instance, during Reconstruction numerous white southerners argued against allowing freedmen to testify. But in Page's hands it is a corrupt judge installed during carpetbag rule who denies Doan's testimony verifying the legitimate inheritance of an ancient southern family. That Doan's testimony is a "ghost story" reinforces the enduring power of the legend of the Indian-killer and his ability to protect his estate for his heirs. Likewise, whereas the original Jacquelin Gray reverted to violence to defend Red Rock, the present Jacquelin Gray, living in what should be a more civilized era, turns to law. Under Reconstruction rule, however, the law can no longer be trusted, as it had been in the antebellum South, to protect civilized order. Once the embodiment of American republican justice, the local courthouse has become a place of corruption, signaled by a failure to maintain established customs. "It had been the practice in the County, when the Judge entered, for the Bar to rise and remain standing until he had mounted the bench, bowed to them, and taken his seat, when they bowed and resumed their places. It was a custom brought from the Supreme Court, before which Mr. Bagby, General Legaie, and others of that bar had practiced in old times" (455). Now, with an African American as sheriff, "not a man rose." Offended by the lack of customary procedures, General Legaie walks out at the start of the trial. In his absence, Judge Bail's biased rulings confirm the old lawyer's quixotic protest.

Nonetheless, General Legaie no more speaks completely for Page than Dr. Cary speaks for him on the question of necessary violence. As noble as both are—Legaie's name evokes the law, Cary's caring—both are relics of another time. When the two journey to Washington, DC, a city where Page lived in a stylish mansion and felt quite at home, they "landed in a city as wholly different from anything they had seen since the war as if it had been a foreign capital" (*RR*, 242). Sympathetic observers think of them as "picturesque" (243). Earlier, they are compared to Don Quixote and Anthony Trollope's Dr. Filgrave (87, 118). Thus, Legaie does not necessarily speak for Page when he thinks of the original trial, "it was not a mere question of title to property he was to argue; it was the question between the old and the new—it was civilization that was on trial" (456). To be sure, a civilization is on trial, but Major Welch's role suggests that it is not simply a conflict between the old and the new. First of all, Welch's action makes it clear that the gentlemanly code of honor is not confined to the South. Second, his transformation from co-defendant with Still to ally with Jacquelin and Steve is Page's acknowledgement that the best aspects of southern civilization can regain supremacy only with aid from the North. With that aid, civilized rule by law can again prevail. But for that to happen, those in the North need to understand that when Reconstruction rule undercut the legal order, violence was temporarily necessary to restore it. In turn, southerners need to accommodate themselves to the results of the war.[1]

In choosing to conclude the book with Steve's trial, Page, through the Welch family, gives northern assent to Steve's Klan activities. He also makes it clear that restoration of civilized order in the South depends upon dismantling the measures passed to enforce Reconstruction rule. The book ends with part of the old order restored. But that order has also been altered—positively with an alliance of the good forces of North and South through the marriage of Steve and Ruth, and negatively through the continued presence of Still. With this new order and hints of a marriage between Jacquelin and Blair Cary, the narration stops. On the one hand, we get a standard North-South marriage. On the other, we get the promised union of a family of former southern Whigs and former southern Democrats.

Page is too often lumped together with advocates of the "Lost Cause." As much as he honors the "Old South," however, *Red Rock* is primarily concerned with the present and future order. At the end of the book, the leaders of the old generation are dead. As noble as they were, neither Dr. Cary nor Mr. Gray speaks completely for Page. Steve, not Dr. Cary, understands the necessity of properly used violence. Likewise, Mr. Gray is partly responsible for the temporary loss of his family's estate because nostalgia caused him to misread Still's character. Telling his son about his will, Mr. Gray assures him not to worry about his debts to Still. "Still was a better man than he was given credit for. A bad manner made those who did not know him well, suspicious of him. But he was the best business man he had ever known, and he believed devoted to his interest. His father, old Mr. Still, had been overseer for Jacquelin's grandfather when Mr. Gray was a boy, and he could not forget him" (*RR*, 47). Despite their flaws, both fathers pass on to the next generation the quality of virtue. Dr. Cary's noble claim that "War cannot plunder virtue" comes from Plutarch's "A Discourse Touching the Training of Children" (246). Jacquelin and Blair's promised marriage proves they have learned their lesson well, and Jacquelin and Steve are positioned to be leaders of a new generation.[2]

Although Jacquelin and Steve inherit virtue from the older generation of gentlemen, Page makes it clear that the inheritance is not automatic. Virtue is always vulnerable. Its stability depends on self-control and the rule of reason over appetite. According to Miss Thomasia, the epitome of virtuous southern womanhood, Steve's father was "the handsomest, most brilliant man I ever saw." But "even he had not been strong enough to resist, even for her sake, the temptation of two besetting sins—drink and gambling." Alcohol undermines virtue by destroying rational control; gambling because it is vulnerable to the wheel of fortune. Steve proves his virtue by promising "not to gamble again" and not to "drink in excess any more" (*RR*, 158). If alcohol and gambling are a threat to individual virtue, commerce, because of its profit motive and its vulnerability to the fortunes of the marketplace, threatens classical republican virtue in an entire society. Indeed, it is Still's association with the negative aspects of commerce that makes him one of the book's villains. His treatment of slaves as commodities causes Steve and Jacquelin to grow up with disdain for him and his son Wash, who also mistreats slaves. Still's behavior reminds us that the Old South was not paradise. Nonetheless, although it included those, like Still, who did not honor virtue, they were, according to Page, controlled by an honorable gentry. With the triumph of the commercial North in the war, those like Still will be even harder to contain. In his romance, however, Page presents leaders capable of wedding virtue with commerce, leading to prosperity and harmony in the New South.[3]

The promise of that prosperity and harmony is not confined to the South. The South might have lost the war, but it can bequeath its tradition of virtue to the entire nation. In his influential chapter "The Americanization of Virtue," J. G. A. Pocock argues that the election of Andrew Jackson and the triumph of classical liberalism and the spoils system spelled the end of republican virtue as a viable ideal in the new republic. Page gives a different account. For him, the ideal survived as a living tradition in the South. With the redemption of the South after radical rule, if the North is willing and the South follows its best leaders, the nation as a whole will be reconstructed on the basis of virtue. On Jacquelin's voyage, "his horizon had widened," and he yearns to see not only his "county" but even more "the flag of the nation" (*RR*, 257–58). The older generation is attached to a piece of land, what Page in the preface calls "'the old County,' or, 'the Red Rock section,' or just, 'My country, sir'" (*RR*, vii). Those of the Old South were loyal to a particular place, a section that is identified as its country. The new generation has learned to subsume the older generation's attachment under a broader loyalty to a united people, a nation, not merely a county or a section. In Constance Fenimore Woolson's "Rodman, the Keeper," the flag commands the loyalty of only Rodman and the dead bodies in the national cemetery over which it flies; in *Red Rock*, the same flag commands the loyalty of all in the region.[4]

In *Gabriel Tolliver,* Harris also seeks harmony of northern and southern interests, but he does not do so through a story about the inheritance of a plot of land. For instance, although it is clear from the start that Gabriel is destined to marry his childhood playmate Nan, his grandmother insists that Nan must marry Francis Bethune because the land she will inherit "joins the land that Bethune will fall heir to someday, and it seems that the two estates should become one" (*GT*,

83–84). An illegitimate child, Harris does not share that "old-fashioned" idea "about marriage" (84). To be sure, through marriage to Nan, Gabriel will inherit the Dorrington estate, but it was not fraudulently dispossessed during Reconstruction. On the contrary, Harris challenges the notion of inheritance by blood. Most people in Shady Dale think that Nan is a blood relative to the Cloptons, the town's founding family. Gabriel's grandmother tells him instead that Nan's

> grandmother was captured by Creeks when only a year or two old. She was the only survivor of a party of seven which had been ambushed by the Indians. She was too young to give any information about herself. She could say a few words, and she knew her name was Rosalind, but that was all. She was ransomed by General McGillvray, and sent to Shady Dale. Under the circumstances, there was nothing for Raleigh Clopton to do but adopt her. Thus she became Rosalind Clopton. She married Benier Odom when, as well as could be judged, she was forty years old. Randolph Dorrington married her daughter, who died when Nan was born. (80)

Nan is not connected to the Cloptons by blood but by Shady Dale's tradition of providing a place of refuge for those in need of succor. Likewise, Gabriel's most important inheritance comes from the Georgian politicians who hold retreats in Shady Dale. Following an antebellum tradition, when Reconstruction made it "necessary to organize a white man's party, the leaders turned their eyes and their steps to Shady Dale" (*GT*, 118). Most prominent among those leaders are Robert Toombs, the first Confederate secretary of state who resigned in protest over Jefferson Davis's abridgement of civil liberties, and Alexander Stephens, the vice president of the Confederacy. "It was Gabriel's acquaintance with Mr. Stephens that first fired his ambition" (119). Stephens, who was "always partial to young men" (119), gave special attention to Gabriel. "Still suffering from his confinement in prison," Stephens accepted Meriwether Clopton's invitation to stay for "a week or more" (121). "During that week, there was hardly a day that Gabriel did not go to the Clopton Place. He went because he could see that his presence was agreeable to Mr. Stephens as well as to Meriwether Clopton. He was led along to join in the conversation which the older men were carrying on, and in that way he gained more substantial information about political principles and policies than he could have found in the books and the newspapers" (121).

Of course, Page also was concerned about having a new generation of leaders inherit a southern political tradition. For him, unlike for Harris, however, that tradition was linked to the landed gentry. Part of the code of virtue that Steve and Jacquelin inherit from their elders is a paternal sense of guardianship for those below them on the social scale. Jacquelin demonstrates his understanding of that code while still a teenager when he saves Andy Stamper from going into debt to Still to buy a horse to join the Confederate army. With full approval from his father, Jacquelin makes a gift of the horse his father had given him. Later, when Jacquelin finally gets word that he is eligible for a prisoner exchange to escape the squalid conditions of Port Lookout, he lets Andy go in his place. In return, Andy gives him proper deference. In contrast, for Harris, the Stampers of the world promise to be the new leaders. Page's New South inherits from the planter class its ideal of disinterested paternal governance that will control the Hiram Stills of the world. Harris's New South is governed by the salt of the earth, like Billy Sanders, himself a former overseer.

III

Like Page, Dixon includes incidents in which white southern families are dispossessed of property because of the tax burden of Reconstruction regimes. Having organized a taxpayers' convention, Dr. Cameron reports to Stoneman, "No such rate of taxation was ever imposed on a civilized people. A tithe of it cost Great Britain her colonies. There are 5,000 homes in this county—2,000 of them are advertised for sale by the sheriff to meet his tax bills" (*CM*, 288). Stoneman is unmoved by the general effects of his policy, but he is touched by a particular case. While in the South, he has been renting from Mrs. Lenoir, a war widow with a beautiful daughter. For the Lenoirs, "The Stonemans' coming was a godsend." The rent they provide pays the Lenoirs' outrageous cotton tax and mortgage. Stoneman even develops a crush on the young Marion. When Dr. Cameron informs Stoneman that the Lenoirs' place and farm is about to be auctioned for tax debt, the carpetbagger is shocked. Preparing the way for Stoneman's miraculous conversion at the end of the novel, Dixon reports that "individual suffering he could not endure" (297). Experiencing the Lenoirs' plight firsthand, he offers to buy the place at twenty times the going rate and let the Lenoirs live in their old home while he seeks another rental. His economic benevolence is, however, undermined by his racial politics. Immediately after the Lenoirs are reinstalled in their home, Gus attacks them and rapes Marion.

Despite incidents of this sort, Dixon's sense of conflict-driven, progressive history does not lend itself to elaborate inheritance plots in the way that Page's sense of tradition does. Nor does it produce a sense of an older generation of politicians passing on its wisdom to the new generation as we get in Page and Harris. On the contrary, the first two works of Dixon's trilogy pay more attention to conflicts between generations than to the inheritance of one generation from another. In *The Leopard's Spots*, the generational conflict is between Charles Gaston, as the representative of the New South, and General Worth, the father of Gaston's lover, as a representative of the Old South. There is even a conflict between Gaston and his former mentor, Rev. John Durham, about the proper vision of a New South. In *The Clansman*, the major generational conflict is between Stoneman and his children, who adopt the South's position and marry into the Cameron family. But there is also a temporary conflict between Ben Cameron and his father over the Ku Klux Klan. In *The Traitor*, however, Dixon does give us a plot about the inheritance of a piece of land. Although, as in *Red Rock*, that plot remedies the dispossession of an old family of the South, it does so with quite different implications.

The book starts with a slightly drunken John Graham, the leader of the Klan, in Independence, North Carolina, forcing his way into his family's former home, now occupied by the scalawag Judge Butler, of the U.S. Circuit Court, who presided over the trial of Jefferson Davis. Butler, whose name evokes the notorious Benjamin Butler, comes from "poor white trash" (*TR*, 16). Butler had married "an aristocrat of aristocrats to her fingertips" (77). Ostracized by her family for the marriage, she gradually comes to recognize her husband for the scoundrel that he is, a recognition that leads to her premature death. Before she dies, however, she helps Butler take over the Graham estate. On twenty-five acres with beautiful formal gardens, the Grahams' house had been built in 1840 by John's eccentric grandfather, son of Colonel John Graham of Revolutionary War fame. The house's architecture is a mixture of Colonial and French, inspired by John's Huguenot grandmother. Continuing the family tradition, John's father distinguished himself in the Mexican-American War. Nonetheless, after the Civil War, Judge Butler orders the confiscation of the estate. At a secret "public" auction Butler's wife buys it for $2,800, even though it is worth $50,000. Dispossessed, John's mother dies, and his father goes mad.

John enters the house with the help of a former family slave, Aunt Julie Ann. Although she despises Butler, she works for him out of loyalty to the house and because she needs money. Confronting Butler, John threatens to oust him with the aid of the Klan, even though John is about to disband it because it has done its job. Instead, he prepares a lawsuit, *Graham v. Butler*, which he never files because the judge is murdered and John is accused of the crime. When the murderer turns out to be a carpetbagger politician, John is acquitted, but he still has to spend time in federal prison for his activities with the Klan. Nonetheless, he regains possession of the house by marrying Butler's beautiful daughter Stella, who takes after her mother, not her father.

John has to win Stella from his rival Steve Hoyle, who is engaged to her when the book begins. As we saw in chapter 3, Steve organizes an illegitimate Klan after John disbands the original group. Under Steve's leadership the Klan perpetuates spiteful and cowardly acts of revenge. Later, Steve becomes a successful scalawag politician and by the end of the book is a federal judge. He inherits his character from his father, who avoided service in the Confederate Army by hiring a substitute. The father emerged from the war a wealthy man, likely having taken advantage of the "infamous Confiscation Act of Congress" to procure cotton and sell it at inflated prices (*TR*, 28). In winning Stella, John restores the estate to its rightful heirs and marks the triumph of "good" forces in the South over the "bad."

The Traitor has enough echoes of *Red Rock* to make them more than coincidental. Both books feature a dispossessed house of a venerable southern family sold at a secret "public" auction. In both, a lawsuit to regain possession is displaced by a trial about the protagonist's leadership in the Klan. Dixon even steals from Page the plot device of having his protagonist marry the woman who can provide evidence against him. Whereas Page portrays a gothic house haunted by the ghost of the Indian-killer, Dixon gives us one with secret passages used by the murderer to accomplish his deed. But Dixon evokes these similarities to make a different point, as evidenced by his choice of the first name of Page's protagonist for that of his villain.

By the book's end, Stella and John decide not to live on the old Graham estate. Instead, they sell it; a new street runs through the former lot, and "a dozen beautiful homes stand on the site of its wide lawns" (*TR*, 330). The couple relocate to a restored mansion called Inwood, "the first house ever built in the state," which was burned by Sherman's army but rebuilt with a new foundation (226). The grounds of their estate extend to the river where "the Graham Brothers' mills are located" (331). Symbols of a new industrial South, these mills are run with the help of the northern transplant and former detective Ackerman.

Dixon's vision of an industrialized New South is in stark contrast to Page's agrarianism linked to a past of plantations. Although, understandably, criticism of *The Clansman* focuses almost exclusively on Dixon's racism, his most famous work also suggests the importance of industry for the South. *Red Rock*'s North-South marriage signals how important northern support is for the new postbellum order of the South, at the same time that the novel has the Welches assimilate into an agrarian lifestyle. *The Clansman* also uses a North-South marriage to stress the importance of northern support, but Phil Stoneman, like Ackerman, does more than assimilate. He brings new economic energy. His future father-in-law, Dr. Cameron, like Page's Dr. Cary, is so devoted to his profession that he treats everyone, even if they have no money. Ben Cameron, like Page's Steve Allen and Jacquelin Gray, is a lawyer but finds few clients who can pay. In contrast, "while the Camerons were growing, each day, poorer, Phil was becoming rich. His genius, skill, and enterprise had been quick to see the possibilities of the water-power"

(*CM*, 277–78). During the war, the local mills had been burned. Phil "interested Northern capitalists, bought the falls, and erected two great mills, the dim hum of whose spindles added a new note to the river's music" (278). Phil is familiar with the importance—and profit—of mills because of his father's iron mills that were burned in the war when Lee moved into Pennsylvania. At the end of the book, we learn that it was while watching his mills burn that Stoneman swore revenge on the South. Dixon primarily uses this incident to contrast Stoneman's character to that of southerners. Whereas numerous southerners accepted wartime destruction, Stoneman responds with spiteful vengeance. But Dixon also uses the symbols of fire and water that these scenes of burning mills bring together to tell a complementary story.

Dixon, the Baptist minister, associates the power of water with purification. The Klan meets in a cave, big enough for "a grand hall eighty feet deep, fifty feet wide, and more than forty feet in height, which had been carved out of the stone by the swift current of the river in ages past when its waters stood at a higher level" (*CM*, 318). Watching his mills burn, Stoneman vows to "ground the South beneath my heel" (372), but the purifying waters of the cave housing the Klan have the power to wear down stone—and Stoneman. This description of the Klan's cave, "lighted by candles placed on the ledges of the wall," occurs in the chapter called "The Fiery Cross." Earlier, in "By the Light of a Torch," the Cameron's barn, "worth more than the house" (259), is set afire, sparking Ben to ask his father's support for the Klan, which fights fire with fire to purify not only the South but also the nation. Indeed, Phil's reconstructed mills, creating a harmonious hum along a southern river, suggest that the South can benefit from Yankee industrial know-how. It can also benefit from northern capital. When Stoneman buys the Lenoirs' farm, he promises to invest their ten thousand dollars in "good Northern securities" (298).[5]

For the South to benefit from northern capital and industry, however, it must be cleansed of the corporate greed that allows Simon Legree in *The Leopard's Spots* to thrive after the war. In *The Clansman*, as the nation's capital celebrates Lee's surrender, "Jay Cooke & Co.'s banking-house had stretched across its front, in enormous blazing letters, the words: 'THE BUSY B'S—BALLS, BALLOTS AND BONDS'" (67). For Cooke, who made a fortune selling governmental bonds to finance the war and whose financial collapse precipitated the Panic of 1873, it is time to dance because the South's defeat will lead to African American suffrage. Later, we learn that the reign of Stoneman, the architect of Radical Reconstruction, is the reign of "the first great Railroad Lobby," the "Cotton Thieves, who operated through a ring of Treasury agents," and the "Whiskey Ring." Dixon, of course, mentions the "*Credit Mobilier* steal" and links corporate corruption to unfair taxes. "The statute-books were loaded with laws that shackled chains of monopoly on generations yet unborn. Public lands wide as the reach of empires were voted gifts to private corporations, and the subsidies of untold millions fixed as a charge upon the people and their children's children" (153–54).

Dixon's indictment of northern capitalist corruption for ruining the inheritance of present and future generations has surprising similarities with the view of his archenemy W. E. B. Du Bois. Hoping to use *The Souls of Black Folk* to build a coalition between the "best" white southerners and the talented tenth of African Americans, Du Bois frequently blames those from the North intent on profit. He insists that the "economic system of the South today which has succeeded the old *regime*" is not progressive but "a copy of that England of the early nineteenth century, before the factory acts,—the England that wrung pity from thinkers and fired the wrath of Carlyle." Those who have inherited the New South are "the sons of poor whites fired with a thirst for wealth and power, thrifty and avaricious Yankees, shrewd and unscrupulous Jews" (*SBF*, 136). Describing the conditions of Reconstruction, he writes:

> The Wizard of the North—the Capitalist—had rushed down in the seventies to woo this coy dark soil. He bought a square mile or more, and for a time the field-hands sang, the gins groaned, and the mills buzzed. Then came a change. The agent's son embezzled the funds and ran off with them. Then the agent himself disappeared. Finally the new agent stole even the books, and the company in wrath closed its business and its houses, refused to sell, and let houses and furniture and machinery rust and rot. So the Waters-Loring planation was stilled by the spell of dishonesty, and stands like some gaunt rebuke to a scarred land. (*SBF*, 109)

For Du Bois, the worst carpetbaggers are Jews. Describing the black belt as the former "Egypt of the Confederacy" (*SBF*, 111), Du Bois invites a comparison between Moses, who led the Jews out of bondage, and present-day Jews who profit by debt. In "Of Our Spiritual Strivings," Du Bois notes that "emancipation was the key to a promised land of sweeter beauty than ever stretched before the eyes of wearied Israelites" (40). But in "Of the Black Belt," "the Jew is the heir of the slave-baron. . . . We see on all sides within the circle of dark forest a Land of Canaan. Here and there are tales of projects for money-getting, born in the swift days of Reconstruction—'improvement' companies, wine companies, mills, and factories; nearly all failed, and the Jew fell heir" (112). Du Bois compares "the lands belonging to Russian Jews," where "the overseers are white" and "the rents are high" to a farm rented by "a plucky white woman" and a plantation with a "Negro overseer" (116). Elsewhere, a fair region "had been ruined and ravished into red waste, out of which only a Yankee or Jew could squeeze more blood from debt-cursed tenants" (113). Describing the "bewilderment of Reconstruction" (111) from the point of view of the freedman, Du Bois blames the carpetbagger, along with the Klan: "The holocaust of war, the terrors of the Ku Klux Klan, the lies of carpetbaggers, the disorganization of industry, and the contradictory advice of friends and foes, left the bewildered serf with no watchword beyond the old cry for freedom" (40).[6]

In different ways, Du Bois's and Dixon's visions of northern capitalist corruption have affinities with the Progressive and New Deal's "Beale thesis" linking Radical Reconstruction to northern big business. To be sure, Dixon and Du Bois tell very different stories about the increasing control of the "Masters of Capital." Whereas Du Bois links the lies of carpetbaggers and the terrors of the Ku Klux Klan, Dixon claims that the Klan freed the South from carpetbaggers and defended a Jewish businessman. For Dixon, politicians like Sumner and Stevens were driving forces behind capitalist and carpetbagger corruption, so much so that he turns his character based on Stevens into a carpetbagger. In contrast, for Du Bois, Sumner and Stevens are exemplary figures whose racial egalitarianism is at odds with the class interests of the capitalists who would come to dominate the Republican Party. As opposed to the Beards, who depicted Radical Reconstruction as the triumph of northern capitalists over the southern planter class, by the time of *Black Reconstruction*, Du Bois saw the egalitarian goals of Radical Reconstruction undermined by a coalition of the planter class with northern capital. "The Northern reform movement," he writes, "had begun to unite itself with Big Business and Super-Finance, and to sympathize with Southern planters" (*BR*, 684). This "left capital, as represented by the old planter class, the new Northern capitalist, and the capitalist that began to rise out of the poor whites, with a control over labor greater than in any modern industrial state in civilized lands" (630).

Du Bois's sympathy was solidly with laborers, so much so that he lumped farm workers together with the proletariat. Dixon had little sympathy for the working class or agrarian laborers, black or white. A crucial question for Beale was: "Why did [the] co-operation between blacks and whites for common ends break down?" For Du Bois, a combination of Dixon's racism and capitalism kept poor whites and blacks from realizing their common class interests. For Dixon, there were no common ends. His heroes were professionals or small, independent manufacturers, who were hurt as much by corporate greed as Du Bois's workers or Harris's "salt of the earth," although not aligned with either. These rugged individuals also had no need for the paternal guardianship of Page's planter class. Moving beyond a tradition of Jeffersonian agrarianism, they become the driving force of Dixon's imagined new southern economy.[7]

IV

Dixon envisions a new southern economy but suggests it in his novels only through background details. The most complicated fictional treatment of the possibilities of the New South comes in George Washington Cable's *John March, Southerner*, which has an inheritance plot as elaborate as *Red Rock*'s. The action of *John March* takes place in the "State of Dixie, County of Clearwater," around the town of Suez "in the heart of what was once the 'Southern Confederacy' "(1). By evoking a general sense of the South, Cable goes against the grain of his reputation as a local-color writer from Louisiana. For physical details he draws on the area of northern Georgia near the Tennessee border. His Georgia setting allows him to continue his 1885 debate with Henry Grady, a Georgian and the most famous advocate of the New South. For readers to understand how different Cable's account of the new southern economy is from Grady's, they need to pay careful attention to the exchange of capital in his novel. After all, according to legend the South took its nickname from ten-dollar bills known as "dixies," issued in Louisiana with the French "dix" on the reverse side.

The fictional area in "Dixie" was first claimed by two cousins, both named Ezra Jaspers. The town of Suez was founded by the cousin who married a woman named Susan. After the development of Suez, all that was left of their original estate was sixty acres, inherited by the beautiful Rose Montgomery. Rose married Rev. John Wesley Garnet. In 1857, the couple established a boy's academy called Rosemont. The other cousin lay claim to a vast estate of 100,060 acres called Widewood. Undeveloped, Widewood descends to John's father, Judge Powhatan March. The judge's first name recalls the Native Americans whose land was taken by the Jamestown settlers and evokes the legend of Pocahontas's marriage to John Rolfe, a legend of cooperation and conflict. When Judge March dies in 1877, soon after Rutherford B. Hayes becomes president, John and his mother, a writer of third-rate sentimental poems praising the South, inherit the estate. As a young boy, John learns from his father why they are land-poor. The judge could have sold parts of it but always refused because doing so "wouldn't a-met the object for which the whole tract has always been held. It was yo' dear grandfather's ambition an' his father's befo' him, to fill these lan's with a great population, p'osp'ous an' happy" (*JM*, 63). John's father acknowledges that such a plan was not "adapted to a slave state. . . . but now, son, you know, all labor's free an' the time come faw a change."

That dream differs from three other plans for developing the South. Garnet and most whites in Suez are intent on recovering and developing the economy while maintaining white domination. In an early, harrowing scene, Major Garnet returns from the war to find that his former slave, the mulatto Cornelius Leggett, has hired his labor to Judge March. Incensed, Garnet viciously whips Leggett, causing an exodus of many of Garnet's servants from his house and terrifying his young daughter Barbara. Another option is set in motion by Gen. Launcelot Halliday, Garnet's commanding officer in the Confederate Army. Immediately after the war, Halliday sells his plantation to the northern officer to whom he surrendered and moves to New Orleans. Possibly modeled on ex-Confederate general James Longstreet, who like him "accepted the situation" (*JM*, 50), Halliday writes an open letter proclaiming, "the King never dies; citizenship never ceases. . . . There are men who, when their tree has been cut down even with the ground, will try to sit in the shade of the stump. . . . Such men are those who, now that slavery is gone, still cling to a civil order based on the old plantation system" (51). When the northern officer's dream of making a profit in the South fails, Halliday recovers his estate by mortgage and establishes "the Negro farm-village of Leggettstown" (53), a development of small, hopefully self-sufficient farms. By 1869, Halliday returns to Suez to live. With scorn, the local paper reprints his open letter of a few years before, including his statement, "If we can't make our Negroes white, let us make them as white as we can," and gives it the signature "Social Equality Launcelot" (54). Leggettstown is, however, "only a clumsy sketch" of a larger plan based on Halliday's "belief in the profound economic value of—'villages of small freeholder farmers'" (53).

Leggettstown is named after Cornelius, who suggests to Halliday what the role for freedmen ought to be. Cornelius goes to a Freedmen's Bureau school and becomes a political leader in the African American community. He represents a third economic possibility. Cooperating with Halliday, he does not limit his economic plan to the Jeffersonian ideal of freeholder farmers. Instead, he supports any measure that might benefit the African American community and simultaneously feather his own nest. For instance, he helps bring in the railroad as long as doing so is coupled with establishing schools for freedmen and a kickback for him.

The difference between Halliday's and Garnet's visions is played out in the political arena. With the support of the African American vote, Halliday, with Garnet as his rival, wins the first election for state representative after the war. With violent suppression of the African American vote in the next election, Garnet unseats his rival. Halliday's defeat is a terrible setback for African Americans politically, but in Cable's complicated portrayal, politically forward-looking Halliday is economically tied to the past. There were two competing visions of the South's agrarian past. One was associated with J. C. Calhoun with plantations producing cash crops of cotton and tobacco. The other was associated with Thomas Jefferson with self-sufficient farmers producing what their families needed to consume. Cable uses Halliday to show the links between the two. Espousing a Jeffersonian vision of self-sufficient farms, the general continues to pay homage to King Cotton. Cotton's reign, as Halliday's first name suggests, helps perpetuate a feudal order. In Du Bois's world, the South's reliance on the cash crop of cotton condemns freedmen to perpetual debt and spoils the land. In his lyrical poem "Corn," Sidney Lanier portrays the cultivation of life-sustaining grain as the agrarian alternative to King Cotton. In Garnet's first encounter with Leggett after the war, the former slave is working for Judge March, trying to repair a wagon "with a half load of corn in the shuck, surmounted by a coop of panting chickens" (*JM*, 17). Later, John's childhood dream of Widewood's "immeasurable wealth" and fairy-tale wonders is marred by the image of "strong weeds and emaciated corn and cotton push[ing] one another down among the big clods" (48). Subservience to King Cotton does more than threaten subsistence agriculture. As the judge tells John, General Halliday's "villages are boun' han' and' foot to cotton fahmin' and can't bring forth the higher industries" (64). If Widewood could attract the best residents from Halliday's villages with a school and church provided for them, capitalists would invest and, "first thing you know, we'll have mines an' mills an' sto'es every *which* away."

On the surface, the economic plan of the politically reactionary Garnet would seem more compatible than Halliday's with Judge March's dream of developing Widewood. For instance, when Garnet first returns from the war, he and the younger Jeff-Jack Ravenel survey the land. Ravenel exclaims, "Law, Major, we've got stuff enough left to make a country of yet." To which Garnet responds, "If they'll let us, Jeff-Jack. If they'll only let us; but will they?" (16). Soon thereafter, when Garnet meets Judge March and his boy, he jokingly proposes uniting the two inheritances of the original Ezras. "Mighty handsome boy, Brother March—stuff for a good soldier—got a little sweetheart at my house for you, sonnie-boy! Rosemont College and Widewood lands wouldn't go bad together" (19). Once this vision is planted in his mind, Garnet cannot let it go. After his election, with "good government" now in place, he discusses developing March's land and makes a deal by which Judge March mortgages part of his land in exchange for John's tuition at Rosemont (79). But developing Widewood will require northern capital.

Cable suggests two sides of the South's efforts to attract investments through two capitalists—one named Gamble, the other Fair. Fat and unattractive, Gamble becomes president of the railroad company that builds a line to Suez a year after Judge March dies. Cable devotes four chapters to describing the town's celebration of the new railroad. The celebration makes John think of "that deep store of earth's largess lying under [the] unfruitful custody" (*JM*, 164) of him and his mother. Because developing Wildwood could bring wealth into the area, Garnet calls John "the hope of Suez!" (162). But John despairs: "He wished his problem was as simple as a railroad question. A railroad can ask for public aid; but fancy him asking public aid to open and settle up his private lands!" (165). John sees two options. The first is suggested by Gamble. With the railroad connection, John should "colonize" his lands by forming a private company. The second option would be to convince Mr. Fair to invest (149). A dignified man from Massachusetts, Fair sends his son Henry, about John's age, to inspect the land. After returning home and consulting with his father, Henry writes John. The Fairs recognize the "latent value" of John's land (222), and they also approve the "spirit" of his plan: "It seeks a common welfare. It does not offer swift enrichment to the moneyed few through the use of ignorant labor unlifted from destitution and degradation, but rather the remuneration of capital through the social betterment of all factors of a complete community" (223). Yet there is a fundamental problem. Far from the "good government" that Garnet claims he has procured, the government of Dixie is "in a state of arrested development" lacking incentives for investors. John's plan has the company paying for and controlling "banks, schools and churches" that elsewhere are provided for by the "community and commonwealth." Furthermore, even if for a time John's plan would succeed, would not Widewood "be an island in an ocean of misunderstanding and indifference? If you should need an act of county or township legislation, could you get it?" It is for these reasons that "capital seeks wider and more distant regions when it would rather be in Dixie" (223). In conclusion, the Fairs encourage John to incorporate ideas put forth by Cornelius Leggett that "would make your scheme as public as you would make it private" (224). Although they are not suggesting an "alliance with Leggett," which would be "out of the question," they could provide "pecuniary support," if John would adopt Leggett's views of how government can spark development.

The thought of taking on ideas put forth by Leggett is difficult for John. He is brought up with the racial attitudes of most southern whites, expressed in his mother's poem, "Slaves to ow [*sic*] own slaves. . . . Neveh." As a young boy John plays war "killing Yankees—colored troops" (*JM*, 43). Furthermore, his animosity toward Leggett is personal. When John is eight, soon after Leggett is whipped by Garnet, the mulatto is charged by Judge March with making sure John gets home. Taking his anger out on the boy, Leggett viciously whips him with the same whip used on himself and makes him promise not to tell anyone, just as Garnet had made Cornelius not tell anyone about his whipping. This traumatic incident understandably colors John's future interactions with the African American politician.[8]

Nonetheless, John does start to change his attitudes. Fair, he tells his mother, is "in with the times. He knows what's got to come and what's got to go." Dismissing her sobbing moan, "My son a Radical!," John realizes that to develop Widewood he will need people to inhabit the land and serve as a workforce (*JM*, 199). One plan is to attract immigrants from the North and abroad. Another is to convince local African Americans to move from Leggettstown. When John tells Halliday this plan, the general exposes his paternalism by responding, ""Would you do such a thing as that?—run off with another man's niggers?" Biting his lip, John answers, "Are they yours, General?" (230). John's dream of development is further complicated by the presence of the "Sandstone County Mountaineers" on the land. Although, like Ruiz de Burton, Cable evokes the label "Squatter Sovereignty" to describe people inhabiting another person's property, Cable's mountaineers are quite different from the acquisitive Yankees in *The Squatter and the Don* (*JM*, 233). Poor and uneducated, they, like African Americans, ride mules, not horses. For years, they have lived on Widewood with the Marches' tacit consent. "To the gentlest of them [John's scheme] would make game scarcer and circumscribe and belittle their consciously small and circumscribed lives; to the wilder sort it meant an invasion of aliens who had never come before for other purposes than to break up their stills and drag them to jail" (213). One warns John, "Ef you bring niggehs we'll kill 'em, an' ef you bring white folks we'll make 'em wish they was dead." According to this squatter, "Grannie Sugg . . . allow ef Johnnie March bring air railroad 'ithin ten mile' o' her, he better leave his medjer 'ith the coffin man" (214). In a scene revealing the underlying violence of Dixie, this squatter later tries to kill John but is mistakenly shot by his own brother, who is attempting to aid him after John has bested him in hand-to-hand combat involving a knife and a gun.

The book's inheritance plot is also linked to its love plot. When he is twelve, John becomes hopelessly infatuated with General Halliday's beautiful daughter Fannie. Fannie, who is four years older than John, is in love with Jeff-Jack, who has taken over as editor of the local newspaper, which exerts substantial control over Suez's political opinions. Later, when Fannie announces her engagement, John feels he has to develop Widewood to impress her, and he forms a company of locals. The day after Fannie's wedding, he heads north to seek investors. His trip coincides with Fannie and Jeff-Jack's honeymoon and Barbara Garnet's journey to attend a northern college. Barbara is accompanied by Mr. and Mrs. Fair, whose son has fallen in love with her. During the long train ride, Jeff-Jack is revealed as a less than an ideal husband; John helps nurse first Jeff-Jack, then Fannie, who become ill one after the other; John and Barbara, without acknowledging it, fall in love; Barbara settles into school in western Massachusetts; and John learns that behind-the-scenes dealing in Suez places his plan to develop Widewood at risk.

Cable describes the scheme to deprive John of his inheritance with meticulous care—so meticulous that it taxes the resources of his reader. John and his mother inherit from the judge not only an estate but also the mortgage on the estate that paid for John's education at Rosemont and is held by Garnet and Ravenel. Unable to attract sufficient northern capital to finance his plans, John agrees to form the Three County Colonization Company, Limited, proposed by Leggett. This company is a joint public-private enterprise, with one third of the stock owned by the company, one third by private parties, and one third by the three counties including and adjacent to Widewood. The company will build improvements, such as dams, to attract settlers and developers. In addition, it will build and staff schools for whites and blacks. In a curious provision, it will also provide a subsidy to Garnett's Rosemont Academy. The three counties' financial contribution will come from a tax that Leggett will steer through the legislature. When a meeting is held for possible stockholders, Leggett gets a special deal, implicitly because of his legislative influence; Garnett gets considerable shares, backed, we are led to believe, by the mortgages he already has on the land; and Ravenel is named one of two trustees for the three counties, with the authority to name the other. John is president of the company but is in position to lose all of his land if the enterprise fails. Although Henry Fair attends the meeting, he holds back from purchasing any shares and afterward expresses concerns to Barbara that some of those present might take advantage of John. Indeed, while John is in the North seeking investors, he learns that a separate construction company has been formed to build the promised improvements. He has not been informed about this plan, even though his company will be billed for the company's costs, costs partially subsidized by a public tax.[9]

With formation of the construction company, Cable alludes to the infamous Crèdit Mobilier scandal. Intent on building a transcontinental railroad, Congress agreed on a generous subsidy to the Union Pacific for every mile of track it laid. The Union Pacific then contracted with the Crèdit Mobilier Company to perform the actual construction. Crèdit Mobilier billed the Union Pacific a lucrative rate for its work, which the railroad company passed on to the government, asking for new legislation when the existing subsidies were exhausted. What the public did not know was that, even though the two companies were separate legal entities, they were owned by the same people. Thus, the public was subsidizing a railroad that was funneling taxpayer dollars into the coffers of a company the railroad executives owned. The only public figures aware of this scheme were some politicians charged with getting subsidy bills through Congress. These legislators got increasingly valuable stock at bargain prices.

In Cable's fictional adaptation of this scheme, the corrupt politician is an African American, who, readers should recognize, has quickly learned methods perfected by national politicians. Furthermore, contrary to prevailing stereotypes, Leggett is not in cahoots with carpetbaggers but with Ravenel, the trustee for the public, and Garnet, who, when he beat Halliday in the second election, gloated, "We've restored public credit and cut the rottenness out of our government" (*JM*, 102). Indeed, John's loss of his inheritance is finalized as Garnet trades his increasingly worthless land company stock for increasingly valuable construction company stock. When the land company goes broke, Garnet and Ravenel buy it at auction and take possession of Widewood, including all of its improvements.

John learns of this betrayal in London, where he is located after a yearlong journey to Europe to seek immigrants to settle in Widewood. The only land he and his mother hold onto is a small bit around their home. John's mother, in the meantime, is secretly engaged to Garnet, whose wife has died. That engagement falls through when Garnet's affair with another company member's wife becomes public. This shareholder had bought stock after convincing his wife to mortgage her estate. He is the one Garnet tricked into exchanging construction company stock for land company stock. Confronted by the enraged husband, Garnet kills him in self-defense but has to leave town and abandon his daughter, who has returned after her northern education. Before he leaves, however, Barbara sees him give Leggett five thousand dollars, after which Leggett also leaves, accompanied by his latest lover.

The scene of Garnet handing money to Leggett jogs Barbara's memory. She recalls as a little girl finding a letter her father misplaced the day he lost the election to General Halliday. Unable to read the document, she had secreted it away. Locating it after many years, she is able to solve numerous mysteries. Rosemont, it turns out, had originally been part of Widewood. Because of confusion over the two Ezras' names, however, it had mistakenly been registered in Montgomery's name. Garnet discovers the mistake while tracking down Rosemont's title, but he keeps it secret. He courts John's mother out of fear that John, controlling what little is left of the March estate, might also discover the mistake. In fact, the one person other than Garnet who knows about Rosemont is Leggett. Relying on his black "Uncle Leviticus's traditions" (*JM*, 508), he researches the local records and begins to bribe Garnet in exchange for silence. Because of the bribery, Leggett has a self-interest in keeping Garnet flush. Former slave and master enter into a secret alliance with Cornelius supporting a law that taxes Rosemont only for its land, not its improvements, and engineering the plan to cheat John out of most of Widewood. Barbara shows John the letter that clears up these mysteries, and the two finally acknowledge their love and, in a contrived but significant ending, marry. Thus, the book fulfills Garnet's jesting early prophecy that the families' two estates will unite with Barbara, not John, bringing much of Widewood to their marriage and John, not Barbara, bringing Rosemont.

John's inheritance of Rosemont is particularly appropriate. His birth coincides with the school's founding, part of Widewood is mortgaged to pay for his tuition, and his father dies at his graduation, which coincides with the start of Hayes's New Departure. After graduating, John himself tries teaching for a year. Most important, John proves capable of being educated. Overcoming romantic dreams, false pride, a strong temper, and racial prejudice, John becomes a model for what a new southern gentleman can be. With Garnet gone, John is the most powerful man in Suez. Fighting backward views, he feels, as a local puts it, that the town doesn't "do the dahkeys justice." Nonetheless, as the same local acknowledges, because of John's leadership, Suez comes "neareh toe it . . . than anywheres else in Dixie" (*JM*, 506).

Through this elaborate inheritance plot, Cable tries his best to portray Reconstruction in all its complexity. Rather than give us a marriage standing for North-South reconciliation, he gives us two southern marriages, with more progressive John marrying the daughter of reactionary Garnet and Garnet's ally Jeff-Jack marrying the daughter of Garnet's political rival General Halliday. Cable also challenges the stereotype that "Negro and carpetbagger rule" was fed by northern corporate corruption. Before *John March, Southerner,* John William DeForest posed his own challenge to that stereotype. *John Vane* (1875) registers the split in the Republican Party between corporate interests and those supportive of African American rights by telling the tale of a naïve politician from New England who goes to Washington intent on abolishing the franking privilege that gave congressmen special access to the mails, a reform once advocated by Charles Sumner. In need of money to satisfy his wife's extravagant tastes, John is corrupted by a Republican insider, who tells him, "Don't go into the war memories and the nigger worshipping; all those sentimental dodges are played out. Go into finance. The great national questions to be attended to now are the questions of finance" (*JV*, 84). Eight years earlier, in *Miss Ravenel's Conversion,* DeForest made it clear that financial corruption during Butler's military rule in New Orleans was not confined to northerners. The most unscrupulous figure in the novel is Mrs. Larue, a beautiful Creole widow, once married to a "lawyer of note and an ultra Southern politician." Working both sides of the conflict, she thrives. Unlike other southerners of her class, "her estate was not in the now worthless investments of negroes, plantations, steamboats, or railroads, but in bank stock; and the New Orleans banks, though robbed of specie by the fleeing Lovell, still made their paper pass and commanded a market for their shares" (*MRC*, 130). To keep her property safe, she decides to go north to invest it. On the boat trip, she has an affair with Colonel Carter, who has married Miss Ravenel. An accomplished officer of the Union Army, Carter is, however, from Virginia. In all things but politics, "he was a true child of his class and state" (149), and he reaps large profits in the illegal cotton trade. When his affair with Mrs. Larue comes to an end, she gains the devotion "of persons who were mightier in counsel and in war than he." Through one of them, she gets permission "to trade for several thousand bales of cotton," which "she sold to a New York speculator for fifteen thousand dollars" (412).

If DeForest highlights corruption on a national scale, Cable concentrates on its manifestations in Dixie, including its racial components. Young Fannie, who like DeForest's Miss Ravenel marries a southerner of dubious morality, points to how complicated the situation in the South is when she tells Ravenel, "It's a war between decency in the wrong and vulgarity in the right" (*JM*, 62). Initially, Cable's portrayal of Leggett supports Fannie's view. Despite Cornelius's obvious vulgarity and corruption, he brings about various positive reforms, especially in the development of public schools. But even Fannie's formulation is too simple for Cable. Despite his evangelical rhetoric, Garnet, who opposes Reconstruction reform, matches Cornelius in his lascivious treatment of women and self-interested, underhanded dealings. Indeed, whereas on the surface former slave and master seem to be on different sides, they in fact form a secret unholy alliance. It is even possible that former master and servant are father and son. We are never told the identity of Cornelius's father, and the two men certainly have enough traits in common. That relationship would give added meaning to Cornelius's brutal beating by Garnet, who later strikes his own daughter. A father and son relationship would also complicate the inheritance plot. Cornelius's suspicion about the proper title to the land from Uncle Leviticus would then become truly a family secret, and Leggett would have bloodline connections to confirm his belief that he is entitled to inherit profits from Rosemont and Widewood.

Unlike proponents of the "Beale thesis," who blame the South's economic woes on northern capitalists, Cable uses this complicated relationship between former master and slave, possible father and son, to show how the South has bred its own corruptions. Early in the book, the narrator proves prescient when he proclaims that "all the corruptions bred by both sides in a gigantic war—and before it in all the crudeness of the country's first century—were pouring down and spouting up upon Dixie their reign of pitch and ashes" (*JM*, 55). Jeff-Jack and Garnet feel there are enough resources in the South to make a country of it, "if they'll only let us" (16), but Cable makes it clear that most of the barriers are self-imposed. Significantly, Cable gives us no carpetbagger politician, corrupt or otherwise. The only carpetbag that appears in the book is the one that breaks as John lugs his possessions to Rosemont Academy for the first time. To be sure, there is the northern officer who buys General Halliday's cotton estate immediately after the war with hopes that he could realize a quick profit. But Cable uses that transaction to counter southern white stereotypes of carpetbaggers exploiting a prostrate South by acquiring ancient estates whose owners could not pay the high taxes imposed to reap illegitimate profit and support the idle habits of freedmen. In Cable's novel, it is the carpetbagger who is forced to surrender his newly purchased estate because he cannot pay his mortgage. Cable also gives us the dubious northern investor, Gamble, who is in league with Garnet and Ravenel in their plan to cheat John out of his inheritance. On one of his trips north to attract capital, John is wired that it is useless to stay because Gamble could not "come to terms with certain much larger railroad owners for the reception of his road into their 'system'" (455). In fact, we soon learn that Gamble "sold his railroad to a system hostile to the fortunes of Suez" (470).

Cable is working against a commonplace account of the times first disseminated nationally by Horace Greeley. Just as before the war Greeley used his *Tribune* to urge young men to go west, so after the war he urged them to go south by touting the "advantages of immigration, the possibility of industrial development, and the potentialities of the South's mineral wealth." What was needed to make the South loyal to the Union was prosperity brought about by an influx of northern capital and industry. The South, Greeley insisted, welcomed this transformation. The Klan's resistance threatened to undermine his argument, and he sent reporters to gather firsthand accounts. The *Tribune* could not deny Klan violence, especially in South Carolina. Nonetheless, it argued that the Klan's atrocities were a reaction to rule by rapacious carpetbaggers. According to Greeley, high taxes and corruption discouraged the immigration of reputable northerners that the South needed and welcomed. Believing that southern prosperity could be achieved only if the Klan and carpetbaggers were driven out together, he launched a press campaign blaming carpetbaggers for the lack of capital investment and industry. As he ran for president in 1872, the journalist insisted that, "had it not been for carpetbag mismanagement, this country today would be filled with millions of Northern or foreign yeomanry carving out farms, or working in . . . iron, copper, coal, and marble." Greeley, of course, lost the election, but his attack on carpetbag misrule and the need for southern home rule gained more and more traction. In modified form, Cable's nemesis Grady took it up in his view of the New South.[10]

To appreciate the extent to which Cable undermines one stereotype after another of "Dixie" laid waste by carpetbagger misrule, readers have to be able to put together details without much help from the narrator. A novelist, Cable believed, should "teach without telling." Cable does not completely refrain from narrative commentary, but when it comes it is almost always complex. For instance, at one point we are told, "The ex-master spurned political fellowship with his slave at every cost; the ex-slave laid taxes, stole them, and was murdered" (*JM*, 61). For the most part, however, Cable leaves it up to readers to make their own connections. Trying to convince Henry Fair to invest in "our new Dixie" (140), Garnet insists that "colored and white" are "treated precisely alike" (141), even though earlier he explains to Gamble "why negroes had to be treated not as individuals but as a class" (83). Garnet also boasts to Fair how "we white folks" helped to build a new colored church, not revealing that his contribution was a meager fifty cents. Pointing to Suez's new sidewalk as a sign of progress, Garnet lets out that "our chain-gang did that" (141). Earlier, we learn that the governor's brother "leases and sublets convicts, five stockades of 'em, and ought to be one himself" (128). The Klan is also present but does its dirty work in the background.[11]

Arlin Turner provides an excellent summary of Cable's technique.

> As in most of Cable's books, the action grows complex, less from intricacy of plot than from the succession of crowded scenes that are presented through a hint here or a snatch of conversation there, with the result that the reader feels at times he cannot bring the background into focus. Into the background are woven all the vexing problems of the postwar South: public education, segregation in public activities, including the churches, Negro suffrage, mob violence, corruption in government and the embezzlement of public funds, immigration, outside capital, natural resources. . . . The book does not argue these questions directly or dogmatically, and no specific solutions are offered. In fact no one character speaks for the author; rather his views come across, as they do in Howells's novels, as the residue from the conversations and actions of all the characters. At the conclusion the problem is still complex, bewilderingly complex, and the grounds for hope are that John March sees the direction in which to seek the solution and recognizes the by-passes lining the way.[12]

As accurate as this description is, Turner does not mention the one notable exception to Cable's narrative strategy. Just after Barbara sees her father give Leggett five thousand dollars, the action is broken by a self-conscious narrative intrusion. We are transported forward in time to New York City, where the narrator, who seems to have come from Suez, meets an old acquaintance, who invites him and his northern wife to dinner to meet Mr. and Mrs. Henry Fair, along with Colonel Ravenel. Across the dining room, they see Garnet, accompanied by his new wife, who is on the lecture circuit, speaking on "Temptation and How to Conquer It" (*JM*, 505). There is an awkward moment when Ravenel refuses to acknowledge that he knows the major, his onetime partner. Otherwise, the conversation is delightful. The narrator's wife especially loves Mrs. Fair, whose southern accent leads us to believe that Henry has successfully courted Barbara. But, having raised our expectations of a North-South marriage, Cable defeats them. Mrs. Fair turns out to be from Chicago. After dinner, the narrator fills out the plot for his wife, including Barbara's marriage to John and all of the mysteries solved by the letter.

This narrative intrusion forces us to recognize that all of the prior action has been told from the point of view of a southern narrator, now living in the North, telling his northern wife about life in "Dixie." Cable's handling of the intrusion is not a complete aesthetic success, but it does answer a charge Grady leveled against the native of Louisiana in their famous 1885 debate. According to Grady, even though Cable had fought for the Confederacy, his love of New England disqualified him from speaking for the South. Grady seemed to gain creditability when, later in 1885, Cable, partly responding to hostility directed toward him and his family for "The Freedman's Case in Equity," moved to the North. In *John March, Southerner*, the narrator, like Cable, is from the South but lives in the North. With loving descriptions of the area around Smith College, the model for Barbara's northern school, he reveals a detailed familiarity with Cable's adopted town of Northampton, Massachusetts. Cable's hero, however, chooses a different path from his narrator. At one point, the Fairs offer to make John's fortune if he moves to the North. Yet John knows that he belongs in the South. By having his sympathetic portrait of a southerner come from a narrator living in the North, Cable establishes his own credentials to speak for the South. To create a truly new and prosperous South, he makes clear, it will take figures like John, who overcomes his prejudice and works for freedmen's justice, not those like Grady, who argued for a black and white division.

Cable's portrait of the New South was not well received. Despite Cable's reputation, he even had trouble getting his ambitious book published. After the success of *The Grandissimes* (1880), Cable was the darling of Richard Gilder, the editor of the *Century Magazine*. But Gilder wanted Creole, local-color fiction and refused *John March*, forcing Cable to go elsewhere for serialization and publication. According to Louis D. Rubin, except for one glowing review, *John March* was "ignored, or else treated indifferently . . . and forgotten thereafter." That situation has not changed much with altered political views of Reconstruction. Even though most people today favor Cable's position over Grady's, in fiction they seek Cable's local-color Louisiana stories. *John March* remains neglected, with Matthew Wilson arguing that its love plot and its economic plot "contradict one another in ideological terms" and Sharon D. Kennedy-Nolle dismissing it in one sentence as fading into "bland generality."[13]

Even Chesnutt preferred Cable's earlier work. In a letter to his former mentor, he remarks, "I have read your *John March, Southerner.* It is a great book, but does not appeal to me for obvious reasons, quite as much as *The Grandissimes* or *Old*

Creole Days. But I realize that the true historian must portray all phases of life, if he would be true to his art." In his 1916 lecture "The Negro in Books," he reveals the source of his reservations: "Mr. Cable's later conception of the reconstructed Negro in the character of Cornelius Leggett, the grafting mulatto politician . . . is less happy and less convincing." Without a doubt, Cable indulges in a number of racial stereotypes of the time, just as his more famous friend Mark Twain does in depicting Jim in *Adventures of Huckleberry Finn*. With his considerable political power, however, Cornelius cannot be accused, as Jim has been, of lacking agency. On the contrary, he is one of the prime movers of the plot. Cable also uses him to counter a stereotype of another order. Tourgée, understandably, rarely portrays a corrupt African American politician. In contrast, Cable wants to acknowledge that they existed. The one serious misjudgment the Fairs from New England make is about Leggett's character. Leggett, however, is not the only African American who moves the plot. The figure Cable most obviously admires is Barbara's companion since childhood, Johanna, whose name echoes that of the novel's hero. Working behind the scenes, Johanna is the first to get word to John about the forces intent on cheating him out of Widewood. Through her knowledge of John and Barbara's true feelings, Johanna also brings the hopelessly hesitant lovers together. Finally, it is Johanna who enables a happy conclusion to the inheritance plot by courageously and hastily driving herself and Fannie from John to Barbara in a buggy harnessed to a fast colt—not to a mule.[14]

In 1881, Gilder proposed that Cable write an essay for the *Century* on Tourgée's fiction, so popular at the time. In turn, Tourgée offered Cable the considerable sum of $7,500 to serialize a novel in one of his journals. Neither of these schemes was realized. Nonetheless, in 1889, Gilder registered the changing mood of the country when he criticized an early draft of *John March* by writing: "I could weep for disappointment. . . . Instead of a return *to* literature, an attempt to fetch everything into literature save & except literature itself. . . . Shades of Tourgée." Gilder was right to recognize that the two novelists shared a number of views, but he, not Cable, betrays a lack of literary sensibility. The editor is so blinded by any criticism of New South ideology that he conflates Cable's and Tourgée's very different literary techniques. Those differences are evident in how they dramatize questions of inheritance.[15]

V

Given their support of freedmen, Cable and Tourgée might be expected to imagine the disinheritance of African Americans in the same way that Page imagines the disinheritance of white planters. In their early work, they do. Set in New

Orleans soon after the Louisiana Purchase, Cable's *The Grandissimes* dramatizes complicated interactions among Creole, Anglo, and African American cultures and shows how Black Codes could lead to the disinheritance of those with African American blood. Likewise, Tourgée's first novel, *Toinette*, rewritten and published as *The Royal Gentleman*, set during slavery and early Reconstruction, depicts an African American woman involved in a love affair with her master and threatened with disinheritance as she becomes entangled in a gothic plot with ghostly hauntings and a secret chamber for sexual trysts. By the end, her daughter, also involved with an aristocratic white man, jointly inherits the plantation with the white wife of her mother's dead lover, who comes from the southern yeoman class. As the white woman explains to Toinette, "The lawyers tell me that we are what they call joint-tenants of it all, with equal rights and powers over it" (*RG*, 454). In this bizarre, yet fascinating, plot, Tourgée imagines a coalition of African Americans and white yeomen inheriting the South from the privileged planter class. Significantly, the joint tenants are both women. Nonetheless, there is a problem: two individuals are due an inheritance accumulated through the collective labor of slaves.[16]

As they more directly addressed the issues of Reconstruction, Tourgée and Cable moved away from plots of mixed-race romance. With the possible exception that Leggett might be Garnet's son, *John March, Southerner* does not raise the specter of mixed-race intimacy. Nor do *A Fool's Errand* and *Bricks without Straw*. Tourgée might have made a strategic choice. Responding to *Toinette*, the Charlotte *Observer* wrote, "*The real purpose of Tourgée was TO POPULARIZE INTER-RACIAL MARRIAGE BETWEEN THE RACES IN NORTH CAROLINA*." To keep from having his point of view dismissed on the basis of that irrational fear, in his next works he avoids the racial question altogether. When he does return to it in his two major Reconstruction novels, he eliminates interracial love and with it the problem of having African Americans promised an inheritance accumulated on the backs of slaves. *A Fool's Errand* and *Bricks without Straw* portray the dispossession of freedmen, but they are not dispossessed of inherited land and property going back to slavery. Instead, time and again, African Americans after emancipation work diligently to accumulate property for themselves, only to have all they have earned through their labor taken from them. As the narrator of *Bricks without Straw* describes it, "They lost at once the labor of their whole life of freedom and were compelled to begin again where slavery had left them" (337). Even a decade later, when he again depicts interracial sexual relations in *Pactolus Prime*, Tourgée has his protagonist bequeath to his daughter, who is passing as white, not a fortune inherited from his slave master (and father) but one Pactolus accumulated under an assumed white name in the Washington, DC, real estate market. Pactolus does calculate the debt the nation owes African Americans for uncompensated labor under two centuries of slavery, but that is about reparations, not inheritance. The elaborate inheritance plots that Tourgée imagines in his major Reconstruction novels, like those of Page and Cable, involve southern whites. More like Page's than Cable's, they are also about possible sectional reconciliation, although for different purposes.[17]

As we have seen, Tourgée felt that North and South were different civilizations. That difference was created by the institution of slavery and the need to legitimate it, not distinct bloodlines. In *A Fool's Errand*, Tourgée uses the marriage plot to imagine the possibility of overcoming those differences in the future. In *Bricks without Straw*, he connects the future with the past. By interweaving an inheritance plot with his love plot of marriage and real estate, he legitimates future reconciliation by showing the two regions' common inheritance from the past. The inheritance plot of *Bricks without Straw* is foreshadowed by a similar plot in *John Eax*, the 1874 companion piece to *Mamelon*.

In *John Eax* and *Mamelon*, Tourgée tries to imagine a New South as a "South without the Shadow" (*JE*, ix). Thus, unlike in Tourgée's other Reconstruction works, race plays a minor role. To be sure, in his preface, Tourgée acknowledges that "the shadow was over all—the shadow of Slavery and its children, Ignorance and War and Poverty" (vi). But he also notes that "there were rifts in the shadow" (vii). The inheritance plot of *John Eax* exploits one of those rifts.

Most of the action of *John Eax* takes place prior to the Civil War. It is about the De Jeunette family, which has dominated its region in the South and whose rule has been more powerful than any written code of law. The De Jeunettes have disdain for labor, none having "condescended, so far as was known, to learn or practice any trade or profession" (*JE*, 29). Charles, however, decides to become a lawyer. Even worse, from his family's point of view, although everyone expects him to marry his beautiful cousin Louise, he falls in love with Alice Bain, the niece of the overseer. When he announces his intentions, he is disinherited, and his mother and father die of shame. With all the influential people in the county against him, he ends up in debtor's prison. Escaping, he goes north, where he marries Alice, who turns out to be the unknown heir of John Eax, a rich British manufacturer from Birmingham. The newlyweds inherit a fortune on the condition that Charles take the name of their benefactor. Rejecting life in Europe, they return to live in one of the new Midwestern states and develop a thriving estate, where they give birth to a daughter, named Louise in honor of Charles's cousin who, Alice reveals, had secretly arranged for Charles's/John's escape from prison. Alice dies young, and when the Civil War breaks out, John raises a regiment and helps defeat the South. At the end of the war, he occupies the region of his childhood and arranges to meet Louise, who is now the local matriarch. She resists meeting a Yankee conqueror but must consent. John reveals his identity and his knowledge of her role in helping him escape prison. When John insists on paying his debt to her, she refuses, lamenting that he has "become a Yankee in fact" (137). Alluding to the currency debate of the time, Tourgée has John jokingly suggest, "Perhaps you want specie" (140). Finally, no longer insisting on repaying his debt, he asks her to marry him instead, which, still in love, she agrees to do.

Tourgée's plot might seem to fit Nina Silber's formula for northern romances of reunion, with a northern man asserting his power by marrying a southern woman who represents the femininity of the conquered region. But we can see how much Tourgée alters that pattern through a brief comparison between *John Eax* and a short story by Constance Fenimore Woolson. Both Tourgée and Woolson are alert to a historical reality. Because so many men died in the war, former plantations were frequently in the hands of women, who, alone, had a hard time making ends meet. As we have seen, southerners used that situation to portray the evils of carpetbag rule, with women losing family estates because they could not pay extravagant taxes. In his response to Dixon's *The Leopard's Spots*, however, Tourgée makes clear—as he does in *John Eax*—that "the great sales of land in that period were due to debts contracted before the end of the war," not because of taxes imposed by Reconstruction governments. In "Rodman, the Keeper," which we looked at in chapter 1, Woolson creates a similar situation. In her 1877 story, Woolson avoids a North-South marriage, and the southern belle is forced to sell the family home to a northerner. In "Old Gardiston," written a year earlier, she includes a North-South marriage.[18]

The title refers to an old southern estate, inherited by Gardis Duke, a girl of seventeen, who lacks the resources to maintain it. When northern troops set up camp nearby, she proudly tries to keep appearances while refusing their help. Then she needs it: "The unhappy state had fallen into the hands of double-faced, conscienceless whites, who used the newly enfranchised blacks as tools for their evil purposes. These leaders were sometimes emigrant Northerners, sometimes renegade Southerners, but always rascals." Those rascals promise each freedman his own planation as soon as the present residents are ejected and the spoils divided. "Out they came, inconsequent and reasonless as ever, to burn Gardiston. But they did not know the United States troops were there" (OG, 666). The troops quickly disperse the unorganized mob, and Gardis finds herself indebted to her former enemy. Obligated to invite the two officers to dinner out of gratitude, she does her best to appear opulent, despite her poverty. When they leave, she burns the faded clothes she wore, declaring, "So perish also the enemies of my country" (668). Afterward she finds herself courted by the young, handsome lieutenant.

Although he is rich enough to help her save Gardiston, she refuses his advances and is forced to sell the family estate to the northern wife of an army contractor. Before the new owner can occupy, however, the house accidently burns down when Gardis, saying goodbye, leaves a lit candle unattended. As Gardis watches the burning house, the older, more reserved captain arrives. With the lieutenant out of the picture, the captain has quietly tried to court Gardis, only to be refused. Now she admits her love, and the two plan to marry. The story ends with Gardiston assuming a voice, satisfied that Gardis is "provided for" and pleased that the "contractor's wife . . . shall have nothing" (674).

Charming in its descriptions of Gardis's comic attempts to preserve appearances, Woolson's story skillfully links the plot with images of fire. After the Union officers save Gardison from freedmen intent on burning it down, Gardis in an act of spite burns the clothes she wore to entertain the officers she considers her enemy, only later unintentionally to burn the house and save it from occupation by a northern woman. Nonetheless, even though, like Tourgée, Woolson criticizes the South's propensity to live in the past, she perpetuates standard stereotypes. Gardis's former slaves are too loyal to abandon her. For them, "emancipation was nothing" (OG, 662), while other freedmen are drunk with their new right to vote and prompted by unscrupulous carpetbaggers and scalawags to render destruction.

Without resorting to such stereotypes, Tourgée matches Woolson's sympathy for the plight of southern women trying to save their family's inheritance. He even complicates the North-South marriage by having his northerner in fact be a southerner. The action of *John Eax*, the narrator tells us, shows that "the old South was dying around us. The new South was springing into life about us—the spirit of the North and the manhood of the South its matchless elements" (144). This is not a story about the masculine North dominating the feminine South. It praises southern manhood and implies that, whereas the birth of a new South will require cooperation with the North, the primary force of change needs to come from the conversion of former southerners. The North and South may be different civilizations, but for Tourgée that difference is, like race, culturally and historically constructed. Thus, we have the homonym linking the De Jeunettes and John Eax. Indeed, although the white South prides itself in its Anglo-Saxon heritage, the De Jeunettes turn out to be descended from French Huguenots, meaning that their Anglo-Saxon pedigree is as adopted as the second John Eax's Yankee loyalty. Likewise, despite their aristocratic pretensions, the De Jeunettes are in fact descended from a family of shoemakers, just as John Eax's adopted family made shovels. That Tourgée intends his story to suggest a myth of origins is made clear when we learn that the English John Eax died in 1783, the year that gave birth to the

United States. In Tourgée's national myth, the nation was built by labor of the sort Eax promoted and that will help create a New South, as shovels till the soil and mine the ore that John discovers on the De Jeunette land. Americans, including those in the New South, become the heirs of the work ethic of that English city "where hammers have forged miracles of progress, and built a metropolis that queens it in the world of mechanic art as easily as Athens once ruled the domain of the beautiful" (108).

Appropriately, the new world Tourgée imagines will be liberated from the archaic system of laws perpetuated in the Old South. For instance, Charles's time in prison allows Tourgée to condemn North Carolina's penal code that not only placed debtors in prison but forced all prisoners, even the ones not yet declared guilty, to suffer unnecessarily. Although the system was not quite as bad as the inquisition, under it, "punishment . . . was inseparably associated with suffering—physical pain. The gallows, the lash, and the branding-iron were its implements and it was considered eminently proper that they should be supplemented by disease and exposure" (*JE*, 11–12). Tourgée had successfully helped reform that inhumane system in North Carolina's 1868 Constitutional Convention.

Of course, the old South's most inhumane law was the law of slavery. By seeking rifts in the shadow it cast, Tourgée is free to imagine a new economic order. As much as novels supporting Reconstruction differ from those condemning it, almost all have one element in common: they portray plantation overseers or their heirs as villains. In *The Leopard's Spots*, Thomas Dixon turns Simon Legree from *Uncle Tom's Cabin* into a postbellum monopoly capitalist who treats his workers worse than slaves. In *Red Rock*, there is the hypocritical Hiram Still. Challenging Dixon and Page on almost every point, African American novelist Charles W. Chesnutt, nonetheless, in *The Marrow of Tradition* makes the son of a former overseer his crudest racist, who acts as a parasite on the economy while enriching himself through the convict-lease system. In contrast, Tourgée and Harris, through Billy Sanders, recognize that the skills of an overseer to make the land productive can contribute to a class alliance against planter domination. The root meaning of "economy" is the management of a household, and Tourgée recognizes that there is something to admire about the way a good overseer can manage an estate.

In "A Conflict Between Church and State," the hard-working, productive southern protagonist is from "what is known as the 'poor-white' class." The son of an overseer, his one ambition is "to start his two boys in life as their own masters."

> Contrary to the usual Northern idea of those in his station, [the father] was one of the most independent and self-respecting of men. Of profound religious conviction and blameless life, he was just, though severe, with those under his

> charge, and allowed no intermeddling with his functions on the part of the owner or anyone else. If at the end of the year the owner were dissatisfied, he could employ another in his place; but during that time there was no appeal from his judgment, and must be no interference with his plans. Though only a salaried foreman, he felt himself responsible for results, and had a reputation which he would not suffer to be imperiled by limitation of his judgment. His boast was that he could "raise more barrels of corn and a greater value of tobacco on fewer acres, with less stock and less labor, and leave the land, stock, and 'niggers' in better condition at the end of the year, than any other man on the Dan." This was not a vain boast nor an unworthy one, but a self-respecting assertion of a thorough agricultural knowledge and high administrative capacity. (GS, 167–68)

In *John Eax,* Tourgée uses an overseer to exploit a rift in the shadow the heritage of slavery cast over Reconstruction. It is through marriage to the overseer's niece that Charles De Jeunette is transformed into the Yankee John Eax, who can fulfill the needs of the standard reconciliation plot by marrying a landed southern lady.

By imagining a world without the shadow of slavery, Tourgée could be accused of neglecting the role of race in the nation's history. In fact, by acknowledging that national reconciliation is much easier to imagine "without the shadow," he emphasizes the role the "race question" played in blocking the birth of a new nation. A product of slavery, the race question is intricately linked to attitudes toward free labor. As the protagonist of *Bricks without Straw* argues, "The very fact of the African being thus degraded led, by natural association, to the degradation of those forms of labor most frequently delegated to the slave. By this means free labor became gradually to be considered more and more disreputable, and self-support to be considered less and less honorable" (421). The reconstructed nation Tourgée imagines must free itself from the heritage of slavery by honoring free labor. The inheritance plot of *John Eax* suggests that the country, North and South, was founded by those adhering to that value.

When Tourgée returns to the issue of race in *A Fool's Errand,* he shows how the book's protagonist tries to bring the nation's founding value of free labor to the South. Confronted with negative stereotypes of unscrupulous carpetbaggers and their greed, he describes the Fool as an immigrant, bringing new values to his new home. Elsewhere, he insists, "Columbus, the Pilgrims, and even Jesus Christ were carpetbaggers." As *A Fool's Errand* demonstrates, however, carpetbaggers had little chance of being welcomed in the South unless they assimilated to white southern values. As a result, just as in *Dred Scott* Justice Taney ruled that US citizenship was reserved for whites because it descended by racial blood from the founders, so the identity of a "southerner" depended on birth and blood. That leaves the Fool without much of a chance of being involved in an inheritance plot in the South. Indeed, by the end, his wife and daughter have relocated to the North, and he dies of yellow fever before he can rejoin them.[19]

The Fool's death evokes the devastating yellow fever epidemic that swept the South in 1878, the year before *A Fool's Errand* appeared. As Edward Blum has shown, the onset of yellow fever fostered the aspects of North-South reconciliation that Tourgée resisted.

> The epidemic was a devastating event, but it also helped northern and southern whites rediscover their commitments to one another. The widespread nature of fear caused by the outbreak created common convictions and shared experiences for whites. Yellow fever evoked sympathy from thousands of northerners, and, as they donated money and prayed for southern whites, northerners collectively expressed feelings of reunion. Northern whites consciously effaced memories of southerners as belligerent evildoers seeking to destroy the Union. Instead, southerners were reconceived as stricken, yet honorable, brothers in need. At the same time, southern whites re-conceptualized northerners and their relationship to the nation. Rather than regarding Yankees as infidel invaders bent on destroying southern civilization, former Confederates now praised them as heroic and Christian patriots.

Northern efforts were not, however, directed at African Americans to the same extent. It is, therefore, fitting that Tourgée's hero is stricken during an epidemic that helps to undermine his egalitarian ideals for reunion.[20]

Without an inheritance plot for his carpetbagger, Tourgée, in his next work, turns to a southern protagonist. *John Eax* is about a former Union soldier; *Mamelon* about a former Confederate soldier. Similarly, the protagonist of *A Fool's Errand* is a former Union soldier, whereas the protagonist of *Bricks without Straw* is a former Confederate soldier. The inheritance plot of *Bricks without Straw* is, like those of *John Eax* and *Mamelon*, about a southern estate. Published six years after these two novels, with slavery still casting its shadow, *Bricks without Straw* is less optimistic than the two earlier works. White planter turned Radical Hesden Le Moyne and his invalid mother, Hester, fiercely proud of her southern ancestors, live at Mulberry Hill. Hesden's father was Casaubon Le Moyne, from Virginia but kin to the Le Moynes of South Carolina with Huguenot ancestry. Casaubon was a Unioner but served in the Confederate Army. He is killed soon after Hesden, also a Unioner, enlists. During the war, Hesden's wife also dies, leaving a young son.

Hesden and his mother's fate gets connected with that of freedmen trying to establish a community at nearby Red Wing, which, except for a small tract of land, along with Mulberry Hill and other properties was once part of a vast estate owned by Hester's grandfather, James Richards. The new community of Red Wing thrives because of the labor and planning of Nimbus and Eliab Hill. The two were born slaves on the plantation of Potestatem Desmit and were childhood friends, with Nimbus becoming Eliab's protector after an illness left Hill paralyzed. When Eliab's mother was hired out to care for Hester, Hesden's father bought mother and son. Illegally taught to read by Hesden and his mother, Eliab is freed to avoid problems with the neighbors and authorities. Thus, Hesden has a personal interest in the affairs at Red Wing.

That interest intensifies when Mollie Ainslee from Massachusetts volunteers to teach at the colored school in memory of her brother Oscar, who served in the Union Army and dies while stationed in the South after the war. Mollie brings with her a powerful black stallion she inherited from her brother. Although she does not know it, the horse had once been Hesden's. In the last battle before Appomattox, while bravely attacking Union lines, Hesden lost his arm and fell off his prized horse, Satan. Oscar takes possession of the abandoned horse and calls him Midnight. Having connected Mollie's brother with her future lover, Midnight/Satan then brings Mollie and Hesden together. When a storm breaks out while she is riding, the horse gallops at breakneck speed to his former home. Almost in shock and becoming sick, Mollie falls from the horse into the one arm of Hesden. As she convalesces under his care, the two, though not acknowledging it, fall in love. Mollie's stay is extended when Hesden's son contracts scarlet fever, and she risks her life to nurse him, to no avail.

With the death of this heir from Hesden's marriage to a fellow southerner, Tourgée opens the possibility of an inheritance plot based on a North-South romance. But the pride of Hesden's lover and his mother complicates that romance. The budding courtship is initially interrupted by the Klan's attack on Red Wing, prompting Mollie to leave without a chance to say goodbye. Back at Red Wing, she is offended that Hesden does not immediately follow her, not knowing that he has another patient to nurse. When Nimbus returns to Red Wing during the Klan attack, he finds Eliab brutally beaten. Before escaping the state for his own safety, Nimbus carries Eliab to Mulberry Hill and enlists Hesden's help in hiding him while he recovers. Cutting a door in a wall in the house for access to the room for curing tobacco, where Eliab is hiding, Hesden discovers a previously unknown will. Rather than reward Hesden for his good deed of protecting Eliab, the discovery of the will threatens to dispossess him and his mother of their estate. The will is that of a cousin of Hesden's grandfather. Both were named James Richards. In the will, the cousin leaves his North Carolina estate to his daughter. That estate turns out to be the same one claimed by Hesden's grandfather, who had been named executor. Hesden's grandfather, it seems, suppressed the will and took possession of the land himself. If that is what happened, then Hesden and his mother have no legitimate title to Mulberry Hill. With no one having made a claim for their land, they could simply destroy the long-hidden will. Too honorable to do that, Hesden vows to renounce his claim if a legitimate heir can be found. He hires the attorney Theron Pardee to try to track down any surviving heirs. While Pardee is in the North trying to locate an heir, Hesden brings a recovered Eliab out of hiding and sends him north for an education. Hesden's mother, like John March's over a decade later, is dismayed to discover that her son has become a Radical. She blames his infatuation with "the little nigger teacher at Red Wing" (*BS*, 376). Hoping he will instead marry his cousin Hetty, she rewrites her will. In it she "devised the plantation to her beloved son Hesden Le Moyne, and her affectionate cousin Hetty Lomax, jointly, and to their heirs forever, on condition that the said devisees should intermarry with each other within one year from the death of the devisor" (363). If either of the two refuses to marry, the entire property goes to the other. Hesden is not yet aware of the new will when Pardee returns from the North.

A lawyer and former Union officer who settles in North Carolina, Pardee is a figure for Tourgée with a significantly different role from that of Comfort Servosse in *A Fool's Errand*. In *Bricks without Straw*, the action does not revolve around its authorial figure. Instead, Tourgée places Pardee in the background from where he facilitates and explicates the action. From the evidence that Pardee uncovers and from Hester's memory of family stories, readers can piece together what happened. There were indeed two James Richards, Hesden's grandfather from Lancaster, Pennsylvania, and his cousin from Marblehead, Massachusetts. They were called "Black Jim" and "Red Jim," respectively. The cousins come from a New England family that had been successful privateers during the Revolutionary War and may have transported slaves. Red Jim was himself a ship captain. After selling his cargo and vessel in Charleston, South Carolina, he headed north to visit his beloved cousin, going from there to Philadelphia. When word came that Red Jim was sick, Black Jim went to Philadelphia, only to find his cousin already dead and almost penniless. According to family legend, Red Jim died of yellow fever, the proceeds of his sale having been stolen before he set out to visit his cousin. The unexecuted will casts suspicion on Hesden's grandfather, especially when Hester tells a story about a later encounter with Hesden's uncle, John Richards. In Hester's youth, John visited Black Jim and showed him Red Jim's distinctive signature. A heated argument ensued. Later, John's body was found in a nearby river. Hester claims that John drowned crossing a ford, but more likely he was killed by his relative after being confronted about the lost will. In fact, Pardee has found an heir who is the legitimate owner of Mulberry Hill.

In holding false title to their estate, Hesden and his mother are in the same position as Nimbus, who, it turns out, bought Red Wing under false pretenses. In desperate need of cash after his stores of turpentine and cotton were burned by Sherman's army during the Civil War, Potestatem Desmit sold Red Wing to his former slave without revealing that he held only a life estate to the land. Desmit dies never telling Nimbus of his deceit, and a local white supremacist buys the title to the land from the true heir who lives in Indiana. Legal proceedings are initiated that will dispossess Nimbus and all the freedmen who bought land from him. Hearing of the suit and in the wake of the Klan attack, many of Red Wing's occupants decide to leave. Mysteriously, however, Pardee buys each holding at full value. The mystery is solved when Pardee reveals to Hesden and Hester that Mollie is Red Jim's heir and the legitimate owner of both Red Wing and Mulberry Hill.

To the great relief of Hester, Mollie, through Pardee, proposes that she will deed Mulberry Hill to Mrs. Le Moyne if the Le Moynes pay to have the claim to Nimbus's land relinquished, a claim that would have no standing in court. This arrangement satisfies Hesden's mother, but he is convinced that they should not lay claim to a property with such a history of deceit. He wants to contact Mollie himself, but that can be done only through Pardee. Mollie, in the meantime, as we saw in chapter 5, has moved to Kansas, wisely invested in real estate, and become rich. In time, Mrs. Le Moyne swallows her pride and admits that Mollie acted more honorably than she. She rewrites her will and ceases her opposition to Hesden seeking Mollie's hand. Reconnected, the two marry, with Mrs. Le Moyne dying shortly after the wedding. Thus, Hesden and Mollie jointly possess Red Jim's/Black Jim's estate, which each wanted the other to own singularly. Adjacent to Mulberry Hill, an African American community is trying to rebuild Red Wing after the destruction heaped upon it.

Like *John Eax*, this novel insists that those of the gentlemanly leisure class are not the rightful heirs and protectors of the commonwealth. It endorses instead the Republican myth of free labor and self-sufficiency, here embodied by Mollie. Similarly, as he does in *John Eax*, Tourgée links *Bricks without Straw*'s inheritance plot to the founding of the nation. On the roads through Red Wing "had marched and countermarched the hostile forces of the Revolutionary period" (*BS*, 136). The long-lost will was signed in 1789. Both novels also suggest the interconnectedness between North and South. That, of course, is not unique to fiction of this period. But by establishing the interdependence of the colonies prior to independence, Tourgée challenges arguments for state sovereignty that described the thirteen original states as descending directly from independent colonies. In *Bricks without Straw*, Hesden's father comes from Virginia but settles in North Carolina and has Huguenot relatives in South Carolina. The two James Richardses with claims to a

North Carolina estate come from a Massachusetts family, with one still a resident of Massachusetts, although conducting extensive trade with the South, while the other lives in Pennsylvania. In *John Eax*, the connection is more general, as both regions have a common origin in free labor. Thus, in both works, a North-South marriage symbolically reunites regions that had been connected prior to the nation's founding. There is, however, a significant difference between *John Eax* and *Bricks without Straw*.

Without the shadow of slavery, *John Eax* gives a positive, democratic sense of the nation's founding. In *Bricks without Straw*, Mollie shares that view; she "worshipped the nation's past" (352). The story of the Richards family is not, however, one to celebrate. The family did help secure independence in the Revolutionary War, but it did so as privateers who possibly profited from the slave trade. Black Jim keeps up the family's relation to piracy, claiming land through deceit. A possible murderer, he is more corrupt than the former slave owner Desmit, who fraudulently sells property to Nimbus. Even Red Jim, who is cheated out of his land, has a suspicious past. The cargo he sells in Charleston could well have been slaves. Whereas *John Eax* links North and South through a common past of free labor, *Bricks without Straw* links the two through their common participation in casting a shadow over the promised land. Such a story of the nation's founding is by no means flattering, and Hester anticipates readers' responses when, listening to Hesden speculate about the family past, she laments, "It is so unpleasant to look back upon one's ancestors and not feel that they were strictly honorable. Don't tell me, please. I had rather not hear it" (*BS*, 335). But Tourgée does tell. When Hesden and Mollie have a young son, the birth of an heir to their North-South marriage raises the possibility of hope. But that optimism is tempered by an underlying pessimism, indicated in the book's title. Denied the resources and support they needed, the freedmen, carpetbaggers, and scalawags trying to reconstruct the South had a task akin to making bricks without straw. As the inheritance plot shows, however, there is another reason for doubt. The nation had to be rebuilt, not on the foundation of a glorious past but on one erected under the shadow of slavery.

-7-

INHERITING A SHADOW AND A DREAM

African American writers did not need to be reminded that slavery cast a shadow over the nation's founding. Frederick Douglass made that point eloquently in "What to the Slave is the Fourth of July?" Before the Civil War, the dream was to overcome the inheritance of slavery through emancipation. After the war, it became increasingly clear that emancipation was not enough. The failure to achieve racial equality through Reconstruction created its own shadow that needed to be lifted. In the first part of this chapter, I look at the plots of three romances, one by Francis Harper and two by Pauline Hopkins, making a political argument that African Americans should get their due inheritance after suffering the evils of slavery. I then turn to three novels by Charles W. Chesnutt making a political argument that African Americans should get their proper inheritance by being able to participate equitably in the social, political, and economic life of the nation.[1]

II

Both Harper and Hopkins incorporate slavery's shadowy past by fashioning plots about African American characters denied inheritance of property accumulated prior to the Civil War. Harper's *Iola Leroy: Or the Shadow Uplifted* starts at the end of the Civil War. The title character, who is a freed slave, can pass as white and serves the Union Army as a nurse. Nine chapters into the book, we have a flashback to explain Iola's heritage. Her father was Eugene Leroy, of French and Spanish descent, who owned a plantation in the French style on the Mississippi River. He married Marie, his former slave, who nursed him back to health during a trip to Europe. On their return, he sent her north for an education. Passing as white, Marie bore her husband three children. Iola and Harry were sent north to school, while little Gracie stayed at home. Suddenly, Eugene died of yellow fever, and his ruthless cousin Alfred Lorraine found a flaw in the marriage document, which reverted Marie back to slavery and turned all of her children into slaves. Taking possession of the plantation, Alfred sent his lawyer to trick Iola into returning from school. After Gracie died of brain fever, Iola and her mother were sold separately as part of the inventory of the estate. With the outbreak of the Civil War, Harry escaped capture and joined a colored regiment of the Union Army. We return to the main action to find Iola courted by a white doctor, who maintains his love even after he learns that she is not "white." After many twists in the plot, Iola, her mother, and her brother reunite, and Iola marries an African American doctor, who can also pass as white but does not. Her brother marries, and both couples dedicate themselves to improving the condition of "coloreds" in the South.

Hopkins's *Contending Forces: A Romance Illustrative of Negro Life North and South* (1900) begins at the turn of the eighteenth into the nineteenth century. Charles Montfort owns seven hundred slaves in Bermuda. When the British government insists that he emancipate them, he moves to Newberne, North Carolina, where he plans to free the slaves gradually on his own terms. He is married to the dark beauty Grace Montfort. The villain Anson Pollock is jealous of Charles's wealth and covets his wife. To procure both he casts "suspicion of Negro Blood in the veins of Mrs. Montfort" and murders her husband. When Grace refuses his advances, he has her whipped (*CF*, 45). She then commits suicide rather than succumb to him, and he takes up with Lucy, Grace's black foster sister and maid. In the meantime, Pollock enslaves the two Montfort sons: Charles Jr. and Jesse. Charles Jr. has the good fortune of being bought by an enlightened Englishman, who plans to free him in England. The two promise to return to help Jesse but then disappear from the action. Jesse escapes on a ship to Boston and seeks shelter as a fugitive slave with the Whitfields, a colored family of Exeter, New Hampshire. He eventually marries the daughter.

At this point, the action flashes forward to end-of-the-century Boston and the African American boardinghouse of Ma Smith. A widow, Ma Smith has two children: William Jesse Montfort and Dora Grace Montfort. Two boarders central to the plot are John Pollock Langley and Sappho Clark. Born into slavery, John is an intelligent lawyer, engaged to Dora. Sappho, who is light skinned, works as a stenographer. She comes from New Orleans and hides a secret past. Will falls in love with her. As the action unfolds, we learn that John wants to marry Dora for "mercenary reasons," while harboring lascivious designs on Sappho (*CF*, 227). "Sensuality," we are told, "was prominent in the phrenological development of his head" (226). John's deficient "moral nature" was "the natural product of such an institution as slavery. Natural instinct for good had been perverted by a mixture of 'cracker' blood of the lowest type on his father's side with whatever god-saving quality might have been loaned the negro by pitying nature" (221). Indeed, although he does not know it at first, "he was a direct descendant of the North Carolina Pollocks" (*CF*, 221–22).

Sappho, it turns out, was raped as a teenager by her white uncle, who left her in a house of prostitution. She bore a son and was rescued by an order of black nuns. Abandoning her son, she starts a new life in Boston. When John discovers Sappho's past, he tries to blackmail her into submitting to him, while still planning to marry Dora. Sappho leaves Boston without a word and embraces her role as a mother back in New Orleans. Protected again by the Convent of the Holy Family, she finds a position working for a rich elderly African American man. In Boston, Dora learns of John's duplicity and is courted by Dr. Arthur Lewis, who is in town for a meeting of the American Colored League. Lewis is modeled on Booker T. Washington and has debates with Will who, in an obvious allusion to W. E. B. Du Bois, is saving to attend Harvard with hopes of later studying in Germany. Lewis is an accommodationist; Will insists that "agitation will do much. . . . It gave us freedom, it will give us manhood" (300). Their debates are observed by Charles Montfort-Withington, MP, who is attending the Canterbury Club Dinner on a visit from England. Montfort-Withington is a wealthy descendent of Charles Jr. With his help, Ma Smith traces her ancestry to Jesse, who had done well until he was ruined financially when he backed a bond for his white employer, who went bankrupt.

Searching for more evidence from the past, Montfort-Withington and Will go to Bermuda, where they discover Grace's ancient maid Lucy, with her daughter and granddaughter, now sixty, all of whom relocated from North Carolina at the end of the Civil War. While in slavery, the granddaughter bore a child whose father was Anson Pollock Jr., a grandnephew of the Anson Pollock who killed Charles Montfort and tried to rape his wife. This child turns out to be John Pollock Langley. Montfort-Withington creates a small annuity for the three women, "to keep them from want" (*CF*, 381). Before Will and his newly discovered relative leave, Lucy dies satisfied that justice is being restored. Indeed, back in the United States, a suit, *Smith v. The United States*, is brought privately before a court composed of "the judges of the Supreme Court of the United States" (383). Mrs. Smith is awarded $150,000 "as the last representative of the heirs of Jesse Montfort. Justice was appeased" (384). With the successful outcome of the suit, Dr. Lewis and Dora marry and settle in New Orleans. Will spends three years studying in Heidelberg, returning with plans to establish "a school which should embrace every known department of science, where the Negro youth of ability and Genius could enter without money and without price. No wife or child would ever be his, he told himself; but he would be a father to the youth of his race" (386). On a visit to his sister, however, he meets Sappho by chance, and their love rekindles. They marry and have a child, while he loves Sappho's first child as his own. With wife and children, Will visits Montfort-Withington in Europe. In the meantime, John, searching for gold, dies in the frozen whiteness of Alaska.

Hopkins's *Hagar's Daughter: A Story of Southern Caste Prejudice*, serialized in 1901–1902 in the *Colored American Magazine*, was intended for an African American audience. Only recently published separately, it has a more bizarre plot than *Contending Forces*. There are again two parts, with the first part taking place at the beginning of secession and the second in 1882, twenty years before the novel was serialized. Wills dominate the action of both parts. The first is that of a dead plantation owner in Maryland with two handsome sons, Ellis Enson and St. Clair Enson. The elder Ellis is honorable, business savvy, and treats his slaves well. St. Clair, compared to a fallen angel from *Paradise Lost*, is so corrupt that his father disinherits him unless his older brother dies "without issue" (*HD*, 21). Trying to reform, St Clair turns to politics, but he cannot help himself. He gambles and, with the help of his loyal and corrupt slave Isaac, succeeds in one confidence game after another. At the beginning of the novel, he is in Charleston joining forces with other southern politicians. While there, he gets word that forty-year-old Ellis has married Hagar Sargeant, the eighteen-year-old daughter of the adjoining estate, who has returned after four years of schooling in the North. The two have an infant daughter. Fearful that he no longer has a chance to inherit his father's wealth, St. Clair works with the uncouth, illiterate slave trader Walker to ruin his brother's marriage. Promised a huge reward if he can help, Walker claims that the wife is a white-looking slave he sold in St. Louis to Mr. Sargeant, who raised Hagar as his daughter. Travelling to Maryland, the two produce the bill of sale, causing havoc in the marriage. At first, Ellis feels he must separate. Then love triumphs, and he works out a plan to take Hagar to Europe, where they and their daughter can live together. Before they can leave, however, Ellis is found dead, a seeming suicide. Hagar and her daughter are sold into slavery. In despair, Hagar escapes and, pursued to a bridge, plunges with her daughter to apparent death into the Potomac River.

The 1882 action introduces readers to California senator Zenas Bowen, his wife, and his twenty-year-old daughter Jewel, who are spending their second year in Washington, DC. Mrs. Bowen is the senator's second wife, his first having died when their daughter was an infant. A loving husband and father, Senator Bowen became a multimillionaire developing Black Hills gold mines. Whoever marries the beautiful Jewel will inherit his fortune. Her beau, Cuthbert Sumner, the son of a rich New England manufacturer, is preparing for a career in politics by working at the Treasury Department. Sumner's boss is the older, handsome General Benson, who is friends with the even older Major Henry Clay Madison, president of a mining company who hopes to strike it rich. The narrator casts suspicion on both. Madison maintains old Confederate views, while Benson has had to spend ten years in exile because he was linked to the Lincoln assassination. His name is an alias, allowing him to get his well-placed job. Believing that "the country owes me a fortune, and I am bound to have it" (*HD*, 79), he concocts a plan with Madison to marry Jewel. Madison has a beautiful daughter a few years older than Jewel. The two women met briefly at a Montreal convent where both were educated. Benson promises Aurelia Madison a million dollars of the Bowen estate if she can seduce Sumner and free Jewel for Benson to marry. In fact, Aurelia and Sumner already had a passionate fling before he met Jewel, whom he truly loves. Nonetheless, Aurelia is artful enough to tempt him and cause Jewel to break their engagement. In a moment of despair, Jewel, who still loves Sumner, impulsively makes a promise to Benson.

Benson departs for a short trip to New York, where Senator Bowen is spending time. He leaves a job for Sumner, which requires him to spend overtime hours with Benson's stenographer Elise Bradford. Elise informs Sumner that five years earlier Benson seduced her and that they have an illegitimate four-year-old son being raised in her home state of Kentucky. Threatening to expose him, she gets Benson to promise to marry her. Elise also reveals that Aurelia, once a mistress of Benson, is a quadroon, the daughter of one of Madison's former slaves. With Jewel once again free, Sumner goes home happy, only to be arrested the next morning for Elise's murder. When word gets to Jewel, she is convinced of Sumner's innocence and marries him in prison. She also hires secret service detective J. Henson to conduct a private investigation into the crime.

The evidence looks bad, especially because the one possible witness, an African American cleaning lady for the Treasury Department, has disappeared. The cleaning lady is Aunt Hennie, a former slave of the Sargeants and an explicit connection to the book's first half. Word also comes that Senator Bowen is struck ill in New York. He comes to Washington, only to die. Allegedly, he wrote a new will in New York, making Madison its trustee and Benson its executor and the guardian of Jewel. Jewel expresses her anger and is soon abducted. With the help of an African American associate and Jewel's maid Venus, Henson recovers Jewel and Aunt Hennie, Venus's grandmother, at the Enson estate. At Sumner's trial, most of the secrets of the plot are revealed. Aurelia's racial status is made public. Benson turns out to be St. Clair Enson. Madison is the slave trader Walker. Mrs. Bowen is Hagar, who survived her plunge into the Potomac and made her way to California. St. Clair murdered Elise, framed Sumner, and arranged for the abduction of Aunt Hennie and Jewel. Most surprising, unless readers have focused on the "H" beginning his name, Henson turns out to be Ellis Enson. St. Clair is sent to prison, where he is killed trying to escape. Walker is convicted of forging Senator Bowen's will and dies in prison. Freed, Sumner is joyful but, displaying his own prejudice, insists that Jewel no longer consider Hagar her mother. In contrast, Ellis, having once before worked through his prejudice, remarries Hagar. Going through her former husband's things, Hagar finds documents and a gold locket revealing that Jewel is in fact her daughter with Ellis, Bowen having adopted her after saving her from drowning. Shocked, Sumner feels ashamed to be married to his beautiful wife. Sharing his shame, Jewel is taken in by her loving parents. The three go for a trip to Europe. To think things over, Sumner does the same. When he returns, his love has overcome his prejudice, and he seeks Jewel at the Enson estate, only to find her grave. Like Henry James's Daisy Miller, Jewel has died of Roman Fever. Hagar, once threatened with disinheritance, ends up inheriting both the Bowen and Enson fortunes with her husband but loses her daughter. The only remaining heir of the Enson family is St. Clair's illegitimate son.

In devising plots about the disinheritance of African Americans under slavery, Harper and Hopkins get caught in a dilemma Tourgée faced in his first novel *Toinette*, revised as *A Royal Gentleman*: the inheritance denied their mixed-race characters was accumulated on the backs of slaves. An unintended implication of such plots is that some African Americans who do well in the post-Emancipation world benefit financially from slavery. Confronted with that dilemma, Tourgée turns to novels that portray freedmen deprived of wealth they accumulate after emancipation. Harper and Hopkins come up with different solutions. To understand the significance of Harper's, we need to compare her romance with two other works about mixed-race women who can pass as white. *Iola Leroy* has frequently been seen as a rebuttal to William Dean Howells's *An Imperative Duty*, in which a woman who can pass as white marries a white doctor and continues to assume a white identity rather than rejecting her suitor and finding and helping her African American relatives. Both works were likely influenced by Tourgée's *Pactolus Prime*, which appeared a short while earlier. *Pactolus* also features a heroine who can pass as white. Unlike Harper's and Howells's steadfast white doctors, her white suitor, a journalist, hypocritically withdraws his offer of marriage when she reveals her "African blood." Neither marrying a white man nor publically revealing that she is "black," Tourgée's heroine escapes to a convent.[2]

Although these works seem to present their mixed-race women with the same choice, the characters' decisions are determined by different circumstances. Howells's heroine is raised as white by her aunt and has never heard about her African American relatives until told the secret. With no emotional bond to those relatives, she can more easily marry a white man rather than try to reconnect with that part of her family. Raised by her mother and growing up with her brother, Iola is committed to acknowledging her racial connection to them and reuniting with them. Like Howells's heroine, Tourgée's is raised as a white orphan. She knows Pactolus her entire life but thinks he is a kindly black servant who cares for her. Only after he dies does she learn that he is her father and has financially supported her through money he made in the Washington, DC, real estate market under an assumed name as a white man. Given her love for her father, she is not ashamed to acknowledge her connection, which she does to her potential suitor. But she also respects her father's wish to pass as white, since he firmly believed that blacks do not have the same opportunities in life as whites. She adopts her father's name, becoming Sister Pactolus, and devotes her life to the cause of improving the situation for African Americans.

The three works also have different inheritance plots. Howells's heroine's connection to the heritage of slavery adversely affects her financially because her father's marriage to a woman of color undercuts his medical practice and renders him poor. She is the heir of the "remnant of the property her [adoptive aunt] had inherited from her husband." But it is so meager that the family of her foster father "willingly, almost eagerly, accepted the conditions of the will" and makes no inquiries about "her purposes or wishes" because they suspect her "colored blood" and do not want to call public attention to their connection to her (*ID*, 112). In contrast, Tourgée's heroine becomes rich as the result of her black father's business acumen, which he can exercise only while posing as a white man. But she donates her inheritance to the advancement of African Americans. In *Iola Leroy*, Harper makes sure that none of Eugene Leroy's descendants inherit wealth from his plantation. Instead, they benefit from another sort of inheritance. Praising the courage of Iola's future husband, Dr. Latimer, for refusing to pass as white, Iola's uncle agrees with Pactolus: "To be born white in this country is to be born to an inheritance of privileges, to hold in your hands the keys that open before you the doors of every occupation, advantage, opportunity, and achievement." Iola responds that "even these advantages are too deeply bought if they mean loss of honor, true manliness, and self-respect." Her future husband would have lost all of these had "he ignored his mother and lived under a veil of concealment, constantly haunted by the dread of detection" (*IL*, 265–66). For Harper, a more important inheritance than financial privilege is that of family cohesiveness.

As portrayed in *Uncle Tom's Cabin* and other works, one of the supreme horrors of slavery was the separation of families. In *Iola Leroy*, the Civil War and freedom enable African American families to reunite. When Harry decides to join the army, he easily could choose to pass as white. But in the biggest "test of his life," he decides to enlist as a colored soldier hoping to find his mother and sister who "were enslaved by a mockery of justice." As his school principal advises him, "I do not think that you should be assigned to a colored regiment because of the blood in your veins, but, you will have, in such a regiment, better facilities for finding your mother and sister" (*IL*, 126). Significantly, Harper appropriates the language of redemption to characterize that reunion. As one character puts it, the Civil War led to "the redemption of a race, and the reunion of severed hearts" (216). To illustrate that redemption, Harper turns the conventions of the "romance of reunion" on their head. Rather than give us the marriage of northern and southern whites to stand for a reunited nation, she offers a chapter called "Delightful Reunions," dramatizing the reunion of Iola's family. Harper does not, however, lose sight of the "redemption" of the nation. According to Iola, "there is but one remedy by which the nation can recover from the evil entailed upon her by slavery." Given the inheritance of slavery, it needs "a fuller comprehension of the claims of the Gospel of Jesus Christ, and their application to our national life" (*IL*, 216). Later, we are told that "for the true reconstruction of the country something more was needed than bayonets and bullets, or the schemes of selfish politicians or plotting demagogues. . . . The South needed the surrender of the best brain and heart of the country to build, above the wastes of war, more stately temples of thought and action" (236). With Iola's family reunited, it can use the education its children inherited from the regime of slavery to contribute to that effort by teaching freedmen "to read the name of the ever blessed Christ" (146). Iola's reunited family is not a symbol for national reunion. Instead, a cohesive black family becomes the basis for successful national Reconstruction.

In *Contending Forces* the inheritance plot is even more complicated. Montfort-Withington's wealth comes when Charles Jr. marries "his rescuer's daughter" (*CF*, 376). Charles Jr. also recovered one hundred thousand dollars in damages when his father-in-law sued the United States government. When that suit was filed, "no trace of Jesse could be found." But "the money was held for him or his heirs by the government" (376). The case of *Smith vs. The United States* shows that Will's previous assertion that "constitutional equity is a political fiction" is wrong (297). His English relative's belief that "you can gain redress from the Federal government" (296–97) proves correct.

Although the main characters in *Contending Forces* get redress for their ancestors' false enslavement, neither the Emancipation Proclamation nor the Thirteenth Amendment personally affects them. All but one of them were born free. Only the villain John is emancipated as the result of the Civil War. In a different novel, someone with his background might have been commended for his efforts to educate himself and become a successful lawyer. But for Hopkins he lacks morality because of bad blood, not from African Americans, but from white "crackers." In *Iola Leroy*, Iola and her mother directly benefit from the Emancipation

Proclamation. Unlike most freedmen, though, both were once free. What allows them to succeed more than most African Americans in the world of Reconstruction is the education they received while they were considered white. Their educational opportunity contributes to one obvious, yet important, point that Harper and Hopkins make: the racialization of slavery meant that being considered "colored" dramatically altered a person's chances in life. Reinforced through the ability of Iola, her mother, and her brother to pass as white, this point is made even stronger by the uncertainty over Grace's racial status. Whether or not she and her sons have black "blood" is less important than that they are perceived as having it.

The uncertainty of race is even more prominent in the plot of *Hagar's Daughter*. The book seems to follow the typical pattern of exposing the injustice of a system that condemns women "in whose veins courses a drop of the accursed blood of the Negro slave" (*HD*, 59). In fact, there is no biological proof that Hagar or Jewel has any black blood. The only evidence is the bill of sale that Walker produces to collect the money St. Clair promises him if he can disinherit Jewel so as to put St. Clair in line for his father's inheritance. Yet Walker could have forged that document the same way he forges Senator Bowen's will in the second half, again to make way for St. Clair's inheritance of a fortune. When Walker produces the bill of sale, Ellis claims, "This paper means nothing" (53). To be sure, Hagar faints when Walker accuses her of being a slave, and later, "as in a dream," she remembers him "vaguely." But her "hideous nightmare" might be shock-induced (57). Or Walker could have falsely sold a white girl into slavery, just as he raises Aurelia, the daughter of a slave, as white. "The only man who could prove the girl's birth," he admits, "is the one I took her from, and he's dead" (55). If, in fact, Hagar has no black blood, then neither does Jewel, and the racial stigma attached to both women is the product of forged documents.

Hopkins reinforces this possibility through subtle allusions to the currency debates of the time. With much of the book's action taking place in the Treasury Department in an era when there was a question whether paper currency could be backed up by specie, Hopkins has her villains profit from paper documents like bills of sale, while associating her protagonists with hard metal. Before she is married, Hagar's duty is "to wash the heirlooms of colonial china and silver" (33). As Ellis falls in love with her, his "dreams were tinged with gold" (35–36). Hagar becomes "the gem he has won" (48). In the second part, Senator Bowen's fortune comes from gold, and he is praised for his "sterling worth" (81, 199). Hagar's daughter is Jewel, and the locket that establishes her identity is on a gold chain. In contrast, Benson and Madison are associated with a speculative economy. Madison is president of a mining company, but its value comes not from actual gold but speculation about finding gold. Both men are experienced gamblers, the hallmark of a speculative economy. They use Aurelia to charm men to their gambling dens. As these examples show, it is the promise of "real" wealth that leads to a speculative economy. The name Aurelia, after all, comes from the Latin for "golden." Indeed, the strict opposition between paper and metal holds no more than the one between blacks and whites. Senator Bowen's major flaw is his love of gambling, which makes him vulnerable to Benson and Madison. And paper can accrue value. Aunt Hennie has a lifetime job at the Treasury Department because one night in 1867 while cleaning she came upon ninety thousand dollars worth of greenbacks and did not steal them but protected them for the government. The president rewarded her with a permanent job at forty dollars a month, an allusion to the promise to freedmen of forty acres and a mule. Bills of sale under slavery as well as the Emancipation Proclamation and the Thirteenth Amendment taught African Americans that paper documents have power. But they also learned that money, metallic and paper, can disappear. As one character laments, "All the money went up in the Freedman's bank" (177).[3]

Linking the theme of racial identity with currency debates, Hopkins shows the influence of African Americans in high places and how the "most distinguished families are not immune from contact with this mongrel race" (*HD*, 266). No doubt, her African American audience enjoyed reading about marriages between allegedly black women and Senator Bowen, former slave owner Ellis Enson, and New Englander Sumner rather than ones between northern and southern whites. Even the racist St. Clair wants to marry Jewel for her inheritance, and the only North-South marriage Hopkins imagines is between Jewel's maid Venus and Sumner's northern valet John Williams.

According to Hazel Carby, Hopkins "created fictional histories with a pedagogical function" to reach an audience that did not read biography or history. Her pedagogical goals invite comparisons with other authors. By setting her action in the political capital of Washington, DC, she follows Tourgeé in *Pactolus Prime* and, even more, William Wells Brown in *Clotel*, from which she steals scenes, including the jump into the Potomac. But her attempt to incorporate historical events causes her to fabricate as much as Dixon. In the first part, she has St. Clair attend a meeting of southern politicians. The speeches of Robert Toombs, John C. Breckenridge, Alexander Stevens (*sic*), Jefferson Davis, and Stephen A. Douglas are as imaginary as the confrontation between Lincoln and Stoneman in *The Clansman*. In fact, as different as the pedagogical goals of Hopkins and Dixon were, the two make some similar points. Hopkins's slave trader Walker tries to profit in the corrupt postbellum capitalist marketplace, just as Dixon's Simon Legree becomes an exploitative corporate capitalist in *The Leopard's Spots* (1902). Hopkins and Dixon are also intent on exposing the limits of "what Puritan New England philanthropy will allow" (*HD*, 271). In *The Leopard's Spots*, Bostonian Everett Lowell is shocked when the mulatto George Harris, whom he has mentored, seeks to marry his daughter. In *The Clansman* (1905), Charles Sumner cannot stand physical contact with African Americans. Likewise, Hopkins's Cuthbert Sumner, who attended Harvard and whose name evokes Douglass's famous friend, cannot conceive of interracial marriages. Hopkins even repeats Thomas Nelson Page's device of having a woman display her devotion by marrying her lover in prison, but with a twist. Jewel, like Page's heroine, willingly sacrifices her reputation to marry Sumner, but when he learns that he has married someone alleged to have black blood, he returns the favor by feeling betrayed. Realizing his mistake too late, Sumner summarizes the book's pedagogical message: "The idolatry of the Molach of Slavery must be purged from the land" (*HD*, 283–84).[4]

That, of course, is clear. It is less clear how the fraternal conflict between Ellis and St. Clair is resolved. On the surface, it seems that Henson/Ellis, the former slaveholder who changes his views and willing marries an allegedly black woman, prevails. At the trial, he exposes the crimes and frauds of Benson / St. Clair, who retains the ideas that made him a loyal Confederate. At the end, St. Clair is dead while Ellis is married to the woman he loves. Although Enson lives and St. Clair dies, however, the racist brother still has a living, if illegitimate, heir. Taken in by Ellis and Hagar, St. Clair's son, the "last representative of the Enson family," will presumably inherit wealth from a slave plantation along with Bowen's considerable estate (284). Slavery might still cast its shadow over the promised land.[5]

Those with possible African blood are not the only ones who occupy high places in the novel. In 1882 Benson / St. Clair, still committed to the Lost Cause, has a governmental office. Even Senator Bowen's position raises questions. Bowen is modeled on Senator Aaron Sargent, who served California until 1879. Sargent's name evokes the Sargeants in *Hagar's Daughter*, and Sargent chaired the Senate committee on mines and mining. Urged by his wife Ellen Clark Sargent, a friend of Susan B. Anthony, the senator introduced the words that years later would become the Nineteenth Amendment. But Sargent also supported the 1882 Chinese Exclusion Act. Early in the novel, Jewell projects a utopian image when St. Clair / Benson conveys that he felt almost like a foreigner upon returning from exile. "'Ah!' she said, with a gentle sigh of pity, 'how dreadful that time must have been. Thank heaven, ours is a united country once more. And you are mistaken, too, in your judgment: we have no foreigners here. We have effaced the word by assimilation; so, too, we have no Southerners—we are Americans'" (*HD*, 121). Hopkins goes so far as ironically to put in Benson / St. Clair's mouth St. Paul's famous phrase "of one blood" (114) evoked by opponents of Chinese exclusion. But, as we saw in chapter 3, California's senator John Miller, who came into office in the same years as the fictional Senator Bowen, justified exclusion by adding "and hath fixed the bounds of their habitation." Hopkins would go on to call a future novel *Of One Blood.* It has a pan-African rather than a national plot. Where Hopkins stood on Chinese Exclusion is not clear. It is also not clear if Hopkins believed that progress was being made toward her utopian ideal. As she wrote *Hagar's Daughter* in 1901–2, the situation for African Americans was, if anything, worse. Repeating with a difference events that occurred about twenty years earlier, the book's second half cannot escape the shadow of slavery cast over its initial action. Likewise, the world twenty years after the book concludes may be condemned to repeat, with a difference, past injustices.

Hagar's Daughter and *Contending Forces* are best described as "sensational melo-drama" (*HD*, 252). Like John William DeForest's *The Bloody Chasm*, they deploy sensational plots to raise serious issues. Whereas DeForest uses events in Paris to unravel the complications of an incredible inheritance plot, Hopkins uses trial scenes. Serving as a deus ex machina, both trials temporarily set things right but lack any aura of verisimilitude. The Supreme Court, for instance, has no authority to meet in private to provide redress as Hopkins imagines. Indeed, in turning to the court for an improbable solution, Hopkins fantasizes intervention by the national government at the time when the court most memorably continued its retreat from living up to the egalitarian promise of the Civil War Amendments. Furthermore, as provocative as Hopkins's melodramas are, they are not as well executed technically as DeForest's. In *Hagar's Daughter,* Hopkins occasionally confuses Aurelia's name as "Amelia." Too often, key elements of the plot, such as Madison's forgery of Bowen's will, are never plausibly explained, only asserted. In his first novel, Charles W. Chesnutt, a technically more accomplished writer, raises some of the same issues as Hopkins but works in a different literary mode.[6]

III

As an aspiring young writer, Chesnutt noted the success of Tourgée's A *Fool's Errand. On* March 16, 1880, he wrote in his journal:

> Now, Judge Tourgee's book is about the south,—The manners, customs, modes of thoughts, etc., which are prevalent in this section of the country. . . . If Judge Tourgee, with his necessarily limited intercourse with colored people, and with his limited stay in the South, can write such interesting descriptions, such vivid pictures of Southern life and character as to make himself rich and famous, why could not a colored man, who has lived among colored people all his life; who is familiar with their habits, their ruling passions, their prejudices; their whole moral and social condition; their public and private ambitions; their religious

> tendencies and habits;—why could not a colored man who knew all this, and who, besides, had possessed such opportunities for observation and conversation with the better class of white men in the south as to understand their modes of thinking; who was familiar with the political history of the country, and especially with all the phases of the slavery question;—why could not such a man, if he possessed the same ability, write a far better book about the South than Judge Tourgee or Mrs. Stowe has written?

Chesnutt did not publish his three novels until about twenty years later, soon after Tourgée lost Homey Plessy's Supreme Court challenge to Jim Crow laws. In 1892, when Tourgée orchestrated Plessy's arrest to initiate the challenge, he hoped to establish a periodical to sway public opinion on the issue. Tourgée wrote to Chesnutt asking him to contribute financially and to serve as an associate editor. Chesnutt hesitated about the contribution, citing his need to support his family, but expressed some interest in the editorship, if he could find time apart from his business as a legal stenographer. The periodical never got off the ground. Nonetheless, Chesnutt followed the *Plessy* case closely. In a speech entitled "The Courts and the Negro," he comments, "The opinion of Plessy vs. Ferguson is as epoch-making as the Dred Scott decision. Unfortunately, it applies to a class of rights which do not make to the heart and conscience of the nation the same direct appeal as was made by slavery, and has not been nor is it likely to produce any such revulsion of feeling." Published in the wake of *Plessy*, all three of Chesnutt's novels try to generate in readers a revulsion of feeling against segregation comparable to that produced against slavery.[7]

His first novel, *The House Behind the Cedars*, takes place in Patesville, North Carolina, a few years after the Civil War. Like Harper and Hopkins, Chesnutt dramatizes racial passing. He also introduces us to his protagonists in the present and later interrupts the narrative with a flashback to explain their heritage. They descend from publicly acknowledged free people of color. Molly Walden's "parents were of the class, more numerous in North Carolina than elsewhere, known as 'old issue free negroes,' which took its rise in the misty colonial period, when race was not so closely drawn, and the population of North Carolina comprised many Indians, run-away negroes, and indentured servants from the seaboard plantations, who mingled their blood with great freedom and small formality" (*HBC*, 156). Until the "growing tyranny of the slave power" erased racial distinctions among people of color, some "attained a considerable degree of prosperity." They even had the "right of suffrage as late as 1835." Molly's father enjoyed prosperity until, in a move reminiscent of Hopkins's Jesse, he "indorsed a note for a white man who, in a moment of financial hardship, clapped his colored neighbor on the back and called him brother" (156). This act of generosity led to the financial ruin and death of Molly's father. "While scarcely more than a child in years," Molly became the concubine of a rich white man, who deeded her the house behind the cedars, where she lived separately. Their first child died young and was buried on the grounds whose cedars are associated with a cemetery. John was born in 1840; Rena eleven years later. When Rena was young, the children's father died, leaving Molly's home, a "store of gold pieces" and "a small piece of real estate in the name of each of the children, the income from which contributed to their maintenance" (158–59). At one point their father had spoken to his lawyer, the honorable Judge Straight, about leaving his children more, lamenting, "I can't give them anything else, but money will make them free of the world" (167). Before writing a will, however, he died. When Judge Straight mentions his intentions to the distant relatives who inherit his large estate, they dismiss both the matter and the lawyer.

As significant as the failure of the father to leave his children money is, Chesnutt makes it clear that he could have given them something else. He could have given "his name to Mis' Molly's children,—to whom it would have been a valuable heritage, could they have had the right to bear it" (*HBC*, 161). Denied his father's name, while inheriting his "patrician features and his mother's Indian hair" (160), John decides to claim his father's whiteness. With the help of Judge Straight, who lets him read his law books while working as an office boy, John at eighteen leaves his home and his state: "With the whole world before him, he had remained in the South, the land of his fathers, where, he conceived, he had an inalienable birthright" (21–22). Following the judge's advice, the white John Warwick settles in South Carolina, where, even if he is discovered, the laws deciding one's color are more liberal. When the war breaks out, John escapes military service and takes over "the management of a large estate left in the hands of women and slaves" (22). After the owner dies in the war, John marries the daughter and after the war is admitted to the bar. Rich through his wife's inheritance, he also prospers as a lawyer, since "many of the good lawyers were killed in the war, and most of the remainder were disqualified" (22). People "had to have lawyers," and they gave John "their business in preference to the carpetbaggers" (22–23). When his wife dies after bearing a son, he visits home and takes Rena, also passing as white, with him. As Rowena Warwick, she is courted by the rich neighbor George Tryon. Although John succeeds in passing as white, Rena fails when Tryon discovers her heritage on a chance visit to Patesville. Rena then succumbs to the plot of the tragic mulatta and dies. Even John's success comes at a cost. As Judge Straight notes, he has built a new life, but to "come back into the old life . . . will weaken the structure" (44). Success requires a break with the past. Indeed, Rena's secret is revealed when she returns to nurse her ailing mother. John may have escaped the "blight of his inheritance" making him "colored" (29). But doing so prohibits him from publicly acknowledging his mother and sister. In this way, he is truly his father's son.

Toward the end of *Contending Forces*, an old gentleman remarks, "It is indeed a fairy tale of love and chivalry such as we read only in books" (398). The romantic elements of *The House Behind the Cedars* would seem to entangle us in a similar world. John takes the name of Warwick from reading Edward Bulwer-Lytton's favorable account of Richard Neville, Earl of Warwick, in *The Last of the Barons* (1843). Aligned with the House of York in the War of the Roses, Warwick is called the Kingmaker because of his role in deposing two kings. Likewise, when Rena starts calling herself Rowena, we are reminded of Walter Scott's *Ivanhoe*. Rowena is first courted by Tryon at a reenactment of a medieval jousting tournament. But the fairy-tale atmosphere is not maintained. There is no improbable court decision or trial providing justice as in *Contending Forces* and *Hagar's Daughter*. Nor is there a miraculous family reunion, as in *Contending Forces* and *Iola Leroy*.

Despite the novel's tragic ending, Chesnutt does not leave us without hope. Intent on using his plot to convince a white audience to overcome its racial prejudices, he calls the second-to-last chapter "The Power of Love." It tracks Tryon as he starts to have second thoughts about abandoning Rena. In the final chapter, perhaps providing a model for Cuthbert Sumner in *Hagar's Daughter*, Tryon decides to find her and make up for his unmanly behavior: "Never in the few brief delirious weeks of his courtship had he felt so strongly drawn to the beautiful sister of the popular lawyer, as he was now driven by an aching heart toward the same woman stripped of every adventitious advantage and placed, by custom, beyond the pale of marriage with men of his own race. Custom was tyranny. Love was the only law. Would God have made hearts to so yearn for one another if He had meant them to stay forever apart?" (*HBC*, 292). But his change of heart comes too late—Rena has died. Tryon's condemnation of the tyranny of custom alludes to the *Plessy* court's justification of Louisiana's Jim Crow law because it adheres to the usages, customs, and traditions of the white southern people. Chesnutt clearly hopes that his white audience will share his white lover's condemnation before it is too late to avoid tragedies similar to the one about which they are reading.

To produce this response in his readers, Chesnutt relies on many of the emotional strategies employed by Harper and Hopkins in their mixed-race romances. All three, for instance, use plots about large estates and star-crossed lovers to show that those classified as white have a much better chance to succeed in life. Employing those strategies, Chesnutt faces the dilemma of having the inheritance denied John and Rena accumulated on the backs of slaves. In an early version, Chesnutt went so far as to report that Molly's father had "even owned a few slaves, as had others of his class." That detail did not make it into the final version, but Chesnutt does have John acknowledge that his father's wealth is indebted to slavery. On a brief boat trip, he converses with passengers who recognize that he is a South Carolina lawyer, not a carpetbagger. When they touch on the "subject of negroes, Yankees, and the righteousness of the lost cause," he finds a way to meet their approval. When one asks, "Did your people lose any niggers?" John replies, "My father owned a hundred" (*HBC*, 42).[8]

Although Chesnutt does not avoid the dilemma faced by Harper and Hopkins, there are significant differences among their stories. Whereas John Walden achieves financial success only by cutting himself off from his family's past, the Smiths in *Contending Forces* become financially secure by discovering their past. Although Iola does not reap the benefits that the Smiths do, she does become a success by reconnecting with her long lost family. For Hopkins and Harper, the color line deprives children of an inheritance due them through marriage. For Chesnutt, the color line deprives children of an inheritance by prohibiting a marriage. The books also give different senses of class. In *Iola Leroy*, racism deprives Iola and Harry of an aristocratic lifestyle into which they were born, whereas in *Hagar's Daughter*, Hagar and Jewel live in luxury. In *Contending Forces*, none of the Smiths are born into an aristocratic way of life, but, given their past, they seem entitled to the same lifestyle as their rich English relative. In *The House Behind the Cedars*, John and Rena also seem entitled to at least some of their father's estate. Nonetheless, they derive not from a plantation owner and one of his slaves but from a plantation owner and free people of color. Those from this class who succeeded did so, like their grandfather, "in spite of galling restrictions," just as, Chesnutt implies, African Americans at the time he is writing about need to do (*HBC*, 156).

Endorsing that rise, he calls attention to a class system within the colored community. Although he succumbs to the conventions of the passing novel, Chesnutt is careful to give attention to those who are not white enough to pass. Harper and Hopkins do as well, but they stress racial solidarity between all shades of color, whereas Chesnutt acknowledges possible tensions. Under slavery, people of color distinguished themselves from "the black mass just beneath them" (*HBC*, 156). This distinction persisted within the African American community after the age of segregation imposed a black and white color line. Chesnutt even notes a distinction within free people of color. As in *Iola Leroy* and *Contending Forces*, *The House Behind the Cedars* gives little attention to characters emancipated under the Thirteenth Amendment, but it does give us a representative of the "black mass" who earned his freedom rather than being born into it.[9]

To help and to protect Molly, her lover built close to her house a cabin in which he "installed a trusted slave by the name of Peter Fowler and his wife Nancy"

(*HBC*, 174). In an earlier version, Peter, then named Fuller, is emancipated by the war. But to emphasize Peter's work ethic, Chesnutt decided to have the skilled mechanic earn enough under slavery to purchase his and his wife's freedom, as well as the house across the street. With their new status, Peter and Nancy "did no work for Mis' Molly save as they were paid for it" (174). Nonetheless, "the two households remained on good terms," even though "Mis' Molly felt herself infinitely superior to Peter and his wife,—scarcely less superior than her poor white neighbors felt themselves to Mis' Molly" (175). Peter's son Frank "had grown up with little Rena." Several years older, "he had watched over her and kept her from harm" (175). As she grows, this representative of the "black mass" silently falls in love with her, but his father counsels him to relinquish impossible dreams: "Now's de time, boy, fer you ter be lookin' rown' fer some nice gal er yo' own color, w'at'll 'preciate you, an' won't be 'shamed er you. You're wastin' time, boy, wastin' time, shootin' at a mark outer yo' range" (125). The primary action focuses on Molly's children, who can pass as white, but Peter's "dark-brown" son turns out to be the most noble character in the book (37). Trying unsuccessfully to protect Rena from her fate, at the book's end he brings her dying body home after others have abandoned her. If in the main plot, Chesnutt follows Harper and Hopkins, who have characters with white blood dispossessed of an aristocratic inheritance, in the subplot he also makes a case for those of Peter and Frank's class having their fair inheritance in the New South, even as the developing economic conditions make that less and less likely.[10]

Chesnutt reinforced the message of the subplot in a short story he published while *The House Behind the Cedars* was being serialized. In "The Sway-backed House," Solomon Grundy, with blue eyes but dark skin, is a freeborn African American in a small North Carolina town, "with a very distinct scorn for ordinary blacks" (SH, 223). He marries a "light-brown woman with a daughter much fairer of complexion than herself" (223). Solomon lavishes great love on his adopted daughter Julia. As a skilled bricklayer and plasterer, he enjoys a good income, and he buys an acre of land with a sizeable two-story house, which he restores. There is only one flaw. The roof sways in the middle. Julia marries and has six children. When she dies, Solomon and his wife take in her daughter Isabella, who replaces Julia as Solomon's favorite, especially when his wife dies. Isabella and Solomon live together even though there is no blood connection and he never adopts her. Beautiful, her value on the marriage market increases because Solomon declares that she is the only heir of his self-accumulated estate. Isabella is courted by Tom Turner, a very dark-skinned blacksmith, and Professor Revels of the grammar school, who is a shade lighter than Turner and looks even lighter through the use of cosmetics. The "ease and grace" of the professor along with his "very remarkable thrift" wins the day, and he and Isabella plan to marry "early in the spring of 187_" (SH, 225).

Then Solomon takes ill and dies. When his will is read, his estate, which consists of the land and house, a little over a hundred dollars, and "three hundred and seventy-five dollars against the defunct Freedman's Saving Bank," which is worthless, will go to Isabella and "the ten children of the decedent's sister, whom he had not seen for years" (227). The professor is visibly disappointed and avoids Isabella, even though their marriage is only a week away. Finally, he tells her that he will still condescend to marry her, assuming that she will work extra hard to make up for what he considers his lost inheritance. Isabella thanks him for his generous offer and informs him that the night before she married the blacksmith, who had treated her with great respect and had no designs on the estate. Chesnutt is not merely mocking the color-consciousness of African Americans. Even though he frequently portrays black professionals and was one himself, as in *The House Behind the Cedars*, he champions a loyal working-class black man over a pretentious schoolteacher.

The plot also recognizes the pull of blood. The professor complains that Solomon, who clearly had a judgment to make, is guilty of "gross injustice" and "unfeeling cruelty" by leaving his property to "distant relatives who had no claim upon him at all" (SH, 230). But as Isabella tells another, "If on his deathbed his conscience smote him because of his poor sister and her children, whom he had neglected so many years, and he felt that he ought to leave something to his own flesh and blood, I surely have no right to complain. They need it quite as much as I, and more" (228). Rena and John's father waited too long to include blood relations in his will. Solomon does not, and his relatives have even more financial need than the Waldens.[11]

IV

Chesnutt's second novel, *The Marrow of Tradition* (1901), avoids the pitfalls of an inheritance plot based on the conventions of the passing novel. Other than one flashback to the days before North Carolina was "redeemed," the action occurs at the end of the nineteenth century in the fictional town of Wellington, including Chesnutt's reenactment of the Wilmington's notorious racial massacre of 1898, an event also evoked in Dixon's *The Leopard's Spots*. The most important figure in the book's inheritance plot is Janet Miller, the mixed-race wife of African American Dr. William Miller. This couple has a young son who is their only heir. The book starts, however, with the southern white couple of Major Philip Carteret and his wife Olivia. Carteret's older brother was killed in the Civil War, and his father returned from the war a broken man who "died not many years later, leaving the major the last of his line" (*MT*, 2). Although the Carterets lost their wealth, Olivia inherited the estate of her father, Samuel Merkell, which included their large house and money to buy a newspaper that the major edits. All that is missing in their lives is an heir. They feel blessed when Olivia becomes pregnant. The first chapter begins with their child's birth in peril and ends with the difficult birth of Theodore Felix: "Theodore was a family name, and had been borne by the eldest son for several generations, the major himself being a second son" (12). Only in the third chapter do we learn that Carteret is using the power of the press to launch a campaign of white supremacy designed to dislodge the coalition government of whites and blacks that prevailed in the last election.

By starting the way he does, Chesnutt relies on a strategy he imagined as a young man. On May 29, 1880, he recorded in his private journal:

> If I do write, I shall write for a purpose, a high, holy purpose, and this will inspire me to greater effort. The object of my writing would be not so much the elevation of the colored people as the elevation of the whites—for I consider the unjust spirit of caste . . . a barrier to the moral progress of the American people. . . . The subtle almost indefinable feeling of repulsion toward the negro . . . cannot be stormed and taken by assault; the garrison will not capitulate; so their position must be mined, and we will find ourselves in their midst before they think.
>
> This work is of a twofold character. The negro's part is to prepare himself for social recognition and equality; and it is the province of literature to open the way for him to get it—to accustom the public mind to the idea; and while amusing them to lead them on imperceptibly, unconsciously step by step to the desired state of feeling.[12]

By evoking our sympathy for the Carterets and raising the possibility that they will lose their long-awaited heir, Chesnutt draws in even prejudiced white readers. Who would not root for the Carterets after the losses the major experienced due to the war? Once readers learn that the person with whom they initially identified is a white supremacist, however, the question is not only if, over the course of the action, Carteret will change but also if prejudiced readers will arrive at the desired state of feeling.

Attentive readers might have been alerted to the possibility of the major's conservative politics by his name. With "Carteret," Chesnutt evokes the British Civil War, as Page and Dixon do in their novels. Whereas the two white southern writers make their founding settlers good Americans by opposing the king, Chesnutt reminds his readers that North Carolina was founded by people intent on restoring the old order to power after republican reform. Sir George Carteret was a royalist on the island of Jersey, who gave the Prince of Wales asylum during the battle with Cromwell. With the execution of Charles I, Carteret proclaimed his guest Charles II and defended Jersey against republican forces. Defeated and exiled,

Carteret returned to England with the restoration of the crown and was appointed treasurer of the navy. He was also named one of eight proprietors of the colony of Carolina, as well as a proprietor for New Netherlands, which he renamed New Jersey after his home island. Carteret County, North Carolina, bears his name. Theodore Felix Carteret is christened with water "from the carved marble font, which had come from England in the reign of King Charles, the Martyr, as the ill-fated son of James I was known to St. Andrew's" (*MT*, 12). Major Carteret, we are told, "believed in the divine right of white men and gentlemen, as his ancestors had believed in and died for the divine right of kings" (34).

Chesnutt contests this view of rightful descent by connecting the black and white inheritance plots. Samuel Merkell, it turns out, is Janet's father as well as Olivia's, and the fates of the half-sisters' families are intricately linked. William Miller's grandfather was a slave who bought his freedom and worked as a stevedore. His son Adam took over his father's business and made money "in the flush turpentine days following a few years after the Civil War" (MT, 50). Investing wisely, he bought the old Carteret mansion. William becomes a doctor and inherits the house while his older brother George carries on the family business. As a result, the Carterets live in the former house of Janet's father, and the Millers live in the former Carteret home. Despite the Millers' prosperity, the color line keeps Janet from receiving any recognition from her sister. Janet's "silent grief" over this lack of recognition "was nature's penalty, or society's revenge, for whatever heritage of beauty or intellect or personal charm had come from her with her father's blood. For she had received no other inheritance. Her sister was rich by right of her birth; if Janet had been fortunate, her good fortune had not been due to any provisions made for her by her white father" (66). Instead, she owes her prosperity to her husband and the labor and business sense of his father.

Later in the book, we learn that in fact Janet had not been neglected by her father. When Olivia's mother died, overbearing Polly Ochiltree had designs on Mr. Merkell, who wanted nothing to do with a woman who had already "buried two husbands" (123). He lived instead with his housekeeper, Julia Brown, who was once a slave of Polly's father. With Olivia sent to live with Aunt Polly, Janet was born to Julia and Sam Merkell. When Janet was quite young, her father was suddenly taken ill. As he was being nursed on his deathbed, Polly intruded into the house and, unseen, overheard Mr. Merkell tell his "dear Julia" that he "kept his promise." He also thanked Julia for saving him "from Polly Ochiltree" (MT 134). Mr. Merkell then told Julia of an envelope in the next room, containing two papers and a letter. Polly sneaked away to procure the envelope, then returned to find Mr. Merkell dead. Falsely accusing Julia of stealing money and a watch, Polly kicked her and Janet out of the house.

Later, Aunt Polly is murdered. Entering her house before the authorities, Olivia finds the hidden envelope and removes it from the crime scene. Inside is her father's will, giving Janet ten thousand dollars and a small tract of land while leaving the bulk of the estate to Olivia. The envelope also contains a marriage certificate for Julia and Mr. Merkell, as well as a letter to her father's friend and attorney Mr. Delamere, explaining Merkell's marriage and asking Delamere to execute the will. Delamere represents the best of the Old South, honorable and a paternalistic protector of African Americans. But he never receives the letter. Olivia burns the documents, only to learn that, in the absence of a will, Janet is entitled to one-third of her father's real estate and half of the balance of the estate. Haunted by a bad conscience, Olivia tries to imagine a way she could give her half sister the ten thousand dollars due her without revealing her knowledge of and destruction of her father's will and marriage certificate. Prior to Olivia's pregnancy, the Carterets lived comfortably off the income of the newspaper business and part of Olivia's "patrimony" invested in a local cotton mill that was paying ten percent (30). With the arrival of their son, they dream of leaving him a rich inheritance, and transfer their investment to speculate in a mine that provides no immediate return but promises immense profits in the future. With much of their property tied up in the mine, "it would have been difficult to procure ten thousand dollars immediately" (272). Olivia, however, thinks of an alternative. "This hospital which had recently been opened was the personal property of her sister's husband. Some time in the future, when their investments matured, she would present to the hospital a sum of money equal to the amount her father had meant his colored daughter to have. Thus indirectly both her father's will and her own conscience would be satisfied" (272).

This inheritance plot is interwoven with the book's other plots, such as its murder plot, its lynching plot, its love plot, and other inheritance plots. Aunt Polly is murdered because Mr. Delamere's decadent grandson, Tom, is in desperate need of money to pay off a gambling debt to Captain George McBane, the son of a former slave overseer and one of Carteret's two white supremacist conspirators. Assuming that Aunt Polly has named him in her will, Tom kills her and steals money he thinks would come to him anyway. Aunt Polly, however, had already disinherited Tom and decided to leave her house and land to Theodore. In murdering Aunt Polly, Tom also frames his grandfather's loyal servant, Sandy, who is then threatened with lynching. Sandy is saved when Mr. Delamere learns of the real murderer from a newspaper reporter, Tom's rival in the book's love plot. Delamere rewrites his will, leaving three thousand dollars to Sandy and the rest of his considerable estate to Dr. Miller in trust for his hospital.

Miller's hospital plays a crucial role in the story's various inheritance plots. It is Miller's way of using the wealth he inherited from his father, plus his own earnings, to help the African American community. It also becomes an ideal recipient of the philanthropic spirit of well-intentioned whites, promising a new order for the South. Appropriately, it is built on a lot once occupied by an old southern family mansion. When Aunt Polly hears of this, she exclaims, "Hugh Poindexter has sold the graves of his ancestors to a negro,—I should have starved first!" In fact, before construction began, Poindexter transferred his grandfather's tombstone to a white cemetery, but in the grave, "there was nothing to remove, except a few bits of heart-pine from the coffin. All the rest was crumpled into dust" (*MT*, 127). Although Aunt Polly is wrong to conclude that "Esau sold his birthright for a mess of pottage," she does suggest the symbolic importance of Miller building the hospital on this piece of land when she laments, "The world is turned upside down" (127). In the end, however, the hospital's fate dramatizes how efforts to reconstruct southern society on a healthier foundation are undermined by proponents of white supremacy. Delamere entrusts his will to General Belmont, one of Major Carteret's fellow white supremacists. Belmont suppresses the will, allowing Delamere's estate to descend to Tom, who is never accused of murder. Then the hospital suffers a fate similar to that of the mansion it replaced. Just as that relic of the old South was "burned during the war" (127), so the hospital is burned in the racial massacre sparked by the white supremacists' press campaign.

As an allegory about who will inherit the South, Chesnutt's second novel is as bleak as his first. For his original audience, it might have seemed even bleaker, due to a change in the time of action. Published at the turn of the century, *The House Behind the Cedars* is set before redemption, with a flashback to the antebellum period. In contrast, the primary action of *The Marrow of Tradition* is closer to its turn-of-the-century moment of publication, while the time soon after the Civil War becomes its background. Much of the book's pessimism comes from the failure to deliver on the promise of the Civil War Amendments and the Reconstruction legislation they inspired. That pessimism is heightened because the primary action takes place at a time when some optimism was reborn, as a fusion government of blacks and whites had taken local control. Furthermore, in the Wellington of *The Marrow of Tradition*, we see a black professional class that was not present in the Patesville of *The House Behind the Cedars*. In that book, John Walden becomes a lawyer only by assuming a white identity, whereas in Chesnutt's second novel, we have a black lawyer, as well as a black physician. Likewise, Molly Walden has transformed into Julia Brown, who, because of laws passed during what the Carterets call the "military occupation" (*MT*, 264, 265), can marry her white lover. Thus, Janet's disinheritance, like that of Iola Leroy, comes from fraud and deceit, not the neglect of her father. Although Janet and her mother experience hard times after they are kicked out of their home, Janet lands on her feet, not by passing as

In 1899, Frances Benjamin Johnston was commissioned to photograph scenes of the Hampton Institute for the US exhibition at the 1900 Paris Exposition. This photograph called "A graduate (dining) at home" captures the professional aspirations of families like the Millers in Chesnutt's *The Marrow of Tradition*. Library of Congress.

white or from the benevolence of whites, but by marrying a prosperous African American. William Miller is a product of the classic American success story that, Chesnutt implies, should have been available to African Americans. The Millers do not come, as the Waldens do, from North Carolina's original free people of color. Instead, like Peter Fowler, Dr. Miller's grandfather bought himself out of slavery through his own labor. His father advanced the family's fortune, cherishing the "proud hope that his children or his grandchildren might be gentlemen in the town where their ancestors had once been slaves" (*MT*, 50). Whereas the name "Carteret" is aristocratic, the name "Miller" implies productive work. Nonetheless, both of Adam Miller's sons, like their creator, have first names of British kings.

Through the Millers' success, Chesnutt rewrites a story that could come straight out of the pages of Page: a noble southern family losing its home to a black family during Reconstruction. In Chesnutt's version, however, the Millers have honorably earned the right to own the Carterets' old home, whereas Olivia Carteret's inheritance of her home is clouded by deceit. In *The House Behind the Cedars*, the Waldens are distinguished from other African Americans, even those who have bought their freedom, by their near whiteness. In contrast, the Millers are marked by their financial success. They start, like the Fowlers, in slavery, but their trajectory after buying their freedom is steadily upward rather than downward. Frank Fowler's father can buy his freedom because he was a good mechanic. Like him, Frank learns a trade, becoming a cooper, but "a barrel factory had been opened in the town, and had well-nigh paralyzed the cooper's trade. The best mechanic could hardly compete with a machine. One man could now easily do the work of Peter's shop" (*HBC*, 126). The Fowlers' economic vulnerability to technological advances is one of several subtle digs Chesnutt makes against Booker T. Washington's formula for African American success. Another comes when Judge Straight momentarily has second thoughts about helping John become a lawyer. "He really must be falling into premature dotage," he thinks. "The proper thing would be to rebuke the lad for presumption and advise him to learn to take care of horses, or make boots, or lay bricks" (*HBC*, 171). Clearly, Chesnutt does not think that it is presumptuous for African Americans to aspire to the professional class. Even having achieved that position, however, Dr. Miller is denied the status of a "gentleman."[13]

A crucial moment in the story's inheritance plots comes when Theodore Carteret's life is in danger and Dr. Miller's former mentor and colleague, Dr. Burns, is called from Philadelphia to operate. For professional reasons, Burns wants Miller to assist him, but Carteret refuses on racial grounds. "With the suave courtesy which was part of his inheritance," Carteret throws himself upon Burn's "magnanimity, as between white men." To Burn's "I am a gentleman, sir, before I am a white man," Carteret replies, "The two terms should be synonymous" (*MT*, 73). Their disagreement is negotiated by Dr. Price, the family doctor who called for Burns and knows Miller. Price concocts an excuse to exclude Miller.

A trained lawyer confined to a job as a legal stenographer, Chesnutt was as alert to discrimination within the professions as he was to discrimination against professionals. Established in 1847, the American Medical Association (AMA) insisted on professionalizing the practice of medicine. That commendable effort was affected by the national debate over race. In 1850, the leaders of the AMA insisted on transcending the politics of racial divide. They did so by promoting sectional harmony at the expense of racial equality. Dedicated to healing, the organization worked to bind "the members of the profession together in one harmonious whole . . . to counteract the centrifugal tendencies of our political system." Leaders were careful to stage annual meetings in the North and the South. Even during the Civil War, there were efforts to have the mission of healing transcend politics. Page's Dr. Cary exemplifies this attitude. "He was as quick to look after a wounded Yankee as after a Confederate. . . . 'A wounded man wasn't an enemy," he had said, 'he was a patient'" (*RR*, 557). One consequence of this noble view was that the profession was careful not to alienate members who supported slavery. This stance carried over to the postbellum period. With emancipation, the biracial National Medical Society was established, based in Washington, DC, with members from the Freedmen's Hospital and the medical department at Howard University. In its 1870 meeting in Washington, the AMA voted to deny admission to members of the society.[14]

In a short story that appeared in the *Atlantic Monthly* shortly after the war, physician S. Weir Mitchell hints at how race underlay this effort to police membership in the medical profession. In "The Autobiography of a Quack," the first-person narrator gives a vivid account of how, to reap a profit, he played on the credulity of people seeking medical care. Expressing the pro-Union views of the *Atlantic*, Mitchell has the Quack, like many carpetbaggers depicted in future southern fiction, avoid military service. The Quack's cowardice is doubly reprehensible. Learning that he can be paid to become a substitute for drafted rich men, he takes the money and then deserts, only to repeat the scheme in another location. At one point, when desertion proves impossible, he fakes epilepsy. Although he won't risk his life for the Union, he is willing to risk his life in another scheme to make a massive profit by running the blockade to deliver desperately needed medical supplies to the South. This episode alludes to the AMA's resolution in 1864 asking Lincoln on humanitarian grounds to lift his ban on the sale of medical supplies to the South. Narrating his story from a hospital bed before he dies of Addison's disease, the Quack describes a "mulatto" mark on his body, a perhaps unintended, but significant, association of the scoundrel with people of color.[15]

In his fiction, Chesnutt pays careful attention to the medical profession. His first book, *The Conjure Woman and Other Conjure Tales*, consists of dialect short stories featuring a woman with healing prowess the AMA would dismiss as unprofessional. With the success of these tales, Chesnutt closed his stenography office to devote himself to life as a professional writer. But he was confronted by a racial stereotype. African Americans were expected to write dialect stories. White readers may have been charmed by African American dialect, but, like W. E. B. Du Bois, Chesnutt did not want dialect to be the voice associated with all African Americans. It is no accident that in his works challenging that stereotype, dialect is the most obvious marker of class within the African American community. Nor is it an accident that in those same works he abandons the figure of the conjure woman and depicts professional doctors. Contemporary critics may delight in pointing out how Chesnutt uses the African tradition of conjuring to undercut the premises of dialect stories by Page and Harris, but Chesnutt was aware of the dangers in that primitivist nostalgia. Conjuring should no more represent all African Americans than dialect speakers should. Professionally trained doctors were needed to serve the community and challenge stereotypes within the profession. In *The House Behind the Cedars,* Chesnutt attacks the scientific racism of the medical profession through Dr. Green. In *The Marrow of Tradition,* superstitious Mammy Jane conjures, while Dr. Miller serves the African American community. Prized by his northern mentor, Miller is betrayed by a southern colleague who accommodates himself to white supremacist thought.[16]

Both Aunt Polly and General Belmont justify disinheriting African Americans by appealing to the "higher law" of white supremacy. Belmont, for instance, suppresses Delamere's will leaving most of his estate to Miller's hospital "by the usual race argument. . . . Mr. Delamere's property belonged of right to the white race, and by the higher law should remain in the possession of white people" (235). A favorite slogan of white supremacists was "Blood is thicker than water," which was used as the title of Rev. Henry Field's reconciliationist account of his travels through the South. Listed today as a proverb, this slogan had been popularized by the naval officer Josiah Tattnall, who evoked it in 1859 to defend his decision to aid a British ship attacked by Chinese, even though doing so violated official US neutrality. When the Civil War broke out, the Georgian Tattnall joined the Confederate Navy. Rather than reject the slogan, Chesnutt appropriates it. On the one hand, Delamere uses it to explain why whites irrationally threaten to lynch Sandy (*MT,* 261). On the other hand, the narrator uses it to describe Janet's desire for recognition from her half sister. If blood is truly thicker than water, Chesnutt insists, then "blacks" and "whites" should equitably share the South's inheritance. Rather than recognize that equitable inheritance, however, white supremacists generate a racial massacre that spills blood on the streets of Wellington.[17]

The massacre affects the inheritance plots in various ways. In addition to showing how racial violence destroys efforts to improve the health of the community, the senseless burning of Miller's hospital renders useless Olivia's plan to have the intention of her father's will fulfilled without acknowledging the legitimacy of her half sister's inheritance—that is, unless Olivia would be willing to help rebuild the hospital that is destroyed as a result of her husband's campaign. Most significantly, in the midst of the bloodshed, an aimless bullet kills Miller's son and sole heir. That tragedy makes it clear that, despite his professional status, Miller is as vulnerable to racial violence as any black person. In the meantime, white leaders

On November 11, 1898, the day after the Wilmington racial massacre, African American leaders, under armed guard, were marched to the railroad station and ordered to leave their businesses, their homes, and their families. They were threatened with physical harm or death if they attempted to return. In contrast, Chesnutt depicts a world in which, without the aid of an African American professional, the heir to a prominent white family is doomed to die.

refuse to take responsibility for the violence. Professionally bound to help the infirm, Dr. Price, anticipating trouble, leaves town to attend a patient, preferring to be "where he could not be called upon to assume any responsibility" (*MT*, 312). Although Carteret is cheered by the mob as "the champion of 'white supremacy,'" he is shocked by the violence that his campaign of hate has unleashed (305). Nonetheless, he insists, "The negroes have themselves to blame,—they tempted us beyond endurance. . . . I am not responsible for these subsequent horrors,—I wash my hands of them" (307).[18]

There is one victory of sorts for African Americans. When violence breaks out, Josh Green pleads with Miller and the black lawyer Watson to assume leadership. When they refuse, Josh rallies African Americans intent on fighting back despite overwhelming odds. During the massacre, he encounters McBane, who as leader of the Klan had murdered Josh's father and driven his mother mad. Absorbing a fatal shot from McBane, Josh buries "a huge bowie knife, a relic of the civil war, which he had carried on his person for many years for a definite purpose . . . in the heart of his enemy" (*MT*, 309).[19]

Josh's vengeance takes place in the third-to-last chapter of the book called "Mine Enemy, O Mine Enemy!" Each of the last three chapters suggests a possible response to white repression of African Americans. With its evocation of the

Old Testament code of an eye for an eye, Josh's response is ultimately unsatisfactory because it will lead to a future of endless violence with no promise of a better future. The next chapter, "Fiat Justitia," suggests a response governed by rule by law, which legal anthropologists of the nineteenth century claimed was developed to contain revenge cycles. Rather than allow individuals to take justice into their own hands, the legal system gives the third party of the state a monopoly on legitimate violence and the authority to mete out justice. As the image of the scales of justice suggests, it promises to do so fairly by balancing competing claims. In this chapter, Carteret, in the midst of the massacre, gets word that his son's life is again at risk. Because Dr. Price is away, the only available doctor to help is Dr. Miller. Carteret is well aware that his wife has refused to recognize Miller's wife as her relative and that he insulted Miller by refusing to let him help during the earlier operation. But he goes to Miller's house anyway, assuming that professional duty will require Miller to treat his son. When Miller instead shows him the body of his own son, "in the agony of his own predicament—in the horror of the situation at Miller's house—for a moment the veil of race prejudice was rent in twain, and he saw things as they were, in their correct proportions and relations,—saw clearly and convincingly that he had no standing here, in the presence of death, in the home of this stricken family" (321). Carteret's lack of standing reinforces the chapter's title and indicates that if the scales of justice are to balance, he has no right to make a claim on Dr. Miller. Nonetheless, Carteret, like Tryon in *The House Behind the Cedars*, becomes a model for Chesnutt's implied readers, who, hopefully, will not need a real tragedy to force them to drop the veil of their prejudices. The problem with this balanced sense of justice is that it leaves neither family with a chance to pass on its inheritance.

Although Theodore and the Miller's unnamed son balance one another in the plot, the inheritances their parents imagine for them have different temporal orientations. The Carterets invest in industries associated with the New South to assure their son a future. Yet, they imagine a future that is a return to the past. They hope that Theodore can "take a place in the world commensurate with the dignity of his ancestors, one of whom, only a generation removed, had owned an estate of ninety thousand acres of land and six thousand slaves" (*MT*, 30). In contrast, the Millers imagine their son's future as part of a new social order, in which he will fulfill his grandfather's dream of having descendants who are "gentlemen in the town where their ancestors were slaves" (50.) With the future of Miller's son denied, Carteret is confronted with the dilemma that, for his son to have a future, he needs the professional help of Miller, whom he has denied the possibility of being a gentleman simply because of his race. That dilemma leads to the third and final possible conclusion.

To put its action into context, we first need to explore Chesnutt's awareness of how difficult it is to lift the veil of prejudice. As we saw in the introduction, the phrase "to see things as they were, in their correct proportions and relations" is an allusion to Howells's description of the formal problem of selection faced by novelists. In *The Rise of Silas Lapham*, the Reverend Sewell castigates popular sentimental fiction. "The novelists," he insists, "might be the greatest possible help to us if they painted life as it is, and human feelings in their true proportion and relation." Chesnutt alludes to this formulation more than once. In "The Sheriff's Children," the sheriff learns that he is the father of a mulatto prisoner he holds in jail and protects from a lynch mob. Confronted with another situation in which a child of mixed-race heritage does not receive the same inheritance as a white sibling, the sheriff lies awake "alone with God" and experiences a "kind of clarifying of the moral faculty, in which the veil of the flesh, with its obscuring passions and prejudices, is pushed aside for a moment, all the acts of one's life stand out, in the clear light of truth, in their correct proportions and relations" (SC, 90). That moment of clarity makes him realize his duty to his son. But it is too late. During the night, the son has killed himself. In *The Marrow of Tradition*, Carteret's epiphany is, if not completely undercut, complicated in a different way. The belief that we can overcome prejudices rests on the assumption that we can distinguish them from the truth. Earlier, however, Chesnutt reminds us how hard that is to do.[20]

When Carteret refuses to let Dr. Miller help Dr. Burns operate on his son, Dr. Burns protests, claiming that he has a professional duty to provide the best care possible and that "principle . . . ought not give way to a mere prejudice." Dr. Price responds, explaining Carteret's position: "He has certain principles,—call them prejudices, if you like,—certain inflexible rules of conduct by which he regulates his life" (*MT*, 71). As much as Chesnutt hates racial prejudices, he recognizes that one person's prejudice is another person's principle. Given that fact of life, rational arguments will rarely convince people to overcome what others see as their prejudices. Chesnutt hopes that a compelling story might have the capacity to accomplish what logic cannot.

To help readers lift their veils of prejudice, Chesnutt uses fiction to pierce the veil between those in the present and memory of a past in which African Americans have been unjustly denied their true inheritance (*MT*, 321). Aunt Polly and Olivia are most directly responsible for denying Janet her inheritance. As Aunt Polly begins to tell Olivia the story of deceit that she has repressed for years, we are told it was "as though memory had thrown aside the veil of intervening years and carried her back directly to the events which she now described" (134). Later, when Olivia discovers the hidden will and marriage certificate, she worries that, so long as Janet is present, she will not "be able to throw the veil of forgetfulness over this blot upon her father's memory" (261).

Josh's past, however, dramatizes the problem with turning to the past to overcome prejudice. What he and numerous African Americans inherit is memory of violent intimidation. The Klan's murder of his father, Josh reveals, "wuz branded on my mem'ry, suh, like a red-hot iron bran's de skin" (111). The metaphor of branded memory alludes to the practice of branding slaves and the legal description of the brands of slavery. Chesnutt uses it to warn his white readers that for many African Americans, as for Josh, remembering the past will cause them to seek revenge for the violence inflicted upon their fathers. Listening to Josh vow revenge for the Klan's violence, Dr. Miller urges him to "put away these murderous fantasies. . . . The Bible says that we should 'forgive our enemies, bless them that curse us, and do good to them that despitefully use us.'" Josh rejects this "Sunday-school" sentiment: "It 'pears ter me dat dis fergitfulniss an' fergiveniss is mighty one-sided. De w'ite folks don' forgive nothin' de niggers does. Dey got up de Ku-Klux, dey said, on 'count er de kyarpit-baggers. Dey be'n talkin' 'bout de kyarpit-baggers ever sence, an' dey 'pears ter fergot all 'bout de Ku-Klux. But I ain' fergot" (113). Josh's attitude will gain more force, Chesnutt suggests, if the history of violent repression is perpetuated through campaigns of lynching and racial massacre. Although Chesnutt does not advocate Josh's violent response, he uses it as a warning to his readers, reminding them that there will not be much of a South to inherit if blacks decide to enact what they consider just revenge. In the midst of the massacre, before learning of his son's death, even the moderate Dr. Miller, "with prophetic instinct . . . foresaw the hatreds to which this day would give birth; the long years of constraint and distrust which would still further widen the breach between two peoples whom fate had thrown together in one community" (291).

Miller's prophecy is yet another allusion to the *Plessy* case. Countering the majority's claim that enforced segregation is consistent with preserving the public peace and good order, Justice Harlan asked: "What can more certainly arouse race hate, what more certainly create and perpetuate a feeling of distrust between these races, than state enactments which, in fact, proceed on the ground that colored citizens are so inferior and degraded that they can not be allowed to sit in public coaches occupied by white citizens?" Most white Americans in 1901 sided with the majority. But most were also appalled at lynchings and racial massacres. By imagining a plot that shows the justification for lynchings and the motives for massacre growing out of the logic of Jim Crow, Chesnutt warns his readers what will happen if segregation persists.[21]

That warning issued, Chesnutt ends with a more hopeful alternative in the final chapter called "The Sisters." Although Carteret acknowledges that he has no standing to ask Dr. Miller to attend to his son, Carteret's wife goes to the Millers and pleads with the half sister she has refused to recognize. Janet, who for years longed for recognition by her white sister, makes it clear that she no longer needs it. She is now psychologically and financially independent, in no need of her white father's bequest, about which she has no knowledge. Nonetheless, she releases her husband to try to save the Carterets' sole heir. Her generous act may seem to evoke the New Testament's message of forgiveness, just as Josh's chapter evokes the Old Testament code of an eye for an eye. Janet, however, is not motivated by forgiveness. She wants to display a higher moral standard than her sister. Having shown how the fates, like the bloodlines, of whites and blacks in the South are interrelated, Chesnutt makes clear that, if white southerners want to pass on a heritage to a new generation, they will need the help and cooperation of blacks. Theodore Felix's first name means the gift of God, but the presence of the word *die* in his nickname of Dodie calls attention to how precarious that gift is. Making a long-term investment at the time of Dodie's birth, his parents confidently think that the "element of time . . . was not immediately important" (*MT*, 30). By the end of the book, however, time is extremely important, not only for Theodore's future but also for the future of the South and the nation, which is threatened by continued violence if whites refuse to recognize African Americans as equals. Appropriately, when Miller arrives at the house in which his wife was born, he asks, "Is the child still alive?" The answer: "There's time enough, but none to spare" (329).[22]

IV

The main character of *The Colonel's Dream* (1905), the last novel Chesnutt published in his lifetime, is Henry French, the last heir of an aristocratic southern family from the small town of Clarendon. In his youth, French joined the Confederate Army and rose to the rank of colonel. Chesnutt's choice of a former Confederate soldier as his protagonist shows his desire to assert his independence as an author. Having first made his reputation as a writer of African American dialect stories, he insisted on expanding his repertoire. Colonel French demonstrates Chesnutt's ability to portray not only a white character but a sympathetic one from the South. Chesnutt's choice of a protagonist has had its costs. Despite the extensive attention paid to Chesnutt in recent years, his novel with a white hero has been relatively neglected. That neglect is unfortunate. Whereas *The House Behind the Cedars* explores the social issue of a possible mixed-race marriage and *The Marrow of Tradition* focuses on the political issue of violent intimidation designed to disfranchise African Americans, *The Colonel's Dream* zeroes in on the economic possibilities of the New South. Like Chesnutt's previous two works, its plot is driven by multiple stories of inheritance.[23]

The action of Chesnutt's first two novels takes place exclusively in the South. The action of *The Colonel's Dream* starts and ends in the North. French's father died in the last year of the war, "having lived long enough to see the conflict work ruin to his fortunes" (17). French, however, was lucky enough to be offered a job in New York "by a relative who had sympathised with the South in her struggle." Starting as a clerk and working his way up, French took his place as the head of the firm when his relative died. The book begins with him sweating out a deal to sell his business and its burlap bag mills in Connecticut to a large corporation. Successful, French makes a substantial profit for himself and his two partners, Mr. Kirby and Mrs. Jarvis, the widow of a former partner. French's wife died early, leaving him with a son, Phil, of five or six years old. For the sake of Phil's health, French travels to Clarendon.

A small, unincorporated town in North Carolina, Clarendon is another of Chesnutt's reminders about the similarities between white "redemption" in the South and restoration of the crown in Great Britain. The Earl of Clarendon, Lord Edward Hyde, was a staunch royalist and Charles II's chief advisor while in exile. Restored to the throne, Charles II named Clarendon his chief minister. The Clarendon Code, with its defense of the Church of England through harsh punishments for dissenters, is a product of his ministry. Clarendon's daughter Anne married Charles II's brother James, later James II, and was the mother of two queens, Queen Mary II and Queen Anne. In 1667, Clarendon was forced to resign on charges of corruption. Exiled to France, he wrote his classic *History of the Rebellion and Civil War in England*. Like George Carteret, who served in the Clarendon ministry, he was one of the proprietors of colonial North Carolina.

Colonel French plans a brief stay in Clarendon but gets involved in trying to vitalize the local economy, held captive by William Fetters, the son of a former slave trader. The same age as French, Fetters has amassed his wealth by leasing convict labor. He holds mortgages on almost all citizens of note in the community. Through the colonel, Chesnutt alludes to Cable, a former confederate soldier who moved north, and Tourgée, with French Huguenot ancestry. Along with his supportive mentors, Chesnutt tries to imagine the conditions for a thriving New South. For Colonel French, "it required no great stretch of imagination to see [Clarendon], a few years hence, a busy hive of industry, where no man, and no woman obliged to work, need be without employment at fair wages; where the trinity of peace, prosperity and progress would reign supreme; where men like Fetters and methods like his would no longer be tolerated" (*CD*, 117–18). French becomes so absorbed in his dream that he decides to stay in Clarendon and proposes to Laura Treadwell, the daughter of a declining southern family. At first, the colonel's dream has the support of the white community. The local newspaper, the *Anglo Saxon*, encourages his investment, since the South's "vast undeveloped resources needed only the fructifying flow of abundant capital to make it blossom like the rose" (86–87). But more than an infusion of capital was needed. Townspeople blame Clarendon's lack of progress on "some outrageous reason . . . the war, the carpetbaggers, the Fifteenth Amendment, the Negroes." Through the colonel's project to buy and rebuild an abandoned cotton mill, Chesnutt shows that "the condition of the town" is "due to causes within itself" (108).

Reconstructing the mill requires bricks. "For most of the period since the war," bricks "had been procured from the ruins of old buildings—it was cheaper to clean bricks than to make them" (152). When new bricks were needed, machine-made ones were imported from the North. French, however, insists that bricks be made locally. "There was good brick clay on the outskirts of the town, where bricks had once been made" (152). In addition, there are numerous unemployed local brick makers, mostly African Americans. Once bricks are made, the work on the factory begins, and a local leader asks the colonel if he plans "to hire white folks to do the work" (153). When the colonel responds that he simply wants good workers, he is told, "You'll have trouble if you hire niggers. . . . You'll find that they won't work when you want 'em to. They're not reliable, they have no sense of responsibility" (153). The colonel answers, "I haven't noticed any unnatural activity of the white men of town." The integrated work force functions smoothly until the white foreman of the masons quits over a disagreement, and French replaces him with an African American. Promoting a colored man causes the immediate resignation of the remaining two white bricklayers and leads to "the thin entering wedge that was to separate the colonel from a measure of his popularity" (191).

Through this incident Chesnutt challenges the portrait of the New South painted by its most famous advocate, Henry Grady. In Chesnutt's 1889 essay "What Is a White Man?," he speculates that Grady originated the phrase "all-pervading, all conquering Anglo-Saxon race" and wonders if Grady meant to exclude "the Celts and Teutons and Gauls and Slavs who make up so large a proportion of our population or even "the Jews . . . whose mortgages cover so large a portion of Southern soil." In *The Colonel's Dream*, we are told that Grady lectured in Clarendon on "white supremacy" (197). More importantly, Chesnutt provides a different picture of how blacks and whites work together. Toward the end of "In Plain Black and White," Grady insists that in the South "the races meet in the exchange of labor in perfect amity and understanding. Together they carry on the concerns of the day, knowing little or nothing of the fierce hostility that divides labor and capital in other sections." Blacks, we are told, "work side by side with the white bricklayer or carpenter in perfect accord and friendliness. When the trowel or hammer is laid aside, the laborers part, each going his own way." Chesnutt makes clear that such harmony exists only when blacks are in a subservient position.[24]

Chesnutt's scene of the making and laying of bricks also engages Booker T. Washington and Tourgée. Trained as a bricklayer, Washington claimed that if African Americans made themselves economically invaluable by mastering skilled labor, social recognition would follow. In contrast, Chesnutt shows that the regime of white supremacy denies African Americans equal economic opportunity. Tourgée had argued that Reconstruction was destined to fail so long as those in favor of it in the South were doomed to make bricks without straw. Chesnutt responds by demonstrating that the material necessities for making bricks—good clay, skilled workers—were readily available. What was lacking was a social attitude that would transform those material resources into something concrete. For Chesnutt, as for Tourgée and Cable, the regime of white supremacy is incompatible with a prosperous New South because it violates a principle of free labor. "The right to work and do one's best work," according to French, "was fundamental, as was the right to have one's work done by those who could do it best" (*CD*, 192). Responding to protests against his choice of a new foreman, he declares, "These people have got to learn that we live in an industrial age, and success demands of an employer that he utilise the most available labour. After Green was discharged, George Brown was the best mason left" (192).

According to Chesnutt, advocates of the New South, like Grady, were willing to sacrifice prosperity to the principle of white supremacy. Addressing a community meeting, Clarendon's mayor declares, "We all appreciate the colonel's worth, and what he is doing for the town. But he has lived at the North for many years, and has got somewhat out of our way of thinking. We do not want to buy the prosperity of this town at the price of our principles. The attitude of the white people on the Negro question is fixed and determined for all time, and nothing can ever alter it" (264).

The issue sparking the mayor's comments is the colonel's burial of the African American Peter in the Frenches' cemetery spot. Peter had been a family slave, entrusted with watching young Henry. When French returns to Clarendon, Peter is unemployed, surviving on part-time handyman jobs. In his ample spare time, he tends to the Frenches' burial spot out of loyalty to the family. He is arrested as a vagrant, and under the corrupt convict-lease system, his labor is sold at a public auction. To save him, French wins the bid and employs him to watch Phil. Late in the book, Peter tries to save Phil, who has walked across a railroad track and is about to be hit by a train backing up to connect with a lone car. Peter is killed immediately, and Phil dies of his wounds. Earlier, Phil had expressed his desire to have Peter buried with him if he ever died. To fulfill his son's wish and to honor Peter's loyalty, the colonel has him buried next to Phil. If in *Red Rock* it is a scandal when Still's purchase of the estate keeps Mrs. Gray from being buried in the family graveyard, in *The Colonel's Dream* the town considers it a scandal when a black man is buried in a white cemetery. The colonel's action marks an end to his dream.

Despite the town's resistance, numerous setbacks, and the loss of his son, "the colonel was beaten, but not dismayed" (*CD*, 278). Deciding to stay in Clarendon and fight, he dozes off, dreaming of a regenerated South, "filled with thriving industries, and thronged with a prosperous and happy people, where every man, having enough for his needs, was willing that every other man should have the same; where law and order should prevail unquestioned, and where every man could enter, through the golden gate of hope, the field of opportunity, where lay the prizes of life, which all might have an equal chance to win or lose." The colonel's dream is interrupted when Peter's dug-up coffin is deposited on his piazza with a misspelled note telling "*Kurnell French*" to "berry yore ole nigger somewhar else" (280).

As bleak as *The Marrow of Tradition* is, when the black servant Sandy is falsely accused of murder, Mr. Delamere is able to save him. In *The Colonel's Dream*, Colonel French cannot protect Peter, even in death. *The Marrow of Tradition* ends with some hope for the heir of an aristocratic white southern family, whereas Colonel French's young son and only heir dies. *The Colonel's Dream* begins with French profiting in a battle with a corporate giant in the North and ends with him admitting defeat in the South. Released by Laura from his commitment to marry, French leaves for the North, burying Phil and Peter in a cemetery where, "sometimes, at night, a ray of light from the uplifted torch of the Statue of Liberty, the gift of a free people to a free people, falls athwart the white stone which marks [Peter's] resting place" (*CD*, 290).

Even the manner of Peter's and Phil's deaths adds to the sense of tragedy. In the novel, railroads are a sign of progress. "Railroads, while they bring in supplies and take out produce, also bring in light and take out information, both of which are fatal to certain fungus growths, social as well as vegetable, which flourish best in the dark" (215). Yet, it is on a railroad line, the symbol of the promise of an enlightened New South, that Peter and Phil die. Although "there was no suggestion of blame" (259) for the accident, Chesnutt suggests a link to a particular genre associated with southern literature. Halfway through the novel, Peter and Phil are fishing when they see a black cat come out of the abandoned mill. When Peter suggests that the cat might be able to speak, Phil expresses skepticism, and Peter reminds him of "Bre'r Rabbit and Bre'r Fox and the yuther creaturs talkin' an' gwine on jes' lak folks" (147). Peter then tells a story about an African American who hopes to make five dollars by spending the night in a haunted house. Waking in the middle of the night, he is confronted by a talking black cat who scares him into running out of the house, forfeiting his pay and knocking over a lamp that burns the house down. "To talk to a black cat," Phil thinks, "would be great fun" (151). Later, he is lured to his death when he sees a black cat on the railroad track and tries to talk to him. An African American mimicking the dialect stories that made Joel Chandler Harris famous has deadly consequences.

Phil's death marks the failure of the French family to pass on its heritage. Indeed, almost all of the various inheritance stories in *The Colonel's Dream* are marked by failure. When the colonel arrives in Clarendon, he learns that his family house was auctioned at a "tax sale at a time of great financial distress, twenty years before, for five hundred dollars" to "a keen-eyed mulatto" barber, "a man of thrift and good sense" (82). Nostalgic about the family memories the house evokes, French buys it for four thousand dollars and fixes it up. When he decides to abandon the South, he contemplates "making over to Miss Laura the old family residence in trust for use as a hospital, with a suitable fund for its maintenance, but it unfortunately caught fire and burned down—and he was hardly sorry" (291).

With the Treadwells, Chesnutt tells another story of the declining fortunes of a southern aristocratic family, a story with echoes of the plot of *Red Rock*. Major Treadwell was one of the few "who weathered the storm of war and emerged financially sound," but he got involved with Fetters "speculating in cotton and turpentine" (*CD*, 52). When the major suddenly died, Fetters foreclosed a mortgage he held upon the family's plantation. Fetters changed the name from Belleview to Sycamore and manned it with convict labor, leaving Laura and her mother poor. To make ends meet, Laura is reduced to giving piano lessons to the barber's daughter, whose mother was once a Treadwell slave. Laura's proposed marriage to French promises to reverse her family's declining fortunes. When this variation of a North-South marriage is called off, Chesnutt does not abandon the Treadwells to poverty. Mrs. Treadwell always believed that "there was something in the wrong" about Fetters's foreclosure on Belleview (53). Sure enough, French discovers "a couple of yellow, time-stained envelopes, addressed on the outside to Major John Treadwell," hidden in his father's desk, which the Treadwells had kept for him (135). They contain "a promissory note from Fetters to Mr. Treadwell, and a contract of certain joint transactions in turpentine and cotton futures" (251) from twenty years ago. Had the note been produced at the time of Treadwell's death, it "would have meant to his survivors the difference between poverty and financial independence." French assumes the note "was barred by the lapse of time" (251).

In North Carolina, however, the statute of limitations is twenty years, and French's lawyer files the note for the Treadwells minutes before it expires. Fetters's payment does not restore the Treadwells' lost plantation, but it allows Mrs. Treadwell to spend her last days in "comfort" and saves Laura from "any fear for her future" (290). A bit of hope in the midst of decline, the Treadwells' reverse in fortune is necessary once Chesnutt decides to have Colonel French abandon the South. Noble as he is, French would never have left the Treadwells in the lurch. Once he is assured of their financial well-being, he is free to return to the North.

The North turns out to offer the only hope for a third decaying aristocratic family. The Dudleys were once "one of the richest and most conspicuous families in the State" (170). In fact, their estate on Mink Run predates the nation's founding. Ancestors include a famous general during the War of Independence and a "distinguished jurist, whose name is still a synonym for legal learning and juridical wisdom" (170). The decline set in with Ralph, a bachelor who sapped his resources to maintain a life of pleasure. He left the estate in charge of his nephew and heir Malcolm. During the Civil War, Ralph took an administrative job with the Confederacy, while Malcolm "kept bachelor hall in the great house," as he already had for ten years with an enslaved housekeeper known as Viney, "a tall, comely young light mulattress, with a dash of Cherokee blood, which gave her straighter, blacker, and more glossy hair than most women of mixed race have, and perhaps a somewhat different temperamental endowment" (171). Worried that his uncle might marry and leave him out of the will, Malcolm begins to court an older rich war widow. They become engaged, but Mrs. Todd calls off the marriage after Viney visits her in private. Angered, Malcolm has his overseer whip Viney, who almost dies and loses her capacity to speak. Malcolm pays for his cruelty. The day after Viney's beating, Malcolm finds a letter from his uncle telling him that he has hidden fifty thousand dollars in governmental gold in the house for safekeeping. Ralph dies in an accident the next day, and the only person who knows where the gold is hidden is Viney, who cannot talk. As a slave, she had not been taught to write, and Malcolm's efforts to teach her fail. Thus, he has no way of knowing where the gold is hidden.

With the end of the war, the estate goes into steep decline: "Part of the land went, at ruinous prices, to meet mortgages at ruinous rates; part lay fallow, given up to scrub oak and short-leaf pine; merely enough was cultivated, or let out on shares to Negro tenants, to provide a living for old Malcolm and a few servants" (176). Viney, however, remains: "After the tragic episode which had led to their mutual undoing, there had been no relation between them but that of master and servant. But some gloomy attraction, or it may have been habit, held her to the scene of her power and of her fall" (176). She helps nurse Malcolm through a bad fever, which reduces his mental capacities. "Absorbed in dreams of hidden gold and in search for it," Malcolm "neglected his business and fell yet deeper into debt" (176). In a plot reminiscent of Hawthorne's "Peter Goldthwaite's Treasure," he tears the house apart but finds no gold. Malcolm's only heir is his handsome orphaned nephew Ben, who lives with him and is in love with Graciella, Laura Treadwell's beautiful orphaned niece. Graciella worries that Ben will never allow her to fulfill her dream of experiencing high society in New York City. Indeed, although Ben is blessed with an inventive mind, he has no talent for farming and spends his life dreaming that his uncle will discover the hidden treasure so he will inherit enough wealth to fulfill Graciella's dream. But his dream proves to be a castle in the air.

After the funeral for young Phil, Ben returns home to find his uncle dying, tended to by Viney, who is chiding him for having her whipped twenty-five years ago. Viney, it turns out, could speak all along but remained silent to take revenge on her former lover. Ralph, she reveals, removed the gold an hour after he hid it, and she has watched as Malcolm ruined his life dreaming of a treasure that did not exist. Apprised of the truth, Malcolm dies, and Viney, her revenge enacted, breaks into tears and covers Malcolm's "emaciated hand" in "fervent kisses" (*CD*, 274). As Ben watches this spectacle, "a veil seemed to fall from his eyes" and "things appeared in their true light" (275). The language recalls Major Carteret's moment of revelation at the end of *The Marrow of Tradition*, but there is a significant difference. Through Carteret, Chesnutt raises the hope, however small, that even a southern white supremacist can overcome racial prejudice. What Ben sees is the futility of life in the South. Fetters will foreclose his mortgage on the Dudley estate, and Ben has "no trade, no profession, no land, and no money" (287). Nonetheless, an opportunity does open up. Ben once showed French a new model for a cotton gin and press. After French returns to the North where invention is rewarded, he sends for Ben to join him, enclosing five hundred dollars and a plan to patent the gin and form a company to manufacture it. With this good news, Graciella can live her dream and accompany Ben to New York. Significantly, however, their happiness does not come from Ben's inheritance. To fulfill their dreams they must abandon the South.

Chesnutt lifts the story of the Dudley estate from his unpublished short story, "The Dumb Witness," featuring Old Julius from *The Conjure Woman* tales. A few changes he made show how bleak his vision had become by the time he wrote *The Colonel's Dream*. Most significant, in the short story there is a treasure that Viney reveals to the young nephew only after Malcolm dies. It includes a will making Malcolm sole heir, "some bonds, and mortgages securing them, on plantations in the neighborhood . . . , also some bonds and other securities of value and your grandmother's diamond necklace" (DW, 159). Other than the necklace, the treasure has little value. When Viney kept Malcolm from discovering the treasure, relatives were legally granted a share of the estate in such a way that "it would be difficult to trace or recover it if the will were found." (161). Likewise, estates on which he assumed he held notes and mortgages were "sold and other wise disposed of" (161). Nonetheless, the treasure's existence lends some credibility to Malcolm's dreams of renewing the Old South. Indeed, the nephew, carrying on the great-uncle's name and possessing a valuable family heirloom, restores the estate to an extent, suggesting hope for a New South. In the novel, however, there is nothing from the Old South for a progressive younger generation to inherit. Controlling the postwar economy, Fetters is the one who profits from cashing in on old notes and mortgages. To be sure, Chesnutt allows for one miracle when French's discovery of a long-lost document allows Laura Treadwell and her old mother to escape Fetter's clutches, but this is merely an instance of the older generation finding a way to survive. Equally important, in the novel, the Civil War plays a much more significant role than it does in the story. In the story, Malcolm courts a Pennsylvania widow who has moved South just before the war, not a southern war widow. In the novel, Chesnutt seems to transfer the promise of a North-South romance to the main plot, but Colonel French is originally from the South. Perhaps more significant, the lost treasure is not a family inheritance but Confederate gold. What Ralph is doing with all of that governmental gold, and whether he has it legitimately, is never made clear. What Chesnutt does make clear is that southern hope for postwar prosperity based on an inheritance from the Confederacy is a castle in the air. No such prosperous heritage exists.[25]

The Dudley's inheritance plot is telling in two other ways. Earlier, Ben pleads with Graciella to have faith that a fortune will eventually be discovered in his family home. She is skeptical even though he shows her the uncle's faded letter about the hidden gold. As the narrator comments, there "it was in black and white, or rather brown and yellow" (*CD*, 127). Through this detail, Chesnutt challenges Grady's assumption that the racial makeup of the nation is one of plain black and white. Of course, belief in the so-called "one-drop rule" allowed people to assume a black and white division. Contrary to popular legend, however, the "one-drop rule" was not the legal norm when Chesnutt was writing. The legal division between whites and blacks varied from state to state. That fact was a crucial part of Plessy's argument about the arbitrariness of the Louisiana Jim Crow law he challenged. As James C. Walker, Tourgée's fellow attorney, pointed out in his brief to the Supreme Court on behalf of Plessy, in South Carolina a court had held that, in doubtful instances, race was mostly for the jury to decide "by reputation, by reception into society, and by the exercise of the privileges of a white man." Judge Straight's advice to John Walden to go to South Carolina in *The House Behind the Cedars* indicates Chesnutt's knowledge of this decision. Walker showed that, in contrast to South Carolina, in North Carolina a "negro" had no less than one-sixteenth black blood, whereas in Michigan a "negro" had one-fourth. In the early twentieth century, the Louisiana Supreme Court distinguished between "white," "colored," and "Negro." All Negroes were colored, but not all colored people were Negroes.

This challenge to black and white thinking is reinforced by Viney. In "The Dumb Witness," the white family calls her "of our blood" (159). Like Molly Walden, she has a mixture of white, African, and Indian blood. Her Cherokee ancestry suggests that she might have been born in the Lumbee River area, where various races intermixed. Out of that intermixture, a group identified itself as the Lumbee Indian Tribe. At one time there was a legend that the tribe was the product of intermarriage between local Native Americans and the English from the Lost Colony of Roanoke. During the Civil War, a number of Indian tribes, such as the Choctaw and the Chickasaw, discontented with their treatment at the hands of the national government, sided with the Confederacy. In turn, the Confederates could use their theory of state sovereignty to promise more independent sovereignty to Indian nations. The Lumbee, however, resisted the Confederate government. Its resistance carried over into Reconstruction, when its opposition to white supremacist regimes placed it in conflict with the Klan. During the Lowrie War, one of the tribe's leaders fought illegitimate Klan violence with illegitimate violence of his own until he was killed. The Lumbee turn out to confirm Chesnutt's challenge to black and white thinking about race even more than he could have known at the time. Although the Lumbee identify themselves as Native Americans, the latest genetic research shows that they have about 47 percent African, 40 percent white, and 13 percent Native American blood. Most likely, they developed primarily out of intermarriage between whites and African Americans in the swampy land that was also home to Native Americans. In the 1950s, the tribe again took on the Klan. It has also found itself caught in a conflict resulting from the US federal system. The Lumbee are recognized as a tribe by the state of North Carolina but not by the US government. The tribe's logo is a circle divided into four sections: white, red, black, and yellow.[26]

As we saw in *The Marrow of Tradition*, whereas Chesnutt would have understood the Lumbees' violent response to white supremacist violence, he hoped for alternatives. For him, there could be hope for the South only if whites gave African Americans the recognition they deserved and if African Americans did not exact revenge for their violent repression in the past. A second way the story of the Dudley estate is important has to do with revenge. Viney's long silence shows the power of mistreated African Americans to destroy the lives and dreams of whites. Complementing Viney's story of revenge in *The Colonel's Dream* is that of Bud

Johnson. Bud's story has the same message as Viney's, with more violent consequences. Bud is an agrarian counterpart to Josh Green. Like Peter, Bud is convicted of vagrancy and fined. To pay his fine, his labor is sold at auction, but Bud has no former owner to save him. His labor is bought by Fetters, and he is forced to endure unbearable conditions during his period of involuntary servitude. He escapes, is hunted down, and has his labor sold again for a significantly longer period. Bud's example so upsets French that he helps to bring a suit that will declare the entire system of convict leasing unconstitutional as a form of peonage, even though "owing to the exigencies of national politics it was not deemed wise, at that time, to do anything which seemed like an invasion of State rights or savoured of sectionalism" (*CD*, 231). When Bud's life is threatened, the colonel realizes that he cannot wait for legal redress and agrees to have his lawyer bribe one of Fetters's guards to let Bud escape again. In hiding, Bud takes revenge by shooting Fetters's son Barclay and the officer who arrested him, now an overseer for Fetters. Both live, but Barclay loses sight in both eyes. Bud is caught and lynched.

Bud's story shows how much bleaker *The Colonel's Dream* is than *The Marrow of Tradition*. Most obviously, in Chesnutt's previous novel a lynching is avoided, whereas in his last one it is not. Of course, Bud is guilty, and Sandy is not. Nonetheless, both novels are opposed to the extralegal violence of lynching. Aware that describing a lynching can generate sensationalism, Chesnutt has the colonel respond to the news of Bud's fate with "Spare me the details. He is dead" (*CD*, 277). The narrator then adds, "A rope, a tree—a puff of smoke, a flash of flame—or a barbaric orgy of fire and blood—what matter which? At the end there was a lump of clay, and a hundred murderers where there had been one before" (277). In *The Marrow of Tradition*, Sandy is saved from lynching, but a racial massacre follows. In *The Colonel's Dream*, Bud's lynching occurs after another lynching is avoided. Initially, Ben is threatened with lynching after he is mistakenly arrested for shooting Barclay, who attended Harvard and is a possible rival for Graciella's hand. Whereas in *The Marrow of Tradition*, Sandy is saved because the white reporter Lee Ellis knows the true criminal—a white man—in *The Colonel's Dream* Ben is saved because the African American teacher Henry Taylor knows the true criminal—a black man. Taylor tells the colonel, who helps in Johnson's arrest, making French partially complicit in the lynching of the man he tried to save from Fetters. Even Fetters, who seems to triumph, does not have a completely successful story of inheritance. Bud, after all, has had a measure of revenge by shooting Fetters's son. Bud's revenge is, however, less successful than Josh Green's. As he is dying, Josh avenges his father's death by killing McBane. In *The Colonel's Dream*, Bud dies, while Barclay is deprived only of his sight. Rather than an eye for an eye, we get an eye for a life.

At the end of *The Marrow of Tradition*, Chesnutt offers an alternative to the logic of the revenge plot; in *The Colonel's Dream*, it prevails and is viewed in racial terms. Bud "had declared a vendetta against the white race" (*CD*, 277). His victim, Barclay, regains his sight in one eye and, "embittered against the whole Negro race by his disfigurement, went into public life and devoted his talents and his education to their debasement" (290–91). Even honest Henry Taylor is victimized by the logic of racial vendetta. When word gets out that he told on Bud Johnson, "The coloured folks wouldn't send their children to [him]," and he loses his job as a teacher (292). In the book's final scene, French, now married to his former silent partner, meets Taylor working as a porter on a train headed for Chicago. French arranges "to find him something better than menial employment, where his education would give him an opportunity for advancement" (293). Taylor's opportunity, like Ben's, will come in the North. Taylor also tells of one more failure in the South. Before leaving Clarendon, French had promised to match money raised to finance an industrial school. Taylor informs him that all plans for the school have been abandoned. Nothing is left of the colonel's dream for a truly equitable New South.[27]

V

In 1905, the same year that *The Colonel's Dream* appeared, Tourgée died. His death and the bleak outlook expressed in Chesnutt's novel mark, for this study, the end of what I have called the era of Reconstruction. The dream of a truly reconstructed nation growing out of the North's victory in the Civil War was over. This is not to say that all hope was lost. In a 1901 letter to Booker T. Washington, Chesnutt acknowledged that he was "on the weaker side in point of popular sympathy," but that, "on the stronger side in point of justice and morality," he thinks he "will win out in the long run." As bleak as the plot of *The Colonel's Dream* is, Chesnutt ends it with a vision of a better future: "White men go their way, and black men theirs, and these ways grow wider apart, and no one knows the outcome. But there are those who hope, and those who pray, that this condition will pass, that some day our whole land will be truly free, and the strong will cheerfully help to bear the burdens of the weak, and Justice, the seed, and Peace, the flower, of liberty, will prevail throughout all our borders" (294).[28]

On November 16, 1905, Chesnutt and Ida B. Wells delivered eulogies for Tourgée at a memorial service in his hometown in upstate New York. A little over two weeks later, on Thanksgiving, members of the Niagara Movement sponsored nationwide memorial services for three "Friends of Freedom": William Lloyd Garrison, Albion W. Tourgée, and Frederick Douglass. The Niagara Movement would transform into the NAACP, founded on February 12, 1909, the one hundredth anniversary of Lincoln's birth. The NAACP would carry on the dream, but its founding also marked a break. To fulfill the dream of racial equality, the nation needed to do more than overcome the shadow of slavery. It also needed to overcome the shadow of legally sanctioned segregation that had been implemented during the counterrevolution to Reconstruction. The constitutional foundation of Reconstruction was ratification of the Civil War Amendments. By 1909, to fulfill its mission, the NAACP had to overcome the Supreme Court's debilitating interpretation of all three: *Hodges v. U.S.* (1906) for the Thirteenth, *Plessy v. Ferguson* (1896) for the Fourteenth, and *Giles v. Alabama* (1903) for the Fifteenth.[29]

Tourgée estimated that the year 2000 was a reasonable date to imagine the end of racism in the United States. He was too optimistic. I hope that this study of the literature of Reconstruction gives us some insight into why that is the case. The task of overcoming the legacy of slavery while reuniting the nation politically after a bloody Civil War taxed the imaginations of lawmakers and men of letters alike. Remedies to promote racial equality threatened to undermine the quest for reunion, and remedies to promote reunion too often sacrificed the quest for racial equality. Both efforts contributed to and were affected by major economic transformations following from the need to finance a war of emancipation that unleashed previously unimaginable destruction. Heirs to policies that sometimes succeeded but too often failed, we face an equally taxing task of imagining ways to finish the job of reconstructing, not simply restoring, the Union. To take one example, in his dissent in the *Plessy* case, Justice Harlan argued, unsuccessfully, for a color-blind Constitution that refused to make distinctions based on color. Today, opponents to the remedy of affirmative action cite the authority of Justice Harlan to promote a color-blind standard. It is no accident that the source for Justice Harlan's color-blind metaphor was Tourgée's brief to the court. It is also no accident that in *Bricks without Straw*, Tourgée uses the same metaphor to call attention to the inability of the nation to see the actual conditions of people of color. Describing how the freedman had been granted rights, the narrator complains, "Right he had in the abstract; in the concrete, none. Justice would not hear his voice. The law was still color-blinded by the past" (*BS*, 106).

Close attention to literature can help us better understand how the utopian possibility of a color-blind society was imagined during the era of Reconstruction. It can also help us better understand how color-blindness to the past can paradoxically foster black and white thinking. After all, those who are color-blind do not have difficulty distinguishing between black and white. They do have difficulty recognizing the subtle shading of colors into one another. Black and white thinking produced by historical color-blindness can result in both arguments for segregation and a naïve belief that there are simple solutions to the shadowy past we have inherited from Reconstruction's inability to remedy racial injustice. As morally reprehensible as the first is, the second makes it almost impossible to redeem the dream. In the era of Reconstruction the quest for racial justice became entangled with so many social, political, and economic forces that the only way to find a solution seems to be to unwind the past.

Literary responses to Reconstruction suggest another daunting problem. We continue to be inspired by Abraham Lincoln's dream that a nation conceived in liberty and dedicated to the proposition that all are created equal can bring about a new birth of freedom. But perhaps the ideals of liberty and equality are inherently contradictory. As we saw in the first chapter, David Blight claims that "the tragedy of Reconstruction is rooted in this American paradox: the imperative of healing and the imperative of justice could not, ultimately, cohabit the same house." Perhaps Reconstruction remains America's unfinished revolution because a house trying to accommodate the ideals of both liberty and equality contains conflicting notions of justice. The only way to guarantee political and civil equality for African Americans, it seems, was through military force inimical to the nation's ideal of liberty. Expansion of national powers that supposedly made the country a beacon of liberty to the world was not enough to overcome some states' resistance to extending equal rights to all. An economic system committed to the free market too often proved incompatible with efforts to advance the interests of freedmen. In a world in which promotion of civil rights continues to come into conflict with the preservation of civil and economic liberties, completion of the revolution will always be deferred into the future. The nation is left with the ongoing task of trying to reconstruct itself based on competing visions of possible worlds and conflicting fabrications of foundational myths.[30]

Notes

Introduction

1. William Dean Howells, "Some Political Novels" *Atlantic Monthly* 47 (January 1881): 119.

2. Laura F. Edwards, *Gendered Strife and Confusion: The Political Culture of Reconstruction* (Urbana: U of Illinois P, 1997), pp. 5, 17, 5.

3. Edwards, *Gendered Strife*, p. 17; Breese, quoted in Harold M. Hyman, "Reconstruction and Political-Constitutional Institutions: The Popular Expression," in *New Frontiers of the American Reconstruction*, ed. Harold M. Hyman (Urbana: U of Illinois P, 1966), p. 1; C. Vann Woodward, *Thinking Back: The Perils of Writing History* (Baton Rouge: Louisiana State UP, 1986), p. 52.

4. Carl Schmitt, *Political Theology: Four Chapters on the Concept of Sovereignty* (Chicago: U of Chicago P, 2006); Eric Foner, *Reconstruction: America's Unfinished Revolution, 1863–1877* (New York: Harper, 1988). The distinction between legitimacy and legality points to my differences with Deak Nabors's fascinating account of the Fourteenth Amendment and American Literature. In addition to an irresistible attraction to counterintuitive readings that align Harriet Beecher Stowe with Justice Taney in *Dred Scott* and Nathaniel Hawthorne with the Fourteenth Amendment, despite the loyal Democrat's skeptical attitude toward federal over state power, Nabors uses literary works to stress what he calls the "victory of law." I use them to stress the important role they play in legitimation. *Victory of Law: The Fourteenth Amendment, the Civil War, and American Literature, 1852–1867* (Baltimore: Johns Hopkins UP, 2006). For the most exhaustive legal histories of the period, see Charles Fairman's somewhat conservative *Reconstruction and Reunion: 1864–88* (New York: Macmillan, 1971), and Harold M. Hyman and William M. Wieck's far more critical *Equal Justice under the Law* (New York: Harper, 1982). Frank J. Scaturro, *The Supreme Court's Retreat from Reconstruction* (Westport, CT: Greenwood, 2000) and Lawrence Goldstone, *Inherently Unequal: The Betrayal of Equal Rights by the Supreme Court, 1865–1903* (New York: Walker, 2011) follow Hyman and Wieck. Pamela Brandwein in *Reconstructing Reconstruction: The Supreme Court and the Production of Historical Truth* (Durham: Duke UP, 1999) and *Rethinking the Judicial Settlement of Reconstruction* (New York: Cambridge UP, 2011) follows Fairman. See also Laura F. Edwards, *A Legal History of the Civil War and Reconstruction* (New York: Cambridge UP, 2015). I cite other sources for specific issues.

5. Alan Trachtenberg, *The Incorporation of America: Culture and Society in the Gilded Age* (New York: Hill and Wang, 1982).

6. Libertarian attacks on Lincoln include Rogers Hummel, *Emancipating Slaves, Enslaving Free Men* (Chicago: Open Court, 1996); Charles Adams, *When in the Course of Human Events* (Lanham, MD: Rowman and Littlefield, 2000); and Thomas J. Dilorenzo, *The Real Lincoln: A New Look at Abraham Lincoln, His Agenda, and an Unnecessary War* (Roseville, CA: Prima, 2003).

7. William Gillette, *Retreat from Reconstruction, 1869–79* (Baton Rouge: Louisiana State UP, 1979), pp. 363, 363–64.

8. *United States v. Cruikshank*, 92 U.S. 542 (1876) at 544; Daun van Ee, *David Dudley Field and the Reconstruction of the Law* (New York: Garland, 1986).

9. David Dudley Field, *United States against William Cruikshank and Two Others: Argument of Mr. David Dudley Field on Behalf of the Defendants* (New York: John Polhemus, 1875), p. 2; Joseph A. Fry, *John Tyler Morgan and the Search for Southern Autonomy* (Knoxville: U of Tennessee P, 1992).

10. James Harvey Robinson, "Editorial Preface" to David Saville Muzzey, *An American History*, rev. ed. (Boston: Ginn, 1920), p. iii; Muzzey, *An American History*, p. 388.

11. Arthur M. Schlesinger and Dixon Ryan Fox, "Editors' Foreword," to Allan Nevins, *The Emergence of Modern America: 1865–1878* (New York: Macmillan, 1927), pp. xviii; Nevins, *Emergence*, pp. 418, 353, 381, 418.

12. Charles and Mary Beard, *The Rise of American Civilization* (New York: Macmillan, 1927); Peter J. Sehlinger and Holman Hamilton, *Spokesman for Democracy: Claude G. Bowers, 1878–1958* (Indianapolis: Indiana Historical Society, 2000), p. 122. Howard K. Beale, *The Critical Year: A Study of Andrew Johnson and Reconstruction* (New York: Harcourt and Brace, 1930). In the 1958 reprint of his book, Beale insists that he had finished it in 1924 and was not influenced by the Beards. "Foreword to the 1958 Edition," *The Critical Year* (1930; reprint, New York: Ungar, 1958), pp. ix–x. Stanley Coben, "Northeastern Business and Radical Reconstruction: A Re-examination," *Mississippi Valley Historical Review* 46 (1959): 67. Coben quotes from socialist William B. Hesseltine, "Economic Factors in the Abandonment of Reconstruction," *Mississippi Valley Historical Review* 22 (1935): 191.

13. Howard K. Beale, "On Rewriting Reconstruction History," *American Historical Review* 45 (1940): 813, 819. An African American dean at Fisk University, A. A. Taylor, who reviewed *Black Reconstruction*, also questioned Du Bois's Marxist framework in "Review," *New England Quarterly* 8 (1935): 608–12. Foner, *Reconstruction*, p. xxi. For an excellent summary of economic criticism and its response to the Beards, see Peter A. Coclanis and Scott Marler, "The Economics of Reconstruction," in *A Companion to the Civil War and Reconstruction*, ed. Lacy K. Ford (Malden, MA: Blackwell, 2005), pp. 342–65.

14. Michael W. Fitzgerald, "Reconstruction Politics and the Politics of Reconstruction," in *Reconstructions: New Perspectives on the Postbellum United States*, ed. Thomas J. Brown (New York: Oxford, 2006), p. 91; Steven Hahn, *A Nation under Our Feet: Black Political Struggles in the Rural South from Slavery to the Great Migration* (Cambridge: Harvard UP, 2003), p. 6.

15. Hans Georg Gadamer, *Truth and Method* (New York: Continuum, 1975).

16. Charles Sumner, "Supplementary Civil Rights Bill, January 15, 1872," in *Charles Sumner, His Complete Works*, ed. George Frisbie Hoar (Boston: Lee and Shepard, 1900), 19:260, 262. For powerful arguments challenging the court's narrow ruling on state action, see Jacobus tenBroek, *The Anti-slavery Origins of the Fourteenth Amendment*

(Berkeley: U of California P, 1951); Michael Kent Curtis, *No State Shall Abridge: The Fourteenth Amendment and the Bill of Rights* (Durham: Duke UP, 1986); and Robert J. Kaczorowski, "To Begin the Nation Anew: Congress, Citizenship, and Civil Rights after the Civil War," *American Historical Review* 92 (1987): 45–68. For an up-to-date contrary view, see Brandwein, *Rethinking*.

17. George W. Cable, "The Freedman's Case in Equity," *Century Magazine* 29 (1885): 409–18; Henry W. Grady, "In Plain Black and White," *Century Magazine* 29 (1885): 910.

18. Cable, "Case in Equity," 417.

19. Michael Les Benedict, "Southern Democrats in the Crisis of 1876–77: A Reconsideration of *Reunion and Reaction*," *Journal of Southern History* 46 (1980): 491.

20. Gregory P. Downs, *After Appomattox: Military Occupation and the Ends of War* (Cambridge: Harvard UP, 2015), p. 34. Even Downs does not note that his realistic assessment was anticipated by William A. Dunning, who Downs claims "portrayed Reconstruction as a foolish failure" in part because of the "reliance upon military force" (245). "Report of the Committee on History and Education for Citizenship," *Historic Outlook* 12 (1921): 214, 215.

21. Foner, *Reconstruction*, pp. 448, 446, 449.

22. Charles Wallace Collins, *The Fourteenth Amendment and the States* (Boston: Little, Brown, 1912), pp. 145–46.

23. Edward A. Pollard, *The Lost Cause: A New Southern History of the War of the Confederates* (Baltimore: E. B. Treat, 1866); Stacey L. Smith, *Freedom's Frontier: California and the Struggle over Free Labor, Emancipation, and Reconstruction* (Chapel Hill: U of North Carolina P, 2013); Jeannine DeLombard, *In the Shadow of the Gallows: Race, Crime, and American Civic Identity* (Philadelphia: U of Pennsylvania P, 2012).

24. Paul H. Buck, *The Road to Reunion, 1865–1900* (New York: Knopf, 1937); Edmund Wilson, *Patriotic Gore: Studies in the Literature of the American Civil War* (New York: Oxford UP, 1962), pp. xxi, 584, 611. Fred Hobson is one of many veteran scholars of southern literature who points to numerous errors and half-truths by Wilson. See *Tell About the South: The Southern Rage to Explain* (Baton Rouge: Louisiana State UP, 1983), pp. 47, 53, 107, 137; Nina Silber, *The Romance of Reunion: Northerners and South* (Chapel Hill: U of North Carolina P, 1993); K. Stephen Prince, *Stories of the South: Race and the Reconstruction of Southern Identity, 1865–1915* (Chapel Hill: U of North Carolina P, 2014).

25. For instance, Foner cites a passage from Tourgée's *A Fool's Errand* without making the important distinction between a biographical author, his narrator, and a character (*Reconstruction*, p. 436).

26. David W. Blight, *Race and Reunion: The Civil War in American Memory* (Cambridge: Harvard UP, 2001), pp. 217–18.

27. Nicolas Lemann, *Redemption: The Last Battle of the Civil War* (New York: Farrar, Straus, and Giroux, 2006), p. 187; Prince, *Stories*, p. 4. See also Louis Gottschalk, ed., *Generalization in the Writing of History* (Chicago: U of Chicago P, 1963). David M. Potter's "Implicit Data and Implicit Assumptions in Historical Study," in Gottschalk, *Generalization*, pp. 178–94, has some poignant comments on Reconstruction.

28. Most literary critics share Ian F. Haney López's view that the one-drop rule turned the law into "a prime instrument in the construction and reinforcement of racial subordination." "The Social Construction of Race: Some Observations on Illusion, Fabrication, and Choice," *Harvard Civil Rights-Civil Liberties Law Review* 1 (1994): 3. For example, Susan Gillman insists that "blood appears as a legal concept in the United

States through the one-drop law of racial identity." *Blood Talk: American Race Melodrama and the Culture of the Occult* (Chicago: U of Chicago P, 2003), p. 46. Paul R. Petrie, introducing a book set in 1883 and published in 1890, speaks of a "series of state laws and judicial rulings imposing the infamous 'one-drop rule'" (*ID*, 17). Julie Cary Nerad criticizes scholars for buying into the one-drop rule in their treatment of passing novels but assumes it was the legal norm in the nineteenth century. "Slippery Language and False Dilemmas: The Passing Novels of Child, Howells, and Harper," *American Literature* 75 (2003): 813–41. Yet, as Daniel J. Sharfstein argues, the one-drop rule "functioned differently from what its unambiguous terms suggest," and today's assumptions prove that "we inhabit a legal regime that is the accretion of centuries of myth and amnesia." "Crossing the Color Line: Racial Migration and the One-Drop Rule, 1600–1860," *Minnesota Law Review* 91 (2007): 601, 603. Many people believed in the one-drop rule or referred to the American regime of race, but only Tennessee enacted a one-drop rule prior to *Plessy*. Even its relic of an 1865–66 black code was short lived and was quickly superseded by more flexible definitions. See Daniel J. Sharfstein, *The Invisible Line: Three American Families and the Secret Journey from Black to White* (New York: Penguin, 2011), pp. 269, 376nn51–52. To be sure, in the early twentieth century with the legalized era of Jim Crow, six southern states and Oklahoma adopted it, but that hardly made it the legal norm. See Ariela J. Gross, *What Blood Won't Tell: A History of Race on Trial in America* (Cambridge: Harvard UP, 2008), pp. 269–71, 288–92. Jeffory Clymer cites Gross. Nonetheless, he goes on to note the "rise to prominence of the 'one-drop rule' in the post-reconstruction era." *Family Money: Property, Race, and Literature in the Nineteenth Century* (New York: Oxford UP, 2012), pp. 168–69n13, 190n33. Clymer relies on F. James Davis, who is frequently misleading. For instance, Davis incorrectly claims that the *Plessy* majority "assumed that a Negro or black is any person with any black ancestry." In fact, because the Jim Crow law in question referred to "coloreds" and "whites," the majority refers to neither Negroes nor blacks. Indeed, those bringing the suit considered themselves people of color but not Negroes. Confronted with Plessy's argument that the definition of who was colored was arbitrary because it varied from state to state, the majority did not uphold the "one-drop rule." It simply ruled that, in our federal system, states got to decide who was colored or not. *Who Is Black?: One Nation's Definition* (University Park: Pennsylvania State UP, 1991), p. 8.

The Fourteenth and Fifteenth Amendments seem to cause special problems for literary critics. Lauren Berlant writes that the Fourteenth Amendment "intended to confer the franchise on all African-American (male) persons." *The Anatomy of National Fantasy: Hawthorne, Utopia, and Everyday Life* (Chicago: U of Chicago P, 1991), p. 14. Gregory Jay writes that "Melville wrote against the backdrop of the debate over the passage of the Civil Rights Act of 1866 and the Fourteenth Amendment, which gave black men the vote." "Douglass, Melville, and the Lynching of Billy Budd" in *Frederick Douglass and Herman Melville*, ed. Robert S. Levine and Samuel Otter (Chapel Hill: U of North Carolina P, 2008), p. 383. Walter Benn Michaels writes, "The Fourteenth Amendment had made it unconstitutional to keep black men from voting because they were black." *The Trouble With Diversity* (New York: Henry Holt, 2006), p. 64. Editors Victoria Brehm and Sharon L. Dean add the endnote about carpetbaggers in *Constance Fenimore Woolson: Selected Stories and Travel Narratives* (Knoxville: U of Tennessee P, 2004), p. 147n10.

29. Trachtenberg, *Incorporation of America*; Kenneth W. Warren, *Black and White Strangers: Race in American Literary Realism* (Chicago: U of Chicago P, 1993).

30. Robert S. Levine, *The Lives of Frederick Douglass* (Cambridge: Harvard UP, 2016); Christopher Hager and Cody Marrs insist on the importance of Douglass's postbellum writings in "Against 1865: Reperiodizing the Nineteenth Century," *J19* 1 (2013): 259–84. Carolyn Karcher is in the vanguard of the Tourgée revival in literary studies. A symptom of how far it has come is that Michael T. Gilmore includes a chapter on him in the midst of ones on canonical figures like Hawthorne, Whitman, Melville, Stowe, Douglass, Twain, and James in *The War on Words: Slavery, Race, and Free Speech in American Literature* (Chicago: U of Chicago P, 2010). Jeannine Marie DeLombard, "The Novel and the Reconstruction Amendments," in *Oxford History of the Novel in English*, ed. Priscilla Wald and Michael A. Elliott (Oxford: Oxford UP, 2014), 5:69–85. Sharon Kennedy-Nolle treats authors that I do not and some—Tourgée, Cable, and Woolson—that I do. Even when we treat the same authors, we almost always focus on different works, which is a sign of how much still needs to be done on the literature of Reconstruction. Kennedy-Nolle adopts the innovative strategy of organizing her book by military districts with one author for each district. As productive as that organization is, it also places a heavy burden on one author to represent a district. For instance, North Carolina and South Carolina were in the same district, but Reconstruction unfolded differently within those states. The same is true of Louisiana and Texas; Alabama, Florida, and Georgia; and Mississippi and Arkansas. Virginia was in a district of its own, but Kennedy-Nolle uses a group of writers from West Virginia to represent it. *Writing Reconstruction: Race, Gender, and Citizenship in the Postwar South* (Chapel Hill: U of North Carolina P, 2015). See also Edlie Wong's forthcoming *Radical Reconstruction: Chinese Exclusion, Black Inclusion, and the Fictions of Citizenship* (New York: NYU P, 2016).

31. Gregory P. Downs, "The Mexicanization of American Politics: The United States' Transnational Path from Civil War to Stabilization," *American Historical Review* 117 (2012): 409; William Shakespeare, *Henry IV, pt II*, Act 4, scene 3, 344–45. Previous scholars were not unaware of the need to see Reconstruction from outside US borders. Five major addresses from a 1965 conference were collected in Harold M. Hyman, *New Frontiers of the American Reconstruction* (Urbana: U of Illinois P, 1966). Three of the talks were by major figures: Hyman, John Hope Franklin, and C. Vann Woodward. The other two were Harry Bernstein, "South America Looks at North American Reconstruction," and W. L. Morton, "Canada and Reconstruction, 1863–79."

32. Jennifer Rae Greeson, *Our South: Geographic Fantasy and the Rise of National Literature* (Cambridge: Harvard UP, 2010), pp. 273–74.

33. Hobson in *Tell* (p. 147n20) refers to evidence that Page had written and revised *Red Rock* at least once before 1885 and that he returned to the manuscript in 1894 when he moved to Washington, DC. Greeson, *Our South*, pp. 279, 282.

34. W. E. Burghardt Du Bois, "The Freedmen's Bureau," *Atlantic Monthly* 87 (1901): 354. The articles did not make up the entire 1901 volume; usually one appeared per issue stretching over parts of two volumes.

35. Thomas Nelson Page, "The Southern People During Reconstruction," *Atlantic Monthly* 88 (1901): 304; "Reconstruction and Disfranchisement," *Atlantic Monthly* 88 (1901): 437.

36. Peter Novick, *That Noble Dream: The "Objectivity Question" and the American Historical Profession* (New York; Cambridge, 1988), p. 77. John David Smith and J. Vincent Lowery, eds., *The Dunning School: Historians, Race, and the Meaning of Reconstruction* (Lexington: U of Kentucky P, 2013); David Donald, "Introduction to the Torchbook

Edition," in William Archibald Dunning, *Essays on the Civil War and Reconstruction* (New York: Harper, 1965), pp. vii–xvi. William Archibald Dunning, *Reconstruction, Political and Economic: 1864–1877* (New York: Harper, 1907), p. xv, "A Critical Period in Foreign Relations," pp. 151–73, with the map between pp. 158–59. Dunning's student Walter Lynwood Fleming published an important set of primary documents for scholarly and pedagogical use. Although the native of Alabama had a southern bias, his selections included more from the North than the South and gave voice to twelve African Americans. *Documentary History of Reconstruction* (Cleveland: Arthur H. Clark, 1906). Convinced of the central role played by freedmen in Reconstruction, he wrote *The Freedmen's Savings Bank* (1927), reprinted in 1970 by the Negro Universities Press. Fleming was close to the Nashville Agrarians, some of whom he taught at Vanderbilt. *I'll Take My Stand* is dedicated to him. Not all of Dunning's students shared his international perspective, but James Wilford Garner did. Having published an account of Reconstruction in Mississippi that Du Bois singles out for its fairness, Garner had a distinguished career. He was named the Hyde lecturer in French universities in 1921 and held a similar visiting position at the University of Calcutta. He wrote a comparative study of the German war code and used his understanding of the Civil War to evaluate Woodrow Wilson's crackdown on civil liberties during World War I, just as Dunning did in a widely read comparison of Wilson and Lincoln. Garner was important enough to be cited by the famous German theorist Carl Schmitt.

37. William Archibald Dunning, *Essays on the Civil War and Reconstruction* (New York: Macmillan, 1898), pp. vii, viii; Henry James, "Democracy and Theodore Roosevelt," in *The American Essays of Henry James*, ed. Leon Edel (Princeton: Princeton UP, 1989), pp. 214–15.

38. Greeson, *Our South*, pp. 273, 273.

39. March 4, 1877, was a Sunday, so the inauguration took place on Monday.

40. John W. Burgess, *Reconstruction and the Constitution* (New York: Scribner's, 1902), p. 103. Gregory P. Downs, "The Dangerous Myth of Appomattox," *New York Times*, April 12, 2015, Opinion 12.

41. Brook Thomas, *Plessy v. Ferguson: A Brief History With Documents* (Boston: Bedford, 1997), p. 10; Arlin Turner, *George W. Cable: A Biography* (Durham: Duke UP, 1956), p. 295; Cable, "The Freedman's Case in Equity," 412; "Reconstruction and Disfranchisement," 434.

42. Woodrow Wilson, *Division and Reunion: 1829–1889* (1892; reprint, New York: Collier, 1961), pp. 213–26. In his history of Texas, the famous western historian Hubert Bancroft, writing in the 1880s, dates his chapter "The Reconstruction Period" as "1865–1871" in *History of the Northern Mexican States and Texas* (New York: Bancroft, 188?) 2:478.

43. William A. Dunning, "The Undoing of Reconstruction," *Atlantic Monthly* 88 (1901): 437, 441, 448. For a 1904 edition this essay replaced the last one in Dunning's 1898 collection, *Essays*. Thomas Dixon, "The Story of the Ku Klux Klan," *Metropolitan Magazine* 22 (1905): 657.

44. Peter Joseph Hamilton, *The Reconstruction Period* (Philadelphia: Barrie, 1905), p. 557.

45. Clarence C. Clendenen, "President Hayes' 'Withdrawal' of the Troops: An Enduring Myth," *South Carolina Historical Magazine* 70 (1969): 240–50; Vincent P. DeSantis, "Rutherford B. Hayes and the Removal of Troops and the End of Reconstruc-

tion," in *Region, Race, and Reconstruction,* ed. J. Morgan Kousser and James M. McPherson (New York: Oxford UP, 1982), pp. 417–50.

46. Clendenen, "President Hayes' 'Withdrawal' of the Troops," 250; Wilson, *Division and Reunion,* p. 236; Hamilton, *The Reconstruction Period,* pp. xxi, 555.

47. In a footnote, Cady claims to date "the action of the novel in the middle 1870's—after the Panic of 1873, and beginning about the time of the end of *The Rise of Silas Lapham*"; see William Dean Howells, *The Shadow of a Dream and An Imperative Duty,* ed. Edwin H. Cady (New Haven: Twayne, 1962), p. 143. Henry B. Wonham and Jeffory A. Clymer agree in Wonham's "Howells, Du Bois, and the Effects of 'Common Sense': Race, Realism, and Nervousness in *An Imperative Duty* and *Souls of Black Folk,*" in *Criticism and the Color Line,* ed. Henry B. Wonham (New Brunswick: Rutgers UP, 1996), p. 129, and Clymer's "Race and the Protocol of American Citizenship in William Dean Howells's *An Imperative Duty,*" *American Literary Realism* 30 (1998): 32.

48. William Graham Sumner, *What the Social Classes Owe to Each Other* (New York: Harper and Brothers, 1883).

49. Thomas J. Brown, Introduction to *Reconstructions,* p. 7; Heather Cox Richardson, "North and West of Reconstruction: Studies in Political Economy," in *Reconstructions,* p. 90; Gregory P. Downs, *Declarations of Dependence: The Long Reconstruction of Popular Politics in the South, 1861–1908* (Chapel Hill: U of North Carolina P, 2011), p. 131. Mark Wahlgren Summers notes, "One could end Reconstruction anywhere," and then lists a variety of options. He also suggests the possibility "that Reconstruction had no end, as long as the issues that it had raised remained incompletely addressed." He finally chooses "Lincoln's Birthday, 1878," when members of both parties celebrated the hanging in the Capitol Building of a painting of Lincoln first reading the Emancipation Proclamation to his cabinet. *The Ordeal of Reunion: A New History of Reconstruction* (Chapel Hill: U of North Carolina P, 2014), p. 398.

50. Heather Cox Richardson, *West from Appomattox: The Reconstruction of America after the Civil War* (New Haven: Yale UP, 2007); Elliott West, "Reconstructing Race," *Western Historical Quarterly* 34 (2003): 7–26, and *The Last Indian War: The Nez Perce Story* (New York: Oxford UP, 2009); Smith, *Freedom's Frontier*; Adam Arenson and Andrew R. Graybill, eds., *Civil War Wests: Testing the Limits of the United States* (Berkeley: U of California P, 2015); Foner, *Reconstruction,* pp. xxvi, 465. See also Brook Thomas, "Turner's Frontier Thesis as a Narrative of Reconstruction," in *Centuries' Ends, Narrative Means,* ed. Robert D. Newman (Stanford: Stanford UP, 1996), pp. 117–37.

51. Frederick Jackson Turner, "The Significance of the Frontier in American History," in Turner, *The Frontier in American History* (New York: Holt, 1920), pp. 15, 27, 27, 24, 2, 25; Henry Grady, "The New South," in *The Life of Henry Grady, Including His Writing and Speeches,* ed. Joel Chandler Harris (1890; reprint, New York: Haskell House, 1972), p. 85; Dudley H. Miles, "The Civil War as Unifier," *Sewanee Review* 21 (1913): 189.

52. Hamilton, *The Reconstruction Period,* p. 526.

53. Albion W. Tourgée, *Undaunted Radical: The Selected Writings and Speeches of Albion W. Tourgée,* ed. Mark Elliott and John David Smith (Baton Rouge: Louisiana State UP, 2010), p. 73.

54. Prince, *Stories,* p. 2.

55. On responses to *A Fool's Errand,* see Elliott, *Color Blind Justice,* pp. 177–82. Kathleen Diffley, *Where the Heart Is Turning Ever* (Athens: U of Georgia P, 1992). Charles

Sumner praises Locke's works for the service they "performed in the war on slavery, and in advancing reconstruction." "Introduction," David Ross Locke, *The Struggles (Social, Financial and Political) of Petroleum V. Nasby* (Boston: L. N. Richardson, 1872), pp. 15, 13.

56. Charles W. Chesnutt, *To Be an Author: The Letters of Charles W. Chesnutt, 1889–1905*, ed. Joseph R. McElrath Jr. and Robert C. Leitz (Princeton: Princeton UP, 1997), p. 167.

57. William Dean Howells, *The Rise of Silas Lapham* (1885; reprint, Bloomington: Indiana UP, 1971), p. 197; William A. Dunning, *Reconstruction Political and Economic: 1865–1877*, pp. xv–xvi.

CHAPTER 1: Reconciliation and Reunion

1. Jay B. Hubbell, *The South in American Literature: 1607–1900* (Durham: Duke UP, 1954), pp. 702–3, 700; Arlin Turner, *George W. Cable: A Biography* (Durham: Duke UP, 1956), pp. 344, 99, 298; Aubrey Harrison Starke, *Sidney Lanier: A Biographical and Critical Study* (New York: Russell and Russell, 1964), p. 451; Sharon Kennedy-Nolle, *Writing Reconstruction: Race, Gender, and Citizenship in the Postwar South* (Chapel Hill: U of North Carolina P, 2015), p. 213; Arlin Turner, "Whittier Calls on George W. Cable," *New England Quarterly* 22 (1949): 92–96. For years, the most influential account of literary reconciliation was in the historian Paul Buck's Pulitzer Prize–winning *The Road to Reunion: 1865–1900* (New York: Vintage, 1937).

2. David W. Blight, *Race and Reunion: The Civil War in American Memory* (Cambridge: Harvard UP, 2001), p. 387.

3. Mark Wahlgren Summers, *The Ordeal of Reunion: A New History of Reconstruction* (Chapel Hill: U of North Carolina P, 2014), p. 3; K. Stephen Prince, *Stories of the South: Race and the Reconstruction of Southern Identity, 1865–1915* (Chapel Hill: U of North Carolina P, 2014), p. 9.

4. Caroline E. Janney, *Remembering the Civil War: Reunion and the Limits of Reconciliation* (Chapel Hill: U of North Carolina P, 2013); John W. Burgess, *The Middle Period: 1817–1858* (New York: Scribner's, 1897), pp. x–xii, and *Political Science and Comparative Constitutional Law* (New York: Baker and Taylor, 1890), 1:44.

5. Janney, *Remembering the Civil War*, p. 5.

6. David W. Blight, *Frederick Douglass' Civil War* (Baton Rouge: Louisiana State UP, 1989), p. 218; William S. McFeely, *Frederick Douglass* (New York: Norton, 1991), p. 291.

7. McFeely, *Frederick Douglass*, pp. 293, 288–89, 289; Vincent P, DeSantis, "Rutherford B. Hayes and the Removal of Troops and the End of Reconstruction," in *Region, Race, and Reconstruction*, ed. J. Morgan Kousser and James M. McPherson (New York: Oxford UP, 1982), pp. 435, 436; Lou Falkner Williams, *The Great South Carolina Ku Klux Klan Trials, 1871–1872* (Athens: U of Georgia P, 1996), p. 129.

8. *Frederick Douglass Papers*, ed. John W. Blassingame (New Haven: Yale UP, 1979), Series 1, 4:484–85, 488–89; William Gillette, *Retreat from Reconstruction, 1869–79* (Baton Rouge: Louisiana State UP, 1979), p. 436n5.

9. McFeely, *Frederick Douglass*, p. 295.

10. Robert S. Levine, introduction to *Martin R. Delany: A Documentary Reader*, ed. Robert S. Levine (Chapel Hill: U of North Carolina P, 2003), pp. 1–22.

11. McFeely, *Frederick Douglass*, p. 293; *Easton Gazette*, November 30, 1878; Frederick Douglass, *Life and Times of Frederick Douglass*, ed. Rayford W. Logan (1892; reprint, New York: Collier, 1962), p. 539.

12. Charles W. Chesnutt, *Frederick Douglass* (1899; reprint, Atlanta: Clark Atlanta UP, 2001), p. 122.

13. Nicholas Lemann, *Redemption: The Last Battle of the Civil War* (New York: Farrar, Straus, and Giroux, 2006), p. 181.

14. John F. Kennedy, *Profiles in Courage* (New York: Harper, 1957), p. 154; Lemann, *Redemption*, pp. 104, 180. Lamar's "Eulogy of Sumner" is reprinted in Dudley H. Miles, ed., *Poetry and Eloquence of Blue and Gray* (New York: Review of Reviews Co., 1911), pp. 292–304. Lamar's explanation to a southern friend of why he made the eulogy is reprinted in Harold M. Hyman, ed., *The Radical Republicans and Reconstruction, 1861–1870* (Indianapolis: Bobbs-Merrill, 1967), pp. 515–19. On opposition to Lamar's appointment to the Supreme Court for his views on African Americans, see Stanley P. Hirshson, *Farewell to the Bloody Shirt: Northern Republicans and the Southern Negro, 1877–1893* (Bloomington: Indiana UP, 1962), pp. 154–56.

15. Kennedy, *Profiles in Courage*, pp. 161, 152–53.

16. Ralph Kishner, *The Class of 1861: Custer, Ames, and Their Classmates after West Point*, foreword by George A. Plimpton (Carbondale: U Southern Illinois P, 2008); James W. Garner, *Reconstruction in Mississippi* (New York: Columbia UP, 1901); Howard K. Beale, "On Re-Writing Reconstruction History," *American Historical Review* 45 (1940): 816.

17. Dudley H. Miles, "The Civil War as Unifier," *Sewanee Review* 21 (1913): 195; Miles, *Poetry and Eloquence*, pp. 322, 326, 328.

18. Edward Everett Hale, "The Man Without a Country," *Outlook* 59 (1898): 117–47; John W. Burgess, *Reconstruction and the Constitution* (New York: Scribner's, 1902), pp. 297–98.

19. David Donald, *Charles Sumner and the Rights of Man* (New York: Knopf, 1970), pp. 563, 564–65; Kennedy, *Profiles in Courage*, p. 152; Summers, *The Ordeal of Reunion*, p. 323; Douglass, *Life and Writings*, p. 302.

20. Severn Teackle Wallis, *Discourse on the Life and Character of George Peabody* (Baltimore: John Murphy, 1870), p. 58; William B. Hesseltine, "Economic Factors in the Abandonment of Reconstruction," *Mississippi Valley Historical Review* 22 (1935): 200.

21. "Reconstruction," illustrated by Horatio Batemen, engraved by J. T. Giles (New York, printed by Francis Ratellier, 1867); H. Bateman, *Explanation of Bateman's National Picture of Reconstruction, Together with the Declaration of Independence and the Constitution of the United States* (New York: Blackwell, 1867); Edward J. Blum, *Reforging the White Republic: Race, Religion, and American Nationalism, 1865–1898* (Baton Rouge: Louisiana State UP, 2005), pp. 1–3; Mark Elliott, *Color-Blind Justice: Albion Tourgée and the Quest for Racial Justice from the Civil War to* Plessy v. Ferguson (New York: Oxford UP, 2006), pp. 26.

22. Miles, *Poetry and Eloquence*, pp. 304–22; Edward E. Hale, *The Man without a Country*, ed. Russell A. Sharp (Boston: Houghton Mifflin, 1923), p. xxi; Henry Grady, "The New South," in *The Life of Henry Grady, Including His Writing and Speeches*, ed. Joel Chandler Harris (1890; reprint, New York: Haskell House, 1972), p. 92.

23. The Library of Congress mistakenly identifies Breckenridge as General P. T. G. Beauregard. See Bernard F. Reilly Jr., *American Political Prints, 1766–1876* (Boston: G. K. Hall, 1991), p. 573. Kennedy, *Profiles in Courage*, p. 161; Duncan Andrew Campbell, *English Public Opinion and the American Civil War* (Woodbridge, Suffolk: Boydell, 2003), p. 106; William J. Cooper Jr., *Jefferson Davis, American* (New York: Vintage, 2001), p. 407.

24. Benjamin F. Butler, *Butler's Book: Autobiographical Personal Reminiscences of Major-General Benj. F. Butler* (Boston: A.M. Thayer, 1892), pp. 139, 145; Hesseltine, "Economic Factors," 195; Stephen Budiansky, *The Bloody Shirt: Terror after the Civil War* (New York: Penguin, 2008), p. 2. Others attributed the phrase "waving the bloody shirt" as referring to Charles Sumner's bloody shirt after his beating in the Senate by Preston Brooks in 1856. Mark Wahlgren Summers cites a sixteenth-century Scottish legend about a parade of widows alleged to have borne the shirts of their murdered husbands to Stirling Castle. Summers, *The Ordeal of Reunion*, pp. 358, 450n29. Scott Romine cites various uses prior to Butler's alleged speech. One in 1868 refers to the bloody shirts of Kansas in 1856, which would reinforce the allusion to Sumner's beating. Romine also cites a reference to France in 1848 by Lewis Cass. See Scott Romine, "Fables of the Bloody Shirt: Narrating Reconstruction Violence," unpublished essay, discussed at University of California, Irvine, May 9, 2014, p. 6.

25. Miles, *Poetry and Eloquence*, 297; Peter Joseph Hamilton, *The Reconstruction Period* (Philadelphia: Barrie, 1905), p. 557.

26. Butler, *Butler's Book*, p. 141; J. Matthew Gallman, "Is the War Ended?: Anna Dickinson and the Election of 1872," in *The Memory of the Civil War in American Culture*, ed. Alice Fahs and Joan Waugh (Chapel Hill: U of North Carolina P, 2004), p. 165.

27. Blight, *Race and Reunion*, p. 57; Hesseltine, "Economic Factors," p. 200.

28. William Dean Howells, "A Sennight at the Centennial," *Atlantic Monthly* 38 (1876): 93.

29. Howells, "A Sennight," 93. La Farge would go on to paint a multicultural mural, "Ancient Lawgivers," including Moses, Lycurgus, Confucius, Justinian, Numa Pompilius, and Mohammed, and his son, the Jesuit priest John LaFarge, S.J., wrote the progressive *Interracial Justice: A Catholic Doctrine of Race Relations* (New York: America P, 1937). Accounts of the 1876 Centennial include Gillette, *Retreat*, pp. 300–334; Robert W. Rydell, *All the World's a Fair* (Chicago: U of Chicago P, 1984); Louise L. Stevenson, *The Victorian Homefront: American Thought and Culture, 1860–1880* (Ithaca: Cornell UP, 1991), pp. 182–99; Gary Nash, *First City: Philadelphia and the Forging of Historical Memory* (Philadelphia: U of Pennsylvania P, 2006); and Michael A. Bellesiles, *1877: America's Year of Living Violently* (New York: New Press, 2010), pp. 9–17.

30. James Russell Lowell, "The World's Fair, 1876," *Nation* 21, Aug 5. 1875, 9; Horace Elisha Scudder, *James Russell Lowell* (Boston: Houghton Mifflin, 1901), pp. 194, 211.

31. Scudder, *James Russell Lowell*, pp. 190, 204, 204. Lowell's efforts at reconciliation did not impress Thomas Dixon. In *The Leopard's Spots*, Dixon repays Lowell's gestures to the South by naming a Bostonian professing to support African Americans, Everett Lowell. When the mulatto George Harris from *Uncle Tom's Cabin* proposes marriage to his daughter, the fictional Lowell unleashes a racist tirade of protest.

32. Starke, *Sidney Lanier*, pp. 244, 242; Raymond B. Nixon, *Henry Grady: Spokesman for the New South* (New York: Knopf, 1943), p. 156; Miles, *Poetry and Eloquence*, p. 191.

33. John Greenleaf Whittier, *The Works of John Greenleaf Whittier* (Boston: Houghton, Mifflin, 1892), 4:207; Starke, *Sidney Lanier*, p. 9.

34. Sidney Lanier, *The Centennial Meditation on Columbia: A Cantata for the Inaugural Ceremonies at Philadelphia, May 10, 1876* (New York: G. Schirmer, 1876), p, 4; Miles, *Poetry and Eloquence*, p. 191; Woodrow Wilson, *Division and Reunion, 1829–1889* (1892; reprint, New York: Collier, 1961), p. 236; Hamilton, *The Reconstruction Period*, p. 537.

35. Gillette, *Retreat*, pp. 307–9; Bellesilles, *1877*, p. 12.

36. Sidney Lanier, *Centennial Edition: Letters, 1874–1877*, ed. Charles R. Anderson and Aubrey H. Starke (Baltimore: Johns Hopkins UP, 1945), 9:297; Lanier, *Meditation*, p. 4.

37. Starke, *Sidney Lanier*, p. 260; Lanier, *Letters*, p. 300.

38. Whittier, *Works*, 3:265–66.

39. Lanier, "Civil Rights," *Centennial Edition: Poems*, 1:40–42.

40. Whittier, *Works*, 3:266.

41. Albion W. Tourgée, "Letter to Martin B. Anderson," *Undaunted Radical: The Selected Writings and Speeches of Albion W. Tourgée*, ed. Mark Elliott and John David Smith (Baton Rouge: Louisiana State UP, 2010), p. 53.

42. Blight, *Race and Reunion*, p. 97; Nina Silber, *The Romance of Reunion: Northerners and the South, 1865–1900* (Chapel Hill: U of North Carolina P, 1993), pp. 6–7, 115–16; Charles Robert Anderson, "James' Portrait of a Southerner," *American Literature* 27 (1955): 309–31. As influential as Silber's work has been, it falls prey to the desire to create a neat narrative of progression. By the end of the century, she argues, the "formula" of a southern woman submitting to a northern man gives way to Dixon's of "southern manhood triumphing over the black menace and over northern women's sentimental attachment to black equality" (186). She uses Page to mark this transition, with him for some inexplicable reason exchanging one formula for another within a few years in *Red Rock* and presaging Dixon's formula. But the reality is more complicated. As I point out, Tourgée, James, and Adams provide counterexamples before Dixon and Page. There are many more. And even Silber's characterization of Dixon and Page is too simple. For instance, in *Red Rock* and *The Clansman*, marriages of northern men with southern women balance marriages of southern men with northern women. The two other novels in Dixon's trilogy have leading southern men marry southern women.

43. Completely missing DeForest's playful irony, Wilson mistakenly believes that Underhill will "receive a large gift from his uncle" only if he "will marry the girl and reunite the two families." That Underhill's financial future is secure no matter what he does makes his willingness to marry all the more absurd. Edmund Wilson, *Patriotic Gore: Studies in the Literature of the American Civil War* (New York: Oxford UP, 1962), p. 702.

44. John William DeForest, "Charleston under Arms," *Atlantic Monthly* 7 (1861): 488–505.

45. Anne Rowe has chapters on Woolson, DeForest, and Tourgée in *The Enchanted Country: Northern Writers in the South, 1865–1910* (Baton Rouge: Louisiana State UP, 1978). By far the best treatments of Woolson and Reconstruction are Kathleen Diffley, ed., *Witness to Reconstruction: Constance Fenimore Woolson and the Postbellum South, 1873–1894* (Jackson: U of Mississippi P, 2011), and Sharon D. Kennedy-Nolle, "Constance Fenimore Woolson and the Tourist Outback of Florida," *Writing Reconstruction*, pp. 25–75.

46. Silber has a chapter called "Sick Yankees in Paradise," in *Romance*, pp. 66–92.

47. Thomas Bailey Aldrich, "Spring in New England," *The Poems of Thomas Bailey Aldrich* (Boston: Houghton, Mifflin, 1885), pp. 210–11.

48. Elizabethada A. Wright, "Keeping Memory: The Cemetery and Rhetorical Memory in Constance Fenimore Woolson's 'Rodman the Keeper,'" *Studies in the Literary Imagination* 39 (2006): 29–54; Francis Miles Finch, "The Blue and the Gray," *Atlantic Monthly* 20 (1867): 369–70.

49. Grady, "The New South," p. 93. On the allusion to Andersonville, see Karen Weekes, "Northern Bias in Constance Fenimore Woolson's *Rodman the Keeper: Southern Sketches*," *Southern Literary Journal* 32 (2000): 102–15, and Martin T. Buinicki, "Imagining Sites of Memory in the Post–Civil War South: The National Cemetery in Woolson's 'Rodman the Keeper,'" in Diffley, *Witness to Reconstruction*, pp. 162–76. That Weekes faults Woolson for her northern bias while others see her as capitulating to the southern point of view indicates that the debate about the politics of reconciliation is far from over.

50. Summers, *The Ordeal of Reunion*, p. 375.

51. Nathaniel Hawthorne, "Chiefly about War Matters," *Atlantic Monthly* 10 (1862): 48.

52. Abraham Lincoln, "First Inaugural," *The Collected Works of Abraham Lincoln*, ed. Roy P. Basler, Marion Dolores Pratt, and Lloyd A. Dunlap (New Brunswick: Rutgers UP, 1953), 4:271.

53. Catherine W. Zipf, "Marking Union Victory in the South: The Construction of the National Cemetery System," in *Monuments to the Lost Cause: Women, Art, and the Landscape of Southern Memory*, ed. Cynthia Mills and Pamela H. Simpson (Knoxville: U of Tennessee P, 2003), pp. 27–45.

54. Henry James, "Miss Woolson," in *The American Essays*, ed. Leon Edel (Princeton: Princeton UP, 1989), pp. 164–65.

55. Albion W. Tourgée, "The South as a Field for Fiction," in *Undaunted Radical*, pp. 204, 205, 207–8; James, "Miss Woolson," p. 165.

56. Tourgée, "From *The Veteran and His Pipe*," in *Undaunted Radical*, pp. 196–97.

57. Tourgée, "From *The Veteran and His Pipe*," p. 192. Gregory P. Downs and Kate Masur, "Introduction: Echoes of War: Rethinking Post–Civil War Governance and Politics," in *The World the Civil War Made* (Chapel Hill: U of North Carolina P, 2015), p. 6.

CHAPTER 2: Federalism

1. In 1897, Edward Everett Hale wrote, "The United States *is* a nation, now. And there is not left any one living in the Northern, Middle, Western, or Pacific States, who ever think that the United States *are* a confederacy." *The Man Without a Country* (Boston: Stillman Smith, 1897), p. iii. Hale's omission of southern states even in 1897 is telling.

2. John W. Burgess, *Reconstruction and the Constitution* (New York: Scribner's, 1902), pp. 4–5.

3. *Texas v. White*, 74 U.S. 700 at 725. On the *Slaughter-House Cases*, see Michael A. Ross, "Justice Miller's Reconstruction: The *Slaughter-House Cases*, Health Codes, and Civil Rights in New Orleans, 1861–1873," *Journal of Southern History* 64 (1998): 649–76; Richard L. Aynes, "Constricting the Law of Freedom: Justice Miller, the Fourteenth Amendment, and the *Slaughter-House Cases*," *Chicago-Kent Law Review* 70 (1994): 627–88; and Michael Kent Curtis, "Historical Linguistics, Inkblots, and Life After Death: The Privileges or Immunities of Citizens of the United States," *North Carolina Law Review* 78 (2000): 1089–1151. On *Texas v. White*, see Harold M. Hyman, *The Reconstruction Justice of Salmon P. Chase: "In Re Turner" and "Texas v. White,"* (Lawrence: UP of Kansas, 1997). The Rehnquist court's revival of antebellum federalism caused a number of legal scholars to return to the Reconstruction era. Norman W. Spaulding tries to orient that scholarship by relying on Michel Foucault's notion of countermemory. The Rehnquist court, he claims, employs "monumental history" to legitimate a "survival the-

sis"; that is, the founders' theory of federalism, which forgets the important changes brought about by the Civil War Amendments. As powerful as Spaulding's argument is, its opposition between "monumentalist memory" and "countermemory" risks perpetuating black and white narratives about the past. Spaulding claims to use countermemory to restore views that have been forgotten, but his method risks obscuring the numerous and complicated narratives in the space between his binary. My method aims at bringing them back into discussion. "Constitution as Countermonument: Federalism, Reconstruction, and the Problem of Collective Memory," *Columbia Law Review* 103 (2003): 1992–2051.

4. William Archibald Dunning, *Essays on the Civil War and Reconstruction* (New York: Macmillan, 1898), p. 109.

5. Dunning, *Essays*, p. 251.

6. John W. Burgess, *Reconstruction*, pp. 60, 245, 246. Du Bois claims that Burgess was a Confederate (*BR*, 718.) In fact, from Tennessee, he bravely fought for the Union.

7. John W. Burgess, "The American Commonwealth: Changes in Its Relation to the Nation," *Political Science Quarterly* 9 (1886): 11; Peter Joseph Hamilton, *The Reconstruction Period* (Philadelphia: Barrie, 1905), p. 556; Frederick Douglass, *The Life and Writings of Frederick Douglass*, ed. Philip S. Foner (New York: International Publishers, 1955), 4:306; John W. Burgess, *Political Science and Constitutional Law* (New York: Baker and Taylor, 1890), 1:224; John W. Burgess, *The Civil War and the Constitution, 1859–1865* (New York: Scribner's, 1901), 1:135.

8. Burgess, *Reconstruction*, pp. 255–56; Edward S. Corwin, *The Commerce Power versus States Rights* (Princeton: Princeton UP, 1936). On Field, see Michael Les Benedict, "Preserving Federalism: Reconstruction and the Waite Court," *Supreme Court Review* 1978 (1978): 39–79. Edward A. Pollard, *The Lost Cause Regained* (New York: G. W. Carleton, 1868), pp. 35, 39. Bostonian James Russell Lowell wrote, "Where currency's debased, all coins will pass." Horace Elisha Scudder, *James Russell Lowell* (Boston: Houghton Mifflin, 1901), p. 206.

9. Hugh Kenner, *The Counterfeiters: An Historical Comedy* (Bloomington: U of Indiana P, 1968). For the monetary history, see Walter T. K. Nugent, *Money and American Society, 1865–1880* (New York: Free Press, 1968). See also Michael Germana, *Standards of Value: Money, Race, and Literature in America* (Iowa City: U of Iowa P, 2010).

10. Walter K. Nugent, *The Money Question* (New York: Norton, 1967), p. 32.

11. Nugent, *The Money Question*, p. 92.

12. Burgess, *Reconstruction*, pp. 279.

13. Albion W. Tourgée, "The Reversal of Malthus," *American Journal of Sociology* 2 (1896): 13–24, and "The Best Currency," *North American Review* 48 (1896): 416–26.

14. See Michael O'Malley, "Specie and Species: Race and the Money Question in Nineteenth-Century America," *American Historical Review* 99 (1994): 369–95.

15. Albion W. Tourgée, "Shall White Minorities Rule?" in *Undaunted Radical: The Selected Writings of Albion W. Tourgée*, ed. Mark Elliott and John David Smith (Baton Rouge: Louisiana State UP, 2010), p. 113; Burgess, *Political Science and Constitutional Law*, 1:44–45; Burgess, *Reconstruction*, pp. 244–45.

16. Burgess, *Reconstruction*, p. 257. The relationship between the Thirteenth Amendment and the Civil Rights Act of 1866 remains controversial. Some argue that the Thirteenth Amendment provides constitutional support for the 1866 act. Others argue that the Fourteenth Amendment was needed to make the 1866 act constitutional. If the Thirteenth

Amendment is the basis of the 1866 act, then the national government has much more power, because national intervention is not restrained by evidence of "state action."

17. Raymond B. Nixon, *Henry W. Grady: Spokesman of the New South* (New York: Alfred A. Knopf, 1943), p. 213; Henry W. Grady, "In Plain Black and White," *Century Magazine* 29 (1885): 910, 909.

18. R. Bruce Bickley Jr., *Joel Chandler Harris* (Boston: Twayne, 1978), pp. 58–59; *Joel Chandler Harris: Editor and Essayist*, ed. Julia Collier Harris (Chapel Hill: U of North Carolina P, 1931), p. 45; *The Life and Letters of Joel Chandler Harris*, ed. Julia Collier Harris (Boston: Houghton Mifflin, 1918), p. 530.

19. On the effect of Twain's Mugwumpery on his literature and vice versa, see Brook Thomas, *Civic Myths: A Law and Literature Approach to Citizenship* (Chapel Hill: U of North Carolina P, 2007), pp. 125–76, and Mark Twain, *Life on the Mississippi* (New York: Limited Editions Club, (1944), p. 274–75. In a chapter called "An Archangel," Twain describes the spellbinding oratory of the self-educated and "erratic genius" Henry Clay Dean, who looked like an "escaped lunatic" but after he spoke was considered an "escaped archangel" (331, 333). Twain does not tell us that Dean wrote *Crimes of the Civil War and the Curse of the Funding System* (Baltimore: J. Wesley Smith, 1869), a polemical indictment of Reconstruction policies, especially those linked to finance, for leaving the "people of the former Confederate States . . . overrun and robbed by predatory invasions, and endangered by the insurrection of domestic savages incited by foreign incendiaries" (2). Harris, "Stalwarts and Strutters," *Editor and Essayist*, p. 73; Thomas Nelson Page, *The Novels, Stories, Sketches, and Poems of Thomas Nelson Page*, the Plantation Edition (New York: Scribner's, 1912), 1:xi. Fred Hobson writes, "Despite his devotion to the Old South, Page was from the first a writer committed to national harmony and reunion." *Tell About the South* (Baton Rouge: Louisiana State UP, 1983), p. 137.

20. Nixon, *Henry W. Grady*, pp. 309–10; Pollard, *The Lost Cause Regained*, p. 211; Harris, *The Life and Letters*, pp. 164–65; Twain, *Life on the Mississippi*, p. 275. Twain reports how people in New Orleans were disappointed to find that Harris was white (274). E. F. Bargainnier reports that "*Red Rock* was the most significant novel published by a southerner in the 1890s" and was the fifth-best seller in 1898. "*Red Rock*: A Reappraisal," *Southern Quarterly* 22 (1984): 44. Theodore L. Gross calls *Red Rock* "the clearest and most elaborate fictional description of Reconstruction from the Southern point of view." *Thomas Nelson Page* (New York: Twayne, 1967), p. 86.

21. Thomas Nelson Page, "The Old South," in *The Old South: Essays Social and Political* (New York: Scribner's, 1892), pp. 25, 51; Nixon, *Henry W. Grady*, pp. 310, 311. Jeremy Wells emphasizes the class differences between Page, Grady, and Harris in *Romances of the White Man's Burden: Race, Empire, and the Plantation in American Literature, 1880–1936* (Nashville: Vanderbilt UP, 2011), pp. 78–79.

22. Hobson, *Tell About the South*, p. 147; William B. Hesseltine, "Economic Factors in the Abandonment of Reconstruction," *Mississippi Valley Historical Review* 22 (1935): 198.

23. Darwin T. Turner, "Joel Chandler Harris and His Old-Time Darkies," *Southern Literary Journal* 1 (1968): 40.

24. Burgess, *Reconstruction*, p. 248.

25. Hilary A. Herbert, "The Conditions of the Reconstruction Problem," *Atlantic Monthly* 87 (1901): 147.

26. Barton J. Hendrick, *The Earlier Life and Letters of Walter Hines Page* (New York: Doubleday and Page, 1922), p. 152.

27. Dudley H. Miles, "The Civil War as Unifier," *Sewanee Review* 21 (1913): 194.

28. K. Stephen Prince, *Stories of the South: Race and the Reconstruction of Southern Identity, 1865–1915* (Chapel Hill: U of North Carolina P, 2014), p. 151; Thomas Nelson Page, "The Old South," p. 50; Thomas Nelson Page, "The Want of a History of the Southern People," in *The Old South*, pp. 268.

29. Prince, *Stories of the South*, p. 151.

30. John G. Sproat, *"The Best Men": Liberal Reformers in the Gilded Age* (New York: Oxford UP, 1968).

31. Harris, *Editor and Essayist*, p. 48; Mark Elliott, *Color-Blind Justice: Albion Tourgée and the Quest for Racial Equality from the Civil War to* Plessy v. Ferguson (New York: Oxford UP, 2006), pp. 304–6; Harris, *Life and Letters*, p. 517; Harris, *Editor and Essayist*, p. 208–9.

32. Thomas Nelson Page, "The Southern People during Reconstruction," *Atlantic Monthly* 88 (1901): 291.

33. Thomas Dixon to Albion W. Tourgée, February 25, 1888, Chautauqua County Historical Society, Westfield, NY. Alluding to the Bible, Tourgée, in *A Fool's Errand*, writes that the Fool "saw that he had expected too much, that he had been simple enough to believe that the leopard *might* change his spots, while the Ethiopian retained his dusky skin" (339).

34. Otto H. Olsen, *Carpetbagger's Crusade: The Life of Albion Winegar Tourgée* (Baltimore: Johns Hopkins UP, 1965), p. 334. See Michael Kent Curtis, "Reflections on Albion Tourgée's 1896 View of the Supreme Court: A 'Consistent Enemy of Personal Liberty and Equal Right'?" *Elon Law Review* 5 (2013): 19–87.

35. Burgess, *Reconstruction*, p. 255; Brook Thomas, "Thomas Dixon's *A Man of the People*: How Lincoln Saved the Union by Cracking Down on Civil Liberties," *Law & Literature* 20 (2008): 21–46; Thomas Dixon, *A Man of the People* (New York: Appleton, 1920), pp. 135–36.

36. Albion W. Tourgée, "The Twentieth Century Peacemakers," *Contemporary Review* 75 (1899): 888.

37. Henry W. Bragdon, *Woodrow Wilson: The Academic Years* (Cambridge: Belknap Press of Harvard UP, 1967), pp. 110–11; Raymond A. Cook, *Thomas Dixon* (New York: Twayne, 1974), p. 41. Cook highlights Dixon's friendship with Wilson. Most of Wilson's biographers tend to downplay it.

38. Woodrow Wilson, *Division and Reunion, 1829–1889* (1892; reprint, New York: Collier, 1961), p. x; Bragdon, *Woodrow Wilson*, p. 240; Burgess, *The Middle Period: 1817–1858* (New York: Scribner's, 1897), p. x; Woodrow Wilson, "Political Sovereignty," in *An Old Master and Other Political Essays* (New York: Scribner's, 1893), p. 94; Woodrow Wilson, "The Reconstruction of the Southern States," *Atlantic Monthly* 87 (1901): 3. See Jennifer Greeson's helpful discussion of Wilson's essay in *Our South: Geographic Fantasy and the Rise of National Literature* (Cambridge: Harvard UP, 2010), p. 275.

39. Wilson, "Reconstruction of the Southern States," 11–12.

40. Burgess, *Political Science and Constitutional Law*, 1:53; Woodrow Wilson, "A System of Political Science and Constitutional Law," *Atlantic Monthly* (67): 695, 697.

41. Burgess, *Political Science and Constitutional Law*, 1:67; Wilson, "Reconstruction of the Southern States," 11, 12.

42. Wilson, "Reconstruction of the Southern States," 12, 14.

43. Burgess, *Political Science and Constitutional Law,* 1:50; Wilson, "Reconstruction of the Southern States," 3, 9; Sumner quoted in Herbert, "The Conditions of the Reconstruction Problem," 154; Wilson, "The Reconstruction of the Southern States," 14–15.

44. Rudyard Kipling, "The White Man's Burden," *McClure's Magazine* 12 (1899): 209–10. On Dixon's imperialism, see *Dixon's Sermons Delivered in the Grand Opera House, 1898–1899* (New York: F. L. Bussey, 1899); Maxwell Bloomfield, "*The Leopard's Spots*: A Study in Popular Racism," *American Quarterly* 16 (1964): 387–401; Raymond Allen Cook, *Fire from Flint* (Winston Salem: John F. Blair, 1968), pp. 91–95, and *Thomas Dixon,* pp. 45–46; Michael Paul Rogin, "'The Sword Became a Flashing Vision': D.W. Griffith's *The Birth of a Nation,*" in *The Birth of a Nation,* ed. Robert Lang (New Brunswick: Rutgers UP, 1994), pp. 254–55; Amy Kaplan, *The Anarchy of Empire in the Making of U.S. Culture* (Cambridge: Harvard UP, 2005), pp. 121–23; Jeffory A. Clymer, *America's Culture of Terrorism, Violence, Capitalism, and the Written Word* (Chapel Hill: U of North Carolina P, 2003), pp. 120–26; Peter Schmidt, "Walter Scott, Postcolonial Theory, and New South Literature," *Mississippi Quarterly* 56 (2003): 545–54. Dixon's publisher, Doubleday, Page, and Co., was also Kipling's publisher in the United States. Walter Hines Page was, like Dixon, an ardent imperialist. While the press was still Doubleday and McClure Co, it had anti-imperialist Charles Eliot Norton write a biographical sketch of Kipling to accompany an edition of his works, but the sketch was commissioned before the outbreak of war. Unlike most scholars at the time, Wilson distrusted German thought, including Hegelianism. Burgess, who was enamored of German thought, despite his sense of Teutonic superiority, opposed the US acquisition of the insular territories from Spain. He argued that practically the country was not ready to take on colonies until it set its own house in order by resolving the Indian, Mormon, and African American problems. He also argued that constitutionally there was no authority for the US government, "at the pleasure of Congress, to go with absolute power into certain places, unattended by the limitations of the Constitution on the behalf of civil liberty" ("The Relation of the Constitution of the United States to the Newly Acquired Territory," *Political Science Quarterly* 15 [1900]: 382). See also Burgess, "How May the United States Govern Its Extra-Continental Territories," *Political Science Quarterly* 14 (1899): 1–18, and "The Decision of the Supreme Court in the Insular Cases," *Political Science Quarterly* 16 (1901): 486–504.

45. Burgess, *Political Science and Constitutional Law,* 1:43; Douglass, *Life and Writings,* p. 222.

46. Untitled articles in *Law Notes* 7 (1903): 19, and *Life* 41 (April 30, 1903): 1070, quoting the *San Francisco Argonaut.* Steven Mailloux first brought Hoar's exchange to my attention. On abolitionist roots, see Paul Goodman, *Of One Blood: Abolitionism and the Origins of Racial Equality* (Berkeley: U of California P, 1998). In *Iola Leroy,* Iola insists that African Americans did not "place the bounds of our habitation. And I believe we are to be fixtures in this country" (249).

47. Thomas Dixon, *Dixon on Ingersoll* (New York: John B. Alden, 1892); Thomas Ingersoll, "Should the Chinese Be Excluded?" *North American Review* (1892): 55. *Fong Yue Ting v. U.S.,* 149 U.S. 698. For the majority, Justice Horace Gray wrote, "the right of a nation to expel or deport foreigners who have not been naturalized, or taken any steps toward becoming citizens of the country, rests upon the same grounds and is as absolute and unqualified, as the right to prohibit and prevent their entrance into the country" (707).

48. Albion W. Tourgée, "A Bystander's Notes," *Our Continent* 3 (February 7, 1883): 187.

49. Olsen, *Carpetbagger's Crusade*, p. 347. Carolyn Karcher provides the most thorough account of Tourgée's support of the Spanish-American War in *A Refugee from His Race: Albion W. Tourgée and the Fight against White Supremacy* (Chapel Hill: U of North Carolina P, 2016).

50. Critical works linking the novel to the Spanish-American War and its aftermath include James Robert Payne, "Afro-American Literature of the Spanish-American War," *MELUS* 10 (1983): 19–32; Kaplan, *The Anarchy of Empire*; Susan Gillman, *Blood Talk: American Race Melodrama and the Culture of the Occult* (Chicago: U of Chicago P, 2003); Peter Schmidt, *Sitting in Darkness: New South Fiction, Education, and the Rise of Jim Crow Colonialism, 1865–1920* (Jackson: U of Mississippi P, 2008); Stephen Knadler, "Sensationalizing Patriotism: Sutton Griggs and the Sentimental Nationalism of Citizenship," *American Literature* 79 (2007): 673–99, and John Gruessen, "Empires at Home and Abroad in Sutton Griggs's *Imperium in Imperio*," in *Jim Crow, Literature, and the Legacy of Sutton Griggs*, ed. Tess Chakkalakal and Kenneth W. Warren (Athens: U of Georgia P, 2013), pp. 49–68. Caroline Levander acknowledges the importance of this work but argues for understanding the book in terms of the fluid border region of Mexico and Texas rather than in relation to internal North-South debates or national expansion to Cuba and the Philippines. See "Sutton Griggs and the Borderlands of Empire," in *Jim Crow, Literature, and the Legacy of Sutton Griggs*, pp. 21–48. Yet, as Gruessen has to acknowledge in a footnote, the crucial ideological debate toward the end of the book, with very minor exceptions, has "no sense of diasporic or hemispheric connections." On the contrary, it is "strictly U.S. centered—and Anglo-Saxon U.S. centered at that" (67n30). As I argued in the introduction, as important as it is to look at works through a transnational or hemispheric lens, we should not necessarily conclude that they advocate a transnational outcome. It takes a selective reading to ignore how important national debates over race were for writers like Griggs. For instance, critics have speculated on why Griggs picks the state of Texas, citing its importance in the nation's history of imperialism and its border region with Mexico. No one, however, has noted that, as Griggs would have known, it was the last of the former Confederate states where hostilities ceased, not ending until August 1866. Bringing the Lone Star state into the Union has a long and complicated history. On the lingering conflict in Texas and the condition of Texas freedmen during Reconstruction, see Jeffrey W. Hunt, *The Last Battle of the Civil War: Palmetto Ranch* (Austin: U of Texas P, 2002); James M. Smallwood, Barry A. Crouch, and Larry Peacock, *Murder and Mayhem: The War of Reconstruction in Texas* (College Station: Texas A&M UP, 2003); Barry A. Crouch, *The Dance of Freedom: Texas African Americans during Reconstruction* (Austin: U of Texas P, 2007); and Gregory P. Downs, "Three Faces of Sovereignty: Governing Confederate, Mexican, and Indian Texas in the Civil War Era," in *Civil War Wests: Testing the Limits of the United States*, ed. Adam Arenson and Andrew R. Graybill (Berkeley: U of California P, 2015), pp. 118–38.

51. Alison La Croix, *The Ideological Origins of American Federalism* (Cambridge: Harvard UP, 2010); William Blackstone, *Commentaries on the Laws of England* (Buffalo: William S. Hein, 1992), 1:105; *Cherokee Nation v. Georgia*, 30 U.S. 1 at 17 (1831); *Downes v. Bidwell*, 182 U.S. 244 at 341–42 (1901).

52. Peter Schmidt, *Sitting in Darkness*, p. 78.

CHAPTER 3: The Ku Klux Klan

1. Andrew L. Slap, *The Doom of Reconstruction: The Liberal Republicans and the Civil War Era* (New York: Fordham UP, 2006), p. 114. On the legal issues, see Michael Kent Curtis, "The Klan, the Congress, and the Court: Congressional Enforcement of the Fourteenth and Fifteenth Amendments & the State Action Syllogism, a Brief Historical Overview," *University of Pennsylvania Journal of Constitutional Law* 11 (2009): 1381–1400.

2. Sidney Lanier, *Centennial Edition: Poems*, ed. Charles R. Anderson (Baltimore: Johns Hopkins UP, 1945), 1:191–92.

3. Charles Sumner, "Violations of International Law, and Usurpations of War Powers," in *Charles Sumner, His Complete Works*, ed. George Frisbie Hoar (Boston: Lee and Shepard, 1900), 19:93–94. Anderson mistakenly identifies the speech Lanier alludes to as another of Sumner's speeches condemning Grant's efforts to annex Santo Domingo: "Naboth's Vineyard," delivered December 21, 1870. Lanier, *Centennial Edition: Poems*, 1:376.

4. Lanier, *Centennial Edition: Poems*, 1:194.

5. *Statutes at Large* (Boston: Little and Brown, 1871), 16:13; Lanier, *Centennial Edition: Poems*, 1:376.

6. Walter Benn Michaels generates an ingenious reading of whiteness based on the mistaken assumption that the Klan uniformly wore white. "Race into Culture: A Critical Genealogy of Cultural Identity," *Critical Inquiry* 18 (1992): 655–85.

7. Elaine Frantz Parsons, *Ku-Klux: The Birth of the Klan during Reconstruction* (Chapel Hill: U of North Carolina P, 2016).

8. William Garrett Brown, "The Ku Klux Movement," *Atlantic Monthly* 87 (1901): 643.

9. J. G. de Roulhac Hamilton, *Reconstruction in North Carolina* (New York: Columbia UP, 1914), pp. 453; Brown, "The Ku Klux Movement," 644.

10. Joel Chandler Harris, *Atlanta Constitution*, April 23, 1890.

11. This unmasking was dramatic enough for Page's illustrator, B. West Clinedinst, to give it a visual rendition. Clinedinst, who also worked with Robert Louis Stevenson and Mark Twain, was such an important illustrator that an award was named in his honor. Pat Oliphant and Norman Rockwell are two of the recipients.

12. In describing Page's myth of necessary violence, I disagree with Scott Romine's claim that "*Red Rock* never fully sanctions resistance outside the law." "Things Falling Apart: The Postcolonial Condition of *Red Rock* and *The Leopard's Spots*," in *Look Away!: The U.S. South in New World Studies*, ed. Jon Smith and Deborah Cohn (Durham: Duke UP, 2004), p. 181. Fred Hobson says that Dr. Cary is Page's spokesperson in *Tell About the South* (Baton Rouge: Louisiana State UP, 1983), p. 149.

13. Alexandra Cook, "Critical Medievalism and the New South: *Red Rock* and *Gone with the Wind*," *South Central Review* 30 (2014): 32–52.

14. Thomas Nelson Page, "The Dragon of the Sea," in *Spanish-American War Songs*, ed. Sidney A. Witherbee (Detroit: Sidney B. Witherbee, 1898), p. 732. See Jeremy Wells's brief discussion in *Romances of the White Man's Burden: Race, Empire, and the Plantation in American Literature, 1880–1936* (Nashville: Vanderbilt UP, 2011), p. 108.

15. Nathaniel Hawthorne, *The House of the Seven Gables*, in *The Centenary Edition of the Works of Nathaniel Hawthorne*, ed. William Charvat, Roy Harvey Pearce, and Claude M. Simpson (Columbus: Ohio State UP, 1965), 2:8. Page even includes a school-

teacher named Dr. Maule. Thomas Nelson Page, "The Want of a History of the Southern People," in *The Old South* (New York: Scribner's, 1892), p. 256.

16. Wells, the only critic to analyze the episode, is so intent on linking Page's belief in white supremacy to the Klan that, despite what is actually written on the page, he has Jacquelin and his friend "don the Klan robes to conduct [their] secret mission." According to Wells, "Denied the opportunity to participate in the first Klan raid because he had not yet returned from China, Jacquelin leaps at the opportunity to do so later when he perceives duty calling" (*Romances*, p. 101). Completely ignoring the fact that at this point in the plot Page condemns the activities of McRaffle's sham Klan and Jacquelin's commitment to rule by law, Wells concocts an ingenious interpretation. Jacquelin's duty, Wells argues, is not to a northern woman who extended kindness to him during the war but to the white race. In Page, the Klan, "which under its hoods represents the South's white citizenry from high to low" (98), stands for white blood in general, not the Old South's familial blood. "Familial blood still matters, but it matters less in the New South than 'white' blood. Once he dons the robes, after all, Jacquelin is less a representative of his family—of the *Grays*, no less—than of the ideals of whiteness" (101). Apparently, Hiram Still and McRaffle no longer qualify as southerners, high or low.

17. Charles Adams in 2000 continued Dixon's argument, claiming that only with the end of military rule did "the Klan become a criminal conspiracy against law and civilized order." *When in the Course of Human Events: Arguing for the Case of Southern Secession* (Lanham, MD: Rowman and Littlefield, 2000), p. 164.

18. Lou Falkner Williams, *The Great South Carolina Ku Klux Klan Trials, 1871–1872* (Athens: U of Georgia P, 1996), pp. 17, 18, 44.

19. Williams, *The Great South Carolina Ku Klux Klan Trials*, p. 124. On Akerman, see William S. McFeely, "Amos T. Akerman: The Lawyer and Racial Justice," in *Region, Race, and Reconstruction*, ed. J. Morgan Kousser and James M. McPherson (New York: Oxford UP, 1982), pp. 395–416.

20. Williams, *The Great South Carolina Ku Klux Klan Trials*, p. 114.

21. *Downes v. Bidwell*, 182 U.S. 244 at 380 (1901).

22. Charles Sumner, "Are We a Nation?" in *Complete Works*, 14:60. Walter Benn Michaels stresses Dixon and Page's anti-imperialism in terms of Reconstruction, seemingly unaware of their support of imperialism in 1898 and after. "Race into Culture: A Critical Genealogy of Cultural Identity," *Critical Inquiry* 18 (1992): 655–85, and "Anti-Imperialist Americanism," in *Cultures of Imperialism*, ed. Amy Kaplan and Donald Peace (Durham: Duke UP, 1993), pp. 365–91. Informed of their pro-imperialism, he makes some minor adjustments to his argument in *Our America: Nativism, Modernism, and Pluralism* (Durham: Duke UP, 1995).

23. Samuel Swett Green, *The Scotch-Irish in America* (Worcester, MA: Charles Hamilton, 1895), p. 24; Carlton Jackson, *A Social History of the Scotch-Irish* (Lanham, MD: Madison, 1982), pp. 121.

24. Jackson, *Social History*, p. 150; John W. Burgess, *The Middle Period: 1817–1858* (New York: Scribner's, 1897), p. ix.

25. Samuel Harden Church, "Cromwell, A Tricentenary Study," *Atlantic Monthly* 83 (1899): 460.

26. Williams, *The Great South Carolina Ku Klux Klan Trials*, p. 128. Rifle clubs are another example of how complicated the legal issues of the time were from a present perspective. In citing them, Dixon suggests that the disarming of whites was a violation

of the Second Amendment. But in the 1871 and 1872 trials, prosecutors claimed that the Second Amendment had been federalized and charged the Klan with depriving African Americans of their right to bear arms.

27. John W. Burgess, *Reconstruction and the Constitution* (New York: Scribner's, 1902), p. 259.

28. The location of Ben's debate with his father over the necessity of violence is another example of the differences between Dixon and Page. Page's debate is conducted in front of the entire white, male community, whereas Dixon's takes place in private.

29. Peter Karsten, "Cromwell in America," *Images of Oliver Cromwell*, ed. R. C. Richardson (Manchester: Manchester UP, 1993), p. 217; Theodore Roosevelt, *Oliver Cromwell* (New York: Scribner's, 1900), p. 99.

30. Roosevelt, *Oliver Cromwell*, pp. 99, 100.

31. Peter Karsten, *Patriot-Heroes in England and America* (Madison: U of Wisconsin P, 1978), pp. 101 and 91; Karsten, "Cromwell," p. 217; Barry Schwartz, *Abraham Lincoln and the Forge of National Memory* (Chicago: U of Chicago P, 2000), pp. 296–97; John W. Burgess, *Political Science and Constitutional Law* (New York: Baker and Taylor, 1890), 1:56.

32. On the anti-imperialists' reliance on *Dred Scott*, see Morris M. Cohn, "The Dred Scott Case in Light of Later Events," *American Law Review* 46 (1912): 548–57; Sanford Levinson, "Installing the *Insular Cases* into the Canon of Constitutional Law," in *Foreign in a Domestic Sense*, ed. Christina Duffy Burnett and Burke Marshall (Durham: Duke UP, 2001), pp. 121–39; and Brook Thomas, "A Constitution Led by the Flag: The *Insular Cases* and the Metaphor of Incorporation," in Burnett and Marshall, *Foreign in a Domestic Sense*, pp. 83–105.

33. Frederic R. Coudert, "The Evolution of the Doctrine of Territorial Incorporation," *Columbia Law Review* 26 (1926): 834.

34. Albion W. Tourgée, "Letter to E. H. Johnson," *Undaunted Radical: The Speeches and Writings of Albion W. Tourgée*, ed. Mark Elliott and John David Smith (Baton Rouge: Louisiana State UP, 2010), pp. 356–78; Emma Tourgée to Thomas Dixon, February 24, 1906; Thomas Dixon to Emma Tourgée, March 4, 1906, courtesy of the Chautauqua County Historical Society.

35. Carolyn Karcher, introduction to Albion W. Tourgée, *Bricks without Straw* (Durham: Duke UP, 2009), pp. 41–42.

36. Otto H. Olsen, *Carpetbagger's Crusade: The Life of Albion W. Tourgée* (Baltimore: Johns Hopkins UP, 1965), pp. 162–65.

37. Walter Benjamin, "Theses on the Philosophy of History," *Illuminations*, ed. Hannah Arendt (New York: Schocken, 1969), pp. 254–55. Richard Wolin describes Benjamin's work as "an aesthetic of redemption" in *Walter Benjamin: An Aesthetic of Redemption* (New York: Columbia UP, 1982). Although he does not cite Benjamin, Christopher Bundrick gives a Benjaminian sense of the force of *Red Rock* when he notes that "it is not the case that the present looks back to an ideal 'then' so much as that the past actively asserts itself into the present, forcing both memory and tribute." "Return of the Repressed: Gothic and Romance in Thomas Nelson Page's *Red Rock*," *South Central Review* 25 (2008): 69.

38. Douglass Southall Freeman, *R. E. Lee: A Biography* (New York: Scribner's, 1935), 1:221; Sumner, "Are We a Nation?" in *Complete Works*, 14:63; Daniel W. Stowell, "Why 'Redemption'?: Religion and the End of Reconstruction, 1899–1877," in *Vale of Tears:*

New Essays on Religion and Reconstruction, ed. Edward J. Blum and W. Scott Poole (Macon: Mercer UP, 2005), pp. 133–46; Lewis P. Simpson, *The Man of Letters in New England and the South* (Baton Rouge: Louisiana State UP, 1973), p. 223; Thomas Nelson Page, "The Old South," in *The Old South*, p. 4.

39. Thomas Dixon Jr., "The Story of the Ku Klux Klan: Some of Its Leaders, Living and Dead," *Metropolitan Magazine* 22 (1905): 660–62.

40. Thomas Nelson Page, "The Southern People During Reconstruction," *Atlantic Monthly* 88 (1901): 304.

41. Charles Fairman, *Reconstruction and Reunion, 1864–88* (New York: Macmillan, 1971), p. 1377. The best account of the Colfax Massacre is Charles Lane, *The Day Freedom Died: The Colfax Massacre, the Supreme Court, and the Betrayal of Reconstruction* (New York: Henry Holt, 2008).

42. *United States v. Cruikshank*, 92 U.S. 542 (1876) at 542–44.

43. Frederick Douglass, quoted in Albion W. Tourgée, *Undaunted Radical*, p. 226. On the changing meaning of "civil rights," see Brook Thomas, *Civic Myths: A Law and Literature Approach to Citizenship* (Chapel Hill: U of North Carolina P, 2007), pp. 105–7; *United States v. Cruikshank*, 92 U.S. 542 (1876) at 544; Michael Les Benedict, "Preserving Federalism: Reconstruction and the Waite Court," *Supreme Court Review* 1978 (1978): 67; Curtis, "The Klan, the Congress, and the Court," p. 1430.

44. Tourgée, "Brief of Plaintiff in Error," *Undaunted Radical*, p. 317.

CHAPTER 4: Of Mules and Men

1. Stephen Crane, *The Red Badge of Courage* (1895; reprint, 4th ed., New York: Norton, 2008), pp. 103, 79, 79, 3. Amy Kaplan shrewdly argues that this "only reference to blacks in the novel" signals Crane's acknowledgement that his story about the Civil War will not be one about "freeing the slaves." She does not, however, make the connection between this opening scene and the later reference to mule drivers. "The Spectacle of War in Crane's Revision of History," in *New Essays on The Red Badge of Courage*, ed. Lee Clark Mitchell (New York: Cambridge UP, 1986), p. 78.

2. Mark Twain to Francis Wayland, December 24, 1885. Reprinted in Edwin McDowell, "From Twain, a Letter on Debt to Blacks, *New York Times*, March 4, 1985, p. G21.

3. Two founding works in American literary studies that look at manhood as a gendered category are Nina Baym, "Melodramas of Beset Manhood: How Theories of American Fiction Exclude Women Writers," *American Quarterly* 33 (1981): 123–39, and David Leverenz, *Manhood and the American Renaissance* (Ithaca: Cornell UP, 1989). Others argue that assertions of manhood after the Civil War respond to the "feminization of American culture," as defined by Ann Douglas in *The Feminization of American Culture* (New York: Knopf, 1977). Notable works of American literary studies linking portrayals of manhood with race and gender include Hazel Carby, *Race Men* (Cambridge: Harvard UP, 1998); Phillip Brian Harper, *Are We Not Men: Masculine Anxiety and the Problem of African-American Identity* (New York: Oxford UP, 1996); and Dana Nelson, *National Manhood: Capitalist Citizenship and the Imagined Fraternity of White Men* (Durham: Duke UP, 1998). Nina Silber and Sharon D. Kennedy-Nolle focus on gender and Reconstruction in *The Romance of Reunion: Northerners and the South, 1865–1900* (Chapel Hill: U of North Carolina, P, 1993) and *Writing Reconstruction: Race, Gender, and Citizenship in the Postwar South* (Chapel Hill: U of North Carolina P, 2015). John Dudley focuses on naturalism in the chapter "Roots of Naturalism in African American Literature,"

in *A Man's Game: Masculinity and the Anti-Aesthetic of American Literary Naturalism* (Tuscaloosa: U of Alabama P, 2004). Gail Bederman provides a cultural historical account of the last part of the period covered in this chapter in *Manliness and Civilization: A Cultural History of Gender and Race in the United States, 1880–1917* (Chicago: U of Chicago, P, 1995). As important as this work has been, opposing manhood to womanhood rather than to childhood has generated a somewhat skewed account of what was at stake in claims for African American manhood after Emancipation. For instance, almost all bringing race and gender together agree with Bederman that "Americans who were trying to reformulate gender explained their ideas about manhood by drawing connections between male power and white supremacy" (20). Thus, assertions of manhood were frequently seen as opposed to women's suffrage and/or a driving force behind American militarism and imperialism at the turn of the century. (See Amy Kaplan, "Romancing the Empire: The Embodiment of American Masculinity in the Popular Historical Novel of the 1890s," *American Literary History* 2 [1990]: 659–90.) But many of the writers I treat strongly supported women's right to vote and opposed American imperialism. Assertions of manhood inevitably have some gendered implications; nonetheless, in this chapter I look at them primarily in relation to the widespread assumption at the time that African Americans were perpetual children. Those sharing that assumption frequently associated African Americans with governmental paternalism, a substitution for the paternal justification of slavery. Many, like Page and Dixon, did indeed link "whiteness to male power" (Bederman, *Manliness*, 20), but they did so to deny African American manhood. In contrast, writers like Cable, Chesnutt, Du Bois, Hopkins, Harper, and Tourgée insisted on African Americans' ability to become responsible adults: self-sufficient workers, dutiful husbands and fathers, and educated citizens fully participating in the civil and political spheres.

4. John S. Haller Jr., *Outcasts from Evolution: Scientific Attitudes of Racial Inferiority, 1859–1900* (Urbana: U of Illinois P, 1971). On Jefferson Davis, see Silber's chapter, "Intemperate Men, Spiteful Women, and Jefferson Davis: Northern Views of the Defeated South," *Romance*, pp. 13–38.

5. Peter Joseph Hamilton, *The Reconstruction Period* (Philadelphia: Barrie, 1905), p. 540.

6. Aviam Soifier, "The Paradox of Paternalism and Laissez-Faire Constitutionalism: The United States Supreme Court, 1888–1921," *Law and History Review* 5 (1987): 249–79. Prior to emancipation, African Americans were most often compared to cattle, linked etymologically to "chattel."

7. *United States v. Rhodes*, 27 FCas. 785 (1866) at 793; George Bancroft, "The Place of Abraham Lincoln in History," *Atlantic Monthly* 15 (1865): 764; Butler, quoted in Eric Foner, *Reconstruction: America's Unfinished Revolution, 1863–1977* (New York: Harper and Row, 1988), p. 533; *Slaughter-House Cases*, 83 U.S. 36 (1873) at 68.

8. William Wells Brown, *Clotel; or, The President's Daughter* (Boston: Bedford, 2000), p. 316; Mark Elliott and John David Smith, introduction to *Undaunted Radical: The Selected Writings and Speeches of Albion W. Tourgée*, ed. Mark Elliott and John David Smith (Baton Rouge: Louisiana State UP, 2010), p. 6; Tourgée, quoted by Kennedy-Nolle, *Writing Reconstruction*, p. 92.

9. Brook Thomas, ed., *Plessy v. Ferguson: A Brief History with Documents* (Boston: Bedford, 1997), p. 58.

10. Dudley H. Miles, ed., *Poetry and Eloquence of Blue and Gray* (New York: Review of Reviews Co., 1911), p. 177.

11. Crane, *Red Badge*, p. 79; Heather Cox Richardson, *West from Appomattox: The Reconstruction of America after the Civil War* (New Haven: Yale UP, 2007), p. 320.

12. Henry M. Field, "Capacity of the Negro—His Position in the North. The Color Line in New England," in Thomas, *Plessy v. Ferguson: A Brief History*, pp. 118–19; Henry Field, *Blood Is Thicker than Water: A Few Days Among Our Southern Brethren* (New York: George Munro, 1886), pp. 17–18. Henry married the former governess for the family of the French nobleman Charles de Choiseul-Praslin, whose suicide to avoid trial for the murder of his wife contributed to the outbreak of France's revolution of 1848. A fictionalized Henry appears as a main character in the 1940 Charles Boyer and Bette Davis film depicting the affair, *All This, and Heaven Too*, based on a novel by Henry's niece and National Book Award winner Rachel Field.

13. Otto Olsen, *Carpetbagger's Crusade: The Life of Albion Winegar Tourgée* (Baltimore: Johns Hopkins UP, 1965), pp. 124–45. See the illustration between pp. 176–77.

14. *Education in America*, ed. Murray N. Butler (Albany: J. B. Lyon, 1900); Thomas Dixon Jr., "Booker T. Washington and the Negro," *Saturday Evening Post* 178 (August 19, 1905): 1–2.

15. Henry W. Grady, "In Plain Black and White," *Century Magazine* 29 (1885): 912; Sidney Lanier, "Civil Rights," *Centennial Edition: Poems*, ed. Charles R. Anderson (Baltimore: Johns Hopkins UP, 1945), 1:41.

16. J. Morgan Kousser, "Making Separate Equal: Integration of Black and White School Funds in Kentucky," *Journal of Interdisciplinary History* 10 (1980): 399–428.

17. Carolyn Hall, unsuccessfully to my mind, tries to read Woolson's story sympathetically in "Poking King David in His Imperial Eye/'I': Woolson Takes On the White Man's Burden in the Postbellum United States," in *Witness to Reconstruction: Constance Fenimore Woolson and the Postbellum South, 1873–1894*, ed. Kathleen Diffley (Jackson: U of Mississippi P, 2011), pp. 177–93. In contrast, Peter Schmidt details its negative portrait of black schools and its condescending attitude toward freedmen in *Sitting in Darkness: New South Fiction, Education, and the Rise of Jim Crow Colonialism, 1865–1920* (Jackson: UP of Mississippi, 2008), pp. 52–54.

18. Heather Cox Richardson, *The Death of Reconstruction: Race, Labor, and Politics in the Post–Civil War North, 1865–1901* (Cambridge: Harvard UP, 2001), p. 208. On Tourgée and the Blair Bill, see Olsen, *Carpetbagger's Crusade*, pp. 304–5n, and Mark Elliott, *Color-Blind Justice: Albion Tourgée and the Quest for Racial Equality from the Civil War to Plessy v. Ferguson* (New York: Oxford UP, 2006), pp. 243–45.

19. Albion W. Tourgée, "Brief of Plaintiff in Error," in *Undaunted Radical*, p. 300.

20. Charles A. Lofgren, *The Plessy Case* (New York: Oxford UP, 1987), p. 166; Thomas, *Plessy v. Ferguson: A Brief History*, p. 55; *Cumming v. Richmond County School Board*, 175 U.S. 528 (1899); Tourgée, "Letter to Martin B. Anderson," *Undaunted*, p. 53.

21. Darwin T. Turner, "Daddy Joel Harris and His Old-time Darkies," *Southern Literary Journal* 1 (1968): 33.

22. Booker T. Washington, "Atlanta Exposition Address," in Thomas, *Plessy v. Ferguson: A Brief History*, pp. 121, 122; Amy Dru Stanley, *From Bondage to Contract: Wage Labor, Marriage, and the Market in the Age of Slave Emancipation* (New York: Cambridge UP, 1998).

23. William Dean Howells, "Some Political Novels," *Atlantic Monthly* 47 (January 1881): 120.

24. Allan Nevins, *The Emergence of Modern America, 1865–1878* (New York: Macmillan, 1927), pp. 358, 19.

25. Louis M. Hacker, *The Triumph of American Capitalism* (New York: Columbia UP, 1940). Roger L. Ransom and Richard Sutch see sharecroppers as renters in *One Kind of Freedom: The Economic Consequences of Emancipation* (1977; 2nd ed., New York: Cambridge UP, 2001). Harold D. Woodman sees them as wage earners in *New South—New Law: The Legal Foundations of Credit and Labor Relations in the Postbellum Agricultural South* (Baton Rouge: Louisiana State UP, 1995). Peter A. Coclanis and Scott Marler provide an excellent summary of the debate in "The Economics of Reconstruction," *A Companion to the Civil War and Reconstruction*, ed. Lacy K. Ford (Malden, MA: Blackwell, 2005), pp. 353–61. Marler makes a compelling case for seeing sharecropping as a hybrid economic form of the type Du Bois suggests. "Fables of the Reconstruction: Reconstruction of the Fables," *Journal of the Historical Society* 4 (2004): 113–37.

26. *Giles v. Harris*, 189 U.S. 473 (1903) at 488. For an account of its immediate reception, see Samuel Brenner, "'Airbrushed out of the Constitutional Canon': The Evolving Understanding of 'Giles v. Harris', 1903–1925," *Michigan Law Review* 107 (2009): 853–79.

27. Charles Lane, *The Day Freedom Died* (New York: Henry Holt, 2008), p. 237; Richardson, *Death*, p. 208; John Tyler Morgan, "The Race Question in America," in Thomas, *Plessy v. Ferguson: A Brief History*, p. 64.

28. *Civil Rights Cases*, 109 U.S. 3 (1883) at 25.

29. *Hodges v. United States*, 203 U.S. 1 (1906) at 19–20. Justice Brewer countered claims that the actions against African Americans stamped them with a badge of servitude by recalling that under slavery "every free Negro was required to carry with him a copy of a judicial decree or other evidence of his right to freedom or be subject to arrest," yet the court failed to prohibit the Geary Act's requirement that Chinese without certificates proving they were legally in the country "might be arrested and deported" (19).

30. *Jones v. Mayer*, 392 U.S. 409 (1968) at 443n78; Robert L. Kobl, "The Civil Rights Act of 1866, Its Hour Come Round at Last: *Jones v. Alfred H. Mayer Co.*," *Virginia Law Review* 272 (1969): 290. In supplanting *Hodges*, *Jones v. Mayer* restored power to the national government. The Rehnquist court, however, undermined the scope of *Jones v. Mayer*. For a response, see Barry Sullivan, "Historical Reconstruction: Reconstruction History, the Proper Scope of Section 1981," *Yale Law Journal* 98 (1989): 541–64. For a more conservative view, see Herman Belz, *Emancipation and Equal Rights: Politics and Constitutionalism in the Civil War Era* (New York: Norton, 1978). See also Alexander Tsesis, *The Thirteenth Amendment and American Freedom: A Legal History* (New York: NYUP, 2004), and Alexander Tsesis, ed., *The Promises of Liberty: The History and Contemporary Relevance of the Thirteenth Amendment* (New York: Columbia UP, 2010).

31. Cleanth Brooks, "The Language of Paradox," *The Well Wrought Urn: Studies in the Structure of Poetry* (New York: Harcourt, 1947), pp. 3–21; Walter Benn Michaels, *The Trouble with Diversity: How We Learned to Love Identity and Ignore Inequality* (New York: Metropolitan, 2006), pp. 61–67. Although she does not engage Michaels, Andreá N. Williams begins her section on *The Marrow of Tradition* with an analysis of the Jim Crow car scene. *Dividing Lines: Class Anxiety and Postbellum Class Fiction* (Ann Arbor: U of Michigan P, 2013), pp. 162–66.

32. Michaels, *Trouble*, p. 63; Henry M. Field, "Capacity of the Negro," p. 118.

33. Barbara Y. Welke, "When All the Women Were White, and All the Blacks Were Men: Gender, Class, Race, and the Road to *Plessy*, 1855–1914," *Law and History Review* 13 (1995): 285–88; Kenneth W. Mack, "Law, Society, Identity, and the Making of the Jim Crow South: Travel and Segregation on Tennessee Railroads, 1875–1905," *Law and Social Inquiry* 24 (1999): 389–92; Kate Masur, *An Example for All the Land: Emancipation and the Struggle for Equality in Washington, D.C.* (Chapel Hill: U of North Carolina P, 2010), p. 231. In addition to the nurse, "a Chinaman of the ordinary laundry type, boarded the train, and took his seat in the white car without objection" (*MT*, 59). This detail alludes to Justice Harlan's dissent in *Plessy* when he makes a case for African Americans at the expense of the Chinese. Chesnutt has a complicated attitude toward those of Asian descent, who, unlike Native Americans, African Americans, and Europeans, were not part of the nation's founding generation. In a speech made around 1892, the year Congress passed the Geary Act, which extended the 1882 Chinese Exclusion Act, Chesnutt warned that unrestricted free trade would reduce American wages to "the European or still worse the Asiatic level." Thus, he praised the Republican Party for supporting "the alien pauper immigration and the alien contract laws." The first restricted the entry of poor immigrants and those likely to become dependent upon public assistance. The second barred the entry of foreigners with prearranged work contracts. On the right of Chinese to occupy white cars, both Harlan and Chesnutt would prove to be wrong. In *Gong Lum v. Rice* (1927), the Supreme Court upheld Mississippi's ruling that Chinese Americans could be classified as colored. Chesnutt, it turns out, criticized the court's decision in a speech acknowledging that "there is more than one race problem in the world." Charles W. Chesnutt, *Essays and Speeches*, ed. Joseph R. McElrath Jr., Robert C. Leitz III, and Jesse S. Crisler (Stanford: Stanford UP, 1999), pp. 95, 96, 496–97.

34. Michaels, *Trouble*, p. 63.

35. Eric Sundquist notes, "Although they are not all developed as characters with equal effectiveness, the blacks of *The Marrow of Tradition* represent a wider range of class and type than any other such fictional group of the period." *To Wake the Nations: Race and the Making of American Literature* (Cambridge: Harvard UP, 1993), p. 447.

36. Michaels, *Trouble*, p. 61.

37. Howard K. Beale, "On Rewriting Reconstruction History," *American Historical Review* 45 (1940): 821.

38. Frederick Douglass, *The Life and Writings of Frederick Douglass*, ed. Philip S. Foner (New York: International Publishers, 1955), 4:544n1.

39. Douglass, *Life and Writings*, 4:544n1, 158.

40. John W. Burgess, *Reconstruction and the Constitution* (New York: Scribner's, 1902), pp. 44–45.

41. Tourgée, quoted in Olsen, *Carpetbagger's Crusade*, p. 260.

42. Schmidt, *Sitting in Darkness*, pp. 55–56. Peter Coclanis argues that today's scholars posit a degree of agency for freedmen that "divinizes rather than humanizes" them. Freedmen trying to act alone "got crushed in the nineteenth century, crushed by overwhelming material, institutional, and ideological power that no subaltern formation anywhere in the world could even begin to match." "Slavery, African-American Agency, and the World We Have Lost," *Georgia Historical Quarterly* 79 (1995): 880, 882. Walter Johnson notes how scholars too often impose their contemporary sense of selfhood retrospectively on the past in trying to account for African Americans' humanity and their resistance to

oppression. "On Agency," *Journal of Social History* 37 (2003): 113–24. See also John C. Rodrigue, "Black Agency after Slavery," *Reconstructions: New Perspectives on the Postbellum United States*, ed. Thomas J. Brown (New York: Oxford UP, 2006), pp. 40–65.

43. William W. Cook, *The Corporation Problem* (New York: Putnam's Sons, 1893), p. 72.

CHAPTER 5: Ruiz de Burton and Railroads

1. In their introduction to *Who Would Have Thought It?*, Rosaura Sánchez and Beatrice Pita, unaware of Sumner's famous "Republicanism v. Grantism" speech, identify Cacklism with Benjamin Butler because of his reputation for corruption. They acknowledge that Butler's support of Grant in 1872 complicates their argument, but they stick with it (WW, xlviii–liii). They also fail to catch Ruiz de Burton's multiple allusions to Secretary of State Seward's alleged claim to be able to violate civil liberties by ringing a little bell (WW, 94, 171, 295). During the Civil War, Seward supposedly told a British lord, "I can touch a bell with my right hand, and order the arrest of a citizen of Ohio. I can touch a bell again and order the imprisonment of a citizen of New York." On the significance of this legend, see Brook Thomas, *Civic Myths: A Law and Literature Approach to Citizenship* (Chapel Hill: U of North Carolina P, 2007), pp. 107–13. On the plan to annex Santo Domingo, see Charles Cullen Tansell, *The United States and Santo Domingo, 1798–1873* (Baltimore: Johns Hopkins UP, 1938), and Eric T. Love, *Race over Empire: Racism and U.S. Imperialism, 1865–1900* (Chapel Hill: U of North Carolina P, 2004). On Douglass's role, see *The Life and Writings of Frederick Douglass*, ed. Philip S. Foner (New York: International Publishers, 1955), 4:64–81, and Robert S. Levine, *Dislocating the Nation: Episodes in Nineteenth-Century American Literary Nationalism* (Chapel Hill: U of North Carolina P, 2008), pp. 179–236.

2. On Ruiz de Burton's disdain for "black" Republicans and her connections with Grant, see, *Conflicts of Interest: The Letters of María Amparo Ruiz de Burton*, ed. Rosaura Sánchez and Beatrice Pita (Houston: Arte Público, 2001), pp. 197, 377.

3. Ruiz de Burton, *Conflicts of Interest*, p. 195.

4. José F. Aranda Jr., "Contradictory Impulses: María Amparo Ruiz de Burton, Resistance Theory, and the Politics of Chicano/a Studies," *American Literature* 70 (1998): 551–79. By the time they edit *Conflict of Interest*, Sánchez and Pita acknowledge Ruiz de Burton's "vacillation and contradiction" (220). This sympathy for the South is complicated by Ruiz de Burton's support of Grant, who presided over Reconstruction but in the book supports the Don against the squatters' claims to his land.

5. José F Aranda Jr., "Returning California to the People: Vigilantism in *The Squatter and the Don*," in *María Amparo Ruiz de Burton: Critical and Pedagogical Perspectives*, ed. Amelia María de Luz Montes and Anne Elizabeth Goldman (Lincoln: U of Nebraska P, 2004), 11–26; US passport, pp. 22–23.

6. Raymond B. Nixon, *Henry Grady: Spokesman for the New South* (Durham: Duke UP, 1943), pp. 167–69; Henry Field, *Blood Is Thicker than Water: A Few Days Among the Southern Brethren* (New York: George Munro, 1886), p. 136.

7. Heather Cox Richardson, *West from Appomattox: The Reconstruction of America after the Civil War* (New Haven: Yale UP, 2007); Elliott West, "Reconstructing Race," *Western Historical Quarterly* 34 (2003): 7–26, and *The Last Indian War: The Nez Perce Story* (New York: Oxford UP, 2009); Stacey L. Smith, *Freedom's Frontier: California and the Struggle over Unfree Labor, Emancipation, and Reconstruction* (Chapel Hill: U of North Carolina P, 2013), and *Civil War Wests: Testing the Limits of*

the United States, ed. Adam Arenson and Andrew R. Graybill (Berkeley: U of California P, 2015). Compare Dixon to Du Bois: "The whole development of Reconstruction was primarily an economic development" (*BR*, 721). Ben Railton provides excellent literary analysis bringing together issues of Reconstruction and the Gilded Age in *Contesting the Past, Reconstructing the Nation: American Literature and Culture in the Gilded Age, 1876–1893* (Tuscaloosa: U of Alabama P, 2007). The western approach to *Squatter* is evident in the notes to both available editions. Jennifer M. Acker's notes for the 2004 Random House edition with an introduction by Ana Castillo provide a fuller account of the Texas Pacific than the 1992 edition, which I reference. But even Acker's account ignores scholars of Reconstruction and relies on an article published in the *Journal of San Diego History*.

8. Vincent Pérez, "Remembering the Hacienda: Land and Community in Californio Narratives," in Montes and Goldman, *María Amparo Ruiz de Burton: Critical and Pedagogical Perspectives*, 27–55. Steven Hahn, "Common Right and Commonwealth: The Stock-Law Struggle and the Roots of Southern Populism," in *Region, Race, and Reconstruction*, ed. J. Morgan Kousser and James McPherson (New York: Oxford University Press, 1982), p. 61.

9. Ruiz de Burton, *Conflict of Interests*, p. 161. There are numerous accounts of the Texas and Pacific by southern historians. I rely mostly on C. Vann Woodward, *Reunion and Reaction: The Compromise of 1877 and the End of Reconstruction*, rev. ed. (Garden City, NJ: Doubleday, 1956), John F. Stover, *The Railroads of the South, 1865–1900* (Chapel Hill: U of North Carolina P, 1955), Mark W. Summers, *Railroads, Reconstruction, and the Gospel of Prosperity* (Princeton: Princeton UP, 1984). Recently, the Texas and Pacific has been treated by the western historian Richard White in *Railroaded: The Transcontinentals and the Making of America* (New York: Norton, 2011).

10. Woodward, *Reunion and Reaction*, p. 163.

11. Jere W. Roberson, "The South and the Pacific Railroad, 1845–1855," *Western Historical Quarterly* 5 (1974): 163–86. Justifying his attempt to get Davis nominated in 1860, Benjamin Butler praised Davis's surveys for making possible "the Union Pacific Railroad, which was built to bind the East and West together as with a chain of steel." Benjamin F. Butler, *Butler's Book: Autobiographical Personal Reminiscences of Major-General Benj. F. Butler* (Boston: A. M. Thayer, 1892), p. 139.

12. Woodward, *Reunion and Reaction*, pp. 98, 282, 98; Summers, *Railroads*, p. 164. A major advocate of Grant's plans for annexation was his private secretary, Gen. Orville Babcock, who was later a central figure in the Whiskey Ring scandal. Ruiz de Burton's support for Grant and his annexation plan, as well as a line along the path of empire, complicates any effort to depict her as anti-imperialist.

13. Joel Chandler Harris, "Mr. Billy Sanders Indulges in Some Political Reminiscences," *Joel Chandler Harris: Editor and Essayist*, ed. Julia Collier Harris (Chapel Hill: U of North Carolina P, 1931), pp. 208–9.

14. Albion W. Tourgée, "Letter to E. H. Johnson?" in *Undaunted Radical: The Selected Writings and Speeches of Albion W. Tourgée*, ed. Mark Elliott and John David Smith (Baton Rouge: Louisiana State UP, 2010), p. 363; Edward A. Pollard, *The Lost Cause Regained* (New York: G. W. Carleton, 1868), p. 196; William Archibald Dunning, *Reconstruction, Political and Economic, 1864–1877* (New York: Harper, 1907), between pp. 224–25; Du Bois, *BR*, 407–8, 475–76, 493, and 531–32; J. G. de Roulhac Hamilton, *Reconstruction in North Carolina* (New York: Columbia UP, 1914), p. 427.

15. Jay B. Hubbell, *The South in American Literature, 1607–1900* (Durham: Duke UP, 1954), p. 793.

16. Henry Field tries to be conciliatory. "The good effect of railroads," he concludes, "was entirely independent of the motives of its builders. . . . Even though their projections might have been animated only by sordid motives, they 'builded better than they knew,' and in the end the country at large reaped the benefit of the great works which they completed." *Blood*, pp. 135–36. Herbert Spencer, *Principles of Biology*, 2 vol. (London: Williams and Norgate, 1864), 1:444.

17. For a different account, see Jennifer S. Tuttle, "The Symptoms of Conquest: Race, Class, and the Nervous Body," in Montes and Goldman, *Critical and Pedagogical Perspectives*, 56–74.

18. Taken in by Ruiz de Burton's version of the dispute between Huntington and Scott, Sánchez and Pita claim that, in *Squatter*, "there are no absolutes, no fixed sites for good and evil" (9).

19. William S. McFeely, "Amos T. Akerman: The Lawyer and Racial Justice," in Kousser and McPherson, *Region, Race, and Reconstruction*, pp. 395–416; Lou Falkner Williams, *The Great South Carolina Ku Klux Klan Trials, 1871–1872* (Athens: U of Georgia P, 1996), pp. 101, 124.

20. Ruiz de Burton, *Conflict of Interests*, pp. 193, 387–88.

21. Gregory P. Downs, "The Mexicanization of American Politics: The United States' Transnational Path from Civil War to Stabilization," *American Historical Review* 117 (2012): 387–409; Ruiz de Burton, *Conflict of Interests*, p. 217.

22. See Ruiz de Burton, *Conflict of Interest*, pp. 100, 377, and *SD*, 347n58. The most extensive recent account of Scott is in White, *Railroaded*.

23. Woodward, *Reunion and Reaction*, p. 255.

24. Hahn, "Common Right and Commonwealth," 57; Jefferson Davis was imprisoned at Fortress Monroe. He and his wife greatly appreciated Burton and his wife's kindness.

25. "Dedication of the Huntington Library," *New York Times*, April 29, 1903. On Armstrong, see Robert Francis Engs, *Educating the Disfranchised and Disinherited: Samuel Chapman Armstrong and Hampton Institute, 1839–1893* (Knoxville: University of Tennessee Press, 1999), and Peter Schmidt, *Sitting in Darkness: New South Fiction, Education, and the Rise of Jim Crow Colonialism, 1865–1920* (Jackson: U of Mississippi P, 2008), pp. 120–23.

26. Smith, *Freedom's Frontier*, p. 218. *In re Tiburcio Parrott*, 1 F. 481 (C.C.D. Cal. 1880), 494. This Ninth Circuit opinion declared this particular anti-Chinese and anticorporate measure unconstitutional. For a discussion of this case, see Brook Thomas, *American Literary Realism and the Failed Promise of Contract* (Berkeley: U of California P, 1997), 236–39.

27. Quoted in Lucy Salyer, "*Wong Kim Ark*: The Contest Over Birthright Citizenship," in *Immigration Stories*, ed. David A. Martin and Peter H. Schuck (New York: Foundation Press, 2005), pp. 70, 71, 71.

28. . Quoted in Salyer, "*Wong Kim Ark*," p. 73. Emphasis added by the attorney.

29. Frederick Douglass, "Southern Barbarism," in *Life and Writings*, 4:440; William E. Birkhimer, *Military Government and Martial Law*, 3rd ed. (Kansas City: Franklin Hudson, 1914), p. 278.

30. See John M. González, "The Whiteness of the Blush: The Cultural Politics of Racial Formation in *The Squatter and the Don*," in Montes and Goldman, *Critical and Pedagogical Perspectives*, 153–68.

31. Mark Wahlgren Summers makes similar comparisons in his chapter "Conquered Provinces," in *The Ordeal of Reunion: A New History of Reconstruction* (Chapel Hill: U of North Carolina P, 2015), pp. 179–203.

32. Quoted in Gerrit L. Lansing, "The Growth and Effect of Railway Consolidation," *Popular Science Monthly* 22 (1883): 581–82. For a comparison of Ruiz de Burton's treatment of Mussel Slough with that of Josiah Royce and Frank Norris, see Forrest Robinson, "Josiah Royce's California," *Western American Literature* 36 (2002): 37–53.

33. Focused on the West in "Returning California to the People," Aranda does not notice the similarity between language defending the squatters at Mussel Slough and rhetoric justifying the Klan. For a discussion of *San Mateo County*, see Morton Horwitz, "*Santa Clara* Revisited: The Development of Corporate Theory," *West Virginia Law Review* 88 (1985): 173–224, and Brook Thomas, *The New Historicism and Other Old-Fashioned Topics* (Princeton: Princeton University Press, 1991), 140–43. Pro-corporate, Justice Field strongly opposed Reconstruction.

34. Lansing, "The Growth and Effect of Railway Consolidation," pp. 581, 589.

35. Alfred H. Kelly, "The Congressional Controversy over School Segregation," *American Historical Review* 64 (1959): 559, 556–7.

36. Woodward, *Reunion and Reaction*, p. 25. For a similar perspective, see David M. Abshire, *The South Rejects a Prophet: The Life of Senator D. M. Key, 1824–1900* (New York: Praeger, 1967).

37. On Woodward's exaggeration of Scott's role in the compromise, see Michael Les Benedict, "Southern Democrats in the Crisis of 1876–77: A Reconsideration of *Reunion and Reaction*," *Journal of Southern History* 46 (1980): 489–524. Charles and Mary Beard, *The Rise of American Civilization* (New York: Macmillan, 1927), 2:111–14. The Beards relied on an account by Roscoe Conklin. Beale disavowed his belief in "Foreword to the 1958 Edition," *The Critical Year: A Study of Andrew Johnson and Reconstruction* (1930; reprint, New York: Ungar, 1958), p. viii. For refutation of the theory, see Howard Jay Graham, "The 'Conspiracy Theory' of the Fourteenth Amendment," *Yale Law Journal* 47 (1938): 371–94, and *Yale Law Journal* 48 (1938): 171–94.

38. Stanley Coben, "Northeastern Business and Radical Reconstruction: A Reexamination," *Mississippi Valley Historical Review* 46 (1959): 87. Walter T. K. Nugent, *The Money Question During Reconstruction* (New York: Norton, 1967), pp. 105.

39. Lorenzo Sherwood, *The Development of Our Industrial Resources* (New York: National Cheap Freight Railway League, 1867).

40. Henry Charles Carey, *The Harmony of Interests: Agricultural, Manufacturing and Commercial* (New York: M. Finch, 1852), *The Way to Outdo England Without Fighting Her* (Philadelphia: Collins, 1865), and *Reconstruction, Industrial, Financial, and Political* (Philadelphia: Collins, 1867).

41. See Mira Wilkins, "Foreign Investment in the U.S. Economy before 1914," *Annals of the American Academy of Political and Social Science* 516 (1991): 9–21, and Dorothy Adler, *British Investment in American Railways* (Charlottesville: University of Virginia Press, 1970). On the laissez-faire, free-trade effects of the move toward a gold standard, see Joseph Schumpeter, *History of Economic Analysis* (New York: Oxford University Press, 1954), pp. 405–6; Milton Friedman and Anna Jacobson Schwartz, *A Monetary History of the United States, 1867–1960* (Princeton: Princeton University Press, 1963); and Richard H. Timberlake, *Monetary Policy in the United States: An Intellectual and Institutional History* (Chicago: Chicago University Press, 1993).

42. William Dean Howells, *The Rise of Silas Lapham* (1885; reprint, Bloomington: Indiana UP, 1971), pp. 79, 261, 262, 261. The West Virginia firm is the Kanawha Falls Company. It most likely would have used Huntington's Chesapeake and Ohio, which ran along the Kanawha River, to ship its paint to market.

43. Hamlin Garland, "The Return of a Private," in *Main-Travelled Roads* (New York: Harper and Brothers, 1922), pp. 119, 120. Carey, *Reconstruction, Industrial, Financial, and Political,* p. 50.

44. Albion W. Tourgée, "Study in Civilization," *North American Review* 142 (1886): 247.

45. Tourgée, "Study," pp. 249, 256, 258, 257.

46. Ruiz de Burton, *Conflict of Interests,* p. 186; John Tyler Morgan, "Mexico," *North American Review* 136 (1883): 409–10. See also Joseph Baylen and John Hammond More, "Senator John Tyler Morgan and Negro Colonization in the Philippines, 1901–1902," *Phylon* 29 (1968): 65–75.

47. Tourgée, "Study in Civilization": 258–61.

48. *Mamelon* and *John Eax* were written in 1874. They were published together in 1882 as *John Eax and Mamelon; or, The South without the Shadow.* Tourgée had a business similar to Paul's which failed because of the Panic of 1873.

49. Otto Olsen, *Carpetbagger's Crusade: The Life of Albion Winegar Tourgée* (Baltimore: Johns Hopkins UP, 1965), p. 111. Jay Cooke got his start through a special deal financing US bonds during the Civil War offered by his friend, Secretary of the Treasury Salmon Chase.

50. Sherwood, *The Development of Our Industrial Resources,* p. 19, quoting from Tourgée's North Carolina *Union Register.*

CHAPTER 6: Working with the Heritage of the Old South

1. In stressing Page's awareness of the need for the South to accommodate itself to the results of the Civil War, I complicate the stereotype of him as the spokesperson for the "Plantation School" of writers who merely perpetuated a nostalgic myth of a lost antebellum civilization. See, for instance, E. F. Bargainnier's claim that Page's primary purpose in *Red Rock* is "creating a myth of what he considered a great lost civilization" ("*Red Rock*: A Reappraisal," *Southern Quarterly* 22 [1984]: 52). Similarly, Kenneth O'Brien argues that such a myth "establishes the framework of the literary and social conventions upon which he will build the novel" ("Race, Romance, and the Southern Literary Tradition," in *Recasting: "Gone with the Wind" in American Culture,* ed. D. A. Pryon [Miami: UP of Florida, 1983], p. 154). In acknowledging the power of the "Plantation School," we need to be careful not to create a simplistic myth about the mythmakers. That tendency persists in even some of today's best critics. John Lowe, for instance, lumps a number of novels and films together as signaling the "triumphant culmination of the Plantation Tradition as America's favorite mythology" ("Reconstruction Revisited: Plantation School Writers, Postcolonial Theory, and Confederates in Brazil," *Mississippi Quarterly* 57 [2003]: 14). See also John Lowe, "Re-creating a Public for the Plantation: Reconstruction Myths of the Bi-racial Family," in *Bridging Southern Cultures: An Interdisciplinary Approach,* ed. John Lowe (Baton Rouge: Louisiana State UP, 2005), pp. 221–53. Jeremy Wells provides a useful summary of "Plantation School" criticism in *Romances of the White Man's Burden: Race, Empire, and the Plantation in American Literature, 1880–1936* (Nashville: Vanderbilt UP, 2011), pp. 33–39. Christopher Bundrick complicates the stereo

type of Page by arguing that *Red Rock* simultaneously "attempts to imagine a South that is capable of moving forward toward modernization and reconciliation while maintaining the sense of timelessness and pastoral calm through which it defined its antebellum iteration" ("Return of the Repressed: Gothic and Romance in Thomas Nelson Page's *Red Rock*" *South Central Review* 25 (2008): 65.

2. *Plutarch's Morals*, introduction by Ralph Waldo Emerson (Boston: Little, Brown, 1878), 1:8. I am indebted to Austin Carter for the reference to Plutarch's "A Discourse Touching the Training of Children."

3. J. G. A. Pocock, *The Machiavellian Moment: Florentine Political Thought and the Atlantic Republican Tradition* (Princeton: Princeton UP, 1975), and *Virtue, Commerce, and History: Essays on Political Thought and History Chiefly in the Eighteenth Century* (Cambridge: Cambridge UP, 1985).

4. Pocock, "The Americanization of Virtue," in *Machiavellian Moment*, pp. 506–52.

5. I am indebted to Alden Wood for pointing out the power of water to wear down stone(man).

6. In 1953 Du Bois retracted his condemnations of Jews. "I did not, when writing, realize that by stressing the name of the group instead of what some members of the group may have done, I was unjustly maligning a people in exactly the same way my folks were then and are now falsely accused" (*SBF*, 266).

7. Howard K. Beale, "On Rewriting Reconstruction History," *American Historical Review* 45 (1940): 822.

8. See J. Robert Payne's psychoanalytic reading of this scene in "George Washington Cable's *John March* and *Gideon's Band*: A (White) Boy Is Being Beaten," *American Literary Realism* 38 (2006): 239–48.

9. John Cleman complains that "the business machinations are difficult to follow and ultimately lack dramatic effect." They do tax the reader's attention, but readers who take the care to follow them should recognize that they have a major dramatic effect. *George Washington Cable Revised* (New York: Twayne, 1996), p. 148.

10. Greeley quoted in William B. Hesseltine, "Economic Factors in the Abandonment of Reconstruction," *Mississippi Valley Historical Review* 22 (1935): 201, 204.

11. Arlin Turner, *George W. Cable: A Biography* (Durham: Duke UP, 1956), p. 93.

12. Turner, *George W. Cable*, p. 294.

13. Louis D. Rubin Jr., *George W. Cable: The Life and Times of a Southern Heretic* (New York: Pegasus, 1969), pp. 238. Rubin gives a positive account of the book but faults the love plot justly if a bit too harshly for not growing "organically" out of the "novel's main problems" (231). Matthew Wilson, *Whiteness in the Novels of Charles W. Chesnutt* (Jackson: UP of Mississippi, 2004), p. 155; Sharon D. Kennedy-Nolle, *Writing Reconstruction: Race, Gender, and Citizenship in the Postwar South* (Chapel Hill: U of North Carolina P, 2015), p. 227. William L. Andrews acknowledges that *John March* is "the first and only serious fictional study of the New South creed before [Chesnutt's] *The Colonel's Dream*." William L. Andrews, *The Literary Career of Charles W. Chesnutt* (Baton Rouge: Louisiana State UP, 1980), p. 299.

14. Charles W. Chesnutt, *To Be an Author: The Letters of Charles W, Chesnutt: 1889–1905*, ed. Joseph R. McElrath Jr. and Robert C. Leitz (Princeton: Princeton UP, 1997), p. 83, and "The Negro in Books," *Essays and Speeches*, ed. Joseph R. McElrath Jr., Robert C. Leitz, and Jesse S. Crisler (Stanford: Stanford UP, 1999), p. 433.

15. Turner, *George W. Cable*, p. 291.

16. See Kennedy-Nolle's excellent discussion of this novel in *Writing Reconstruction,* pp. 76–122.

17. Otto Olsen, *Carpetbagger's Crusade: The Life of Albion Winegar Tourgée* (Baltimore: Johns Hopkins UP, 1965), p. 216.

18. Albion W. Tourgée, "Letter to E. H. Johnson," in *Undaunted Radical: The Selected Writings and Speeches of Albion W. Tourgée,* ed. Mark Elliott and John David Smith (Baton Rouge: Louisiana State UP, 2010), p. 364).

19. Quoted in J. G. de Roulhac Hamilton, *Reconstruction in North Carolina* (New York: Columbia UP, 1914), p. 640.

20. Edward J. Blum, *Reforging the White Republic: Race, Religion, and American Nationalism, 1865–1898* (Baton Rouge: Louisiana State UP, 2005), p. 147.

CHAPTER 7: Inheriting a Shadow and a Dream

1. All three authors, especially Chesnutt, have experienced a major revival after years of neglect. The reissue of Harper's and Hopkins's works by the Schomburg Library of Nineteenth-Century Black Women Writers sparked their revival. Nonetheless, some critics still fault their contrived plots. See Houston A. Baker, *Workings of the Spirit: The Poetics of Afro-American Women's Writing* (Chicago: U of Chicago P, 1991), pp. 24–28, and, more sympathetic, Mary Helen Washington, *Invented Lives: Narratives of Black Women, 1860–1960* (New York: Doubleday, 1987). The two most influential positive assessments are Hazel Carby, *Reconstructing Womanhood: The Emergence of the Afro-American Woman Novelist* (New York: Oxford UP, 1987), and Claudia Tate, *Domestic Allegories of Political Desire: The Black Heroine's Text at the Turn of the Century* (New York: Oxford UP, 1992). The first collection of essays on Hopkins was *The Unruly Voice: Rediscovering Pauline Elizabeth Hopkins,* ed. John Cullen Gruesser (Urbana: U of Illinois P, 1996). On inheritance, see Julie Cary Nerad, "'So Strangely Interwoven': The Property of Inheritance, Race, and Sexual Morality in Pauline E. Hopkins's *Contending Forces,*" *African American Review* 35 (2001): 357–73. Jeffory Clymer compares inheritance in Chesnutt's novels and Hopkins's *Hagar's Daughter* in his chapter "The Properties of Marriage in Chesnutt and Hopkins," *Family Money: Property, Race, and Literature in the Nineteenth Century* (New York: Oxford UP, 2012), pp. 123–47. I am indebted to his readings, although, like all of us who want to talk about race while insisting that it is socially constructed, he gets caught in some paradoxes. He examines fictional inheritance plots in which racial prejudice and the law disable blacks from inheriting family money. At the same time, he rightly points out that in Chesnutt's and Hopkins's works, the "blackness" of alleged "black" characters is frequently unclear. If so, in these cases, it is not blacks but alleged "blacks" who are disinherited. Such are the complications of living in a world that is not simply black and white.

2. The paradox of African Americans inheriting wealth from a slave economy complicates Mikko Tuhkamen's evocation of the trauma of slavery to explain the bizarre plot of *Hagar's Daughter.* Its repeated action, he argues, "invokes a haunted history that cannot be put behind us because it is ceaselessly passing into the present, suspended and unacknowledged." I would simply add that the complication of potentially rewarding African Americans in the present through wealth accrued on the basis of slave labor also haunts Harper's and Hopkins's fictional imagination. "'Out of Joint': Passing, Haunting, and the Time of Slavery in *Hagar's Daughter,*" *American Literature* 79 (2007): 337.

On Howells and Harper, see Kenneth W. Warren, *Black and White Strangers: Race and American Literary Realism* (Chicago: U of Chicago P, 1993); Henry B. Wonham, "Howells, Du Bois, and the Effects of 'Common-Sense': Race, Realism, and Nervousness in *An Imperative Duty* and *Souls of Black Folk*," in *Criticism and the Color Line: Desegregating American Literary Studies*, ed. Henry B. Wonham (New Brunswick: Rutgers University Press, 1996), pp. 126–39; Cathy Boeckmann, A *Question of Character: Scientific Racism and the Genres of American Fiction, 1892–1912* (Tuscaloosa: U of Alabama P, 2000); Debra J. Rosenthal, "The White Blackbird: Miscegenation, Genre, and the Tragic Mulatta in Howells, Harper, and 'Babes of Romance,'" *Nineteenth-Century Literature* 56 (2002): 495–517; Michelle Birnbaum, *Race, Work, and Desire in American Literature, 1860–1930* (New York: Cambridge UP, 2003); Kathleen Pfeiffer, *Race Passing and American Individualism* (Amherst: U of Massachusetts P, 2003; Julie Cary Nerad, "Slippery Language and False Dilemmas: The Passing Novels of Child, Howells, and Harper," *American Literature* 75 (2003): 813–41; Stephanie P. Browner, *Profound Science and Elegant Literature: Imagining Doctors in Nineteenth Century America* (Philadelphia: U of Pennsylvania P, 2005); and Steven J. Belluscio, *To Be Suddenly White: Literary Realism and Racial Passing* (Colombia: U of Missouri P, 2007). For *An Imperative Duty*'s response to *Pactolus Prime*, see Brook Thomas, *American Literary Realism and the Failed Promise of Contract* (Berkeley: U of California P, 1997), pp. 198–99.

3. My financial reading of *Hagar's Daughter* is indebted to Brian Fonken.

4. Hazel Carby, introduction to *The Magazine Novels of Pauline Hopkins* (New York: Oxford UP, 1988), p. xxxv.

5. Clymer makes a similar point and concludes that "the possibility for blacks to control previously white family money is radically delimited by the lingering effects of racial prejudice" (*Family Money*, p. 145).

6. According to Clymer, "The courtroom thus becomes the place where interracial marriages are put back together, where identities that in the past led to dramatic ruptures are reclaimed in the hope of rekindled love" (*Family Money*, p. 145). William E. Moddelmog, links *Contending Forces* to the campaign for a national antilynching law in *Reconstituting Authority: American Fiction in the Province of the Law, 1880–1920* (Iowa City: U of Iowa P, 2000), pp. 106–13. Laura H. Korobkin focuses on issues of federalism that literary critics rarely attend to in "Imagining State and Federal Law in Pauline Hopkins's *Contending Forces*," *Legacy* 28 (2011): 1–23. Jeannine Marie DeLombard looks at the resolution in relation to torts in "The Novel and the Reconstruction Amendments," *Oxford History of the Novel in English*, ed. Priscilla Wald and Michael A. Elliott (Oxford: Oxford UP, 2014), 5:84–85.

7. Charles W. Chesnutt, *The Journals of Charles W. Chesnutt*, ed. Richard Brodhead (Durham: Duke UP, 1993), pp. 124–25; Charles W. Chesnutt, "The Courts and the Negro," in *Plessy v. Ferguson: A Brief History with Documents*, ed. Brook Thomas (Boston: Bedford, 1997), p. 157. A major work sparking the widespread revival of interest in Chesnutt is William L. Andrews, *The Literary Career of Charles W. Chesnutt* (Baton Rouge: Louisiana State UP, 1980). Earlier, John Edgar Wideman published "Charles W. Chesnutt: *The Marrow of Tradition*," *American Scholar* 42 (1973): 128–34. Dickson D. Bruce did pioneering work in *Black American Writing From the Nadir* (Baton Rouge: Louisiana State UP, 1989. Eric Sundquist followed with extensive treatment of Chesnutt's short stories and *The Marrow of Tradition* in *To Wake the Nations: Race in the Making of American*

Literature (Cambridge: Harvard UP, 1993). Since then, Chesnutt has benefitted from too much excellent scholarship to cite exhaustively.

8. Charles Chesnutt Papers, R-252, p. 42, Fisk Special Collections, John Hope and Aurelia E. Franklin Library, Nashville, Tennessee. Erin Sweeney alerted me to Chesnutt's revision. Darryl Hattenhauer points out how John's success depends on wealth accumulated from exploitation of his wife's slaves in "Racial and Textual Miscegenation in Chesnutt's *The House Behind the Cedars*," *Mississippi Quarterly* 47 (1993): 27–45.

9. Andreá N. Williams offers a compelling analysis of how postbellum African Americans represent class: "Chesnutt represents the black middle class as neither an object of mockery, as in minstrelsy and mulatto-bashing, nor as an idealized model of selfless racial leadership, as in Frances Harper's *Iola Leroy*." *Dividing Lines: Class Anxiety and Postbellum Class Fiction* (Ann Arbor: U of Michigan P, 2013), pp. 161.

10. Charles Chesnutt Papers, R-252, p. 54. On Frank, see Trudier Harris, "Chesnutt's Frank Fowler: A Failure of Purpose?" *CLA Journal* 22 (1979): 215–28.

11. Moddelmog links "The Sway-backed House" with *The House Behind the Cedars* through an interest in "the relationship between race and property" (*Reconstituting Authority*, p. 136). "The Sway-backed House" complicates Clymer's argument about family money being steered to whites. Chesnutt is also alert to how class-consciousness within the African American community affects inheritance.

12. Chesnutt, *Journals*, pp. 39–40.

13. Matthew Wilson sees Chesnutt writing in dialogue with Page's *Red Rock* and Dixon's *The Leopard's Spots* but simplifies the tradition of the Plantation School. *Whiteness in the Novels of Charles W. Chesnutt* (Jackson: UP of Mississippi, 2004), pp. 120–27.

14. Douglas Melvin Haynes, "Policing the Social Boundaries of the American Medical Association, 1847–70," *Journal of the History of Medicine and Allied Sciences* 60 (2005): 184.

15. S. Weir Mitchell, "The Autobiography of a Quack," *Atlantic Monthly* 20 (1867): 466–75, 586–97.

16. Richard Brodhead, introduction to Charles W. Chesnutt, *The Conjure Woman and Other Tales* (1899; reprint, Durham: Duke UP, 1993), pp. 1–26. As Brodhead puts it, his publisher "tells Chesnutt that he cannot be an author—or that he can be one, but only on terms of their, not his, devising. More particularly, Chesnutt is told that he can be published on the condition that he write in one form: the vernacular dialect tale he had long since chosen against" (17).

17. On Tattnall, see Brook Thomas, *Civic Myths: A Law and Literature Approach to Citizenship* (Chapel Hill: U of North Carolina P, 2007), pp. 83, 260n84.

18. There are hints that Sandy may be Mr. Delamere's son, but they are not conclusive.

19. Calling Josh's death "heroic," Walter Benn Michaels argues that it is "a lesson in how to build up racial sympathy and solidarity, a sort of sentimental education for blacks required to live under Jim Crow laws." He goes on to compare Chesnutt's effort to evoke racial solidarity that transcends class with Dixon's effort to do the same, as exemplified by his depiction of racial solidarity in the Klan. This reading distorts both Dixon and Chesnutt. For Dixon, the Klan does claim to represent the white race, but it has a clear class hierarchy in its organization. Chesnutt, while understanding Josh's motives, does not endorse his method. For the book to create the effect Michaels claims it has, its target audience would have been black. But, as we have seen, Chesnutt targets a predominately

white audience. Clearly, he hopes that audience will have sympathy for blacks, but it is sympathy across the color line, a line he goes out of his way to undermine. After all, the book itself ends with an act of interracial cooperation. Walter Benn Michaels, *The Trouble with Diversity: How We Learned to Love Identity and Ignore Inequality* (New York: Metropolitan, 2006), p. 62. To a certain extent, Andreá Williams agrees with Michaels on Chesnutt's lesson but distinguishes his tales in the North and the South. Although Chesnutt acknowledges "intraracial tensions" in *The Marrow of Tradition*, "his greater focus on interracial conflict indicates how racial solidarity generally supersedes the importance of class differences in the South," as opposed to his "Blue Vein" stories, like "The Wife of His Youth," set in Ohio (*Dividing Lines*, p. 169). But Chesnutt's Ohio also had to deal with lynchings and racial prejudice.

20. William Dean Howells, *The Rise of Silas Lapham* (1885; reprint, Bloomington: Indiana UP, 1971), p. 197.

21. *Plessy v. Ferguson: A Brief History*, p. 58. Chesnutt wrote his novel in Ohio, where he had recently helped pass a state antilynching law, supported by then-governor William McKinley, who had become president. John Cyril Barton has convincingly shown how Chesnutt intended his novel to affect the campaign for a national antilynching law. " 'The Necessity of an Example': Chesnutt's *The Marrow of Tradition* and the Ohio Anti-Lynching Campaign," *Arizona Quarterly* 67 (2011): 27–58. Trinyan Mariano relates Chesnutt's lynching plot to torts in "The Law of Torts and the Logic of Lynching in Charles Chesnutt's *The Marrow of Tradition*," *PMLA* 128 (2013): 559–74.

22. I am indebted to Brandon Wild for pointing out the pun in Dodie's name.

23. Notable exceptions to the neglect of *The Colonel's Dream* include Brook Thomas in *American Literary Realism*, pp. 173–90, and "The Legal Argument of Charles W. Chesnutt's Novels," *Law and Literature*, issue 18 of *REAL*, ed. Brook Thomas (Tübingen: Narr, 2001), pp. 311–34; Gary Scharnhorst, " 'The Growth of a Dozen Tendrils': The Polyglot Satire of Chesnutt's *The Colonel's Dream*," in *Critical Essays*, pp. 271–80; Dean McWilliams, *Charles W. Chesnutt and the Fictions of Race* (Athens: U of Georgia P, p. 2002); Wilson, "*The Colonel's Dream*: The Eccentric Design of Charles W. Chesnutt's New South Novel," in *Whiteness*, pp. 148–82; Ryan Simmons, "*The Colonel's Dream*: Reconsidering a Radical Text," *Chesnutt and Realism: A Study of the Novels* (Tuscaloosa: U of Alabama P, 2006), pp. 113–30). As Simmons points out, both McWilliams and Scharnhorst fault the novel's literary execution (p. 177n1). A paperback edition finally came out from a division of Penguin/Random House with an introduction by Ishmael Reed, *The Colonel's Dream* (1905; reprint, New York: Harlem Moon, 2005). Reed argues for the book's contemporary significance in a chapter on Chesnutt in his *Mixing It Up* (Philadelphia: De Capo, 2008).

24. Chesnutt, "What Is a White Man?" *Essays and Speeches*, p. 68; Henry W. Grady, "In Plain Black and White," *Century Magazine* 29 (1885): 916, 914.

25. Thomas analyzes the significance of Chesnutt's revisions from unpublished story to novel in *American Literary Realism*, pp. 184–88. Wilson, without acknowledgment, makes a few of the same points in *Whiteness*, pp. 170–71. Clymer structures his "Coda: 'Race Feeling' " around a discussion of "The Dumb Witness," with only passing mention of *The Colonel's Dream*. He needs to give priority to the story because his thesis demands that there be some "family" money to pass on. As probing as Clymer's account is, its focus causes him to miss some details of the story. For instance, he does not note that the widow is from the North and that a diamond necklace is in the treasure. More important

for a coda, he does not address the political significance of changes Chesnutt made from the version of the story in an unpublished work to the version in his last published novel.

26. W. William Evans, *To Die Game: The Story of the Lowry Band, Indian Guerillas of Reconstruction* (Baton Rouge: Louisiana State UP, 1971).

27. Reed confuses the schoolteacher Taylor with a barber, ignores how he is abandoned by the colored community, and inaccurately writes, "The black middle class success story in *The Colonel's Dream,* a barber, is reduced to the status of a porter as the result of white mob violence" (*Mixing It Up,* p. 54).

28. Charles W. Chesnutt, *To Be an Author: The Letters of Charles W. Chesnutt, 1889–1905,* ed. Joseph R. McElrath Jr. and Robert C. Leitz (Princeton: Princeton UP, 1997), p. 167.

29. Otto H. Olsen, *Carpetbagger's Crusade: The Life of Albion Winegar Tourgée* (Baltimore: Johns Hopkins UP, 1965), p. 352.

30. David W. Blight, *Race and Reunion: The Civil War in American Memory* (Cambridge: Harvard UP, 2001), p. 57. For a more extensive explanation of how contradictory civic ideals generate national myths, see Thomas, *Civic Myths.*

Index